Black Crescent

Beginning with Latin America in the fifteenth century, this book gives a social history of the experiences of African Muslims and their descendants throughout the Americas, including the Caribbean. It examines the record under slavery and the postslavery period into the twentieth century. The experiences vary, arguably due to some extent to the Old World context. The book also discusses Muslim revolts in Brazil, especially in 1835, by way of a nuanced analysis. The second part of the book looks at the emergence of Islam among African-descended people in the United States in the twentieth century, with successive chapters on Noble Drew Ali, Elijah Muhammad, and Malcolm X, with a view to explaining how orthodoxy arose from various unorthodox roots.

Michael A. Gomez is Professor of History at New York University. He is the author of *Pragmatism in the Age of Jihad: The Precolonial State of Bundu* (1992), *Exchanging Our Country Marks: The Transformation of African Identities in the Colonial and Antebellum South* (1988), and *Reversing Sail* (Cambridge, 2005). His research, teaching interests, and publications include the African Diaspora, Islam, and West African history. He currently serves as Director of the Association for the Study of the Worldwide African Diaspora.

Black Crescent

The Experience and Legacy of African Muslims in the Americas

MICHAEL A. GOMEZ

New York University

CAMBRIDGE UNIVERSITY PRESS

CAMBRIDGE UNIVERSITY PRESS
Cambridge, New York, Melbourne, Madrid, Cape Town, Singapore, São Paulo

Cambridge University Press
40 West 20th Street, New York, NY 10011-4211, USA

www.cambridge.org
Information on this title: www.cambridge.org/9780521840958

© Michael A. Gomez 2005

First published 2005

Printed in the United States of America

A catalog record for this publication is available from the British Library.

Library of Congress Cataloging in Publication Data

Gomez, Michael Angelo, 1955–
Black crescent : the experience and legacy of African Muslims in the Americas / Michael
A. Gomez.
   p. cm.
  Includes bibliographical references and index.
  ISBN 0-521-84095-3 (hardcover) – ISBN 0-521-60079-0 (pbk.)
1. African Americans–History. 2. Africans–America–History. 3. Muslims–America–History.
4. Islam–America–History. 5. Africans–America–Religion–History. 6. African Americans–
Religion–History. 7. Muslim, Black–America–History. 8. Slavery–America–History.
9. United States–Race relations. 10. America–Race relations. I. Title.
  E185.G615 2005
  305.6′97′0899607–dc22   2004027722

ISBN-13 978-0-521-84095-8 hardback
ISBN-10 0-521-84095-3 hardback

ISBN-13 978-0-521-60079-8 paperback
ISBN-10 0-521-60079-0 paperback

Contents

v

Acknowledgments

This project began taking shape in 1994. I appreciate all those who read various versions of the manuscript, especially Claude W. Clegg III and Paul Lovejoy, and all the unnamed evaluators used by Cambridge University Press. Thanks to Lew Bateman as well – it's good to work together again.

Many contributed in one way or another over the years to help this work come to light. Among them are João Reis (who did not read any of the manuscript, but who was very helpful during my stay in Salvador), Robert Hill, Sterling Stuckey, Kathleen Phillips Lewis, Fitzroy Baptiste, Brinsley Samaroo, Amir al-Islam, and Alfred Muhammad. The chapter on Muslims in New York came out of a larger study completed for the New York African Burial Ground Project, under the direction of Michael Blakey, and I thank him for his encouragement and support. The staff at the Schomburg Center for Research in Black Culture were also helpful with materials on Noble Drew Ali. Significant portions of Chapter 5, "Founding Mothers and Fathers of a Different Sort," originated in an article published by the *Journal of Southern History,* LX (November 1994).

My wife Mary and my daughters Sonya, Candace, and Jamila are to be commended for their patience.

As always, I thank Almighty God.

Prologue

In 1492, Christopher Columbus crossed the Atlantic, and with him came Islam. Among his crews were Muslims who had been forced to profess the Christian faith; it is highly probable that Islam remained embedded in their souls. To these and others similarly stationed throughout the western hemisphere in the fifteenth and sixteenth centuries were added enslaved Africans, some of whom were also Muslim. Through the nineteenth century, the number of African Muslims transported to the Americas continued to grow. What follows is a history of these Muslims and their descendants in the Americas, the latter a category composed of the genealogically related as well as the African-descended who would convert to Islam.

The book is divided into two sections. The first discusses the presence of African Muslims in the Americas through periods of enslavement. It provides the context for the second part's examination of Islam's development in the United States, where, through a progression of ideas, communities transitioned from variation to orthodoxy and the adoption of the faith's five pillars. These are the formulaic profession of God's Oneness and Muhammad as His messenger; daily prayer; almsgiving; pilgrimage; and fasting Ramadan. The second part of the book also examines the embrace of the seventh-century Qur'ān and the acceptance of Muhammad as seal of the prophets. The principal argument here is that subsequent orthodoxy owes much to earlier variegation.

Put succinctly, enslaved African Muslims were distributed throughout the Americas, and they were either more numerous or more organized as a community in the Caribbean and Brazil than in what became the United States. Islam as an African importation faltered in the first two regions, going into total eclipse in many cases, whereas it emerged as an important social and political force in the United States. The experience in the Caribbean, Brazil, and Latin America can be explained by severe political repression, in combination with exclusionary practices on the part of Muslim communities and various campaigns to repatriate to West Africa. Stated differently, African Muslims in these areas were very visible and, in the case of Brazil, threatening, receiving corresponding attention in kind from the state. In contrast, Muslim communities in the United States were comparatively quiet and compliant; their legacy survived a temporal interim until the early twentieth century, when the fortunes of Islam were revived by way of the rise of nationalist sentiment. Although by no means the only ones to do so, early leaders of Islamic-like movements forged indissoluble bonds with nationalist expressions, providing a vehicle through which certain Islamic ideas could be introduced and disseminated. Regarded as unorthodox by many, such movements reached the height of their popularity under Malcolm X, whose eventual embrace of orthodoxy in the form of Sunni Islam paved the way for many to follow. As I will explain, closure of the circle and reattachment to a form of Islam more closely resembling the religion of African forebears owes much to the pioneers of theologies at variance with the conventional.

The present discussion of Islam in the United States turns on leading figures and major movements; it is therefore far from an exhaustive study of Islam and African Americans. Research into the myriad facets and principals contributing to the complex texture of African American Muslim communities is, in many ways, in its infancy. In particular, three areas of inquiry remain for subsequent study: Islam and African American musicians, particularly jazz musicians; Islam and African Americans in the penal system; and a contextual study of Arabic manuscripts written by enslaved Muslims, which would include such materials from all over the Americas.[1]

All in due season.

---

[1] An example of an important research project that delves into the little-known history and experience of African American Muslims is Robert Dannin's ethnography, *Black Pilgrimage to Islam* (New York: Oxford University Press, 2002). Its discussion of musicians and the prison experience, as well as certain pioneers in the faith, is critical; though it is largely confined to the New York area, it provides avenues of analysis that would facilitate further inquiry.

PART ONE

I

Ladinos, Gelofes, and Mandingas

On the lush island of Hispaniola in 1522, Admiral Diego Columbus, governor and son of the explorer, received a most unusual gift early Christmas morning. At the sound of the second cockcrow, some twenty enslaved persons, heretofore proscribed within what was a sizeable *ingenio*, or sugar mill and its environs, lay aside their fears and set upon a path of alteration. Intent on spreading sedition throughout the island, the insurrectionists moved to mobilize an equal number of coconspirators on neighboring establishments. Machetes in hand, they literally dismembered plantation personnel and livestock as they proceeded, initiating a "wild and bloody expedition under dawn's early light." In their wake lay torched houses and fields, while "here and there in the open ground lie the decapitated bodies of unfortunate whites who [the insurgents] were able to catch off-guard." On December 28 they reached the cattle ranch of Melchoir de Castro, some thirty miles from the island's capital of Santo Domingo, upon which they may have been planning an assault. By then, however, they no longer enjoyed the element of surprise; a mixed force of Europeans and indigenous persons under Melchoir de Castro's leadership, both militia and volunteers, attacked the desperate band of Africans, effectively ending the revolt. Those not immediately killed took to the hills, only to be captured within a week. When the dust settled, some fifteen bodies were recovered, including those of at least nine Europeans; Diego Columbus reflected that if the uprising had not been quickly quelled, many more "Christian" lives would have been lost. Thus began the first collective insurrection of Africans in the Americas, a movement largely composed of Senegambians, a significant proportion of whom were probably Muslim.[1]

[1] See Carlos Federico Gulloit, *Negros rebeldes y negros cimarrones: Perfil afroamericanos en la historia del Nuevo Mundo durante el siglo XVI* (Montevideo, Argentina: Fariña Editores, 1961), 79–84; Franklyn J. Franco, *Los negros, los mulatos y la nación dominica* (Santo Domingo: Editora Nacional, 1969), 14–15; Leslie B. Rout, Jr., *The African Experience in Spanish America: 1502 to the Present Day* (Cambridge, England: Cambridge U. Press, 1976), 104–05. Also see Brent Singleton, "The

The insurgence was not the first act of rebellion on record by Africans in the New World. To be sure, there were, all along, so many occurrences of individual and composite rebellion – from mutinies and suicides aboard the slavers to poisonings, sabotage, work stoppages, thefts (or reappropriations), and an assortment of culturally informed responses to captivity. The first recorded instances of resistance were in 1503, when Nicolás de Ovando, Hispaniola's first royal governor, wrote to Isabella requesting that she prevent further shipments to the colony of enslaved *ladinos*, or persons possessing knowledge of Spanish or Portuguese languages and cultures, but who also often had connections to either Senegambia, Islam, or both. De Ovando had arrived earlier in April of 1502 and was already complaining that the ladinos on the island were "a source of scandal to the Indians, and some had fled their owners," establishing maroon communities in the mountains.[2]

While many resisted their enslavement, other ladinos served as personal attendants to the early Spanish colonists, and they constituted a significant number by the second quarter of the sixteenth century; "a perusal of the early accounts of the exploits of the conquistadores will reveal the fact that the Negro participated in the exploration and occupation of nearly every important region from New Mexico to Chile." With chasms of discrepancy between their treatment as prescribed in *Las Siete Partidas* (regulations originally developed in the thirteenth century that provided the basis for subsequent slave laws) and their actual experience, Africans taken from Cuba along with natives of the island carried the artillery of Hernan Cortés in his campaign in Mexico, and they were among those sent by Velásquez to punish Cortés for insubordination in 1520. In 1534, Pedro de Alvarado, the lieutenant of Cortés, brought 200 enslaved Africans on his expedition to Quito (Ecuador), most of whom died in the snows of the Andes, while a number of Africans carried the baggage of Diego de Almagro and Rodrigo Orgoñez through the Andes from Cuzco to Chile, often paying the ultimate price. Hernando Solano marched with four Africans, one of whom was a woman; Diego de Pantojas had an African in his company; and so on.[3] The list of Africans so engaged is rather extensive, but perhaps the

Ummah Slowly Bled: A Select Bibliography of Enslaved African Muslims in the Americas," *Journal of Muslim Minority Affairs* 22 (2002): 401–12, for a helpful list of sources on the general subject of African Muslims in the Americas. Sources listed by Singleton that were not useful to this study are not cited. Further, citations to the same sources sometimes differ in form between Singleton and the present work. Finally, while a number of sources listed by Singleton have applicability beyond this chapter, this will be the only citation to the Singleton compilation.

[2] See Rolando Mellafe, *La introducción de la esclavitud negra en Chile: tráfico y rutas* (Santiago: Editorial Universitaria, 1984), 10–11; Rout, *African Experience in Spanish America*, 22.

[3] See J. Fred Rippy, "The Negro and the Spanish Pioneer in the New World," *Journal of Negro History* 4 (1921): 183–89; Gonzalo Vial Correa, *El africano en el reino de Chile: Ensayo histórico – jurídico* (Santiago: Instituto de Investigaciones Historicas, 1957). *Las Siete Partidas*, compiled between 1256 and 1265, was a "compendium of Justinian law and local custom which became a reference point in all legal matters of Spain and its later colonial empire. The rights and obligations of those enslaved were enumerated in *Las Siete Partidas*, and in this manner, the institution of slavery was recognized as an integral part of the Spanish society and was given a legal basis." See

most distinguished of them all was "Estevánico, or Estévan, an Arabian black from Azamor, in Morocco," who, if a historical figure, was quite the swash-buckler and agent of Spanish imperialism in what would become New Mexico and Arizona.[4]

As opposed to anglophone North America, where the meeting of Africans and the English was so novel and startling as to be a nearly cataclysmic event, the engagement between Africans and Europeans in what would become Latin America was in many ways an extension of an interaction begun hundreds of years earlier in Iberia, North Africa, and elsewhere in the Mediterranean.[5] Muslim expansion into Iberia in 711 initiated a prolonged period of occupation that lasted nearly 800 years, culminating with Grenada's fall in 1492. Muslim conquerors introduced (or reintroduced in some instances) scientific, religious, and classical studies, along with architectural innovations and a quality of civilization both unique and superior to much of what was current in Europe, The Portuguese and Spanish became well acquainted with Muslims, a diverse assembly of differentiated unequals that included Arabs, Berbers, Arabo-Berbers, and West Africans. Together, they comprised the unwieldy and heterogeneic category referred to as "Moors" by Europeans. Spanish use of the term *Moor* in the sixteenth century, therefore, was not necessarily a reference to race as it is currently understood. Indeed, Berbers and Arabs had had such extensive "contact with Negroes" that they had "absorbed a considerable amount of color." Rather, *Moor* referred to a *casta* (as opposed to *nación*), a designation that "did not intend to imply a racial factor but rather a cultural characteristic – Islam."[6]

Africans were therefore present in al-Andalus (Iberia) since Islam's arrival there, but they actually seized political control with the coming of the Almoravids in the eleventh century. The emergence of the Almoravids signaled the dawn of a new dispensation: North Africa achieved unification under the authority of an indigenous regime, having had extensive experience with occupational forces, from the Carthaginians to the Romans to the Byzantines to the Arabs. The Sanhaja Berbers, in a feat similar to the prophet Muhammad's consolidation of the Arabian peninsula under a central government, initially extended their influence south to the Senegal River and the dominant power of

---

Frederick Marshall Rodriguez, "Cimarrón Revolts and Pacification in New Spain, the Isthmus of Panama and Colonial Colombia, 1503–1800" (Ph.D. diss., Loyola U. of Chicago, 1979), 14.

[4] See Frederick W. Hodge, Jr., "The Narrative of the Expedition of Coronado, by Pedro de Castañeda," in J. Franklin Jameson, ed., *Original Narratives of Early American History: Spanish Explorers in the Southern United States, 1528–1543* (New York: Charles Scribner's Sons, 1907), vol. 11; Woodbury Lowery, *The Spanish Settlements Within the Present Limits of the United States, 1513–1561* (New York and London: G. P. Putnam's Sons, 1911), 278–82.

[5] See, for example, Winthrop Jordan, *White Over Black: American Attitudes Toward the Negro, 1550–1812* (Chapel Hill: U. of North Carolina Press, 1968), and compare with Bernard Lewis, *The Muslim Discovery of Europe* (New York and London: Norton, 1982).

[6] See Gonzalo Aguirre Beltrán, "Tribal Origins of Slaves in Mexico," *Journal of Negro History* 31 (July 1946): 276–77.

legendary Ghana (to the river's east), and they may have played a role in the kingdom's demise. The Sanhaja then crossed Gibraltar, thereby effecting an empire that connected auriferous West Africa to the markets of southern Europe, establishing a formidable presence in the western Mediterranean in the process.[7]

Almoravid control of al-Andalus was achieved by military conquest. A significant proportion of the Almoravid army, in turn, was West African.[8] In employing West African soldiers in Iberia, the Almoravids were continuing a practice begun by the Umayyads at least since the reign of al-Hakam I (796–822), when they were among the palace guard and the garrisons.[9] While denying them rank and promotion, Abd al-Rahman III (who reigned 912 – 961), al-Hakam II (who reigned 961–76), and al-Mansur (who reigned 976–1002) also used "black" troops, who formed a so-called black honor guard under al-Hakam III. Enslaved, these soldiers comprised an *'abīd* or servile army, although many were eventually manumitted and merged with other categories of Andalusian Muslim society. The long and extensive interaction between North and West Africans, bond and free, both in Africa and al-Andalus, was such that the distinction between "black" and "white" Africans was often devoid of biological meaning, though it was maintained as part of very real social conventions.

Notwithstanding the importance of West African recruits as soldiers, the majority of those involuntarily transported from West into North Africa and beyond the strait were female, true for most components and periods of the entire transsaharan slave trade. It is therefore appropriate to speak of the transsaharan trade as predominantly a trade in women and young girls, who were multiply exploited in that even those purchased for domestic labor were just as vulnerable sexually as were those recruited as concubines. Because the progeny of slaveholding fathers and enslaved mothers followed, when acknowledged by the former, the status of their fathers in keeping with Islamic law, individuals from such backgrounds could achieve degrees of social distinction.

The volume of the early transsaharan trade, which was gender specific, was low. Indeed, the lofty empires of Ghana, Mali, and Songhay, while engaged in a modicum of slave trading, were far more renowned for their supplies of gold. The Lake Chad area was an exception to this characterization, featuring a long and close association with the slave trade across the Sahara. Even so, the number of West Africans enslaved in Iberia, to either Muslims or Christians, was not very significant in the early stages of the Muslim presence in al-Andalus. The end of Moorish rule in Portugal in 1250 brought with it a significant decrease in

---

[7] See Jamil M. Abun-Nasr, *A History of the Maghrib in the Islamic Period* (Cambridge and New York: Cambridge U. Press, 1987).

[8] See John O. Hunwick, "African Slaves in the Mediterranean World: A Neglected Aspect of the African Diaspora," in Joseph E. Harris, ed., *Global Dimensions of the African Diaspora*, 2nd ed. (Washington, DC: Howard U. Press, 1993), 303.

[9] See E. Lévi-Provençal, *Histoire de l'Espagne musulmane*, 3 vols. (Paris: G.P. Maisonneuve, 1967), especially vol. 3; also see Rout, *African Experience in Spanish America*, 13–14.

the availability of manual labor, as many Muslims fled the realm for Grenada, while the cessation of conflict also meant the discontinuation of a ready supply of war captives. The Portuguese therefore sought to augment their labor force with West Africans, purchasing them from Muslim traders at Guimarães in northern Portugal. Merchants at Barcelona also purchased captives at Tunis and North African markets from the eleventh through the fifteenth centuries, and, from the late fourteenth century, Africans bought in North Africa were sold in Cádiz. However, these *sarracenos negros*, or black Muslims (in anticipation of C. Eric Lincoln), were quite expensive as a result of the costs of transsaharan commerce, and they remained more the exception than the rule in thirteenth and fourteenth-century Portugal.[10]

The African's fate would begin to change in the fifteenth century with the convergence of maritime innovations, New World "discoveries," and the Great Dying of aboriginal populations in the Americas. The Atlantic would begin to supplant the Sahara, bringing Europe directly into contact with subsaharan Africa. The Portuguese onslaught can be said to have begun with Prince Henry "the Navigator" (who navigated little of anything), who, in his command of Portuguese forces at Ceuta (Morocco) in 1418, set in motion attempts to take the North African (Barbary) coast and to explore further south along West African shores in search of both Prester John (imagined by Europeans to be a powerful Christian ruler and potential ally in the struggle against the "Saracens") and the Rio de Ouro (River of Gold). In 1441, Nuno Tristão and Antão Gonçalves reached Cape Blanc, where they took prisoner eleven *azenagues* (Tuareg) and one "black" woman. The captives were first brought to Portugal and then returned to West Africa and exchanged for ten "blacks," gold dust, and ostrich eggs. By 1444, Lançarote de Freitas, having helped found the Lagos Company, returned to Portugal from the West African coast with 235 azenague and "blackmoor" captives, where most were sold in Lisbon or Lagos. The designation *blackmoor* suggests that the Portuguese identified these West Africans as Muslims remarkable for their skin color. Because they are assigned neither an ethnic nor a place-name comparable with that of *azenague*, the origins of these particular blackmoors are uncertain; they could have been trade captives from south of the Senegal River or members of the various Sudanese enclaves found throughout the area north of the Senegal, or they may have already been enslaved to Tuareg slaveholders and therefore progenitors of the *bella*, transhumant communities in perpetual subjugation.[11] If they originated south of the Senegal, not all would have been Muslim before leaving West Africa, but they may have subsequently converted in Europe, a speculation about which more will be stated later.

---

[10] See Rout, *African Experience in Spanish America*, 3–12.

[11] See Edmond Bernus, *Touaregs nigériens. Unité culturelle et diversité régionale d'un peuple pasteur* (Paris: Editions de l'office de la recherche scientifigue et technique outre-mer, 1981); Claude Meillassoux, ed., *L'ésclavage en Afrique précoloniale* (Paris: F. Maspero, 1975).

Nuno Tristão did not stop there. Later in 1444 he reached the Senegal River itself, followed by Dinis Dias's voyage to Cape Verde the following year. Having finally reached "the land of the blacks," or "Guinea," the Portuguese soon learned that negotiation and trade were preferable to violence. Establishing commercial stations on Arguin Island, Cape Verde, points along the coast of Sierra Leone, and on the Gambia and Geba Rivers between 1445 and 1460, the Portuguese exchanged wheat, textiles, horses, and weapons for gold dust, spices, ivory tusks, and human beings. Interestingly, the Tuareg made the transition from trade bait to trade partners, and in 1445 the Lagos Company began purchasing West Africans from the Tuareg. Three years later, some 1,000 had been shipped to Portugal, and in the fifty years between 1450 and 1500, 700 to 900 captives were imported into Portugal and Madeira annually.[12] This dramatic rise in the West African trade could not go unnoticed, and, in the absence of official war with West Africa, it was justified with Hamitic discourse: Gomes Eanes de Zurara, who himself participated in a slave raid sometime before 1448, argued that the enslavement of ten Muslim captives brought to Portugal in 1442 was "in accordance with ancient custom which after the Deluge, Noah laid on his son Cain [Canaan] cursing him in this way: that his race would be subject to all the other races of the world."[13]

By 1462, the Portuguese had become veritable slave trading entrepreneurs and were supplying Spain with captives as well. Their dependability was such that in 1479 they reached the Treaty of Alcáçovas, granting Portugal the right to supply Spain with African captives. The Portuguese brought "cheap" West African captives into Cádiz and Barcelona as well as Valencia and Seville. Importation estimates are uncertain, but Valencia may have received some 5,200 captives between 1477 and 1516, while a 1616 census in Cádiz reveals that West African captives outnumbered Berbers and North Africans by more than 20 percent. Seville, however, had the largest concentration of enslaved Africans by 1565 – some 6,327 out of a municipal population of 85,538, and some 6 percent of a 100,000 total estimate of enslaved persons in Spain. The percentage of West Africans in this total estimate is unknown, but it is clear that the slave trade, after the 1503 establishment of the Casa de Contratación (a maritime council administering trade with the American colonies) in Seville, had in sixty years contributed to the population and was a factor in Seville becoming both a "thriving metropolis" and Spain's largest city.[14]

Most of the West Africans sold by the Portuguese in Spain after 1462 were known as *negros de jalof*, and they were also referred to as *gelofes*. This is clearly a

---

[12] See Rout, *African Experience in Spanish America*, 3–12.
[13] Ibid., 12; Gomes Eanes de Zurara, *Chronique de Guinée* (Dakar: IFAN, 1960), 93–94.
[14] See Ruth Pike, *Aristocrats and Traders: Sevillian Society in the Sixteenth Century* (Ithaca and London: Cornell U. Press, 1972), 1; Rout, *African Experience in Spanish America*, 15–16; Colin Palmer, *Slaves of the White God: Blacks in Mexico, 1570–1650* (Cambridge, MA: Harvard U. Press, 1976), 7–9; Celestino López Martínez, *Mudéjares y moriscos sevillanos* (Seville: Editorial Renacimiento, 1994); Emiliano Endrek, *El mestizaje en Córdoba: Siglo XVIII y principios del XIX* (Córdoba: Universidad Nacional de Córdoba, 1966).

reference to the empire of Jolof near the Senegal River, but, given the Portuguese area of operation, the reference must include all persons recruited from the Senegal to Sierra Leone (see Map 1). By the end of the fifteenth century, *mandingas* (Mande-speakers) from the same general area were also being marketed, while West Central Africans from around the Congo River, called *bantu* by the lusophones, began arriving in Iberia in 1513. Whatever their origin, these persons were brought to Spain to live and work. Women served as domestics and sexual objects; men as "footmen, coachmen, and butlers, while others functioned as stevedores, factory workers, farm laborers, miners, and assistants to their owners in crafts."[15] Others were purchased by the crown and used in the galleys in construction projects, and although not all galley slaves were West Africans, many were.[16] Interestingly, the 1522 Santo Domingo rebellion is attributed to negros de jalof.

Jolof was an empire more or less contiguous with the northwestern portion of the contemporary state of Senegal. Founded in the thirteenth century, it was composed of a number of vassal states, including Waalo, Cayor, Siin, Salum, Baol, and Takrur (which later became Futa Toro). A multiethnic composite inhabited by Wolof, Mande speakers, Fulbe (or *hal pulaaren*, "speakers of Pulaar," who were further subdivided into settled, at times ethnically mixed, Tukulor communities and Fula or Fulani pastoralists), and the Sereer, Jolof in its pluralism foreshadowed the majesty of imperial Songhay in the interior of the West African savannah. Fourteenth- and fifteenth-century references to negros de jalof therefore refer to multiple ethnolinguistic groupings, among whom the Wolof may have been prominent.

After the middle of the fifteenth century, a number of arguably interrelated events eventually led to the disintegration of Jolof into its constituent components. The old Malian empire, whose outer western provinces included polities in Senegambia, went into decline (though it lingered in atrophied condition through the seventeenth century), leaving a power vacuum in the upper and middle Niger valleys filled by imperial Songhay. The transition from Mali to Songhay, however, encouraged vassal states in Senegambia to also consider independence. With profits to be made from trading with the slaving Portuguese along the coast, and an obligation to protect the citizenry from falling prey to that very traffic, vassal states asserted their interests. Between 1490 and 1512, Futa Toro broke away from Jolof suzerainty under a new, nominally Muslim Denyanke dynasty. Siin soon followed, and, by the middle of the sixteenth century, coastal Cayor gained its independence, effectively ending a 100-year process during which Jolof's imperial status (and very existence) steadily dissipated.

It was therefore out of an atmosphere charged with warfare, political transition, and social volatility that many of the negros de jalof were taken into Iberia.

---

[15] See Rout, *African Experience in Spanish America*, 15–16.
[16] See Charles Verlinden, *L'esclavage dans l'Europe médiévale*, 2 vols. (Bruge: De Tempe, 1955), vol. 1, 842.

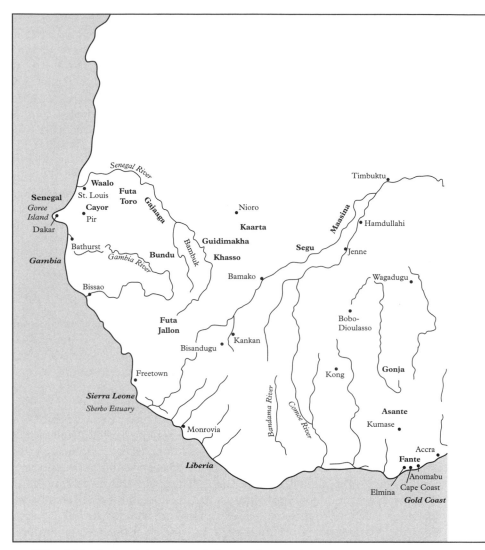

MAP 1. West Africa in the eighteenth and nineteenth centuries.

While many were certainly Muslim, it is likely that most were not. Islam had moved into the West African savannah through the Sahara by the beginning of the ninth century and as a result of Berber and Arab commercial activity. Some subsaharan African (or "Sudanese") merchants living in the savannah and the *sāḥil* (or sahel, literally "shore" or transition zone between the desert and the savannah) began to convert, so that Islam became associated with trade, especially long-distance networks of exchange. In some societies, political rulers also converted to the new religion with varying degrees of fidelity, so that Islam became a vehicle by which alliances between commercial and political elites were

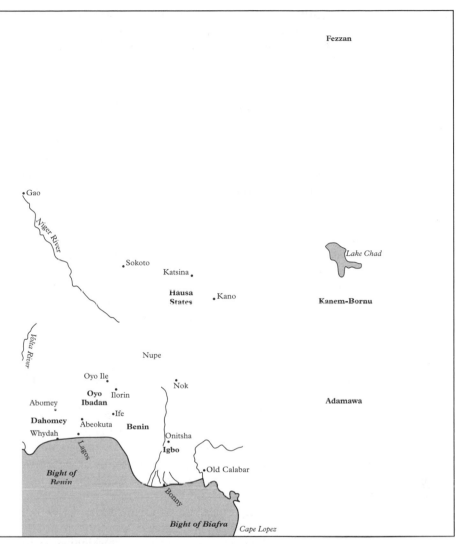

MAP 1. Continued.

forged. One source, for example, stated in 1455 that the religion of the "Zilofi" kingdom of "Senega" (a reference to the Wolof and other constituent groups of the Jolof empire) was "Muhammadanism: they are not, however, as are the white Moors, very resolute in this faith, especially the common people."[17] For many centuries thereafter, Islam in Senegambia (and elsewhere in West Africa) remained the religion of merchants and rulers, the faith of the elite, who seldom interfered in the beliefs of the peasantry. Generally speaking, reformers

[17] See G. R. Crone, ed. and trans., *The Voyages of Cadamosto* (London: Hakluyt Society, 1937), 31.

in the fifteenth and sixteenth centuries sought to correct the unorthodoxy of the court, but fundamental, widespread religious transformation did not take place until the eighteenth and nineteenth centuries, upon the heels of numerous, reverberating *jihāds*, or holy wars. Whether Muslim or not, however, the majority in fifteenth-century Senegambia were quite familiar with Islam given its presence since the ninth century. Captives brought to Iberia, site of a flourishing Islamic culture, were made to work alongside Berbers in the galleys and elsewhere, where they soon came to realize that the monotheistic expressions of Christianity, Islam, and Judaism were the only faiths valued in their new surroundings. Although many received the Christian rite of baptism, others were deeply influenced by contact with North African Muslims, converting in some cases while repenting in others. The so-called ladino, therefore, was in some instances an undercover Muslim practicing the delicate art of dissimulation, permissible under certain circumstances in Islam.[18] The New World provided an opportunity to unmask.

Evidence for the West African Muslim presence comes from a number of sources, including records from the Portuguese Inquisition. Accounts of enslaved West African Muslims attempting to flee Lisbon by sea include that of the gelofe Zambo (a name to be discussed later), who attempted to abscond by land the following year (1566). Under examination, he revealed that he was a Muslim before his capture in West Africa, and that he continued to practice Islam even after his forced Christian baptism in Lisbon.[19] Beyond the anecdotal, however, there is significant indication in Pike's discussion of sixteenth-century Seville that many captive West Africans underwent a counter acculturative experience in Spain, actually strengthening their allegiance to Islam. In 1492 and 1502, Isabella issued edicts requiring Moors and Jews to either convert to Christianity or suffer exile. The *mudéjares* (originally a term of derision for Muslims in northern Iberia who made pacts with and worked for Christians) submitted to conversion rites between 1502 and 1505 and saw their mosque turned into a church and the old *morería* (walled Moorish quarters), the Adarvejo, dismantled. Forcibly converted and subsequently called moriscos ("Christian Moors"), they remained a tightly knit community, maintaining their own language (*algarabía*) while abstaining from wine and swine. Numerically a minority in Seville with a population of about 6,000, their success in adhering to Islam was such that in 1588 the Sevillian official Alonso Gutiérrez "claimed that they were real Moslems like those in North Africa and that, they exercised the Christian religion only when forced and for purposes of subterfuge." Dominguez Ortiz likewise maintains that, in contrast to Africans who were born in Spain and became sincere Christians, Moors "seldom abandoned Islam," and that, following the fall of Grenada, although they were "theoretically converted," the moriscos, "descendants of the ancient Moors, [were] in reality Spaniards

---

[18] See, for example, Qur'ān *sūra al-Nahl*, v. 107.

[19] See James H. Sweet, *Recreating Africa: Culture, Kinship, and Religion in the African-Portuguese World, 1441–1770* (Chapel Hill and London: U. of North Carolina Press, 2003), 89–91.

of the mahometan religion." Pike concurs, observing that most of the period's official documents were of the opinion that the moriscos were endogamous in order "to preserve Moslem rites and practices and to prevent any real religious assimilation... and available evidence seems to verify it."[20]

Muslims had controlled parts of al-Andalus for nearly a millennium. The depth of their resistance to the rise of Castile and Aragon can be measured by the unsuccessful Alpujarras rebellion (1568–70) and its aftermath in the 1570s and 1580s, when a deluge of refugees from Grenada poured into Seville. In 1580, a morisco conspiracy was uncovered in Seville, in which Fernando Muley, otherwise known as Fernando Enríquez, was alleged to have held clandestine meetings in his home with moriscos from Cordova, Ecija, and other towns, in which they purportedly plotted to take Seville and then move through the rest of al-Andalus with North African and Turkish aid. The morisco community was placed under severe restrictions, as they were again in 1596 when it was feared that the English attack on Cádiz would lead to a morisco uprising. With the exception of enslaved persons, the moriscos would eventually be expelled from Seville in January of 1610.

Although the vast majority of the moriscos of sixteenth–century Seville were free and only a minority enslaved, most of the free moriscos were impoverished and unskilled, working as stevedores, carriers, and as farm hands on occasion. It is very probable, then, that the lives of the slave and the free morisco were not very different, since they essentially performed the same tasks and worked in close proximity. Although the Moorish and morisco slaves were distinguished as *esclavos blancos*, "Negro, Moorish, and Morisco slaves made up a sizable and conspicuous part of the population of Seville," with West Africans in the servile majority. There was similar interaction between various Muslim communities in Portugal. Examples include the 1554 case of the gelofe "Francisco," who unsuccessfully plotted to escape by sea with so-called Turkish slaves "Antônio" and "Pedro," and the 1564 attempt of the gelofe "Antônio" and two other "Turks," which was equally unsuccessful.[21]

With the "discovery" of the New World and increased importation of West Africans into Seville, it became second only to Lisbon as a slave entrepot. In fact, the first enslaved West Africans to enter the Americas came from Seville, some having been born there. It is therefore the case that many of these captives, among whom negros de jalof featured large, had undergone a different kind of seasoning (or preseasoning) in Iberia in that they had ostensibly become Christians, but in all probability they had moved more firmly into the Muslim camp.

The last thing the Spanish wanted was for the New World to evolve into another theater of war in their protracted and costly struggle with Islam. A

---

[20] See Pike, *Aristocrats and Traders*, 154–175; Antonio Dominguez Ortiz, "La esclavitud en Castilla durante la edad moderna," in *Estudios de historia social de España* (Madrid: Instituto Balmes de Sociologia), vol. 2, 373, 394–95.

[21] See Sweet, *Recreating Africa*, 90–91.

1501 decree therefore banned Jews, Moors, heretics, and "New Christians" from entering the Americas.[22] The same decree, however, allowed for the passage of those "born in the power of the Christians." The distinction between new converts and individuals born into a condition of subservience reflects difficulties in Iberia with the unanticipated acculturative experience of persons who became ladinos after having been Muslims (or Jews or something else). However, the exception made for those "born in the power" meant that an unspecified number of "black and mulatto servitors" made the April 1502 landing in Hispaniola with Nicolás de Ovando. The 1501 royal proclamation also did not categorically rule out sufficiently socialized ladinos originally born in West Africa, and de Ovando's cook, a ladino with twenty to thirty indigenous assistants, modeled preferable behavior. The story goes that whenever one of the assistants complained about anything, the cook "took a dagger and stabbed the person in the neck. When asked why he did such a thing, the Negro responded that it was only a 'little slap.' This cynical response led to a proverb in Spain that [was] fashionable during this period: 'God protect you from the little slap of the Fulani *loro*.'"[23]

Notwithstanding de Ovando's Fulani (Pullo) cook, the creation of maroon communities by 1503 suggests that the attempt to screen or filter slave imports was ineffective, and that ladinos with counter-acculturative experiences were indeed arriving. De Ovando's 1503 request to halt further shipments of ladinos was partially premised on the notion that indigenous labor could be satisfactorily exploited, but death and resistance soon redirected his attention. Hispaniola's estimated autochthonous population of 100,000 in 1492 declined to 30,000 by 1514, and it would drop further still to 500 by 1570. Shipments of Africans therefore resumed, with seventeen esclavos negros arriving in January of 1505 to either work in the gold mines or in the fields. Evidence that contraband Africans were continuing to arrive can be found in Ferdinand's 1506 order to de Ovando "concerning the expulsion of all Berber slaves, reiterating that he allow to enter the island neither a rebellious slave nor one raised with moriscos." In 1510 another 250 West Africans were shipped to work the mines, so that by 1514 some 1,000 so-called blacks and ladinos outnumbered the 689 Europeans in Hispaniola.[24]

---

[22] See Carlos Larrazabal Blanco, *Los negros y la esclavitud en Santo Domingo* (Santo Domingo: Postigo, 1975), 13–14; Rout, *African Experience in Spanish America*, 22–24.

[23] See Carlos Esteban Deive, *La esclavitud del negro en Santo Domingo (1492–1844)* (Santo Domingo: Museo del Hombre Dominico, 1980), 268: "Dios, te garde de la bofetafilla de fulano loro." The term *loro* is defined by Scelle as a person with a "red or chestnut color bordering on black." Also see Georges Scelle, *La traite négrière aux Indes de Castille: contrats et traités d'assiento* (Paris: Librairie de la Société du Recueil J. B. Sirez et du Journal du Palais, 1906), vol. 1, 221–22.

[24] See Larrazal Blanco, *Los negros y la esclavitud en Santo Domingo*, 13–14; Rout, *African Experience in Spanish America*, 22–24; Mellafe, *La introducción de la esclavitud negra en Chile*, 11; Carlos Esteban Deive, *La esclavitud del negro en Santo Domingo (1492–1844)* (Santo Domingo: Museo del Hombre Dominico, 1980), 23–26.

The 1516 appeal of Dominican friar Bartolomé de Las Casas to prohibit enslavement of Native Americans while promoting the captivity of Europeans and Africans had the effect of reinvigorating commerce in the latter.[25] Charles I restarted the shipment of Africans in 1517 that had been briefly halted the previous year. Up until this time the crown had resisted the notion of direct slave trafficking between Africa and the New World, fearing certain Africans were antagonistic to Christianity and would contaminate the indigenous population. "It was for this reason that only blacks born in the power of Christians, or who had at least resided on the Peninsula long enough to be baptized, were permitted in America."[26] However, the *asiento* or exclusive rights system was introduced in 1518, a year that also witnessed the beginning of direct shipments from Africa to the New World. In addition to economic considerations, the direct shipments were the result of a growing demand for unacculturated, non-Spanish-speaking Africans, called *bozales*, who were believed to be "more submissive and stronger than [the ladinos], who had already proven their capacity to rebel when confronted with degrading work. For the Spanish, the *bozal* was free of the contamination of the vices and bad habits of the western world."[27] What the authorities apparently did not fully appreciate, however, was that the ladinos and the bozales often enough shared the same West African background, bonds subject to even greater strengthening when both groups were reduced to a similar fate of bondage, toiling at the same tasks, struggling on the same physical site. The indigenous population also resisted, and at some point prior to 1522 a local named "Enriquillo" led a revolt and established a maroon society. This community was receptive to absconding Africans, who daily added to their numbers. It did not take long for all of the elements to come together and for "the yolofes to act on their own behalf." The result was the 1522 Santo Domingo rebellion.[28]

In conceding the need for direct shipments from Africa, the crown had attempted "to exclude slaves suspected of Islamic leanings, such as the notorious *esclavos Gelofes* (Wolofs) of the Guinea area, many of whom not only were infidels but were prone to insubordination as well."[29] The gelofes (Senegambians) had established a reputation as "indomitable, disobedient, and ready to rebel."[30] While described as "blacks of excellent appearance, tall and athletic, their limbs slender and strong, with shiny, jet-black skin," Senegambians came to be seen as the premier examples of "evil-natured blacks, the true 'bête noir' of the trade, the bills of slave sale plainly stating their origins to avoid future complaints: 'The jelofe I sell you' – declares a slave trader to a buyer ... – 'with

---

[25] See Mellafe, *La introducción de la esclavitud negra en Chile*, 11; Palmer, *Slaves of the White God*, 8–9.
[26] See Frederick P. Bowser, *The African Slave in Colonial Peru, 1524–1650* (Stanford, CA: Stanford U. Press, 1974), 27–28.
[27] See Esteban Deive, *La esclavitud del negro en Santo Domingo*, 35.
[28] See Guillot, *Negros rebeldes y negros cimarrones*, 79–80.
[29] See Bowser, *African Slave in Colonial Peru*, 28.
[30] See Scelle, *La traite négrière aux Indes de Castille*, vol. 1, 222–23.

the understanding that he is a drunkard and a thief and a gambler, and is sick and demon-possessed.'"[31]

In putting down the 1522 Santo Domingo revolt, authorities concluded that it had been waged by "a combination of Muslim-influenced *gelofes* and disgruntled *ladinos*," and they reissued decrees in 1530 and 1532 to ban the importation of enslaved Moors, Jews, whites, and ladinos into the New World; only African bozales who were not gelofes were to be accepted.[32] "But," Esteban Deive points out, "as the regime of exploitation was the same for one as for the other, the *bozal* would soon imitate the slave rebelling or resisting slavery by various means. In the ordinances of 1528, sent to prevent and remedy the running away of black slaves, it is said that most of the runaways were *bozales*."[33] Therefore, while a number of the enslaved were Muslim and were responding out of an offended Islamic sensibility and within the context of a long-running conflict with Christian Iberia, others were neither Muslim nor Christian. The Muslim element was important in the resistance of the enslaved in Hispaniola, but it was not the only factor.

Senegambians continued to participate in acts of rebellion in Hispaniola through the middle of the sixteenth century, after which they gradually begin to disappear from the record. Even so, "it would still be possible to find some yolofe leader in the chronicles of the rebellions, leading slaves from another area of origin."[34] The ongoing Senegambian presence can be seen in the 1547 public auction of Hernando Gorjón's sugar mill or ingenio on the outskirts of Azua, for example, when the following persons were among those being sold: Juan Bran, Pero Bran, María Bran, Ana Jolofa, Gonzalo Mandinga, Mandinga, Pedro Zape, Juan Zape, and Diego Jolofo. Mandinga and Diego Jolofo were both over seventy years of age, having labored as a shepherd ("pastor") and cowhand, respectively. The *cofradías* or brotherhoods in sixteenth-century Hispaniola were organized around African ethnicity, and the fact that Nuestra Señora de la Candelaria was partially composed of mandingas is further demonstration of Senegambian strength. A September 1587 census of Santo Domingo lists Pedro Gómez, a free black, along with "Fulano Ceballos, mulatto, shoemaker," the latter a probable Pullo (pl. Fulbe) and therefore possible Muslim, with features akin to those of mixed-race persons (and very typical of the Fulbe). In the early seventeenth century, thirty-two Africans captured in the mountains of the Baoruco, who had become a "gang of warriors," included Juan Faula, Juan Mandingo, Beatriz Mandinga, María Mandinga, and Francisco Mandinga. Another so-called gang of eight runaways included Antón Xolofo and Ana Mandinga. Even into the eighteenth century, there is evidence of Senegambians who may have been Muslims, including Vincente Mandinga, who was married to Luisa Mandinga in 1717. In 1726, Damián Castillo was described as a free black of the "casta *mandinga*." As late as October of 1796, Fermin Jara (whom

[31] See Guillot, *Negros rebeldes y negros cimarrones*, 24–25.
[32] See Rout, *African Experience in Spanish America*, 24.
[33] See Esteban Deive, *La esclavitud del negro en Santo Domingo*, 35.
[34] Ibid., 98–99, 234–38, 260; also see Guillot, *Negros rebeldes y negros cimarrones*, 26.

Deive claims came from Bornu, a Muslim land), Valentín Senegus, Lorenzo Senegui, and Basilio Sengui were among thirty-one people arrested after a revolt on the hacienda of Boca Nigria. The surnames of the last three reflect a change in the way Senegambians were identified almost 300 years after their initial introduction to the island, but their residence suggests that the Muslim presence on the island spans the partition of Hispaniola into Santo Domingo and Saint Domingue.

When Senegambians were not busy revolting, they were involved in the early colonial economy. With the importation of bozales, slaveholders were positioned to differentiate between them and the ladinos on bases other than religion and culture. In particular, slaveholders became aware of the particular skills Senegambians brought with them, and there were conscious efforts to match those skills with tasks in the colony. Thus, "it is perhaps no wonder that all the *vaqueros* and *ganaderos* (cowboys) on the mid-sixteenth-century Hispaniola estates were not only Africans but from Wolof, Fula, and Mandinga areas, where there was a strong equestrian and cattle-raising tradition."[35] Indeed, Juan de Castellanos (1522–1607), having traveled through Puerto Rico, Venezuela, and Colombia, wrote a song depicting the prestige of the Senegambian "cowboy," first published in 1586, part of which is as follows:

> They have as much land as they like
> Temperate and fecund,
> Their numbers grow greatly,
> Increasing rapidly,
> So much that now they appear in Guinea,
> Haiti, Cuba, Saint Joan and Jamaica;
> Among them are the warlike Gilosos
> With the vain arrogance of gentry.[36]

---

[35] See John Thornton, *Africa and Africans in the Making of the Atlantic World, 1400–1680* (Cambridge, England: Cambridge U. Press, 1992), 135, endnote 17.

[36] See Juan de Castellanos, *Elegíade varones ilustres de Indias* (Bogotá, Colombia: Gerardo Rivas Moreno, 1997), 100, elegy 5, canto 2. The song is as follows:

> Destos cada cual es un señorío,
> Gentil y principal heredamiento;
> Tienen necesidad de gran gentío
> Para tener cabal aviamiento;
> Faltaba ya de indios el avío
> Por el universal acabamiento,
> De suerte que hay en estas heredades
> Negros en escesivas cantidades.
>
> Tienen la tierra tal cual se desea
> En temple y abundancia cosa rica,
> En grande aumento va cada ralea,
> Y con gran vigor se multiplica,
> Tanto, que ya parecen ser guinea,
> Haiti, Cuba, Saint Joan y Jamaica;
> Destos son los Gilosos muy guereros
> Con vana presuncion de caballeros

This process of labor differentiation was repeated elsewhere in the Americas. It was critical to the genesis of "class" distinctions among the enslaved, about which more will be stated later.

Hispaniola was not the only New World site of rebellion in the early sixteenth century. Revolts broke out wherever the enslaved were present: Puerto Rico in 1527, Colombia in 1529, the Panamanian town of Acla in 1530, Panama City in 1531, the Venezuelan town of Coro in 1532, and San Pedro, Honduras in 1548.[37] The revolt in Puerto Rico is of particular interest in that Senegambians were implicated as the principal troublemakers. Nicolás de Ovando, governor of Hispaniola, may have been responsible for introducing the first Africans to the "island of San Juan" in 1509, when he sent a group from Santo Domingo to Ponce. By the following year, an unspecified number of Africans were on the island along with 200 Europeans. It was not long before the *boricua* or native population began to decline, and "coinciding with the rapid indigenous extinction was the exhaustion of the few sources of gold available on the island." Colonists, faced with the choice of either abandoning the island or developing an alternative source of income, chose the latter and began growing sugarcane. "It quickly became apparent that successful sugarcane production required the use of many arms," and Africans were identified as the necessary source. Tomás de Castellón began the first ingenio on the grasslands of San Germán (contemporary Añasco) in 1523, and "many African slaves took active part in the cultivation and production of sugarcane on this *ingenio*." Sugarcane plantations began to develop elsewhere in Puerto Rico after de Castellón's success, ending the brief mining period of the island's history around 1530 while initiating its agricultural phase.[38]

The 1530 royal decree of Charles V, banning "Berber slaves of the caste of Moors, Jews, or mulattoes" from entering the Americas, was therefore issued in response to events in both Hispaniola and Puerto Rico and for the purpose of suspending "the sending of black jelofes and berbers." However, as Senegambians continued to arrive and the legislation proved ineffective, another royal decree was issued in 1531, forbidding the trade in enslaved Berbers to the Spanish colonies. It was the royal proclamation of September 1532, according to Diaz Soler, that identified the Senegambians as the party responsible "'for the revolts of the blacks in the island of San Juan and others,'" as the "'Gelofe slaves are arrogant, disobedient, rebellious, and incorrigible,'" and that again attempted to prohibit their entry into Puerto Rico without special permission. As if to erase any doubt, Governor Francisco Manuel de Lando sent a representative to the court of Charles V two years later, "accusing the *jelofes* with the insurrections taking place in the Antilles." All of these measures were

---

[37] See Rafael López Jiménez, *Rebeldá esclava en el Caribe* (Veracruz: Gobierno del Estado de Veracruz, 1992), 50–51.

[38] See Luis M. Diaz Soler, *Historia de la esclavitud negra en Puerto Rico* (Rio Piedras: Universidad de Puerto Rico, 1974), 28–53.

MAP 2. P. Latin America, 1820 (after the Wars for Independence).

futile, however, since slavetraders continued to bring Africans into the colonies with little concern for their origins.[39]

Sources for Africans bound for what would become Latin America would change in the third quarter of the sixteenth century, resulting in many more from West Central Africa, but West African Muslims continued to find their way into Puerto Rico (see Map 2). Planters on the island, lacking the resources

[39] Ibid., 203–04; also see Guillot, *Negros rebeldes y negros cimarrones*, 26.

to import sufficient numbers of enslaved agriculturalists, began depending on a clandestine trade with English traffickers who exchanged persons for tobacco, salted meat, and hogs. The trade also provided planters a means to avoid exorbitant taxation. By the third quarter of the seventeenth century, the island was importing "blacks coming from Senegambia, known as *mandingas*. The illegal commerce reached such a peak that in 1678 the governor of the island, Don Juan de Robles Lorenzana, decided to appoint a war captain to put an end to the contraband that the English and other nationalities were bringing in from the lesser Antilles."[40] The mention of the mandingas or Mande-speakers is significant because, although not all Mande were Muslim, a great many were, especially by this period in time. Some of the Mande groups constituted the core of the old Malian empire established in the thirteenth century, and they had therefore enjoyed a long affiliation with the faith. That these more recent Muslims were no longer referred to as negros de jalof reflects both the demise of the West African kingdom of Jolof and the fact that it was the Mande who would come to be universally associated with Islam in the Americas. Of course, the Mande were always a part of the Senegambian contingent, where they were concentrated along the Gambia and Casamance Rivers, but there were also Mande-speaking populations in the upper Niger valley as well. The non-Muslim Susu and Bambara of Segu and Kaarta dominated the latter area into the early nineteenth century, and they eventually converted to Islam.

However, the Mande were also in "Sierra Leone," or what is now Guinea, Guinea-Bissau, Sierra Leone, and portions of Liberia, where many, such as the Jallonke of the Futa Jallon massif, began to convert to Islam in the eighteenth century in the course of a bitter holy war. Apolitical, Muslim, nonproselytizing Mande trading communities known as the Juula connected West Africa from the savannah to the forest, and from the Atlantic to Lake Chad. It is therefore the case that many of the Mande were viewed as staunch Muslims, and it is the Mande, not the Wolof or Sereer or even the Fulbe, who occupy the most prominent (and notorious) place in early Latin America's memory of the Muslim presence. About this there will be much more to say.[41]

---

[40] See Diaz Soler, *Historia de la esclavitud negra en Puerto Rico*, 83.

[41] On the Mande, see J. Suret-Canale and Boubacar Barry, "The Western Atlantic Coast to 1800," in J. F. A. Ajayi and Michael Crowder, eds., *History of West Africa*, 2nd ed. (New York: Colombia U. Press, 1976), vol. 1; Jean Boulegue and Jean Suret-Canale, "The Western Atlantic Coast," in J. F. A. Ajayi and Michael Crowder, eds., *History of West Africa* (New York: Longman, 1985), vol. 1; Walter Rodney, *A History of the Upper Guinea Coast, 1545–1800* (Oxford, England: Monthly Review Press, 1970; Boubacar Barry, *La Sénégambie du Xve au XIXe siècle: Traite négrière, Islam et conquête* (Paris: L' Harmattan, 1988); Boubacar Barry, *Le royaume du Waalo: le Sénégal avant le conquête*, rev. ed. (Paris: Editions Karthala, 1985); Ivor Wilks, "Wangara, Akan and Portuguese in the Fifteenth and Sixteenth Centuries," *Journal of African History* 23 (1982): no. 2, 333–49 (Part I) and no. 4, 463–72 (Part II); Richard Roberts, *Warriors, Merchants, and Slaves: The State and the Economy in the Middle Niger Valley, 1700–1914* (Stanford, CA: Stanford U. Press, 1987); James Searing, *West African Slavery and Atlantic Commerce: The Senegal River*

In addition to Hispaniola and Puerto Rico, there was also a Senegambian presence in early-sixteenth-century Costa Rica and Panama. There is little specific information on the former, but it is recorded that the only African known by name in the colony before 1574 was a Pedro Gilofo, also known as Pedro Fulupo. The two monikers reinforce the observation that "Gilofo," a form of the term *jelofe* or *gelofe,* does not really refer to a specific group but rather to the area of Senegambia. "Fulupo," in contrast, strongly suggests that Pedro was Fulbe, a group that increasingly becomes identified with Islam throughout West Africa. On September 1, 1540, in the town of Orisco, local official Hernán Sánchez de Badjoz sentenced Pedro to die for having spent twenty days away from the property of his holder Alonso García and in the territory of "indios de guerra." With the revolts of Hispaniola and Puerto Rico and elsewhere as context, officials determined to preempt any potential mass uprising in Costa Rica. Pedro the Fulbe was boiled alive.[42]

Of course, Africans of various backgrounds would arrive in Costa Rica in the course of the seventeenth and eighteenth centuries, including groups from Cape Verde, Dahomey, West Central Africa, and Gold Coast. The area of "Guinea" included Senegambia and Sierra Leone and contained Muslim groups, as did the "Sudanese" category. Because groups from these areas and categories arrived in Costa Rica, where they developed differing reputations, it is highly likely that Muslims were among them. Thus, Duncan and Meléndez write that "those from Guinea were also more highly esteemed by the Spanish, so that their value was greater than that of the others, as they were sharp-witted, beautiful and well-disposed. The Sudanese were also very appreciated, not like the mandingo, who although tame were considered prone to theft."[43] This disparagement of the Mande is the beginning of a mantra, as will be seen.

Resistance was apparently a bit more organized in sixteenth-century Panama. There had been a number of complaints about runaway communities, or "Isthmian cimarrones," prior to 1556, but by that year the area's problems in this regard fully surfaced. One "Ballano" had established himself as the head of a maroon community, having been able "to attract both ladino and bozal Blacks by virtue of his royal African descent." Ballano's community constituted a threat to the interests of the Spanish, who subsequently succeeded in convincing Ballano to attend peace talks at a banquet site. In anticipation of Toussaint L'Ouverture's experience with the French, Ballano was captured and eventually taken to Spain; unlike Toussaint, Ballano was given a royal pension and allowed to live out his days in Seville.

Most of Ballano's followers, after some initial trepidation, proceeded to settle for peace with the Spanish in 1574 and 1579; in exchange, they received their

Valley, 1700–1860 (Cambridge, MA: Cambridge U. Press, 1993); Charlotte A. Quinn, *Mandingo Kingdoms of the Senegambia* (Evanston, IL: Northwestern U. Press, 1972).

[42] See Quince Duncan and Carlos Meléndez, *El negro en Costa Rica* (San José, Costa Rica: Editorial Costa Rica, 1976), 19–20, 25; Rout, *African Experience in Spanish America,* 101.

[43] See Duncan and Meléndez, *El negro en Costa Rica,* 21–24.

freedom, possession of their land, assurances of nonbelligerence, and a degree of autonomy. About 200 in number, they founded a new town called Santiago del Principe, only to relocate later in an area near Nombre de Dios. They finally moved to Porto Bello in 1585 along with the rest of the population of Nombre de Dios.[44]

There were, however, those who did not go along with the peace, and in a "region formerly controlled by Ballano," a new community of about 300 persons formed. Led by Antón Mandinga, the maroons began to harass and otherwise threaten the security of the area. That the community was led by a Mande-speaker who was possibly Muslim suggests that others were Muslim or at least familiar with Islam. The extent to which Islam may have informed the activities of this breakaway group cannot be determined, but there apparently was considerable debate over how the community should respond to the English presence in a land claimed by Spain. The schism is discussed in the correspondence of Diego de Trias Trejo to the Spanish crown, and, based on intelligence supplied to him by a captured *cimarrón* (runaway), it depicts a leader isolated and on the run by May of 1578.[45] By 1581, with or without Antón Mandinga as leader, the cimarrones were able to negotiate their own freedom, lands, and other concessions with the Spanish.

*   *   *

While Muslims and others of African descent were raising literal and figurative cane in Hispaniola, Puerto Rico, Panama, and Costa Rica, they were also arriving in Central America in considerable numbers. There is evidence of a Muslim presence there as late as the early nineteenth century, when Charles Napier Bell claimed to have learned the traditions of the Mosquitos of Nicaragua from an old woman who was both Mande and Muslim.[46] Most of the evidence, however, comes from Mexico.

Notwithstanding activity in Hispaniola and elsewhere in the New World, Mexico and Peru were in fact the two largest importers of captives in the

---

[44] See Rodriguez, "Cimarrón Revolts and Pacification in New Spain," 138–51.

[45] The document says the following:

> [The captured *cimarrón*] said that there are great disagreements and differences among the negroes. They complain of Anton Mandinga, who gave admission and favour to the English; and he says they are resolved to kill him, maintaining that because of him there came upon them the evils and damage which have been done them. This same thing have I understood from the other negroes whom I hold prisoners, and from the one who surrendered. And Anton Mandinga himself must have comprehended as much, for after I fell upon his village and burned it and destroyed it and captured his women and children, he had been so overcome by fear that nothing is certainly known concerning him, nor has he rejoined the other blacks.

> Document no. 67, "Diego de Trias Trejo to the Crown, Panama, 15 May 1578," in Irene A. Wright, ed., *Spanish Documents Concerning English Voyages to the Spanish Main, 1569–1580* (London: Hakluyt, 1932), 217.

[46] See Peter Linebaugh and Marcus Rediker, *The Many-Headed Hydra: Sailors, Slaves, Commoners, and the Hidden History of the Revolutionary Atlantic* (Boston: Beacon Press, 2000), 165.

sixteenth and seventeenth centuries; between 1521 and 1639, Mexico alone imported around 110,525 Africans, who were subsequently auctioned at the various *feria de los negros*. By the time of formal emancipation in 1827, some 200,000 Africans had labored in Mexico. Their contributions were critical in light of the Great Dying, which saw the native population of Central Mexico plummet from an estimated 27,650,000 in 1519 to 1,075,000 by 1605.[47]

Palmer has divided the African experience of enslavement in Mexico into three phases. The first was a period of gradual numerical increase, beginning in 1519 when the first enslaved person "arrived in the service of the Conquistadores" and ending in 1580 following a four-year devastating plague (probably typhus). The second phase, 1580 to 1650, witnessed a "meteoric rise" in both demand and importation of enslaved labor; the final period, from 1650 to 1827, was characterized by the diminution of the enslaved population and a partial recovery of the native contingent. The initial labor shortage created by the Great Dying was compounded by the abolition of Native American enslavement in 1542, and it led to the increased use of Africans in the silver mines, which opened in 1534, and in the cane fields a few years earlier. Africans had experience working in the mines and galleys of Spain and Portugal, where they also served as domestics, refuse collectors, and porters. The New World was therefore in some sense more of the same for these ladinos, who continued in the silver mines of Zacatecas and Durango as well as in all of the other previous roles, to which were added new ones: dyers and other textile workers, gilders, blacksmiths, personal attendants, hospital and slaughterhouse workers, sugarcane cultivators, and ranchers (*rancheros*).

Urban areas had a higher proportion of enslaved persons than did the rural districts, where the larger haciendas were composed of ten to twenty captive persons (and some held many more). The practice of *jornal*, or hiring out per diem, could be found in the countryside as well as the towns. Partially as a result of these differing labor assignments, enslaved society experienced stratification: Persons attained elevated status "by the possession of certain valuable skills, such as sugar processing (sugar master), and through their prior status in Africa." Social layering was also informed by degrees of acculturation, so that the ladinos were seen as superior to the bozales and were therefore found in more highly valued skilled jobs with greater frequency, notwithstanding their common origins and capacity to coalesce. Multiracial categories, phenomena familiar to Iberia, were further complicated by the indigenous factor and the absence of European women, and they also contributed to the hierarchical arrangement: The so-called *mulatto* (European–African), *mestizo* (European–indigenous), and *castizo* (mestizo–European) were joined by the morisco (in this context, a "mulatto"-European issue) and the *zambo*, the result of an indigenous and African union. The *zambo*, or *sambo*, was also employed in Lima, Peru, where such a person was described as having a "stronger taint, with nappy

---

[47] See Palmer, *Slaves of the White God*, 1–4, 27–29; Philip Curtin, *The African Slave Trade. A Census* (Madison: U. of Wisconsin Press, 1969).

hair and thick lips." Qualifying descendants of these unions, however, could eventually obtain *cédulas de gracias al sacar*, or certificates declaring the purchaser "cleansed" of "impure origins."[48] Those who could not erase the taint remained relatively privileged, for "it was the mulatto bastards and *criollos morenos*, for example, who were generally taught to be blacksmiths, cobblers, brick masons, carpenters, or tailors."[49] The term *zambo* is of some interest in that its pronunciation is very similar to *Sambo*, often a corruption of *Samba* meaning "second son" in Pulaar, the language of the Fulbe. Since the foregoing categories of racial admixture are based on phenotype, it is possible that indigenous–African progeny were so called because of their analogous appearance to the Fulbe. Suffice it to say at this juncture that, although this particular word may reflect the influence of the Fulbe in Mexico, additional evidence verifies their presence. Again, many of the Fulbe were Muslim.

Until 1570, Senegambia, or "Upper Guinea" as it was called by the Spanish and "Guinea of Cape Verde" by the Portuguese, was the principal source of African captives for the Americas by virtue of its physical proximity to Iberia. The *castas de rios de Guinea* or "nations of the River of Guinea" tended to be divided into three constituents: gelofes, mandingas, and *biafras*.[50] The arrival of competition in the form of English, French, and Dutch slavers resulted in higher prices for Senegambian captives, encouraging the Portuguese to move further south. After 1570, São Tomé became a leading entrepot for the enslaved, called "castas de San Tomé," who hailed from West Central Africa and were distinguished as *loandas*, *benguelas*, *congos*, and *manicongos*, a mix of place and group names. Individuals from both Senegambia and West Central Africa are therefore reflected in mid-sixteenth-century Mexico. Palmer has calculated a representative sample of 196 African-born "Afro-Mexicans" from 1545 to 1556, and the results show the predominance of Senegambians: 80.1 percent were from Senegambia (including Guinea-Bissau), 12.3 percent were from elsewhere in West Africa, 7.1 percent hailed from West Central and southern Africa, and 0.5 percent were from North Africa. This accords well with Boyd–Bowman's analysis of 84 Africans (for whom origins are recorded out of a total of 167) in Puebla de los Angeles (Mexico) from 1540 to 1555, in which 90 percent were from Senegambia and the remaining 10 percent from West Central Africa. Riley's figures for the Cuernavaca area from 1522 to 1549, showing only 43 percent hailing from Senegambia, differ because the total includes persons of unknown origin.

[48] See Max Radiguet, *Souvenir de l'Amérique espagnole* (Paris: Librairie Nouvelle, 1874), 57–58; Palmer, *Slaves of the White God*, 3–7, 36–44; Rout, *African Experience in Spanish America*, 126–61. Rout discusses multiple racial variations.

[49] See Rout, *African Experience in Spanish America*, 78.

[50] Ibid., 28–30. Peter Boyd-Bowman, in his "Negro Slaves in Early Colonial Mexico," *The Americas* 26 (October 1969): 142, cites Murdock on the *biafra*, stating there is "a tribe called *Biafada*, *Biafar*, or *Bifra*, in the Senegambia region.... Tempting though it would be to identify these *Biafra* with the present-day Biafrans of S. E. Nigeria, the evidence, alas, is against it." See George P. Murdock, *Africa, Its People and Their Culture History* (New York: McGraw-Hill, 1959), 111–21.

Palmer demonstrates that, from 1615 to 1640, there was a dramatic shift in the export pattern from Senegambia to São Tomé, so that three out of four slavers listed "Angola" as their destination, consistent with a study of 402 Africans in the seventeenth century revealing that 75.4 percent were from West Central Africa and 20.9 percent from West Africa, thus reversing the sixteenth-century trend. Of the 196 Africans that Palmer surveyed in the mid-sixteenth century, 27 were gelofes and 14 were mandingas, accounting for 21 percent of the total. This compares with 13 "Jolofo" and 5 mandingas, or 22 percent, in Puebla de los Angeles, and, interestingly, 11 gelofes and 5 mandingas, again 22 percent, for the Cuernavaca area.[51]

Aguirre Beltrán's study of Africans in Mexico is a rather thoroughgoing discussion of African ethnicity. That is, drawing on archival materials that include bills of sale, which were required (but often enough failed) to provide the origin, age, and sex of captives, Aguirre Beltrán is able to present a plausible and proportional sketch of the various groups arriving in Mexico. For example, he writes that "the Bambara entered our country under the name of Bambura." Of those who could have been Muslim, Aguirre Beltrán mentions the "Tucuxui," whom he identifies as the Tukulor, who, as has been pointed out, were Pulaar speakers as were the rest of the Fulbe or Fula: "The Fula, often mentioned, entered the country confused by the slavetraders with the Mandingos. They formed a completely different group, originally Caucasoid, but by being in contact with black peoples they absorbed a large amount of color. The Fula frequently appear in the slave manifests of the slave ships, but almost always by a different designation." Aguirre Beltrán's last statement is applicable to the whole of the Americas and not just Mexico, as he makes clear in the next sentence: "In Haiti, for example, they were known by the names Peul, Poulli, and Poulard; in Brazil they were called Fulani, Filanins, Fulbes and Fulas. They were divided into two classes: those called 'pretosfulos' and those called 'fula-fula,' the first being a mix of Fula and black while the second were pure Fula."[52] It is therefore possible that while the atypical features of the Fulbe (an observation repeatedly made all over the New World) may explain the term *zambo*, there can be no doubt that many of the Fulbe, including those in Mexico, were Muslim, some of whom made up part of the negros de jalof or gelofes.

Though the number of Fulbe arriving in Mexico would have steadily decreased (per Palmer's schema), their entrance into the Americas as a whole would have proceeded from at least three major zones of supply: Senegambia, Sierra Leone, and the Bight of Benin. In the interiors of all three areas, the Fulbe were engaged in a series of holy wars or jihāds, beginning with Futa

---

[51] See Palmer, *Slaves of the White God*, 20–23; Boyd-Bowman, "Negro Slaves in Early Colonial Mexico," 140–41; G. Michael Riley, "Labor in Cortesian Enterprise: The Cuernavaca Area, 1522–1549," *The Americas* 28 (January 1972): 278–87.

[52] See Gonzalo Aguirre Beltrán, *La población negra de México: Estudio ethnohistórico*, 2nd ed. (Mexico, D. F.: Fondo de Cultura Economica, 1972), 109–10.

Jallon (Sierra Leone) in the 1720s, through the conflict in Futa Toro (middle Senegal valley) in the 1770s, and erupting into truly large-scale activity with the 1818 jihād of Seku Amadu in Maasina (upper Niger valley) and the campaigns of *al-ḥājj* ʿUmar Tal in Senegambia and the upper Niger beginning in 1852. There were a number of other such conflicts; one of the most important centered in what is now Nigeria, and it will be examined in the chapter on Brazil. The Fulbe, together with other groups involved in such activity, were subject to capture just like everyone else, and therefore they show up from time to time in the fields, but particularly in the houses, of planters throughout the Americas. Their experience is most poignant in the American South, where they played an important role in the rise of social stratification among the African-derived.

The Wolof also entered Mexico in noticeable numbers up to the end of the sixteenth century, after which their representation dwindled, possibly as a result of their identification with revolts in Hispaniola and elsewhere.[53] It is very possible that the *yelofe* with whom William Collins became friends in 1572 was in fact Wolof. Collins, or Guillermo Cabello as he was known in Spanish, had sailed with Sir John Hawkins (slavetrader and plunderer of Spanish galleons) and had been captured and confined to the mines of Tasco along with about 1,000 Africans and twice as many Native Americans. Collins was something of a scholar and loved to converse with the Africans, "especially Juan Gelofe... bright and rebellious," who became quite taken with Collins upon learning from the latter that slavery did not exist in England, and that the English queen would soon send a fleet to rescue them and free the enslaved and empower them. "The yelofe, a leader well-informed of the sentiments of the slaves, assured him [Collins] that they would look forward to his wholehearted support." It would appear that the English rescue never took place.[54]

It was not the Wolof, however, with whom the Fulbe were confused in Mexico, but the Mande, for even though the Wolof gained a reputation as rebellious, their presence in Mexico and other parts of the New World was significant only in the sixteenth century, whereas various Mande-speakers arrived just as early and continued to arrive throughout the Americas and in larger numbers. Thus, it was the Mande, the so-called mandinga, who came to represent the typical African Muslim in many places. Aguirre Beltrán goes further, arguing that of all the various African groups, Muslim and non-Muslim, who came through Arguin in the sixteenth century, "those who formed the great Mande group were, without a doubt, the ones who exercised the greatest influence in Mexico, during the entire 16th century. They entered under the general designation of Mandingos and left as a souvenir of their presence in Nueva España a number of geographical places which bear their name and the survival of the tribal name as a popular designation of the devil." The equating of the Mande with Satan is, at one level, a reflection of the Iberian attitude toward Islam as well as the Spanish experience with African Muslims both in al-Andalus and the Americas. Notwithstanding the Spanish loathing of Islam,

[53] See Aguirre Beltrán, "Tribal Origins of Slaves in Mexico," 292–94.
[54] See Guillot, *Negros rebeldes y negros cimarrones*, 122.

they had centuries of experience whereby they had also come to respect it, such that in Mexico "it was soon seen that not all [Africans] were as wild or savage as had been preferred, but some possessed a level of highly developed culture: they knew Islamic writings and religion, such as the *mandingas*, or they were frankly resistant to slavery, as was true of the *gelofes*." Antagonism between Spaniard and Muslim can be observed in the redefinition of another word in Mexico, *marabout*, which originally referred to a Muslim holy man but also came to denote the devil. Though adversarial, the relationship between Spaniards and Muslims does not diminish the Mande contribution to the African sojourn in Mexico (and other places); indeed "it is easy to prove in colonial archives the role they played in the integration of the patterns of culture of the colony and the persistence of their influx will surely be recognized when ethnographic investigations motivated by the Negro groups which still live in Mexico are undertaken."[55]

Vincente Rossi adds another dimension to the origin of the negative characterization of the Mande in the Americas. Having somewhat erroneously established that the mandinga were from a "powerful kingdom" (they hailed from numerous polities), he writes that their leaders "were bribed by the Christians" into selling their war captives. This led to greater Mande involvement in warfare, resulting in an odious reputation among neighboring, victimized groups. It was church officials, Rossi argues, who were "the main traffickers in slaves," clandestinely working together with government officials and others to purchase captives from the slavetraders:

[The church] spread grotesque suspicions, using the unfortunate race's terror of the mandingo in order to produce a great fear of the devil, declaring him to be of mandingo nationality, which reawakened in the naive believers the vague memory of a horrible occurrence, which tore them away from a place where there were no white torturers.... And they fervently worshiped the High God to escape the perversity of the devil, a mandingo![56]

While perhaps placing too much emphasis on the role of the church in this matter (Africans captured by Muslims would need no help in remembering the experience), Rossi is useful in pointing out that the Spanish disdain for Muslims found resonance with certain African groups, thus helping to explain why pejorative connotations of the term *mandinga*, including such modifiers as "rebellious" "evil," and "naughty," were so pervasive.

Aguirre Beltrán found that the African presence in Mexico was not limited to West and West Central Africans. Somewhat surprisingly, he uncovered a number of Nguni-speakers from what is now South Africa – including the Xhosa, Zulu, and Sotho – who were sold in Sofala and carried to Mexico: "Of these tribes only the Xhosa who entered with the spelling Zoza, were known in

---

[55] See Aguirre Beltrán, "Tribal Origins of Slaves in Mexico," 280–81; Aguirre Beltrán, *La población negra de México*, 105–07, 160–61. Aguirre Beltrán defines *marabut* as "religious Moorish tribes." The term is also used to refer to the grave sites or shrines of holy men in Tunisia.

[56] See Vincente Rossi, *Cosas de Negros* (Buenos Aires: Librería Hachette, 1958; orig. pub., 1926), 222–23.

Mexico by their particular name." The reference to Sofala, however, refocuses attention on the theme of Islam in that Sofala was a major entrepot connecting East Africa and the Swahili coast with the Indian Ocean and the Persian Gulf. Concerning the Swahili city-states, where Islam had been long established at least since the tenth century, Aguirre Beltrán writes that Africans "from at least two of these sultanates appear on the inventories of slaves of the 16th century. The first, termed of Melin nationality, were taken from Melinda, today called Malinda.... The other sultanate from which Negroes were taken bound for Nueva España was that of Mozambique." Inclusion of the Mozambican dimension recalls that the slave trade was not confined to the Atlantic but also involved the Pacific, as early in the trade a small number of Mozambicans were shipped over the Pacific to Acapulco, Mexico, where they were inexplicably called "Chinese." Speculating that "Zibalo" or "Cibalo" groups came from Zanzibar, Aguirre Beltrán remarks that, whatever their prominence in the sixteenth century, by 1645 the Mozambicans "were few in Nueva España. In spite of this, they seem to have been somewhat numerous in the district of Queretaro, where cultural survivals point to the influence which they exerted: Mozambique was considered as a synonym for the devil."[57] That Muslims were concentrated in a particular area heightens the possibility that there may have been some corporate expression of their beliefs, constituting a threat to colonial authorities. It is very probable, then, that Mozambicans and the Swahili in general were identified as devils because they were Muslims, an approach with which the Mande were familiar. This all suggests that the Spanish in Mexico (and elsewhere in Spanish-held territories) waged a deliberate and aggressive cultural war against Muslims in order to contain the spread of Islam, a campaign that met with a certain receptivity among those West Africans victimized by Muslim raiding and warfare.

It is with New Spain, or what would become Mexico, that a discussion of so-called esclavos blancos is informed by more substantial evidence. Reference has been made to the fact that North and West Africans were in the company of the conquistadors. As has been demonstrated, because they were "intractable and rebellious" as well as "agents of Islam," Moorish captives were repeatedly banned from entering the New World. A 1543 cédula required the expulsion of all enslaved Moors, whose numbers, although unknown, probably did not "exceed a few score." In 1577 the crown renewed the ban, "a tacit admission that the earlier prohibition had been violated." The following year, authorities reported that they had expelled two enslaved Moors and "would shortly be expelling more. By 1597, the number of Moorish slaves in New Spain [Mexico] was negligible."[58]

Though numerically inferior, North Africans or Moors had an impact on the trajectory of early colonial development in the Americas through their participation in sedition and by their influence with West African Muslims, resulting in the alteration of African import patterns. They also left an undeniable legacy

[57] See Aguirre Beltrán, "Tribal Origins of Slaves in Mexico," 344–46.
[58] See Palmer, *Slaves of the White God*, 120.

in the New World that can be traced, and Aguirre Beltrán provides the context for understanding the Moorish experience in the Americas. Nearly 100 years after the fall of Ceuta in 1415, the Portuguese captured Zafi (or Azafi) in 1507, in what is now Morocco (north of Cape Guer). An entrepot of significance through the end of the sixteenth century, Zafi supplied slaves as well as various merchandise to Genoese and Venetian markets in the area, which facilitated their movement to Mexico. They therefore entered the New World under the designation of *Cafí*:

[T]heir introduction was limited to the century of the conquest. The slaves taken in Zafi were the direct result of the war against Islam, from which place the principal contingent was composed of natives from Morocco and Fez – Moors, Bereberes (Berbers), Jews and Loros – who passed to the West Indies in the company of their master-settlers or conquerors, under the common designation of "white slaves."

The need to establish the primacy of the "Santa Fe Cathólica" led to the issuance of royal proclamations to either prohibit or expel the so-called esclavos blancos in 1501, 1506, 1509, 1530, 1531, 1543, and 1550, whose very repetition reflects a lack of compliance. As a result, "small groups of white slaves entered our country and America in general."[59]

To reiterate, the assignment of 'race' to the Moors is a difficult enterprise. The Berbers were Africans, many of dark hue, others of traceable linkage to subsaharan African ancestry. Aguirre Beltrán himself, after acknowledging that the Moors had long and extensive interaction with "blacks" and were therefore "mixed," goes on to make the argument that the Arabo-Berbers of Zafi maintained a three-tiered society, the lowest level of which was occupied by the "Negro-Berbers" from whom were probably recruited most of the captive Cafí. It is therefore the case that these esclavos blancos were "white" only in a relative sense, that many were of subsaharan ancestry, and that most in the final analysis were African.

Most were African, but not all. The now-extinct Gomera or Guanches of the Canary Islands were imported into Mexico in very small numbers at the end of the fifteenth century from Zafi. If they were arguably African, others clearly were not. Various captives from the Mediterranean were occasionally brought to Mexico:

Of these slaves, the most highly esteemed were those of Greek origin. During the Mussulman rule in Spain an uninterrupted stream of Greek beauties and eunuchs from the Orient satisfied the needs of Moorish harems.... That slaves of this nationality entered Mexico seems to be proven by the affirmation of Mota y Escobar who, in the *Memoirs of the Archbishop of Tlaxacala*, in 1609, points out the existence of Greek residents, dedicated to fishing and married to Negroes and mulattoes in the town of Medellin, near Vera Cruz.[60]

---

[59] See Aguirre Beltrán, "Tribal Origins of Slaves in Mexico," 274–79; Aguirre Beltrán, *La población negra de México*, 103–05.

[60] See Aguirre Beltrán, "Tribal Origins of Slaves in Mexico," 277–79. Aguirre Beltrán located Mota y Escobar's *Memoirs* in the Archivo del Museo Nacional de México, MS.

The presence of these few Europeans, however, does not significantly alter the preceding qualifications of the concept of esclavos blancos in Mexico.

To speak of *esclavas blancas* entering Mexico would be more accurate, since most in this category were female. This observation is supported by licenses issued to such persons as Rodrigo Zimbrón in 1535, the bishop of Oaxaca in 1539, Inés de las Casas in 1540, and D. F. B. Marin in 1692: "There exists the suspicion that these slaves – who appear to have been designated for domestic service – were in reality dedicated to prostitution."[61] The sexual exploitation of esclavas blancas was not limited to Mexico but could be found throughout the colonies in the sixteenth century. In 1543, when the decree calling for the expulsion of enslaved Moors was issued, colonists in Hispaniola requested its annulment "because slaves and free persons from this background were few and very useful in a variety of occupations," so the order was rescinded in November of 1550. Very prominent among these occupations was prostitution, for which licenses were granted to individuals who transported "fallen women" (*mujeres publicas*) from Iberia to ostensibly perform domestic work, licenses provided by royal officials who 'closed their eyes' to what was really going on. This activity was to some extent informed by King Fernando's 1512 order to send *esclavas blancas y cristianas* to the Americas in order to avoid "carnal relations between the colonists and the native women." In turn, the order itself was conditioned by realities in Spain, where in Seville, for example, "near the humble abodes and port districts, in shipyards, beaches and fishing areas, no particular attention was called to the branded, half-dressed slave, the mulatto woman, the *bozal* woman, or the free man ridiculously and gaudily dressed, all of which made up part of the fauna picaril."[62] Although Spaniards continued to 'traffic' with indigenous women and the king's order failed to achieve the desired effect, "what is clear is that *casas públicas* were established in the Indies from the very beginning of colonization." The *mujer morisca* would from time to time, through the vehicle of marriage to prominent *peninsulares* (Spaniards born in Spain), play an influential role in local developments, or as mothers facilitate the union of their children with those of notable families. Through these and other means, certain of the esclavas blancas were "absorbed" into the Spanish category.[63]

*   *   *

Moors were therefore in New Spain as both enslaved and free persons, but their experience in the New World was not limited to these two categories. They also occupied a third category, that of the *forzado*, and such persons regularly appear in New World registries. Forzados had been convicted of crimes in Spain

[61] Ibid., 276.
[62] See Guillot, *Negros rebeldes y negros cimarrones*, 18.
[63] See Fernando Romero, *Safari Africano, y compraventa de esclavos para el Péru (1412–1818)* (Lima: Instituto de Estudios Peruanos, 1994), 91–92; Scelle, *La traite négrière aux Indes de Castille*, vol. 1: 221–31.

and elsewhere, and, rather than receive floggings, banishments, and fines for minor offenses and capital punishment for major ones as was customary during medieval times, they were subsequently given sentences averaging four to six years but in actuality ranging from two years to life; by 1653, the standard punishment had become ten years. Capital crimes were punished with "penal servitude at hard labor on the galleys," a policy introduced by Ferdinand and Isabella, who presided over a rising, powerful nation-state with the means to force compliance with the growing demand for labor. In particular, Spain required a standing galley fleet to protect its interests along its southern coast and in the Mediterranean, and it elected to employ a "servile rowing force" rather than depend on free oarsmen (*buenas boyas*). By the end of the sixteenth century, buenas boyas had almost completely disappeared from the Spanish galleys.[64]

Galleys had become the principal means of exploiting convicted males in Spain by the seventeenth century, so that slaves and the forzados, who were illegally required to continue working beyond the completion of their sentences, were the two major components of galley labor. Since Christians could not serve on galleys, sources for the enslaved included North African Muslims purchased or captured in war as well as others who were from subsaharan Africa. Concerning the Moors, many were war captives seized from North African vessels and they were professional seamen and corsairs; upon capture, they became property of the monarch or *esclavos del rey*, and they were placed in the galleys. The Spanish crown's policy was so successful that, in the 1580s, the galleys were completely full and could not accommodate additional persons. As time progressed, the percentage of the enslaved increased relative to that of the forzado; in 1612, some 26 percent of the oarsmen were enslaved, whereas in 1668 the enslaved accounted for 41 percent of the total, "almost all of whom were Moslems." Enslaved persons who had converted to Christianity were allowed to serve as guard assistants, while both Christian converts and Muslims served as personal attendants to galley officials. Certain Muslims, however, in particular the *arraeces* or corsair captains, were considered highly dangerous, and they were restricted to manning the oars. Mutinies and escapes were therefore relatively few, but they "usually involved a conspiracy between forzados and Moslem slaves."[65]

One of the best examples of the Muslim forzado presence in the New World can be found in a 1595–96 document from Havana, Cuba. It is self-described as the "account of the *forzado* oarsmen, slaves, and free oarsmen from the galley named San Agustin, taken from its manifest on 28 February 1595. Those who remain are serving your majesty, some of them in the labor crews of this city and the others in the aforementioned galley." Ten years earlier, the galley San Agustin had arrived in Havana with 149 persons on board and divided into the following categories: 18 forzados "for life" (*perpetuo*); 18 forzados for

---

[64] See Ruth Pike, *Penal Servitude in Early Modern Spain* (Madison: U. of Wisconsin Press, 1983), 3–9.
[65] Ibid., 9–25; Rout, *African Experience in Spanish America*, 16–20.

whom there were neither sentences nor licenses (*asientos*), suggesting they were stowaways; 7 free oarsmen; 61 forzados with limited sentences; and 45 Moorish slaves.[66] Of the 149, nearly 30 percent, or 44 persons, have names that are either clearly or conjecturally Muslim, African, or both:

Amado Hernande de Uliestes [Amadu, or Mahmud]
Juan Garcia del Aljarafe [region that includes Seville]
Ysayn de Metexeli [Husayn]
Ramadan de negro Ponte
Atia de Telez
Alicarali de Drahaman
Hamete de Tunez [Hamid, or Ahmad]
Hemete de Meliana
Almançor de Marruecos [al-Mansur]
Lorenço Lanis morisco
Mami de negro Ponte
Ysufe de Anadolia [Yusuf]
Mostafa de Rodas [Mustapha]
Ata Vies de Escandaria
Ramadan muladin
Brahen de Aglipoli [Ibrahim]
Ysmael de Vila [Isma'il]
Alonso Gallego morisco
Sebastian de Melo
Rexefe de Anadolia
Yçayn de Anadolia [Husayn]
Cassimo de Fez
Hamete de Constantina
Amar negro de Fez [Umar]
Yçayn de Marruecos
Hassan de Xexuan
Masmi alias por otro nombre Antoño renegado portugues
Hamete de Fez
Hamu de Mostagani
Mami de Rodas
Ali de Arjel
Albequerin de Cela
Osman de Arjel [Usman]
Hamete de Fez
Hamete Mendaz

---

[66] See Documento XII, "Relación de los esclavos forcados que quedaron de la Galera San Augustin de la Havana," in César García del Pino and Alicia Melis Cappa, *Documentos para la historia colonial de Cuba: siglos xvi, xvii, xviii, y xix* (La Habana: Editorial de Ciencias Sociales, 1988), 63–67.

Hazan de Alcasar [Hassan]
Ali de Miquinas
Beli de Anadolia
Hamon de Selen
Peri Bosne
Ale de Mostagan
Dargute del Mar Negro
Brahen de Anadolia
Antoño Negro de Lisboa

A number of individuals, at least five, were from the Ottoman heartland ("Anadolia"); others were from Morocco (Fez, Marrakesh); and one hailed from the Black Sea ("del Mar Negro"). The report went on to state that all of the forzados had completed their terms and had been granted their freedom, with the following exceptions: those with life sentences, those for whom there were no licenses, and those who had committed crimes since their arrival in Cuba, necessitating additional sentences. Therefore, even sixteenth-century Cuba had a Muslim presence.

In fact, with Cuba it becomes possible to extend the discussion of Islam to Latin America into the eighteenth and nineteenth centuries. To begin, a source based on records through 1578 demonstrates that 70 percent of nearly 169 Africans arriving in Cuba and Mexico were from "Upper Guinea" (Senegambia and Sierra Leone), while only 12 percent were from West Central Africa; it is logical to assume that Muslims were arriving in Cuba in proportions similar to those in Mexico.[67] That Cuba never developed a reputation as a Muslim haven requires some explanation, especially in light of developments in Brazil (discussed in Chapter 3).

Part of that explanation lies in the fact that, with the exception of Havana, there were no large concentrations of Africans in Cuba prior to the eighteenth century.[68] The trade in slaves was irregular, and those who managed to arrive were used for diverse tasks. The island's planter class would be encouraged, however, by England's transformation of Barbados into a sugar colony based on slave labor, the English seizure of Jamaica in the mid-seventeenth century for the same purpose, and the corresponding establishment of the French in Saint Domingue. The cultivation of sugarcane was unevenly developed until the 1740s, when the Spanish crown lifted all taxes on Cuban sugar entering Spain at a time when the world market was paying more for sugar. From 1750 to 1761 the number of ingenios increased from sixty-two to ninety-six, and the following year England occupied Havana for a summer, effectively ending the asiento system and opening up the island to intensified importation of Africans, most

[67] See Rout, *African Experience in Spanish America*, 31.
[68] This section is based on Laird W. Bergard, Fe Iglesias García, and Marcía del Carmen Barcia, *The Cuban Slave Market, 1790–1880* (Cambridge, England: Ortiz Cambridge U. Press, 1995), 23–36.

of whom hailed from non-Muslim areas in Africa. From 1763 to 1792, some 70,000 Africans entered the island, compared with 325,000 between 1790 and 1820. Technological innovation, coupled with the Haitian Revolution, resulted in skyrocketing sugar production in Cuba; the number of ingenios tripled from 529 in 1792 to 1,531 by 1861. A concomitant rise in coffee production also drew heavily upon enslaved labor, which by 1827 was 64 percent male. By 1862, when there were "more blacks than whites in Cuba," the island held 368,550 slaves, 60 percent of whom were male, working on sugarcane and coffee plantations as well as on *sitios* (small-scale farms), *vegas* (tobacco farms), and *potreros* (cattle ranches).[69]

It is likely that further research will uncover more information on Muslims in Cuba. Anecdotal evidence provides some clues. For example, there is the 1747 case of the *cimarrones* or runaways of El Portillo, some of whom were captured and brought to trial. It became clear during the judicial procedures that El Portillo was a heterogeneous community in the sense that Africans from very different backgrounds were welcomed there. Individual names demonstrated the diversity, such as "the Congo Joaquín Eduardo," the Congo Gregorio," "the Carabali Miguel," "the Carabali Mariana," the Mina María," and so on. Included among the captured was "the Mandingo Salvador," who had been absent from his holder Joseph Lopez for five years. Salvador, who was sixty years old at the time of his hearing, further testified that he had been brought to the island forty years earlier, having been sold from an English sloop off the coast of Manzanillo along with many other Africans. In giving his testimony he had taken a Christian oath, but it is very possible that he was Muslim, having matured in West Africa at the turn of the eighteenth century.[70]

A tabulation of numbers and average prices of enslaved persons who can be identitifed "by African nationality" from 1790 to 1880, compiled by Bergard, Iglesias García, and del Carmen Barcia, also reveals a probable presence of Muslims in Cuba.[71] Based on records for Havana, Santiago, and Cienfuegos, the study reveals that the specific makeup of the nationalities was subject to minor changes from year to year, but among the various categories the Mandinga were constant until 1870, as were such groups as the Mina, Carabali, Congo, Lucumí, and Arará. Besides the Mandinga, other groups closely associated with Islam who make the list are the Wolof, who appear in 1793, 1829, and 1846; and the Fula or Fulbe, who show up in 1823. Table 1.1 calculates the total number of persons under consideration, with the percentage of Mandinga, Wolof, Fulbe, and potential Muslims in parentheses.

Of course, any attempt to draw definitive conclusions from such a small pool of data is unwarranted, but perhaps some tendencies can be discerned. From

---

[69] See Fernando Ortiz, *Hampa afro-cubana: Los negros brujos a puntes para un estudio de ethnología criminal* (Miami: Ediciones Universal, 1973; orig. pub. 1906), 12.

[70] See Gabino La Rosa Corzo, *Los palenques del oriente de Cuba: Resistencia y acoso* (Havana: Editorial Academia, 1991), 54–60.

[71] See Bergard, Iglesias García, and del Carmen Barcia, *Cuban Slave Market*, Table B.5, 199–206.

TABLE 1.1. *Enslaved Persons and Percentages of Potential Muslims in Cuba, 1790–1880*

Year	Number (%)	Year	Number (%)
1790	47 (12.8)	1830	67 (7.5)
1791	14 (7)	1831	92 (8.7)
1792	19 (0)	1832	48 (4.2)
1793	63 (12.7)	1833	87 (10.3)
1794	132 (6.8)	1834	72 (2.8)
1795	65 (7.7)	1835	111 (9.9)
1796	59 (14)	1836	222 (4.5)
1797	79 (1.3)	1837	312 (6.4)
1798	73 (12.3)	1838	118 (7.6)
1799	69 (10)	1839	311 (4.2)
1800	65 (9.2)	1840	484 (8.6)
1801	52 (9.6)	1841	351 (4.5)
1802	43 (13.9)	1842	229 (6.5)
1803	44 (13.6)	1843	244 (10.2)
1804	9 (33)	1844	432 (7.8)
1805	24 (20.8)	1845	103 (1)
1806	16 (6)	1846	363 (8.2)
1807	25 (16)	1847	379 (6.6)
1808	40 (27.5)	1848	257 (5)
1809	74 (24.3)	1849	135 (11)
1810	35 (14.2)	1850	136 (1.5)
1811	36 (25)	1851	38 (2.6)
1812	47 (17)	1852	139 (3.6)
1813	41 (24.3)	1853	185 (5.9)
1814	28 (17.8)	1854	85 (3.5)
1815	52 (28.8)	1855	44 (6.8)
1816	32 (21.9)	1856	119 (.8)
1817	79 (16.5)	1857	53 (0)
1818	99 (17.1)	1858	34 (0)
1819	64 (10.9)	1859	61 (4.9)
1820	83 (16.9)	1860	68 (4.4)
1821	108 (10.2)	1861	46 (4.3)
1822	115 (13.9)	1862	58 (0)
1823	131 (14.5)	1863	29 (17.2)
1824	100 (14)	1864	19 (5.2)
1825	35 (11.4)	1865	28 (0)
1826	46 (15.2)	1866	12 (16.7)
1827	71 (9.8)	1867	9 (0)
1828	41 (17)	1868	28 (0)
1829	68 (8.8)	1869	3 (0)

1790 to 1800, the percentage of potential Muslims hovers around 10 percent. That number more than doubles between 1808 and 1816, and it averages near 10 percent through 1829. The period 1835 to 1853, for which there is a larger pool of information from which to draw, tends to place the figure of possible Muslims below 10 percent. From 1853 to 1869, it does not appear that the potential Muslim population was significant.

It is inconceivable that the Mande, Fulbe, and Wolof in Cuba did not include Muslims. The probability that most were in fact Muslim is enhanced by the fact that 1790 to 1869 was a period in West Africa of Islamic reform, holy wars, and intensified rates of conversions. It is also possible that some of the Lucumí or Yoruba were Muslim, but there is little evidence that confirms a strong sense of Islamic identity among them. The case of the Yoruba is particularly curious, given the major role they apparently played in Muslim revolts in Brazil. There is little to suggest comparable activity in Cuba, suggesting that events in Brazil and connections with what became southwestern Nigeria require reexamination.

There is, however, the turn-of-the-century, problematic scholarship of Fernando Ortiz that views the presence of Muslims in Cuba as a given, and that attempts to connect that presence with the Lucumí. Characterizing African religions in Cuba as "underworld witchcraft" informing criminal activity, Ortiz argued that the catholicized *afro-cubano* continued to practice "fetishism," and that "from the natural struggle between African religions there triumphed in Cuba, as in Brazil, the religion of the Yoruba or Nago blacks, despite being mistreated by the common enemy of them all, Catholicism. These blacks are those who entered Cuba as *lucumís*." According to Ortiz, Lucumí religion features an unapproachable highest god known by a number of names: Olorun, Olodumare, Oga-ogó, Oluwa, Oba-ogó, Obañgidzi, Eledá, Elemi, and so on. Followers call on the *orisha*s, approachable deities, among whom the most prominent are Obatalá, Shangó, and Ifá. The androgynous Obatalá, the greatest of the three, is also called Orish-nlá ("the great *orisha*"), Alamorere ("the one from the good clay"), and Alabalasé ("the one who predicts the future"). Central to all of these names is "Ala," which represents Islamic influence as far as Ortiz is concerned: "The Islamic religion left indelible marks upon the theology of the blacks from the African regions.... Plenty of Muslim slaves (*mandingas*, *yolofes*, *fulas*, *macuás*, etc.) entered Cuba, and those who probably referred to the god Olorun as Alá were from the Yorubas." Ortiz went on to comment that the continuing presence of amulets in early-twentieth-century Cuba was also a consequence of Muslim influence:

[S]ome amulets consisted of written prayers that were worn hanging from the neck, and placed on walls, behind doors, etc. This type is on the highest level on the amulet scale, so to speak. [These amulets] are based on the same concept that leads certain Mohammedans in Africa to consider as *gris-gris* anything written on paper, especially if it contains verses from the Koran drawn by a *marabout*, so that it was not difficult, especially by means of the *mandingas*, for this superstition to have arrived in Cuba.

Though inferential, Ortiz's evidence for Muslims in Cuba is plausible, as is his attempt to identify Islamic influence among the Lucumí.[72] These apparent efforts to merge elements of Islam and Yoruba religion, or perhaps more accurately to create connective spaces between them, may be similar to a phenomenon in North Africa, where in Morocco, Tunisia, and Algeria, the descendants of subsaharan Africans (and North Africans, for that matter) practice Islam along with *bori*, a cosmology concerned with the spirit world's interaction with the corporeal. Bori is a mixture of spirits – infants, nature gods, spirits of deceased Muslim leaders, Muslim *jinn* (spirits), and so forth – who cause illness and who are appeased through offerings, sacrifice, and dance possession. West African communities practicing bori, such as the Songhay, Bambara, and Hausa, were distinguished in North Africa at least through the mid-twentieth century.[73]

There is additional evidence that the Mande and other potential Muslims were arriving in Cuba, and that as late as the second half of the nineteenth century, in the story of Esteban Montejo, a self-styled "criollito" born in December of 1860. He states that his godfather was "Gin Congo," his father's name was "Nazario," and that he was a lucumí, all of which reveal a keen sense of ethnicity in Cuba. He went on to say that he learned about the African religions in the *barracones* or settlement areas, and that the two major religions were those of the lucumí and the *conga*, of which the latter was more important. There is no specific discussion of Islam in his biography, but there is mention of the Mande:

On the *ingenios* there were blacks from different *naciones*. Each one [*naçion*] had its own look. The *congos* were black, although there were a lot of *jabaos* [persons of mixed European and African ancestry]. They were usually little (*chiquitos*). The *mandingas* were of medium color. Tall and strong. As far as my mother was concerned, they were a bad influence and criminals. They always stayed to themselves. The *gangas* were good people. Little with freckled faces. Many were *cimarrones*. The *carabalís* were like the *congos musungos*, fierce.[74]

The Mande's religion is not mentioned, but the fact that they kept to themselves may have been because of their Islamic beliefs, surrounded as they were by an overwhelming number of 'polytheists.' Interestingly, Montejo's mother's sentiments towards the Mande are consistent with the association of the word

---

[72] See Ortiz, *Hampa afro-cubana*, 27–53, 156. The idea that Obatalá is a "yorubized" reference to Allah is also discussed in Sylviane A. Diouf, *Servants of Allah: African Muslims Enslaved in the Americas* (New York: New York U. Press, 1998), 186–88.

[73] Concerning *bori*, see Mohammed Ennaji, *Serving the Master: Slavery and Society in Nineteenth-Century Morocco*, trans. Seth Graebner (New York: St. Martin's Press, 1998); Émile Dermenghem, *Le culte des saints dans l'islam maghrébin* (Paris: Éditions Gallimard, 1954); Vincent Crapanzano, *The Hamadsha: A Study in Moroccan Ethnopsychiatry* (Berkeley: U. of California Press, 1973); A. J. N. Tremearne, *The Ban of the Bori: Demons and Demon-Dancing in West and North Africa* (London: Heath, Cranton, and Ouseley, 1914); and Janice Boddy, *Wombs and Alien Spirits: Women, Men, and the Zār Cult in Northern Sudan* (Madison: U. of Wisconsin Press, 1989).

[74] See Esteban Montejo, *Biografía de un cimarron* (Madrid: Ediciones Alfaguara, 1984), 24–45.

mandinga with the devil in Mexico. This association is repeated in other parts of the Spanish-speaking Americas.

Another part of the biography raises the possibility that the Fulbe or Fula were a known quantity early in Cuba's history. Montejo states that women were a major topic of discussion among men. "One went to talk with friends, actually acquaintances, and they told him everything that happened with women. I was never disposed to tell my business. Every man should learn to be discreet. But these braggarts would say very calmly: 'Listen, *Fulano*, you know that tomorrow I'm going to take [inference, 'have sex with'] *Fulanita*.'" *Fulano* should probably be read as "so-and-so," but it is tempting to wonder if the term initially entered the language from interactions with the Fulbe and was somehow transformed into an idiom of nonspecific reference with a connotation of disparagement, not inconsistent of the use of the term mandinga. Montejo also makes mention of "a person called *Fulanito Congo*," whom he called "Faustino."[75]

The Fulbe presence in Cuba as possibly indicated by an admittedly speculative reading of Montejo is, in contrast, verified by Fredrika Bremer's eyewitness account in 1851. Writing from Mantanzas, she states that "there is here a negro of the Fellah tribe, a little man, with delicate features, and the long, black, shining hair which is said to be peculiar to this tribe." The Fulbe reference followed her observation that "the Luccomées and Mandingoes...are tall of stature, with handsome and often remarkably regular, even noble features, the expression of which is grave. The negro preachers and fortune-tellers are principally of the Mandingo tribes." While it is possible that Bremer was describing Christian minsters and seers, it is fascinating to consider that she may have been misinterpreting what were actually Muslim activities.[76]

It is clear from the foregoing discussion that Muslims from North and West Africa were present in Cuba from at least the sixteenth century late into the nineteenth, although the extent to which they influenced Cuban culture and society remains an open question. It would also appear that Muslims entered Venezuela, although even less is known about their experience there. The first few Africans to arrive in Venezuela did so in 1528 or 1529, and even though the rate of imported captives intensified in the final decades of the sixteenth century, Venezuela remained a "poverty-stricken outpost" of Spanish imperialism, primarily a source for aboriginal labor and pearls. By the eighteenth century, however, it had become "the most profitable non-mining economy in Spanish America" as a result of the cultivation of cacao. The slave trade, "languishing" until then, registered a "record number" of captives between 1730 and 1780, who produced, in addition to cacao, sugar and indigo and hides. Pearl divers of African descent also distinguished labor in Venezuela (and Colombia). The end of the "cacao boom" around the turn of the century led to the tapering off and eventual termination of the trade in 1810, by which time there were some

---

[75] Ibid., 124.
[76] See Fredrika Bremer, *The Homes of the New World; Impressions of America*, trans. Mary Howitt (New York: Harper and Brothers, 1853), vol. 2, 313–14.

60,000 enslaved persons in Venezuela. Coffee had gained importance by that time, and it began its own boom in 1830. By 1844, however, less than 2 percent of the population was still enslaved; the institution was abolished in 1854.[77]

Acosta Saignes writes that "there were Wolof or Jolofes in Venezuela in the middle of the seventeenth century, but due to the repulsion generated by the events of Hispaniola, which led the Crown to the aforementioned prohibition, owners frequently asked for [slaves] of other tribes." The Senegambians therefore entered Venezuela in small numbers, and, while they were found in various places, they were well represented in the mines of Cocorote in the mid-seventeenth century (mining having begun there in 1620). Although Acosta Saignes identifies them as Wolof, it is likely that by the seventeenth century there were many Mande and others within this aggregate, with the Mande being referred to as both "Mandinga" and "Gangá." The "Folopo," who were either Fulbe or Juula, also show up on documents concerning the slaves.[78]

The evidence that the Mande brought to Venezuela were Muslim is derivative from both the West African background and the scarce anecdotal information. An example of the latter suggests that the person in question was Muslim, but it is not a certainty. Acosta Saignes relates that, in 1607, Don Francisco Ortíz and Doña Inés del Basto built a chapel (*ermita*) in Maracaibo.

There were many Christians, they had several slaves and they taught them catechism. Every day at the sound of the Angelus [litany traditionally recited morning, noon, and evening in celebration of the angelic visitation to Mary, announcing the miraculous conception of Jesus], they gathered all the servants in the place mentioned and they prayed the rosary. The sources state that Doña Inés had among her slaves a very lively young black man (*negrito*) with shiny eyes who, when she rang for the rosary, made some excuse and went to the corral to avoid being present and taking part in the prayer. Doña Inés, seeing that he always did this, set out to make him pray and one day surprised him and, while he was inside [the corral], told him that he would have to pray the rosary, and wanting him to recite the short prayers with the others, forced him to do what she wanted, holding him tightly; however, she had to release him because at the recital of the "Ave María," he struggled and got away. The *negrito* ran very quickly and disappeared from view forever, which why today the street is called 'Carabobo' ('foolish face'?), as he left behind such a strong smell of sulfur. . . . He was a Mandinga.[79]

We can only speculate that the young man was a Muslim and therefore wanted no part of the Christian prayers. Acosta Saignes further comments that it "is well known that slaves from this tribe presented serious problems to the slave holders," and that although the Mande were "intelligent, industrious, and enterprising," they were also "rebellious, clever, disobedient, unruly, and were quick to run away. They were judged to be so bad that the name Mandinga was

---

[77] See John V. Lombardi, *The Decline and Abolition of Negro Slavery in Venezuela, 1820–1854* (Westport, CT: Greenwood Publishing, 1971), 3–35, 95–123; Miguel Acosta Saignes, *Vida de los esclavos negros en Venezuela* (Caracas: Ediciones Hospécides, 1967), 24.

[78] See Acosta Saignes, *Vida de los esclavos negros en Venezuela*, 131–41, 252.

[79] Ibid., 189.

given to every dangerous, cunning, sneaky, violent individual. And that is how the devil obtained the nickname 'Mandinga.'"[80] In addition to the symmetric association of the Mande with the devil in Mexico, Acosta Saignes' observations raise the possibility that Africans could be mislabeled as *mandingas* as a function of their attitude and behavior toward the slaving regime. It is also plausible, however, that Venezuelans of the period bore in mind the distinction between a sociocultural identity based on connections to West and West Central Africa and a political identity informed by the posture toward enslavement. In any event, it would appear that the Mande, and by extension Islam, came to constitute a paradigmatic response to enslavement and thus influenced the terms of religious and social discourse in Venezuela.

The traffic in enslaved persons in Colombia was very much tied to activity elsewhere in the "Spanish Indies" as a result of the importance of the port of Cartagena. Following the schema of del Castillo Mathieu, the first period of the traffic extended from 1533 to 1580, during which time there was a predominance of so-called Wolof in the enslaved population, at least until the middle of the century, after which other groups become dominant. Using data from Mexico and Peru, del Castillo Mathieu proposes "a relative predominance of the Wolof in Cartagena." By 'Wolof' he actually means Senegambians, which is clear when he writes the following: "It is very possible that a good part of these *yolofos* were in reality *fulas* or *fulupos*," a reference to the Fulbe. In fact, he speculates that "it would not be out of the question to suppose, therefore, that the *fulani* language (or the *yolofa*) played a role of lingua franca . . . because of the high cultural level of the *fulas* and the *yolofes* and the political role of the *yolofo* empire [Jolof], where the *fulani* and the *yolofo* were distinguished as languages of major importance." It follows that many of these persons were Muslim.[81]

From 1580 to 1640, the Portuguese held the asiento, and Cartagena became the leading center of the traffic; captives destined for Lima arrived initially in Cartagena, as did many Africans headed for Puerto Rico and Santo Domingo during this period. As for those who remained in Colombia, there is little information on the numbers or experiences of potential Muslims. Commenting on the seventeenth century, Borja writes the following:

[T]he presence of black Muslims in Cartagena is indisputable. The Spaniard was accustomed to the threatening presence of Islam. But Islam and blackness were truly a dangerous combination. These elements reinforced the image of the savage, about which Sandoval [the priest Alonso de Sandoval] is a witness: "There are four major sources from where blacks ordinarily come to the city of Cartagena of the Indies. Among them

---

[80] Ibid.

[81] See Nicolas del Castillo Mathieu, *Esclavos negros en Cartagena y sus aportes léxicos* (Bogotá, Colombia: Publicaciones del Instituto Caro y Cuervo, 1982), 23–159; Jorge Pal, Palacios Preciado, *La trata de negros por Cartagena de Indias* (Tunja, Colombia: Ediciones La Rama y El Aguila, 1973); María del Carmen Borrego Pla, *Palenques de negros en Cartagena de Indias a fines del siglo xvii* (Seville: Escuela de Estudios Hispano-Americanos de Sevilla, 1973).

are the *iolofes*, *berbesíes* [probably Sereer], *mandingas*, and *fulos* who usually understand each other well, even though the languages and cultures are different, because of the great communication they have due to all these nations having commonly received the accursed sect of Muhammad."

As far as the priest was concerned, these people were overwhelmingly Muslim; however, his testimony is impressionistic, and a quantitative sense of the Muslim population cannot be extracted from it. Indeed, a mid-century census of Chocó records 3,918 slaves, of which only 23 were listed as "Mandingas."[82]

Captives on their way to Peru stopped first at Cartagena; they then voyaged nine to ten days to Portobelo. From there they crossed the isthmus, "a short but hard journey through the lush vegetation of the tropical rain forest," which took two days. Healthy captives walked, while the sickly and mothers with infants were transported by either mule or barge down the Chagres River. Some required a month-long convalescence in Panama before continuing on to Callao, Lima's port of entry. Royal treasury officials inspected their movement at Cartagena, Portobelo, and Panama, and perhaps they made note of the high mortality rate visited upon the process. In light of this experience, to refer to the traffic as the transatlantic slave trade is something of a misnomer.[83]

Africans began to arrive in Peru as early as 1529, usually from other Spanish settlements. Although 600 Spaniards and 400 Africans left Panama for Peru in 1535, a number that assuredly included Senegambians, Peru's early development mostly relied on indigenous labor, especially in light of the 1536 victory over the Inca. Africans were recruited to work the silver mines, but operations remained on a much smaller scale than planned. By mid-century, the African population in Lima was near 3,000, reaching 4,000 in 1586 and 6,690 by 1593. By 1640, there were probably 20,000 Africans in Lima, one-half of the city's population and two-thirds of the 30,000 Africans in the whole of Peru. This was in some sense a response to the much more precipitous decline of the native population, from 6 million in 1525 to 1.5 million by 1571.[84]

The entire Peruvian economy benefitted from the increased African numbers, but agriculture was the major beneficiary. Olives, plantains, oranges, sugarcane, wheat, and barley were all cultivated by Africans, who also worked to produce sugar and wine. Africans cared for the cart-pulling oxen and mules, and they could be found fulfilling various roles in trade and shipping along the Pacific coast. They were prominent as masons, carpenters, shipwrights, bricklayers, blacksmiths, and tailors, and they were hired out as *jornaleros* (day wage workers). Notwithstanding the importance of these occupations, Africans were "perhaps most conspicuous as retainers and household servants in the urban

---

[82] See Jaime Borja, "Barbarización y redes de indoctrinamiento en los negros – Cosmovisiones en Cartagena. Siglo XVII y IIVIII," in *Contribución africana a la cultura de las Américas* (Bogotá, colombia: Instituto Colombiano de Antopologia, 1993), 249; Alonso de Sandoval, *Un tratado sobre la esclavitud* (Madrid: Alianza, 1987).

[83] See Bowser, *African Slave in Colonial Peru*, 62–66.

[84] Ibid., 3–18, 62–80.

TABLE 1.2. *Potential Muslims in Peru, 1560–1650*

	Jolofo	Mandinga	Fula
1560–95	80	89	4
1600–50	40	195	4
TOTAL	120	284	8

areas along the coast and in many parts of the highlands. This was particularly true of Lima, where blacks were employed on a lavish scale."[85]

There is some information on potential Muslims in Peru during the sixteenth and seventeenth centuries. Using notarial records, Bowser was able to chart the "ethnic origins of Afro-Peruvians" from 1560 to 1650, listing some twenty-two groups from West Africa. Table 1.2 is extracted from his data. Bowser's figures represent a total of 5,278 persons for the ninety-year period, so that the percentage of potential Muslims for the time span is 7.8 percent.[86] Again, the Jolofo category actually represented multiple groups from Senegambia, the majority of whom may have been Wolof, while the Mandinga category was subject to arbitrary expansion. Nevertheless, these figures, as paltry as they are, are consistent with the overall perspective that, with the progression of time, the Mande presence in Peru and elsewhere in the Spanish colonies became dominant among potential Muslim categories.

As Table 1.2 shows, in spite of Spanish efforts to expel Moors and gelofes from their American possessions by a series of *cédulas reales* or royal decrees, "Wolofs were still being offered for sale in Lima in the 17th century."[87] The presence of the Wolof is also indicated by the "exceedingly painful" testamentary declaration of an artisan's Spanish widow, who "stated that she wished to free Isabel Mulata (age eight), who she knew to be her dead husband's daughter by her slave Francisca Jolofa." However, as the estimates also suggest, the Mande would grow much larger in the seventeenth century, a fact indirectly (and unintentionally) supported by Bowser's discussion of interracial relations. Sexual contact between Spanish men and African women, as indicated in the example of Francisca Jolofa, was "widespread and persistent throughout the colonial period. One seventeenth-century observer noted maliciously that the Spanish men of Peru seemed to prefer black women over their own.... Whatever the reason, the black women of the colony, and particularly the mulatas, seem to have held an overpowering attraction for the Spanish, and even the Indian male." Presented in context, the major problem with the preceding statement is its failure to contest the exoticism prevalent in the discourse

[85] Ibid., 88–146.

[86] Ibid., 40–41. I am not including the Folupo category here, as it may refer to the Fulbe but it may also refer to others. There were 237 such persons, all of whom arrived in Peru from 1605 to 1650. If they are added to the potential Muslim column, it raises the potential Muslim percentage of the total to 10.8 percent.

[87] Ibid., 360, footnote 7.

over white male–black female relations in Latin America, and it glosses over the rape and violence and degradation that surely accompanied many, if not most, of these liaisons. Nevertheless, the author proceeds to the more germane point: "As Ricardo Palma says, of the ethnic composition of the Peruvian population, 'Él que no tiene de Inga tiene de Mandinga' [he who is not descended from an Inga, i.e., Inca, is descended from a Mandinga]." Of course, the Mande may have been chosen for this little ditty purely out of an artistic sense of rhyming, although other group names ("Casanga," "Balanta," "Mina," "Angola," etc.) would have sufficed just as well. Rather, the use of the Mande more probably illustrates their relative prominence and somatic desirability. Mande women are the focus of these comments, many of whom were probably Muslim.[88]

The African presence continued in Peru into the eighteenth and nineteenth centuries, but the estimates alone reveal a harsh and difficult existence.[89] In 1791 there were 40,000 slaves and 41,398 "mulattoes and free blacks" in Peru; by 1821 there were still 41,228 slaves, 33,000 of whom were agriculturalists. The figures for 1791 and 1821 are arresting when it is recalled that some 65,747 captives were imported into Peru between 1790 and 1802, with another large influx in 1814. To be sure, many probably passed into the ranks of the "mulattoes" and free persons, but others were worked to death. By slavery's abolition in 1854, there were about 17,000 enslaved persons in Peru; an 1876 census estimated the black population at 44,224, indicating a continuing downward spiral in the African-derived population.

One French traveler to Peru in the nineteenth century, encountering the *cofradías* or brotherhoods in Peru that were organized into differentiated groups on the basis of African lineage, opened a partial vista onto the suffering of the enslaved. Sunday was a day of rest, he wrote, when "the slaves benefitted from the hours of leisure afforded them by the master in order to banish from their thought the sadness and troubles of their real lives, and to lose themselves entirely in their memories and illusory dreams. They recaptured the rank they occupied in their country before, betrayed by the fate of arms or victims of some drama where love played a terrible role, they were brought to die in a strange land. . . . [T]his one became an emperor, this one a king, another a prince or great person of this or that rank." Remembering and dreaming invariably lead to storytelling, and on this particular Sunday our traveler was treated to a most intriguing account, one directly related to the experience of Muslims in the New World:

In these brotherhoods, which receive members from diverse African societies, interest is often captured by strange, marvelous, and original stories. For example, the *Mandingue* savant, voyager, the Caucasian of Africa, will reveal to you forgotten or unpublished versions of the Koran or the Bible.

---

[88] Ibid., 286–88.
[89] See Mario C. Vázquez, "Immigration and *Mestizaje* in Nineteenth-Century Peru," in Magnus Morner, ed., *Race and Class in Latin America* (New York: Colombia U. Press, 1970), 83–84.

One day, when I was allowed to go to this spirit out of curiosity, an old *marabout* [holy man], no doubt, recounted for me the dispersion of the sons of Noah, whom he maintained to be a man of the black race and the father of mankind.

Hence, the first man was born black. Three was the number of his sons, who were black like their father. The patriarch, drawing near his end, gathered his progeny and said: 'Children, my life is close to its end, and soon we will be separated; the hour has therefore come that I reveal to you the marvelous power of a cistern that I am going to open. That one among you who plunges right in will come out with a complete transformation. You are from this moment free to try it.'

He spoke; the three brothers conferred, and the eldest, Ham probably, decided to live in the same form and with the same clothes as his father. Shem followed his older brother's example; but Japheth, who already felt in his heart the ambition that he passed on to his descendants, plunged resolutely into the miraculous cistern. The metamorphosis was immediate; he reappeared before the astonished eyes of his brothers in the form of a handsome, adolescent Caucasian. A duet of recriminations rose immediately against Noah, during which the sound began to quickly and strangely diminish. Shem had changed his mind, leaving Ham to go it alone, and had gone down to the water that was now almost depleted, taken a handful of the wet soil, and rubbed it all over his body. This small application was sufficient to change the ebony black of his skin to ochre. Seeing this, Ham stopped his lamentation, hurled himself with a single bound to the bottom of the cistern, landing on his hands and feet, and exhausted himself trying to drink one drop of the miracle water. Too bad! The earth in his hands was dry; only the bottoms of his feet, the palms of his hands, and his large lips retained the color of Japheth he so envied. 'Cruel Father,' he cried in his dialect (*patois*), 'you aren't able to say anything to me, to me your first-born? . . . How will I now live next to my brothers, for whom I have become an object of derision?' . . .

His paternal instincts were moved, and Noah said: 'You will have another chance to be the one to determine your destiny. God gave me the power to distribute gifts among you three – wealth, independence, and wisdom – and I give you the choice as my first-born.' Alas! Who lost out again? It was poor Ham; he chose gold, Shem independence, and to Japheth's handsome features he added wisdom, which allowed him to dominate his older brothers.

Isn't this an original paraphrase of the verse of Scripture which, following to the curse of Ham, says: 'May God bless Japheth, may he dwell in the tent of Shem, and may Canaan be their servant'?[90]

To be sure, there are very many folktales in the world that attempt to explain the origins of human differentiation, and the "curse of Ham" legend has multiple versions. This particular story, however, is somewhat unique in that it operates at multiple levels and was told by someone who was clearly identified as an African Muslim, Mande-speaking, with some measure of learning. Whether the story was formed in West Africa or somewhere in the Americas (or in between) is uncertain, but its inconsistencies suggest formation, or at least completion, in an atmosphere that challenged the self-perspective of the African. Adam and Noah are both black, but the preferability of whiteness is clear from the reactions of Ham and Shem to Japheth's somatic transformation. Ham's loyalty to his

[90] See Radiguet, *Souvenir de l'Amérique espagnole*, 136–39.

father, a laudable attribute, prevents him from entering the magical cistern, a regrettable decision in the end. Shem stands by Ham for a moment, but his loyalty is limited, and he quickly abandons his brother. The story therefore not only explains how Shem's skin became lighter but also seeks to examine his character. The inescapable implication is that, although Shem is closer to Ham, he is not to be trusted. While certainly not a commentary on Islam, which presumably issued from the progeny of Shem, the tale may reflect difficulties with Arab and North African enslavement of subsaharan Africans.

Noah is grieved, and he makes every effort to rescue his firstborn by guaranteeing him first choice of three divine gifts. Ham makes the wrong decision again, and by implication greed and shortsightedness are the culprits that lead him astray. Japheth, therefore, is the de facto beneficiary of choices made by others, and he arrives at a place of advantage quite by accident and through a process that unfolds over many, many years. History is collapsed; the very long and distinguished glories of Africa are of little consequence in the eyes of this enslaved Muslim. Rather, the principal concern is to explain the present circumstance. In the end, the African is subject to the European because of both the former's bad choices and something innate, something "already in the heart" of Japheth long before he deceitfully broke ranks with his elder brothers (they had conferred) and took the plunge. Implicit in all this is the notion that whiteness is an aberration and the result of some fundamental, sinister drive to control and dominate. Interestingly, such ideas will again surface in the nineteenth and twentieth centuries and would again be promulgated by men and women associated with Islam in one fashion or another. This time, though, the venue would be North America.

The examination of Spanish-speaking America ends in the Rio de la Plata, where both de Carvalho-Neto and Pereda Valdés mention the presence of the Mande as a possibility, but their observations are largely based on the scholarship of Vincente Rossi. As was true of Mexico and Venezuela, the term *mandinga* was synonymous with "black devil," and Pereda Valdés argues that the practice of labeling any mischievous or rebellious person a *mandinga* is sufficient proof of their prior existence in the area, a circuitous but reasonable assumption. There is also evidence of persons in Uruguay from Mozambique, a few of whom could have been Muslim. Pereda Valdés is on more secure terrain, however, when the argument is fastened to the fact that early-nineteenth-century Montevideo was both officially and in practice the port through which southeastern slave trafficking was "obliged" to come before going on Buenos Aires and even Peru. Some would of course remain in Uruguay, and from 1770 to 1810 about 2,691 Africans were imported into the port. Interestingly, and in contrast to Peru, by 1843 the African-derived population in Uruguay had increased to 4,344, out of a total of 31,189 residents. It is plausible that a modicum were Muslims. What is also interesting is that de Studer found that, from 1742 to 1806, about half of the enslaved persons entering the Rio de la Plata came from Brazil, while the other half sailed from Africa. She further states that captives from Congo and Angola were preferred because they were "robust and good workers," whereas it was believed that "those who had spent time with the Moors brought many traces (*pegados muchos*) of their errors and all the stubbornness of the Mohammedan race."[91] This is a reference to Senegambian Muslims, but it could also include Muslims from what is now Nigeria, namely the Hausa, Fulbe, Kanuri, and Yoruba, as such a large proportion were coming from Brazil.[92]

[91] See Ildefonso Pereda Valdés, *El negro en el Uruguay: pasado y presente* (Montevideo: Revista del Instituto Histórico y Geográfico del Uruguay, 1965): 19–47; Ildefonso Pereda Valdés, *Negros esclavos y negros libres: Esquema de una sociedad esclavista y aporte del negro en nuestra formación nacional* (Montevideo: Ministerio de Instrucción Pública y P. Social, 1941), 26; Paulo de Carvalho-Neto, *El negro uruguayayo (hasta la abolición)* (Quito: Editorial Universitaria, 1965), 64–71; Elena F. Sheüss de Studer, *La trata de negros en el Río de la Plata durante el siglo xviii* (Montevideo: Libros de Hispanoamerica, 1984, orig. pub. 1958), 323; Carlos M. Rama, "The Passing of the Afro-Uruguayans from Caste Society into Class Society," in Morner, *Race and Class in Latin America*, 48–50; Josefina Plá, *Hermano negro: La esclavitud en el Paraguay* (Madrid: Ediciones Paraninfo, 1972).

[92] Raymond Delval, *Les musulmans en Amérique Latine et aux Caraïbes* (Paris: Éditions L'Harmattan, 1992), provides some discussion of African Muslims in both Latin America and the Caribbean during slavery, but he is much better with data on Muslims, especially those from India, Lebanon, Syria, and so on, from the late eighteenth century forward.

2

Caribbean Crescent

Between 1662 and 1867, some 37 percent of all Africans imported into the killing fields of the Americas arrived in that part of the Caribbean in which the English and French languages would achieve qualified dominance (transformed as they were by African inflection, syntax, and vocabulary), a figure that towers above the 10 percent estimate for the Spanish-speaking Caribbean.[1] In general, there is more specific and descriptive information on Muslims in the anglophone sector, necessitating a demographically driven argument for the presence of Muslims under French domination. Data of an anecdotal nature can found for numerous locations throughout the region, but truly discernible patterns, about which some analysis can be sustained, are at this stage of the research visible only for the islands of Jamaica, Trinidad, and Saint Domingue. These three sites are therefore taken in that order to determine the quality and implications of an Islamic presence in the Antilles (see Map 3).

It is probable that the English-speaking Caribbean received some 80 percent of all Africans transported by British carriers. It therefore stands to reason that the importation patterns for the whole of the British trade are especially reflective of the situation in the West Indies.[2] Between 1700 and 1807, Senegambia and Sierra Leone, the regions of origin out of which most Muslims would have come, supplied 6.2 percent and 15.5 percent of the total British trade, respectively. While the great majority of this 21.7 percent share would have adhered to a variety of religious beliefs at variance with Islam, there is little doubt that some unquantifiable number of Muslims were imported among the rest.

It is with some irony that a palpable Muslim presence is documented for Jamaica, given that Curtin's earlier projections for the respective contributions

---

[1] See David Eltis and David Richardson, eds., *Routes to Slavery: Direction, Ethnicity and Mortality in the Transatlantic Slave Trade* (London: Publisher, Frank Cass 1997).

[2] See Philip D. Curtin, *The Atlantic Slave Trade: A Census* (Madison: U. of Wisconsin Press, 1969), 136–48; David Richardson, "Slave Exports from West and West-Central Africa, 1700–1810: New Estimates of Volume and Distribution," *Journal of African History* 30 (1989): 13.

The Caribbean

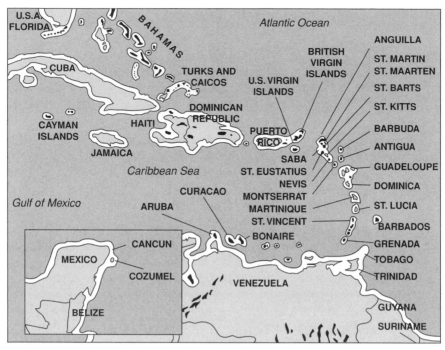

MAP 3.

of Senegambia and Sierra Leone to the island reduce the estimates to 3.7 and 10.9 percent.[3] The English would spread to Jamaica in 1655, having established their presence in St. Kitts (St. Christopher) in 1624, Barbados in 1627, Nevis in 1628, and Montserrat and Antigua in the 1630s.[4] Because of limited arable land, St. Kitts, Nevis, Montserrat, and Antigua could not compete with the productive capacity of Barbados, the "richest and most populous" of the English colonies in the seventeenth century. With a high percentage of cultivable land originally covered by thick tropical growth, Barbados, with neither mountains or rivers, was cleared within the first forty years of foreign occupation for sugarcane agriculture. The exactions of sugarcane, however, combined with the territorial limitations of the land, eventually resulted in the soil's exhaustion.

The larger island of Jamaica (see Map 4), in contrast, was characterized by a relative abundance of arable flat land and by numerous mountains and rivers,

[3] See Curtin, *Atlantic Slave Trade*, 158–62.
[4] See Richard S. Dunn, *Sugar and Slaves: The Rise of the Planter Class in the English West Indies, 1624–1713* (Chapel Hill: U. of North Carolina Press, 1972), xiii–39; B. W. Higman, *Slave Populations of the British Caribbean, 1807–1834* (Baltimore, MD: Johns Hopkins U. Press, 1984), 1–54; Orlando Patterson, *The Sociology of Slavery* (London: MacGibbon and Kee, 1967), 15–52.

Jamaica

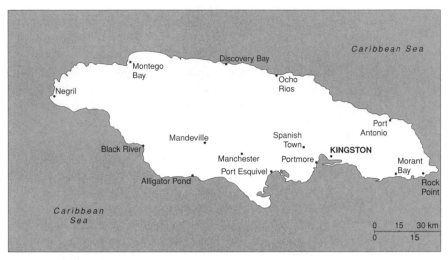

MAP 4.

and it was to early English occupiers "the most fascinating of the Caribbean islands."[5] The Spanish had maintained a minimal presence for 150 years before the 1655 English takeover, by which time there were only 1,500 Spaniards, Portuguese, Jews, Arawaks, and "blacks" dispersed throughout the island. Indeed, by 1611 only 74 Arawaks had survived the Spanish "cruelty."[6] English-speaking Jamaica, in turn, was "founded in blood," a characterization of the island's seizure from the Spanish by an "undisciplined gang of soldiers."[7] It served as the principal port for buccaneering operations against the Spanish until the end of the seventeenth century, when the island transitioned to large-scale plantation agriculture. In concert with agricultural expansion was an exponential rise in the population of black enslaved persons, soaring from 514 in 1661 to 9,504 in 1673. The servile population doubled between 1730 and 1762 to 146,805, reaching a total of 291,000 by 1795. The year 1817 saw some 345,252 enslaved in Jamaica, largest in the British Caribbean, by which time many persons of African descent no longer shared that status.[8] With slightly less than one-half of all the enslaved working on sugar plantations by 1832 (the rest on coffee plantations and in other capacities), Jamaica had one of the most diversified economies in the region.[9]

---

[5] See Dunn, *Sugar and Slaves*, 39.

[6] Ibid., 149–55; also see Patterson, *Sociology of Slavery*, 15.

[7] See Dunn, *Sugar and Slaves*, 149–57; Patterson, *Sociology of Slavery*, 94–96.

[8] Ibid.

[9] See Patterson, *Sociology of Slavery*, 52; also see B. W. Higman, *Slave Populations*, 54; B. W. Higman, *Slave Population and Economy in Jamaica, 1807–1834* (Cambridge, England: Cambridge U. Press, 1976), 13–23.

Jamaica would develop a reputation as the preserve of the Akan from the Gold Coast, and deservedly so; it is rather mystifying, however, why persons and cultural tendencies imported from the Bight of Biafra into Jamaica, an importation nearly as great if not greater than that of the Akan, have yet to receive much scholarly attention. Accounting for the origins of as much as 62 percent of all Africans coming to Jamaica, those from the Gold Coast and the Bight of Biafra would have enjoyed such numerical strength as to wield considerable cultural and social influence among the African-derived population.[10] Even so, there remained room for the divergent experience, the exceptional case. While it is certainly possible, and no doubt factual, that Muslims came to Jamaica out of areas other than Senegambia and Sierra Leone (a region that includes the Windward Coast in this study), it is from these two regions, accounting for 10 percent of the African total, that Muslims were most likely to have come. They came as early as 1730, when London's Society for Promoting Christian Knowledge received a letter from the Reverend William May of Kingston that included Arabic writings by a "Mandingo negro." The Arabic manuscripts were shown "to some of our gentlemen who understand that language and they allowed it to be passages from the Alcoran."[11]

Perhaps the most famous Muslim in Jamaica was Muhammad Kaba.[12] Born around 1756 in the difficult-to-locate place of Bouke or Bouka, which was perhaps near Timbo, capital of the Muslim theocracy of Futa Jallon in the historical region of Sierra Leone (or present-day Guinea), or in the nearby area of Bambuk (east of the Faleme River in what is now eastern Senegal–western Mali), Kaba grew up in an era of tremendous change and upheaval in West Africa. It was a time during which the forces of radical Islamic reform gained the ascendancy, setting the stage for subsequent movements that would reverberate throughout the whole of the West African savannah (and parts of the adjacent forest) in wave after wave of reformist activity during the eighteenth and nineteenth centuries. The mountainous area of Futa Jallon was at the epicenter of it all, an area where migrations of Fulbe pastoralists from Maasina in the fifteenth, seventeenth, and eighteenth centuries led to conflicts with the autochthonous Jallonke, Mande-speaking agriculturalists. By the early

---

[10] See Curtin, *Atlantic Slave Trade*, 158–62; Eltis and Richardson, *Routes to Slavery*; David Eltis, Stephen D. Behrendt, David Richardson, and Herbert S. Klein, *The Trans-Atlantic Slave Trade: A Database on CD-ROM* (Cambridge, England: Cambridge U. Press, 1999), hereafter called the *Du Bois CD-ROM Database*.

[11] See K. E. Ingram, *Sources of Jamaican History, 1655–1838* (London: Inter Documentation Company, 1976), vol. 1, 496–97. For an overview of Muslims in Jamaica, see Sultana Afroz, "The Unsung Slaves: Islam in Plantation Jamaica," *Journal of Muslim Minority Affairs* 15 (1994): 157–70; also under the same title in *Caribbean Quarterly* 41 (1995): 30–44.

[12] See R. R. Madden, *Twelve Months Residence in the West Indies*, 2 vols. (Philadelphia: Carey, Lea and Blanchard, 1837), vol. 2, 196–98; also mentioned in Ivor Wilks, "Abū Bakr al-Siddīq of Timbuktu," in Philip D. Curtin, ed., *Africa Remembered: Narratives by West Africans From the Era of the Slave Trade* (Madison: U. of Wisconsin Press, 1967); Yacine Daddi Addoun and Paul Lovejoy, "The Arabic Manuscript of Muhammad Kabā Saghanughu of Jamaica, c. 1823," available online at http://yorku.ca/nhp/shadd/kaba/index.asp.

eighteenth century, tensions between the Muslim Fulbe and the mostly non-Muslim Jallonke became intolerable for reasons contested in the literature, and sometime between 1725 and 1728 a jihād was launched at Fugumba. Initially a pan-Muslim enterprise, the reformist ranks included both Fulbe and Jallonke constituents under the legendary leadership of the cleric Karamoko Alfa. The ensuing war in Futa Jallon was long and arduous, and although Muslim forces were able to consolidate their gains in 1747 with an important victory at Talansan, significant fighting continued through the end of the eighteenth century. Muhammad Kaba's arrival in Jamaica is a direct consequence of these hostilities.[13]

There were at least two factors fueling the combat in Futa Jallon. The first had to do with internal squabbles among the Muslims. Having established in 1747 an *almaamate* or Muslim theocracy under *sharīa* (Islamic law) led by Muslim clerics, the interethnic quality of the alliance fell apart with the advent of Ibrahima Sori to power in the 1770s; the reform movement was henceforth a Fulbe-dominated affair, and fighting between Muslims resulted in a number of Jallonke captives. The second factor, however, was perhaps of greater consequence and concerned the counter-jihād of non-Muslim forces, in particular the campaigns of Kundi Burama of Wassulu, who wreaked havoc in Muslim-controlled territories from the 1760s into the 1780s. As a result, this twenty-year period has been characterized as the "most violent" phase of Futa Jallon's interminable war, and it was responsible for an increase of more than 100 percent per year in slave exports from the coasts of Sierra Leone.[14] Indeed, Rodney has estimated that 75 percent of all Africans sold from the region in the second half of the eighteenth century hailed from the interior, which is precisely where all of the fighting took place.[15] Significantly, it was around 1777–78 that Muhammad Kaba "fell into the hands of robbers and was carried off to the coast to be sold."[16]

Muslim contemporaries of Muhammad Kaba in Jamaica would have included at least two of Bryan Edwards's slaves, both of whom were mentioned in the latter's history of the colonial Caribbean.[17] "An old and faithful Mandingo servant, who stands at my elbow while I write this," Edwards relates, was captured and brought to Jamaica as a youth. Although he claimed to have

[13] See, for example, Thierno Diallo, *Les institutions politiques du Foûta Djalon au XIXe siècle* (Dakar: Université de Dakar, Institut Fondamental d'Afrique noire, 1972); Boubacar Barry, *Le royaume du Waalo: Le Sénégal avant le conquête* (Paris: Editions Karthala, 1985); William Derman and Louise Derman, *Serfs, Peasants, and Socialists: A Former Serf Village in the Republic of Guinea* (Berkeley and Los Angeles: U. of California Press, 1973); Alfa Ibrahim Sow, *Chroniques et récits du Foûta Djalon* . . . (Paris: C. Klincksieck, 1968).

[14] See Paul Lovejoy, *Transformations in Slavery: A History of Slavery in Africa* (Cambridge, England: Cambridge U. Press, 1983), 59.

[15] See Walter Rodney, *A History of the Upper Guinea Coast* (Oxford, England: Oxford U. Press, 1970), 244–55.

[16] See Madden, *Twelve Months*, vol. 2, 196–98; Wilks, "Abū Bakr al-Siddīq," 164.

[17] See Bryan Edwards, *The History, Civil and Commercial, of the British Colonies in the West Indies, in Two Volumes*, 2nd ed. (London: John Stockdale, Piccadilly, 1794), vol. 2, 61–63.

forgotten a great deal, the elderly man still remembered "the morning and evening prayer," which he demonstrated for Edwards in a "shrill tone, a sentence that I conceive to be part of the Alcoran, *La illa ill illa!* [There is no God but God]." In addition to the aged servant, Edwards also had "another Mandingo servant, who could write, with great beauty and exactness, the Arabic alphabet, and some pages from the Alcoran."

Edwards apparently had opportunity to observe other enslaved Muslims as well, for he characterizes them as a group who "pride themselves greatly among the rest of the slaves; over whom they consider that they possess a marked superiority." Edwards was able to distinguish these Muslims not only (or even primarily) by their religion and bearing, but by their "complexions and persons." Referring to all African Muslims as "Mandingoes," Edwards was particularly intrigued by "the tribe among them (called also the Phulies) [Fulani, or Fulbe] that seems to me to constitute the link between the Moors and Negroes properly so called." Describing Fulbe skin as "less glossy black" and their hair as "soft and silky to the touch" (though "bushy and crisped"), he averred that they were "not well adapted for hard labour." The elevation of the Mande and Fulbe above their fellows slaves, and their association with less demanding labor, are recurrent themes throughout the French- and English-speaking Caribbean and North America.

A number of these Muslims were similar to Muhammad Kaba in that they enjoyed substantial privilege while in Africa. As described to R. R. Madden, an Irish special magistrate sent to Jamaica to facilitate the 1833 Emancipation Act whereby the enslaved in British territories were to enter a four-year apprenticeship period prior acquiring their "full" freedom, Muhammad Kaba's father, Abu Bakr al-Qadiri, was a "substantial yeoman, possessing 140 slaves, several cows and horses, and grounds producing quantities of cotton, rice, and provisions."[18] The holdings of his father, combined with the fact that Kaba received his education from both his father and his uncle Muhammad Batul, suggests that wealth had been in Kaba's family long enough to provide the material basis requisite for the pursuit of scholarship. In fact, his full name, Muhammad Kaba Saghanughu, as revealed in an Arabic document he wrote some time before 1824, suggests that he was Jakhanke, a Mande community of related families engaged in both commerce and scholarship throughout Senegambia.[19] Indeed, the pre-1824 document also reveals an education

---

[18] See Madden, *Twelve Months*, vol. 2, 196–98.

[19] See Addoun and Lovejoy, "Arabic Manuscript of Muhammad Kabā Saghanughu," 5–6. On the Jakhanke, see Lamin O. Sanneh, *The Jakhanke: The History of an Islamic Clerical People of the Senegambia* (London: International African Institute, 1979); Thomas Hunter, "The Development of an Islamic Tradition of Learning Among the Jahanka of West Africa," (Ph.D. diss., U. of Chicago, 1977); Ivor Wilks, "The Transmission of Islamic Learning in the Western Sudan," in Jack Goody, ed., *Literacy in Traditional Societies* (Cambridge, England: Cambridge U. Press, 1968), 161–97. Originally thought to be passages from the Qur'ān, the document is deposited with the Baptist Missionary Society papers, Angus Library, Regent's Park College, University of Oxford. Addoun and Lovejoy have named the document *Kitāb al-Ṣalāt* ("The Book on Praying").

in West Africa related to the Qadiriyya *ṭarīqa*, a Sufi brotherhood in competition with several others in West Africa. Kaba refers to the *Ṣaḥīḥs* of al-Muslim and al-Bukhāri, two canonical texts of the *ḥadīth* or traditions of Muhammad, as well as the scholarship of 'Abd Āllāh b. al-Mubārak, *Shaykh* (master teacher) Bābā'l-Fakīru, and Abū Maydan (d. 594/1198), all of which suggests a Qadiriyya connection, as does his father's name.[20] Having reached adulthood in Africa, Kaba's sudden misfortune of capture and subsequent exportation may simply underscore the complex and unpredictable character of warfare at the time.

Muhammad Kaba was 78 years old in 1834, and he had spent some 56 years in Jamaican slavery on a property in coffee-producing Manchester. Renamed Robert Tuffit (or Robert Peart), he is significant for a number of reasons, the first of which is he was one of the oldest Muslims the special magistrate Madden encountered on the island (as it turns out, much of what is known about individual Muslims in Jamaica has filtered through Madden's recollection of his personal contact with them). As a result, it is particularly instructive to determine if Kaba's relationship to Islam had changed, as he had been so long severed from his origins. In response to this question, it would appear that "the old African" retained, at the very least, a very special place in his heart for Islam, and in all probability he remained a Muslim while feigning conversion to Christianity. Madden's commentary on an 1834 letter written by Kaba to another African Muslim in Jamaica, Abu Bakr as-Siddiq (henceforth Abu Bakr; called "Donlan" in the quote), supports this interpretation:

The curious part of the case is this: he writes a letter, in Arabic, to Donlan, and states... that the purport of the letter is to convert Donlan from Mahometanism to the Christian faith; and for this purpose the old African requests of me to be the medium of communication between them. But what is my surprise at finding the letter of the old man, who is so anxious to convert his countryman from the Mussulman creed, commencing in these terms, "In the name of God, merciful and omnipotent, the blessing of God, the peace of his prophet Mahomet!" So much for the old African's renunciation of Islamism.[21]

Kaba, who had "always borne an irreproachable character, and maintained a high place in the estimation of his employers," was alleged to have converted to Christianity some twenty years prior to writing this letter, in 1812, after thirty years of Jamaican bondage, proclaiming that he did "not regret his captivity, as it was the means of bringing him to the knowledge of Christ."[22] Baptized, he became a member of the Moravian Mission at Carmel, and would go on to

[20] See Addoun and Lovejoy, "Arabic Manuscript of Muhammad Kabā Saghanughu," 3–10. Also see John O. Hunwick, "Toward a History of the Islamic Intellectual Tradition in West Africa Down to the Nineteenth Century," *Journal of Islamic Sciences* 17 (1997): 9.

[21] See Madden, *Twelve Months*, vol. 2, 133–37; see also Allan D. Austin, *African Muslims in Antebellum America: A Sourcebook* (New York and London: Garland Publishing, 1984), 541.

[22] Ibid.

become a Moravian "helper" or elder.[23] His correspondence indicates, however, both a twenty-year exercise in dissimulation and a very complicated relationship to the Christian church. Abu Bakr's reply is equally instructive, as will be demonstrated shortly. It is important to note here, however, that Muhammad Kaba may have very well attempted to codify his message to Abu Bakr by using a referential device that will also be used elsewhere, namely the United States, by other African Muslims. The chapter on Muslims in the American South, therefore, includes a closer examination of written communication as artifice.

Muhammad Kaba is also significant for the revelation of the existence of a clerical letter, or *wathīqa*, that had circulated among Muslims in Jamaica some time prior to 1834. "About three years ago," or around 1831, Muhammad Kaba "received from Kingston, by the hands of a boy, a paper written in Africa forty-five years previously. He knew it to be of this date, as the paper was purported to have been written in the forty-third year of the age of the King, Allaman Talco, who was thirty-five years old when he (Robert Peart) left the country. The paper exhorted all the followers of Mahomet to be true and faithful, if they wished to go to Heaven, etc."[24] The dating of the letter has been contested, so that it may have been composed around 1827 or 1828, as opposed to 1786.[25] However, the question of the wathīqa's date should not obscure its larger potential significance; namely, that Muslims in Africa were aware of their enslaved coreligionists in the Americas, and they were exhorting the latter to remain faithful. In contrast, it is also possible that the letter was composed for Muslims in Africa without any thought of the New World, and that it was transported, conceivably smuggled, to Jamaica with other paraphernalia that somehow made the transoceanic crossing. However, events on the island would lead to the letter's destruction by Kaba's wife in 1832, at a time when servile insurrection made possession of the letter dangerous.

The "Baptist War" of 1831–32, so named because of the leadership of Baptist missionaries and independent ministers in the uprising, was not as readily embraced in Manchester Parish, where Kaba lived, as it was in other parts of the island. This may have been because of Kaba's apparent opposition to the revolt; in any event, a number of plantations in Manchester did not participate, and it is speculated that those enslaved on the Manchester plantations did not rise up largely in response to Kaba's leadership.[26] The symmetry between this response

---

[23] See J. M. Buchner, *The Moravians of Jamaica: History of the United Brethren's Church to the Negroes in the Island of Jamaica, From the Year 1754 to 1854* (London: Longman, Brown, 1854), 33, 50–52, 56–66, 69–75; Addoun and Lovejoy, "Arabic Manuscript of Muhammad Kabā," 12–15.

[24] See Madden, *Twelve Months*, vol. 2, 198.

[25] See Wilks, "Abū Bakr al-Siddīq," 163–64.

[26] See John Clark, W. Dendy, and J. M. Phillippo, *The Voice of Jubilee: A Narrative of the Baptist Mission, Jamaica, From its Commencement; With Biographical Notices of its Fathers and Founders* (London: John Snow, 1865), 55–66; Buchner, *Moravians of Jamaica*, 84–112; Addoun and Lovejoy, "Arabic Manuscript of Muhammad Kabā," 15–17. Sultana Afroz has characterized the

and the active opposition to insurrection by Muslim leaders in the Georgia Sea Islands (North America) is striking, and it will be discussed in Chapter 5.

The enduring presence of Muhammad Kaba, the pastoral circular, and the reaction to the events of 1831–32 speak to a third aspect of the old African's significance. That is, there was necessarily a community of Muslims in Jamaica who were aware of each other's presence and who clearly enjoyed the advantages of close proximity and regular fellowship. The enslaved who did not rise up out of loyalty to both Kaba and the Moravian Mission must have included Muslims. The boy bearing the letter from Kingston had to have some idea of the person to whom he was delivering it. In his October 1834 letter to Abu Bakr, Muhammad Kaba related that news of the former's manumission was a "heartfelt joy . . . for many told me about your character." The "many" may have very well included Muslims who knew Abu Bakr. Nevertheless, the role of the special magistrate Madden is also instructive in this context, for it was also through his contacts with individuals like Muhammad Kaba that further information about Muslims in Jamaica is revealed. Thus, Madden writes of the Sunday morning visit of three "Mandingo negroes, natives of Africa" who could "all read and write Arabic; and one of them showed me a Koran written from memory by himself."[27] One of the three visitors was Anna Musa (literally, "I am Musa") or "Benjamin Cochrane," who developed a salutary reputation as a physician, shared by some white doctors in Kingston. Musa's two companions are unidentified, but they could well have been "Benjamin Larten" and "William Rainsford," who are named in a separate document. Additional confirmation of a Muslim community is provided by an encounter with an unidentified elderly Muslim, who addressed Madden "with the Muslim *salaam* in Arabic; he was a native African, and he presented a pair of ducks. . . . He seemed to think I was a friend of his countrymen, and he wished to prove to me that he was grateful for it."[28]

Given the fact that most of these persons, including Abu Bakr and Muhammad Kaba, professed to have converted to Christianity, it cannot be asserted with certainty that none of these claims was in fact true. However, given the example of Muhammad Kaba, and in anticipation of the discussion of Abu Bakr and others elsewhere in the Americas, it is very possible if not probable that most if not all remained true to their Muslim beliefs and only affected Christian conversion, a posture not unlike that alleged of the moriscos of sixteenth-century Seville.[29] Indeed, ostensible Christian conversion was apparently a recent phenomenon in Jamaica, given that by 1788 "practically no attention had been paid to the conversion of Negroes," with the result that "some Mandingo Negroes

revolt as a jihad; see "The Jihad of 1831–1832: The Misunderstood Baptist Rebellion in Jamaica," *Journal of Muslim Minority Affairs* 21 (2001): 227–43.

[27] See Madden, *Twelve Months*, vol. 1, 98–102; see also Austin, *African Muslims in Antebellum America*, 547–50.

[28] See Madden, *Twelve Months*, vol. 2, 207.

[29] See Austin, *African Muslims in Antebellum America*, chapter 6, for a discussion of these "Six African Muslims in Jamaica."

retained vestiges of Mohammedanism."[30] Even a genuine embrace of Christianity was apparently negotiated through Islamic cognitive office, leading Madden to make this remark: "I do not mean to say there was any hypocrisy in the new profession. . . . I only mean to state my belief, that all the proselytes I have seen in Mahometan countries, have rather ingrafted the doctrines of Christianity on the stem of Mahometanism, than plucked up the latter, root and branch, to make way for the former."[31]

When he first met Madden, and in contrast to Muhammad Kaba, Anna Musa was technically a "free negro" with at least one slave of his own: "As an Arabic scholar, his attainments are very trifling, but his skill as a negro doctor, one of the English physicians of Kingston assured me was considerable," an assessment derived in part from Musa's success in curing a young white woman's serious illness. Musa's Sunday visits to Madden's home, where he would hold forth on "medical plants and popular medicine," led the latter to conclude that "a more intelligent and respectable person, in every sense of the word, I do not know." Musa had actually begun studying the effects of plants and herbs on cattle while a lad in Africa, where Madden places him "in the Mandingo country," while Musa himself identifies his home as the "Carsoe nation," which was probably Khasso, a partially Islamized polity located in the upper Senegal valley that combined both Fulbe and Malinke populations. With his capture, Musa was initially taken to Tortola, then Jamaica, then Antigua, again back to Jamaica, and then to Barbados via a bewildering set of scenarios that saw him exit and reenter enslavement (or an unfree status in the guise of serving in a West Indian regiment) several times. It was in Barbados that he served aboard a vessel commanded by a Lord Cochrane and apparently sailed with him to the West African coast nearest his homeland ("I was in a place called Senegal") for an unspecified period. Consistent with his bizarre story, there is no indication that he was aware of the irony and sought to escape. Instead, he completed his service in Jamaica and became a free man.[32] Perhaps Anna Musa is the rarity, an African Muslim who preferred exile to home.

Notwithstanding the laudable qualities of Muhammad Kaba and the strange tale of Anna Musa, it was Abu Bakr with whom Madden was most fascinated. Born in Timbuktu around 1790, Abu Bakr subsequently lived from ages two to nine in Jenne, where he received his initial education. He then began traveling in regions more southerly, all the while under the care of a tutor. In particular, he spent a year in the Juula town of Kong, after which he spent the rest of his days in Africa in "Bouna," another Juula town. These and other entrepots linked such savannah towns as Jenne and Ja to gold and kola nut-producing lands to the south, most importantly the Akan goldfields under the sway of

---

[30] See Frank Wesley Pitman, "Slavery in the British West India Plantations in the Eighteenth Century," *Journal of Negro History* 11 (1926): 663.

[31] See Madden, *Twelve Months*, vol. 2, 135–37.

[32] Ibid., vol. 1, 98–102. On Khasso, see Michael A. Gomez, *Pragmatism in the Age of Jihad: The Precolonial State of Bundu* (Cambridge, England: Cambridge U. Press, 1992).

imperial Asante with its capital at Kumase. Warring factions within Asante, no doubt related to the growth of Muslim power and its implications for control of the gold and kola trades, led to the reassertion of non-Muslim authority and the targeting of Muslim forces and their commercial allies. Bouna was attacked, and Abu Bakr was one of those captured and taken first to Kumase and then to Lago port (just east of Accra and west of Cape Coast), where he was sold to an English slaver around 1805. He was thus part of the comparatively large percentage of Africans who sailed for Jamaica from the Gold Coast.[33]

By the time special magistrate Madden came across Abu Bakr in 1834, he had been been "owned" by three persons. He was initially the "property" of a stonemason named Donellan, from whom he was purchased by one Haynes, who baptized Abu Bakr as "Edward Donellan" (also spelled Donlan and Doulan). In 1823 he was purchased by Alexander Anderson, who came to recognize Abu Bakr's literacy skills and used him as his record keeper, a task Abu Bakr performed in Arabic. It was in this capacity that Abu Bakr first came to Madden in September of 1834. He had been sent by slaveholder Anderson "as a constable on his master's property." Madden "discovered, by mere accident of seeing the man sign his name in very well written Arabic, while I was swearing in his comrades, that he was a man of education, and, on subsequent inquiry, a person of exalted rank in his own country."[34] It is possible that Abu Bakr was trained in calligraphy, as one member of the House of Assembly exclaimed "I had often heard, too, of the beauty of his penmanship; but the idea I had formed of it fell infinitely short of the specimen you [Madden] had put into my hands."[35] Subsequent visits by Abu Bakr led Madden to observe the following:

[H]is attainments, as an Arabic scholar, were the least of his merits. I found him a person of excellent conduct, of great discernment and discretion. I think if I wanted advice, on any important matter, in which it required extreme prudence, and a high sense of moral rectitude to qualify the possessor to give counsel, I would as soon have recourse to the advice of this poor negro as any person I know.[36]

So impressed was Madden, and perhaps also motivated by Abu Bakr's potential as a commercial agent in West Africa, that he began negotiating with Anderson for Abu Bakr's freedom within days of their first encounter. Anderson's initial refusal was hardly a surprise, given that "the accounts of the whole of his vast business were kept by him [Abu Bakr] – in short, that no sum of money which could be awarded to him could compensate him for the loss of the man's services." However, Anderson reversed himself several weeks later under public pressure and manumitted Abu Bakr without compensation, since he "had been a good servant to him – a faithful and good negro."

[33] See Wilks, "Abū Bakr al-Siddīq," for background information.
[34] See Madden, *Twelve Months*, vol. 2, 108–09.
[35] Ibid., vol. 2, 130–33.
[36] Ibid., vol. 2, 108–9.

Upon his return to England in 1835, Madden appealed to the Royal Geographic Society to consider Abu Bakr for a voyage to West Africa, but was rebuffed out of concern for Abu Bakr's long absence from Africa and hence questionable suitability. Even so, Abu Bakr was brought to England in 1835 by another special magistrate Captain Oldrey, whereupon Madden persuaded one John Davidson to take Abu Bakr along with him to Timbuktu. It did not go well for Davidson, who after leaving for Morocco in September of 1835 was killed in a raid in November of the following year en route to Timbuktu. Communication with Abu Bakr was lost until 1841, when the British vice-consul at Morocco learned that Abu Bakr had arrived safely in Jenne. He was one of the few to actually achieve the return.

Abu Bakr is best known for his autobiography. In fact, he wrote three versions of it: The first was completed for Madden in 1834 while both were still in Jamaica; a second was penned on the passage from Jamaica to England; and a final redaction was recorded in England in 1835. All three were written in Arabic, with the first translated orally for Madden and the latter two given to G. C. Renouard. The first and last translations have survived, whereas all three Arabic originals have yet to surface.[37]

It is clear from the autobiography that Abu Bakr hailed from a privileged background. Claiming to be of sharifian heritage, that is, a descendant of the prophet Muhammad, his father was called "Kara [Karamoko?] Mūsa the Sharīf," and was a *tafsīr* or expert in Qur'ānic exegesis (from the Arabic *mufassir*). He married Abu Bakr's mother "in the land of Katsina and Bornu," suggesting that the woman was Fulbe (or Hausa) or Kanuri. As one result, Kara Musa continued to send to his father-in-law gold from the Akan fields, along with horses, other beasts of burden, and "valuable silks from Egypt, with much wealth." The gold was gathered, according to Abu Bakr, by his father's slaves, and their trip to Kong, and then Bouna, was facilitated by his father's slaves. Kara Musa in fact visited his brothers in these towns, which may indicate that the brothers were merchants. That they may have been merchants in Juula towns strongly implies that they themselves were Juula; that is, Muslim, non-proselytizing Mande-speaking trading communities dispersed widely throughout West Africa. If Abu Bakr's father was Mande, it would mean that at least Abu Bakr and Muhammad Kaba were Mande-speakers, linguistically related to the mandingas of the Spanish-speaking colonies. However, in nineteenth-century Jamaica and in contrast to their image in Spanish-speaking areas, these mandingas were much more favorably viewed.

One of the principal reasons for this favorable rating was that, in contrast with many Muslims in sixteenth-century Hispaniola and elsewhere, none of the

---

[37] In addition to Madden's *Twelve Months*, see Wilson Armistead, *A Tribute for the Negro* (Manchester, England: W. Irwin, 1848), 245–47 and G. C. Renouard, "Routes in North Africa by Abú Bekr as Siddík," *Journal of the Royal Geographical Society* 6 (1836): 102–07. For a discussion of all of this, see Wilks, "Abū Bakr al-Siddīq."

Muslims encountered by Madden in Jamaica was in any way associated with subversive behavior; on the contrary, like Muhammad Kaba, who apparently did not support a slave uprising, these Muslims were seen as progressive and well suited for the slaveocracy, respectful of authority and reliable, "faithful and good negroes" like Abu Bakr. In return, such Muslims were often rewarded with vocationally skilled positions or placed in positions of responsibility over others similarly enslaved. Patterns of privileging Muslim individuals would develop all over anglophone America, and they stand out in sharp relief against the anti-Muslim mania of the Spanish and Portuguese domains. The reasons for the different experiences and policies are several.

First, the periods in which Muslims were seen as threatening Spanish dominion (a justified fear for the most part) tended to be earlier, when Muslims from Senegambia, for example, arrived in substantial numbers and could galvanize their followers (of course, Brazil's experience was somewhat divergent). In Jamaica and Trinidad and North America, however, Islamic communities were engulfed by seas of African non-Muslim traditions. Second, African Muslims were seen by whites (especially anglophones) as superior to other Africans, a conviction internalized at times by the Muslims themselves. This idea of superiority originated from their possession of literacy, their adherence to monotheism, and their membership in ethnolinguistic groupings of preference (issues receiving greater scrutiny in subsequent chapters). All of these elements can be observed in Madden's reflection that "the Mandingoes are said to be superior in intelligence to the other classes. Many of them read and write Arabic; and my own experience confirms the account of Bryan Edwards as to their priding themselves on their mental superiority over the other negroes."[38] Third, the reputation of Muslims in Jamaica and Trinidad as loyalists developed around the time and within the context of apprenticeship; with qualified emancipation in sight, an accommodationist strategy would certainly have its advantages. Fourth, it is not clear that privileged individuals such as Abu Bakr and Muhammad Kaba, who themselves owned slaves in West Africa (while Anna Musa owned at least one in Jamaica), were necessarily abolitionists. It is true that Abu Bakr testified to having "tasted the bitterness of slavery . . . and its oppressiveness" in Jamaica, but this did not mean that he was unalterably opposed to the institution itself. Finally, there was a history and tradition of conflict between Christians, Muslims, and Jews in Iberia, a conflict that was in many ways transported to the New World. England had no such tradition, and therefore had no reason to anticipate religious hostility in any a priori fashion.

It can also be argued that Abu Bakr's embrace of fatalism, a conviction not universally shared by Muslims, was hardly the basis for insurrectionary activity, his articulation of *maktūb* ("that which is [already] written")

---

[38] See Madden, *Twelve Months*, vol. 1, 98–100. Also see Bryan Edwards, *The History, Civil and Commercial, of the British Colonies in the West Indies*, 2nd ed. (London: printed for John Stockdale, 1794), vol. 2, 65.

scarcely the stuff of incendiary discourse. Hence, his reflections on becoming enslaved:

But praise be to God, under whose power are all things. He does whatsoever He wills! No one can turn aside that which He has ordained, nor can anyone withhold that which He has given. As God Almighty himself has said: Nothing can befall us unless it is written for us (in his book)! He is our master: in God, therefore, let all the faithful put their trust![39]

Abu Bakr's reference to the Qur'ān, while betraying his convictions as a Muslim, also sprang from a deep well of personal experience in West Africa, revealing familiarity with mechanisms of power and therefore constituting a validation, not necessarily of his own enslavement, but of the idea of servitude itself. At the same time, however, it must be remembered that his autobiography was written for an audience that included Madden, so that by referencing the Qur'ān he was also making an interior statement that exposed a core of cultural autonomy in his thinking. That Islam was integral to his integrity is evidenced by a nuanced, coded letter to Christian clergy after his alleged conversion to Christianity:

I beg leave to inform you that I am rejoiced and well pleased in my heart for the great boon I have received in the Testament, both of the old and new law of our Lord and Saviour, in the Arabic language. I am now very anxious to get a prayer-book, the psalms, and an Arabic grammar – also a copy of the Alcoran.[40]

While the request for the Qur'ān may simply represent a nostalgic moment, it is more probably the key to unveiling of Abu Bakr's actual disposition, a conspicuous inconsistency in an otherwise plausible display of dissembling. A similar strategy (and interpretation) may be observed in his October 1834 response to Muhammad Kaba, who begins his letter with the statement, "This is from the hand of Mahomed Caba, unto Bekir Sadiki Scheriffe," and ends the correspondence by asking Abu Bakr "to give me a good answer, 'Salaam aleikoum.'" Abu Bakr's reply confirms his Muslim identity by echoing Kaba's salutation:

Dear Countryman, I now answer your last letter, my name, in Arabic, is Abon Becr Sadiki, and in Christian language, Edward Doulan, I born in Timbuktu, and brought up in Jenne; I finished read the Coran in the country of Bouna, which place I was taken captive in war.[41]

In the absence of the actual Arabic correspondence, we are in some ways proscribed by Madden's apparently errant translation, but the essentials of the exchange are sufficient to establish that thirty years of Jamaican captivity were insufficient to dislodge Abu Bakr's tenacious hold on an African Muslim identity. The rest of the letter, while consistent with a kind of sociopolitical conservatism, more probably simply reveals elation over his personal manumission

---

[39] See Wilks, "Abū Bakr al-Siddīq," for the manner in which he combines elements from both the Madden and Renouard translations.
[40] See Madden, *Twelve Months*, vol. 2, 136–37.
[41] Ibid., vol. 2, 198–99.

and pending repatriation, as well as recognition of the roles of Madden and slaveholder Anderson in those processes:

My master's name in this country is Alexander Anderson. Now my countryman, God hath given me a faithful man, a just and a good master, he made me free; and I know truly that he has shown mercy to every poor soul under him. I know he has done that justice which our King William the Fourth commanded him to do (God save the king) and may he be a conqueror over all his enemies, from east to west, from north to south, and the blessing of God extend over all his kingdom, and all his ministers and subjects. I beseech you, Mahomed Caba, and all my friends, continue in praying for my friend, my life, and my breadfruit, which friend is my worthy Dr. Madden, and I hope that God may give him honour, greatness, and gladness, and likewise his generation to come, as long as Heaven and Earth stands... Dear countryman, I also beseech you to remember in your prayers my master Alexander Anderson, who gave me my liberty free and willingly; and may the Almighty prosper him, and protect him from all dangers.[42]

* * *

European occupation of Trinidad (see Map 5) began July 31, 1498, and for the next 300 years the island languished under Spanish domination.[43] This would change with the cédula of 1783, by which migration and the expansion of slavery were encouraged through the offer of land:

At the heart of the Cedula were the provisions for settling the land. Any national of a state friendly to Spain, being a Roman Catholic, who went to the island, and took the oath of allegiance to Spain, would be entitled to free land. If a white male or female, the personal allotment was ten carreaux, with an additional five carreaux for each slave imported into the island. Free black and free coloured settlers were entitled to half the entitlement of land given to whites. The land granted was without cost and could be held forever, provided that the grantees settled in the island for at least five years.[44]

The 1783 cédula was apparently crafted to "attract wealthy French planters," since the terms of the decree meant that "settlers would be almost exclusively French, for only the French planters could fulfill the requirement of Roman Catholicism and alliance with Spain."[45] Together with the soon-to-commence

---

[42] Ibid.; see also Wilks, "Abū Bakr al-Siddīq," 163–66.
[43] See James Millette, *Society and Politics in Colonial Trinidad* (Curepe, Trinidad: Omega Bookshops, 1970, 1985), 1.
[44] Carl Campbell, *Cedulants and Capitulants: The Politics of the Coloured Opposition in the Slave Society of Trinidad, 1783–1838* (Port of Spain, Trinidad: Paria Publishing, 1992), 91–92. The conversion is as follows: 1 carreau = 3.2 acres. See also Donald Wood, *Trinidad in Transition: The Years After Slavery* (London and New York: Oxford U. Press, for the Institute of Race Relations, 1968), 31–32.
[45] Bridget Brereton, *A History of Modern Trinidad, 1783–1962* (Port of Spain, Trinidad: Heinemann, 1981), 14. Also see V. S. Naipaul, *The Loss of El Dorado* (London: Andre Deutsch, 1969); Eric Williams, *History of the People of Trinidad and Tobago* (New York: Praeger, 1964); Gertrude Carmichael, *The History of the West Indian Islands of Trinidad and Tobago, 1498–1900* (London: Redman, 1961); Lionel Mordaunt Fraser, *History of Trinidad*, 2 vols. (Port of Spain, Trinidad: Government Printing Office, 1891 and 1896; 1971).

Trinidad

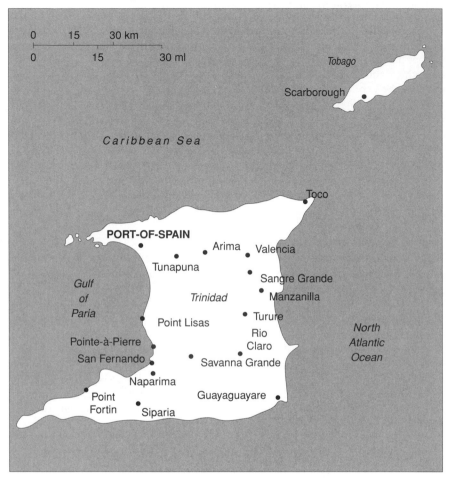

MAP 5.

French Revolution, the cédula had the effect of encouraging not only the wealthy but those of various strata from the francophone world. By 1784, only one year after the proclamation, the island was "'a French colony in all but name',"with the French outnumbering the Spanish twenty to one.[46] In that same year, immigrants from Grenada, Martinique, Guadeloupe, St. Lucia, and Cayenne began to arrive in significant numbers, establishing the dominance of the French and Creole languages. Of course, among the new arrivals were enslaved persons; some 3,000 to 4,000 arrived in 1792 from Martinique alone.[47]

In contrast to Jamaica, Barbados, and other Caribbean islands, the arrival of substantial numbers of enslaved Africans in Trinidad was relatively late. Before

[46] See Wood, *Trinidad in Transition*, 32; Millette, *Society and Politics in Colonial Trinidad*, 24–25.
[47] See Brereton, *A History of Modern Trinidad*, 22; Wood, *Trinidad in Transition*, 32.

1783, Trinidad's population had never exceeded more than "a few hundred"; for example, in 1777, by which time Jamaica's population had exceeded its 1762 mark of 146,805 (and would reach 291,000 by 1795), there were only 200 enslaved blacks, 870 free "mulattoes," and 340 whites in Trinidad. In 1782, the population stood at 2,813, but by 1789 the figure had increased sixfold to 18,918, an estimate that included 2,200 indigenous survivors, 10,100 enslaved persons, 4,467 free "coloreds," and 2,151 whites.[48] The importation patterns are striking: as high as 63 percent of enslaved Africans imported directly from Africa to Trinidad were from the Bight of Biafra, and as high as 18 percent from West Central Africa. The Gold Coast, Senegambia, Sierra Leone, and the Bight of Benin, areas from which Muslims would have come, contributed the remaining 19 percent.[49]

The rapid development of labor allowed Trinidad to quickly "step into line as a major producer of West Indian staples," and by 1797 and the takeover of the island by the British, sugar had become the island's most important crop.[50] A "third-phase" sugar-producing colony, Trinidad had over 150 sugar estates by 1797, serviced by 130 mills that produced 7,800 hogheads of sugar per annum.[51] Sugar production reached an initial peak in 1805, a level not again achieved until 1826, after which there was rapid expansion of sugarcane cultivation. By 1832, 90 percent of the total value of Trinidad's exports was provided by sugar and its by-products. By that time, it is estimated that 70 percent of the enslaved population labored on sugarcane estates.

While the sugar industry was clearly important in Trinidad, it was by no means the only industry of significance. Like Jamaica, Trinidad boasted a "relatively diversified agricultural economy," typified by considerable investment in cocoa, coffee, and cotton production. Cocoa in particular remained an important crop from the Spanish period, but as a smallholder's specialty it was principally cultivated by the numerous free "colored" (of mixed racial ancestry) and black populations and was not as dependent on slave labor. In 1810, at least 20 percent of Trinidad's population was free and colored, owning 37.3 percent of all estates and 31.5 percent of all enslaved persons.[52] Even so, the overwhelming majority were smallholders; only two free coloreds owned sugar estates with over 100 enslaved persons.

While the 1783 cédula led to the swift peopling of the island and the emergence of a bustling export economy, adjustments in the British Caribbean labor market led to yet another phase of significant immigration into Trinidad. With the 1807 British abolition of the slave trade as context, the response to the

---

[48] See Millette, *Society and Politics in Colonial Trinidad*, 15; Wood, *Trinidad in Transition*, 32.

[49] See the *Du Bois CD-ROM Database*. The percentages are as follows: Gold Coast, 10.4 percent; Senegambia, 2.29 percent; Sierra Leone, 1.96 percent; and Bight of Benin, 4.49 percent.

[50] See Millette, *Society and Politics in Colonial Trinidad*, 18–19; Brereton, *A History of Modern Trinidad*, 17.

[51] See Higman, *Slave Populations of the British Caribbean*, 58–62; Brereton, *A History of Modern Trinidad*, 17–18.

[52] See Brereton, *A History of Modern Trinidad*, 64.

disparities in shifting labor needs and values was an intercolonial redistribu-
tion of servile labor, wherein some 20,000 enslaved workers were moved from
place to place within the Caribbean between 1813 and 1825.[53] Trinidad absorbed some 6,000 of these workers, while Demerara-Essequibo also registered notable gains in imported labor. The period of 1813 to 1825, the only
time span for which origins of exported workers are so far available, saw Dominica, Berbice, and the Bahamas as the overall leaders in exporting labor.
The principal suppliers to Trinidad, however, were Dominica and Grenada, accounting for some 39 percent of the total number. The Virgin Islands also sent
"significant numbers," along with Barbados, St. Vincent, and the Bahamas,
whereas Anguilla, Nevis, and Montserrat's contributions were "modest." Once
in Trinidad, the new workers were concentrated in the western portion of the
island, rimming the Gulf of Paria, together with the existing servile population.
The introduction of imported labor also effected a steady progression toward
a balanced sex ratio, resulting in a change from 123.9 males to 100 females in
1817, to 112.6 males to 100 females by 1832. The question of African origins
in Trinidad, therefore, is challengingly complex.

With the conclusion of the Napoleonic Wars, the British government set
about the task of demobilizing their African and African-descended troops.
One experiment involved resettling these and others who had allied with the
British cause. Among the latter were American freedpersons who between 1812
and 1815 had either fought in the Corps of Colonial Marines on the side of
the British or had been "set free" by British forces during the course of the
war.[54] Originally disbanded in the Bahamas, some eventually settled in Nova
Scotia, while others were sent to Trinidad after 1815, where the population at
the time was only 30,000. There they were settled in eight "Company villages"
near Port of Spain in Laventille and Caroni, and then in the southern part of
the island in Naparima, 15 miles south of San Fernando, as well as near Princes
Town in the Savanna Grande region. The villages, named according to their
companies, contained about eighty men each, and each man was given sixteen
acres of land. Such privileging necessarily resulted in advantages; the notion
that the freedpersons' example "could not but produce a profound social effect
on their fellow Negroes in the island, stimulating a greater spirit of independence" does not reflect all of the dynamics at play.[55] The "Americans," as
they were called, apparently achieved some level of agricultural success, and by
1824 there were 923 in the villages, their numbers augmented by "liberated"
African women (about whom more will be stated shortly) sent to correct the imbalanced sex ratio. However, even with the post-1826 expansion of sugarcane

---

[53] See Higman, *Slave Populations of the British Caribbean*, 72–90, 118–22.
[54] See K. O. Laurence, "The Settlement of Free Negroes in Trinidad Before Emancipation,"
Caribbean Quarterly 9 (1963): 26–52; Brereton, *A History of Modern Trinidad*, 68; Wood, *Trinidad
in Transition*, 38.
[55] See Carlton R. Ottley, *Slavery Days in Trinidad: A Social History of the Island From 1797–1838*
(Trinidad: C. R. Ottley, 1974), 66–67.

cultivation and their gradual absorption into Trinidadian society, the Americans managed to maintain a sense of unique identity late into the nineteenth century. To a large degree, the perpetuation of this identity was made possible by the retention of their religious tradition. Theirs was a "highly emotional Baptist worship.... Their services were apocalyptic and noisy, and caused concern to the staid English Baptist ministers who visited them." In fact, it may be that religion was the Americans' small contribution to Trinidadian culture, as they "started a fashion in the religious life of Trinidad that has persisted, in spite of official disapproval, until the present day."[56]

In contrast to the American Baptist legacy, quite a different tradition was being established elsewhere in the island. Between 1818 and 1825, demobilized troops from the Third and Sixth West India Regiments were settled between Arima and Manzanilla in northern and eastern Trinidad.[57] The ranks of the West India Regiments had been initially filled by free and enslaved blacks specifically purchased from slaveholders throughout the Caribbean, but the need for more troops saw the British establish a center in 1812 at Bunce Island, Sierra Leone, where either indigenous persons or those liberated from slavers were recruited. Many in the Regiments were therefore African born. Interestingly, members of the Trinidad-based Third West India Regiment strongly opposed repatriation to West Africa, so that resettlement in sparsely populated Trinidad seemed a logical solution.[58] In February of 1825, some 376 men, 35 women, and 34 children from the Third Regiment settled in villages on a line east of Arima stretching to the east coast, and they were spaced in such a way as to facilitate communication from Port of Spain across northern Trinidad. In contrast to the Americans at Naparima, single men in villages at Manzanilla, Quaré (apparently what is now Valencia), Turure, and La Seiva, areas relatively isolated through the 1830s, were given eight acres each (sixteen for families) and received no additional funds (the Americans were paid annual quit rents of $1.56). Even so, settlements such as Quaré were making "good progress" by 1825, with houses "'much more spacious, comfortable and cleaner than the houses of slaves.'" Settlements in northern and eastern Trinidad, though initially productive agriculturally, would suffer from chronic transportation problems, as maintaining roads proved exceedingly difficult. There is evidence, however, that to some extent roads were not maintained to maximize autonomy and to keep colonial influence at bay. Colonial authorities responded by regularly threatening to withhold alcoholic allotments if work was not performed on the roads.[59]

The religious practices of the northern and eastern settlements were of some interest to British authorities and missionaries. In the 1820s, when there were no regular clergy assigned to the settlements, it is estimated that there were

[56] See Wood, *Trinidad in Transition*, 38–39.
[57] See Laurence, "Settlement of Free Negroes in Trinidad," 26–27.
[58] Ibid., 27.
[59] Ibid., 30–35.

"perhaps 200 Methodists and 20 Muslims."[60] It is difficult to know the effect on religious life of colonial efforts to correct sexual imbalances. However, from 1817 to 1828, parcels of women from Africa (captured from slavers), Halifax, and Antigua were occasionally brought into the settlements, where by the latter year some 150 men at Quaré and Manzanilla were estimated to have remained "unattached." By 1834, when the Moravians decided to establish what would be an unsuccessful mission at Quaré and Manzanilla, the imbalance persisted at 443 men, 91 women, and 151 children. Six years later, schools were established at the two villages.[61]

It is all the more remarkable, therefore, that after visiting Quaré and Manzanilla in 1841, the Reverend J. H. Hamilton, rector of the Church of England over Tacarigua, Arouca, and Arima, gave the following report:

I am sorry to say that their moral and religious state is most deplorable. From the entire want, for a long series of years, of clerical instruction, even the outward form of Christianity has almost disappeared amongst them; indeed, melancholy to relate, many of them have relapsed into the errors of Mahometanism, under the guidance of three Mandingo priests established amongst them. One of their number can write, and has copied portions of the Koran, which he reads to his assembled followers, and to whom they seem to look up with the greatest reverence.[62]

Several of the Regiments' exsergeants had been described as "Mandingo Muslims," and a number of factors had apparently combined to reify both their leadership and Islam: the absence of any sustained missionary efforts; the relative isolation of the settlements; a shared desire for autonomy; and the advantages they enjoyed as former officers, as all the settlements were organized according to military protocol and discipline. Perhaps resentment over the withholding of alcohol also contributed to their ascendance, but Hamilton's testimony strongly suggests that there was a functioning Muslim community in Quaré and Manzanilla that consisted of not only Muslims born in Africa but Muslims converted in Trinidad. Just a few months before his May 1841 testimony, Hamilton had written to the Governor that many of the Muslims in Manzanilla and Turure were "nominally Mohammedans (!) who are under the influence and guidance of five (so called) Mandingo priests by whom they are instructed in portions of the Koran; one only of this number can write, to whom they seem to look up with great reverence." Hamilton identified this leader as

---

[60] See the evidence of William Wright before Committee of Council, enclosure in no. 629, PRO CO 295/66; also in Laurence, "Settlement of Free Negroes in Trinidad," 36. Compare this with the testimony of Robert Mitchell before the same committee, who stated that while there was no government-supported clergy in the settlements, "they have about five Anabaptist preachers amongst themselves, who occasionally lecture on Sundays." Asked about the "religious persuasion" of the settlers, Mitchell estimated that "the great body are Anabaptists, about one fourth Methodists, and perhaps twenty Mahomedans." Robert Mitchell, Esq., Extracts of the Minutes of Evidence Taken by the Committee, Tuesday, December 14, 1824, PRO CO 295/66.

[61] See Laurence, "Settlement of Free Negroes in Trinidad," 37–38.

[62] See Rev. J. H. Hamilton, Minutes of Evidence Taken by the Sub-Committee of the Agricultural and Immigration Society, PRO CO 295/134.

"Seyimah Brock," who "appears to possess an extraordinary influence over the settlers of that faith."[63] By 1841, therefore, Quaré and Manzanilla were "predominantly Muslim," and the language of the settlements was "Manzanillan," a blend of English, French, and African languages.[64]

Ultimately, the Muslim community in such places as Quaré and Manzanilla was undermined by the withdrawal of government support. Difficult to sustain in the first place, these settlements were financed by whatever produce they could get to market, and by the pensions of the former soldiers. When the Treasury in England discontinued pension payments as part of an effort to trim expenditures, the colonial government also began disengaging from the settlements themselves. Reports from the area in 1841 describe an unraveling situation: while rice, yams, corn, plantains, and ginger were yet being produced and marketed, the housing and living conditions of the inhabitants were characterized as "very inferior," quite a contrast with conditions in 1825. The remainder of the 1840s saw the total abandonment of the settlements by the government, which, together with the constant flooding of the Quaré River and new opportunities presented by emancipation, encouraged settlers to relocate elsewhere in Trinidad.[65] The isolation of the few who remained was perforated in the late 1860s with the completion of a permanent road linking Arima to the coast, thereby facilitating both commerce and the spread of Christianity. In the end, Islam had achieved paramountcy in at least two of these villages and was probably influential among the others. Research is currently underway into the material culture left behind by these Muslims.[66]

In fanning out from the failed settlements of northern and eastern Trinidad, some Muslims came into contact with coreligionists in Port of Spain, the other locus of Islamic activity in Trinidad. One such Muslim was Muhammad Sisse (Sisei). Born between 1788 and 1790 in Niani-Maru on the Gambia River to parents Abu Bakr and Aisha, Sisse "belonged to the class of Muslim traders," a possible reference to the Jakhanke.[67] Having married, he "settled down to

---

[63] See the Letter from Rev. Hamilton, March 19, 1841, PRO CO 295/34. The reference to "Seyimah Brock" is in a report immediately following that of March 19, but in a different handwriting. Regarding the March 19 report, Hamilton added: "I enclose a specimen of his writing with the translation as dictated by himself for Your Excellency's inspection." There is no enclosure, however; see folios 275–82. Also see Brinsley Samaroo, "Early African and East Indian Muslims in Trinidad and Tobago," in David Dabydeen and Brinsley Samaroo, eds., *Across the Dark Waters: Ethnicity and Indian Identity in the Caribbean* (London: MacMillan Education, 1996).

[64] See Wood, 37–38; Brereton, *A History of Modern Trinidad*, 68–69.

[65] See Laurence, "Settlement of Free Negroes in Trinidad," 38–47.

[66] The author is grateful to Dr. Brinsley Samaroo, who shared information from archaeological digs in the region in the summer of 2003. He has prepared a video presentation on the topic, entitled "Some Early Muslims in Trinidad: A Lecture in the Valencia Forest" (Infovision). He has also prepared an abstract, entitled "Archeological Study of Muslim Heritage in Trinidad."

[67] A Jakhanke center existed in Niani. The clan name *Sisse*, in turn, is a very old maraboutic clan appellation that can be associated with the Serrakhole of the region. See Michael A. Gomez, *Pragmatism in the Age of Jihad: The Precolonial State of Bundu* (Cambridge, England: Cambridge U. Press, 1992), 24, 29, 116–18.

sedentary life of a school-teacher" in Niani-Maru prior to his capture some time after 1810. Sold to a French slaver that was interdicted by a British antislavery squadron, Sisse was taken to Antigua, mustered into the Third West India Regiment, and renamed Felix Ditt. Once stationed in Barbados, he saw action against the French in Guadaloupe. Arriving in eastern Trinidad in 1816 after his regiment's demobilization, Sisse is said to have helped to strengthen those already in the faith while working to convert others, such that "a complete regiment was converted to Islam in Trinidad," possibly a reference to Manzanilla, Quaré, or other such villages. However, Sisse "somehow had neither land nor pension" in eastern Trinidad, and he eventually drifted to Port of Spain. There, Sisse would join forces with coreligionists to unsuccessfully petition the British government several times to assist their return to West Africa. Determined, Sisse borrowed $144 "from another Mandingo" and purchased passage for himself, his wife ("a creole woman from Grenada" he had married in 1831), and a young child to England in 1838. There, his cause was taken up by Captain John Washington, secretary of the Royal Geographical Society, who questioned him concerning Mungo Park's report before taking his case to the Colonial Office. Washington was so impressed with Sisse, who "knew the Koran well" and who wrote his native language "indifferently in Arabic characters," that he had a portrait of him made. Agreeing to act as a commercial agent for the British (and completely analogous to the experience of Ayuba Sulayman in North America), he returned to the Gambia and possibly Niani-Maru in 1838, after which he disappears from the record.[68]

Two other Muslims who had been in Quaré before connecting with the Port of Spain Muslims were Muhammad Hausa, also known as Philip Finlay, and "Jackson Harvey." Arriving in Quaré in 1818, the two men wrote their own petition in 1837, in which can be found reference to both their service in the West India Regiment and their relationship with Muslims in Trinidad:

Therewith, that Memorialists are Native Africans and were brought from there in the year 1809 as recruits for His Majesties Third West India Regt.

That in the year 1818 the Left Wing of that Regt having been disbanded, memorialists were discharged and some years afterwards formed the design of returning to their native country.

That in order to effect this Memorialists submitted with they of their countrymen a petition to the Gov't of Trinidad, praying His Majesties Gov't to provide a vessel to carry them to Africa, but that the prayer of their petition was not favorably received.

That Memorialists being still anxious to return to their native land have paid the amount of their passage to ___ from Trinidad, at the cost, exclusive of provisions, for the voyage, of seventy dollars each for themselves and wives.

[68] See Austin, *African Muslims in Antebellum America*, 37–38; Carl Campbell, "Mohammedu Sisei of Gambia and Trinidad, c. 1788–1838," *African Studies Association of the West Indies Bulletin* 7 (1974): 29–28. Most of the information on Cissé is derived from Captain John Washington, who interviewed Cissé in 1838. See John Washington, "Some Account of Mohammedu Sisei, a Mandingo, of Nyani-Maru in the Gambia," *Journal of the Royal Geographical Society* 8 (1838): 449–54.

That Memorialists humbly submit, that the nation to which they belong – Mandingoes – were enabled previously to the 1ˢᵗ August 1834 [reference to the start of the Apprenticeship and end of slavery] to set free by purchase every individual of that Nation in Trinidad, *with a few in some of the other islands*, thereby showing their peaceable and industrious habits.

That Memorialists humbly implore your Lordship to take their case with your gracious consideration, that you would be pleased to grant to them and to their wives a conveyance to Sierra Leone, and that your Lordship would be further pleased to consider the case of their countrymen whom they have left behind with a view to their return also and as in duty bound they will ever pray.[69] [italics added]

The characterization of the Muslim community as industrious is important (and will be examined). Reference to contact with Muslims on "other islands" is incredibly suggestive, and it recalls the wathīqa that surfaced in Jamaica. However, given the interisland circulation of persons both free and enslaved, it is entirely possible if not probable that Muslims were able to maintain some level of contact between islands. In any event, this specific petition was answered in September of 1837, after which the two and their wives went on to Sierra Leone and the Bight of Benin via Badagry, following a possible audience with Queen Victoria. That they traveled together and both went to the Bight of Benin strongly suggests that both were Hausa.[70]

In contrast to the American refugees, Muhammad Sisse, Muhammad Hausa, and many others from the Third West India Regiment were African born. Their regular contact with the rest of Trinidadian, African-derived society meant that they experienced points of significant correspondence. The census of 1813, for example, listed 25,696 enslaved persons, of whom 11,633 were creole or born somewhere outside of Africa, while the majority of 14,063 were born in Africa. Of the latter group, some 2,863 or 20 percent are estimated by de Verteuil to have been Igbo, a figure considerably less than the 41.2 percent share Higman attributes to the Bight of Biafra. In either case, the Igbo are presented as the largest ethnicity in Trinidad by 1813, followed by those from West Central Africa (19.1 percent according to Higman), with the Senegambians constituting the third largest category (12.2 percent according to Higman), estimates that accord well with more recent data.[71]

---

[69] See The Honorable Memorial of Philip Finlay and Jackson Harvey, Natives of Africa, July 21, 1837, PRO CO 295/119.

[70] See Carl Campbell, "John Mohammed Bath and the Free Mandingoes in Trinidad; The Question of Their Repatriation to Africa, 1831–38," *Journal of African Studies* 2 (1975–76): 482–84; Christopher Fyle, "Four Sierra Leone Captives," *Journal of African History* 2 (1961): 82. Fyle refers to both men as "Hausa," whereas Campbell identifies them as "Mandingoes."

[71] See Higman, *Slave Populations of the British Caribbean*, 127; Anthony de Verteuil, *Seven Slaves and Slavery: Trinidad, 1777–1838* (Port of Spain, Trinidad: Scrip-J Printers, 1992), 9; the *Du Bois CD-ROM Database*. See footnote 49. Interestingly, it is with the Senegambian contingent that Higman and de Verteuil converge, for the latter claims that 1,421 or 10 percent of the African born were "Mandingo"; 171 or 1.2 percent were Fulbe; and 109 or 1 percent were Hausa. Thus, it is likely that, by the second decade of the nineteenth century, at least 12 percent of the enslaved Trinidadian population came from regions in Africa that had been Islamized for

In fact, there is strong evidence for a sizeable Muslim community of people who, under the leadership of an *imām*, attempted to inhabit a proscribed autonomy within which their affairs were governed by sharīa. By 1838, there were approximately 140 persons in this community, living in the Port of Spain vicinity. Their leader, Muhammad Bath, also known as Leonas Bath and Jonas Barth, had been brought to Trinidad in either 1804 or 1805, having been initially captured by "Caffres" (unbelievers) in Africa. While an autobiography in the fashion of Abu Bakr as-Siddiq has yet to surface, there are documents extant from the period that succeed in illuminating aspects of the larger community of the faithful, if not Muhammad Bath himself.[72]

War between England and France was fortuitous for Muhammad. Fort George, or La Vigie, was envisioned to defend the island, and Governor Hislop determined to use enslaved workers in its construction. Hislop, "observing that Jonas Bath was a man of rank among the 'colonial Negroes,' put him in charge of the slaves hastily constructing Fort George." Muhammad had been "discovered to be a person of eminence" not long after his arrival in Trinidad, and he swore on the Qur'ān that he was a "Prince in his own Native Country." His position as driver (in essence) on the fort project "contributed greatly to the performance of work by the slaves," and it is an example of the use of Muslims in supervisory roles, an example that will be encountered again in North America. Interestingly, he apparently had access to a Qur'ān, whereas Abu Bakr of Jamaica could only wish for one.[73]

The reference to "colonial Negroes" calls attention to the anomalous nature of Muhammad's captivity. Owned by the British government, Muhammad believed that "it was the king of England who had bought him." To occupy such a category was thought to be a mark of higher status among the enslaved population. "Colonial Negroes" in Port of Spain also interacted closely with so-called free coloreds or people of mixed racial ancestry, a category numerically superior to free blacks. It was therefore the case that, in the person of Muhammad, there gathered various insignia of distinction: nobility of birth, natural leadership talent, differentiation from "common Negroes" through the British crown, affiliation with mixed-race persons, and an urban lifestyle. Muhammad's literacy in Arabic and apparent knowledge of Islamic law were the coups de grace. Muhammad's rise to "power" was rapid, if not spectacular.

It is not clear when Muhammad achieved his freedom, but, by 1812, no more than eight years after initially setting foot in Trinidad, he had become magistrate over his "fellow tribesmen" (at least in the eyes of the attorney general, Henry Fuller). Because the "Mandingoes" swore on the Qur'ān and signed their names in Arabic, some method had to be found to certify

considerable periods of time. Of course, data from the *Du Bois CD-ROM Database* allow for a figure as high as 19 percent.

[72] See Campbell, "John Mohammed Bath," 467–68; Wood, *Trinidad in Transition*, 39–40. Campbell's is the best discussion to date on Muhammad Bath and the Muslims in Trinidad.

[73] See Campbell, "John Mohammed Bath," 468–70.

certain legal documents. Fuller, who knew Muhammad personally, solved the dilemma by having Muhammad countersign "Mandingo" statements, suggesting that Muhammad had also acquired some level of literacy in English as well.[74]

Beyond simply interfacing with British authorities, though, Muhammad was patriarch of a vibrant Muslim society. While in contact with free coloreds, the Muslims nevertheless lived clustered together in a particular neighborhood of Port of Spain. The pattern of their self-segregation was even obvious to an outsider like Sir Andrew Halliday, who, visiting Trinidad in 1835, observed that the Muslims "formed a distinct society of themselves strictly bound together by their Mohammedan faith." Muslims were engaged in commerce as traders and hucksters, and they at least gave the appearance of enjoying relative prosperity, convincing Halliday that several of their number were wealthy.[75]

A principal reason for Halliday's impression was the fact that Muhammad had organized the Muslims into a cooperative in a manner similar to the *cabildos* of Cuba and *irmandades* of Brazil. The major objective of the mandingo society was, of course, the manumission of its members, so that part of the earnings from trading as well as from agricultural profits went into the general coffer for the purpose of purchasing each individual's freedom. Muhammad himself obtained his freedom by buying another slave for $500 and then presenting that person to the British government as his substitute, and he may have been an early beneficiary of the system, although this is unknown. The aforementioned Muhammad Sisse stated that he personally knew of twenty Mande who had purchased their freedom through the cooperative. One year earlier, two other Muslims had managed to reach England, where they maintained that from 1814 to 1834, over fifty Muslims had been manumitted through the efforts of the society. Buying the freedom of at least seventy persons was costly; it was Muhammad Sisse who estimated that each person's redemption ranged from $300 to $700. If the costs are averaged to $500 a person, then the Muslim community necessarily raised at least $35,000 to manumit seventy persons, a remarkable feat. By August 1, 1834, it was Muhammad Bath's boast that "very few, if any, of their tribe ... remained in slavery to partake of the beneficent and humane achievement of the British nation."[76]

The Port of Spain Muslims not only collectively saved to purchase each other's freedom but also borrowed from one another to finance commercial and agricultural ventures. According to Muhammad Bath, they had joined the smallholding circles of Trinidad through ownership of cocoa and coffee estates and slaves, while maintaining houses in town. Beyond the need to resolve inevitable disputes, there is also the suggestion of an attempt on the part of the Muslims to order their collective lives in accord with Islamic prescription. Thus, Muhammad Bath assumed the responsibilities of a *qāḍī* or judge, adjudicating

[74] Ibid., 470–71.
[75] See Andrew Halliday, *The West Indies*, 321–22.
[76] Campbell, "John Mohammed Bath," 472–75.

cases on the basis of religious or secular law as required. In summarizing his role, he stated the following:

[He] hears and decides all differences and disputes in relation to debts, property or otherwise, that all the people of that faith and nation obey and observe all the orders, directions and decisions which he makes upon matters in dispute between them, that are brought under his notice, whether in his character of priest or of magistrate.[77]

Perhaps the most striking aspect of the Muslim sojourn in Trinidad is that, despite the Muslims' commercial gains, prosperity, and elevated standing, their most fervent desire was to return to West Africa. On at least three separate occasions between 1831 and 1838, the Port of Spain Muslims sent written petitions to the British government requesting assistance in repatriation. This is significant, as the petitions were devised precisely during the period when the apprenticeship was beginning and slavery was ending. The fact that the initial petition was submitted in 1831, prior to apprenticeship, suggests that the Muslims' motivation for seeking repatriation was principally driven by a longing for home. From the succeeding petitions, however, it is also possible to argue that they were reacting as property owners, anxious about the security of their investments. For whatever reasons, it is clear that these Muslims, like coreligionist Abu Bakr of Jamaica, wanted no part of postemancipation Trinidad. See the June 28, 1833 petition, addressed to "His Most Excellent Majesty William IV – King of Great Britain and Ireland":

Allah huma sally allah Mamohed wallah ah ah Mohamed salla la hu adahs wa salla ma [transliterated in English in the petition, should be "In the name of God, the Compassionate, the Merciful. May God bless His Prophet, our master Muhammad, and His Family and Companions, and grant them peace."]
    The humble petition of Jonas Mahomed Barth, Sultan of Yullyallhad [or Fullyallhad], Almani, Chief of the Negroes of the Mohammedan religion in the island of Trinidad on behalf of himself and others.
    May it please your most sacred Majesty.
    We embrace the opportunity afforded by the departure of our friend and dutiful subject James McQueen for Europe to send you these lines invoking the one and only true God of Christians and Mahommedans that they may find you and all your Royal Family in health and prosperity. ___ of God be with you all!
    We the followers of Mahomet the prophet of God place all confidence in your Majesty – for, being made prisoners of war in Africa by Caffres, we were sold as slaves in this island, where we are now free.
    But we cannot forget our country. Death alone can make us to do so. For two years past we have petitioned your Governor, General Grant, without success, to send us to Senegal or Gambia from which we can easily reach our country.
    When slaves we did not spend our money in liquor as other slaves did, and always will do. We knew its value. We hid it, and honourably and honestly bought our freedom.

---

[77] Ibid., 471.

If your Majesty doubts what I say about myself and the free Mandingoes here, pray ask General Hislop, Colonel Cassidy late 1st West India Regiment, and Capt. Holmes, for my character and that of my Nation.

I was bought by Your Majesty's father, the good King George, the Third. He would not sell me but gave me freedom, on my first having paid $500, for another slave as my substitute, which slave was lately emancipated by the Governor, though my money has not been returned to me. Thus by my own exertions I became free. All my country men have done so. All slaves here might have been free, if they had followed our example.

We know your Majesty is all powerful under God. We know your goodness towards us is as certain as we must die. We know you can send us in your ships to our country. But permit us to say according to the law of Mahomet, which we revere, a person that owes money and cannot pay it, is a slave. We owe money here. We want to sell our cocoa and coffee plantations and our slaves, and our houses in town. But there are no purchasers to be found here. We, therefore, beg your Majesty to buy them for a fair price, so that we may pay our debts which we cannot do otherwise. We owe for the maintenance of our slaves, who have the same cloathes and same table as ourselves. Notwithstanding all this, they will not work for they say they are free. So we are now become their slaves, and they our masters.

We write this letter – if any words displease Your Majesty, forgive us. We know after God is You.

For the Mandingoes and Fullah Nations, by their Chief and Almamy.[78]

The 1833 petition is signed in Arabic "Ana Yunas ibn Ibrahim," or "I am Jonas son of Ibrahim," and it provides multiple windows into the lives and thoughts of the Port of Spain Muslims. First of all, there is no feigning of conversion to Christianity here, no hint of dissembling. The Muslims very proudly claimed to be so, suggesting that by dint of hard work they had achieved such a level of recognition and quality of reputation that they did not feel threatened or hindered by the profession of their religion. They were practicing Islam openly, signing their names in Arabic, swearing upon the Qur'ān, sharing their resources in close quarters. Unfortunately there is no testimony as to their diet or ritual activities, but there is every indication that they adhered to Islamic dietary proscriptions and conducted corporate prayer. Nothing is said of their dress, but Muhammad Bath is known to have "always appeared in public in the dress of a Moslem priest."[79] Some sort of Islamic educational system may have even been maintained; there is no reason to assume that everyone writing in Arabic learned to do so in West Africa.

Second, it is clear that by 1833 the Muslims were experiencing financial difficulties. While Halliday was persuaded otherwise two years later, Muhammad Bath makes it clear in this petition that the Muslim debt was mounting, and that relief was not in sight. No doubt, the large sum of money required to manumit the faithful, though a source of tremendous pride, had drained the community. With the implementation of apprenticeship, slaveholders would be compensated for the loss of their workers. As slaveholders, the Muslims were

[78] See PRO CO 295/100.
[79] See Campbell, "John Mohammed Bath," 467–68.

simply asking for their compensation in advance, in addition to the purchase of their properties. In other words, they were not asking for a government grant, but for an exchange of property for passage to Africa. Aboard British vessels, they would be protected from recapture by slavers still in operation.

The second point is related to the third. That is, the 1833 petition reveals that the Muslims were very conscious of their differences with the enslaved. The former were Muslims; the enslaved were not. The thriftiness of the Muslims had allowed them to purchase their own freedom; those enslaved remained so because of their frivolity and lack of understanding. In a real sense, Muhammad Bath was equating the "Caffres" who captured him in Africa with those he encountered in Trinidad, an interesting reflection on the fact that the majority of the island's enslaved population was African born. What is more, there is no condescension to the British, although they are no more Muslim than other Africans. Rather, Muhammad Bath appeals to the British as a kind of peer, as someone who also owns Africans and who also has difficulties with their lack of productivity. The statement that the enslaved of the Muslims "have the same cloathes and same table as ourselves" may refer to a benign regime, but it may also reflect the likelihood that the enslaved had been converted to Islam and had to receive decent treatment and a certain level of support, according to Islamic prescription.[80]

In sum, the 1833 petition is not so much antislavery as it is prorepatriation. Muhammad Bath, as sultan of Yullyallhad or Fullyallhad (a term resisting identification) and chief of the Muslims, wanted to return his entire community to West Africa. Mention of Senegal and Gambia suggests that most were in fact Mande (Muhammad Bath himself was reportedly Susu, a Mande-speaking people), but not all were "Mandingo," as Muhammad Hausa and Jackson Harvey were both probably Hausa, and the petition specifically mentions the Fulbe.[81]

The British government refused the 1831 and 1833 petitions, setting the stage for the appeal of January 11, 1838, addressed to the "Right Honourable Lord Baron Glenelg, Her Majesty's Principal Secretary of State for the Colonial Department":

The Memorial of the undersigned African Subjects of her Most Gracious Majesty the Queen of Great Britain and Ireland humbly sheweth unto your Lordship:

That your Memorialists are natives of Africa and of the Nation or Tribe called Mandingo; that during the existence of the Slave Trade Your Memorialists were torn from their beloved Country, their friends and relations, delivered into the hands of Slave Merchants, who imported Your Memorialists into the West Indies and sold them as Slaves.

That Your Memorialists, resolving to extricate themselves and others of their Nation, from the cruel and degraded state to which they had been reduced, formed themselves

---

[80] On the treatment of slaves in Islam, see John O. Hunwick's "African Slaves in the Mediterranean World: A Neglected Aspect of the African Diaspora," in Joseph E. Harris, ed., *Global Dimensions of the African Diaspora* (Washington, DC: Howard U. Press, 1993), and R. Brunschvig,'s "Abd," in *The Encyclopedia of Islam* (Leiden: Brill, 1960).

[81] See Campbell, 482–84; Fyle, "Four Sierra Leone Captives," 82.

into a Society in this Island; and as the earnings of their honest industry accumulated, gradually redeemed themselves and their Countrymen from the House of bondage; hence on the memorable first day of August one thousand, eight hundred and thirty-four, a day which will always live in the annals of Nations, and which will ever be remembered with feelings of the highest gratitude by the black man – Your Memorialists can safely, and with truth, assert, very few, if any of their tribe in the Island of Trinidad remained in Slavery to partake of the beneficent and humane achievement of the British Nation. – No! – Your Memorialists had long before unfettered themselves, their tribe and their families, by the fruits of their joint and industrious efforts.

That Your Memorialists have always behaved themselves as quiet and peaceable members of this Community; that they are proud of the name of British Subjects and feel grateful for the protection and benevolence which they have experienced from the Government.

That your Memorialists are anxious to return with their families to their dear Native Country.

That many generous and praiseworthy attempts have been made by the enlightened of Europe to introduce and establish civilization in Africa, but that such attempts have hitherto proved vain or but very partially successful. That Your Memorialists feel confident that could they but reach the shores of the land that gave them birth, their efforts, as heads of their tribe, would ensure success in propagating Civilization, the benefits of which they so deeply feel themselves, and would give them an opportunity of proclaiming to their Nation the liberality of the British Government.

That there are no means of direct communication between this Island and any of the British Settlements on the Coast of Africa, and if there were, the greater number of Your Memorialists have not the means to defray the necessary expenses attendant upon going there; besides which, Your Memorialists are greatly afraid, that if they were to venture upon the open sea, in any other than a British Armed vessel, they would be exposed to the imminent danger of being captured and again sold into the Iron hands of bondage by the Nations that still carry on the Slave Trade.

Upon these grounds, and under these fears, and also upon the assurance of their Countryman Mohammed Houssa, otherwise called Philip Finlay, who visited England last year and was introduced into the presence of Her Most Gracious Majesty who was pleased to grant him a passage to Sierra Leone in one of her Majesty's ships, and upon his prayer, Her Majesty was further most graciously pleased to promise she would send one of her ships to this Island to convey your Memorialists to Sierra Leone, whence they would be enabled to reach their Country, and also relying upon the well earned reputation for generosity and liberality of the British Government, Your Memorialists have respectfully ventured to address your Lordship and to pray that your Lordship would be pleased to lay their case at Her Majesty's feet, and intercede on their behalf to obtain one of her Majesty's Armed Vessels to convey themselves and their families to Sierra Leone.

And that the merciful God of the Mahommedans and of the Christians will be pleased to grant their Most Gracious Sovereign the blessings of a long, happy and prosperous reign is and ever will be the prayer of Your Memorialists.[82]

Twelve signatures in Arabic, on behalf of the entire Muslim community, accompany the petition: those of Muhammad Bath, one Saliha (or Charles Alexander),

---

[82] See PRO CO 295/120. An incomplete version can be found in Carmichael, *History of the West Indian Islands of Trinidad and Tobago*, 414–16.

Muhammad Waatra (also Muhammadu Maguina, also known as Auguste Bernard), Muhammad Habin (otherwise called Muhammad Littledale), Muhammad Sissri (Sissei, or Felix Ditt), Fonta Ture (also Sampson Boissière), Abu Bakr Ture (or Joseph Sampson), Ibrahima ("Brahima," also Adam Balthazar), Hammadi Turuke (or Louis Modeste), Muhammad Balliah (or Chrsitopher Picka), Samba N'jai ("Samba Jaiih," or Michael Sylvestre), and Malik Ayuba ("Malick Job," or Thomas Jones).

The 1838 appeal represents a completely new approach; the Muslims must have received counsel in view of the British denial of the petition in 1833. Five years later, the appeal reads much more like an antislavery document; the abolition of slavery is lauded, and the Muslims identify with "the black man" rather than slaveholding interests. In fact, there is no mention of property at all. Although the Muslims remain very proud of their self-liberation, they no longer make disparaging statements about enslaved persons. In a fascinating tactical shift, the Muslims instead present themselves as ideal agents in the great civilizing mission of Africa. As British subjects, they had imbibed western culture and were prepared to disseminate its superior qualities throughout West Africa. Of course, there remained the fundamental problem of religion; Christianity was part and parcel of the civilizing effort. To their credit, the Muslims made no attempt at dissembling; they would remain true to their faith.

In the end, the 1838 effort was no more successful than those of 1831 and 1833. Lieutenant Governor Hill met with Muhammad Bath on April 23, 1838 to deliver the government's rebuff; the Muslims resubmitted the appeal two days later, but this time it was accompanied by only six signatures. Muhammad Sisse, no longer willing to wait for his coreligionists, sailed to England by the middle of the year. Muhammad Bath, his vision of repatriating an entire community unfulfilled, died that September. Fourteen years later, in July of 1852, centenarian Muhammadu Maguina passed away. One of the twelve signatories of the 1838 petition (as Muhammad Waatra), his obituary called him the "patriarch of the free Africans," suggesting that leadership of the Port of Spain Muslim community had fallen to him after Bath's death.[83]

Not much more is presently known about the subsequent history of the original Port of Spain Muslim community. Some may have indeed followed Muhammad Sisse and made the return voyage. However, the story of African Muslims in Trinidad does not end with Muhammadu Maguina's death. Rather, their saga continues with yet another mass movement of persons into Trinidad. Between 1839 and 1867, some 36,120 so-called postemancipation Africans from Sierra Leone and St. Helena, most of whom had been rescued from Atlantic slavers, were distributed throughout the British-held Caribbean. Recruited as indentured workers for the sugarcane fields, over 7,000 came to Trinidad.[84]

---

[83] See Campbell, "John Mohammed Bath," 487–92; Wood, *Trinidad in Transition*, 40.
[84] See Maureen Warner-Lewis, *Guinea's Other Suns: The African Dynamic in Trinidad Culture* (Dover, MA: The Majority Press, 1991), 14–15; Wood, *Trinidad in Transition*, 66–80.

Warner-Lewis interviewed the children and grandchildren of these immigrants between 1966 and 1972. Her findings speak to a wide range of interests regarding the African experience in Trinidad, an experience that included Muslims. Among her informants, the Fulbe ("Fula"), "Yoruba Muslims," and Hausa were well remembered, the Hausa even more so than the Mande or "Mandingoes." This probably reflects the circumstances in the Bight of Benin during the first half of the nineteenth century, in which holy war produced Muslim and non-Muslim captives alike. In any event, the Mande among these immigrant descendants were associated with East Indians and called "Injun from Africa." This may refer to the "silky hair textures of the savanna peoples," or their similar facial bone structures, but it may also derive from the similar veiled headdresses of Indian and Mande women.[85] The interviews also reveal that Muslims, at least those arriving from 1841 on, distinguished themselves by dress and adornment. In addition to the women's veils, Mande and Hausa men sometimes wore their hair in plaits, and one Hausa man plaited his beard in two. The Hausa males wore kaftans, humorously referred to as "nightgowns" by Trinidadian-born blacks and coloreds.

One interview is of particular interest. Jane-Ann Joseph, born in the 1880s in Mayo, Trinidad, was both a twin and the tenth child of a Hausa father and part-Hausa mother.[86] The father, Auta ("last child" in Hausa), was originally brought to Tobago where he may have been enslaved and was called "Alejandro Murray." In Trinidad, where he was renamed "John Joseph," he and several other Hausa men were able to purchase land to grow cocoa and sugarcane. Auta died around the turn of the century while Jane-Ann was a teenager.

The details of Auta's life in Trinidad reveal that African Muslim fortunes were beginning to change in the second half of the nineteenth century:

Although an Anglican, Auta practiced Muslim rites at home. In observing *salla* (prayers), most likely for Id-al-Fitr and Id-al-Kabr, he would bathe first thing in the morning and, with palms raised and facing the sun, recite the Koran, after which he would sprinkle water three times on the ground.[87]

Auta's position was therefore very different from that of Muhammad Bath; the influx of Africans of other faiths, combined with the pressures of Christian conversionists, resulted in the cloaking of Auta' true beliefs, through which he kept the two religions separate as opposed to attempting some form of synthesis. Like Auta, other Muslims retained the integrity of their core beliefs, but they "found it necessary to conform to the religious norms of an officially Christian island."[88] The head of the Muslims in Mayo was one "Alhaji," suggesting he had made the pilgrimage to Mecca and Medina. There was also a

[85] See Warner-Lewis, *Guinea's Other Suns*, 7–8, 16–19, 24–27. See also Maureen Warner, "Africans in 19th Century Trinidad, Part I," *African Studies Association of the West Indies Bulletin* 5 (1972): 39.

[86] Ibid., 69–70.

[87] Ibid.

[88] Ibid., 48–49.

mallam (from the Arabic *'ālim*, or "learned one") called "Bia-bia" who read the Qur'ān and had a book with Hausa translations in English. Although Auta did not read Arabic, he clearly sought to set an example for his offspring, giving Muslim names to at least some of his children. For instance, his first son was named Idi, and his first daughter Fatuma. Muslim names were passed on to his grandchildren as well, such as Zainabu and Asetu.

Another feature of Islamic life in Mayo and elsewhere in Trinidad was the giving of a *sadaka* (Hausa) or *sàrákà* (Yoruba). According to Warner-Lewis, the Yoruba *sàrákà*, borrowed from the Muslim Hausa, is described as follows.

[This] is an event mounted for the purpose of ancestor commemoration. It was put on by a family on an annual basis and was intended to revere the memory of family members who had died and to placate their spirits. It was also given to obtain special favor in times of crisis; to offer thanksgiving for financial or career achievement, as well as for recovery from illness. The ceremony took the form of a communal feast and dancing to drum accompaniment.

Auta presented the sadaka every New Year's Day, a tradition that was still observed by Jane-Ann and her daughter as late as 1972. In addition to the ritual slaughter of goat, sheep and fowl are also used along with a glass of sweetened milk, *akara* (fried balls of flour and water), and white rice. Having soaked overnight, half of the rice is made into *gumba* by mixing it with water and sweetening it with milk and sugar; the other half is used to make *waina*, which is rice and white sugar served on top of the akara.[89] Such preparations are remarkably similar to traditions found in the North American sea islands off the Georgia and South Carolina coasts in the nineteenth century, and they bear witness to the transplantation of African Islamic cultural practices in the Americas.

An important aspect of the Hausa Muslims at Mayo was that they were overwhelmingly male. This may explain why Auta was responsible for observing the sadaka as opposed to a woman, as was the custom in the Georgia and Carolina coastal areas. The absence of Hausa or other Muslim women meant that female partners had to be found elsewhere, which raises the interesting question about conversions among female spouses. It would appear that Jane-Ann Joseph, whose mother was part Hausa, benefitted from a unified Muslim familial culture, but this was not necessarily true of other unions formed with Muslim men. Indeed, the perpetuation of Islam would have hinged upon the degree to which mothers consented to the Islamization of their children. In the case of Jane-Ann there happened to be considerable consent, and it is interesting, perhaps instructive, that she and her daughter were the ones to continue the tradition of the sadaka.

Compounding the difficulty of Muslim males finding suitable marriage partners was the problem of religious and ethnic rivalries. In a discussion of Hausa–Yoruba tensions that has direct implications for the next chapter's

[89] Ibid., 5–6, 69–70, 115–16.

examination of Islam in Brazil, Warner-Lewis maintains that, as a result of the early-nineteenth-century jihād of Usuman dan Fodio in what is now Nigeria, the following was true:

[M]ost of the Hausa slaves were therefore likely to have been war captives of the Yoruba. Not much love was lost between these two tribes, for there is evidence in Trinidad that Yoruba and Hausa tried (certainly in the early stages of their settlement) to keep as far apart from each other as possible. Intermarriage was taboo; each was excluded from the other's social occasions; and the Hausa sang scathing songs which emphasised the religious superiority of their monotheism over the polytheistic creed of the Yoruba. Despite this, there is linguistic and social evidence that there was creative interaction between the two nations.... One reason for this interaction was, of course, the fact that some Yoruba were also Moslem, and proudly so, to judge from the manner in which their descendants recall this.[90]

It was therefore the case that the mid-nineteenth-century importation of labor was very important to the continuation of Islam among the African-descended in the aftermath of the Port of Spain Muslims' failed attempt at repatriation en masse. By the 1850s, "Mandingo" squatters were sighted on Crown lands in the southeastern corner of the Montserrat district. In 1868, government land commissioner Robert Mitchell, in passing through Montserrat, reported he came into contact with "Mandingoes," "Foulahs," "Honnas" (Hausas), "Yarribas," and others. The "Mandingoes" were also found clustered in Moruga in the late nineteenth century.[91] According to de Verteuil, the "Mandingoes" were still a "recognizable tribe" in Trinidad through the 1880s, when a number of them, "including some ex-soldiers and their families, lived just outside the city [Port of Spain] boundary at the corner of Belmont Circular Road and Belmont Valley Road." This is consistent with Warner-Lewis's correlation between spatial patterns and ethnicity:

Thus, the tendency to tribal settlement in Trinidad, as in Jamaica, was spontaneously organized *by the Africans themselves* and not by officialdom.... Particular tribes apparently monopolised whole settlements: the Hausa – Tortuga and Mamural in Central Trinidad; the Yoruba dominated Caratal and Gasparillo in Montserrat; Yarraba Woods and St. Marys in Carapichaima; together with Yarraba Village.... There were several Congo enclaves throughout Moruga Wood.... There was a Mandingo colony in the Mandingo Road area of Moruga. In some cases, however, various nations settled in particular "blocks" of the same village.[92] [italics added]

Such specificity will, it is hoped, assist future research in determining with greater accuracy the history of African Muslims in late-nineteenth-century and early-twentieth-century Trinidad, and in particular help illuminate the lines of interaction between the various Muslim communities on the island. Such

[90] See Warner, "Africans in 19th Century Trinidad, Part I," 42.
[91] See Campbell, "John Mohammed Bath," 492–93; Wood, *Trinidad in Transition*, 239–40.
[92] See Maureen Warner, "Africans in 19th Century Trinidad, Part II," *African Studies Association of the West Indies Bulletin* 6 (1973): 13–37.

information will aid in the task of detailing Islam's demise by the late nine-teenth century, when, "there was a resurgence of traditional African practice among Trinidad Moslems in that some of them drank liquor and ate pork. And although noticeably resistant at first . . . they eventually submitted to a Christian in place of an Islamic monotheism."[93]

While the Islam introduced by Africans would eventually go into eclipse in Trinidad, the fact remains that the African Muslim presence there consti-tutes one of the largest, most organized, most vibrant, most enduring, and most influential African Muslim communities in all of the Americas prior to the twentieth century, perhaps rivaled only by their coreligionists in Brazil. Their presence and contributions were recognized by East Indian Muslims ar-riving in Trinidad after 1845, such that in 1946 the esteemed Indian elder Syad Mohammed Hosein recalled that, during his childhood, he had been shown an Arabic Qur'ān by a person whose father had received it as a gift from a "Mandingo."[94] It does not appear, however, that African and East Indian Muslims coalesced during the second half of the nineteenth century, when the number of Muslims from both communities would have been significant.[95]

Although they disdained relations with other, enslaved blacks and generally assumed a nonthreatening, cooperative posture with the colonial and slavehold-ing interests (and indeed became part of those interests), it must also be rec-ognized that, in another, very substantial way, the Trinidadian African Muslim community registered a definitive rejection of western civilization in that they wanted neither western religion nor life under western authority. Having achieved positions of advantage in Trinidadian society, they nevertheless pre-ferred the culture and civilization of their West African homelands. Perhaps this refusal of assimilation into a European cultural mode represents the ultimate revolt against colonialism. The decision by those with means to return to West Africa to remain in Trinidad alongside those without such means speaks to the cohesion of the Muslim community, and to its highly developed spirit of self-sacrifice and commitment. As will be seen in the next chapter, however, the Muslims of Brazil would pursue the implications of their need for autonomy in a very different manner.

Of course, there are other accounts of Muslims on British-controlled lands here and there, anecdotal information insufficient to construct a more compre-hensive picture of life for African Muslims in these particular locales. There is the case of Muhammad, purchased in 1798 from a slaver by Daniel Hill in Antigua. In a relatively short period of time, and in manner reminiscent of Abu Bakr of Jamaica, Hill discovered that Muhammad was possessed of "a considerable share of Arabic literature," with the result that Muhammad was thereafter treated "with particular indulgence." Muhammad lived his life openly as a Muslim, something slaveholder Hill respected as he "paid the utmost

---

[93] See de Verteuil, *Seven Slaves and Slavery*, 270; Warner-Lewis, *Guinea's Other Suns*, 48–49.
[94] See Samaroo, "Early African and East Indian Muslims in Trinidad and Tobago," 205.
[95] See Warner, "Africans in 19th Century Trinidad, Part II," 26.

attention to the religious scruples of his slave," suggesting, for example, the observance of dietary proscriptions and regularized prayer. In time, slaveholder Hill had granted Muhammad both his freedom and the means to begin his return to West Africa, so that after a three-month stay in Liverpool in 1811, Muhammad obtained additional funds from the Director of the African Institution in London to sail for Gorée Island, "the nearest point to the residence of his family in Africa." Arriving safely at Gorée, Muhammad was supposedly reunited with his native village eventually, "to the great joy of himself and his friends," a story whose ending sounds suspiciously fraudulent.[96] In any event, again we encounter the theme of a gifted (literate) Muslim who is deemed above enslavement by the slaveholder and therefore sent back to West Africa.

There is the brief mention of "Bob" of Demerara, a colony that along with Essequibo and Berbice were formerly under Dutch control and over which European flags changed a number of times in the late eighteenth century before the British takeover. Under the British, Demerara's enslaved population doubled between 1792 and 1802. Initially committed to coffee and cotton, Demerara by the beginning of the nineteenth century had begun to derive much of its wealth from sugar. By 1823, half of the colony's east coast was growing sugar, though not exclusively. It was also in 1823, however, that 10,000 to 20,000 slaves rose up in a revolt that was quickly repressed, and in which over 200 persons were killed. At the time of the revolt the percentage of African-born persons among the enslaved population was 46 percent; many of the leaders of the rebellion were therefore born in Africa and were "Coromantee" or Akan-speakers, fighting at a time during which there were considerable efforts to proselytize the enslaved. "Tensions between Muslims and Christians" were exemplified by "Bob" the driver, known as the "Mahometan. He clearly opposed the rebellion, and was quite ready to supply the authorities with a list of names of the rebels who had come to his plantation."[97] In Bob we therefore find familiar elements of conservatism, privilege, and dissociation from other Africans and their descendants. These elements have been and will be encountered elsewhere, encouraged by the confluence of circumstances in the absence of which the behavior of Muslims could be very different.

* * *

It is with Saint Domingue (see Map 6) that windows into a fairly significant African Muslim community are reopened, and it is with Saint Domingue that we return to the divided island of Hispaniola. Ceded to the French in 1697, Saint Domingue soon came to dominate the production of sugarcane.[98] In

---

[96] See Folarin Shyllon, *Black People in Britain, 1555–1833* (London, New York, and Ibadan: Oxford U. Press, for the Institute of Race Relations, 1977), 60.

[97] Emilia Viotti da Costa, *Crowns of Glory, Tears of Blood. The Demerara Slave Rebellion of 1823* (New York: Oxford U. Press, 1994), passim, 195.

[98] In 1697, Hispaniola was split into the Spanish-held section of Santo Domingo and the French-controlled Saint Domingue. Santo Domingo was briefly held by the French between 1795 and

Saint Domingue (and Dominican Republic)

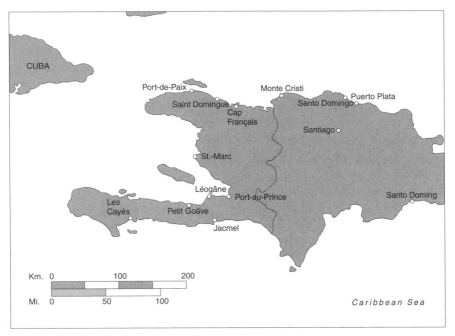

MAP 6.

1791, the year that marked the beginning of its revolution (lasting until 1804), Saint Domingue's 500,000 enslaved laborers produced 79,000 metric tons of sugar, compared with the 60,900 metric tons of Jamaica's 250,000 enslaved population. France reexported rather than consumed most of the 1791 sugar crop from all of its colonies, supplying 65 percent of the world free market in sugar, 50 percent of which came from Saint Domingue. In contrast, Britain consumed most of its Caribbean territories' production of sugar, and it only reexported 16,186 metric tons per year between 1788 and 1792, or 13 percent of the world free market.[99]

The Haitian Revolution instigated a "dramatic transformation" of the world sugar market. The "destruction of the world's largest and most efficient producer and the effective withdrawal of Haitian sugar from the market opened the way for rival producers. Sugar cultivation was intensified in existing areas and expanded into new ones," with Jamaica and the British isles as the initial beneficiaries. Cuba would emerge as the leading sugar producer in the 1820s, and although Brazil would also produce sugar, its outdated technology

1808, at which point it became Spanish territory again. In 1822, Santo Domingo was reunited with Haiti, but in 1844 it declared its independence as the Dominican Republic.

[99] See Dale W. Tomich, *Slavery in the Circuit of Sugar: Martinique and the World Economy, 1830–1848* (Baltimore, MD: Johns Hopkins U. Press, 1990), 16–18.

and inadequate transport allowed Cuba to continue dominating world sugar production through the second half of the nineteenth century.[100]

Between the sixteenth and the nineteenth centuries, approximately 6.85 percent of the Africans imported into Saint Domingue were from Senegambia; another 4.5 percent hailed from Sierra Leone; and slightly under 4 percent were from Mozambique. These zones represent the areas from which Muslims were most likely to come to Saint Domingue, in declining order of likelihood. It is probable that Muslims also came out of the Gold Coast (which contributed 4.35 percent of the total for the years cited), and certainly there were Muslims exported from the Bight of Benin (accounting for 27 percent of the total), although in the latter case the captive-producing holy war of Usuman dan Fodio in what would become northern Nigeria would only begin in 1804, so that it would be several years before the number of Muslims coming from the Bight of Benin would be significant. It is therefore reasonable to assume that Muslims in Saint Domingue could have been no more than 10 percent of the enslaved population, and was probably far less.[101] It was Debien's finding that Muslims – "Poulards," "Haoussas," "Malés," "Mandingues," and "Sénégals" – were minorities in the 1780s and 1790s, and the Hausa were always male; not a single Hausa woman is ever identified.[102] Further substantiation of his observations, although crude, can be found elsewhere in his research: of 14,167 enslaved people in Saint Domingue between 1796 and 1797 for whom there are proper names, 6,188 are of African origin – 1,651 West Central Africans ("Congos"), 736 Yoruba ("Nagos"), 544 Arada, 519 Igbo, 224 Bambara, 124 Hausa, 95 Wolof, Sereer, and Fulbe ("Senegals"), 67 Susu, 26 Fulbe ("Poulards"), 26 Mandinga, and 3 other Mande-speakers ("Malles"). Beginning with the Hausa, the succeeding groups can be associated with Islam. Assuming all of these individuals were Muslim, the total of 341 persons renders the representation of Muslims in the African-born population at slightly over 5 percent. For the entire named population of 14,167, the percentage of Muslims drops to 2.4.[103]

While evidence of sizeable Muslim communities of the order of those in Trinidad has yet to materialize, it is nonetheless clear that Muslims were by no means unusual in Saint Domingue. In fact, it can be observed from the number of instances in which they are discussed that there was a strong

---

[100] Ibid., 21, 23–63. Cuba also experienced a decline in sugar prices resulting from the rise of the French beet sugar industry between 1827 and 1847.

[101] Percentages are taken from the *Du Bois CD-ROM Database*. See also Curtin, *Atlantic Slave Trade*, 163–203, especially Table 60 on p. 200. The pioneering study in all of this was Gabriel Debien, "Les origines des esclaves des Antilles," *Bulletin de l'Institut Fondamental d'Afrique Noire* 23 (1961): 363–87; 25 (1963): 1–41, 215–66; 26 (1964): 166–211, 601–75; 27 (1965): 319–71, 755–99; 29 (1967): 536–58. See also Jean Fouchard, *Les marrons de la liberté* (Paris: Éditions de l'École, 1972), for a representation of the number of shipments of captives from the various African supply zones from 1764 through 1791.

[102] See Gabriel Debien, *De l'Afrique à Saint Domingue* (Port-au-Prince, Haiti: Revue de la Société Haïtienne d'Histoire et de Géographie, 1982), 7.

[103] See Gabriel Debien, *Les esclaves aux Antilles Françaises (XVIIe–XVIIIe siècles)* (Paris: Société d'Impressions Caron-Ozanne, 1975), 67.

association between Muslims and relative privilege in the island. Fouchard, whose body of work represents a sustained critique of slavery and racism, nevertheless betrays a preoccupation with western culture by the manner in which he situates the Muslim as carrier of superior civilization. After briefly tracing Islam's development in the western Sudan, he writes that "some of the groups of slaves imported into Saint-Domingue had incontestably benefitted from this stream of civilization." That some of the enslaved had spent many years learning Arabic was also indisputable, since "it is only by this influence that it can be explained that a small number among them knew how to read and write, before having been carried away by those evil slavetraders stationed along the paths of servitude." In light of this fact, Fouchard argues, it is not astonishing that "sénégalais, quiambarras, mandingues, bambaras, dioulas, peuls" were all beneficiaries of "this stream of civilization and were distinguished from the unfortunate herd of the plantations by their obvious intelligence, as a result of contact with a life more refined than the ardent and almost animal struggle in the bush."[104] Fick concurs, writing that "numerous slaves considered illiterate by the undiscerning white could read and write their own language and were fully educated in their own culture."[105]

As a result of their perceived greater intelligence, Muslims were often and disproportionately assigned to more "prestigious," less backbreaking tasks that either used their existing skills or provided training in such skills. The "Senegalese" for example, who were both "Muhammadans and circumcised," were "better suited for domestic service," which, "in the eyes of the colonist indicated a superior level of intelligence."[106] Debien goes a bit further, differentiating among some of the Muslim groups according to ethnicity or region of origin. For example, the Mande were viewed in Saint Domingue as "good Muslims," even though it was understood that "they were not good for everything. Great producers of rice, with long experience, they did not make very sturdy plantation workers. Colonists estimated that it would take two years for a driver to succeed in making them passable field workers (*negres de terre*). Like the Senegalese, they were principally employed as domestics." Relative to the masses of non-Muslim slaves, the Muslim Fulbe were also "an exception. They were often employed as herders of livestock."[107]

While the majority of the African-born Muslims were apparently male, there were Muslim women among them, and it is probable that as Muslims and members of certain ethnicities they experienced privilege along with the men. "A fact even more curious," wrote Fouchard, "is that Moors were counted among the slaves of Saint Domingue." A Moorish woman named "Ahyssa"

---

[104] See Jean Fouchard, *Les marrons du syllabaire* (Port-Au-Prince, Haiti: Éditions Henri Deschamps, 1988; orig. pub. 1953?), 14–18.
[105] See Carolyn E. Fick, *The Making of Haiti: The Saint Domingue Revolution From Below* (Knoxville: T U. of Tennessee Press, 1990), 39.
[106] See Fouchard, *Les marrons du syllabaire*, 19.
[107] See Debien, *Les esclaves aux Antilles françaises*, 44–45.

(Aisha), "born on the banks of the Senegal [River], arriving in Saint Domingue as a slave, having been brought by an English vessel, was declared free by the will of her master. This decision by the owner was approved by decree of the le Cap Council and following the ordinance of the administrators on July 27, 1776, Aisha . . . was declared free and officially manumitted."[108] The specific reasons for Aisha's manumission are not provided, but the context and language of the case suggest that the reasons are related to her uniqueness as a Moor and a woman. Her story recalls that of "Madeleine" in French Guiana (Cayenne):

[She was] originally named Aoua (Awa) and nicknamed Victoire, an attractive Fula slave on the Remire plantation in 1690. Her first master, the *sieur* Gaudais, had treated her as a wife (and nicknamed her Piaquenine, perhaps a form of "pickaninny"), as had two subsequent Frenchmen, Boudet and Dupuis. All the while, though, she was also married to a slave named Etienne (originally Bony), a Bambara who came on the same ship with her. Goupy des Marets, who recorded these details, believed that she might be a good worker, but as she had served as wife to three Frenchmen, she was "good for nothing at all today except to play the lady [*faire la demoiselle*]".[109]

Awa's situation perhaps epitomizes the plight of Muslims in the French Caribbean. Relatively isolated vis-à-vis their coreligionists in Trinidad (or even Jamaica), they were forced to make unsavory adjustments to survive. It would have been difficult if not impossible for Awa to have adhered to Islamic law while "married" to four men, none of whom were Muslim (including or especially the Bambara fellow). In this instance, as could have been the case with Aisha, it was the perceived beauty of Awa that explains her privilege (such as it was) as opposed to her likely Muslim identity.

From a variety of sources, Fouchard has culled examples of individual runaways who are good candidates for Muslim status. "Jean Baptiste," for instance, was a Hausa with a slightly reddish complexion ("un peu rouge de peau"); and "Jean-Pierre Belaly" (from Bilali) a Mandinga, as were "Orcan" and Bacha." "Salomon" was Senegalese and escaped from the schooner *Little Lily* ("La Petitie Lise"), as was "Harry," a Senegalese sailor who had taken his leave from the English vessel *The Catherine*. The Igbo "Dalman" and the Mandinga "Jean" had also run away, but in this instance with American sailors rather than from them, all headed to Port-au-Prince from Saint Marc. In examples that reflect the advantages that could accrue to those from preferred backgrounds, "Joseph," a Pullo ("Poulard"), ran away by himself while still in his blue livery jacket, while ten or twelve Mandinga, between twenty-two and twenty-six years of age, had absconded together. In the latter case, they were described as bricklayers ("maçons"), bakers ("boulangers"), and confectioners ("confiseurs").[110] That the dozen or so skilled workers were together prior

---

[108] See Fouchard, *Les marrons du syllabaire*, 18.
[109] See John Thornton, *Africa and Africans in the Making of the Atlantic World, 1400–1680* (Cambridge, England: Cambridge U. Press, 1992), 163, 181.
[110] See Fouchard, *Les marrons de la liberté*, 21, 287, 397, 402–03, 405, 412, 415.

to and during their flight suggests they may have comprised a community of believers, a conjecture at most.

The given names of the individuals make their association with Islam uncertain (with the exception of Jean-Pierre Belaly), but Fouchard was able to locate unmistakable Muslim names: "Sometimes some of the negroes bore Muhammadan names. From random research in the inventories of colonial slave owners or from the announcements concerning the slaves in the newspapers of Saint Domingue, we have found [the names of] Ali, Tamerlan, Muhammad, Ibrahim ("Evahim"), Mustapha, Umar and other names with Arab connections."[111] One Tamerlan in particular constitutes the focus of an encounter recorded by a French officer in Saint Domingue:

> But an even more curious account is that of the colonel Malenfant who for a little while was in command of the Gouraud plantation in Plaine du Cul-de-Sac [just north of Port-au-Prince]. In Saint Domingue he had the opportunity to meet a slave named Tamerlan, who had been a teacher for the son of a king in Africa, [as well as] a priest and a writer.

What follows next in the colonel's memoirs are comments that relate to events in the Haitian Revolution. In order to get at the full implications of his recollections, however, one must disassemble and rearrange the precise sequence of his statements, continuing with the description of the meeting with Tamerlan and returning a bit later to the substance in between. Picking up the narrative, and in the course of reading one of his own letters, Malenfant noticed that a black fellow was seemingly reading right along with him:

> After having read my letter, I said to him: Do you know how to read? – No sir, he replied. – Why, then, were you looking at what I was reading? – Forgive me, I do not know how to read French. – Then, you do know how to read? – Yes sir, and [I know how] to write the language of my country, and that of people who are like mulattoes with long hair. – Write something for me. He took a pen and began to write from right to left: his letters were well-made, and he wrote quickly. What did you write? I do not know this language, I believe it is Arabic: is this what you call it? – No, he responded. – Well, what did you write? – It is a prayer.

The approximately forty-four-year-old black man, Tamerlan, had written over twenty lines. The "mulattoes" are no doubt a reference to Arabo-Berbers who both lived in and frequented the West African savannah. Either he did not understand Malefant's question about the language he wrote, or he was indeed writing an African language using Arabic script, such as Fulfulde (Pulaar, language of the Fulbe, in written form). This possibility alone is sufficiently intriguing; but what is more is the date of the encounter – June of 1791. Within two months, the famed Haitian Revolution would break out in all of its terror and carnage.[112] Perhaps Tamerlan's had written a supplication for the overthrow of slavery.

---

[111] See Fouchard, *Les marrons du syllabaire*, 22.

[112] See the classic, C. L. R. James, *The Black Jacobins: Toussaint L'Overture and the San Domingo Revolution* (New York: Vintage Books, 1989; orig. pub., 1963).

Or perhaps the writing represented something else altogether. Between his introduction of Tamerlan and his retelling of their conversation, the colonel encapsulated his experience in fighting against the forces of the Revolution.

There is still a large quantity of blacks from the interior of Africa, whose language is not known by the negroes along the coast.... In the wars that I was forced to wage, often there was found in the sacks of a few negroes who were killed, pieces of paper on which there was writing. The Patriots [the pro-France faction in the Revolution] exclaimed when the dragoons brought these papers: see, behold the correspondence of the aristocrats. These writings were not understood by anyone. It was Arabic.[113]

It is instructive that reactionary forces believed the writings to be the correspondence of the Revolution's leaders. Although plausible, it is more probable that these papers were amulets. The use of Qur'ānic verse as amulet was (and is) widespread and of considerable vintage throughout Islamic Africa. It is clear from the colonel's comments that Muslims made common cause with others of African descent in the complicated undertaking that was the Haitian Revolution, both as soldiers and as mallams or holy men who called upon the forces of the Islamic sciences in pursuit of their cause. Although the role of amulets is briefly discussed in what remains of this chapter, a more detailed exploration awaits analysis of their use in Brazil.

The unveiling of Muslim amulets in the course of the Revolution forms a predicate upon which a number of speculations may be suggested. First, there may have been a modicum of communication between Muslim individuals, as presumably the amulets were not meant for the manufacturers alone. To be sure, there were probably plenty of non-Muslims who used the amulets as well, as was the case in West Africa; but even so, there is no reason to dismiss the possibility of Muslim-to-Muslim contact. Second, it would appear that, Muslim interaction notwithstanding, the Islamic faithful lived within a context in which the vast majority of the African-descended practiced other religions. When the moment of truth arrived in 1791, the only meaningful factions were the blacks, the "mulattoes," and the whites; the Muslim community simply was not viable, and those who adhered to the faith had to make a decision. Of course, the full spectrum of the kinds of choices Muslims made must await further research, but it is certain that autonomy was out of the question. Third, despite the enchantment of some French with literate Muslims, there has yet to emerge any indication of French humanitarianism equivalent to that of those few British who supported Muslim repatriation to West Africa. It is almost certain, therefore, that the fate of Muslims in Saint Domingue was primarily a function of racial conflagration.

In any analysis of Haitian Revolution precursors, the role of François Makandal must figure prominently. There are two aspects of his life that relate most directly to the present study: Makandal's background and upbringing in West Africa, and the manner in which he informed and was influenced by what he

---

[113] Ibid., 20–21.

would learn and experience in Saint Domingue. Regarding the former, there is no reason to question the idea that Makandal was raised a Muslim in West Africa. He was born in "Guinea," which could have been anywhere in West Africa, but, given the pattern of French slaving operations off the West African coast, it is probable that he hailed from the interior of either Sierra Leone or Senegambia. He was from a notable family, and at the least attended *madrasa* or Qur'ānic school where he would have memorized parts of the Qur'ān by heart, after which he would have engaged preliminary studies in the Islamic sciences or *'ilm*. As a result, he necessarily developed some facility in Arabic. The report that while in West Africa he "possessed a remarkably inquisitive mind and, introduced to the arts, displayed a keen interest in music, painting, and sculpture, while having acquired a considerable knowledge of tropical medicine, despite his young age" may be exaggerated since he became a prisoner of war at the age of twelve, at which point he was sold into the trade and shipped to Saint Domingue.[114] Either before or after having a hand amputated, either by way of sugar mill machinery or in a contest with a slaveholder over a "young and beautiful Negress," he chose the life of a maroon, developing a following in the North, and for six years he nurtured plans for the overthrow of the slaveocracy. In particular, he gained remarkable facility in the art of poisoning, having "acquired considerable knowledge of herb medicine." Makandal used poison to eliminate enemies white and black, and he was determined to poison the water supply of the provincial capital of Cap-Français, the initial step in the slaughter of all whites.[115]

The conspiracy was underway in the 1750s. By then, Makandal was "an orator, in the opinion of a white contemporary equal in eloquence to the European orators of the day, and different only in his superior strength and vigour." He presented himself to his followers as a "prophet or sorcerer," and he was also a gifted organizer, not unlike Denmark Vesey in South Carolina. "He claimed to predict the future; like Mahomet he had revelations; he persuaded his followers that he was immortal and exercised such a hold over them that they considered it an honour to serve him on their knees; the handsomest women fought for the privilege of being admitted to his bed." Makandal's libido proved to be his undoing, as he fell victim, inebriated, to an ambush set by slaves whose wives had been so "appropriated," and was delivered to colonial authorities. Upon discovery of his scheme to destroy whites and slavery, he was judged, condemned to death, and burned alive at the stake in 1758.[116]

C. L. R. James's association of Makandal with Muhammad was James's method of indicating that he was aware of Makandal's Muslim background. That James chose to sublimate that background evinces the correct judgment

---

[114] See Fick, *The Making of Haiti*, 60–63; Fouchard, *Les marrons de la liberté*, 494–98; Thomas Madiou, *Histoire d'Haïti*, 3 vols. (Port-au-Prince, Haiti: Département de l'Instruction Publique, 1922), vol. 1, 35–36.

[115] See Fick, *The Making of Haiti*, 60; James, *Black Jacobins*, 20–22.

[116] Ibid.

that Makandal, in the New World, was no longer living life as a Muslim, or at least as an orthodox one. Indeed, it is clear that Makandal absorbed a number of non-Muslim influences, and he emerged as the quintessential *houngan*, or priest of *voudun*. Makandal arguably represents, therefore (and perhaps ironically), the very antithesis of monotheistic Islam, and he forms the epicenter, along with Boukman, of folklore celebrating the ideal of the houngan:

As a legendary figure, his name became identified with almost all forms of fetishism, with poisoning, sorcery, and slave dances. Thereafter, the *houngan*, or voodoo priests, were often referred to as "makandal"; to possess certain powers or simply to practice voodoo was to be a "makandal"; his name was ascribed to certain voodoo dances; voodoo talismans were thereafter often referred to as "makandals" and strictly forbidden.[117]

This is probably not the kind of legacy a Sunni or orthodox mallam would want to leave behind, but it is highly instructive and emblematic of the kinds of forces at work in prerevolutionary Saint Domingue. Makandal, clearly a gifted man, chose to reinvent himself and get in front of the curve.

Further evidence that Makandal had abandoned his orthodoxy was the nature of the *wanga* or *ouanga*, the charm or poison used to harm enemies. First, Muslim amulets were generally not manufactured to harm but to protect. Second, the wanga was not a pouch into which was placed Qur'ānic verse on paper, the customary form of a Muslim amulet. Rather, the operative ingredient of the wanga were the roots of the tree *figuier maudit*, a West African variety, portions of which must have been smuggled into the Caribbean, where it still grows. Along with banana tree roots, cemetery bones (baptized children were best), holy water, holy bread, nails, and holy candles, the roots of the figuier maudit were ground and placed into a covered iron pot and boiled, over which an incantation was pronounced. The incantation, which pronounced the name "Allah, Allah," several times along with the invocation of the Christian God and Jesus Christ, is alleged to have been used by Makandal himself and passed down to successive generations of houngans.[118] Whatever the veracity of the tradition, everything about Makandal's life points in the direction of religious synthesis. The pronunciation of "Allah" may have been of redemptive value to Makandal, but his association of Islam with other religions and practices would be interpreted as *shirk* (attributing associates to God) by Sunni Muslims.

It has also been suggested that another great leader of the Haitian Revolution, the houngan Boukman, was in some way associated with Islam.[119]

---

[117] Ibid., 63.

[118] This information was provided by means of correspondence with Gwendolyn Midlo Hall, October, 1999, and it should be supported by the following documents: "Mémoire pour servir à l'information des procès contre les nègres devenu sorcier, et empoisonneur, 1758" F3 88, *Archives Nationale* (Paris); "Order of the Superior Council of New Orleans, 9 July 1763," C13a 43, fol. 304, 308, *Archives Nationale* (Paris).

[119] See Sylviane A. Diouf, *Servants of Allah: African Muslims Enslaved in the Americas* (New York: New York U. Press, 1998), 152–53.

Boukman, also apparently born in "Guinea," came to Saint Domingue from Jamaica, where he was Boukman Dutty. The idea here is that Boukman was an appellation derived from "book man" in the English and simply transliterated into the French, thereby pointing to West African literacy as the source of the name. Even if this were true, however, the same kinds of difficulties present themselves as were encountered by the examination of Makandal. Interestingly, one of the participants in the August 1791 Bois-Caïman ceremony, in which Boukman and Jean-François solemnized the beginning of the Revolution, was Cécile Fatiman, a "green-eyed mulatto woman with long silken black hair, the daughter of a Corsican prince and an African woman." The name *Fatiman* sounds suspiciously like *Fatima*, and, given the woman's description, she may very well have been of Muslim heritage and Arabo-Berber extraction. Whatever her background, she, like Makandal and Boukman, would have difficulty explaining her behavior to Muslim reformers of eighteenth- and nineteenth-century West Africa, as "she herself was a *mambo*, a voodoo high priestess."[120] In contrast, their activities may have been somewhat analogous to the bori cult of North Africa, mentioned in the previous chapter's discussion of Lucumí and Islam in Cuba.

$$* \quad * \quad *$$

In sum, Islam in Saint Domingue was not only competing with alternative faiths but with a movement to overhaul the social and political apparatus. Various ideas, including those stemming from the French Revolution, were in the air and up for debate. Whatever angle is used, the numerically weak and geographically scattered, African-born bearers of Islam would be swept up (and away) by the events of 1791 to 1804. Theirs was a very different experience from their counterparts in Trinidad and Jamaica, and their journey certainly diverged from that of their coreligionists in Brazil, to which the inquiry now turns.

[120] See Fick, *The Making of Haiti*, 93.

3

Brazilian Sambas

Brazil may well represent the land of slavery par excellence, perhaps having imported some 40 percent of all Africans transported through the transatlantic slave trade.[1] With males accounting for nearly 68 percent of those imported, the initial major preoccupation was the cultivation of sugarcane.[2] More specifically, the second half of the sixteenth century through the seventeenth saw the steady expansion of sugarcane in northeastern Brazil, especially in the provinces of Bahia and Pernambuco. The late-seventeenth-century discovery of gold and diamonds in southwestern Brazil led to the intensification of captive imports, with most going to the provinces of Minas Gerais, Mato Grosso, and Goiás. Sugar production caught its "second wind" between 1787 and 1820, and the enslaved people were again brought into coastal areas, following the weakening of the gold and diamond boom after 1760. The rise of coffee and the diversification of crops in central and southern Brazil in the 1820s furthered the continuation of the slave trade, so it is no exaggeration to conclude that Brazilian society was founded on the backs of African and indigenous labor.

Of all the Africans imported into Brazil, it would appear that some 73.2 percent were taken from West Central Africa, largely Congo and Angola, where Muslims were few indeed. Muslim populations were certainly among those emerging from the Swahili coast and its environs, which contributed some 17.3 percent to the total number of imported captives, while the Gold Coast, another region from which some were probably Muslim, made up only

---

[1] See David Eltis and David Richardson, eds., *Routes to Slavery: Direction, Ethnicity and Mortality in the Transatlantic Slave Trade* (London: Frank Cass, 1997). The database is weak for Brazil, so all estimates are qualified by this fact.

[2] See David Eltis Stephen D. Behrendt David Richardson, and Herbert S. Klein, *The Trans-Atlantic Slave Trade: A Database on CD-ROM* (Cambridge, England: Cambridge U. Press, 1999), hereafter called the *Du Bois CD-ROM Database*; Katia M. de Queirós Mattoso, *To Be a Slave in Brazil, 1550–1888*, trans. Arthur Goldhammer (New Brunswick and London: 1986; orig. pub., 1979).

2.5 percent of the total. It is therefore striking that Muslims in Brazil, as will be demonstrated, would achieve a degree of renown entirely out of proportion to their actual numbers. It is even more remarkable that the region from which the more prominent hailed, the Bight of Benin, only contributed 4.54 percent of the import total.[3]

In May of 1891, a government official ordered the archival records on Brazilian slavery burned.[4] Even so, data regarding the Brazilian servile estate in general and the experiences of Muslims in particular have steadily developed. In addition to the account of Mahommah Gardo Baquaqua, a Muslim exported from the Bight of Benin and whose biography may represent the "only known Brazilian slave narrative," there is also substantial information about African Muslims in various Brazilian locales, including Rio de Janeriro and Bahia, cohering around the famous 1835 *malê* revolt in the city of Salvador in the latter.[5] The subject of a number of studies, the most authoritative and rigorous treatment of the revolt remains that of João Reis.[6] The spectacular nature of the insurrection explains its centrality here, but the history of Islam in Brazil goes beyond the confines of Salvador, reaching Rio de Janeiro and other urban centers as well as rural areas. With that understood, the present chapter offers an interpretation of events in Bahia that, while by no means novel, represents a departure from that of Reis, to whom much of what follows is indebted.

As was established in the first chapter, the Iberian experience with Islam was lengthy and complicated, resulting in the former's considerable familiarity with the latter. Gilberto Freyre's notions about the relatively benign character of Brazilian slavery, an argument long since disputed, is to some extent driven

[3] See the *Du Bois CD-ROM Database*. Again, these numbers are offered with the caveat that they should be revised, as the data for the Brazilian sector of the Atlantic slave trade are insufficient.

[4] See Nilda Beatriz Anglarill, "Acerca de los esclavos musulmanes de Bahia (Brasil) y la revuelta de 1835," *Scripta Ethnologica* 13 (1990–91): 75–90.

[5] See Robin Law and Paul E. Lovejoy, eds., *The Biography of Mahommah Gardo Baquaqua: His Passage from Slavery to Freedom in Africa and America* (Princeton, NJ: Wiener, 2001). Hailing from Djougou (contemporary northern Benin), Baquaqua was captured and brought to Pernambuco ca. 1845, where he was eventually sold to a ship captain in Rio de Janeiro. In 1847, Baquaqua accompanied the ship to New York City, where he obtained his freedom through the intervention of the abolitionist New York Vigilance Society. He then spent two years in Haiti under the auspices of the American Baptist Free Mission Society, returning in 1849 to the United States, where he enrolled in New York Central College in McGrawville, from 1850 to 1853. In 1854 we find him living in Chatham, Canada West (Ontario) where and when he recorded his memoirs. In early 1855, six months after his autobiography was published, he moved to Britain, where in 1857 his trace grows cold. He was therefore only a slave in Brazil. Law and Lovejoy do a impressive job of historical excavation. See Samuel Moore, *An Interesting Narrative. Biography of Mahommah G. Baquaqua, a Native of Zoogoo, in the Interior of Africa. (A Convert to Christianity.) With a Description of that Part of the World; Including the Manners and Customs of the Inhabitants* ... (Detroit: George E. Pomeroy, 1854).

[6] See João José Reis, *Slave Rebellion in Brazil: The Muslim Uprising of 1835 in Bahia*, trans. Arthur Brakel (Baltimore and London: Johns Hopkins U. Press, 1993).

by the recognition of this earlier encounter.[7] The purported Brazilian propensity for the homogenization of racial difference was "the general result of the long contact of the Spanish and Portuguese peoples with the Arabs, the Moors, and the Jews," a process producing an "integration, or balance, of contending elements rather than segregation or sharp differentiation of any of them."[8] An example of such balance was the alleged exaltation of "brown Moorish women"; it was the "Moorish brown girl" who came to be regarded by Portuguese males as "the supreme type of beauty and of sexual attractiveness; the Moors are considered superior, and not inferior, to the purely white Portuguese."[9] The protracted engagement with "the Saracens" in Iberia led to an intensification of sexual desire for the "enchanted Moorish woman," objectified as "a charming type, brown-skinned, black-eyed, enveloped in sexual mysticism, roseate in hue, and always engaged in combing out her hair or bathing in rivers or in the waters of haunted fountains."[10] This male obsession with possessing an exoticized imaginary no doubt stemmed from very real political, cultural, and at times military struggles, and it is certainly consistent with a perspective valorizing the theft of foreign lands and subjugation of their inhabitants. Brazil, one of those lands, would become another site for the sexual veneration of the "brown-skinned woman," at times indigenous but often a female of mixed racial ancestry, thus resulting in a correspondence of propriety, desire, and labor: "white woman for marriage, mulatto woman for f___, Negro woman for work."[11] Missing, of course, is the Portuguese female view of the brown Moorish male, an absence suggestive not only of the limitations and prohibitions of the times' conventions, but of its anxieties as well.

Beyond the sexual dynamics of the Moorish presence in Iberia was its cultural influence, and, as has already been mentioned, one of its New World legacies was that the colonizing Portuguese "knew that a brown people may be superior to a white people, as the Moors had been in Portugal and Spain."[12] While not enamored of Islam, the Portuguese had nonetheless learned to respect it, so it is not surprising that African Muslims were viewed differently than non-Muslim Africans. Freyre writes the following:

Some of those imported into Brazil were from areas of the most advanced Negro culture. This explains why some Africans in Brazil – men of Mohammedan faith and intellectual training – were culturally superior to some of their European, white, Catholic masters. More than one foreigner who visited Brazil in the nineteenth century was surprised to find that the leading French bookseller of the Empire's capital had among his customers Mohammedan Negroes of Bahia; through him these remarkable Negroes, some of them

---

[7] See Gilberto Freyre, *The Masters and the Slaves (Casa-grande e senzala); a study in the development of Brazilian Civilization*, trans. Samuel Putnam (New York: Knopf, 1964); _____, *New World in the Tropics: The Culture of Modern Brazil* (New York: Knopf, 1966).

[8] See Freyre, *New World in the Tropics*, 43.

[9] Ibid., 54–55.

[10] See Freyre, *Masters and Slaves*, 12–13.

[11] Ibid., 13–14.

[12] See Freyre, *New World Tropics*, 56.

ostensibly Christian but actually Mohammedan, imported expensive copies of their own sacred books for secret study. Some of them maintained schools, and the Mohammedan Negroes in Bahia had mutual-aid societies through which a number of slaves were liberated.[13]

References to sacred book purchases, instruction, and mutual-aid societies will be taken up with greater detail later in the chapter, their inclusion at this point serving to underscore the ways in which the Muslim community in Brazil was distinguished from all others, including many (if not most) of the Portuguese and their descendants, who in general were either semi- or completely illiterate.[14]

The common embrace of Islam among these Africans resulted in their being seen at times as a single community by the slaveholding society, but their actual backgrounds were more variant. For example, from the beginning of the seventeenth century to the dawn of the nineteenth, most enslaved Muslims in Brazil were Mande-speakers, referred to as "mandingoes" in Bahia (recalling the nomenclature used in Spanish-speaking lands), presumably from Senegambia, Sierra Leone, and to a lesser extent the hinterlands of the Gold Coast.[15] With the beginning of the nineteenth century, however, Muslims exported through the Bight of Benin began to arrive in Bahia in much larger numbers, so that within the century's first three decades, the clear majority of those arriving were from such groups as the Hausa, the Yoruba (called *Nagôs*, a Fon term for the Yoruba), and the Nupe (also called *Tapas*), many of whom were Muslim. Mahommah Gardo Baquaqua's background further illustrates the point: He was from a family in Djougou (contemporary Benin) that can be associated with the Wangara network of merchants; his mother was Hausa (from Katsina) and his father was possibly of Arab descent.[16]

These Muslims, whatever their more precise origins, were differentiated by slaveholders from non-Muslims. There is a consensus among the sources that, as was true of the Caribbean and, as demonstrated in the next two chapters, what certainly was true in colonial and antebellum North America, slaveholders in Brazil developed patterns of preference for the various African "ethnic" types. That is, an association between the perceived natural abilities and tendencies among ethnolinguistic groups, hailing from certain regions of Africa, and their use in divergent labor assignments was not at all uncommon in Brazil. Thus, those from West Central Africa, so-called Angolas or Bantus, were seen as docile and predisposed to agricultural labor as cultivators and mill operators, as they were said to possess more significant "mechanical inclination." In contrast, the *Minas*, a designation in the Brazilian context that actually referred to populations exported through the Slave Coast and the Bight of Benin – the Hausa,

[13] Ibid., 117–18.
[14] See Freyre, *Masters and Slaves*, 298.
[15] See Reis, *Slave Rebellion in Brazil*, 93.
[16] See Law and Lovejoy, eds., *Mahommah Gardo Baquaqua*, 17–35.

Fulbe, Yoruba, Nupe, Kanuri, Ewe, and Fon (many of whom, with the exception of the latter two groups, were Muslim) – were "regarded as more enterprising and intelligent than 'Angolas' and as poor plantation hands at the same time."[17] Prized as "household slaves and in the trades and skills," the Minas were "urban slaves" par excellence.

There was no iron law in this connection and exceptions appear to have been frequent, but most of the "Angolas" tended to "find" their way into the engenho [mill and surrounding plantation], where they operated mill machinery with the expected dexterity and worked in the fields in relative isolation from influences outside the plantation. The "Minas," conversely, tended to concentrate in towns, especially in the capital of Bahia itself, as domestic servants and negros de ganho. The negro de ganho stood somewhere between the domestic slave and the manumitted.[18]

Like the jornaleros in Spanish-speaking lands, the negros de ganho or ganhadores were hired out to work in such capacities as "stevedores and porters, smiths and tailors, masons and carpenters, printers and sign painters, and sculptors in wood and stone," with the understanding that they would turn over an agreed upon portion of their earnings to their owners. It would appear that, prior to the nineteenth century, both Hausa and Yoruba composed many if not most of urban Bahia's negros de ganho. By the late 1820s, though, the Yoruba were the dominant urban group, while more of the Hausa found themselves working in the rural engenhos. In any event, the Hausa, Fulbe, and Yoruba who were Muslims were viewed "either as mandingueiros, sorcerers capable of creating trouble, or as men of 'non-Negroid' features, somehow 'whiter' and 'superior' and 'more intelligent' than the 'pagan African.'"[19] One could therefore postulate that the perception of the Muslim as an evil sorcerer or mandingueiro, the dominant view of the Mande in Spanish territories, was mitigated by the relatively larger numbers of Muslims arriving in Bahia and by their utility and literacy.

Among the Minas, Francis de Castelnau in the 1840s made further differentiations, describing the Hausa as generally "greatly superior, with respect to intellectual development, to the Negroes along the coast; they are also blessed with great physical strength, but in general they are less submissive and resigned to their position of captivity than are the Nagos." As for the Fulbe, referred to as the "Fulanis, Fulas or Fullatas," de Castelnau claimed they were "descendants of the ancient Egyptians" and "conquerors of central Africa." "Even in captivity," he wrote, "they exercise tremendous influence over the Negroes. It's rare that they allow themselves to be taken in captivity... therefore there are

---

[17] See R. K. Kent, "African Revolt in Bahia: 24–25 January 1835," Journal of Social History 3 (1970): 339–41.

[18] Ibid. Baquaqua's experience was divergent. Though he tried to differentiate himself by abstaining from alcohol, he was treated so severely that he attempted to escape, while eventually turning (ironically) to alcohol. See Law and Lovejoy, eds., Mahommah Gardo Baquaqua, 159–61.

[19] See Kent, "African Revolt in Bahia," 341; Roger Bastide, African Civilizations in the New World, trans. Helen Sebba (Baltimore and London: Johns Hopkins U. Press, 1978), 105.

very few of them in Bahia. All of them know how to read and write; as Muslims
they are intolerant and vindictive."[20]

Ramos echoes these findings, stating that the "Sudanese Negroes" (Yoruba,
Ewe-Fon, and Akan) and the "Moslem Negroes" (Hausa, Fulbe, and Nupe)
were two of the "three great Negro peoples" who arrived in Brazil (the third
having been those from West Central Africa). In Bahia, according to Ramos,
the Yoruba came to be most preferred, as they were "tall, robust, courageous
and hard-working, better tempered than the others and noted for [their] intelligence." The somatic ideal of the Yoruba was complemented by similar
characteristics of the non-Yoruba Muslims, also described as "tall, well built
and hardy." The Muslim males were further distinguished by "a stubby beard,"
and they maintained their social distance from enslaved non-Muslims, "refusing to mix with them," choosing instead to lead "rigorous and even austere
lives."[21] To Ramos's comments can be added the observations of the infamous
Gobineau, the French representative in the Brazilian court of Dom Pedro II for
eighteen months between 1869 and 1870:

There is, however, a certain category of blacks found mainly in Bahia and its surroundings, who in a remarkable way stand out from the crowd of other individuals from the
same race. These are the Minas from the area of Gabon. These slaves are taller and more
robust than their companions in servitude. They are also considered more intelligent,
but at the same time more obstinate, less obedient, and capable of resistance: the police
on occasion have had to watch them closely.[22]

As previously noted, over two-thirds of all Africans imported into Brazil were
males, and, as will be seen in connection with insurrectionary activity, a similar
sexual imbalance prevailed in the first several decades of nineteenth-century
Bahia. However, some of these Muslims were also female; indeed, Freyre maintains that the distinctive dress of the *baianas*, women vendors selling food and
drink in urban Bahia and described as "tall, heraldic-appearing, aristocratic in
bearing," reflects Muslim influence in the use of the *rodilha* or "Mussulman
turban on their heads."[23] Freyre further argues that some females exported
out of the Bight of Benin, a number of whom were Muslim, became the lovers
and wives of whites, the latter transfixed by the legacy and reputation of the
"Moorish brown girl," so that the Muslim element contributed not only culturally but genetically to even the elite strata of Brazilian society:

And this importation of culturally advanced and aesthetically attractive Negroes from
the African areas most influenced by Mohammedan civilizing power explains why in

[20] See Francis de Castelnau, *Renseignements sur l'Afrique Centrale et sur une nation d'hommes a queue
qui s'y trouverait, d'après la rapport des nègres du Soudan, esclaves à Bahia* (Paris: Chez P. Bertrand,
1851), 8–9.

[21] See Arthur Ramos, *The Negro in Brazil*, trans. Richard Pattee (Philadelphia: Porcupine Press,
1980; orig. pub., 1939).

[22] See Georges Raeders, *Le comte de Gobineau au Brésil* (Paris: Nouvelles éditions latines, 1934),
74–76.

[23] See Freyre, *Masters and Slaves*, 319.

Brazil, probably more commonly than in any other American colony, beautiful Negresses became the famous mistresses of wealthy and prominent Portuguese merchants in Bahia, Ouro Preto, Rio, and Recife. Some of them surpassed their white or Amerindian rivals in prestige. In Minas Gerais, more than one became rich and married her daughters to socially important young men, European or Brazilian white. One such was Jacintha de Siqueira...; many a Brazilian now prominent in political or professional life has her blood in his veins.[24]

As culture bearers and corporeal exemplars, African Muslims disproportionately endured relatively less inhumane treatment in slavery than did their non-Muslim coworkers. The reasons for their frequent rebellions are therefore not necessarily self-evident.

Muslim rebellion in the nineteenth century centered in Bahia, whose capital and port of Salvador was surrounded by an area of "fertile, well-drained wetlands" known as the Recôncavo, site of a number of lucrative engenhos that made Bahia one of the leading producers of sugar in the Americas through the early 1820s. The demographic composition of Salvador and thirteen parishes in the Recôncavo in 1808 reveals a land that simultaneously featured severe economic extremes and significant social fluidity. Of a total population of 249,314, some 37 percent (93,115) were enslaved, but 41.8 percent (104,285) were blacks and persons of mixed ancestry who were either free or manumitted, while whites (a qualified category since racial "purity" was a dubious distinction in this time and place) accounted for 20.2 percent (50,451). The indigenous population was nearly negligible at 1,463. In the city of Salvador, however, the picture is estimated to have been different by 1835, in that the percentage of the enslaved population was higher (42 percent, or 27,500) and the free and manumitted blacks and persons of color significantly lower (29.8 percent, or 19,500) than the 1808 figures for the province. In turn, so-called whites composed 28.2 percent (18,500) of the 65,000 total in Salvador, a greater percentage than the 1808 estimate of whites for the province as a whole.[25]

Nineteenth-century Bahia appears to have been stratified in every conceivable way, a circumstance driven to no small degree by economic decline. Bahia's war of independence against the Portuguese in 1822–23 resulted in the flight of Portuguese commercial expertise and capital (anticipating a similar reaction following the independence of Angola and Mozambique in the 1970s), a disastrous development as the Portuguese controlled the most important commercial ventures, including trading in slaves and exchanging slave-produced primary products for European commodities. Competition from sugar production in

[24] See Freyre, *New World in the Tropics*, 151.
[25] See Reis, *Slave Rebellion in Brazil*, 3–6; João José Reis and P. F. de Moraes Farias, "Islam and Slave Resistance in Bahia, Brazil," *Islam et sociétés au sud du Sahara* 3 (1989): 41–66. Readers may also want to consult with Clyde Ahmed Winters, "The Afro-Brazilian Concept of Jihad and the 1835 Slave Revolt," *Afrodiaspora: Journal of the African World* 2 (1984): 87–91; and Yusuf A. Nzibo, "The Muslim Factor in the Afro-Brazilian Struggle Against Slavery," *Journal of Muslim Minority Affairs* 7 (1986): 547–56.

Cuba and sugar beet production in Europe combined to help promote the downward spiral in Bahia's economic fortunes, further facilitating drought, counter-
feit currencies, and inflation. The constriction of opportunity helped solidify
widely divergent extremes, such that 10 percent of Salvador's residents owned
67 percent of the wealth (with ten individuals alone accounting for 37 percent
of that wealth), a category that included leading planters and merchants, high-
ranking state and military officials, and church prelates. Intermediate categories
consisted of similar officials at lower levels, together with professionals and artisans. Restricting the analysis to the free population beneath the upper echelons
of society, Reis affirms that the overwhelming majority lived "on the brink of
poverty." Such poverty did not necessarily preclude owning slaves, however,
as many of the 40 percent of the free, slaveholding population were poor, yet
owned at least one slave.[26]

Bahia's economic misfortunes necessarily deepened widespread impoverishment: "The many vagabonds, beggars, aged and abandoned slaves... had their
ranks enlarged by the artisans dismissed from the military arsenals, the soldiers
mustered out of the army, and peasants fleeing the droughts in the interior and
heading for the city."[27] The rise of general and pervasive discontent produced
multiple social eruptions in the form of revolt and social agitation, further revealing the divisive nature of Bahian society. Politically ideological splits were
manifest in the revolts of 1832 and 1833, including the Sâo Felix uprising of
the former year, when proponents of federalism fought against the advocates
of an independent nation-state. In addition to political philosophy (which no
doubt was also informed by the economic crisis), Bahia was also disaggre-
gated by pro- and anti-Portuguese sentiments, and although Reis notes that
all nonslave revolts in Bahia were anti-Portuguese, the rioting that occurred in
the streets of Salvador in 1823 and 1831 was particularly virulent in its anti-
Portuguese sentiment. Affixing blame for spiraling costs to local Portuguese
merchants, black and so-called mulatto soldiers, together with an "urban un-
derclass" said to be led by radical "anarchists," perpetrated violence against
Portuguese property and persons, beating and killing them while protesting in
the streets.

To political divergence and incipient "nativism" can be added problems in
the military. In an arrangement paralleling that of Haiti, the Bahian military was
divided into white, black, and mixed-race units, and, in October of 1824 the latter, possibly with the involvement of black soldiers as well, took over and occupied Salvador when their commandant was dismissed, signaling their imminent
breakup and ensuing unemployment. Known as the *Periquitos* or parakeets (for
the soldiers' green uniforms), these soldiers of color were opposed by black
troops known as the *Batalhâo dos Henriques*, named for seventeenth-century
hero Henrique Dias, who defended public buildings against the Periquitos. It
was therefore the case that, by the third decade of the nineteenth century, Bahia

---

[26] See Reis, *Slave Rebellion in Brazil*, 10–18.
[27] Ibid., 19.

in particular and Brazil in general were engulfed by "rivalry and competition among different regions of the same country; divisions within the ruling class; conflicts between federalists and centralists, liberals and conservatives, republicans and anarchists."[28]

We will return to the question of the relationship between Bahian tumult in general and Muslim-led rebellion in particular, but let us pause here to further underscore the considerable extent to which Brazilian society was divided. To be more specific, it would seem that "race" in early-nineteenth-century Brazil, or at least in Bahia, was something nearly exclusively in the mind of the European born and derived, and that its meaning or significance among those of African descent was quite unstable. That is, African-descended people, in their own minds, not only occupied varying statuses but were distinct constituencies, forming alliances or pursuing animosities between them as expediency dictated. The foregoing discussion of the military's involvement is suggestive of this point, as differences between blacks or *crioulos* and those of mixed ancestry, called *pardos* ("tan") and *cabras* (between crioulos and pardos), were accentuated and institutionalized by the creation of segregated military units. At times they came together to pursue a common interest, as was the case in some of the *mata-marotos* or anti-Portuguese urban uprisings, but at other times they fought against each other (as in the Periquitos vs. the Batalhâo dos Henriques). Enslaved individuals participated in the various rebellions, but their cause was impeded by the reality that every free segment of Bahian society, "regardless of caste or color" and including those of African descent, was generally and ultimately repulsed by the idea of equality and fraternity with the slaves. Every free segment, that is, save the African born.[29]

The size of the African-born population in Salvador in the 1830s was considerable, as some 60 to 65 percent of all slaves were from the continent, meaning that one-third of Salvador's entire population was born in Africa. "Such a concentration of large groups of Africans created an ideal environment for the development of a strong slave culture and the reinstatement of ethnic and slave solidarity."[30] Stated differently, the African-born population, always called *pretos*, had an agenda of their own, often different from that of Brazilian-born people of African descent. In fact, an examination of revolts led by the Muslim African-born in Brazil often reveals not only a strong hatred of whites but also very powerful antipathies toward the Brazilian born of African descent. Furthermore, affinities among the African-born cut across the slave–free divide, and they tended to be confined to those of same or similar ethnolinguistic background. Indeed, African ethnic identity in Bahia was rather pronounced: "African slaves turned their past into an instrument of identity and transformation. Ethnic identity was strengthened early by interaction among people of the

---

[28] Ibid., 21–38. On the Haitian military, see Carolyn E. Fick, *The Making of Haiti: The Saint Domingue Revolution From Below* (Knoxville: U. of Tennessee Press, 1990).

[29] See Reis, *Slave Rebellion in Brazil*, 5–6, 22–38.

[30] See Reis and de Moraes Farias, "Islam and Slave Resistance in Bahia," 43.

same nation. Africans refused to be treated as a homogeneous, uniform group of human beings."[31]

Perhaps the most important institution giving tangible expression to the African-born's sense of community, a community related to yet separate from that of the Brazilian born, was the *canto* arrangement. Literally meaning "corner," the canto was the place where each group in Salvador, called *naçoes* or "nations," would regularly gather and conduct business. The basis for the cantos were the negros de ganho or ganhadores, whose mobility allowed them to meet and discuss employment opportunities as well as try to establish consistent rates for their wages. In ways that mimicked the self-manumitting practices of Muslims in Trinidad, Muslims in Bahia maintained freedom clubs, or *juntas de alforria*. A critical achievement for the cantos, members of the juntas de alforria helped one another purchase their freedom through pooling their resources: "On a revolving basis members would be entitled to the amount necessary to buy their freedom, but they continued to pay whatever they owed until they paid off their debt plus whatever interest was necessary owing to inflation."[32] Examples of the nation-specific juntas de alforria, also known as "brotherhoods" or *irmandades*, include the Brotherhood of Our Lady of Solitude Protectress of the Abandoned People (*Irmandade de Nossa Senhora da Soledade Amparo dos Desvalidos*), founded in 1832 and changing its name in 1848 to *Sociedade Protectora dos Desvalidos*, a brotherhood that involved Muslims (to be discussed later in the chapter); *Nossa Senhora da Boa Morte* (Our Lady of Good Death), formed by Yorubas from Ketu (in what is now Nigeria); and the Angolan-based *Venerável Ordem Terceira do Rosario de Nossa Senhora das Portas do Carmo* (Third Sacred Order of the Rosary of Our Lady of the Gates of Carmo).[33] The Catholic associations of the various names meant that members of the juntas were often practicing Catholics to varying degrees, but many also continued to adhere to African-derived traditions, including Islam.

The Bahian black world was therefore highly differentiated, the consequence of both self-determination and the machinations of the servile regime. The Count of Arcos, Governor of Bahia (1810–18), for example, enlisted culture as a means of keeping the African-born from uniting: "He believed Africans should be permitted to practice their religions, play their music, and dance traditional dances, since the free expression of African traditions would exacerbate ethnic differences."[34] Incongruities between Brazilian-born and African-born blacks were also cultivated in ways that promoted divergence. The labels of *crioulo* and *pardo* gained concrete meaning and significance in the relative privileges afforded the latter and in such stratifying strategies as segregated military units. Similarly, differences between African-born Muslims and African-born

---

[31] See Reis, *Slave Rebellion in Brazil*, 154.

[32] Ibid., 161–65; Kent, "African Revolt in Bahia," 340.

[33] See Pierre Verger, *Trade Relations Between the Bight of Benin and Bahia from the 17th to 19th Century*, trans. Evelyn Crawford (Ibadan: Ibadan U. Press, 1968): 457, 464–65.

[34] See Reis, *Slave Rebellion in Brazil*, 45.

non-Muslims would have been accentuated by the asymmetric treatment they received by the slaveholding community; Muslims (along with non-Muslims who hailed from the same areas and were phenotypically similar) dispro-portionately experienced relative privilege, resulting in a heightened sense of exceptionalism. A community unto themselves, it is not surprising that they aggressively pursued their own interests, culminating in spectacular events.

Although relatively privileged, African-born Muslims would have neverthe-less regarded enslavement as an indignity and an affront. Their qualified privi-leges would have been further eroded by the proportionate increase of Muslim importations into Bahia during the first third of the nineteenth century, when thousands arrived from the Bight of Benin.[35] It is therefore not surprising that Muslims, who already maintained their own enclaves and worked together to maximize their economic capacities, would also take up arms and fight for their interests: "[T]he Africans in Bahia worked, prayed, played and eventually rebelled on the basis of ethnicity."[36] In so doing, they created even further dis-tance between themselves and both Brazilian-born persons of African descent and other African-born naçoes. This is a point for us to keep in mind when we examine issues of motivation and objectives later.

There is a long history of slave insurrection and maroon formation in Brazil, going back to Palmares and the creation of *quilombos* or maroon communi-ties (in the case of Palmares, a breakaway state) in the seventeenth century.[37] The specific history of Muslim revolt in Brazil, however, apparently begins in the early nineteenth century, when waves of mostly males from the Bight of Benin arrived in such numbers that, by 1835, groups hailing from the region (including the Yoruba, Hausa, Kanuri, Nupe, and the non-Muslim Fon and Ewe) together constituted nearly 60 percent of the entire African-born, en-slaved community.[38] By May of 1807, an uprising apparently largely planned by the Hausa near Salvador was betrayed and its leaders taken captive. A group that probably included Fulbe (as they both lived in close proximity in northern Nigeria and intermarried extensively), the Hausa would have had more Mus-lims among them than other groups from the Bight of Benin, and although significant numbers of Hausa did not convert to Islam until the eighteenth cen-tury, their powerful, autonomous city-states had begun undergoing degrees of Islamization as early as the fifteenth century.[39] The purported 1807 scheme

---

[35] Ibid., 93.

[36] See Reis and de Moraes Farias, "Islam and Slave Resistance in Bahia," 43.

[37] See, for example, João José Reis and Flávio dos Santos Gomes, *Liberdade por um fio: história dos quilombos no Brasil* (São Paulo: Companhia das Letras, 1996); R. K. Kent, "Palmares: An African State in Brazil," in Richard Price, ed., *Maroon Societies: Rebel Slave Communities in the Americas* (Baltimore, MD: Johns Hopkins U. Press, 1979). Also see Clovis Moura, *Rebeliões da senzala* (São Paulo: Edições Zumbi, 1959); Luis Luna, *O negro na luta contra escravidão* (Rio de Janeiro: Editôra Lectura, 1967).

[38] More accurately, this is 57.3 percent. See Reis, *Slave Rebellion in Brazil*, 139.

[39] The literature is extensive. One could begin with the following: Mervyn Hiskett, *The Develop-ment of Islam in West Africa* (London and New York: Longman, 1984); Mahdi Adamu, *The Hausa*

to commandeer ships and return to West Africa is not beyond credulity, as it accords well with such attempts elsewhere in the Americas.[40] Just as interesting, and more germane at this point, was the fact that both enslaved and free Hausa participated, highly suggestive that the participants were operating out of an exclusive vision of liberation. Less than two years later, in January of 1809, nearly 300 insurgents, mostly Hausa slaves but this time accompanied by *Jejes* (Ewe-Fon) and Nagôs (Yoruba), unsuccessfully attacked the town of Nazaré das Farinhas in search of food and supplies, having participated in a massive organization of collective flight from Salvador and various engenhos in the Recôncavo. Insurrectionary activity had spread from the Hausa, suggesting that Islam was becoming an umbrella under which non-Hausa from the Bight of Benin found refuge, or with which they could identify to some degree, as not all who joined the rebellion were Muslims. A revolt in February of 1814 was similarly led by Muslim Hausa and joined by Nagôs and others; one month later, the "Hausas attacked again" in Iguape, where Bahia's largest engenhos were located. Again, what is striking about these uprisings is their exclusionary nature; Brazilian-born slaves are not involved, and only Africans from the Bight of Benin are identified as participants.[41]

The period between 1814 and 1835 was one of incessant upheaval and unrest, often the product of African discontent. The year 1816 witnessed a serious conflagration in the towns of São Francisco do Conde and Santo Amaro, leading to the torching of several engenhos. Three revolts erupted during Bahia's war of independence in 1822, followed in 1824 by an uprising on a plantation in Santana that resulted in the creation of a quilombo on the site. Two years later in August of 1826, yet another revolt erupted in the Cachoeira district, and in December of that year Africans and enslaved persons rose up at a quilombo called Urubu ("Vulture") outside Salvador. The revolt there is very instructive in that it consisted of more than fifty men and women who were led by one Zeferina, who upon her capture disclosed a plan that envisioned reinforcements arriving from Salvador, followed by a march upon the city and destruction of all

Factor in West African History (Zaria and Ibadan: Oxford U. Press, 1978); R. A. Adeleye, *Power and Diplomacy in Northern Nigeria, 1804–1906* (London: Longman, 1971); Murray Last, *The Sokoto Caliphate* (London: Longman, 1967); Umar b. Muhammadu Bukhari, *Tanbīh al-Ikhwān fī amr al-Sūdān*, trans. Muhammad Isa Talata Mafara (Sokoto: Sidi Umaru Press, n.d.); Beverly B. Mack and Jean Boyd, *One Woman's Jihad: Nana Asma'u, Scholar and Scribe* (Bloomington and Indianapolis: Indiana U. Press, 2000).

[40] There are too many accounts of the enslaved running away and heading for bodies of water, and attempting to seize vessels with the intent of returning to Africa, for the phenomenon to be readily dismissed. For example, see several reports of such activity in Michael A. Gomez, *Exchanging Our Country Marks: The Transformation of African Identities in the Colonial and Antebellum South* (Chapel Hill and London: U. of North Carolina Press, 1998).

[41] See Reis, *Slave Rebellion in Brazil*, 40–48; Reis and de Moraes Farias, "Islam and Slave Resistance in Bahia," 44–46; Stuart B. Schwartz, "Cantos e Quilombos numa Conspiracão de Escravos Hausás: Bahía 1814," in Reis and dos Santos Gomes, *Liberdade por um Fio*, 373–406; Raimundo Nina Rodrigues, *Os africanos no Brasil* (São Paulo: Companhia Editora Nacional, 1932, 1977), 43–49.

the whites. Perhaps what was more important was that "Queen" Zeferina revealed that most persons at Urubu were Nagôs, both enslaved and free. Although some Hausa were also involved, paraphernalia seized during the revolt's suppression are consistent with Yoruba indigenous religion, and this suggests that the Urubu rebellion was one expression of non-Muslim Yoruba indignation.[42]

Small-scale slave revolts continued between 1827 and 1831, including one in 1830 that was unique in that it was generated from within Salvador. It is with the 1835 revolt, however, that Muslim involvement again becomes central to developments. Although referred to as the "revolt of the *malês*" (a term possibly derived from *imale*, the Yoruba designation for Muslim, which may have, in turn, been a corruption of *Mali* and appropriated from Mande speakers), it would appear that Muslims in Bahia found the term *malê* pejorative, and they called themselves *musulmīn* or *mussurumin* instead.[43] The 1835 revolt, a much better documented affair that involved as many as 500 African insurgents, provides important insight into the state of affairs between Muslims and non-Muslims; more specifically, it suggests the extent of African Muslim antipathies toward African-born non-Muslims and Brazilian-born blacks. Concerning the former, very few non-Muslim Africans who were imported from regions outside of the Bight of Benin participated; only 3 percent of those arrested in the 1835 uprising were from West Central Africa (so-called Congos and Angolas), although they made up 24 percent of enslaved Africans and 13.4 percent of free Africans in Salvador. The participation of Brazilian-born blacks was similarly anemic, as only two pardos and three crioulos were arrested in conjunction with the revolt, although Brazilian-born blacks and persons of mixed ancestry composed 40 percent of Salvador's population.[44] While such small percentages may indicate that it was the non-Muslims who rejected alliances with Muslims, anecdotal evidence affirms the existence of Muslim intolerance prior to the

---

[42] See Reis, *Slave Rebellion in Brazil*, 44–69; Ann M. Pescatello, "*Prêto* Power, Brazilian Style: Modes of Re-Actions to Slavery in the Nineteenth Century," in Ann M. Pescatello, ed., *Old Roots in New Lands: Historical and Anthropological Perspectives on Black Experiences in the Americas* (Westport, CT: Greenwood Press, 1977), 83. Also see Décio Freitas, *A revolução dos malês: insurreições escravas* (Porto Alegre: Editôra Movimento, 1985); Clovis Moura, *Rebeliões da senzala* (São Paulo: Edições Zumbi, 1959); Howard M. Prince, "Slave Rebellion in Bahia, 1807–1835," (Ph.D. diss., Columbia U., 1972). Pedro Calman's *Malês; a insurreição das senzalas* (Rio de Janeiro: Pro Luce, 1933), is written as a kind of novel.

[43] See Ramos, *The Negro in Brazil*, 87–88; Reis, *Slave Rebellion in Brazil*, 96–97; Reis and de Moraes Farias, "Islam and Slave Resistance in Bahia," 47; Sir Harry Johnston, *The Negro in the New World* (New York: Johnson Reprint, 1969; orig. pub., 1910), 94. Records of the 1835 revolt can be found in "Peças processuais do levante dos Malês," *Anais do Arquivo do Estado da Bahia* 40 (1971); and "Devassa do levante de escravos ocorrido em Salvador em 1835," *Anais do Arquivo do Estado da Bahia* 38 (1968), 50 (1992), 53 (1996), and 54 (1996). See Paul Lovejoy, "Background to Rebellion: The Origins of Muslim Slaves in Bahia," *Slavery and Abolition* 15 (1994): 151–80, footnote 12 for divergent explanations for the derivation of *malê*. Also see Nei Lopes, *Bantos, malês e identidade negra* (Rio de Janeiro: Universitária, 1988).

[44] See Reis, *Slave Rebellion in Brazil*, 141, 148.

revolt. Carlos, an enslaved Yoruba, testified that "'the Nagôs who can read, and who took part of the insurrection, would not shake hands with nor respect outsiders. They even called them *gaveré*," possibly a corruption of the Arabic *kāfir* or "unbeliever." Likewise, those Africans and their descendants who converted to Catholicism were ridiculed by Muslims for "'going to Mass to worship a piece of wood on the altar, because images are not saints.'" In fact, in an interview conducted with an elderly Pullo man in Bahia in the late 1840s, the informant stated that he refused to enter the house of "Christian dogs," a characterization remarkable in that it was repeated in an entirely different context thousands of miles to the north, in what would become the United States, in a similar reference by an African-born Muslim to black Christians (as will be discussed subsequently).[45] It would therefore appear that there was considerable distance between African Muslims and the Brazilian-born of African descent, as the dynamic of Islam added another dimension to general tensions between the African-born and Brazilian-born communities. "To put it mildly," Reis summarizes, "relations between Afro-Brazilians and Africans were strained," indicated by the nearly nonexistent creole (used here to refer to those both Brazilian born and African descended) participation in the more than twenty slave revolts prior to 1835.[46] The Brazilian-born of African descent led their own revolts.

As the preceding discussion indicates, part of the African Muslim aversion to non-Muslim creoles had to do with religion, and with the Catholics' veneration of saints and extensive use of images. Perhaps even more important were the issues of policing and privilege. Creoles formed most of the military, paramilitary, and auxiliary forces used to enforce the servile estate, and they could be counted on to subscribe to a nascent Brazilian identity by which they consistently sided with the slaveholders against both Africans and the Portuguese. Concerning privilege, creoles disproportionately served as domestics and in jobs requiring greater vocational training.[47] It is no wonder then, that while some testimony charged that the 1835 conspirators planned to kill not only whites but blacks and mixed-race persons as well, other evidence suggests that those of mixed race were not to be killed but rather reenslaved.[48] This all makes for an untidy analysis of the 1835 revolt, the object of which, based on such information, is far from evident.

That privileged creoles would be the object of African Muslim hostility is not without its own irony, as some who achieved such privilege were themselves descendants of earlier arriving African-born Muslims, attracting inordinate attention to themselves for reasons already mentioned. The apparent absence of a discernible Islamic heritage, combined with the behavior of the 1835 insurrectionists themselves, who it would seem targeted only the African-born

---

[45] See the interview of "Mohammad-Abdullah-Filani," in Castelnau, *Renseignements*, 46.
[46] See Reis, *Slave Rebellion in Brazil*, 141.
[47] Ibid., 143–49.
[48] Ibid., 116–21.

population in Brazil for purposes of proselytization, indicates that intragenerational efforts to transfer Islam as a coherent tradition prior to the nineteenth century were minimal and, in any event, not very successful. This pattern may help to explain, along with considerations to follow, the eventual diminution of the Muslim profile in Brazil.

The actual events of the 1835 revolt can be succinctly summarized. Planned to begin early on January 25, a Catholic holiday that also coincided with the end of Ramadan, the insurrection was in fact largely over by dawn's early light. Alerted to the conspiracy the day before, authorities surprised the participants on the morning of January 25 by attacking a group meeting in the *loge* or basement of a two-story house.[49] Fighting broke out all over Salvador, and after several hours over seventy people were dead, some fifty of them Africans, while an untold number were wounded. The ensuing investigation, from which a wealth of information on Islam in Bahia was garnered, consisted of over 200 hearings conducted in an atmosphere of widespread fear and panic. Concerned that other conspiracies were in the making, authorities, as a deterrant, embarked on a zealous prosecution of those captured. This campaign led to the execution, flogging, imprisonment, or deportation of more than 500 persons. The enslaved who survived the floggings (one leader was sentenced to 1,000 lashes) were returned to slaveholders on the condition that they were to henceforth either wear foot shackles and chains or sport a neck chain with an attached cross.[50] Conceived as an urban rebellion that would quickly connect with those in the countryside, the brevity of the 1835 revolt means that its significance derives more from its broader implications and potential.

The analysis of the role of Islam in the 1835 revolt begins with the characterization that it was an overwhelmingly African-born movement of mostly Nagôs, Muslim and non-Muslim, under the leadership of Muslims, most of whom were Nagôs.[51] Nagôs were 68.1 percent of all those who went to trial as defendants, although they only constituted 26 percent of the African-born in Salvador. Concerning the Muslim leaders, at least four of the seven most important were Nagôs, and three of the Nagô leaders were enslaved at the time of the revolt. Ahuna or Aluna, a mason whose holder lived near Pelourhino Square, may have been the principal leader of Bahia's Muslims, and in any event he was very popular and beloved "by all his Brethren." Next in influence and stature was perhaps Pacífico Licutan, or Bilal as he referred to himself, an elderly Nagô tobacco roller enslaved to a physician who twice refused to accept the necessary payment from Licutan's junta de alforria for his manumission. Learned in the Islamic sciences, Bilal was a *mestre* (Portuguese for "teacher") or *alufá*, a Yoruba designation that in Bahia came to replace the Hausa *malām* or

---

[49] The *loge* was an "urban slave quarter," otherwise a storage room (*armazém*), where people were crowded together under unhealthy, poorly lit, poorly ventilated conditions (Ibid., 178).

[50] Ibid., 73–92; also see Verger, *Trade Relations*, 305–17.

[51] See Reis, *Slave Rebellion in Brazil*, 121–54.

malomi, a corruption of the Arabic *mu 'allim* or "learned one."[52] Luís was also an enslaved Nagô and tailor, an elderly man to whom many paid deference, and who may have made clothing for the Muslim community. In any event, he was not a major figure in the conspiracy itself. In contrast to Ahuna, Bilal, and Luís, Manoel Calafate (in any way relating to "caliphate"?) was a Nagô freedman, an alufá and caulker by trade who fought and died in the rebellion. Indeed, his house was an important Muslim meeting place and was the site of the revolt's beginning. A fifth leader was Nicobé, or Sule, whose ethnicity is unknown but who was a teacher of Arabic and was depicted by one slave as "the captain of them all" one month prior to the uprising. The last two significant persons were Sanim, otherwise known as Luís, an elderly Tapa (Nupe) who was a enslaved tobacco roller; and Dandará, or Elesbão do Carmo, a freed Hausa malãm who lived with an enslaved Nagô woman named Emereciana. Dandará, advanced in age, owned a tobacco shop that also served as school and mosque.

In the 1890s, Nina Rodrigues interviewed an elderly alufá who maintained that one Mala Abukar or Mala Mubakar (malãm Abu Bakr) was the *almaami* or supreme leader of all Muslims in Bahia.[53] Perhaps this Mala Abukar, also called "Tomé," was either Manoel Calafate or Nicobé, but the problem is that contemporary evidence for his existence is very thin.[54] The designation *almaami* has serious implications, as it was a title taken by a head of state in various Muslim reformist politics in nineteenth-century West Africa, and in that sense has some bearing on the discussion to come of Muslim political intentions. In any event, Rodrigues states that Mala Abukar was later deported back to Africa.

Other important figures in the revolt, who were not necessarily in the top rung of leadership, included "the well-known Islamic militant" Belchoir da Silva Cunha, a Nagô freedman in whose house Muslims regularly met and where alufá Sanim, or Luís, held classes. Belchoir shared his house with Gaspar da Silva Cunha, another Nagô and manumitted tailor who, together with Belchoir, had been previously "owned" at the same time by Manoel da Silva Cunha. Both Gaspar and Belchoir were flogged for their involvement in the revolt, after initially receiving capital punishment as a sentence. One Aprígio, identified as a malê, may have also played an important role, as he shared a residence with Manoel Calafate and was "accused" of teaching others how to read.[55] Traditions gathered in the late twentieth century maintain that malê women

---

[52] See Reis and de Moraes Farias, "Islam and Slave Resistance in Bahia," 46. Could the term *alufá* be related to *alfa*, a designation used in Senegambia for a particular level of scholarly achievement?

[53] See Rodrigues, *Os africanos no Brasil*, 61–62, 95,109–10. Also see Robert Ricard, "L'Islam noir à Bahia d'après les travaux de l'école ethnologique Brésilienne," *Hespéris* 35 (1948), 64.

[54] See Reis, *Slave Rebellion in Brazil*, 117–18. Reis raises the possibility that Mala Abukar never actually existed.

[55] See Reis, *Slave Rebellion in Brazil*; Verger, *Trade Relations*, 297–317.

such as Luiza Mahim and Isaura and Sabina da Cruz also participated in the revolt as leaders.[56]

Much of the evidence identifying these individuals as Muslim leaders came from witnesses testifying against them. However, an important, incontrovertible source of information verifying Islam's presence in Bahia was the documents written in Arabic, often taken from the bodies of those slain in the uprising, or otherwise found on the persons of those suspected of collaboration. The various documents can be divided for purposes of analysis into such categories as Qur'ānic verses, prayers, and amulets, with the caveat that they are all more or less intimately related. The scriptures were either complete chapters or *sūras*, or excerpts thereof, and include the following verses or *ayāt*: 1:106, 107, 109, 110, 112, 113, 114; 2:255; 6:59; 9:128, 129; 11:6. The writing was orthographically Maghribian (found in North and West Africa), and it ranged in degree of command from polished to novitiate, with the various grammatical errors an indication of both the nominal nature of the embrace of Islam by some and the overall difficulties of sustaining the Islamic sciences in a place such as Bahia.[57]

That pursuit of the Islamic sciences was at least attempted in Bahia is strongly suggested by the level of religious activity recorded in the contemporary records. The urban setting, combined with the ganho system, afforded coreligionists a degree of mobility whereby they were able to gather in their cantos and corporately pray twice a day, while learning Arabic along with the Qur'ān. The homes and personal businesses of free Muslims served as venues of worship and education, as well as for more conspiratorial exercises; Manoel Calafate's house and Dandará's shop were used for such purposes. The Englishman Abraham allowed his Muslim slaves, James and Diogo, to build a structure on his land that became perhaps the most important Muslim meeting place in Bahia. Others rented rooms in downtown Salvador (called *machachalis* or *machacalis* or "private mosques"), where they could conduct their meetings in seclusion. Significant differentiation in writing skills, combined with such reports as that of the French consul, who claimed that Africans who were ostensibly being proselytized were in fact being recruited for the revolt, suggest that conversions to Islam were also taking place. Materials confiscated following the 1835 rebellion included dozens of wooden writing boards or slates, called *wala* or *pataku* in Yoruba and *allo* in Hausa, upon which students would write with an ink made from burnt rice.[58] While such activity is indirect, the totality of it points to the

---

[56] See Antônio Monteiro, *Notas sobre negros malês na Bahia* (Salvador, Bahia: Edições Ianamá, 1987), 47–53.

[57] See Rolf Reichert, *Os documentos árabes do arquivo do estado da Bahia* (Salvador, Bahia: Centro de Etudos Afro-Orientais, Universidade Federal da Bahia, 1970); Vincent Monteil, "Analyse des 25 documents arabes des Malês de Bahia," *Bulletin de l'Institut Fondamental d'Afrique Noir* (or *BIFAN*) 29 (1967): 88–98; Rolf Reichert, "L'insurrection d'esclaves de 1835 à la lumiere des documents arabes des Archives publiques de l'État de Bahia (Brésil)," *BIFAN* 29 (1967): 99–104.

[58] See Ramos, *The Negro in Brazil*, 88–89; Reis, *Slave Rebellion in Brazil*, 104–06, 114.

probable conducting of *madrasa* or Qur'ānic school, where students learned the Arabic alphabet, from whence they progressed to memorization of the Qur'ān and possibly even *tafsīr* (Qur'ānic exegesis). The study of *ḥadīth* (traditions of the Prophet) is a more remote probability, as access to the collections of the traditions would have been necessary.

The foregoing discussion paints a picture of a robust Islam in Bahia prior to 1835 that, while not the leading religion among Africans in Bahia, was nonetheless "a heavyweight contender in a cultural free-for-all that also included the Yoruba orisha cult, Aja-Fon Voodum, the Angolan ancestor spirit cult, among other African religious manifestations." Reis further argues that Islam had acquired significant prestige in Bahia: "To be known as a Malê was an honor. It meant being respected for Malês' written culture and magical powers, or merely for membership in a group known to express strong African identity."[59] As alluded to earlier, and as subsequently discussed further, the prestige of Islam among non-Muslims was very much related to its unique production of amulets, which often consisted of Qur'ānic verses written on paper and placed in a pouch or container and worn on various parts of the body. The ink with which Qur'ānic verses were recorded on writing boards was also viewed as containing supernatural power, and it was at times consumed in the water used to wash the writing slates. The site of "magical powers," Muslim amulets were very popular in West Africa among Muslims and non-Muslims alike precisely because of the belief that the written word had especial efficacy. Such amulets, called *mandingas* (suggesting that they were initially introduced by Mande-speakers in Brazil in the eighteenth and nineteenth centuries) and *tiás* (from the Yoruba *tira*), were also recovered in the wake of the 1835 revolt, and they were a clear source of Muslim notoriety.[60]

Muslim dress and diet in Bahia were also distinctive, as they were in coastal Georgia and South Carolina. Regarding the former, mention has already been made of the rodilha of the baiana as a possible Muslim legacy. Greater certainty informs the significance of the all-white *agbada* or *aqbada*, transferred from what is now southwestern Nigeria to Bahia. There it became known as the *abadá*, and it was worn privately by Muslims except for the occasion of the revolt in 1835, when Muslims came out to do battle in abadás and skullcaps. In addition, males wore silver or iron rings in conformity with the Muslim custom proscribing males from wearing gold. Placed on the third or fourth finger and thumb of the left hand, the rings constituted the primary symbol of Muslim status, and they were discarded as such following the 1835 uprising. As for diet, although difficult, it would appear that Muslims in Bahia at least attempted to follow *ḥalāl* guidelines, as "Ezequiel, an African freedmen, criticized the Malês for not eating pork and said of their life of self-denial: 'They all want to be priests.'" Mutton was eaten frequently, and communal meals were a regular

---

[59] Ibid., 97, 114.
[60] Ibid., 98–99; also see Reis and de Moraes Farias, "Islam and Slave Resistance in Bahia," 45.

feature of Muslim life in Salvador.[61] In the nineteenth century in general, the end of Ramadan was celebrated with the ritual killing of a sheep and the exchange of gifts, called *saká*, bringing to mind the similar exchange of *sadaka* or *sàrákà* in Trinidad.[62]

That a revolt occurred in Bahia in 1835, and that the revolt was led by Muslims, is established in the literature. The purpose of the revolt, however, remains a subject of speculation. The work of Raymundo Nina Rodrigues, Arthur Ramos, Pierre Verger, Roger Bastide, Jack Goody, Luis Luna, and Paul Lovejoy conjunctively argues for a continuity of purpose between events in northern Nigeria and northeastern Brazil during the first third of the nineteenth century.[63] That is, the 1804–12 jihād of Usuman dan Fodio (or 'Uthmān b. Fūdī) that resulted in the creation of the Sokoto Caliphate, a theocracy in northern Nigeria modeled after the Baghdad-centered Abbasid Caliphate (750–1258), was a struggle exported into Bahia along with captives from the area. Hence, much of the unrest between 1807 and 1835 was in fact the prosecution of holy war. However, Reis's considerable scholarship has complicated the discussion of the various revolts between 1807 and 1835, leaving the jihadist thesis very much in doubt.

Jurema in fact preceded Reis in rejecting the explicatory value of jihād, arguing in a Marxist polemic that the causes of the revolt are to be located solely in the servile conditions obtaining in Bahia.[64] Pescatello also anticipated Reis by pointing out the multifaceted nature of the various ethnolinguistic African communities and their corresponding religious configurations:

> Granted, many rallied to the cause of a *jihad*, and religious and cultural values did play an extremely important part in the development or destruction of slave society per se. But it must be recognized that the movements were too complex to have been motivated solely for a religious purpose and that these rebellions were not singular in intent.[65]

Reis, in turn, provides a much more exhaustive context for the nineteenth-century revolts in his discussion of the politics of the period, the military unrest, the anticolonial and anti-Portuguese movements, the federalist rebellions, land disputes, and so forth, all of which help to explain the climate

---

[61] See Reis, *Slave Rebellion in Brazil*, 107–10.

[62] See Bastide, *African Civilizations*, 104–05.

[63] See Nina Rodrigues, *Os africanos no Brasil*, 66–68; Jack Goody, "Writing, Religion, and Revolt in Bahia," *Visible Language* 20 (1986): 318–43; Roger Bastide, *As religiões africanas no Brasil*, 2 vols. (São Paulo: Editora Pioneira and Editora da Universidade de São Paulo, 1971), Vol. 1, 150–55; Ramos, *The Negro in Brazil*, 30–123; Verger, *Trade Relations*, 286–317; Luis Luna, *O negro na luta contra escravidão* (Rio de Janeiro: Editôra Lectura, 1967), 131–32; Lovejoy, "Background to Rebellion: The Origins of Muslim Slaves in Bahia." Also see Etienne Ignace, "A Revolta dos malês (24 para 25 de janeiro de 1835)," *Revista do Instituto Histórico e Geográfico Brasileiro* 14 (1907): 129–49.

[64] See Aderbal Jurema, *As insurreições da senzala* (Recife: Edições da Casa Mozart, 1935), 28–30, 48. The problem here is that the author offers no documentation.

[65] See Pescatello, "*Prêto* Power, Brazilian Style," 81–82.

within which arose the nineteenth-century revolts, particularly that of 1835, and the circumstances by which they were conditioned. As a result, Reis is far less sanguine on the applicability of the jihadist explanation to the events of 1835.[66]

Such a position is difficult to get around in that it acknowledges and subsumes the jihadist argument while transcending it. Nonetheless, there is a need to reassess the marginal assignment of the northern Nigerian context. The qualification here is that the West African jihadist tradition was temporally lengthy, socially transformative, and territorially expansive, reaching even into Yorubaland in significant ways. That it may have had transoceanic implications, affecting developments as far away as Brazil (and even North America to a lesser extent, as discussed in Chapter 5), is incredibly fascinating and deserving of renewed consideration. In the end, notwithstanding and in appreciation of all of Reis's qualifications, the northern Nigerian context probably merits a place more proximate to the center of the Bahian collective political and social maelstrom than the periphery.

Succinctly, the history of Islamic reform in West Africa harkens back to at least the late fifteenth century and the rise to power of *Askīa al-ḥājj* Muhammad Ture, ruler of imperial Songhay (1493–1529).[67] Indeed, reform swept into northern Nigeria, in Hausaland, where contemporaries Muhammad Rumfa of Kano (1463–99) and Muhammad Korau of Katsina (1463–99) joined *Askīa* Muhammad of Songhay in enacting legislative measures that brought into being structures of government and jurisprudence in conformity with *sharī'a* (Islamic law), even though the majorities of their respective constituencies were either non-Muslims or nominally Muslim. Non-Islamic customs would again surge in certain of the Hausa city-states in the sixteenth and seventeenth centuries, coterminous with the rise of Katsina as a center of Islamic learning, but it was in the last quarter of the seventeenth century that the emergence of a new type of Islamic reform movement, one led by Muslim clerics demanding more thoroughgoing reforms at the level of the state, combined with their insistence on a more exacting embrace of Islam among a broader base of the masses, assumed proportions of significance. Beginning in southern Mauritania, and extending into the eastern reaches of what is now Senegal, the new reform movement seized the language and legitimizing power of the jihād to sweep

---

[66] See Reis, *Slave Rebellion in Brazil*. Reis's position finds support in Rosemarie Quiring-Zoche, "Luta religiosa o luta política? O levante dos malês da Bahia segundo uma fonte islâmica," *Afro-Ásia* 19–20 (1997): 229–38.

[67] The literature is extensive. One can begin with Mervyn Hiskett, *The Sword of Truth: The Life and Times of Shehu Usuman dan Fodio*, 2nd ed. (Evanston, IL: Northwestern U. Press, 1994); David Robinson, *The Holy War of Umar Tal: The Western Sudan in the Mid-Nineteenth Century* (Oxford, England: Clarendon Press, 1985); Lansiné Kaba, *The Wahhabiyya: Islamic Reform and Politics in French West Africa* (Evanston, IL: Northwestern U. Press, 1974); Yves Person, *Samori: une revolution Dyula*, 3 vols. (Dakar: IFAN, 1968–75); Michael A. Gomez, *Pragmatism in the Age of Jihad: The Precolonial State of Bundu* (Cambridge, England: Cambridge U. Press, 1992).

into the mountainous areas of contemporary Guinea, and back into the flood plain of the middle Senegal River by the end of the eighteenth century, before extending its reach to northern Nigeria. In the wake of ever-expanding holy wars, theocratic governments were established under almaamies (Muslim rulers). Usuman dan Fodio (1754–1817), a Pullo and descendant of Fulbe who had migrated from lands further west, became aware of regional jihadic activity and the precedents of *Askīa* Muhammad and the Abbasids at Baghdad. Further influenced by the Wahhabi movement in the Arabian peninsula, the *Shehu* (teacher) Usuman dan Fodio launched his own jihād after a period of intense, peripatetic teaching from 1774 to 1804, becoming an important link that would subsequently connect to such luminaries as *Seku* Amadu Lobbo (d. 1844) of Maasina, al-ḥājj ʻUmar Tal (d. 1864) of Senegambia, Samori (d. 1900) in the Volta, and others. Muslim luminaries even fought each other, as was the case in Bornu, where al-Kanemi defended Bornuese sovereignty against the claims of Sokoto; or as was true in Timbuktu, where the Kunta shaykhs led a polemical war against al-ḥājj ʻUmar Tal that became quite physical. These were vast movements creating massive, theocratically premised empires, constituting an enormous territorial expanse stretching across virtually the whole of the West African savannah while reaching south into many parts of the forest areas. A number of these leaders would eventually square off (or collaborate) with the French and British, but the legacy of their movements invariably reverberates to this day.

The struggle in Hausaland was once portrayed as a conflict between Islamized Fulbe pastoralists and an urbanized Hausa population, the latter vacillating between Islam and indigenous tradition. It is now increasingly clear that there was extensive intermarriage and cultural interaction between Hausa and Fulbe, and that the Hausa Islamic tradition is storied and substantial, so that the jihād of Usuman dan Fodio called on a complex of resources. In the process of fighting for and establishing the Sokoto Caliphate, both Fulbe and Hausa jihadists fought against existing governments, with the result that both Hausa and Fulbe, both Muslim and non-Muslim, were captured in the process. Representatives from all four possible combinations would find themselves in Brazil, so that not all Hausa and Fulbe were necessarily Muslims, or much further beyond the nominal condition. However, they were all certainly familiar with Islam.

Antecedent Islamic activity and subsequent jihād in northern Nigeria eventually reached southwestern Nigeria and the Yoruba, where they connected with an already-existing tradition of Islam.[68] The Yoruba, organized into autonomous towns similar to the Hausa, were an urban people who maintained their own dialects and local customs. Although they did not necessarily view themselves as participants in a broader, pan-Yoruba culture, their religious

---

[68] See T. G. O. Gbadamosi, *The Growth of Islam Among the Yoruba, 1841–1908* (London: Longman, 1978); Patrick J. Ryan, *Imale: Yoruba Participation in the Muslim Tradition* (Cambridge, MA: Harvard U. Press, 1978).

traditions recognized common *orishas* (deities) and the antiquity and cultural and spiritual prominence of the towns Ife and Oyo Ile ("home" Oyo, its original site). While it is not clear when Islam entered Yorubaland, it had become a permanent fixture during the seventeenth century, and by the end of the eighteenth century Yoruba Muslims were proselytizing along the coast and as far west as Dahomey. By that time, Muslim communities were thriving in Owu, Badagry, Iseyin, Ikoyi, Igboho, Ogbomoso, and especially Ketu, where they comprised a significant proportion of the army. However, it was in Oyo, achieving imperial status by the beginning of the seventeenth century, that a small but vibrant Muslim community experienced the greatest influence.

All of the important Islamic communities were located in the Oyo empire, heterogenous groups made up of Yoruba, Hausa, Kanuri, and Nupe elements among others. Such was the Muslim presence in Oyo, Igboho, Ogbomoso, and Osogbo that a special office, that of the *Parakoyi*, was created to help regulate their affairs and to lead them in war. War indeed became a major preoccupation of imperial Oyo, and Islam played some role in its eventual demise. With such seismic activity taking place in Hausaland in the early nineteenth century, the "intense Muslim evangelization and reformist preaching" that spread to Yorubaland could not go unnoticed, such that there was a strong traditionalist reaction against it. The struggle was particularly heightened at Ilorin, where in 1797 Afonja revolted against the *Alafin* of Oyo and joined forces with a leading Muslim mu 'allim, al-Salih. By 1823, Muslim Ilorin, inspired by the Sokoto example, brought Oyo imperial control to an end. Muslim Yoruba began flocking to Ilorin as both citadel and refuge from rising traditionalist persecution elsewhere. Oyo's empire was crumbling; Dahomey broke away in 1823, and between 1831 and 1833, Muslim Ilorin either destroyed or defeated most of imperial Oyo's important towns. The final battle between Oyo and Ilorin was frontal and saw the destruction of imperial Oyo and the abandonment of Oyo Ile. Ilorin's victory was short lived, however, as the Muslim community there became embroiled in factional fighting between advocates of local control and those taking their cues from Sokoto. The struggle for the succession to imperial Oyo lasted from 1837 to 1878, with Ibadan emerging as victor. Along the way to imperial status, Ibadan had defeated Ilorin at the Battle of Osogbo in 1840, leaving Islam among the Yoruba in a state of momentary disarray.

From the foregoing discussion, it should be clear that Yoruba and Hausa captives exported out of the Bight of Benin during the first three decades of the nineteenth century were well acquainted with war, both in its jihadic form and otherwise. Furthermore, these captives constituted a mix of Muslim and non-Muslim persons, within both Yoruba and Hausa groups as well as others, so that while the number of non-Muslim Yoruba captives was undoubtedly much higher, there were certainly Muslim Yoruba among them as well. Between 1801 and 1825, some 113,839 captives left the Bight of Benin (75.7 percent of them male); possibly 35.6 percent landed in Bahia, by far the leading New World destination of captives from the Bight of Benin for this twenty-five-year period.[69] Many of them, no doubt, were caught up in the jihād of either Sokoto or Ilorin, fighting either for or against.

The pervasive nature of jihād in West Africa during this period is illustrated in two separate sets of slave testimonies conducted in nineteenth-century Brazil. In 1819, six Hausa and Nupe individuals interviewed in 1819 by d'Andrada all attributed their capture to jihād.[70] Similarly, holy war or other conflicts involving Muslims produced a number of Muslims interviewed in Bahia in the late 1840s by Francis de Castelnau. Concerning the latter set of interviews, one Adam, a Hausa known as "Braz" in Bahia, was a war captive, as were Karo (or Manoel), Abu (Aba) Hama, Sulayman, and Ali, Kanuris from Bornu taken by Hausa soldiers in possible instances of "Muslim-on-Muslim" hostility. Muhammad of Katsina, known as Manoel in Bahia, was also taken captive by (fellow) Muslims, only Fulbe (or Fulani) in his particular circumstance. In a reversal of fate, it was the Pullo Muhammad Abdullah who was taken in combat against the Hausa of Katsina, for whom his contempt was second only to his low regard for Christians:

This old man, who has been in Bahia for about thirty years, is free from slavery by his own work, and continues today working as a carpenter. He is educated, and knows not only how to read and write in his own language, but in Portuguese as well. He is, moreover, very intolerant, very fanatical, and by every means tries to convert me. And even though I have treated him well, given him money, and so on, he refuses to return to my house, telling another black man he does not want to go to the house of a Christian dog. He is perhaps 66 years old. He was a teacher and made the pilgrimage to Mecca.... [H]e belittles many of the Hausas who, he says, wear goatees because they think it makes them look like men.[71]

Muhammad Abdullah was about thirty-six years old when he was captured in a war with the Hausa, which must have taken place between 1815 and 1819, precisely during the period of Sokoto consolidation. He therefore arrived in Bahia as a mature, well-educated, jihād-tested leader, as others, even the Hausa in Bahia, looked up to him.

While a quantification that could inspire confidence is elusive, the conjunction of the West African context and the testimony of a number of captives brought to Bahia strongly suggests that a significant percentage of captives from the Bight of Benin were in some way connected with the Islamic reform movement. Of those who clearly led the 1835 revolt, the Hausa Dandará admitted to having been "a teacher in his Land."[72] Even if individuals were

[69] See the *Du Bois CD-ROM Database*.
[70] Menèzes de Drumond, "Lettres sur l'Afrique ancienne et moderne," *Journal des Voyages* 32 (1826), 203–05.
[71] See Castelnau, *Renseignements*.
[72] See Reis, *Slave Rebellion in Brazil*, 133.

not directly connected with martial events in what is now Nigeria, news of such developments certainly reached them once they landed in Bahia. Verger writes the following:

Wars were raging in West Africa and the pressure of Islam on the Yoruba world brought about political transformations and inter-tribal wars which procured many captives for the slave-traders along the coast. News of events in Africa arrived regularly in Bahia with each arrival of slaves from the Bight of Benin. This was commented upon and transmitted to the black stevedores of *cantos* in Corpo Santo Street, to palanquin bearers, the majority of whom were Hausa, and to the dock workers who loaded the merchandise for the trade aboard the slave vessels; it came from the African slave sailors on board these vessels who had time during the long crossings to learn about what was going on in their native land.[73]

The qualification that the Nagôs had largely replaced the Hausa as the majority urban workers in Salvador by the 1820s, with the Hausa relegated to the Recôncavo in greater numbers, does not detract from the probability that many West Africans who may not have had anything to do with war (a less than likely status) nevertheless remained abreast of such developments in their native land.[74] Living in a physical Bahia, they were yet experiencing an imagined West Africa informed not only by reliving the past but by keeping apace with the present.

Consistent with the foregoing discussion is Lovejoy's examination of data for 117 individuals, from which he concludes that the jihād of Usuman dan Fodio contributed to a significant change in the ethnic configuration of Africans entering Bahia from the last decades of the eighteenth century into the first of the nineteenth. As the jihād was responsible for a "significant proportion" of those exported out of the Bight of Benin, militant Islam was able to emerge in Bahia precisely because the jihād deposited a high concentration of Muslims there.[75]

In light of this information, it is difficult to imagine persons taken out of a context of reform, who proceed to adapt to a new environment in ways consistent with their religion, and who then respond in militaristic ways to their changed circumstances, without serious meditation on the meaning of their actions in light of that same religion. That the 1835 revolt was planned to begin in the final days of Ramadan, in fact on the day after *Lailat al-Qadr*, the "Night of Power," an annual celebration of the beginning of the Prophet's reception of divine revelation through the angel Jibril, is a critical point (and, again, an insight provided by Reis's scholarship). It therefore follows that even if the revolt was not conducted as a sharī'a-prescribed jihād, the West African

---

[73] See Verger, *Trade Relations*, 286.
[74] See Kent, "African Revolt in Bahia," 340.
[75] See Paul E. Lovejoy, "Jihad e escravidão: as origens dos escravos muçulmanos," *Topoi: Revista de Historia* 1 (2000): 11–44; this is also available online at http://www.yorku.ca/nhp/publications/topoi/001.htm.

precedent must have been uppermost in the minds of a significant proportion of the revolt leaders, at the least.[76]

The heavily male, imbalanced sex ratio among the Nagôs (and others) no doubt contributed to their discontent, as did the hellish conditions of slavery. The observation that Muslim pride was assaulted by the interruption of the November observation of *Lailat al-Mirāj*, a celebration of the Prophet's nocturnal ascensions to heaven, that Muslims were insulted by the arrests of Pacífico Licutan and Ahuna, and that they were further outraged by the public destruction in November of the Vitória "mosque," up to that point a very visible sign of Muslim prominence in Bahia, showed that these were clearly very important developments, and they likely precipitated the revolt.[77] However, once the planning of the revolt began, it would have necessarily drawn from an ideological well much deeper than slights and indignities. Uprisings and mass movements of any kind tend to be very complicated anyway; conflicts fought under the banners of jihād and crusade have often been much more informed by antagonisms arising from economic concerns or conflicts over resources, yet they remain part of the discourse on holy war. In the actual working out of the principle, away from the fervor and erudition of the theoretician, holy war has invariably been an unreconcilable contradiction in terms, wherever it has made its claims known.

That non-Muslim Nagôs fought under Muslim leadership in the 1835 revolt is not necessarily an impediment to recognizing its Islamic import; non-Muslim Fulbe fought under Usuman dan Fodio. Indeed, the apparent alliance between Muslim and non-Muslim Nagôs engenders the speculation that Muslim leaders had come to recognize not only the necessity of such a partnership but also the parallel nature of Muslim and non-Muslim cosmologies among the Yoruba. Islam had very clearly taken on cultural elements unique to the Yoruba, a phenomenon true of the symbiosis between most religions and their host societies. In turn, and in a manner similar to the aforementioned experience in Cuba, orisha-based religion among the Yoruba made room for the Muslim deity, not only acknowledging but highly valuing Muslim spiritual prowess. Worshipers of the orishas, who continued to practice such worship after conversion to Catholicism in a syncretic or dualistic tradition that has come to be known as *Candomblé*, viewed Muslims as "the sons of Oxalá," or Orisalá, and they regularly consulted the alufás for guidance.[78] However, not all non-Muslim Nagôs were receptive to the alliance, or at least they sought to create that impression (for obvious reasons) during the investigation following the 1835 revolt. João Ezquiel did not care for the austere Muslim lifestyle and was not anxious to give up pork. Antonio emphasized the autonomous quality of the Yoruba city-state,

---

[76] Concerning waging a legal jihād, see Rudolph Peters, *Islam and Colonialism: The Doctrine of Jihad in Modern History* (New York and The Hague: Mouton, 1979); Rudolph Peters, *Jihad in Medieval and Modern Islam* (Leiden: Brill, 1977).

[77] See Reis, *Slave Rebellion in Brazil*, 109–15.

[78] See Bastide, *As religiões africanas*, vol. 1, 216–17; Reis, *Slave Rebellion in Brazil*, 123–25.

stating that "even though they were all Nago, each one had his own country." Feliciano, an elderly man who had been in Brazil for so long that he apparently was viewed as an *assimilado*, was simply not trusted.[79]

The fact that the participants in the 1835 revolt were overwhelmingly born in Yorubaland suggests, fundamentally, a preference for things African and a rejection of things Brazilian. That the Hausa composed 13.5 percent of the participants, while those from West Central Africa (the so-called Bantu-speakers) only accounted for 3 percent, indicates a more specific desire for things *West African*, especially from the Bight of Benin. Although operating in an urban environment, the Muslim community apparently made every effort to preserve its distinctive character. Emerging out of a conjoined West African environment, about which they were continually informed by the steady means of the slaver, Muslims met regularly in their houses and cantos, keeping alive their languages, foods, and customs. That is, the Muslim community was clearly recreating West African conditions on foreign soil. Although there is no indisputable evidence linking their activities to jihād and the creation of a theocracy, there may equally be a lack of evidence establishing direct connections between their revolts and the overall political climate of turmoil in Bahia. As it is reasonable to assume that the general character of Bahian turmoil made its way into the Muslim mind, it is just as logical to expect that the West African context played some role in the business of revolution, a role that escapes the margins.

Finally, what would have been the next step of the Muslims had they taken Salvador and substantial parts of Bahia? A government of some sort would have been a rational expectation. From what source would the principles for such a government have come? Just what were the objectives of the revolts, especially that of 1835? While it is possible to characterize 1835 as a slave revolt, the fact that many participants were not slaves, that they did not solicit the assistance of the enslaved community in general but were quite selective, and that there was some discussion (though admittedly minor and possibly inconsequential) of actually enslaving those of mixed ancestry suggests that 1835 may not have been an attempt to overthrow slavery as an institution at all (indeed, Gaspar da Silva Cunha, a Nagô leader, already owned "Congo" José as a slave). Rather, it may have been a Muslim and Yoruba grab for power, in the successful aftermath of which slavery may have well continued on. Mala Abukar's title of *almaami* suggests that the concept of a Muslim-controlled state was seen as both plausible and desirable, and it is entirely consistent with events in northern and southwestern Nigeria during the nineteenth century.

Although it did not bring Islam to an end in Brazil, the suppression of the 1835 revolt was thoroughgoing. In addition to those condemned to death, prison, forced labor, and flogging, hundreds were deported from Bahia, some all the

---

[79] See Verger, *Trade Relations*, 459–60.

way back to West Africa. For freedpersons undesirous of returning to West Africa, this was an onerous sentence; for enslaved persons, deportation often meant deepening instability as they were sold to slaveholders elsewhere in Brazil. Others returned to West Africa voluntarily, and between October and December of 1837 around 800 passports were issued. The measures were largely successful in preventing the repeat of a major insurrection; except for unsubstantiated rumors of a malê uprising in Salvador in 1844 and a slave conspiracy in the Recôncavo the following year, there were no further significant disturbances. Muslims went underground for a period, and militant Islam took a hiatus.[80]

Paradoxically, the 1835 revolt did not have much of an impact on the importation of persons from the Bight of Benin; in fact, importation into Bahia from this particular zone of supply actually increased. Of the 11,131 captives estimated to have embarked from the Bight of Benin between 1831 to 1835, some 14 percent disembarked in Bahia. Between 1836 and 1840, the export figure increased to 22,383, with Bahia's share increasing to 25.4 percent. Over the next five years (1841–45), Bahia received 40 percent of the 17,098 persons departing the Bight of Benin, a percentage that only increased to 60.7 percent of some 26,776 persons between 1846 and 1850.[81] Either slaveholder fears of insurrection have been overestimated, or such concerns were satisfactorily addressed by the heavy-handed nature of the state's reaction to the events in Salvador. Muslims therefore continued to arrive in Bahia after 1835, helping to explain their lingering presence in the early twentieth century.

In the decade following the 1835 revolt in Bahia, however, Muslims appear only periodically on the radar screen. In 1846, the visitor Thomas Ewbank interviewed a Bahian planter, who described Salvador's slaves as predominantly "Mina" and "shrewd and intelligent," maintaining their native language and separate juntas, havens from which they plan "schemes of revolution . . . Some write Arabic fluently, and are vastly superior to their masters."[82] Castelnau's interviews of Bahian Muslims in the late 1840s focuses on their homelands (while evincing a bizarre interest in the "Niam-Niam," a reference to the fantasy of non-Muslim "primitives" with tails – "hommes à queue").[83] The interview with the Hausa "Mahammah" of Kano (called Manoel in Bahia) may be of use to Africanists as he provides details about his life and travels, including ventures to Bornu and Agades. Another Hausa, Muhammad of Katsina (called Manoel in the land of his captivity), was over eighty years old and is described as a *marabout* or cleric (or alufá), wearing a distinctive green turban. Finally, fear of the reprisals of 1835 are evident in the behavior of four Muslim men, all from Bornu, who trembled while speaking with Castelnau and refused to provide any

---

[80] See Goody, "Writing, Religion and Revolt in Bahia," 326; Reis, *Slave Rebellion in Brazil*, 189–232.
[81] See the *Du Bois CD-ROM Database*.
[82] See Thomas Ewbank, *Life in Brazil; or, A Journal of a Visit to the Land of the Cocoa and the Palm* (New York: Harper and Brothers, 1856), 439.
[83] See Castelnau, *Renseignements*.

details about their previous lives. Notwithstanding all of the reprisals, however, Islam in Bahia would survive into the twentieth century, as will be seen.

The Muslims of Salvador fled the persecutions of 1835 in multiple directions, with some winding up in places such as Rio de Janeiro, Pernambuco, and Alagoas. In Rio they joined an apparently smaller number of Muslims already there, referred to as "Minas" in the police correspondence (the major source for what is known about them prior to 1850), who along with others had been transferred from Bahia to the South from 1830 to the 1870s to meet the labor demands of the coffee boom. Karasch reports that whereas the Muslim Nagôs appear to have been recent converts, the Muslim Hausa after 1850 developed "a fairly distinct religious community in Rio."[84]

In 1852, travelers Candler and Burgess were asked to meet with a delegation of about ten freedmen who, in contrast to many freedmen forcibly expelled from Bahia following the 1835 revolt, and in conformity with the pattern of Muhammad Bath and the Muslim community in Trinidad, were anxious to leave Brazil and return to West Africa:

> To this we readily assented, and met them, in strict privacy, at the office of a ship-broker, an Englishman, who possesses their confidence, and acted as an interpreter between us. They gave us their history. They were of the Mina tribe of Africans, from the coast of Benin, torn away many years since by the ruthless man-stealer, and brought and sold into slavery. They had earned money enough by very hard labour to buy themselves of their master, and were now wishing to return to the land they came from. They could pay their passage back again across the ocean, but waited to know whether the coast was sufficiently free from the slave-traders to warrant their making the attempt.

This pattern of self-manumission and repatriation had been established the previous year, when sixty-three of their "companions" paid for their passage from Rio to Badagry, a transaction verified by the charter agreement:

> Charter Party
> Rio de Janeiro
> On the 27th of November, 1851, it is agreed between George Duck, Master of the British brig called the Robert, A1, and Raphael Jose de Oliveira, free African, that the said ship shall receive in this port, sixty-three free African men (women and children included in this number) and their luggage, and shall proceed to Bahia, and remain there if required fourteen days, and then proceed to a safe port in the Bight of Benin on the coast of Africa, not south of Badagry (the port of destination being decided in Bahia), and deliver the same on being paid freight, here in this port, the sum of eight hundred pounds sterling, to be paid before the sailing of the next British packet. The master binds himself to provide for the said passengers, sixty pounds of jerked beef, two and a half alquierés of farinha, and half an alquieré of black beans daily; a cooking-place and the necessary fire-wood to be furnished by the captain, half a pipe, say sixty gallons, of water to be supplied daily. The master is allowed to take any cargo or passengers and luggage that

[84] See Mary C. Karasch, *Slave Life in Rio de Janeiro, 1808–1850* (Princeton, NJ: Princeton U. Press, 1987), 284. Also see Alberto Da Costa E Silva, "Buying and Selling Korans in Nineteenth-Century Rio de Janeiro," *Slavery and Abolition* 22 (2001): 87.

may offer at Bahia for the benefit of the ship. Passengers and luggage to be on board on or before the 15th of December, 1851, and disembark within forty-eight hours after the ship's arrival at the port of destination.

Penalty for non-performance of this agreement, five hundred pounds sterling.

George Duck
Raphael Jose de Oliveira

The fact that Candler and Burgess received a letter from the delegation a few days after their meeting, "beautifully written in Arabic by one of their chiefs, who is a Mahommedan," strongly suggests that most if not all of these so-called Minas were Muslims. Further research is required to learn the final outcome of these negotiations.[85]

Some thirteen years later, another quite remarkable window is provided into the Muslim communities of Rio, Salvador, and Pernambuco by one 'Abd ar-Rahman al-Baghdadi, who, as his *nisba* (last part of the name indicating place of origin or status) indicates, was originally from Baghdad.[86] Educated in Damascus, al-Baghdadi was drawn to Constantinople from where, in 1865, he was commissioned to travel to Basra with two steamships. Contrary winds took them to Rio instead, where he would meet with Muslims and teach them the correct way of pursing Islam "for the sake of the Lord of the Worlds."[87]

Muslims in Brazil were attracted to al-Baghdadi because of his distinctive Muslim dress. They approached him cautiously at first, coming to his ship in a small group after most other visitors had left, and addressing him with the Muslim greeting "as-salaam 'alaykum." As al-Baghdadi and others prayed, the small contingent of blacks followed their lead: "We stood to pray and all of them stood with us. They made their ablutions and prayed just like us. We became convinced that they were Muslims and that they believed in the unity of God."[88] Astounded that Muslims were in this part of the world, the Ottoman Muslims warmly embraced their African coreligionists, although they had serious difficulties communicating with them.

A translator, who later accompanied an even larger group of Brazilian Muslims to the ship, explained to al-Baghdadi that "these blacks came from *Bilād al-Sūdān* [literally "land of the blacks"]," and went on to discuss how they were captives from various wars in Africa. When asked, the translator estimated that there were 5, 000 Muslims (either in Rio or Brazil as a whole;

---

[85] See John Candler and Wilson Burgess, *Narrative of a Recent Visit to Brazil to Present and Address on the Slave-Trade and Slavery* (London: Marsh, Friends' Book and Tract Depository, 1853), 38–39.

[86] Abd al-Raḥmān al-Baġdādī, *The Amusement of the Foreigner*, trans. Yacine Daddi Addoun and Renée Soulodre-La France (Toronto: Nigerian Hinterland Project, York University, 2001). This is a draft version of the translation, which together with the Arabic text can be viewed at www.yorku.ca/nhp/shadd/baghdadi.pdf. For an annotated translation in German, see Rosemarie Quiring-Zoche, "Bei Den Malé Brasilien Das Reisebuch des 'Abdarrahmān al Baġdadī," *Die Welt des Islams* (40) 2000: 196–273.

[87] Ibid., 6.

[88] Ibid., 7.

the text does not specify), and that "their hearts are sick of ignorance. Because they left their country when they were very small, none of them have learned the religion of the Chosen Prophet."[89]

Al-Baghdadi decided to visit their homes, where he observed that they were not praying properly (they were not performing bows and prostrations in the prescribed order, they were not using prayer mats, and so on). After two weeks of trying to correct them, al-Baghdadi suspected the translator, who was also their leader, was an imposter; he would later claim that the translator was in fact a Moroccan Jew who purposely misled the Muslim community in Rio.

Having learned some Portuguese, al-Baghdadi later returned to the domiciles of the Muslims and began teaching the fundamental tenets of Islam and Islamic practice, including how and when to fast Ramadan. He was also able to end the requirement of converts paying a fee for their conversion. He noted, however, that the Muslim women were rather resistant to his reforms: "Their women have no desire to fast [Ramadan]. They do whatever they want just like Christian women who spend their time sleeping. They go to the markets without covering themselves; they drink what is forbidden."[90] Al-Baghdadi further complained that the Muslim women were very much opposed to his efforts to reform their inheritance practices, as such changes would reduce their share. All of this reflects in part the fact that African Muslims entering Brazil were disproportionately male, and that their wives were necessarily recruited from non-Muslim populations, who had their own views of such matters.

As a consequence of living in a society in which the Catholic Church was embraced by the state, and as a result of prior conflict between Muslims and the state that culminated in the 1835 outbreak in Bahia, Muslims in Rio were very secretive about their religion, worshiping clandestinely while going to such lengths as to have their children baptized. Fearing his distinctive clothing would alert authorities to their true religious disposition, the Rio Muslim community insisted that al-Baghdadi dress differently when in their company, as discovery of the truth would lead to certain persecution and possibly death.[91]

From Rio, al-Baghdadi went to Salvador, Bahia, where he estimated that there was an even greater number of Muslims. "But," he recorded, "they are not as eager to learn. Their ignorance is the same as in the first town." He went on to write of his apparently successful effort to end the particularly offensive practice of men "trying out" prospective wives by living with them before marriage. As was true of Rio, Muslim women in Salvador were "like the Frank [Christian] ones; they do not veil themselves." The women also gave alms to the church, and al-Baghdadi essentially blamed them for their children becoming Christians rather than Muslims.[92]

[89] Ibid., 7–8.
[90] Ibid., 16–17.
[91] Ibid., 19–20.
[92] Ibid., 28–29.

Finally, al-Baghdadi visited Pernambuco, where he found the Muslims to be even "more alert and dynamic than in the first town [Rio]." He went on to say that "their conditions in praying and fasting are like the others, except for the fact that they are more inclined to magic geomancy and prophecy," an apparent reference to amulets and methods of divination. Al-Baghdadi remained in Pernambuco for six months. For his extended stay and service, his passage back to Constantinople was paid by the Muslims in Brazil.[93]

Just a few years after al-Baghdadi's visit to Brazil, another significant report concerning the Muslim community in both Bahia and Rio de Janeiro was provided by the French ambassador Gobineau, in Brazil for eighteen months during 1869 and 1870. After stating that most of the Minas were in Bahia, and that they were physically and intellectually superior to others who were enslaved, Gobineau discussed their ongoing mutual aid clubs and common treasury, and that they purchase their freedom through their savings and collective efforts. While in years past they "often" returned to West Africa, a statement that accords well with events in Rio in 1851 and 1852, the rate of repatriation had declined in recent years, in conjunction with growing numbers of freed Muslims ("Minas"). Rather than return to West Africa, Muslims were remaining in Bahia and Rio, where they successfully plied their trades and "created a small fortune."[94]

By 1869, according to Gobineau, most if not all Muslims were "Christians on the outside but Muslims in fact," adopting European names after having been baptized, a facade made necessary by the state's intolerance of Islam. Like Muhammad Kaba and Abu Bakr in Jamaica, or for that matter the *moriscos* of sixteenth-century Seville, these Minas were ostensibly Christian but in actuality devout Muslims, studying Arabic to understand the Qur'ān. In Rio, about 100 copies of the Qur'ān were sold on an annual basis by the French bookstores Fauchon and Dupont. Impoverished slaves made "the greatest sacrifices" to purchase the book, often taking a year to amass the funds (fifteen to twenty-five millereis, or thirty-six to fifty francs) to acquire it, paying in installments. In addition, Arabic grammar texts, edited in French, were also purchased by Muslims.[95] The practice of selling such materials may have begun in 1865, when the aforementioned al-Baghdadi entered a "small shop" in Rio and found a Qur'ān. He asked the proprietor to order more, giving the owner a deposit that he recouped once the Qur'āns arrived and Rio Muslims began purchasing them.[96] This all suggests a cautious, quiet, and dedicated Muslim community entering the last quarter of the nineteenth century that was more and more committed to remaining in Brazil, the reasons for which may have had as much to do with developments in West Africa as circumstances in Brazil.

[93] Ibid., 32–35.
[94] See Raedes, *Le comte de Gobineau au Brésil*, 74–76.
[95] Ibid.; also see Da Costa E Silva, "Buying and Selling Korans," 83.
[96] al-Baġdādī, *The Amusement of the Foreigner*, 16.

In Rio, the machacalis or mosques from the late nineteenth into the early twentieth centuries were most likely the homes of the alufás, with the main machacali located at Borão de São Félix Street. The informality of the arrangement obviously helped to conceal what had become a suspect religion, but it was also against the law to build public mosques; indeed, it was only after 1870 that public Protestant churches were built in Brazil.[97] To become an alufá required a period of "great study," so that the books purchased from the French bookstore were not merely emblematic but also critical to Islam's pursuit. There also appears to have been a hierarchy of authority among the alufás, with those of greater status held to possess the power to control the *jinn* (spirits good and bad) and the rain.[98]

There is evidence that, as late as 1906, Muslims in Rio attempted to maintain distance from non-Muslims, including the orisha-worshiping Yoruba.[99] The mussulmis are said to have "despised" Candomblé and its adherents, while the latter "mocked" the observances of the Muslims. Such Muslims prayed at least twice a day (at dawn and dusk) and when they bathed, praying the *tessubá* or *tecebá* (or Muslim "rosary," called "praying on the bead" in North America). They fasted Ramadan, avoided pork, and worked at Arabic literacy, continuing to use writing boards. However, the picture in early-twentieth-century Rio could not have been so cut and dry. Though their clandestine ways inspired mistrust, Muslims were also respected as serious, hard-working people. The potential for a camaraderie transcending religious affiliations was especially high among Bahian immigrants in Rio, resulting in intermarriages and alliances that ultimately diluted the singularity of Islam.

In addition to Rio, there is also information on the late-nineteenth-century and early-twentieth-century Muslim community in such places as Alagoas and Pernambuco. A malê conspiracy is reported to have taken place in Alagoas as early as 1815.[100] The Muslim community there apparently endured into the early twentieth century, when Moraes Filho wrote about "A Festa dos Mortos" ("Feast of the Dead") in the city of Penedo, site of one of the largest black populations in Alagoas. Rodrigues and Duarte identify it as a Muslim

[97] João do Rio (Paulo Barreto), *As religiões no Rio* (Rio de Janeiro: Organizaçao Simões, 1951; orig. pub., 1906), 5–8, 23; Da Costa E Silva, "Buying and Selling Korans," 84–89; Karasch, *Slave Life in Rio*, 285.

[98] The foregoing is in some conflict with the characterization by Rodrigues of conditions in Rio. While he did not believe Rio Muslims to be as organized as those in Bahia, the former did not suffer the same degree of state repression, so that Rio Muslims were able to observe their rituals ("festas solenes") publicly and with great pageantry ("com grandes pompas"). Rodrigues explains this apparent anomaly as the consequence of the presence of "Arab" Muslims in Rio, into whose assemblies "negros malês" were admitted. See Rodrigues, *Os africanos no Brasil*, 68.

[99] See João do Rio (Paulo Barreto), *As religiões no Rio* (Rio de Janeiro: Organizaçao Simões, 1906, 1951), 5–8, 23; Da Costa E Silva, "Buying and Selling Korans," 84–89; Karasch, *Slave Life in Rio*, 285.

[100] See Abelardo Duarte, *Negros muçulmanos nas Alagoas (os malês)* (Maceió, Alagoas: Edições Caeté, 1958), 42–50.

observance (or an Islamically influenced rite in the view of the latter), involving as it did prayers and long periods of fasting, abstinence from alcohol, the co-ordination of rites with phases of the moon, the donning of long white tunics (recalling the Nagô *abadá*), and the sacrifice of sheep. Just north of Alagoas, Freyre saw women in Recife dancing with bands of yellow cloth on their throats in a fashion resemble those participating in Muslim fasts in Bahia. Elsewhere in Pernambuco, ceremonies did not proceed before the removal of shoes and slippers, and they included the drinking of ink-filled water from writing boards. "Prayer-papers" everywhere operated as amulets, worn around the neck or nailed to doors and windows "to deliver the body from death and the house from thieves and malefactors."[101]

Despite the repression of 1835, therefore, Islam in Brazil endured, though lowering its profile. Even in 1869, when the dynamics of importation began to undermine the health of Islam in Brazil, Muslims fought to retain their tradition. The data for slave imports into Brazil, though incomplete, reveal a precipitous plunge in the number of captives from the Bight of Benin arriving in Brazil, falling from 43 percent of 3,270 who disembarked between 1851 and 1855, to zero percent of the total of 9,525 from 1856 through 1875.[102] This drastic decline in the number of Muslims entering Brazil would have an impact, underscoring the extent to which Islam in Brazil was premised upon an African-born population and, indeed, largely restricted to them.

However, the arrest of Muslim importation, though eventually calamitous, did not result in the immediate deterioration of Islam in Brazil; it resulted in the gradual erosion of that community's vibrancy. By the beginning of the twentieth century, the Abbé Ignace Étienne Brazil reported that Muslims remained "fanatical" and antagonistic toward whites and Catholicism. The early-twentieth-century Muslim community in Brazil retained structure, with Imam Hassoumanou of Bahia as head of all the coreligionists in Brazil. There was an *alkali* (from the Arabic *al-qāḍī*), a judicial office whose existence suggests that Muslims in Brazil were still attempting to adjudicate their own affairs according to Muslim law. Prayer five times a day (*ṣalāt*), fasting during Ramadan, and giving alms (*zakāt*), three of the five pillars of Islam (*shahāda* or the confession of faith in God and Muhammad as Prophet, and performing the pilgrimage or *ḥajj* are the other two) were all practiced, as were the avoidance of pork (presumably, therefore, ḥalāl meals were prepared), the use of a lunar calendar, abstinence from alcohol, and the consumption of water made of sūra-replicating ink from writing boards. However, some decline is indicated in the observation that, while Muslims still spoke Yoruba, they could no longer

---

[101] Ibid., 50–55; also see Freyre, *Masters and Slaves*, 31, 315–18; Rodrigues, *Os africanos no Brasil*, 68; Mello Moraes Filho, *Festas e tradições populares do Brasil* (Rio de Janeiro: F. Briguiet, 1946), 333.

[102] See *the Du Bois CD-Rom Database*. From 1851 to 1855, some 26.3 percent of the 3,270 slaves who disembarked from the Bight of Benin arrived in Southeast Brazil, and 16.7 percent of the total landed in Pernambuco.

read Arabic, relying instead on a Portuguese translation of it.[103] The loss of Arabic was no doubt the result of the fall in importations and the difficulties of negotiating Islam through at least four languages (Yoruba, Arabic, Portuguese, and French), but there were exceptions to this assessment by the Abbé, as will be noted.

Abbé Étienne's observations accord well with those of Nina Rodrigues, who also undertook an investigation of Muslims in Bahia during the first decade of the twentieth century. The office of the Abbé's Imam Hassoumanou is probably the same one referred to as that of the "Imã" or almaami by Rodrigues, a figure otherwise called the *limamo*. The limamo at the time of Rodrigues's research was the Nagô "Luís," a tall and robust man bent over with age. "Although no one told me he has a harem," wrote Rodrigues, "he has numerous offspring." His current wife was a thirty-something-year-old Brazilian-born woman who had converted to Islam while living in Rio de Janeiro. Well-versed in scripture, she read and wrote Portuguese but not Arabic, while the limamo's abilities were just the reverse; each therefore had a Qur'ān in the language of their literacy. To the limamo reported "numerous priests," the alufás, such as the Hausa "Jatô" on Taboão Street and the Nagô "Derisso" (on the same street), the "old Nagô Antônio" in Pelourinho Square, a Hausa on Alvo Street, another on Fogo road, and so on. To these offices Querino added that of the "xerife," a reference to those claiming descent from Muhammad.[104]

Rodrigues was witnessing the beginning of the end of orthodox Islam as it had been known in Bahia. He described the limamo Luís and his wife as "embittered" by the ingratitude of the Brazilian-born children of African-born Muslims, who "preferred the fetishist life of the blacks who followed the saints [Candomblé] or the Yorubas, or to convert to Catholicism." In fact, the couple was greatly afraid of the ridicule, contempt, and even violence that could be visited on them by others ("população crioula"), who could mistake them for the followers of Candomblé or other African religions.[105] As a consequence of these circumstances and the residual "terror" left by the repression of the 1835 revolt, the pursuit of Islam in the first few years of the twentieth century was taken with the utmost caution, away from public view.[106] Muslim worship took place, for example, in the inner chamber of a modest house on the Rua da Alegria in Salvador. There Muslims gathered every Friday for prayer and

[103] See Ignace Étienne Brazil, "La secte musulmane des Malês du Brésil et leur révolte en 1835," *Anthropos* (Basel) 4 (1909): 99–105, 405–15; _____, "Os Malês," *Revista do Instituto Histórico e Geográfico Brasileiro* 72 (1909): 69–126.

[104] See Rodrigues, *Os africanos no Brasil*, 61–62; Ricard, "L'Islam noir à Bahia," 64. The unspecified responsibilities of the "office" of *sherîf* could only be undertaken by the advanced in age ("pessoa idosa"). In fact, Querino ranks this position above that of the limamo. See Querino, *Costumes africanos no Brasil*, 67–68.

[105] It is not clear to whom Rodrigues refers when he writes "população crioula." Is he referring to Brazilian-born whites, or to all the Brazilian-born people who did not adhere to African religions?

[106] See Rodrigues, *Os africanos no Brasil*, 62–63.

a communal meal. Located in the home's study were religious texts, writing tablets, inkpots, special quills, and so on. On the walls hung portraits of Mecca with Arabic inscriptions. Muslim funerary rites were conducted by the alufás, who fasted an additional thirty days to those required during Ramadan. As in West Africa, Muslims, Catholics, orisha-worshipers, and practitioners of other African religions (none of these categories are mutually exclusive) all sought Muslim amulets or mandingas.[107]

Difficulties with the Brazilian-born began to fray, but did not immediately unravel, the fabric of a Muslim society that continued to enjoy a measure of cohesion. Marriages contracted between Muslims, for example, remained very solemn commitments. Those getting married first consulted with the limamo, who would not sanction the union if both parties did not consent. Infidelity (on the part of the woman) carried the penalty of total rejection and abandonment by the Muslim community. Muslims maintained their own networks of mutual assistance, and impoverished Muslims (a relative concept, no doubt) were assisted by their coreligionists, refusing to accept public charity.[108]

While they were under suspicion and had to conduct their observances clandestinely, Rodrigues estimated that as many as one-third of the old, surviving Africans in Bahia were "muçulmi ou malê," that of this group the Nagôs were the most influential, and that of the Nagôs from such urban centers as Oyo, Ilorin, and Ijesha, almost all were "muçulmis, malês ou muçulmanos." The Nupe ("Tapas"), greatly reduced in number, were also Muslims, mostly women who still spoke their native tongue, as did the Nagôs. The same was true of the Mande-speakers and the "Bornus" (Kanuri) and "adamauás" (probably a reference to Fulbe, Hausa, and Kanuri persons from the Islamic amirate of Adamawa in what is now northern Cameroon, rather than non-Muslims from such groups as the Duru or Mbum from the same area), Muslims who were nearly "extinct" in Bahia. "Pure" Fulbe, "black people of the white race," were remembered by the living as having once been in Bahia, identified by their "copper red color and nearly straight, undulating hair." Rodrigues's numerical estimate is consistent with the report of Djinguiz, who maintained that as many as 100,000 African-descended Muslims remained in Bahia and Rio de Janeiro as late as 1907.[109]

A lack of information concerning the methods by which such estimates were obtained, combined with the secretive nature of the Muslim community in general, can only enfeeble the reliability of quantitative assessments. Statistical ambiguity regarding Brazilian Muslims in the beginning of the twentieth century, however, only continues for the next several decades, such that by the late 1940s,

---

[107] Ibid.

[108] See Querino, *Costumes africanos no Brasil*, 69–70.

[109] See Rodrigues, *Os africanos no Brasil*, 61, 109–14. Djinguiz's estimate should be taken with a grain of salt. See Mohammed Djinguiz, "L'Islam dans l'Amérique centrale et dans l'Amérique du Sud," *Revue du Monde musulman* 6 (October 1908).

the status of Muslims as a distinct community of faith is far from certain.[110] Earlier in the century, Rodrigues had predicted that Islam in Brazil would essentially disappear, observing that Islam was confined to the elderly, African-born population, and that there were no efforts to convert either Brazilian-born blacks or those of mixed ancestry.[111] However, the scholarship of Pierre Verger and the assertions of Antônio Monteiro leave the accuracy of Rodrigues's prognostication in some doubt. Monteiro maintains he interviewed the *mestres* ("teachers") Gibirilo, or Manoel do Nascimento Santos Silva (son of Tibúrcio Souto), José Maria Mendonça, and Artur Costa e Leodegário Ludogério de Souza in Salvador, who he claims were leading *malês* in the 1970s and 1980s. Monteiro's objective was to identify the descendants of African-born Muslims and their achievements and contributions; a number of those discussed were highly educated or otherwise professionally trained. Very guarded in conversation, mestre Gibirilo, Monteiro's major source, owned a velvet-covered green notebook in which were Arabic inscriptions. Verger also knew some of these individuals personally, stating that they were the scions of African-born individuals. What is not clear is what Monteiro means by the term *malê*; were the informants practicing Muslims, or was the term simply a signifier for a cultural inheritance? Verger, in contrast, is unambiguous, stating that mestre Gibirilo and others were in fact Muslims who also belonged to such societies as the previously mentioned Irmandade de Nossa Senhora da Soledade Amparo dos Desvalidos: "They simultaneously adhered to Catholicism and Islam with the same sincerity, but observed the greatest reserve in manifesting their Muslim faith. The *Malê* who had escaped police investigations during the previous century after the revolts and uprisings, especially the '*Malê* war' of 1835, had acquired habits of prudent distrust, which they had transmitted to their children." This simultaneous embrace of both Islam and Christianity (the former more fervently than the latter) finds an echo in the late-nineteenth-century to early-twentieth-century observations of Querino, who spent significant time in Bahia and recorded that the *malês* recognized only two superior beings: *Olorum-u-luá* (Creator God) and Mariama (mother of Jesus).[112] In this instance, however, the former appellation not only suggests Christian–Muslim interpenetration but the inclusion of the Yoruba orishas as well. Monteiro maintained that the *malês* also organized exclusive recreational clubs like Clube da Barra and Ladeira da Praça, and he concurred with Verger that *malês* (specifically, alufá Manoel Victor Serra) were responsible for founding Irmandade de Nossa Senhora.[113]

---

[110] See Reis and de Moraes Farias, "Islam and Slave Resistance in Bahia," 62, note 32.

[111] See Rodrigues, *Os africanos no Brasil*, 61.

[112] See Querino, *Costumes africanos no Brasil*, 66. The term *Olorum-u-luá* is Nagô, not Mande.

[113] See Monteiro, *Notas sobre negros malês na Bahia*, 13–19, 63–74; Verger, *Trade Relations*, 457–58. Verger identifies Gibirilu as the son of Ife-born José Maria do Santo Silva – is this the José Maria Mendonça mentioned by Monteiro? The velvet-covered notebook is said to have been lost in a fire at the Liceu de Artes e Ofícios. Zaid Abdul-Aleem wrote his master's thesis on this topic, having interviewed over fifty scholars and descendants of the *malês* in Bahia in 1996. His work

However, just as Christianity had an impact on the pursuit of Islam, and as will be demonstrated in the chapters concerning North America, Islam also left an impression on Christian traditions. Freyre has written that the bias of some against Catholicism, opting instead for Protestantism, is probably informed by an Islamic residue of ridicule.[114] Another example of Muslim influence is the church of *Nossa Senhora da Conceição da Lapinha* (Our Lady of the Conception of Lapinha), currently located in Lapinha Square in Salvador (Liberdade-Salvador). The church was designed and built in the 1860s and 1870s by mestre Manoel Friandes (1823–1904), whom Querino identifies as an imale or Muslim. Friandes, an architect and builder of renown, was commissioned by the Catholic Church to erect a number of buildings. The interior of Lapinha church follows a morisco pattern, and around the edges of the ceiling, over the Moorish arches, and over the nave is an Arabic inscription that reads, "Behold, This is the Miracle of God and This is the Door of Heaven."[115]

Despite the repression of 1835, therefore, Islam as the heritage of African slaves continued in Brazil at least through the mid-twentieth century, and arguably into the 1980s, though by then its followers were greatly reduced numerically. The apparent strategy of promoting the religion only among the African-born, combined with the hostility of the state and Christianity, help to explain its diminution. In a land where Islam had clearly made its greatest impact, and where Muslims boasted their largest numbers, the religion went into eclipse; perhaps a Nigerian Muslim mission in operation in Salvador since the 1990s will revive its fortunes. It is an inescapable irony that, in another land, where Islam's presence was not as extensive, that religion would indeed flourish throughout the twentieth century and into the twenty-first, gaining new life and adherents at the precise moment when Islam had assumed atrophic form in Brazil. To that land and the origins of the Muslim community in its midst we now turn our attention.

supports Monteiro's claims, locating Gibirilo's Qur'ān in the Centro Estudos Afro-Orientais. See Zaid Abdul Aleem, "African Muslim Survival and Adaptation in Salvador, Bahia" (M. A. thesis, Duke U., 1996).

[114] See Freyre, *Masters and Slaves*, 315–16.

[115] See Manuel Raimundo Querino, *Artistas Bahianos* (Rio de Janeiro: Imprensa Nacional, 1909), 206. According to literature I obtained while visiting Lapinha, the church was actually founded in the 1770s, while construction of the current edifice began in 1925.

4

Muslims in New York

It has been demonstrated that African Muslims were already acquainted with Iberians prior to their removal to what would become Brazil and Latin America, so that what transpired between them in the New World was in a real sense a prolongation of the familiar. In latitudes much further to the north, however, the engagement of European and African, Muslim and non-Muslim alike, was much more novel an experience. This was particularly true of the territory subsequently and most famously known as New York. While meager, indirect, and deductive, the evidence for the presence of Muslims in this area remains deserving of investigation.

Englishman Henry Hudson's search for a new route to Asia, undertaken to promote the interests of the Dutch East India Company, brought him to what became the Hudson Valley in 1609. The area was called "New Netherlands" as early as 1614, but the first permanent settlement of Europeans, about thirty families of French-speaking Walloons, disembarked from the *Nieu Nederlandt* and established "New Amsterdam" on the island of Manhattan in 1624. The Dutch West India Company, by means of Governor Peter Minuit, "purchased" the island from "the Indians" in 1626; by 1630, some 300 Europeans, mostly Walloons, were already there. The English would seize the colony in 1664, but in the final two decades of Dutch rule the population soared to around 9,000. Concentrated in or near a few towns, the settlers were largely farmers, half of whom were non-Dutch – Germans, Frenchmen, Danes, Swedes, Fins, Englishmen, and so on. Between 1638 and 1648, some eighteen European languages were spoken in the colony. It was into this kaleidoscope of mostly northern Europeans that Africans were introduced.[1]

At some point in 1625 or 1626, the first Africans arrived in New Amsterdam by means of the Dutch West India Company. Eleven men of African descent stepped ashore with surnames indicating either place of origin, subsequent

---

[1] See Allison Blakely, *Blacks in the Dutch World: The Evolution of Racial Imagery in a Modern Society* (Bloomington and Indianapolis: Indiana U. Press, 1993), 24–25.

places of habitation, or group or personal features with which they were associated. The whole lot, in fact, could have been "captured seamen" from Portuguese or Spanish vessels. Thus, Paulo Angola, Big Manuel, Little Manuel, Manuel de Gerrit de Reus, Simon Congo, Anthony Portuguese García, Little Anthony, Jan Fort Orange, John Francisco, Peter Santomee, and Jan Primero began their careers as slaves of the company. In 1628, three enslaved African women were imported "for the company's Negro men," and, together with other Africans, they served the company for twenty years, performing such "heavy manual labor" as the construction and maintenance of Fort Amsterdam (on land now occupied by the Battery) and the wall built to defend against Native Americans (that would eventually mark the site of Wall Street).[2] Enslaved laborers were also used as stevedores and deck hands in connection with the fur trade, and they could be found tending the livestock and farms of the company, where they grew crops for the garrison at New Amsterdam. Critical to agricultural success in the Hudson Valley beyond New Amsterdam, Africans were even called to "take up arms and help protect the lives and property of their masters."[3]

Slavery in New Netherlands was perhaps atypical for North America in that slaves could legally marry; own land, livestock, and other property; and file lawsuits and petitions. Because there was some flexibility in the demands on African labor early in the colony's existence, and because of the need to secure African loyalties against the Native American threat, the company responded to a petition for freedom from the original eleven Africans to land in the colony by granting them "half-freedom" status on February 25, 1644, whereby they could work for themselves but were required to pay the company "22½ bushels of maize, wheat, or corn and one fat hog . . . or be re-enslaved," while remaining available to work for the company whenever needed. Eight of the original eleven would go on to achieve "full freedom."[4]

[2] Reference to the conscription can be found in such sources as the colony's council minutes of February 12, 1652: "The director-general approves the request of the community and promises to have the necessary forts cut and furnished by his own servants or Negroes, with the commonality bearing the expenses of putting up the palisades enclosing [the fort]." Charles T. Gehring, trans. and ed., *New York Historical Manuscripts: Dutch. Volume V: Council Minutes, 1652–1654* (Baltimore, MD: Genealogical Publishing Co., 1983), 11.

[3] See Thomas J. Condon, *New York Beginnings: The Commercial Origins of New Netherland* (New York: New York U. Press, 1968); M.A. Harris, *A Negro History Tour of Manhattan* (New York: Greenwood Publishing, 1968), 5–6; James Weldon Johnson, *Black Manhattan* (New York: Arno Press and the New York Times, 1968; orig. Pub. 1930), 4–5; Sherrill D. Wilson, *New York City's African Slaveowners: A Social and Material Culture History* (New York and London: Garland Publishing, 1994), 23–24, 37; Edgar McManus, *A History of Negro Slavery in New York* (Syracuse, NY: Syracuse U. Press, 1966), 5–6; Oliver A. Rink, *Holland on the Hudson: An Economic and Social History of Dutch New York* (Ithaca and London: Cornell U. Press, 1986), 70; Leo H. Hirsch, Jr., "New York and the Negro, From 1783 to 1865," *Journal of Negro History* 16 (1931): 383.

[4] See Wilson, *New York City's African Slaveowners*, 24–39; Thelma Wills Foote, "Black Life in Colonial Manhattan, 1664–1786" (Ph.D. diss., Harvard U., 1991), 9–14. The land granted to the "African eleven" was in fact located in what is now Greenwich Village, the colony's northern boundary during the Dutch period. Each of the eleven received between one and twenty acres

   Angolans formed the largest and most identifiable black contingent in New
Netherlands early in its history, but, as the Dutch period progressed, most
came from the Caribbean, although many were probably born in Africa and
"seasoned" in the West Indies.⁵ The characterization of Angolans as "proud
and treacherous," and of Angolan women as "thievish, lazy, and useful trash,"
contributed to the preference for "seasoned" captives out of the Caribbean,
who arrived in small parcels of ten or fewer by way of privateers, perhaps

---

(Big Manuel was deeded much of contemporary Washington Square Park); the "Negro" tracts
were more or less contiguous and close to the wagon road, as were preceding and subsequent
grants to Africans and their descendants. As much is suggested by an April 1647 land grant to
Evert Duyckingh that was bounded on the west "by the lot owned by the Negroes," and by
a March 1647 grant to Lourens Pietersz Noorman, whose property was similarly adjacent to
"the lot of the Negroes." In addition, there was Domingo Anthony, "Negro," who received five
morgens of land (slightly over ten acres) along the wagon road in July of 1643, while on the
same date "Catelina, widow of Jochem Antony, Negro," was granted property "north of the
wagon road, extending along the aforesaid wagon road south west 66 rods until the land of
Domingo Antony." Becoming a widow may have been one of the few, if not sole avenues to
landownership by women, as Catelina was joined in her new status by Anna "Negerinna," a
"free" black and widow of Andries d'Angola. One "Francisco Negro," possibly John Francisco,
acquired land in March of 1647 bounded on the north by Gerrit Hendricksz and on the south by
Anthony Congo, whose possessions also ran along the wagon road as did those of "Jan Negro,
who came with the Captain," (an apparent reference to Jan Fort Orange). As a final example,
there was the September 1645 grant to "Anthony Portugies, Negro," presumably one and the
same with Anthony Portuguese García, who would be indirectly related to the question of the
Muslim presence in what becomes New York. Anthony Portuguese's land was adjacent to that
of Manuel Trumpetter (or Trumpeter or Trompeter), a half-free black by 1643. See Charles T.
Gehring, trans. and ed., *New York Historical Manuscripts: Dutch. Volumes GG, HH, and II, Land
Papers* (Baltimore, MD: Genealogical Publishing Co., 1980), 20, 24, 34, 36, 48, 50, 55–58; Wilson,
New York City's African Slaveowners, 38–39.
⁵ Africans such as the Angolans tended to marry other Angolans at least through the middle of the
seventeenth century, and in death their children were adopted by surviving Angolans. A possible
exception to this pattern was Maria d'Angola, who married and survived Gratia d'Angola, a
"free" man who had received some ten acres in 1644. Maria went on to marry Christoffel
Santomee in October of 1667, who presumably had some connection of significance with São
Tomé (but who also could have originated in Angola). Records from the Dutch Reform Church
show that, from 1639 to 1652, fourteen marriages involving Africans were contracted, some 28
percent of all marriages performed during this period, including the union of an Angolan woman
and a European male. Apparently the first all-African marriage took place in May 1641 between
the widow Lucie d'Angola and the widower Anthony Van Angola. Lucie d'Angola had been
previously married to the late Laurens d'Angola, whereas the designation "widower" can only
be applied with qualification and skepticism to Anthony Van Angola, also known as Anthony
of Angola, Cleyn or Little Antonio (presaging Little Anthony and the Imperials of the 1950s and
1960s), and Anthony the Blind Negro, as he married Lucie on the same day that his wife Catalina
(Katalina) Van Angola died. Little Anthony and Lucie, in turn, both died shortly after their son
Anthony was baptized in the Dutch Reform Church on August 3, 1643, although their deaths
are not recorded until after December 30, 1644. The son was immediately adopted by his "free"
godmother Dorothy d'Angola (also known as Clara Creole, Etoria, or Retory). See Richard
Dickerson, "Abstracts of Early Black Manhattanites," *New York Genealogical and Biographical
Record* 116, no. 2 (April 1985): 100–04; no. 3 (July 1985): 169–73. Also see Peter R. Cristoph,
"The Freedmen of New Amsterdam," *Journal of the Afro-American Historical and Genealogical
Society* 4 (Winter 1983): 140–41.

accounting for one-third of New Amsterdam's enslaved imports.[6] McManus's claim that the African-born slaves "turned out to be unsatisfactory to most users of labor" and were "almost immediately" reexported to plantation colonies appears exaggerated, however, since landholding and marriage records reveal that many Africans remained in New Netherlands for the duration of their short lives. Calculating the size of the enslaved and "free" black population of New Netherland is difficult, but a modest estimate suggests that by 1664 there were at least 700 Africans in Manhattan, perhaps 40 percent of the island's residents and 10 percent of New Netherland's total population.[7]

New York's heterogeneous African-descended communities, arriving from West and West Central Africa as well as from the Caribbean, were very much part of the rough-and-tumble, frontier-like conditions of New Netherlands. One of the most prominent among them was Anthony Jansen Van Salee, also known as Anthony Jansen Van Vaes, who contributed greatly to the colony's loutish ambience.[8] He was often called "Anthony the Turk," an appellation commonly applied to North Africans at the time, and property records would continue to refer to land bearing his name as the "Turk's land." Anthony

[6] See J. Franklin Jameson, ed., *Narratives of New Netherland, 1609–1664* (New York: Charles Scribner's Sons, 1909), 127; Rev. James Michaëlius to the Reverend Adrianus Smotius, August 1628, in John R. Broadhead and E.B. O'Callaghan, eds., *Documents Relative to the Colonial History of the State of New York* (Albany, NY: Weed, Parsons and Co., 1854), vol. 2, 768.

[7] Following their initial advent in 1625–26, it is possible that Africans were brought to the colony in 1635 aboard the *Eendracht*, after which arrived the *Tamendare*, a slaver that sailed from either Curaçao or Brazil (or both) to New Amsterdam by way of Barbados in 1646 with a cargo of captives. In September of 1655, the *Witte Paert* carried 300 Africans directly from Africa, as did the *Bontekoe* the following year after an initial stop in Curaçao. During the last five years of Dutch control, at least six slavers made port in New Amsterdam bearing at least 400 enslaved persons (170 females and 230 males): the *Sphera Mundi* with five captives, the *Eyckenboom*, the *New Netherland Indian* (two voyages, one with thirty-six captives), the *Sparrow* with forty captives, and finally the *Gideon* in 1664, two weeks before the English took over, with 270 to 290 "half-starved Negroes and Negresses." See Broadhead and O'Callaghan, *Documents*, vol. 2, 430; Oliver A. Rink, "The People of New Netherland: Notes on Non-English Immigration to New York in the Seventeenth Century," *New York History* 62 (1981): 33; Rink, *Holland on the Hudson*, 163; Roi Ottley and William J. Weatherly, eds., *The Negro in New York: An Informal Social History* (New York: New York Public Library, 1967), 6–7; McManus, *History of Negro Slavery in New York*, 5–12; Wilson, *New York City's African Slaveowners*, 37–39; David Kobrin, *The Black Minority in Early New York* (Albany: U. of the State of New York, 1971), 4; Foote, "Black Life in Colonial Manhattan," 6–14; Thomas J. Davis, "Slavery in Colonial New York City" (Ph.D. diss., Columbia U., 1974), 34–35; Joyce D. Goodfriend, "Burghers and Blacks: The Evolution of a Slave Society at New Amsterdam," *New York History* 59 (1978): 128–39; Elizabeth Donnan, *Documents Illustrative of the History of the Slave Trade to America* (New York, Octagon Books, 1965), vol. 1, 75–76, 141–45; vol. 3, 405–33; Vivienne L. Kruger, "Born to Run: The Slave Family in Early New York, 1626 to 1827" (Ph.D. diss., Columbia U., 1985), vol. 1, 34–45.

[8] See Leo Hershkowitz, "The Troublesome Turk: An Illustration of Judicial Process in New Amsterdam," *New York History* 46 (1965): 299–310; Hazel Van Dyke Roberts, "Anthony Jansen Van Salee, 1607–1676," *New York Genealogical and Biographical Record* 103, no. 1 (January 1972): 16–28. Unfortunately, the language of the latter article exhibits an animus against people of African descent.

was described as "a mulatto noted for his size and strength and one of the more interesting characters of New Amsterdam. Seemingly he was born at the seaport-town of Salé, headquarters of the buccaneer Jan Jansen, who married a Mohammedan and became the Sultan's Admiral of the Fleet." One author suggests that Anthony issued from the marriage of this "Mohammedan" with Jan Jansen (renamed Morat Rais); another, that Anthony did not have a "Moor" for a mother, since he was born around 1607 and Jan Jansen was not captured by Algerian pirates in the Canary Islands until 1618 (and therefore did not arrive in North Africa until eleven years after Anthony's birth). The denial, however, does not detract from the concession that Jan Jansen was Anthony's father, nor from the probability that Anthony was a Muslim prior to his arrival in New Amsterdam. In all likelihood, his mother was African, North or otherwise, as Anthony and related persons were consistently viewed as "mulattoes."

Anthony, according to one source, made "an unfortunate choice of a wife" in marrying Grietje Reyniers, five years his senior, aboard a ship bound for New Netherlands in 1629. On one hand, it was perhaps "the preference of Anthony, either a Mohammedan then, or influenced by that religion, to be married by a sea captain rather than by a Dutch minister"; on the other hand, the marriage may have been contracted in this way out of consideration for Grietje, who had supposedly acquired a "reputation," having been previously fired for "improper conduct" as a "waiting girl" in an Amsterdam tavern. However, what is known about Grietje comes from detractors who, in accordance with male hypocrisy, typically sought to sully women's characters to their advantage. To the extent Grietje in fact suffered social dishonor, the knowledge of such, together with Anthony's probable Muslim upbringing, may have been the principal contributors to a colorful, rather combustible career in New Netherlands after their arrival in 1630. Anthony went on to establish himself as both an "excellent and prosperous farmer" and "one of the largest landowners on Manhattan" prior to 1639, when he first bought a farm between what is now Maiden Lane and Ann Street. He and Grietje were constantly at odds with those around them, however, and their story is a source of some of the most salacious material to come out of the Dutch period.

Of the approximately fifty civil suits and forty-three criminal cases argued before the colonial court between 1638 and 1639, a number featured Anthony and his wife Grietje as litigants in opposition to the Domine Everardus Bogardus of the Dutch Reform Church and his second wife, Anna Jans. The context of the first 1638 proceeding was the request by Anthony's next-door neighbor Peter de Truy and fellow ministerial salary collector Wolphest Van Couwenhoven that he "pay money toward the salary of the Reverend Mr. Bogardus." Anthony's emphatic and profane refusal was a serious affront to both the minister and the authority of the church. Tensions led Anthony and the Domine to sue each other in court for debts, with the court ruling that the Domine owed Anthony seven guilders while Anthony was required to pay court fees. True to character, Anthony refused to pay the fees, and Grietje upped the ante by calling the minister a liar. Insulted, the Domine asked witnesses to appear before the court and recount injurious statements made by Anthony and Grietje. The two salary collectors testified to having heard Anthony say that "I had rather lose my head than pay him in this wise, and if he insist on [having] the money, it will yet cause bloodshed." Anthony spoke up, demanding that the minister declare that he and his wife were honorable, for "if I should clear the minister and remain myself in disgrace what would be the result?" The Domine's response was far from charitable, however, as he produced yet another character witness, midwife Lysbert Dircks, who maintained that, after delivering Grietje's baby, Grietje asked if the infant resembled Anthony or Andries Hudden, provincial council member. "If you do not know who the father is," she answered, "how should I know? However, the child is somewhat brown."

On October 7, 1638, the Domine again brought Anthony and Grietje to court for slander and scandalizing his congregation, and again the strategy was to impugn Grietje's character. Witnesses alleged that, upon arrival in New Amsterdam, Grietje declared the following: "I have long enough been the whore of the nobility; from now on I shall be the whore of the rabble." She was further accused of lifting her petticoat and showing her backside to sailors. On October 16 and 21, 1638, both Anthony and Grietje were forced to apologize to the minister, with Grietje admitting to issuing lies about him. In view of the situation's volatility, the court further forbid Anthony from carrying arms other than a knife and an axe within certain boundaries.

By December of 1638, it was clear that Anthony and Grietje's social difficulties were no longer confined to the Domine; they were defendants in at least eight suits between October of 1638 and March of 1639, losing almost all of them (one of these suits was brought in December of 1638 by Anthony the Portuguese, who sought damages after Anthony's dog attacked his hog). Finally, in April of 1639, the court reviewed all of the cases against the couple, including the accusation that Grietje had at one time "in her house measured the male members of three sailors on a broomstick." Required to again apologize and make back payments to Reverend Bogardus, the couple were branded "troublesome persons" and given six months to leave New Netherlands forever. Following Anthony's appeal to the director of the Dutch West India Company, however, the couple was permitted to settle in Long Island on a 200-acre tract after selling their property in New Amsterdam, thus pioneering the towns of Utrecht and Gravesend. Anthony not only went on to become one of the "largest and most prominent" landowners in Long Island, but he also bought a house on Bridge Street in New Amsterdam as early as 1643, defying the court's decision. Furthermore, he became a merchant and creditor within New Amsterdam, where he continued to experience friction with the residents, this time winning a few court cases. All four of Anthony and Grietje's daughters married into "respectable" New Amsterdam families. Grietje died sometime before 1669, after which Anthony married the widow Metje Grevenraet and returned to live in the Bridge Street house in what had become New York City. Anthony died in 1676.

Anthony's lifelong difficulties may simply be attributable to personality or to economic rivalries and jealousies. It is abundantly clear that many did not care for Grietje. However, his Muslim, North African background cannot be discounted as a factor in either his defiant attitude toward authority, particularly the church, or the treatment he received from other settlers. The fact that "neither he and nor his wife were zealous church going inhabitants" is indirect evidence of Islamic sensibilities, although there is no evidence that he actually practiced Islam in the West. That a descendant later sold "a beautiful copy of the Koran" is important in that it reveals an ongoing reverence for the religion and strengthens the suspicion that his actions and decisions were influenced by an Islamic upbringing. In any event, Anthony would not be the only Moor to reach North America, and thus he becomes a part of a Moorish legacy that extends to the present.

Another possible Muslim presence in New Netherlands was Abraham Van Salee, part owner of the privateer *La Garce* along with Jan Jansen and Philip Jansen. Abraham was apparently Anthony's full or half-brother, and he was also called "Turk" and "the mulatto."

In 1658, he was fined twelve guilders for refusing to help financially support the Reverend Mr. Polhemus, claiming that he did not understand Dutch. He died the following year, leaving his property with a woman of African descent and their son, born in the year of Abraham's death. One source speculates that the son was Frans Abramse Van Salee, for although there were a number of men named Abram or Abraham Jansen, there was only one called "Abraham Jansen alias the Mulatto." Frans married as Frans Abrahamszen to African-descended Lucretia Hendricks, daughter of Anna Maria, in November of 1680. He later married a second wife, Isabel Frans, daughter of Francois d'Angola and Barbara Manuels. The various marriage patterns suggest the principals were all of African descent.[9]

With the beginning of the English period, the evidence for Muslims in New York becomes even more indirect and speculative. Between 1700 and 1774, at least 6,800 enslaved persons were imported into New York City, 41.2 percent of whom were born in Africa.[10] Before 1742, 70 percent came from the West Indies and American sources, with "thousands" arriving from Barbados and Jamaica. A minority therefore came directly from Africa, usually "occasional shipments of African children under the age of thirteen." After 1742, however, the relative percentages were inversely proportionate, so that 70 percent came from Africa, and between 1750 and 1756, New York City became a "regular

[9] Ibid.; also see Henry B. Hoff, "Frans Abramse Van Salee and His Descendants: A Colonial Black Family in New York and New Jersey," *New York Genealogical and Biographical Record* 121, no. 2 (April 1990): 65–71. Also see vol. 121, no. 3 (July 1990): 157–66 and 121, no. 3 (October 1990): 205–11.

[10] See James Lydon, "New York and the Slave Trade, 1700–1774," *William and Mary Quarterly* 35 (1978): 375–94; Wilson, *New York City's African Slaveowners*, 40–41; Edwin Olson, "Social Aspects of the Slave in New York," *Journal of Negro History* 26 (1941): 66–77; Kruger, *Born to Run*, 79–83; McManus, *A History of Negro Slavery in New York*, 28–30.

port of call." This turnabout was related to the revocation of the asiento after 1750, when Spanish markets were closed to English slavers. Traders responded by flooding New York and other English colonies with captives until some time after 1770, when the New York market collapsed. The demographics reflect these changes: at the beginning of the eighteenth century, 14.5 percent of the city's population was of African descent, a figure that peaked in 1746 at 20.8 percent and declined to 7.2 percent, or 2,369 persons, by 1790 (reflecting in part the relocation of black British loyalists to Canada following the American War of Independence). In addition to loading and unloading cargo at the docks, slips, and warehouses along the East River, slaves worked in the shipbuilding and construction industries and ferried between Long Island farms and the city, engaged in any number of public works projects and domestic services. They were especially skillful in the marketplace, with so many selling produce in the city streets that the Common Council had to curb their activities in 1740.

The sources tend to be rather unspecific with regard to the supply areas in West Africa from which captives were taken. One can assume that there must have been a modicum of Muslims among them, but there are only anecdotal and indirect references to support this assumption. The relationship between New York and West Africa of course dates back to the Dutch, who in 1617 "pur chased" Gorée Island from the "natives" and proceeded to build two small forts there in addition to establishing a presence at Rufisque on the mainland (the Dutch also took Elmina and Fort St. Anthony at Axim from the Portuguese in 1637 and 1642, respectively).[11] Although there is nothing to suggest that the Dutch recruited heavily from Senegambia or Gorée, some Senegambians may have filtered into New Amsterdam. For the English period, however, there are instances in which Senegambia is specifically cited as the source of captives. For example, about 500 Africans, "many of them directly from Gambia," were transported to Philadelphia in 1762 at the peak of that city's participation in the slave trade; some probably found their way to New York City. Even more likely to have reached the city were some who arrived in New Jersey in May 1762, concerning whom a notice read as follows: "Just imported from the River Gambia in the Schooner *Sally* . . . a parcel of likely Men and Women Slaves, with some Boys and Girls of different Ages."[12] The background of the legendary Ira Aldridge, luminary Shakespearean actor and thespian of the African Com- pany, whose performances were held at the African Grove (corner of Bleecker and Mercer streets), may also include a Senegambian heritage. Born in July of 1807, Aldridge was at times described as the son of a "full-blooded negro pastor in New York City," Daniel Aldridge, who in turn was purported to have been "the son of a Senegalese chief." Daniel, according to this account, was

---

[11] See Donnan, *Documents*, vol. 1, 75–76; Ira Berlin, "From Creole to African: Atlantic Creoles and the Origins of African-American Society in Mainland North America," *William and Mary Quarterly* 53 (1996): 251–88.

[12] See Gary B. Nash, *Forging Freedom: The Formation of Philadelphia's Black Community, 1720–1840* (Cambridge, MA: Harvard U. Press, 1988), 10; Donnan, *Documents*, vol. 3, 455.

Senegalese born but brought to North America by missionaries in order to return to Senegal "as a Christian ruler." Because Daniel's father was overthrown, Daniel settled instead for the Presbyterian pastorate. Such accounts are competing and fanciful, perhaps intended to add to the stature of Ira Aldridge, but there may be a kernel of factuality involved. However, given that Islam made steady advances in Senegambia in the eighteenth and nineteenth centuries, the story of Ira's grandfather may not reflect an Islamic background but just the opposite, and the grandfather may have been swept away in an era of Muslim reform.[13]

It is also reasonable to speculate that names associated with Africans could reflect a Muslim identity. The name *Sambo* or *Samba*, for example, may be a Pulaar name meaning "second son" in that language, so that at least some of those so designated may have been of Fulbe origin and quite possibly Muslim. The name was very popular in the New York area, as was the case in November of 1763 with a runaway "who calls himself Sambo" and who spoke English "indifferently," strongly suggesting that Sambo was his actual, African-given name. Two years later, another Sambo escaped from Hunterdon County, Jersey bearing a "single Mark on his Right Cheek; he is also a New Negroe and can speak but little English; he is apt to speak the Words that are spoke to him again."[14] Perhaps the most curious account of a Sambo in the New York area was written in 1799 by an anonymous white woman living near Mount Pleasant in Westchester County. The Sambo in question suffered tremendously under the hands of the slaveholder for having committed various infractions: stealing geese and liquor, spending all of his money while out on a "Lusslin frollick," running away for days at a time, on so forth. In each instance, he received 70 to 100 lashes, at one point enduring the penalty of 100 lashes for three successive Saturdays. In each instance, he was forced to remove his new clothing, clothing he obtained with money he earned as an outhire, and put on clothes provided by the slaveholder. This clearly indicates a struggle over Sambo's identity and sense of ownership, the conflicting claims represented in the apparel of choice. Sambo also took considerable time to maintain his hair in braids, and his plaits were removed and his head shaved as punishment in one instance. As noted in Chapter 2, Mande and Hausa men often plaited their hair, and although it is not known if Sambo was Muslim, he certainly fought to maintain an identity counter to the one provided by the slaveholder.[15]

West Africa may not have been the only region from which most Muslims came to New York City. Some could have also come out of the Madagascar trade, with which New York had extensive involvement. Captives from the Madagascar sector arrived in North America in two brief spans of time: from

[13] See Johnson, *Black Manhattan*, 78–83.

[14] See the *New-York Gazette*, November 7, 1763; *Pennsylvania Gazette*, July 11, 1765.

[15] See *Major Samuel S. Forman Papers, BV Forman Papers*, vol. 1, no. 55, New York Historical Society; Shane White, *Somewhat More Independent: The End of Slavery in New York City, 1770–1810* (Athens: U. of Georgia Press, 1991), 203–05.

the 1670s to 1698, when the lucrative trade was halted by an act of Parliament; and for five years between 1716 and 1721, after which the legal traffic was terminated. Although the British East India Company had exclusive rights to trade from the Cape of Good Hope east to Cape Horn, "unlicenced English and colonial slavers were resorting to Madagascar as early as the 1670s." The costs of conducting business in Madagascar were far less than along the West African coast, where three and four pounds in goods had the equivalent purchasing power of ten shillings in Madagascar. Between 1682 and 1687, eleven slavers carried 1,741 captives from Madagascar to Barbados, while Jamaica received 345 captives from Madagascar aboard three ships. New York, in turn, accepted several ships from Madagascar in the 1680s and 1690s, "many of them dispatched by the prominent merchants Stephen Delancey and Frederick Philipse." The latter two shipped "liquor and gunpowder to the Red Sea pirate lairs at Madagascar and nearby islands in exchange for slaves.... Records concerning this trade are scant, but New Yorkers apparently raided ashore to gather slaves, as well as trading for them with local chieftains." Such trafficking saw these and other New York merchants financing trips to Madagascar and the East African coast, where pirates facilitated the acquisition of hundreds of captives for the New York market. Firearms, Bibles, and food were supplied in addition to gunpowder and liquor; in return, gold, silver and East Indian manufactures accompanied humans.[16]

The year 1698 "was a banner year for the New York slave trade. In addition to the usual trickle of slaves from the West Indies, Van Cortlandt informed a correspondent in April of "3 vessels Coming in hier whith Slaves two from mardagsr [Madagascar] and one from gieny [Guinea]." One month later he observed that the "great quantity of slaves that are come from Madagasca makes slaves to sell very slow especially these that are ould (old)," further qualifying that "no negro above 25 or 30 years of age sell well ... but from 15 to 25 years sell commonly for 30 or 40 pond as they are likely." Frederick Philipse, the most prominent slave merchant in the city, brought two shipments of about 400 "East Africans" from Madagascar into the city that year, a quantity "large by New York standards." He would go on to explain his involvement in the Madagascar sector: "It is by negroes that I find my cheivest [chiefest] Proffitt. All other trade I only look upon as by the by." Although the East India Act of 1698 brought most of New York trade with East Africa to an end, slavers continued their proscribed activities, and, in 1721, a slaver was caught in New York attempting to smuggle in another 117 captives from Madagascar.[17]

---

[16] See Lydon, "New York and the Slave Trade," 376; Virginia Bever Platt, "The East India Company and the Madagascar Slave Trade," *William and Mary Quarterly* 26 (1969): 548–50; Donnan, *Documents*, vol. 3, 406, 442; Brodhead and O'Callaghan, *Documents Relative to the Colonial History*, vol. 4, 623.

[17] See Joyce B. Goodfriend, *Before the Melting Pot: Society and Culture in Colonial New York City, 1664–1730* (Princeton, NJ: Princeton U. Press, 1992), 112–13; Foote, "Black Life in Colonial Manhattan," 33–36; B.V. Van Cortlandt, Jr., *Letter Book of Jacobus Van Cortlandt, 1698–1700*, New York Historical Society.

It would appear that pirates in league with New York financiers were based on the island of Sainte Marie, off the east coast of Madagascar, from which point they raided vessels and locations in the Red Sea and Indian Ocean. One Captain Adam Baldridge established himself in Sainte Marie as "the chief manager of the trade in plundered goods and pirate supplies." In 1691 he wrote to Frederick Philipse that "he could supply him with a shipload of 200 slaves at a per capita cost of thirty shillings," well below similar costs along the West Africa coast. Enticed and persuaded, Philipse began sending vessels in 1693. As a result of his and others' efforts, "New York became notorious as a pirate haven and the center for supplying the Indian Ocean pirates. Its streets and alehouses were filled with buccaneers, and its citizens were kept awake by their lewd activities with prostitutes. 'Turkey' and 'Araby' gold and strange coins of all kinds added to the city's diverse currency." Parliamentary intervention in 1698, interdiction, and Frederick Philipse's death in 1702 halted that family's participation for another decade or so, until the period of 1715 to 1717, when Frederick Philipse II and the Van Horne family led New York's merchants in the Madagascar trade, this time bypassing the pirates and trading directly in the sector.[18]

While most of those exported from Madagascar were non-Muslim, some may have been Muslim. Evidence for what is admittedly speculative comes from what is known about Madagascar in the seventeenth and eighteenth centuries. The information is not new, but scholars of the slave trade tend to pass over the Islamic factor in Madagascar. Islam moved into Madagascar as early as the twelfth century, if not sooner, and was very much associated with foreign domination, amalgamations of various sorts and to varying degrees, and trafficking in human beings. An initial wave of foreigners dates back to around 1100 and to Iharana or Vohémar in the northeast, where archaeological excavations uncovered the remnants of a culture dominated by Arabic-literate merchants. This first foreign settlement apparently consisted of Indianized Arabs called *Karamatians* (the Bātinī), who left the Malabar coast of India in the tenth century, then departed the port of Mangalore by the beginning of the twelfth century, and ended up in northeastern Madagascar. One group that may have been related to or influenced by the Muslim presence were the Onjatsy, who occupied the northernmost province of the island and, while enjoying a loose affiliation with Islam, evinced no indication of literacy. A more concrete example of the mixture of foreign-born Muslims and the indigenous population were the Zafi Raminia, or descendants of Raminia. In the first half of the fourteenth century, the Zafi Raminia were forced to begin moving down the eastern littoral by Sunni Muslims from Malindi and Mombasa, persons of Arab lineage who established two major entrepots at Boina

[18] See Foote, "Black Life in Colonial Manhattan," 34–36; Jacob Judd, "Frederick Philipse and the Madagascar Trade," *New-York Historical Society Quarterly* 55 (1971): 354–74; Robert C. Ritchie, *Captian Kidd and the War Against the Pirates* (Cambridge, MA: Harvard U. Press, 1986), 38; Broadhead and O'Callaghan, *Documents Relative to the Colonial History*, vol. 4, 552.

Bay in the northwest and at Bimaro, site of ancient Iharana. By the middle of the seventeenth century, the eyewitness Flacourt indicates that while the Raminia were not devout Muslims in any sense, they nevertheless "neither ate nor drank from the rising to the setting of the sun" during Ramadan. The Portuguese, meanwhile, had begun trading with the "Moors" of Boina Bay and Bimaro in the early sixteenth century. The exchange with Europe paled, however, in comparison with the much larger exchange between the Swahili coast and Madagascar. East Africa exported gold, textiles, and silver principally for the rice grown in Madagascar. Captives, cattle and beeswax were also involved.[19]

Some time after the beginning of the sixteenth century, yet another group of Muslims from either the Swahili coast or the Comoro Islands came to northwest Madagascar. This last group, however, was decidedly Muslim and literate, forming "Arabico-Malagasy communities known collectively as Antalaora, or overseas people." They were also called "Silamo," meaning "Muslims," by the Malagasy, and at least part of them, the Anteimoro, relocated to the southeastern portion of the island. It was the Anteimoro who composed the *Sora-bé*, or "Great Writings" or "Sacred Books," using Arabic script for a Malagasy language. There is much to suggest a serious pursuit of Islam here, including the fact that the tradition of literacy was preserved over generations by *kitabi*, or "book-men," and that a kind of religious brotherhood, the *ombiassa*, was maintained on the island. Such was the influence of Anteimoro Islam that even the powerful, non-Muslim Sakalava rulers of Menabé were using Muslim scribes by the eighteenth century.

The Sakalava were the first to achieve empire in Madagascar. It was the Sakalava state of Menabé, established perhaps in the early seventeenth century, that maintained a trade in captives with Europeans, and it was Menabé that received at least two ships from New York City prior to 1703 for the purpose of trafficking. While the trade in captives would culminate in the

[19] See Raymond K. Kent, *Early Kingdoms in Madagascar, 1500–1700* (New York: Holt, Rinehart & Winston, 1970), 16–17, 27–28, 69, 88–115, 160–91, 205–18; E. de Flacourt, *Histoire de la Grande Ile Madagascar 1661*, reprinted as vol. 8, *Collection des ouvrages anciens concernat Madagascar* (Paris: Comité de Madagascar, 1913), 244; Gabriel Ferrand, *Les Musulmans à Madagascar et aux îles Comores* (Paris: Ernest Leroux, 1891–1902), 3 vols.; Mouren and Rouaix, "Industrie ancienne des objets en pierre de Vohémar," *Bulletin de l'academie Malgache* 12 (1913): 3–13; Alfred Grandidier, *Ethnographie de Madagascar* (Paris: L'Imprimerie Nationale, 1908), vol. 1, 103–65; Alfred Grandidier, Charles-Roux, Cl. Delhorbe, H. Froidevaux, and G. Grandidier, *Collection des ouvrages anciens concernant Madagascar* (Paris: Comité de Madagascar, 1904), vol. 2, 14, 311–12, 315–17, 333, and vol. 3 (1905), 655; Auguste Toussaint, *La route des îles: Contribution à l'histoire maritime des Mascareignes* (Paris: École Parctique des Hautes Études, 1967); Maurice Bloch, "Modes of Production and Slavery in Madagascar: Two Case Studies," in James L. Watson, ed., *Asian and African Systems of Slavery* (Berkeley and Los Angeles: U. of California Press, 1980); Gwyn Campbell, "Slavery and Fanompoana: The Structure of Forced Labour in Imerina (Madagascar), 1790–1861," *Journal of African History* 29 (1988): 463–86; Gwyn Campbell, "Madagascar and the Slave Trade, 1810–1895," *Journal of African History* 22 (1981): 203–27.

nineteenth century, the exchange with New York represented a surge that had been developing since the third or fourth decade of the sixteenth century, by which time the captive trade had superceded rice in relative importance. Raiding into the interior gradually escalated, accounting for the majority of presumably non-Muslim captives. However, local states along the coast also fought occasionally, resulting in Muslim war captives. Given the spread of Muslim influence and populations along the coastal areas and reaching into the interior, it is plausible that some percentage of persons brought to New York City from Madagascar was Muslim.

While clear connections with an Islamic heritage are lacking, there are relatively numerous references to the Malagasy in the documentation, especially in the runaway slave advertisements. These tend to focus on the divergent phenotype of the Malagasy. Thus, in July of 1738, James Thompson of Piscattaway, New Jersey reported missing "a lusty Madagascar man, of yallowish Complexion" who "talks good English." In May of 1749, Samuel Morse and Francis Bloodgood of Woodbridge, New Jersey also sought the return of Mando, a "young black fellow," who had absconded with a forty-year-old "yellow Madagascar Fellow named Tom." Such was the association of "yellowness" with the Malagasy that Arent Bradt of Schenectady described in October of 1735 his runaway indentured servant William Smith as appearing "in colour like the Madagascar." Finally, John Willet, Jr. of Flushing published a notice in the May 19, 1746 edition of the *New York Weekly Journal*, in which he discussed twenty-one-year-old Primus, who "alters his Name frequently, he is about 6 feet high, and well-proportioned, he is of a Malagasco complexion and it is observed that he will lye so that he is not to be believed or depended upon in that respect."[20]

It would appear from the shipping data that the majority of captives from Madagascar were males; the few references to women in the runaway slave ads support this, and they include the search by Johannes Van Houten of Bergin, New Jersey, for a Dutch-speaking "Malagasco Negro wench, aged about 41 years." Almost all of the runaway references indicate that those absconding did not live in New York City but in more rural areas in neighboring places, suggesting the Malagasy were seen primarily as agricultural workers. Thus, a "Malisgasco Negro Man" escaped from Cornelius Van Horne on the Rariton River (in the Philadelphia area) in September of 1724, while in the preceding year a "Madagascar Negro" named Jack had run away from Gabriel Stelle of Shrewsbury (also closer to Philadelphia). However, it is not clear where some were located, as in the case of the "Native of Madagascar" Cato, twenty years of age and conversant in English and Dutch, who escaped with literate and

---

[20] See the *New-York Gazette*, July 24, 1738; *New-York Gazette, Revived in the Weekly Post-Boy*, May 1, 1749; *New-York Weekly Journal*, October 6, 1735; *New-York Weekly Journal*, May 19, 1746. For more examples, see Graham Russell Hodges and Alan Edward Brown, eds., *"Pretends to Be Free": Runaway Slave Advertisements From Colonial and Revolutionary New York and New Jersey* (New York and London: Garland Publishing, 1994).

skilled Johnny (who could speak English, Dutch, and French and was a "very good cooper") and Delaware-born John Watson, a "servant man."[21]

There is also evidence of Muslims to the north of New York City, in Canada, including one Richard Pierpoint (d. 1837). Born around 1742 in the West African, Muslim state of Bundu, he entered the Americas in 1760, after which he fought on the side of the British in the American War of Independence. He later fought against the Americans in the War of 1812, after which he settled in the Niagra, Canada area.[22]

Consideration of the *Amistad* affair of 1839 arguably returns the focus to New York, as the postmutinous ship drifted near Long Island in August before being commandeered by the U.S. navy later that month. Of the thirty-six Africans brought to port in New London, Connecticut, at least one, "Gilabaru," was unquestionably Muslim, as the "people in his country could read and write from 'right to left' in Arabic."[23] As others were Mende, it is probable that more

[21] See *The American Weekly*, August 1, 1723 and September 17, 1724; *New-York Weekly Journal*, May 10, 1736 and September 27, 1742. Angolans, Senegambians, and the Malagasy have so far featured large in the discussion of New York City. Of course there were other groups, such as those who played prominent roles in the New York City rebellion of 1712, when "'some Negro slaves of ye Nations of Carmantee and Pappa plotted to destroy all the White[s] in order to obtain their freedom.'" Included among these groups were "Spanish Negroes" who had been taken "in a Spanish prize" or sailing vessel and brought to New York by privateers to be sold as slaves. They appealed to Governor Hunter in 1712 for their release, claiming to be free men and Spanish subjects; the governor, who "secretly pittyed their condition," did not free the "Spanish Indians" as they were also called, "haveing no other evidence of what they asserted then their own words." The insurrection may not have been a direct result of their discontent, but an insurrection did take place, killing nine and wounding five or six before it had run its course. Twenty-one persons were executed by use of a variety of methods – some were hanged, others burned, one broken at the wheel; six who were never captured ended their own lives. The conspiracy of 1741 was also alleged to have had the involvement of "Spanish Negroes" taken from the sloop *La Soledad*; these persons also insisted that they were free and subjects of Spain. They were promptly enslaved in New York, however, and once the purported plot came to light in which some 2,000 enslaved persons were believed poised to torch the city, they were seen as primary suspects, having remained "outspoken and recalcitrant" about their enslavement. Suspicions of an enslaved man named Juan were particularly high; he and his fellow ladinos would be collected and interrogated. In the end, sixteen blacks and four whites were hanged; thirteen blacks were burned at the stake, and seventy-one were banished from the city. It could be that none of these ladinos had the slightest connection to Islam, but given the discussion in the first two chapters, some may have been Muslim. See Goodfriend, *Before the Melting Pot*, 114, 123; Davis, "Slavery in Colonial New York City," 34–35, 117–18; Thomas J. Davis, *A Rumor of Revolt: The "Great Negro Plot" in Colonial New York* (New York: The Free Press, 1985), 18–20, 79–80; Rev. John Sharpe, "Proposals for Erecting a School, Library and Chapel at New York," March 11, 1713, in *Collections of the New-York Historical Society* (1880), 351; David T. Valentine, *History of the City of New York* (New York: G.P. Putnam and Co., 1853), 270; Kruger, "Born to Run," 83; Brodhead and O'Callaghan, *Documents Relative to the Colonial History*, vol. 5, 342.

[22] See Peter Meyler and David Meyler, *A Stolen Life: Searching for Richard Pierpoint* (Toronto: Natural Heritage Books, 1999). In the American War of Independence, Pierpoint served in a unit called Butler's Rangers.

[23] See Helen Kromer, *Amistad: The Slave Uprising Aboard the Spanish Schooner* (Cleveland: Pilgrim Press, 1973), 11. See also Howard Jones, *Mutiny on the Amistad: The Saga of a Slave Revolt and Its*

were Muslim. While their return to West Africa prevented any organic contribution to subsequent Muslim communities in North America, their experience
and example certainly fired the imagination of all those left behind to struggle
for freedom.

Impact on American Abolition, Law, and Diplomacy (New York: Oxford U. Press, 1987); B. Edmon
Martin, *All We Want is Make Us Free: La Amistad and the Reform Abolitionists* (Lanham, MD:
U. Press of America, 1986); Mary Cables, *Black Odyssey: The Case of the Slave Ship "Amistad"*
(New York: Viking Press, 1971); William Owens, *Black Mutiny: The Revolt on the Schooner
Amistad* (Baltimore, MD: Black Classics Press, 1953; Iyunolu Folayan Osagie, *The Amistad
Revolt: Memory, Slavery, and the Politics of Identity in the United States* (Athens: U. of Georgia
Press, 2000).

5

Founding Mothers and Fathers of a Different Sort

African Muslims in the Early North American South

From the foregoing discussion it is clear that African Muslim communities in what is now Latin America and the Caribbean could be numerous and prominent, and at times they directly informed the direction of the regions' historical development. That African Muslims of lesser aggregation and influence could be found in climes as far north as New York City and Canada has also been demonstrated, but the epicenter of the African Muslim community in colonial and antebellum North America (see Map 7) shared something of the character of both North America and the Caribbean in that it was located along the Georgia and South Carolina coasts, comprising both islands and the immediate mainland vicinity. Long viewed as the source and reservoir of Gullah culture, it has become apparent that coastal islands such as Sapelo, St. Simons, St. Helena, and their environs were also the collective site of the largest gathering of African Muslims in early North America, establishing a legacy that continues into the present day. The Georgia–South Carolina Muslim community is therefore the focus of this chapter, and it is discussed in some detail following preliminary observations.

In general, data concerning Muslims in the American South support arguments more tentative than conclusive. Nonetheless, the consistency of the evidence allows for several statements. First, their numbers were significant, probably reaching into the thousands. Second, Muslims made genuine and persistent efforts to observe their religion, and, even though the continuation of their faith took place primarily within their own families, there were instances in which others may have been converted. Third, cultural phenomena found in segments of the African American community, such as ostensibly Christian worship practices and certain artistic expressions, were probably influenced by these early Muslims. Fourth, the perception and treatment of Muslims in the American South very much informed the contours of subsequent African American social stratification. Finally, as discussed in the second part of this book, certain aspects of twentieth-century Islamic movements among African Americans are arguably directly related to the experiences of these pioneers.

North America

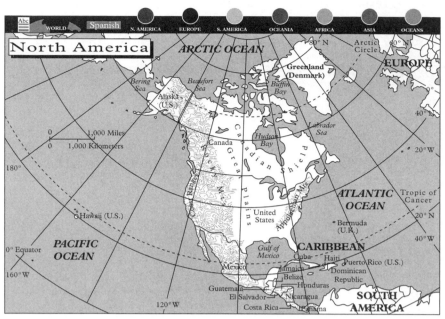

MAP 7.

Evidence for the existence of Muslims in the early American South comes from both sides of the Atlantic. On the American side, several types of sources provide insight into the presence and activities of these Muslims: the appearance of Muslim names in slaveholder ledgers and in the runaway slave advertisements of newspapers; references to Muslim ancestry in interviews with formerly enslaved individuals and with the descendants of Muslims; stated preferences for certain somatic types by the slaveholding community; recorded instances of Islamic activity; and profiles of those Muslims who had crossed a threshold of white notoriety, a category that includes documents written in either Arabic script or language by these Muslims. On the African side, research has produced detailed information concerning the ethnic and cultural elements that characterized those regions from which American-born captives emanated, and it provides a reasonably clear picture of the political and social contexts out of which they were extracted. An examination of the African side of the argument will follow discussion of the Georgia–South Carolina Muslim community.

To be sure, the Muslim presence in the American South antedates the arrival of the English. Spanish Florida's St. Augustine (and nearby Fort Mose) featured a significant black population.[1] By the middle of the eighteenth century,

---

[1] See Jane Landers, "Gracia Real de Santa Teresa de Mose: A Free Black Town in Spanish Colonial Florida," *American Historical Review* 95 (1990): 9–30. Works ranging in quality that address this and other aspects of the African Muslim experience in the Americas include Clyde Ahmed

the third largest African group in this metropolitan area were the Malinke or Mande-speakers, among whom Muslims were certainly present.[2] As was true of the Spanish in Florida, the French in Louisiana also imported Muslims, especially from Senegambia, along with non-Muslims from Whydah and Congo–Angola.[3] The Muslim population, although unquantifiable, must have been significant. The runaway notices for Louisiana would support this probability, as they are absolutely replete with references to the Senegalese.[4] Midlo Hall has commented that the "slaves of French Louisiana often kept their African names, many of which were Islamic. Some slaves with French names had Baraca, an Islamic religious title, as a second name."[5]

The Muslim population in Louisiana was by no means confined, however, to Senegambians. There are a number of references to northern Nigeria in the newspapers as well. For example, New Orleans' *Moniteur de la Louisiane* called for the return of a runaway from the Hausa nation ("nation Aoussa") in October 1807.[6] The following September, twenty dollars was offered for the return of two individuals of the Hausa nation who had been recently purchased from a slaver.[7] The next month, an auction by Patton and Mossy featured four men and six women "from the Congo, Mandinga, and Hausa nations, in the country eight months, from 11 to 22 years of age."[8] As a final example, "le Nègre HENRY, nation Aoussa" appeared in the runaway notices.[9] The dates of these publications fall within the 1804–12 period of the jihād of Usuman dan Fodio in northern Nigeria, so it is probable that most of these Hausa, as was discussed in the case of Brazil, were war captives, both Muslim and non-Muslim.

Winters, "Afro-American Muslims from Slavery to Freedom," *Islamic Studies* 17 (1978): 187–205; Winters, "A Survey of Islam and the African Diaspora," *Pan-African Journal* 8 (1975): 425–34; Abdullah Hakim Quick, *Deeper Roots: Muslims in the Americas and the Caribbean from before Columbus to the Present* (London: Ta-Ha, 1996); Amir N. Muhammad, *Muslims in America: Seven Centuries of History, 1312–2000: Collections and Stories of American Muslims*, 2nd ed. (Beltsville, MD: Amana, 2001).

[2] See Jane Landers, "Black Society in Spanish St. Augustine, 1784–1821" (Ph.D. diss., U. of Florida, 1988), 27–28.

[3] See Gwendolyn Midlo Hall, *Africans in Colonial Louisiana: The Development of Afro-Creole Culture in the Eighteenth Century* (Baton Rouge: Louisiana State U. Press, 1992), 10–35; also see James A. Rawley, *The Transatlantic Slave Trade: A History* (New York: Norton, 1981), 114–15.

[4] See for example, *Moniteur de la Louisiane*, September 11, 1802, and July 30, 1806.

[5] See Midlo Hall, *Africans in Colonial Louisiana*, 166. This is based on the apparent use of the term *baraka* as an appelation in Louisiana, a practice that will also surface in coastal Georgia–South Carolina; otherwise, *baraka* is an Arabic term that conveys the sense of "communicable spiritual power." For more on *baraka*, see E. Westermarck, *Pagan Survivals in Mohammedan Civilization* (London: Macmillan, 1933), 87–144; J. O. Hunwick, "Religion and State in the Songhay Empire, 1464–1591," in I. M. Lewis, ed., *Islam in Tropical Africa*, 2nd ed. (Bloomington: International African Institute in association with Indiana U. Press, 1980).

[6] See *Moniteur de la Louisiane*, October 10, 1807.

[7] Ibid., September 17, 1808.

[8] Ibid., October 19, 1808.

[9] Ibid., February 25, 1809.

While the existence of Islam in what is conventionally considered Spanish-and French-speaking North America (Native Americans and Africans were speaking their own languages) is important and merits further investigation, the preponderance of the evidence concerns "English-speaking" North America. The anglophone slaveholding society regularly distinguished between the various groups within the larger African community.[10] The enslaved from Senegambia and Sierra Leone (regions about which more will be stated later in the chapter), often simply called "Mandingo" by whites, were generally viewed by slaveholders as preferable to others.[11] Within the categories of Senegambia and Sierra Leone was the bulk of the Muslim imports, and as was true of Latin America, terms like *Mandingo* and *Mandinga* were equated with Muslims by the nineteenth century.[12] Although all of these Mande-speakers may not have been Muslim, such association suggests that a substantial percentage must have been. The North American preference for the Mandinka (one component of the Mande or Malinke world and certainly among those dubbed *Mandingo* by whites) is reflected in the activity of eighteenth-century North American shippers, who, although not responsible for the majority of slave importations into North America, nevertheless confined their activities to those areas of West Africa of greatest interest to planters, and for that reason obtained the vast majority of those they enslaved from Senegambia and Sierra Leone.[13]

Advertisements for enslaved runaways in the American South contain unique and substantial information on individual ethnic and cultural traits, and they conveniently transport the discussion to the Georgia and South Carolina coastal area. These advertisements are important in part because they occasionally provide names that are clearly Muslim but rarely identified as such.[14] Names

---

[10] See Philip D. Curtin, *The Atlantic Slave Trade: A Census* (Madison: U. of Wisconsin Press, 1969), 156–57; Ulrich Bonnell Phillips, *American Negro Slavery* (Baton Rouge: Louisiana State U. Press, 1918), 42–44; Darold D. Wax, "Preferences for Slaves in Colonial Louisiana," *Journal of Negro History* 58 (1973): 390–97; Melville Herskovits, *The Myth of the Negro Past* (New York and London: Harper and Brothers, 1941), 50; Marguerite B. Hamer, "A Century before Manumission: Sidelights on Slavery in Mid-Eighteenth Century South Carolina," *North Carolina Historical Review* 17 (1940): 232–36; Rawley, *Transatlantic Slave Trade*, 272–73; Elizabeth Donnan, "The Slave Trade into South Carolina before the Revolution," *American Historical Review* 33 (1928): 816–17.

[11] See, for example, David Duncan Wallace, *The Life of Henry Laurens* (New York and London: G. P. Putnam's Sons, 1915), 76–77; Allan D. Austin, *African Muslims in Antebellum America: A Sourcebook* (New York and London: Garland Publishing, 1984), 29.

[12] See Austin, *African Muslims*, 21. Midlo Hall, of course, argues that these terms were synonymous as early as the eighteenth century in Louisiana (*Africans in Colonial Louisiana*, 41–42).

[13] See Michael A. Gomez, *Exchanging Our Country Marks: The Transformation of African Identities in the Colonial and Antebellum South* (Chapel Hill: U. of North Carolina Press, 1998), 1–68; David Richardson, "Slave Exports from West and West-Central Africa, 1700–1810," *Journal of African History* 30 (1989): 16; Paul Lovejoy, "The Impact of the Atlantic Slave Trade on Africa: A Review of the Literature," *Journal of African History* 30 (1989): 374.

[14] For examples of names that probably have African origins, see Charles Lyell, *A Second Visit to the United States of America*, 2 vols. (New York: Harper and Brothers, 1849), vol. 1, 263. For discussions of names as ethnic markers, see John C. Inscoe, "Carolina Slave Names: An Index

such as Bullaly (Bilali), Mustapha, Sambo, Bocarrey (Bukhari, or possibly Bubacar from Abu Bakr), and Mamado (Mamadu) are regularly observed in the advertisements for runaway slaves. Unless slaveholders clearly understood the origin of these names, they would not necessarily associate them with Islam.[15] A good example of this concerns the name Sambo or Samba, which can mean "second son" in the language of the Hausa and Fulbe.[16] The January 9–12, 1782 publication of Charleston's *Royal Gazette* sought the return of Sambo, or Sam, described as having a "yellowish complexion . . . and his hair is pretty long, being of the Fulla country."[17] The connections between Sambo, Islam, and the Fulbe become even more apparent when the preceding advertisement is juxtaposed with another notice in which a decidedly Muslim name is identified with the same ethnicity: the June 17, 1766 edition of Charleston's *South-Carolina Gazette and Country Journal* features an ad in which Robert Darrington sought the return of one "Moosa, a yellow Fellow . . . is of the Fullah Country.[18] Although the association between the name Sambo and Islam is strong in these examples, it is not the contention here that the name was the exclusive property of Muslims. Rather, it is more reasonable to conclude that a significant number of African-born males with this name may have been Muslim.

* * *

The May 24, 1775 edition of Savannah's *Georgia Gazette* ran a notice for three missing men, including twenty-two-year-old Sambo, reportedly "of the Moorish country."[19] This association with the Moorish country may be more a reference to Sambo's Muslim identity than to his actually having hailed from North Africa, but it should be borne in mind that Moors, or Arabo-Berbers from Mauritania and elsewhere in North Africa, were in fact imported into North America as they had been into Spanish-held territories, with a legacy in North America that endures (the focus of subsequent chapters).[20] One such notable

---

to Acculturation," *Journal of Southern History* 49 (1983): 527–34; Cheryll Ann Cody, "There Was No 'Absalom' on the Ball Plantations: Slave-Naming Practices in the South Carolina Low Country, 1720–1865," *American Historical Review* 92 (1987): 563–96.

[15] See Lathan Windley, comp., *Runaway Slave Advertisements: A Documentary History from the 1730s to 1790*, 4 vols. (Westport, CT: Greenwood Press, 1983); Inscoe, "Carolina Slave Names," 533–35.

[16] In Mende and Vai, however, the name Sambo implies disgrace. See Lorenzo Dow Turner, *Africanisms in the Gullah Dialect* (New York: Arno Press and the New York Times, 1969; orig. pub. 1949); Keith E. Baird and Mary A. Twining, "Names and Naming in the Sea Islands," in Michael Montgomery, ed., *The Crucible of Carolina: Essays in the Development of Gullah Language and Culture* (Athens: U. of Georgia Press, 1994).

[17] Windley, *Runaway Slave Advertisements*, vol. 3, 593.

[18] Ibid., vol. 3, 605.

[19] Ibid., vol. 4, 64.

[20] For example, some of the evidence for Moors in America comes from Midlo Hall's reseaerch, in which the appellation Nar, a Wolof term for Moor, is used to characterize a number of enslaved persons in Louisiana. See Gwendolyn Midlo Hall, *Slavery and Race Relations in French, Spanish, and Early American Louisiana: A Comparative Study* (Chapel Hill: U. of North Carolina Press, forthcoming).

person (discussed in the preceding chapter) was Anthony Jansen Van Salee of New Amsterdam. Another individual, less controversial but certainly no less interesting, was the figure of "S'Quash."[21] S'Quash, "a grown man of splendid muscle and build," was brought into Charleston in December of 1807, just before the ban on the slave trade went into effect on the first of January, 1808. He was purchased by Joseph Graham of western North Carolina, who together with several other "gentlemen" had sent $5,000 in gold and two wagons to Charleston to purchase "Negroes." Sixteen boys between twelve and sixteen years of age were taken from the slaver while S'Quash, kept below deck until the others were displayed and purchased, was thrown into the deal for good measure. Four men were needed to secure S'Quash, a process described as struggling "up with a massive human burden, 'hog-tied,' and dangerously quiet." The likelihood that S'Quash had attempted mutiny is increased by the captain's refusal to untie him while aboard the ship, as "he has been loose on the ship one and that was once too often." When he was finally allowed to stand, "in spite of the cramps, galls, and filth of constant confinement, he was a commanding figure. His clear-cut, aquiline features were extremely dark, like a Moor, and his straight black hair and beard, matted and foul from neglect, were not kinky. He was obviously not a Negro." The captain could not provide any specific information on the Muslim giant's origins, speculating instead that he was an Arab slavetrader against whom an "old score" had been settled. A descendant of S'Quash's original purchaser would later maintain that the titan was "an Arab of a family long educated of his day and class in that he had been to Cairo and could read Greek as well as Arabic. Greek was probably his first means of communication, as that language was then a part of a gentleman's classical education."[22] As will be seen, S'Quash's posture toward the slaveholding regime would soon undergo a dramatic and diametric reversal.

Yet another example of a North African brought into North American captivity was "Selim," who was taken prisoner aboard a Spanish privateer while en route from "Algiers" to Istanbul, where he was pursuing his education. The son of "wealthy and respectable parents," Selim was transferred to a French slaver and carried to New Orleans, where his status becomes unclear. Plausibility is an issue in that, after he was sent "up the rivers Mississippi and Ohio to the Shawnee towns" and left as a "prisoner of war with the Indians," he claims to have escaped and walked all the way to Virginia, where he was discovered hiding atop a tree "in a most wretched and pitiable condition" near the close of war between France and England in 1755, so-called Braddock's War. The story becomes even more curious in that, following his being provided a Greek New Testament and his subsequent conversion to Christianity, he returned to "Algiers" where he was disowned by his family as a result of his conversion.

---

[21] See Allan D. Austin, *African Muslims in Antebellum America: Transatlantic Stories and Spiritual Struggles* (New York and London: Routledge, 1997), 34.

[22] See Paul B. Barringer, *The Natural Bent: The Memoirs of Dr. Paul B. Barringer* (Chapel Hill: U. of North Carolina Press, 1949), 3–13.

Some years later, Selim was found back in Virginia and "in a state of insanity," with moments of lucidity. While the details are in question, his actual existence is supported by the preservation of his likeness by Charles Wilson Peale.[23]

Evidence of North Africans in the slaveholding South also comes from legal motions filed on behalf of those claiming to have been illegally enslaved. In 1753, for example, "Abel Conder" and "Mahamut" petitioned South Carolina's royal council in "Arabick," requesting their release from Daniel LaRoche, for whom they had labored for fifteen years along with enslaved Africans. They claimed to come from "Sali on the Barbary Coast," where they were initially captured by the Portuguese after a military engagement and then sold to a Captain Henry Daubrig, who brought them to Carolina.[24] The royal council's ruling on this matter has not been found, nor is there information on the final resolution of a petition filed before the South Carolina General Assembly in 1790 by Francis, Daniel, Hammond, and Samuel, and their spouses Fatima, Flora, Sarah, and Clarinda, who as "free Moors" sought the legal rights of whites. The men claimed to have been taken captive in Morocco and brought to Carolina, where they were enslaved before purchasing their freedom. Just two years earlier, two men "dressed in the Moorish habit" caused a stir in Charleston, to where they had traveled from Virginia, having alleged to have come from Algeria. A final example concerns Joseph Benenhaly (Ben Ali), who may have been a pirate and who wound up in Sumter County, South Carolina, where he could have participated in the American War of Independence. A North African, Benenhaly is the alleged progenitor of the "Turks" of Sumter County.[25]

* * *

The appearance of incontestably Muslim names in the runaway slave notices is relatively infrequent. More commonly, slaveholders seeking the return of runaways associated them with particular regions of origin (for example, Gambia

[23] See Rev. Benjamin H. Rice, "History of Selim, the Algerine Convert," in Bishop William Meade, ed., *Old Churches, Ministers, and Families of Virginia* (Bowie, MD: Heritage Books, 1992; orig. pub. Philadelphia: J. B. Lippincott, 1857), 341–48. Selim made a trip to Philadelphia with Governor Page, who was a member of Congress, where he met with Peale. The portrait was in the possession of Robert Saunders of Williamsburg as late as 1857. If verifiable, this would be the second portrait of an African Muslim painted by Peale, the first being the 1819 portrait of Yarrow Mahmud, discussed later in this chapter.

[24] See James W. Hagy, "Muslim Slaves, Abducted Moors, African Jews, Misnamed Turks, and an Asiatic Greek Lady: Some Examples of Non-European Religious and Ethnic Diversity in South Carolina prior to 1861," *Carologue: A Publication of the South Carolina Historical Society* 9 (1993): 12–13, 25–27. This information is derived from the *South Carolina Council Journal*, note 21, pt. 1, pp. 298–99, March 3, 1753, South Carolina Department of Archives and History. Sali may have been Salé, Asilah, or Safi, all in Morocco.

[25] See Hagy, "Muslim Slaves, Abducted Moors," 26–27. Hagy also mentions the intriguing case of Billy Simmons, a slave purportedly from Madagascar who claimed to be a Jew. This claim was supported by two cantors as well as other authorities in the 1850s. "Billy the Jew," however, was also a scholar "in Hebrew and Arabic," which raises some questions about his religious loyalties.

or Senegal) or provided an ethnic identity (such as Mandingo or Fula). The *Charleston Courier*, for example, advertised the finding of a "new Negro BOY, of the Fullah nation, says his name is Adam."[26] In the case of either supposed region of origin or ethnic derivation, one cannot conclusively argue that the individual in question is Muslim, but – given both the African background and the tendency among American planters to conflate Muslims, ethnicity, and region of origin – the probability that many of these persons were Muslims is high.

The fact that examples of Muslim runaways come overwhelmingly from South Carolina and Georgia, especially along the coast, and to a lesser degree from colonial Louisiana is probably due to the fact that Charleston (and Savannah) was a preeminent slave port, surrounded by major slaveholding areas devoted to rice and indigo cultivation.[27] Senegambians and Sierra Leonians, in great demand for their agricultural skills, tended to come from areas in which there was a Muslim presence. Given their preference for enslaved persons from these areas and distaste for Africans from the Bight of Biafra, South Carolinian and Georgian planters paid close attention to ethnicity. In contrast, Virginians may not have been as discriminating, and their alleged indifference to ethnicity, as opposed to any actual disproportion, may explain the relative absence of references to Muslims from Senegambia and Sierra Leone.[28]

Further examples of advertisements that more clearly refer to Muslims include the notice for "two Gambian Negroes...the one his Name is Walley [Wali] the other's Bocarrey."[29] In this notice, a connection is established between Gambia and Muslims. At times a geographic or ethnic affiliation is not given, only the name, as was the case in 1757, when a "negro man named Mamado" escaped from Rachel Fairchild; or again in 1772, when William Wood of Santee advertised for a "Negro fellow named Homady [Amadi, from

---

[26] See the *Charleston Courier*, May 1, 1809.
[27] See Gomez, *Exchanging Our Country Marks*, 1–113. The author has only partially reviewed early Mississippi and Louisiana newspapers, so the assessment is subject to revision. Also see Charles Joyner, *Down by the Riverside: A South Carolina Slave Community* (Urbana: U. of Illinois Press, 1984), 14–15; Peter H. Wood, *Black Majority: Negroes in Colonial South Carolina* (New York: Knopf, 1974), 58–62; Daniel C. Littlefield, *Rice and Slaves: Ethnicity and the Slave Trade in Colonial South Carolina* (Baton, Rouge: Louisiana State U., 1981), 76–98.
[28] See Curtin, *Atlantic Slave Trade*, 156–58; Rawley, *Transatlantic Slave Trade*, 334–35. Littlefield (*Rica and Slaves*, 31–32) disagrees with the view that Virginian planters were unconcerned about ethnic origins. To the contrary, Littlefield maintains not only that Virginians were concerned but also that they preferred the Igbo and others from the Niger delta [Littlefield's position is predicated upon Darold D. Wax, "Preferences for Slaves in Colonial America," *Journal of Negro History* 58 (1973): 374–75]. Rawley, in turn, states that Virginians preferred those from the Gold Coast and Windward Coast, accepted the Igbo in large number, and disliked those from Angola. See also Judith Ann Carne, *Black Rice: The African Origins of Rice Cultivation in the Americas* (Cambridge, MA: Harvard U. Press, 2001).
[29] See the *South Carolina Gazette*, October 19, 1738, in Windley, *Runaway Slave Advertisements*, vol. 3, 35.

Ahmad]."[30] Enough time had passed for John Graham of Augustin's Creek and John Strobhar of Purrysburgh to learn the names of their absconded slaves and to seek the return of Mahomet and Mousa respectively, whereas John Inglis of Charleston could only state that three "new" men and one woman had escaped, and that "two of the fellows are of a yellow complection and Moorish breed."[31] Then there is the 1805 report concerning Sambo, of "grave countenance," who "writes the Arabic language."[32]

In North Carolina in 1808, 100 dollars was offered for the apprehension of Arthur Howe, a white man who had taken away enslaved Mustapha, commonly called "Muss," described as "polite and submissive" and a "handy fellow with most tools or about horses."[33] That same year, Charlestonian R. Heriot suspected that "an African wench named Fatima," who was about twenty years old and spoke very little English, may have been "enticed away" and "harboured by some worthless person or persons."[34] However, most enslaved Muslims, as was true of the enslaved population in general, were quite capable of stealing away on their own, as reflected in Godin Guerard's report from Georgia in 1792: "A Moor slave man, about 25 years of age, named Mahomet who is badged by that name, but passes by the name Homady in common."[35]

The matter of absconding obviously involves the question of destination. Muslims were no different than others in that, among other places, they sought refuge among Native Americans. In 1781, "Hommady" had been absent from the slaveholder's property for three weeks and was "suspected to be harboured among the Indians."[36] Similarly, someone matching the description of the previously mentioned Mahomet of John Graham's Augustin's Creek had "been seen at a settlement near the Indian Line on Ogechee very lately," three years after his initial flight.[37] While Native American communities may have provided safe havens for enslaved people on occasion, some Muslims were interested in taking matters a step further by leaving America altogether, and in this way they shared the aspirations of their coreligionists in Trinidad, Jamaica, and Brazil. The case of the "new Negro Fellow, called Jeffray, sometimes, Bram, or Ibrahim" illustrates the point: "From some hints given by himself and others it is suspected he will endeavor to get on board some vessel."[38]

---

[30] See the *South Carolina Gazette*, June 23, 1757 and March 1, 1773, in Windley, *Runaway Slave Advertisements*, vol. 3, 155, 320.

[31] See the *Georgia Gazette*, September 7, 1774, March 15, 1781, and August 17, 1774, in Windley, *Runaway Slave Advertisements*, vol. 3, 56, 89, 54–55.

[32] See the *Charleston Courier*, February 9, 1805; quoted in Hagy, "Muslim Slaves, Abducted Moors," 25–26.

[33] See the *Edenton Gazette and North Carolina Advertiser*, June 23, 1808.

[34] See the *Charleston Courier*, June 19, 1808.

[35] See the *Gazette of the State of Georgia*, June 7, 1792.

[36] See the *Royal Georgia Gazette*, October 4, 1781.

[37] See also *Georgia Gazette*, August 31, 1774.

[38] See the *Gazette of the State of Georgia*, December 8, 1791.

The evidence suggests that African Muslims were also residing on various coastal plantations to the south of South Carolina and Georgia. For example, thirty-six enslaved persons were abducted from Amelia Island, Florida, in 1813 by white "patriots."[39] Of the thirty-six, the following may have been Muslim: Jack and Samba and their two children, Saluma and Pizarro; Adam and Fatima and their one-year-old child, Fernando; and thirteen-year-old Ottemar or Otteman. The four adults were African born, and from the names Samba, Saluma, and Fatima it is probable that these two families were wholly Muslim. Furthermore, fifteen of the thirty-six were African born, so that even more may have been Muslim. However, the names given to them by their holders, such as Hamlet, Neptune, and Plato, make it impossible to know their ethnic or religious affiliation.

The relationship between Muslim identity and naming patterns becomes even more intriguing in the case of the John Stapleton plantation at Frogmore on St. Helena Island, South Carolina.[40] In May of 1816, a list of the 135 enslaved persons on the Frogmore estate was drawn up, on which the following individuals appear: Sambo, eighty-five years old and African born; Dido, a fifty-six-year-old "Moroccan"; Mamoodie and his wife Eleanor, both African born and age twenty-eight and twenty-nine, respectively; and the family of Nelson, Venus, and child Harriett. Sambo and Dido were probably Muslim. Mamoodie and Eleanor had a child named Fatima in 1814 (who died in infancy), so they were very likely Muslim also. The more interesting individuals are Nelson and Venus, who were twenty-nine and twenty-seven, respectively, and both African born. In a subsequent enslaved list drawn up in 1818, their child Hammett appears. *Hammett* (Hamid or Ahmad) is a Muslim name, which would suggest that one or both of the parents were Muslim. Again, the remaining names on the 1816 list are not African, but twenty-eight people are listed as African born. It is therefore possible that others were Muslim, as Nelson or Venus may have been, but the absence of a corroborating Hammett prevents any such identification. Based solely on what has been presented thus far, then, at least thirty persons from coastal Carolina through northern Florida (excluding St. Augustine) have been individually named and identified as probable Muslims. There were many more so identified, as shall be demonstrated.

* * *

Consistent with the preponderance of runaway notices featuring Muslims in South Carolinian and Georgian newspapers is the quantitatively greater amount of information available on Muslims and their descendants living along the Georgia coast, both on the various sea islands and on the mainland near Savannah. The data provide a rare glimpse into the lives of African-born

[39] See the *Augusta Herald*, November 11, 1813.

[40] See the John Stapleton Papers (South Caroliniana Library, U. of South Carolina, Columbia), microfilmed on reels 6 and 7, series A, pt. 2, *Records of Ante-Bellum Southern Plantations from the Revolution through the Civil War*, Kenneth M. Stampp, gen. ed.

Muslims, their progeny, and the associated community of believers. What emerges is an incomplete but substantive picture of individuals who pursued their religion with diligence and purpose, and this in an atmosphere charged with Christian catechism and the allure of competing African religions. Further, there is possible evidence of non-Muslims converting to Islam. Finally, the manner in which the grandchildren and subsequent progeny of these African-born Muslims relate their stories betrays considerable pride and admiration, suggesting a strong and clear identification with an Islamic heritage, if not an actual embrace of the religion.

To begin, it would appear that the number of enslaved Muslims in this area was significant indeed. In May of 1802, for example, two Muslim men named Alik and Abdalli escaped from Sapelo Island; it is likely that both men were African born, as one spoke "bad English" and the other's facility in the idiom was only slightly better.[41] Toney, Jacob, and eighteen-year-old Musa also escaped from Sapelo Island in March of 1807, contesting the proprietary claims of one Alexander Johnston.[42] Conceivably, all three men were Muslim.

Reference to Sapelo Island underscores the fact that Sapelo, along with St. Simons Island, was the conjoined site for the most important Muslim community in Georgia–South Carolina and, arguably, the whole of antebellum North America. The famous Hopeton plantation on St. Simons was one of a number (both on the island and along the Altamaha River) owned by John Couper (1759–1850) and his son James Hamilton Couper (1794–1866). In an 1827 document detailing the sale of Hopeton by John Couper to James Hamilton (a close friend) and his son James, 381 names of the enslaved are listed.[43] Of these names, Fatima is repeated six times, Mahomet twice, and there is one Maryam, all probably Muslims. However, the principal Muslim on the plantation was Salih Bilali, who is listed as "Tom" in the document. How many more Muslims there were at Hopeton cannot be discerned from the available data, but it is probable that there were others whose Islamic identities are hidden behind such anglicized monikers. Indeed, James Hamilton Couper himself wrote that "there are about a dozen negroes on this plantation, who speak and understand the Foulah language; but with one exception, they appear not to have been native born Foulahs, and to have acquired the language, by having been for sometime in servitude among that nation."[44] Hamilton's conjecture that many individuals speaking Pulaar had been first enslaved in West Africa, although speculative, is quite possible.

Salih Bilali, in some contrast to other Muslims who received a measure of notoriety in North America, remained a devout Muslim his entire life. Born

---

[41] See the *Columbia Museum and Savannah Advertiser*, May 11, 1802.

[42] Ibid., March 27, 1807.

[43] See the State of Georgia Archives, GRG2-009 and GRG2-029 (Georgia Department of Archives and History, Atlanta).

[44] See the letter from James Hamilton Couper, in William Brown Hodgson, *Notes on Northern Africa, the Sahara, and Soudan* (New York: Wiley and Putnam, 1844), 68–74.

around 1765, he grew up in Maasina, along the upper Niger valley.[45] Initially captured around 1790, a period in which the Bambara were consolidating their control over the upper Niger, Salih Bilali was eventually taken south and sold at Anomabu, along the Gold Coast. That he exited West Africa from Anomabu rather than the Senegambian coast, the anticipated site of embarkation for captives from the upper Niger, suggests the variety of options available to those trafficking in such captives.[46] Arriving in the Bahamas, he was repurchased around 1800 and brought to Hopeton plantation on St. Simons, where by 1816 (at the age of 51) he was the head driver at Cannon's Point plantation. His acclaim arose from his considerable managerial skills; such were his abilities and his reliability that the plantation owner left Salih Bilali in charge of the entire plantation for months at a time, absent any other supervision. The date of Salih Bilali's death is uncertain, but it may have been in the late 1850s.

Ben Sullivan was eighty-eight and living on St. Simons when interviewed by the Works Progress Administration (WPA) in the 1930s.[47] He was the grandson of Salih Bilali, and his father's name was "Belali," an indication of the grandfather's desire to pass on his Islamic identity. In addition to his father and grandfather, Ben Sullivan (Bilal ibn Sulayman?) remembered two other Muslims in the community, "Ole Israel" and Daphne. Concerning the former, Ben reported this: "Ole Israel he pray a lot wid a book he hab wut he hide, and he take a lill mat an he say prayuhs on it. He pray wen duh sun go up and wen duh sun go down. He alluz tie he head up in a wite clawt an seem he keep a lot uh clawt on hand." The book to which Sullivan refers may well have been the Qur'ān. Daphne also prayed regularly, bowing "two aw tree times in duh middle uh duh prayuh," a clear reference to prescribed Muslim prayer in which *rak 'a* and *sujūd* (bowing and prostration) are performed. Daphne, described as having a visage that was "shahp-feechuh . . . an light uh complexion," also wore a veil.

On nearby Sapelo Island was the large plantation of Thomas Spalding (1774–1851), the driver of which was Salih Bilali's coreligionist and contemporary Bilali (d. 1859, pronounced "Blali" in the Sapelo community), also referred to as "the Old Man."[48] Otherwise known as known as "Ben Ali," Bilali originated somewhere in "Guinea" and, like Salih Bilali, may have spent time in the

[45] See Ivor Wilks, "Salih Bilali of Massina," in Philip D. Curtin, ed., *Africa Remembered: Narratives of West Africans from the Era of the Slave Trade* (Madison: U. of Wisconsin Press, 1967); Austin, *African Muslims*, 309–16.

[46] See Philip D. Curtin, *Economic Change in Precolonial Africa* (Madison: U. of Wisconsin Press, 1975), 159–68.

[47] See the Georgia Writers' Project, *Drums and Shadows: Survival Studies among the Georgia Coastal Negroes* (Athens: U. of Georgia Press, 1940), 178–83.

[48] See the Cornelia Bailey interview, July 1992. Cornelia Walker Bailey was born in Bell Marsh on June 12, 1945. Bilali is her great-great-great-grandfather through his daughter Bentoo (Arabic "Binta"). Bailey presently lives in Hog Hammock Community on Sapelo with her husband and family. The interview was taped, and notes were taken during the interview. Both tapes and notes are in the author's possession. For more on Sapelo Island, see William S. McFeely, *Sapelo's People: A Memory of Slavery, an Appointment with Freedom* (New York: Norton, 1994).

Bahamas before he was brought to Sapelo (perhaps the two met in the Bahamas, if not before).[49] Also like Salih Bilali, Bilali was a dependable driver who was called on to manage the Sapelo plantation of 400 or 500 enslaved persons.[50] He is perhaps most noted for an extant collection of excerpts from an Islamic, Maliki legal text known as the *Risāla* of Ibn Abī Zayd.[51] Bilali also served as the model for Joel Chandler Harris's caricature "Ben Ali."[52]

As one observer stated in 1901, based on her memories of the late 1850s, Bilali's large family of twelve sons and seven daughters all "worshiped Mahomet."[53] Some details of their religious practices are provided by Katie Brown, who at the time of the WPA interviews was "one of the oldest inhabitants" of Sapelo Island.[54] She was also the great-granddaughter of Bilali, or "Belali Mahomet." She enumerated Bilali's seven daughters as "Margret, Bentoo, Chaalut, Medina, Yaruba, Fatima, and Hestuh," most identifiably Muslim names. Margaret was the grandmother of Katie Brown, who went on to say this:

Magret an uh daughter Cotto use tuh say dat Bilali an he wife Phoebe pray on duh bead. Dey wuz bery puhticluh bout duh time dey pray and dey bery regluh bout duh hour. Wen duh sun come up, wen it straight obuh head an wen it set, das duh time dey pray. Dey bow tuh duh sun an hab lill mat tuh kneel on. Duh beads is on a long string. Belali he pull bead an he say, "Belambi, Hakabara, Mahamadu." Phoebe she say, "Ameen, Ameen."[55]

Margaret also wore a head covering that extended to her shoulders, a practice emulated by Katie (whose head covering, however, was not as elaborate). In addition to such observances, it would seem that Bilali adhered to Islamic prescriptions concerning marriage, as Brown remarked: "Magret she say Phoebe he wife, but maybe he hab mone one wife. I spects das bery possible."[56]

---

[49] Allan D. Austin, *African Muslims: Transatlantic Stories*, 6. Katie Brown maintained that Bilali's wife Phoebe "come by Bahamas. She speak funny words we didn know." Whether or not Phoebe was African born is therefore unclear, but Brown maintains that by the time Bilali and Phoebe and their daughters arrived in Sapelo, the "whole fambly wuz mos grown up." This conflicts with the testimony of Shad Hall, who claims that "Belali an all he fambly come on same boat frum Africa." See the Georgia Writers' Project, *Drums and Shadows*, 161–62, 166.

[50] See Lydia Parrish, *Slave Songs of the Georgia Sea Islands* (New York: Creative Age Press, 1942), 27–28; Austin, *African Muslims*, 265–68.

[51] The manuscript is entitled "The Ben-Ali Diary" and was held by the Georgia State Law Library until 1997, when it was transferred to the University of Georgia Library in Athens. See also Joseph H. Greenberg, "The Decipherment of the 'Ben-Ali Diary,' a Preliminary Statement," *Journal of Negro History* 25 (1940): 372–75; B. G. Martin, "Sapelo Island's Arabic Document: The 'Blali Diary' in Context," *Georgia Historical Quarterly* 78 (1994): 589–601.

[52] See Joel Chandler Harris, *The Story of Aaron (so named), the Son of Ben Ali* (Boston: Houghton Mifflin, 1896).

[53] See Parrish, *Slave Songs*, 28, note 22.

[54] See the Georgia Writers' Project, *Drums and Shadows*, 158–60.

[55] Ibid., 161.

[56] Ibid.

It would also appear that there was some attempt to adhere to Islamic dietary proscriptions. Information is rather meager on this question, but Cornelia Bailey offers a glimpse with her observation that Bilali's children would not eat "wild" animals or "fresh" meat, and that seafood such as crab was avoided, as were certain kinds of fish.[57]

Taken together, the testimonies of Ben Sullivan, Cornelia Bailey, and Katie Brown provide the essential contours of Muslim life in early Georgia – prayer mats, prayer beads, veiling, Qur'āns, dietary regulations, and daily, ritualized prayer. The composite picture is consistent with a serious pursuit of Islam.

Nothing is known about Bilali's twelve sons, which suggests either a breakup of the family in the Bahamas (assuming they were there) or an idealization resulting from iconographic forces that helped shape his memory. However, his daughters are verifiable persons who were possibly African born and forced into captivity along with their parents, and who were just as religious.[58] Shad Hall of Sapelo, another descendant of Bilali through his grandmother Hestuh (Esther?), describes the daughters as follows: "Hestuh an all ub um sho pray on duh bead. Dey weah duh string uh beads on duh wais. Sometime duh string on duh neck. Dey pray at sun-up and face duh sun on duh knees an bow tuh it tree times, kneelin' on a lill mat."[59]

A sense of a closely knit community emerges from these interviews. Katie Brown refers to Salih Bilali of St. Simons as "cousin Belali Sullivan." Shad Hall states that his grandmother Hestuh bore a son called "Belali Smith," who in turn was Phoebe Gilbert's grandfather, also a Sapelo resident.[60] Phoebe Gilbert's other set of grandparents were Calina and Hannah, both of whom were Igbo. Sapelo inhabitant Nero Jones was also related to "Uncle Calina and An Hannah" and says that they were "mighty puhticuluh bout prayin. Dey pray on duh bead. Duh ole man he say 'Ameela' and An Hannah she say 'Hakabara.'"[61] The last quote is fascinating, for it strongly suggests that Calina and Hannah converted to Islam in America, as the Igbo of southeastern Nigeria were not Muslim.[62] Furthermore, the Igbo population in early America was substantial but never identified with Islam.

Sapelo also provides evidence of cultural practices primarily associated with Muslim women that were derivative of West African Islamic societies. The

---

[57] See the Cornelia Bailey interview, July 1992.

[58] Although Bilali was African born, his wife and children may not have been. According to Bailey, his wife Phoebe was "from the islands" (the Caribbean), meaning that she was either West Indian-born or "seasoned" there. Because Bilali came with his entire family (except for his alleged twelve sons) to Sapelo, the family may have developed in the Caribbean rather than Africa. See the Cornelia Bailey interview, July 1992.

[59] See the Georgia Writers' Project, *Drums and Shadows*, 165–68.

[60] Ibid., 164.

[61] Ibid.

[62] In response to a direct question about this, Bailey responded that Calina and Hannah were indeed Muslims and that they came to Sapelo via the Caribbean. Thus, they could have converted to Islam while in the Caribbean; see the Cornelia Bailey interview, July 1992.

evidence centers around the production and significance of "saraka" cakes, which, according to Diouf, are often distributed during Ramadan in fulfilment of the requirement to pay alms or *zakāt*. Diouf makes this further argument:

[T]here is little doubt that these words [*sakara–saraka*] are slight corruptions of the Arabic word *sadakha*. *Sadakha* are voluntary alms that the believer offers to acquire merit with Allah.... The Sea Islands *saraka* and the Brazilian *saka* are the exact transportation to America of an African Muslim custom. The rice ball is the traditional charity given by West African women on Fridays.... The cake is still made in West Africa in the same way that Bilali's daughter made hers.... The confection of the rice cakes represents the only recorded example of Islamic behavior specifically expressed by slave women. As slaves, as women, as Africans, and as Muslims, Muslim women did not receive much attention during and after slavery.[63]

Such tradition appears to relate to previously mentioned customs recorded in Trinidad and Brazil, where (at least in Trinidad) a portion of the prepared foods included rice sweetened with sugar.[64] At least two of Bilali's daughters, Margaret and Hestuh, participated in his hemispheric-wide custom. The following is according to granddaughter Katie Brown:

[Margaret] make funny flat cake she call "saraka." She make um same day ebry yeah, an it big day. Wen dey finish, she call us in, all duh chillun, an put in hans lill flat cake an we eats it. Yes'm, I membuh how she make it. She wash rice, an po off all duh watuh. She let rice sit all night, an in mawnin rice is all swell. She tak dat rice an put it in wooden mawtuh, an beat it tuh paste wid wooden pestle. She add honey, sometime shuguh, an make it in flat cake wid uh hans. "Saraka" she call um.[65]

Shad Hall's "Gran Hestuh" also made a "strange cake, fus ub ebry munt. She call it 'saraka.' She make it out uh meal an honey.... Sometime she make it out uh rice." Those times during which saraka was prepared were clearly special occasions, the Islamic nature of which was underscored by Hestuh's invocation of "Ameen, Ameen, Ameen" prior to the cake's consumption.[66]

Islam along coastal Georgia was by no means confined to the descendants of Bilali and Salih Bilali. The WPA interviews of Ed Thorpe of Harris Neck, Rachel and Alec Anderson and Rosa Grant of Possum Point, and Lawrence Baker of Darien reveal that their ancestors were also Muslim.[67] Like the Bilali families, these early Muslims prayed three times daily, ending their prayers with "Ameen, Ameen, Ameen." In fact, Rosa Grant says of her grandmother Ryna that "Friday wuz duh day she call huh prayuh day." This is not a reference to daily prayer, for Grant had already stated that her grandmother's prayers began "ebry mawnin." Rather, this is a reference to the Muslim observance

[63] See Sylviane A. Diouf, *Servants of Allah: African Muslims Enslaved in the Americas* (New York: New York U. Press, 1998), 64–66.

[64] See Maureen Warner-Lewis, *Guinea's Other Suns: The African Dynamic in Trinidad Culture* (Dover, MA: The Majority Press, 1991), 5–6, 115–16.

[65] See the Georgia Writers' Project, *Drums and Shadows*, 162.

[66] Ibid., 166–67.

[67] Ibid., 120–21, 144–45, 154–56.

of Friday prayer, at which time Muslims congregate in the early afternoon. Whether Grant and others actually gathered for the prayer is not known, but she at least attempted to keep alive the significance of the day.

There is also the possibility that other Muslims contemporary with Bilali, with names similar to his, lived in other areas along the Atlantic coast. Speculation on this point arises from the possible Muslim ancestry of Frederick Douglass. His great-great-grandfather was named "Baly," and his grandparents were Betsy and Isaac Bailey of Talbot County along Maryland's Eastern Shore. It was Betsy Bailey's daughter Harriet who gave birth to Frederick Augustus Bailey. McFeely writes this:

In the nineteenth century, on Sapelo Island (where Baileys still reside), there was a Fulfulde-speaking slave from Timbo, Futa Jallon, in the Guinea highlands, who could write Arabic and who was the father of twelve sons. His name was Belali Mahomet.... "Belali" slides easily into the English "Bailey," a common African American surname along the Atlantic coast. The records of Talbot County list no white Baileys from which the slave Baileys might have taken their name, and an African origin, on the order of "Belali," is conceivable.[68]

Because Betsy Bailey was born around 1772, she was essentially Bilali's contemporary and therefore unlikely to have been his descendant. However, McFeely's point concerning the structural similarities between Belali and Bailey, coupled with the absence of white Baileys in Talbot County, is an intriguing one, such that the possibility of Muslim antecedents in this particular lineage cannot be ruled out.

A major source of substantial corroboration for the presence of a sizeable Muslim community in coastal Georgia–South Carolina continues to be the underused, path-breaking work of Lorenzo Turner. Three-fourths of the personal names he collected during his fifteen-year study, which began in 1932, were collected in coastal Georgia, principally in St. Simons, Sapelo, Harris Neck, and the vicinity of Darien; the remainder were gathered in coastal South Carolina, including the islands of Edisto, St. Helena, Hilton Head, Johns, James, and Wadmalaw. Of the hundreds of names in the study, some 274 have a possible Muslim connection or derivation. These names, of which 122 or nearly 45 percent are female, convey a variety of meanings. Some are male day names, such as Alahadi ("Sunday," Mandinka), Jumo ("Friday," Mandinka), and Sibiti ("Saturday," Mandinka); others are female day names, including Limo ("Sunday," Hausa), Altine ("Monday," Wolof), Araba ("Wednesday," possibly Mandinka), Laraba ("Wednesday," Hausa), Aramisa ("Thursday," Mandinka), Arajuma ("Friday," Mandinka), and Jumare ("Friday," possibly Pulaar). Some of the names refer to periods of the day, such as the female Laila (from the Arabic for "night"), the female Lisha ("evening," Hausa), the female Nange ("daytime," Pulaar), and the female Somanda ("morning," Mandinka); other names represent seasonal change, such as the male names Sanjano ("period

[68] See William S. McFeely, *Frederick Douglass* (New York: Norton, 1991), 3–5.

after the rains," Mandinka) and Rani (Hausa for "hot season"), and the female names Kaule (Mandinka for "the intermediary season") and Klema ("the hot season," Mandinka). Some appellations even express various times of prayer, such as the female Alansaro ("three o'clock prayer time," Mandinka), the male Fitiro (Mandinka for "six o'clock prayer"), and the female Luha ("morning prayer, between 8 and 9 o'clock," Pulaar).[69]

While not all of the foregoing are incontestably Muslim names, such are to be found in the Turner collection. These include Adamu, Ali, Amina, Aminata, Ayisata, Bakari, Baraka, Bilali, Binta, Bintu, Birahima, Birama, Fatimata, Fatima, Fatuma, Gibril, Haruna, Hasana, Mamadi, Mamadu, Male, Mare, Mori, Moriba, Musa, and Safiyata. As has been pointed out, Sambo may also refer to a Muslim male. Interestingly, Turner encountered the name Shaitan, or Satan; how this name was used is not specified – perhaps it was used by Muslims in reference to certain non-Muslims. The linguistic evidence also suggests that Muslim amulets were widely distributed; for example, the Hausa female name Makari bears a relationship to amulets (literally "an antidote" or "protection"), and it is consistent with other terms found by Turner such as *juju*, used throughout Senegambia for amulets of various sorts (including non-Muslim varieties), and *kafa*, possibly derived from Hausa as the name for a "charm" of some kind.[70]

In addition to Muslim names, Turner gathered data constituting a wealth of information relating to rank and caste. These names are both Muslim and non-Muslim, and they could possibly shed light on the vexing and elusive question of the transfer of "class" statuses from Africa to North America. Such information would greatly aid the effort to examine African identities and the transformation of those identities in New World settings in all of their complexities, an undertaking that must await subsequent inquiry as it lies beyond the present scope.

The Muslim presence in coastal Georgia–South Carolina (and possibly elsewhere along the Atlantic) was therefore active, vibrant, and compelling. Clearly, the history of Africans along this corridor is more complicated than previously understood; its study can no longer be limited to the Gullah language and associated handicrafts and artifacts, notwithstanding their importance.

* * *

Despite the vitality of the Islamic tradition and the strength of their bonds, Muslims in early Georgia–South Carolina faced certain distinct challenges to the preservation of their faith: Although they may have gathered in small numbers and clandestine places to pray, they could neither openly maintain Qur'ānic schools (or madrasas), nor have access to Islamic texts. It was inevitable that their collective memory would eventually falter. As an example, Bilali, author of

---

[69] See Lorenzo Dow Turner, *Africanisms in the Gullah Dialect* (New York: Arno Press and the New York Times, 1969; orig. pub. 1949), 41–190.
[70] Ibid., 190–208.

the "Ben-Ali Diary," put together passages from Ibn Abī Zayd's *Risāla* in such a haphazard way that Nigerian clerics, upon reviewing the document, declared it to be the work of jinn (spirits).[71] Likewise, Salih Bilali, although claiming to possess a Qur'ān, apparently could not write Arabic coherently.[72] Allowing for exceptional cases such as Bilali's, the gradual loss of Islamic knowledge, combined with the parochial application of Arabic to religious discourse, constituted a blow to the continuation of Islam in the early American South.

Additional challenges to Islam include the fact that it was in competition with other African religions, especially prior to the nineteenth century. In the American South, most Africans adhered to non-Islamic beliefs. The host society, although at times amused by religious variations, became increasingly concerned with controlling the religion of its captive population as the nineteenth century progressed. The gradual increase in the number of Christian converts among African Americans resulted from both their own desire to embrace an Africanized version of Christianity and a campaign within the post-1830 militant South to use religion as a means of social control. As Africanized Christianity slowly became a force, Islam would have suffered.

The process by which Christianity began to compete with and eventually overtake Islam can be viewed in the Sapelo community. The progeny of African-born Muslims (who tended to restrict their social interactions with non-Muslims) eventually began attending the Tuesday, Thursday, and Sunday night "prayer houses" held by each community on the island, while continuing with their own Muslim gatherings. With the establishment of the First African Baptist Church in May of 1866, however, the open and collective pursuit of Islam became increasingly rare, although it is difficult to say when, exactly, it ended on the island.[73]

In addition to the impact of Christianity, it should be noted that ethnocentricity, combined with other cultural differences, probably restricted efforts at proselytization among non-Muslims. As was true of Brazil, continuity of the Islamic tradition was heavily dependent on a cultural transfer within existing Muslim families and over generations. This was a formidable task, especially as the importation of non-Muslims into North America greatly exceeded that of Muslims in the late eighteenth and early nineteenth centuries; many Muslims had little choice except to marry non-Muslims. Further, African-born Muslims may have been unable to effectively communicate with their children and grandchildren and would have been frustrated in their attempts to convey the tenets of Islam adequately.[74] Enslavement itself introduced structural impediments to such matters as a formal education, circumcision, the

---

[71] See Greenberg, "Ben-Ali Diary," but also see Ronald A. T. Judy, *(Dis) forming the American Canon: African-Arabic Slave Narratives and the Vernacular* (Minneapolis: U. of Minnesota Press, 1993) for an alternative analysis.

[72] See Austin, *African Muslims*, 321.

[73] See the Cornelia Bailey interview, July 1992.

[74] Indeed, in the Georgia coastal area, none of the descendants of African-born Muslims claim to be Muslim themselves in the WPA interviews.

formation of brotherhoods, the maintenance of moral proscriptions, and the observance of basic dietary rules. The children of African Muslims would have been socialized within the context of the larger, non-Muslim slave culture and deeply influenced by this process. In short, Muslims would have had great difficulty in preserving Islam within their families, assuming a stable enslaved family. With Louisiana as a possible exception, such an assumption is most unwarranted.[75]

It is therefore with the children and grandchildren of African-born Muslims that questions concerning the resilience of Islam take on significance. While it cannot be established with certainty that the progeny were Muslim, the Islamic heritage was certainly there; individuals bore Muslim names and retained a keen memory of the religious practices of their ancestors. However, their reluctance to be unequivocal on the question of their own adherence to Islam can be observed in the responses of Georgian coastal blacks to queries posed by WPA interviewers. Indeed, a careful review of these interviews reveals considerable anxiety among the informants, understandable given the politics of the time. If they were practicing Muslims, they were certainly not going to tell it to whites in the rural South of the 1930s.[76]

One account given by the interviewers underscores the ambiguity of religious affinities and supports the contention that the informants did not reveal all. It concerns one Preacher Little, who was encountered on Sapelo Island and whose physical appearance, demeanor, and dress were initially described as "Mohammedan looking."[77] Although the interviewers were subsequently assured that the minister was Christian (and they went on to witness the minister preside over a religious service), their first impressions are instructive, especially as this encounter took place after the interviews with the descendants of Salih Bilali and Bilali. Preacher Little may have been a Muslim who dissembled in the interviewers' presence, but he could have also been the embodiment of a certain Islamic–Christian synthesis. Indeed, this possibility is enhanced by the reflections of Charles Jones in 1842, who wrote that African-born Muslims related Yahweh to Allah and Jesus to Muhammad.[78] His observation contains a number of potential meanings, including the possibility that Africans, while ostensibly practicing Christianity, were in reality reinterpreting Christian dogma in light of Islamic precepts, a phenomenon not unlike the Cuban fusion of Islam and Yoruba religion discussed by Ortiz. If Jones was correct, such correlations were probably more Muslim than Christian in their worldview, since Islam had already shaped their perspective. It is therefore

---

[75] Following Midlo Hall, colonial Louisiana pursued a slave policy that provided for some sense of familial security. See Midlo Hall, *Africans in Colonial Louisiana*, 168.

[76] For example, Rosanna Williams of Tatemville, Georgia, became so alarmed at the questions of the interviewers that she asked, "Wut yuh doin? Is yuh gonuh sen me back tuh Liberia?" See the Georgia Writers' Project, *Drums and Shadows*, 71.

[77] Ibid., 169–70.

[78] See Charles C. Jones, *The Religious Instruction of the Negroes* (Savannah, GA: Thomas Purse, 1842), 125.

conceivable that their descendants may have continued this kind of syncretism (or dissimulation).

A further example again comes from Sapelo and the descendants of Bilali.[79] Cornelia Bailey's grandmother would tell the former about the life of Harriet Hall Grovner, Bailey's great-grandmother and the granddaughter of Bentoo, Bilali's daughter. Harriet was a practicing Muslim until the First African Baptist Church was organized in 1866, at which time she joined. Although she became very active in the Sunday school, it is possible that, because she frequently retreated into the woods to pray, she was also practicing Islam, since she would have had no reason to continue her clandestine activities unless she was praying something other than Christian prayers. The fact that Harriet died in 1922 and may have still been practicing Islam at such a late date and as a direct legacy of an African Islamic tradition is highly significant, because in this way she would have been an organic link to an African Muslim past while at the same time contemporaneous with the dawn of Islamically informed movements among African Americans in the early twentieth century.

* * *

Evidence for the Muslim presence in the American South is also supported by a consideration of the African background. As was true for parts of the Caribbean and Hispaniola and other sites in what would become Latin America, but in contrast to Bahia, Senegambia was the major source of Muslims for the early American South. In fact, Senegambia may have supplied as much as 21 percent of the entire trade volume to North America, second only to West Central Africa and especially concentrated in Maryland and Louisiana.[80] However, Senegambia is an immense region, within which were at least three staging areas from which Africans were procured: the coastal area, from the lower Senegal to the lower Casamance valleys; a midrange area, encompassing the middle and upper Senegal and Gambia valleys; and the middle and upper Niger. The presence of Islam within this vast stretch of territory was relative to specific lands and periods of time.

It has already been observed that, within the coastal area, most of the Wolof remained unconverted to Islam before the end of the eighteenth-century. By the early nineteenth century, however, Islam had become a major force in Cayor. Along the lower Gambia and the Casamance, the various Mande-speaking populations, along with the Sereer, were also turning to Islam, facilitated by the presence of Muslim merchants among them.[81]

[79] See the Cornelia Bailey interview, July 1922.

[80] See David Eltis, Stephen D. Behrendt, David Richardson, and Herbert S. Klein, *The Trans-Atlantic Slave Trade: A Database on CD-ROM* (Cambridge, England: Cambridge U. Press, 1999), hereafter called the *Du Bois CD-ROM Database*. For Louisiana and Maryland, the estimates of those from Senegambia are 60.8 percent and 49.4 percent, respectively.

[81] See Jean Suret-Canale and Boubacar Barry, "The Western Atlantic Coast to 1800," in J. F. Ade Ajayi and Michael Crowder, eds., *History of West Africa*, 2nd ed. (New York: Columbia U. Press, 1976), vol. 1, 466; Jean Boulègue and Jean Suret-Canale, "The Western Atlantic

Concerning the Senegambian midrange, a substantial proportion of the population was Muslim. The middle Senegal valley produced a strong Muslim polity as early as the eleventh century, followed by a sixteenth-century dynasty of fluctuating Islamic loyalty that was overthrown in 1776 by the militantly Islamic theocracy of Futa Toro, an ethnically Fulbe or Tukulor state (as the latter term has been used to distinguish the Muslim, sedentary, and sometimes ethnically mixed portion of the Fulbe from the pastoral, non-Muslim segment). The upper Senegal and Gambia valleys contained proportionately fewer Muslims (and lower population densities), but the Islamic factor had been present for several hundred years by the eighteenth century, largely because of the far-reaching Malian empire, resulting in the Muslim-led state of Bundu in 1698.[82] The midrange therefore represents a focus of Muslim power that only increased through the duration of the transatlantic trade.

Far into the interior lay the western reaches of the Niger River, a mixture of Muslim and non-Muslim populations from the time of imperial Songhay (1464–1591) to the early nineteenth century, when the area known as Maasina fell to the armies of militant Fulbe Muslims. Before then, the area witnessed intense warfare as the non-Muslim Bambara of Segu established control of the upper Niger in the eighteenth century. Muslim and non-Muslim alike were among the war captives, many of whom were eventually transported to the western hemisphere.[83]

From the fifteenth through the mid-nineteenth century, then, Senegambia gradually became Islamized, more dramatically in the nineteenth than in previous centuries, with the majority of the population becoming Muslim during the nineteenth. By virtue of its location vis-à-vis Europe, Senegambia

Coast," in J. F. Ade Ajayi and Michael Crowder, eds., *History of West Africa*, 3rd ed. (New York: Longman, 1985), vol. 1, 519; Paul Lovejoy, *Transformations in Slavery: A History of Slavery in Africa* (Cambridge, England: Cambridge U. Press, 1983), 58. Regarding written accounts, Mollien observed that "Mahometanism is making daily progress, and will soon become the only religion of the country of Cayor," while Jobson's early-seventeenth-century description of "Marybuckes" (*marabouts*, or Muslim clerics) and Islam along the Gambia is echoed by Smith and Moore's early- and Park's late-eighteenth-century observations, demonstrating Islam's growing influence. See G. Mollien, *Travels in the Interior of Africa to the Sources of the Senegal and Gambia* (London: H. Colburn, 1820), 61; Richard Jobson, *The Golden Trade, or a Discovery of the River Gambra, and the Trade of the Aethiopians* (London: Dawsons of Pall Mall, 1968; orig. pub. 1623, London), 78–99; Frances Moore, *Travels into the Inland Parts of Africa* (London: E. Cave, 1738), 12–26; Mungo Park, *Travels in the Interior Districts of Africa* (London: W. Bulmer, 1799), 15–35; William Smith, *A New Voyage to Guinea* (London: Cass, 1967; orig. pub. 1744, London), 26–27.

[82] Eyewitness written accounts include Saugnier's report in 1784 that the Serrakole's religion was "nearly allied to Mahometanism, and still more to natural religion"; by 1821, Gray and Dochard essentially said the same: "From a state of Paganism these people are progressively embracing the Mahometan faith." See M. Saugnier and M. Brisson, *Voyages to the Coast of Africa* (London, 1792; reprint, New York: Negro Universities Press, 1969; orig. pub. 1792, London), 220; Major William Gray and Surgeon Dochard, *Travels in Western Africa, in the Years 1818, 19, 20, and 21* (London: J. Murray, 1825), 266.

[83] Lovejoy, *Transformations in Slavery*, 72–73.

simultaneously became a principal supplier of captives early in the Atlantic trade.[84] The Wolof states along the Atlantic coast were deeply affected by the trade before the last quarter of the seventeenth century; the masses sought asylum in a politicized Islam, resulting in increasing captives from further in the interior, in the middle and upper Senegal and Gambia valley.[85] Although the relative contribution of Senegambia to slave trafficking declined after 1750, the bulk of captives continued to come from the midrange and the upper and middle Niger, where Islam was relatively more widespread. After 1750, traders operating in the upper and middle Niger simply redirected war captives to other points along the coast of West Africa.[86]

In addition to Senegambia, Sierra Leone was a source of the enslaved population for early America and the American South in particular, supplying 17 percent of the total number imported.[87] For our purposes, Sierra Leone stretches from the Casamance River to Assini and was contiguous with what is now Guinea-Bissau, Guinea, Sierra Leone, Liberia, and the Ivory Coast. Late-seventeenth-century and early-eighteenth-century accounts agree that Mande-speaking Muslim populations were in the numerical minority along the coast, and from the middle of the sixteenth century through the seventeenth, the region's principal sources for the slave trade were littoral, non-Muslim

---

[84] Curtin, *Atlantic Slave Trade*, 96–126; Lovejoy, *Transformations in Slavery*, 35–37.

[85] This shift is indirectly confirmed by the rise of Bundu and Futa Toro, in part the response of Muslims to their victimization in the trade. See David Robinson, "The Islamic Revolution in Futa Toro," *International Journal of African Historical Studies* 8 (1975): 185–221; Michael A. Gomez, *Pragmatism in the Age of Jihad: The Precolonial State of Bundu* (Cambridge, England: Cambridge U. Press, 1992); Abdoulaye Bathily, "La traite atlantique des esclaves e ses effets économiques et sociaux en Afrique: La cas du Galam, royaume de l'hinterland sénégambien au dix-huitième siècle," *Journal of African History* 27 (1986): 269–93; compare with Curtin, *Economic Change*.

Regarding earlier events, evidence from a clerically led revolt along the coast in the 1670s, known as the *tubenan* movement, supports this contention. The term *tubenan* is from the Arabic *tawba*, or "to repent"; the Wolof word *tub* essentially carries the same meaning. The Moor Nasir al-Din gained the support of the Wolof peasantry by condemning the participation of the Wolof elite in the slave trade, declaring that "God does not allow kings to plunder, kill or make their people captive." When the lieutenants of Nasir al-Din in turn betrayed the trust of the peasantry and began selling them into slavery, they were quickly overthrown. Their ouster suggests the presence of effective opposition to the trade within the coastal area. For more on *tubenan*, or "la guerre des marabouts," see Philip D. Curtin, "Jihad in West Africa: Early Phases and Inter-Relations in Mauritania and Senegal," *Journal of African History* 12 (1971): 11–24; Boubacar Barry, "La guerre des marabouts dans la region du fleuve Sénégal de 1673 à 1677," *Bulletin de l'Institut Fondamental* (formerly *Français*) *d'Afrique Noire* 33 (1971): 564–89; Suret-Canale and Barry, "Western Atlantic Coast," vol. 1, 470; P. Cultru, *Premier voyage du Sieur de la Courbe fait à la Coste d'Afrique en 1685* (Paris: É. Champion, 1913), 30.

[86] For example, as Raffenel reported that the non-Muslim Bambara of Segu were renowned warriors, "greatly superior to their neighbors in the art of war, the Bambara are truly fearsome," a number of Muslims were necessarily fed into the trade as captives of war. See Anne Raffenel, *Voyage dans l'Afrique occidentale... exécuté, en 1843 et 1844* (Paris: A. Bertrand, 1846), 299. Also see Gomez, *Exchanging Our Country Marks*, 17–64.

[87] See the *Du Bois CD-ROM Database*. I combine estimates for Sierra Leone and the Windward Coast.

populations.[88] However, for the second half of the eighteenth century, the vast majority of those sold into the trade were from the interior, indicating that such captives arrived in North America in similar proportions.[89] The largest polity in the Sierra Leone interior was Futa Jallon, whose jihadic long durée has been discussed. As a consequence of this protracted war, both Muslims and non-Muslims found themselves on plantations not only in Jamaica and elsewhere in the Caribbean, but in the American South as well. It should be kept in mind, however, that some captives could have also been procured through the considerable commercial activity of Muslims from Kankan (Guinea) to Kong (Ivory Coast).[90]

The Gold Coast was the next region, supplying some 12 percent of the total trade to North America.[91] Adjoining Sierra Leone, it occupies what is essentially present-day Ghana. European traders arrived along this coast as early as the fifteenth century. Originally an exporter of gold and a net importer of the enslaved, the Gold Coast became a net exporter of captives by the early seventeenth century.[92] In the first decade of the eighteenth-century, Africans were exported from the region at a rate of 2,500 per year; by the 1740s, the trade peaked at 9,100 per year. The escalation of the trade was a consequence of rising demand and the expansionist behavior of Asante, which pursued an imperial policy from 1680 (the approximate date of its founding) to 1750.[93] One of the polities defeated by the power of Asante was the province of Gonja, a Muslim territory vitally connected to the middle Niger valley via Muslim commercial networks leading through Kong, Dagomba, Wa, and Mamprussi. In addition, Muslim traders from as far east as Hausaland conducted business on a regular basis in the capital of Kumase.[94] The Islamic presence in the interior "was strong, providing commercial connections with the far interior, so that the Akan states were involved in continental trade on a scale that was at least equal to Oyo, Dahomey, and Benin and was perhaps even greater."[95] All of this

---

[88] See, for example, John Matthews, *A Voyage to the River Sierra Leone* (London: Cass, 1966; orig. pub. 1788, London), 17–18; compare with Joseph Corry, *Observations upon the Windward Coast of Africa* (London: Cass, 1968; orig. pub. 1807, London), 41–44.

[89] Walter Rodney, *A History of the Upper Guinea Coast* (Oxford, England: Oxford U. Press, 1970), 95–113, 244–55.

[90] Gray and Dochard's emphasis on Futa Jallon's strict observance of Islam is echoed by Callié's depiction of its people as "extremely fanatical," underscoring the seriousness of the jihād. See Gray and Dochard, *Travels in Western Africa*, 39–40; René Callié, *Travels through Central Africa to Timbuctoo* (London: H. Colburn and R. Bentley, 1830), 222.

[91] See the *Du Bois CD-ROM Database*.

[92] See Lovejoy, *Transformations in Slavery*, 56.

[93] See Ivor Wilks, *Asante in the 19th Century: The Structure and Evolution of a Political Order* (Cambridge, England: Cambridge U. Press, 1975); Lovejoy, *Transformations in Slavery*, 56.

[94] See Wilks, *Asante in the 19th Century*; Peter B. Clarke, *West Africa and Islam* (London: Edward Arnold, 1982), 50–60; Melville Herskovits, *The Myth of the Negro Past* (New York: Harper and Brothers, 1941); and Melville Herskovits, *The New World Negro* (Bloomington: Indiana U. Press, 1966), 90–93.

[95] See Lovejoy, *Transformations in Slavery*, 56–57 (quotation on 57).

implies that Muslim captives constituted some percentage of the supply from the Gold Coast.

The Bight of Benin was the next supply zone, contributing nearly 3 percent to North America's total volume.[96] Reaching from the Volta to the Benin River and corresponding to what is now Togo, Benin, and southwestern Nigeria, the area witnessed a series of struggles in the 1780s and 1790s that produced numerous captives, to whom were added those captured in the course of Yoruba resistance to the ultimately successful expansion of Muslims from Ilorin. The latter were inspired by the previously discussed 1804 jihād and subsequent caliphate of Usuman dan Fodio of Sokoto; the point to be made here is that Muslims from what is now northern Nigeria were not only brought to Brazil and the Caribbean via the Bight of Benin, but also to North America. While evidence of northern Nigerians (the Hausa and perhaps some of the Fulbe) in what would become the American South, specifically Louisiana, was already provided earlier in the chapter, it is reinforced by the words of a Mississippi planter, who registered his preference for Africans "of the Bornon, Houssa, Zanfara, Zegzeg, Kapina, and Tombootoo tribes."[97]

A consideration of these regions, which comprise the zones from which the overwhelming majority of Muslims would have come to the American South, provides some sense of the proportion of Muslims among those imported from Africa. These four regions, in which Islam was of varying consequence, supplied approximately 53 percent of all those imported to North America. This means that of the estimated 481,000 Africans imported into British North America during the slave trade, nearly 255,000 came from areas influenced by Islam. It is therefore reasonable to conclude that Muslims arrived in North America by the thousands, if not tens of thousands.[98]

It would be a mistake to focus solely on the Muslim population, however, as Islam's influence in West Africa was not confined to the converted, practicing community. On the contrary, many non-Muslims were acquainted with a number of its tenets through the activities of Muslim traders and clerics. The Muslim trading networks, through which the Juula, Yarse, and Hausa merchants supplied disparate West African communities with goods from as far away as the Mediterranean, also linked the savannah with the forest area, from Senegambia to Lake Chad. Their apolitical, nonproselytizing code of conduct also helps to explain the receptivity of many Muslim and non-Muslim communities to their commercial endeavors.[99]

---

[96] See the *Du Bois CD-ROM Database*.

[97] See Charles Sackett Sydnor, *Slavery in Mississppi* (New York: Appleton-Century, 1933), 141.

[98] See Gomez, *Exchanging Our Country Marks*, 65–67; Curtin, *Atlantic Slave Trade*, 83–89; Paul Lovejoy, "The Impact of the Atlantic Slave Trade on Africa: A Review of the Literature," *Journal of African History* 30 (1989): 363–94; James A. Rawley, *The Transatlantic Slave Trade: A History* (New York: Norton, 1981), 428.

[99] For more on the Juula, see Timothy F. Garrard, *Akan Weights and the Gold Trade* (London: Longman, 1980); Ivor Wilks, "Wangara, Akan and Portuguese in the Fifteenth and Sixteenth Centuries," *Journal of African History* 23 (1982): 333–49 (pt. 1); 463–72 (pt. 2).

In addition to, and often in conjunction with, the activities of Muslim traders was the role of Muslim clerics throughout West Africa. Far removed from the lofty positions of the erudite in cities such as Kano and Jenne, numerous clerics of a more utilitarian calling were spread across the region's expanse. Literate in Arabic, these men performed religious and diplomatic services for royal courts and commoners alike. In particular, they provided amulets for both Muslims and non-Muslims; in fact, Muslim amulets, often containing Qur'ānic inscriptions encased in sealed pouches, were very popular among non-Muslim populations, as it was believed that writing possessed particular efficacy.[100] Mosques and madrasas, or Qur'ānic schools, were invariably established in the Muslim part of town or in the nearby Muslim village. As a result, many West Africans practicing indigenous religions were nonetheless familiar with and influenced by Islam, having been exposed to Muslim dress, dietary laws, and overall conduct.

By the same token, it was not unusual for those who had converted to Islam to retain certain aspects of their previous beliefs; Islam in West Africa underwent a number of reforms in an effort to achieve orthodoxy.[101] However, to the degree that these non-Islamic tendencies were not in conflict with the fundamental tenets of the faith (one God, Muhammad as God's messenger, daily prayer, fasting Ramadan, and so on), the integrity of these practitioners and the veracity of their confession is not open to challenge.

Muslims who achieved some notoriety in the American South can sometimes be traced to one of the preceding regions, thereby strengthening the argument that significant numbers of Muslims were imported. For example, Ayuba b. Sulayman, or Job Ben Solomon, was born around 1702 in the upper Senegal valley (in Bundu). Ironically, it was during a excursion to the upper Gambia to sell captives that he himself fell victim to other slave traders, who ultimately carried him to the Atlantic coast. Captured and sold along with him was Lamine Njai, or "Lahamin Jay." Arriving in Maryland in 1732, Ayuba b. Sulayman was a free man and en route to West Africa by 1733 as a result of the benevolence of a Royal African Company officer who was moved by Ayuba's petition for liberty in Arabic. Lamine Njai also eventually returned to West Africa.[102]

---

[100] Regarding the role of clerics and amulets, see Jack Goody, ed., *Literacy in Traditional Societies* (Cambridge, England: Cambridge U. Press, 1968), and Mervyn Hiskett, *The Development of Islam in West Africa* (New York: Longman, 1984).

[101] For an introduction to this discussion, see I. M. Lewis, ed., *Islam in Tropical Africa*, 2nd ed. (Bloomington: International African Institute in association with Indiana U. Press: 1980), or Nehemiah Levtzion, ed., *Conversion to Islam* (New York: Holmes and Meier, 1979).

[102] See Gomez, *Pragmatism in the Age of Jihad*, 47, 61–62, 68–70; Thomas Bluett, *Some Memoirs on the Life of Job* (London: R. Ford, 1734); Moore, *Travels into the Inland Parts*; Philip D. Curtin, "Ayuba Suleiman Diallo of Bondu," in Curtin, *Africa Remembered*. See also Douglas Grant's condescending *The Fortunate Slave: An Illustration of African Slavery in the Early Eighteenth Century* (London: Oxford U. Press, 1968); J. M. Gray, *A History of the Gambia* (Cambridge, England: Cambridge U. Press, 1940) 211–12.

Another arrival in North America in the 1730s was Yarrow Mahmud, or "Yarrow Mamout." His origins are unspecified, but his physical appearance, preserved by Charles Wilson Peale's 1819 portrait when Yarrow Mahmud was living in Georgetown, reveals features consistent with those of the Fulbe, so that he may have also come out of the middle or upper Senegal valley as had Ayuba b. Sulayman.[103]

Yet another Muslim, who received perhaps the greatest amount of attention as a result of both his Arabic literacy and his possible conversion to Christianity, was Umar b. Said, or "Omar ben Said" (ca. 1765–1864). Umar b. Said, who was also Fulbe, was born in Futa Toro, along the middle Senegal River, and he was captured and sold in the beginning of the nineteenth century. In his important autobiography, he records that at the age of thirty-one, "there came to our place a large army, who killed many men, and took me, and brought me to the great sea, and sold me into the hands of the Christians," a development both representative of the many conflicts of the middle and upper Senegal valleys and demonstrative of Muslim susceptibility. Umar b. Said, who came to be known as "Prince Moro" or "Moreau," was brought to Charleston, South Carolina along with "two of his countrymen." Upon entering a difficult work regime under a second slaveholder, he absconded to Fayetteville, North Carolina, where he eventually met up with a more sympathetic slaveholder in the person of one James Owen. He would soon come into possession of an Arabic Bible, and he subsequently engaged in a campaign to send such Bibles to West Africa in cooperation with another African Muslim of some renown, Lamine Kaba, or "Lamen Kebe."[104]

Lamine Kaba, renamed "Old Paul" in America, originated in the Sierra Leone region but differed from Ayuba b. Sulayman and Umar b. Said in that he was not Fulbe, but, like Muhammad Kaba of Jamaica and (possibly) Muhammad Sisse of Trinidad, hailed from the clerically oriented community of the Jakhanke, along the southern reaches of Futa Jallon. Having previously accompanied a Muslim force that attacked non-Muslims somewhere along the western reaches of the Niger ("Jaliba") River "to convert them to Islamism," Lamine Kaba would himself fall victim to slaving activities years later. His place of capture and point of departure are not specified, but it was his search for writing paper along the coast that led to his enslavement. The need for writing paper is consistent

---

[103] See Austin, *African Muslims*, 68–70. Austin includes Peale's comments on Yarrow Mahmud in this account. For an accessible photograph of Peale's *Yarro Mamout (1819)*, see the Library of Congress's *Civilization* 2 (March–April 1995): no. 2, 16.

[104] See "Autobiography of Omar ibn Said, Slave in North Carolina, 1831," *American Historical Review* 30 (1925): 787–95 (quotation on 793); Dr. Bedell, "Prince Moro," *Christian Advocate* (1825): 306–07; Austin, *African Muslims*, 445–59; Austin, *African Muslims: Transatlantic Stories*, 129–56. Austin estimates that Umar arrived in Charleston in 1807, which means that the "large army" is probably a reference to the combined armies of Bundu, Kaarta, and Khasso, who invaded Futa Toro in 1806 to 1807. See David Robinson, *Chiefs and Clerics: Abdul Bokar Kan and Futa Toro (1853–1891)* (Oxford, England: Oxford U. Press, 1975), 15–18; Robinson, "Islamic Revolution of Futa Toro."

with the clerical nature of the Jakhanke, and his capture again illustrates the insecurity that prevailed in the Sierra Leone region. Held in captivity in at least three southern states, Lamine Kaba was the source for a publication on the Serrakole or Soninke language. His participation in the Bible dissemination strategy was a major factor in his manumission and repatriation to Liberia in 1835, after nearly forty years of enslavement.[105]

Like Lamine Kaba, Ibrahima Abd ar-Rahman was also from the Sierra Leone region, but, unlike him, he was Fulbe, born in Futa Jallon in 1762 and claimed to be the son of Almaami Ibrahima Sori, one of the most illustrious leaders in Guinean history. In the course of a military campaign under his command, he and his army were routed and captured. What immediately followed is uncertain, but at least some of the captives were sold to the Malinke along the Gambia River, including Abd ar-Rahman. Eventually, he and fifty of his former soldiers were traded to an English slaver and transported to the western hemisphere. Abd ar-Rahman's personal path led to the Gambia, whereas others formerly under his charge were possibly taken to the Sierra Leone coast. In any event, Abd ar-Rahman's account underscores the volatility of the region and supports the contention that many Muslims from Futa Jallon became captives of war and involuntary participants in the transatlantic trade. Nothing more is said of the other Muslims captured with Abd ar-Rahman, except for Samba, or Sambo, who was aboard the same slaver as his former commander.[106]

Abd ar-Rahman and Samba arrived in New Orleans in 1788 and eventually wound up on the same Natchez farm together. In Mississippi, Abd ar-Rahman was known as "Prince," and among the several remarkable stories with which he became associated was one that brought him national fame. As life would have it, he encountered a white man in Mississippi whom he had previously befriended in West Africa. Upon the man's identification of Abd ar-Rahman as royalty, a series of events were set into motion that ultimately led to Abd ar-Rahman's return to Africa in 1829, where he died within months of arrival. This motif of sudden, unexpected intervention leading to revelation of the enslaved's noble status mirrors the experience of Ayuba b. Sulayman, and it contributes to the observation that it was the extraordinary or unusual circumstance that explains the relative prominence of these persons, as opposed to the lone fact that they were Muslims. Indeed, many of the accounts concerning such individuals

---

[105] See Austin, *African Muslims*, 409–11; Theodore Dwight, Jr., "Condition and Character of Negroes in Africa," *Methodist Quarterly Review* (January 1864): 77–90; Theodore Dwight, Jr., "On the Sereculeh Nation, in Nigrita. Remarks on the Sereculehs, an African Nation Accompanied by a Vocabulary of the Language," *American Annals of Education and Instruction* 5 (1835): 451–56. For more on the Jakhanke, see Lamin O. Sanneh, *The Jakhanke: The History of an Islamic Clerical People of the Senegambia* (London: International African Institute, 1979), and Thomas Hunter, "The Development of an Islamic Tradition of Learning among the Jahanka of West Africa" (Ph.D. diss., U. of Chicago, 1977).

[106] See Terry Alford's very fine *Prince Among Slaves* (New York: Oxford U. Press, 1977); Cyrus Griffin, "The Unfortunate Moor," *African Repository* (February 1828): 364–67; Austin, *African Muslims*, 121–32.

refer to other enslaved Muslims who, because they did not share in the special circumstance, do not receive recognition. Focused attention on a handful of Muslims is therefore potentially misleading if it leads to the conclusion that Muslims were numerically inconsequential.

Consistent with the foregoing discussion is the observation that Abd ar-Rahman and Samba were not the only Muslims in Natchez. On his journey to New Orleans in 1822, Thomas Teas recorded the following concerning an encounter in Natchez:

This evening a Moorish Slave came on board [the ship], and I had a long conversation with him. He stated himself to be the son of a Moorish prince – that he was taken prisoner in an incursion he made with a small body of men, into the territories of a neighboring chief, and that he was carried to Timbuctoo, and sold to a slaver, who brought him to the coast, and disposed of him to a Spanish ship, which brought him into New Orleans, about 10 years ago. The capital of his father's dominions he says, is Tombuc; a town on the Niger.... He retains the faith of his fathers. He appears well educated, writes and speaks the Arabic with apparent fluency and ease. I got him to write the Mahometan creed: "There is but one God – Mahomet is his Prophet, and Ali his priest."[107]

This unnamed "Moor" was probably West African and not Arabo-Berber, given his origins on the Niger River. That he was illegally introduced to New Orleans via Timbuktu around 1812 rules out the possibility that this could have been Abd ar-Rahman or Samba. Both pride in his cultural inheritance and internal conflict over his failure to adhere to the standards of that inheritance are provided in his impromptu confession to Teas:

He lamented in terms of bitter regret, that his situation as a slave in America, prevents him from obeying the dictates of his religion. He is under the necessity of eating pork, but denies ever tasting any kind of spirits. He has one wife. He will not allow that the Americans are a polite and hospitable people as the Moors – nor that they enjoy a tenth part of the comfort they do – and that for learning and talents they are far behind them.

The unnamed Moor's removal to Natchez follows the pattern of Abd ar-Rahman and Samba, and it suggests that further investigation into the river port as a site of Muslim numerical significance may be warranted.

* * *

It remains to examine both the viability and impact of Islam in the colonial and antebellum American South beyond what has been discussed for the Georgia–South Carolina coast. With regard to the former, it is not always easy to know the extent to which these Muslims had opportunities to engage in corporate expressions of faith. At first glance, it would seem highly improbable

[107] See Thomas S. Teas, "A Trading Trip to Natchez and New Orleans, 1822: Diary of Thomas S. Teas," *Journal of Southern History* 7 (1941): 378–99 (quote on 387–88). This account is mentioned in Austin, *African Muslims: Transatlantic Stories*, 35.

that the host society would allow Muslims to assemble, for example, to pray. Nevertheless, evidence suggests that such assemblies in fact took place. First, there are recorded instances of individual Muslims praying, or performing ṣalāt. In some cases such prayer was conducted in a hostile environment. Ayuba b. Sulayman, for example, was chased and otherwise harassed while praying.[108] In other instances, Muslims were allowed to pray in the prescribed manner by slaveholders. Thus Ayuba, after his initial difficulties, was afforded privacy. The record from the Georgia–South Carolina coast is replete with references to individuals praying regularly, such as "Ole Israel," Daphne, and the Igbo couple Calina and Hannah; presumably there were times when they prayed together. Salih Bilali of St. Simons was a devout Muslim who fasted Ramadan; Bilali of Sapelo wore a fez and kaftan, prayed daily (facing the east), and also observed the Muslim feast days, practices observed by his wife and daughters as well as others among the faithful along the Georgia–South Carolina coast.[109] It would appear that Abd ar-Rahman continued to practice Islam and that, after either a flirtation with Christianity or a conscious strategy of dissimulation (to gain support for his repatriation), he immediately reaffirmed his Muslim beliefs upon returning to Africa.[110] Charles Ball, enslaved in Maryland, South Carolina, and Georgia for forty years, also witnessed certain Muslim observances among fellow enslaved persons, for he wrote that "I knew several who must have been, from what I have since learned, Mohammedans; though at that time, I had never heard of the religion of Mohammed."[111] Ball took particular interest in one Muslim in South Carolina who prayed "five times every day, always turning his face to the east," and records his account of life in the West African sāhil, where he was captured as a lad by Tuareg (Arabo-Berber inhabitants of the desert) and served for two years as *bella* (slave) before his ultimate transfer to the Atlantic trade. Ball, like other observers, took note of Muslim behavior but did not know enough to recognize what he saw.

Individual examples of adherence to Islam suggest that many enslaved persons practiced the religion, perhaps clandestinely, or perhaps in full view of undiscerning eyes such as Ball's. In any event, the possibility that Muslims congregated for prayer is enhanced by a second factor: the general tendency among the enslaved to steal away into secluded areas for religious and social purposes. It has generally been assumed that stealing away involved the enslaved's pursuit of their particular brand of Christianity, or indigenous African religions, but there is absolutely no reason to preclude Muslims from similar activity. Thus, we have the example of Harriet Hall Grovner of Sapelo Island, who found it necessary to regularly seek refuge to pray as late as 1922. The probability

[108] See Grant, *Fortunate Slave*, 82–84.
[109] See Austin, *African Muslims*, 265, 321.
[110] See Alford, *Prince Among Slaves*, 57–58; Austin, *African Muslims*, 6–7.
[111] See Charles Ball, *Slavery in the United States* (New York: Negro U. Press, 1969; orig. pub. 1837), 164–65, 167–86.

that Muslims gathered in groups to pray is increased when the question of contact between Muslims is considered. Bilali and Salih Bilali, residing on plantations on neighboring sea islands, were considered the best of friends and were in contact with others who were Muslim, many apparently Fulbe. As has been demonstrated, the sea island Muslim community of Sapelo and St. Simons was significant, a conclusion further supported by Bilali's statement and leadership when called upon to defend the island against the British in 1813: "I will answer for every Negro of the true faith," he announced, and proceeded to muster a force of eighty men.[112] Religion and religious observances must have constituted an important, if not central, component of Muslims' bond. Abd ar-Rahman and Samba, his fellow Pullo (singular of Fulbe) enslaved on the same farm, were able to associate closely with each other, and the two communicated with at least one other Muslim, a Mandinka in this instance, from Natchez.[113] As coreligionists, they surely sought opportunities to recreate sacred space in corporate prayer.

It would also appear that Muslims not only struggled to maintain their bonds with each other but also attempted to preserve Islamic education, particularly the knowledge of Arabic and the Qur'ān. One Dr. Collins, who wrote a manual on the medical treatment of the enslaved, stated that many individuals from Senegal "converse in the Arabic language, and some are sufficiently instructed even to write it."[114] LeConte recalled "an old native African named Philip," a Muslim who during the antebellum period demonstrated the outward expressions of the religion "by going through all the prayers and prostrations of his native country."[115] Abd ar-Rahman would write the *Fātiḥa* (opening sūra, or chapter, of the Qur'ān) for whites who believed they were receiving the "Lord's Prayer" in an exotic hand.[116] The unnamed Moor of Natchez discussed by Teas wrote the *shahāda* (statement of belief in one God and Muhammad as God's messenger) for him, while S'Quash was reported to have been fluent in both Arabic and Greek. And of course, Umar b. Said penned his autobiography in Arabic.

Many Muslims struggled not only to preserve their traditions but also to pass them on to their progeny. Thus Bilali bestowed Muslim names upon most, if not all of his daughters, and apparently taught all but the youngest Pulaar (language of the Fulbe) and possibly Arabic, as they regularly communicated with one another in a "foreign tongue."[117] Samba, the companion of Abd ar-Rahman,

[112] See Austin, *African Muslims*, 268, 313, 324–25.

[113] See Alford, *Prince Among Slaves*, 43–44, 77.

[114] See Dr. Collins, *Practical Rules for the Management and Medical Treatment of Negro Slaves* (1811), quoted in Grant, *Fortunate Slave*, 81.

[115] See William Dallam Armes, ed., *The Autobiography of Joseph LeConte* (New York: D. Appleton, 1903), 29–30.

[116] See Austin, *African Muslims*, 129; see note 64.

[117] Ibid., 265, 272–75. Cornelia Bailey maintains that Arabic was not taught but that "some African" was spoken.

had at least three sons, and he gave them all Muslim names.[118] In 1786 Sambo and Fatima escaped Edward Fenwicke of John's Island; Sambo was "of the Guinea country" and probably Muslim, but Fatima was described as country born, so she may have either converted to Islam or had at least one Muslim parent.[119] The recurrence of Muslim names among American-born enslaved people is corroborative evidence of the desire among many to keep their religion and culture alive.[120]

* * *

One of the more interesting aspects of the Muslim experience in the early American South was the impact of this religious community on the process of stratification within African and African American society. Given that it was largely a society of enslaved persons, such stratification began with the perception of the slaveholders. Vis-à-vis other Africans, and consistent with the record in Brazil and the Caribbean, Muslims were generally viewed by slaveholders as "more intelligent, more reasonable, more physically attractive, more dignified people."[121] Phillips has written that planters found the Senegalese to be the most intelligent, as they "had a strong Arabic strain in their ancestry."[122] William Dunbar, a prominent Natchez planter, specifically preferred Muslims from what would become northern Nigeria over Senegambians, but the former were Muslims nonetheless.[123] The belief in the superiority of the "Mohammedans" was a consistently held view throughout the colonial and antebellum periods. As an example, Salih Bilali is described as "a man of superior intelligence and higher cast of feature."[124] To a great extent, this view of the Muslim was informed by the physical appearance of the Fulbe and certain Mande speakers, whose features were believed to be phenotypically closer to Europeans than other Africans.[125] European travelers invariably commented upon Fulbe features: Gray and Dochard described them as "much resembling the European," as did Callié, whereas Jobson stated that the Fulbe were "a Tawny people, and have a resemblance right unto those we call Egyptians."[126]

As a result of their experience and perceived advantage, as well as for reasons to be explored shortly, many Muslims in the early American South were given more responsibilities and privileges than other slaves, an occurrence consistent

---

[118] See Alford, *Prince Among Slaves*, 77–78. Two of the sons were named *Sulimina* (but called "Solomon" and "Samba").

[119] See the *State Gazette of South Carolina*, July 31, 1786, in Windley, *Runaway Slave Advertisements*, vol. 3, 400.

[120] See Windley, *Runaway Slave Advertisements*, passim.

[121] See Newbell N. Puckett, *Folk Beliefs of the Southern Negro* (Chapel Hill: U. of North Carolina Press, 1926), 528–29; Lyell, *Second Visit*, vol. 1, 266.

[122] See Phillips, *Negro Slavery*, 42.

[123] See Sydnor, *Slavery in Mississippi*, 141.

[124] See Puckett, *Folk Beliefs*, 528–29; Lyell, *Second Visit*, vol. 1, 266.

[125] See Collins, *Practical Rules*, 37; Austin, *African Muslims*, 81.

[126] See Gray and Dochard, *Travels in Western Africa*, 40; Callié, *Travels through Central Africa*, 222; Jobson, *Golden Trade*, 42.

with the treatment of Muslims in Jamaica and Trinidad. Alford writes that Muslim slaves were used as "drivers, overseers, and confidential servants with a frequency their numbers did not justify."[127] The quintessential example of this was the experience of S'Quash in North Carolina, who, soon after arriving on the plantation, "was given work around the 'big house,' in order to acquire some English and the pattern of living in this strange land. Such was his ability that he ultimately became headman on the plantation, succeeding in time the white overseer." Such was the distinction achieved by S'Quash that, according to the tradition of the family that claimed ownership of him, he served as a long-distance manager in several drives of the enslaved from North Carolina to Mississippi; in fact, he supposedly made one such drive entirely on his own. Contemplation of the implications of this tradition led one member of the slaveholding family to write the following: "If this last be true, it was an extraordinary and ironical achievement for an African trader to have achieved a similar position of authority in his transplanted existence and without his freedom."[128]

The privilege did not end with S'Quash but was extended to other Muslims and to his progeny on the 800-acre plantation. Regarding the former, there lived on the same plantation an "Uncle Abram," probably a generation younger than S'Quash. Abram was a headman who possessed a "rich and deep" voice and was "immensely proud of his skill in calling the hands together for work every morning." While it is not evident that Abram was Muslim, the observation that, in contrast to the "Guinea nigger," the "tall, light-colored Mandingo with rich tenor voice was nearly always held in the house" clearly resonates with Abram's baritone delivery and level of responsibility, the association of the Mandinka and Islam an underlying factor. Concerning descendants, "Old Phyllis" was the daughter of S'Quash and was described as "a great power on the plantation," whereas her daughter, also named Phyllis, was a nurse to one of the slaveholder's children, her son a white child's playmate. Such was the legacy of S'Quash that his granddaughter Phyllis would crush any challenge to her authority by issuing the following warning: "Lemme 'lone now, doan you know I'se de gran-chile uv S'Quash!"[129]

Further examples of Muslim privilege include the careers of Bilali and Salih Bilali, who were both placed in positions of high authority and used that authority to jointly quell a slave insurrection. Zephaniah Kingsley, Jr., a slaveholder who advocated the "benign" treatment of slaves, recorded that along the Georgia coast during the War of 1812, there were "two instances, to the southward, where gangs of negroes were prevented from deserting to the enemy [England] by drivers, or influential negroes, whose integrity to their masters and influence over the slaves prevented it; and what is still more remarkable,

---

[127] See Alford, *Prince Among Slaves*, 56.
[128] See Barringer, *The Natural Bent*, 13.
[129] Ibid., 9, 24–27.

in both instances the influential negroes were Africans; and professors of the Mahomedan religion."[130] This is an apparent reference to Bilali and Salih Bilali, whose behavior anticipated Muhammad Kaba's opposition to the 1831–32 "Baptist War" in Jamaica. Not only did they crush the revolt but, as previously mentioned, Bilali defended Sapelo Island in 1813 with eighty armed slaves, preventing access to the English. It is likely that the great majority of these eighty persons were Muslim, given the extensive nature of Islam in the Georgia–South Carolina coastal corridor, combined with Bilali's statement that he could depend only upon fellow Muslims, as opposed to the general enslaved population whom he characterized as "Christian dogs."[131]

Old Zephaniah would have known something about the privileged slaves of African descent, and he may have been somewhat familiar with Islam. In 1806 he went to Havana and purchased thirteen-year-old Anta Majigeen Naji, a Wolof girl from Cayor (in Senegal) who had been captured and shipped out of Gorée Island. He brought Anta back to Laurel Grove in Spanish East Florida, where she became his "wife" and thereafter known as Anna Magigine Jai Kingsley. Thirty years her senior, Zephaniah at first made her his household manager and then, in 1811, he manumitted her. A man of many slave mistresses, Zephaniah was apparently particularly fond of Anna, with whom he had three children. Establishing a new home at Fort George Island, he thereafter ventured to Haiti, where Anna joined him in 1836. With his demise in 1843, Anna returned to Duval County, Florida. It is entirely possible that Anna had been raised a Muslim prior to her enslavement; perhaps such a background, in addition to her physical qualities, helps to explain her elevation in Zephaniah's eyes, a development consistent with slaveholder preferences.[132]

Anna had entered a status combining freedom with property holding, including human beings, and was as far removed from the servile quotidian as possible. Bilali and Salih Bilali were also distinguished from the rank and file; they appear to have served as models for a character named "Old King" in an otherwise crude apologist literature published in 1853.[133] Old King had come to a North American coastal island as an enslaved adult and as a "Mahomedan," and he was subjected to both the company of "pagan negroes" and the authority

---

[130] See Zephaniah Kingsley, *Treatise on the Patriarchal or Co-operative System of Society as it Exists in some Governments, and Colonies in America and in the United States under the Name of Slavery, with Its Necessity and Advantages* (n.p.: 1829), 13–14. See also Parrish, *Slave Songs*, 25; Austin, *African Muslims*, 268.

[131] See Ella May Thornton, "Bilali – His Book," *Law Library Journal* 48 (1955): 228–29. Cornelia Bailey disagrees with the idea that the Muslims of Sapelo enjoyed advantages over non-Muslim slaves and maintains that slaveholders treated both groups the same (see the Cornelia Bailey interview, July 1992).

[132] See Daniel L. Shafer, "Shades of Freedom: Anna Kingsley in Senegal, Florida and Haiti," *Slavery and Abolition* 17 (1996): 130–54.

[133] See David Brown, *The Planter: Or, Thirteen Years in the South, by a Northern Man* (New York: Negro U. Press, 1970; orig. pub. 1853), 120–28. I discovered this reference in Austin, *African Muslims: Transatlantic Stories*, 37.

of "Christian dogs," a phrase resonating with preceding testimony as well as
the sentiment of Muhammad Abdullah of Bahia in the 1840s. He soon became
a "lord of the Isle," who in "retirement" carried himself with the "dignity of
a retired field-marshal, and the authority of a patriarch," having served as a
driver during his productive years. Such was his prestige and elevated status
that even the slaveholder treated him with respect, demonstrated by an imagined conversion in which the slaveholder deferentially asks him to show an
overseer how to prepare a field (appropriately named King-field). In the conversation, Old King addresses the holder by his first name, and initially replies,
"I'll think about it Jacob, and let you know in the morning." The slaveholder
is greeted the next day by King's deliberation: "I am sorry to disappoint you,
Jacob, but I have concluded not to go to King-field this morning," to which the
holder eventually responded, "Really, King, I thought certainly you would be
more obliging." The holder's disappointment turns to cheer when King elects to
compromise. Such an embellishment of the Bilali–Salih Bilali legacy, whereby it
assumed mythlike proportions, was premised upon the very real phenomenon
of Muslim privilege, and for that reason it enjoyed more than a sliver of
plausibility.

As the careers of Bilali and Salih Bilali suggest, there were certain tensions
between Muslim and non-Muslim slaves, whether the latter were African born
or not. In the first place, there is evidence that some American-born slaves
condescended to newly arrived Africans.[134] To the extent that African Muslims
encountered such a reception, they would have experienced pressures to modify
or discontinue their Muslim–African practices in order to conform to what was
acceptable in the new setting, or they would have found the resolve to remain
faithful to their convictions. The evidence shows that, despite pressure from
Christianity and African indigenous traditions, the majority resisted coercion
to abandon their faith.[135] Stories of Muslim piety and determination include
that of Salih Bilali, described by his owner as "the most religious man that he
had ever known"; another depicted him as a "strict Mahometan" who refused
alcohol, holding "in great contempt, the African belief in fetishes and evil spirits."[136] Contrasting examples are few in number and include Abd ar-Rahman,
whose supposed conversion to Christianity is contradicted by his immediate
recommitment to Islam upon repatriation to Africa. Furthermore, although it
is true that Lamine Kaba and Umar b. Said both professed Christianity, serious
reservations surround the conversion of the latter.[137] For example, shortly before his death, Umar b. Said allegedly wrote the following: "Salaams to all who
believe on the Lord Jesus Christ. I have given my soul to Jesus the Son of God.
O, my countrymen Bundah, and Phootor, and Phootdalik [Bundu, Futa Toro,
and Futa Jallon], give salaams to Muhammad Said and Makr Said . . . and the

---

[134] See, for example, Puckett, *Folk Beliefs*, 58–29.
[135] See Blassingame, *Slave Community*, 73.
[136] See Austin, *African Muslims*, 316, 321.
[137] Ibid., 448.

rest."[138] However, Umar b. Said continued to implore the help of Allah and the prophet Muhammad with invocations found even within the margins of his Christian Bible.

With all of the foregoing information in mind, it is not surprising to read of Bilali's characterization of his fellow (or actually subordinate) slaves as Christian dogs. Neither is it startling to read of Abd ar-Rahman's comments to Cyrus Griffin, in which "he states explicitly, and with an air of pride, that not a single drop of negro blood runs in his veins."[139] This attitude was confirmed by the children of Bilali, all of whom were Muslims, and who were described as "holding themselves aloof from the others as if they were conscious of their own superiority."[140] Bailey essentially verifies this, stating that not only did Bilali "keep his distance" from others because he "did not like mixing" with them, but that Muslims and non-Muslims as a whole tended to "keep to themselves," although they generally "got along" and could work together for specific purposes or special occasions.[141] Such detachment was certainly consistent with S'Quash's comportment, who "held himself completely aloof from the Negro slaves and would neither live nor mate with them, staying in a hut by himself." S'Quash in fact would eventually find a mate on another plantation, someone who met his standards, and for whom his owner would have to pay the "top price" of $3,000.[142] Such behavior is strikingly similar to that of the Muslims of Jamaica, Trinidad, and Bahia, who in the latter case also "refused to mix with the other slaves." It may provide the principal clue into the identity of Charles Ball's African-born grandfather, who was imported into Calvert County, Maryland around 1730.[143] Eventually known as "Old Ben," Ball's grandfather "always expressed great contempt for his fellow slaves, they being, as he said, a mean and vulgar race, quite beneath his rank, and the dignity of his former station." The old African never attended church services, depicting "the religion of this country" as "altogether false, and indeed, no religion at all; being the mere invention of priests and crafty men." In contrast, Ball's grandfather recalled the genuine religion of his West African home, delivered by a "holy man" whose heavenly revelations had been recorded in "a small book, a copy of which was kept in every family," which, among other things, proscribed "drunkenness." Although much of what he related about his

---

[138] See George E. Post, "Arabic-Speaking Negro Mohammedans in Africa," *African Repository* (May 1869): 130–31. The letter was originally written in Arabic and placed in the library of Andover Theological Seminary.

[139] See Griffin, "Unfortunate Moor," 365–67. See Austin, *African Muslims: Transatlantic Stories*, 65–80. Austin argues that Cyrus Griffin played a prominent role in transforming Abd ar-Rahman into a Moor.

[140] See Georgia Bryan Conrad, *Reminiscences of a Southern Woman* (Hampton, VA: Hampton Institute Press, 192–?, n.d.), 13.

[141] See the Cornelia Bailey interview, July 1992.

[142] See Barringer, *The Natural Bent*, 13.

[143] See Arthur Ramos, *Negro in Brazil*, trans. Richard Pattee (Philadelphia: Porcupine Press, 1980; orig. pub. 1939), 26; Ball, *Slavery in the United States*, 15–16, 21–24.

religion diverges from Islam, the concept of a single religion, a prophet, a holy written revelation, and his utter disregard for both western Christianity and his enslaved fellows strongly suggests that Ball's grandfather was a Muslim with a fanciful, perhaps failing memory of the faith.

The attitude of Muslim superiority must first be explained within the context of the West African background. The fact that these people themselves had been slaveholders in the Old World influenced their view of the enslaved; Umar b. Said, for example, claimed to have owned seventy slaves in West Africa.[144] Their African experience was shaped along the lines of highly stratified societies in which the servile population was seen as inferior. The ethnic factor is relevant here as well, in that there are considerable data on the ethnocentricity of the Fulbe.[145] Originating long ago in present-day southern Mauritania, many of the Fulbe claim descent from the Arab general 'Uqba b. Nafi', who in 667 led Muslim armies as far south as Kawar in the Fezzan.[146] This clear fiction reflects the larger truth of their mixed ancestry, resulting, in some instances, in the view of the non-Fulbe as inferior. Park remarked on this attitude, stating that "the Foulahs of Bondou ... evidently consider all the Negro natives as their inferiors, and when talking of different nations, always rank themselves among the white people."[147] It is instructive that Wyatt-Brown, in discussing three related yet distinct psychological responses by men to enslavement, cites Ibrahima Abd ar-Rahman as a prime example of a Fulbe man who, by virtue of his exclusionary early socialization vis-à-vis other ethnicities, embodies the first category of response, which was characterized by a "ritualized compliance in which self-regard is retained." That is, Ibrahima maintained his culturally inculcated dignity and pride as he reconciled himself to enslavement by remembering his *pulaaku*, the essence of the distinctive Fulbe character and prescriptive code of behavior. Hence, he never descends to the second category of response, which "involves the incorporation of shame," or to the third category, described as "samboism" and "shamelessness."[148] Indeed, to Ibrahima's way of thinking, the internalization of enslavement could only be characteristic of the lesser non-Fulbe.

---

[144] See Brown, *The Planter*, 219.

[145] For the Fulbe in West Africa, see Paul Riesman, *Freedom in Fulani Social Life* (Chicago: U. of Chicago Press, 1977); Victor Azarya, *Aristocrats Facing Change: The Fulbe in Guinea, Nigeria, and Cameroon* (Chicago: U. of Chicago Press, 1978); Marguerite Dupire, *Organisation sociale des Peuls* (Paris: Plon, 1970); Marguerite Dupire, *Peuls nomades: étude descriptive des WoDaaBe du Sahel Nigérien* (Paris: Institut d'ethnologie, 1962); Paul Marty, *L'Islam en Guinée: Foûta-Diallon* (Paris: E. Leroux, 1921); G. Vieillard, *Notes sur les coutumes des Peuls au Foûta Djallon* (Paris: Larose, 1939); Claude Rivière, *Mutations sociales en Guinée* (Paris: M. Rivière et Cie, 1971); M. Z. Njeuma, *Fulani Hegemony in Yola (Adamawa), 1809–1902* (Yaoundé, Cameroon: Publishing and Production Centre for Teaching and Research, 1978).

[146] See Paul Irwin, *Liptako Speaks: History from Oral Tradition in Africa* (Princeton, NJ: Princeton U. Press, 1971), 46–77.

[147] See Park, *Travels in the Interior District*, 59.

[148] See Bertram Wyatt-Brown, "The Mask of Obedience: Male Slave Psychology in the Old South," *American Historical Review* 93 (1988): 1228–52 (quotations on 1232).

A second factor in explaining Muslim attitudes of superiority concerns Islam itself. To live as a Muslim in eighteenth- and nineteenth-century West Africa was to live in an increasingly intolerant society. This was the period of jihād, of the establishment of Muslim theocracies, of self-purification and separation from practices and beliefs seen as antithetical to Islam. Abu Bakr as-Siddiq of Jamaica summarized the perspective of the Muslim:

> The faith of our families is the faith of Islam. They circumcise the foreskin; say the five prayers; fast every year in the month of Ramadan; give alms as ordained in the law; marry four free women – a fifth is forbidden to them except she be their slave; they fight for the faith of God; perform the pilgrimage to Mecca, i.e. such as are able to do so; eat the flesh of no beast but what they have slain for themselves; drink no wine, for whatever intoxicates is forbidden to them; they do not keep company with those whose faith is contrary to theirs, such as worshippers of idols.[149]

It is clear, then, that fundamental differences between Islam and other religions could have further militated against a uniform experience of enslavement, along with such considerations as regional differences, urban versus rural conditions, and so on.

However, a third factor in Muslim attitudes of superiority is as important as the first two – namely, a number of these enslaved Muslims were from prominent backgrounds in West Africa. For example, Abd ar-Rahman was a scion of Almaami Ibrahima Sori. Ayuba b. Sulayman's father was a leading cleric in the upper Senegal valley. Several Muslims, including Lamine Kaba, Bilali, and Umar b. Said, boasted of extensive educations in West Africa. In fact, it was more common than not that West African Muslims were recipients of an Islamic education and were therefore literate, and the various documents that concern notable Muslims invariably comment on the fact that they could write in Arabic (or in Arabic script). From the observer's vantage point, this was quite incredible. However, it should be appreciated that literacy within the West African Muslim community was widespread; most Muslim villages and towns maintained madrasas (or Qur'ānic schools), to which children from ages seven to fourteen, both boys and girls, went for instruction. With madrasa began memorization of the Qur'ān by heart, and Arabic grammar was introduced. From madrasa, young men (and occasionally young women) of sufficient means moved on to more advanced studies, often requiring travel from one town to another in order to study under the appropriate shaykh, or master teacher of a specific curriculum. The more advanced students went on to renowned centers of learning, such as Pir and Jenne, where there were concentrations of scholars. Thus the educational process was well established, with a tradition reaching back to at least the fourteenth century.[150] Reducing such an educated elite to the

---

[149] See Wilks, "Abu Bakr al-Siddiq," 162–63.
[150] See Marty, *L'Islam en Guinée*, 108–47; Jean Suret-Canale, "Touba in Guinea: Holy Place of Islam," in Christopher Allen and R. W. Johnson, eds., *African Perspectives* (Cambridge, England: Cambridge U. Press, 1970); Gomez, *Pragmatism in the Age of Jihad*, 26–28.

status of slaves – a status shared with those of humble birth – was particularly demeaning.

It is important to note that, reflecting the pastoral background of many Africans and referring to considerations of differentiation within the servile condition, some of the enslaved Muslims, such as Ayuba b. Sulayman, were completely unaccustomed to agricultural labor, which became evident very quickly.[151] Dr. Collins remarked that the Muslims of Senegambia "are excellent for the care of cattle and horses, and for domestic service, though little qualified for the ruder labours of the field, to which they never ought to be applied."[152] The doctor's observations accord remarkably well with both the similar treatment of Muslims in Brazil and the Caribbean as well as the 1903 report of a French official in Guinea, who wrote that "the Fula is poorly endowed by nature for physical labor, puny and sickly... with no resource other than cultivation by his slaves."[153] The aristocratic or pastoral background of some West Africans, combined with the aforementioned agricultural expertise of others, meant that Muslims were, in the eyes of the host society, better suited for domestic or supervisory roles, a determination that widened the schism between Muslim and non-Muslim. The early twentieth century provides evidence that Fulbe slaveholders viewed agricultural work as servile and beneath them; it may be that this attitude was present as early as the eighteenth century, so that decisions by North American planters to place the Fulbe and other Muslims in nonagricultural positions may have also been influenced by such sensibilities.[154] This planter notion of Muslim superiority is demonstrated in "African Humanity," published in 1789 in the *Gazette of the State of Georgia*:

A MOORISH slave, having been severely beaten by his master, resolved on taking vengeance, which he executed in the following way: During the gentleman's absence he secured the gates (the house being in the country) in the strongest manner; and having fast bound his mistress and her three children conveyed them to the roof of the house, where he sat with the greatest composure. The gentleman returning, and ringing for admittance, was surprised at seeing the slave in that situation, and threatened him with the severest punishment, if he did not open the gate immediately. The slave tauntingly replied, "He would soon make him alter his language." Then taking up two of the children, and bidding them go open the gate, he flung them over the battlements. The father, in the greatest consternation, promised him not only pardon for the two murders, but even freedom and money, if he would spare his wife and third child. "I will never believe you," exclaimed the slave, "unless you convince me you are in earnest by cutting off your nose." This injunction being complied with, the villain immediately flung down the child and mother, and on hearing the piercing outcries of his master, advised him to

---

[151] See Grant, *Fortunate Slave*, 81.
[152] See Collins, *Practical Rules*, quoted in Grant, *Fortunate Slave*, 81.
[153] See the quote from Paul Guebhard, found in Martin Klein, *Slavery and Colonial Rule in French West Africa* (Cambridge, England: Cambridge U. Press, 1998), 141.
[154] Ibid., 182–83, 217.

go hang himself, as his only resource. To complete his savage triumph, he threw himself after them, and expired without a groan.[155]

Given its melodramatic character and implausible reconstruction of events, the account likely represents an embellishment at the very least, if not a complete fabrication. In either case, the didactic quality of the narrative is evident, warning slaveholders of both excessive punishment and excessive trust. The slaveholder's family had been left alone with a trusted "Moor," suggesting that by 1789 Muslims had established a reputation for reliability. The story therefore issues a caution: Even a privileged Muslim, epitomizing the very best of "African humanity," could not be fully trusted, so have a care for nonprivileged African-born slaves, as they are particularly dangerous.

Finally, it is probable that some Muslims were deeply affected by racist views of whites toward other Africans, views that included a vision of the Fulbe as fundamentally different from and superior to others similarly enslaved, views consistent with "Lord" Lugard's 1903 assessment of domestic slavery in what would become northern Nigeria, where the enslaved populations in "the towns of Kano and Sokoto are ruled by *an alien race* who buy and sell the people of the country in large public slave markets."[156] In 1844, Hodgson wrote this unequivocally:

The Foulahs are *not* negroes. They differ essentially from the negro race, in all the characteristics which are marked by physical anthropology. They may be said to occupy the intermediate space betwixt the Arab and the Negro. All travelers concur in representing them as a distinct race, in moral as in physical traits. To their color, the various terms of *bronze, copper, reddish*, and sometimes *white* has been applied. They concur also in the report, that the Foulahs of every region represent themselves to be *white* men, and proudly assert their superiority to the black tribes, among whom they live.[157]

While acknowledging that the Fulbe's nappy hair placed them among the "oulotric" ("wooly haired") populations of the world, Hodgson insisted that this was an inconsequential feature.[158] In view of such sentiments, the Fulbe and other Muslims would have been encouraged to distance themselves from the average African and descendant of Africans, even to the point of denying any kindred relationship to them. Thus, Abd ar-Rahman's claim that he had no "negro" blood. In fact, Abd ar-Rahman, if he did not initiate the idea, certainly

---

[155] See the *Gazette of the State of Georgia*, April 23, 1789.
[156] In Paul E. Lovejoy and Jan S. Hogendorn, *Slow Death for Slavery: The Course of Abolition in Northern Nigeria, 1897–1936* (Cambridge, England: Cambridge U. Press, 1993), 27.
[157] See William Brown Hodgson, *Notes on Northern Africa*, 49–50.
[158] Hodgson (p. 50) maintained that the Fulbe were the descendants of Arab fathers and "Taurodo" mothers, the latter an apparent reference to subsaharan communities living in the sāḥil and in contact with the Arabo-Berber populations of Mauritania. Hodgson's remarks relate to the Fulbe claim of descent from the Arab general 'Uqba b. Nafi' discussed in the text. The *Torodbe* (singular *Torodo*) of Futa Toro were in fact a clerical community who rose from humble origins to provide leadership for various theocratic states in Senegambia.

did not dispute the claim that he was a Moor; on the contrary, he placed "the negro in a scale of being infinitely below the Moor."[159] Mark Twain's view of Abd ar-Rahman, however, underscores the dilemma of those seeking an accommodation with such racism: the inescapability of blackness, and the unattainability of whiteness. Learning of Abd ar-Rahman's return to West Africa, the irascible Twain offered the following good wishes:

I, for one, sincerely hope that after all his trials he is now peacefully enjoying the evening of his life and eating and relishing unsaleable niggers from neighboring tribes who fall into his hands, and making a good thing out of other niggers from neighboring tribes that are saleable.[160]

The matter of claiming Moorish or Berber ancestry was not unique to Abd ar-Rahman, and, as was mentioned in conjunction with unnamed Muslims in Louisiana, S'Quash of North Carolina, Anthony Jansen Van Salee of New Amsterdam, and Selim of Virginia, it was not entirely without foundation. In fact, the question of Moorish ancestry, whether plausible or wholly putative, is a significant site of inquiry for the presence of Islam in North America; it is examined in subsequent chapters. Given the validity of some claims, incredulity over the 1937 statement of centenarian Silva King of Marlin, Texas issues into uncertainty: "I know I was borned in Morocco, in Africa, and was married and had three children befo' I was stoled from my husband. I don't know who it was stole me, but dey took me to France, to a place called Bordeaux, but drugs me with some coffee, and when I knows anything 'bout it, I's in de bottom of a boat with a whole lot of other niggers."[161]

Although there is evidence of strained relations between Muslims and non-Muslims, there are also instances of cooperation. Charles Ball mentions his acquaintance and friendship with a number of Muslims.[162] Abd ar-Rahman himself, in an ironic twist, married a Baptist woman in 1794 (perhaps a concession to necessity), had several children by her, returned to Liberia with her in 1829, and expired in her arms a few months later. However, it was Muhammad 'Ali b. Said, or Nicholas Said, who perhaps best exemplifies the Muslim who made common cause with others. Born around 1833 in the Islamic state of Bornu near Lake Chad (bordering Hausaland), he was taken captive around 1849, whereupon he began a most circuitous voyage to the United States. After initially crossing the Sahara, he was sold in Tripoli to owners in Mecca, then Turkey, then Russia, after which he traveled to various European destinations before his tour of the Americas as a free man between 1860 and 1862. By 1863 he had become a teacher in Detroit, Michigan, as he was fluent in French and Italian, and

---

[159] See Griffin, "Unfortunate Moor," 365–67.
[160] See Mark Twain, "American Travel Letters, Series 2," *Alta California* August 1, 1869, final letter.
[161] See Rawick, *American Slave*, vol. 4, 290.
[162] See Austin, *African Muslims*, 127–31; Ball, *Slavery in the United States*, 164–65, 167, 186; also see Charles Ball, *Fifty Years in Chains, or the Life of an American Slave* (New York: H. Dayton, 1858).

probably English. He then joined the 55th Regiment of Massachusetts Colored Volunteers and served until his exit from the Union Army in South Carolina in 1865. Marrying, he subsequently died in Brownsville, Tennessee in 1882.[163]

Muhammad 'Ali b. Said was one of the few African-born blacks in North America by the outbreak of the Civil War. His experience further diverges from the majority of those of African descent in that he did not pass through American slavery. In fact, his sojourn was experientially closer to Muslims in Bahia than those in the American South in that he also came out of a context of holy war, but in this instance it was an internecine conflict between the Sokoto Caliphate and al-Kanemi, clerical leader of Bornu. In a declamation that resonates with the scholarly invectives of the time, Muhammad 'Ali b. Said characterized Usuman dan Fodio as a "false prophet." Given his anomalous circumstances, it is noteworthy that he chose to fight against slavery, which suggests an identification with those from whom others of similar faith sought to create distance.

There are several avenues of inquiry regarding Islam that lay beyond the scope of this project but require further investigation. To begin, the research of Thompson on the relationship between African and African American art and philosophy has revealed that, at least in the area of quiltmaking, Africa Americans exhibit what are clearly Mande influences.[164] The Mande world contained many Muslims (in addition to non-Muslims), so that such evidence points to the possible continuity of an Islamically influenced cultural heritage, if not the religion itself. Such a possibility may also be supported by intriguing archaeological testimony.[165] In any event, it represents a promising area of exploration.

Second, a study of the potential impact of Islam on African American Christian practices in certain areas or communities would be instructive. On Sapelo Island, for example, the congregation always prays to the east, which is the direction in which the church is pointed.[166] Regarding personal prayer, individuals are taught to pray toward the east because the "devil is in the other corner." The deceased are also buried facing the east.[167] Such details reveal substantial influence indeed, which may even be reflected in the teachings and beliefs of the church. Islam may have experienced a nadir as a complete and coherent system of belief by the late nineteenth century, but some of its constituent elements may yet guide and sustain ostensibly Christian tradition.

---

[163] See "A Native of Bornoo," *Atlantic Monthly* (October 1867): 485–95; Austin, *African Muslims: Transatlantic Stories*, 173–85.

[164] See Robert Farris Thompson, *Flash of the Spirit* (New York: Vintage Books, 1983), 218–23.

[165] See Theresa A. Singleton, "The Archaeology of the Plantation South: A Review of Approaches and Goals," *Historical Archaeology* 24 (1990): no. 4, 75.

[166] See the Cornelia Bailey interview, July 1992.

[167] See Washington Creel's *"Peculiar People,"* 320. Washington Creel maintains that the Gullah buried their dead so that the body faced the east; the practice may not, therefore, reflect a Muslim influence but a West Central African one. Little has been written on the subject, however, and additional research is warranted.

Finally, the qualitative testimony is consistent in its view that the Muslim–non-Muslim distinction played a role in social divisions among the enslaved population.[168] Not all lighter-skinned house servants and skilled workers were the result of African–European sexual unions in North America; some were Fulbe and other Africans with "atypical" features. A process of socialization that began in West Africa was in all probability reinforced in the early American South, so much so that somatic divergence was translated into labor differentiation among Africans. Any sense of Muslim superiority carried by Africans into the American South would have met with deeply racialized ideological forces resulting in the strengthening of such notions. Such was the paradox that issued into a discernible pattern of Muslim exceptionality, a pattern that would continue to characterize Islam's reemergence among the African-descended in the twentieth century. The road to such subsequent developments, however, takes many surprising twists and turns through the terrain of the nineteenth century, beginning with the strange and murky worlds of the Melungeons and related communities.

---

[168] For an analysis of the relationship between African "difference" and social stratification in the African-derived communities of North America, see Gomez, *Exchanging Our Country Marks*.

Interlude

Into a Glass Darkly – Elisive Communities

The preceding chapter has demonstrated a significant Muslim presence in eighteenth- and nineteenth-century North America, a presence with organic, cross-generational extensions into the twentieth century and beyond. It would appear, however, that in addition to an African and African-descended Muslim community in dynamic tension and direct exchange with a larger black population, there may have also been Muslims, both North and West African, who entered the North American mainland in much smaller numbers, intermingling with Native American and European populations at various historical junctures to create transracial, polycultural formations in the hinterlands and in isolation. Given the difficulty of producing definitive statements concerning the historical processes through which such formations passed, it must be stressed here that the present chapter is speculative in the extreme; information on the subject is almost entirely derivative. However, the possibility of a Muslim isolated presence is such that it elevates the discussion to the realm of plausibility and thereby warrants some analysis, with the expectation that further research will render a much less indeterminate approximation.

To begin, there are a number of communities both along the eastern littoral and stretching into the southern and even midwestern interior that have been categorized as ethnically and culturally anomalous, referred to at times as "triracial isolates." Its people a composite of varying degrees of African, Native American, and European ancestry, the category includes such groups as the Brass Ankles of South Carolina; the Cajans and Creoles of Alabama and Mississippi; the Guineas of West Virginia, Maryland, and Ohio; the Carmel Indians of Ohio; the Brown People of Virginia; the Turks of Sumter County, South Carolina; the "Cubans" of North Carolina and Virginia; the Croatans or Lumbees of North and South Carolina and Virginia; the Red Bones of Louisiana; the Issues of Virginia; the Wesorts of southern Maryland; the Moors and Naticokes of Delaware and New Jersey; and the Jackson Whites of New Jersey and New York. Shrouded in mystery and mythology, the circumstances by which these groups came into being are poorly understood, notwithstanding a rather sizeable literature.[1]

Individual North African Muslims discussed in the previous chapter, for instance, may or may not be related to these clusters; Joseph Benenhaly, as purported progenitor of the Sumter County Turks, may be the lone clear example of the former. Of all such groups, two are of greatest interest here: the Melungeons of Tennessee, Kentucky, and Virginia, and the Ishmaelites of Kentucky, Indiana, and Illinois. While there is some evidence of an early Muslim presence among the former, there is a more discernible Islamic influence among the latter. Perhaps what is more important is that there is a linkage between the Ishmaelites and the movement of Noble Drew Ali, thereby possibly representing at least one uninterrupted chain of transmission of Islamic influence from the eighteenth century into the twentieth.

We begin with the Melungeons, who, according to one estimate, totaled over 200,000 people in 1997, "most...unaware that they carry Melungeon blood."[2] A number of factors distinguish them from other groups, beginning with their physical appearance. A late-twentieth-century description refers to them as a "dark-skinned, frustratingly European-looking people," while in an observation recorded thirty years before they were said to "have dark skin and straight hair. Yet, their skin is neither copperish nor blackish...rather, it has an olive-like darkness to it."[3] These portraitures tend to mask an expanse of attributes, as a report filed in 1946 maintained that the Melungeons "vary in color from white to black...brothers and sisters may range from the blackest Negro to a blonde, blue-eyed fair-skinned person, with all the shades in-between. Some are perfect Negroes, while others have a marked Indian look."[4]

---

[1] The literature is extensive and uneven; it includes scholarly investigations, pseudo-scientific discussions, journalistic treatments, and folklore. To begin, see William Harlen Gilbert, Jr., "Memorandum Concerning the Characteristics of the Larger Mixed-Blood Racial Islands of the Eastern United States," *Social Forces* 24 (1946): 438–47; ____, "Mixed Bloods of the Upper Monongahela Valley, West Virginia," *Journal of the Washington Academy of Sciences* 36 (1946): 1–13; Calvin Beale, "American Triracial Isolates," *Eugenics Quarterly* 4 (December 1957): 187–96; E. Franklin Frazier, *The Negro Family in the United States* (Chicago: U. of Chicago Press, 1940), 226–40; Horace M. Bond, "Two Racial Isolates of Alabama," *American Journal of Sociology* 36 (1931): 552–67; Guy B. Johnson, "Personality in a White-Indian-Negro Community," *American Sociological Review* 4 (1939): 516–23; Frank G. Speck, "The Jackson Whites," *The Southern Workman* (February 1911): 104–07; C. A. Weslager, *The Nanticoke Indians: A Refugee Tribal Group of Pennsylvania* (Harrisburg: Pennsylvania Historical and Museum Commission, 1948); James W. Hagy, "Muslim Slaves, Abducted Moors, African Jews, Misnamed Turks, and an Asiatic Greek Lady: Some Examples of Non-European Religious and Ethnic Diversity in South Carolina prior to 1861," *Carologue: A Publication of the South Carolina Historical Society* 9 (1993): 12–13, 25–27.

[2] See N. Brent Kennedy, *The Melungeons: The Resurrection of a Proud People – An Untold Story of Ethnic Cleansing in America* (Macon, GA: Mercer U. Press, 1997), xv. Kennedy's book is more a personal account of his family's history and is not a professional history. Nevertheless, he succeeds in bringing together the various theories regarding Melungeon origins and development, and he is one of the better sources on this topic.

[3] Ibid., xiv; also see Henry R. Price, *Melungeons: The Vanishing Colony of Newman's Ridge* (Cookeville, TN: n.p., 1966), 1–2.

[4] See Gilbert, "Mixed Bloods," 4.

Consistent with this variegation is another contemporary portrayal: "Some have black, kinky hair and dark oily skin; others have black, straight hair and coarse, bronze-colored skin and dark eyes. Yet another group of them are fair-complexioned with blue or grey eyes, and a fourth have an almost Oriental appearance with smooth, yellowish skin."[5] Notwithstanding the various combinations, the bottom line was that, throughout and by the end of the twentieth century, Melungeons were atypical in appearance. More than 100 years earlier, the Melungeons were essentially depicted the same way: "a colony of dark-skinned, reddish-brown complexioned people, supposed to be of Moorish descent, who affiliated with neither whites nor blacks, and who called themselves Malungeons, and claimed to be of Portuguese descent."[6] Such "difference" is strikingly consistent through two centuries, for as early as 1784 John Sevier (who organized the state of Franklin, forerunner to Tennessee) entered what are now Hancock and Rhea counties in Tennessee and came upon "'a colony of dark-skinned, reddish-brown complexioned people' supposed to be of Moorish descent, who were neither Indian nor Negro, but had fine European features and claimed to be Portuguese."[7]

The notion of being both "Moorish" and Portuguese constitutes the crux of Melungeon relevance to this study. Before these claims can be more thoroughly examined, however, additional, verifiable historical context is needed. To that end, it would appear that by the time of Sevier's 1784 encounter, the Melungeons were an established community and had been around for at least 100 years. Indeed, in a 1674 expedition through what would become Tennessee, James Needham recorded that he met with "a white people which have long beards and whiskers and weare clothing," and who "talkes he knowes not what. They have many blacks among them."[8] The unfamiliar language could very well have been Portuguese, but it is unclear who these "many blacks" could have been. In their midst was a bell tower over six feet high, around which "a great number" would gather at the morning and evening soundings, and toward which all would bow. The derivation of this practice is uncertain, but it may have some association with Catholicism.[9] By the 1750s, when English and Irish-Scots began to pour through the Valley of Virginia, they found a group of people who claimed to be of Portuguese ancestry and, to a lesser extent, descendants of Spaniards and "Turks," who were "speaking a broken form of Elizabethan English and carrying English surnames as well."[10] These people were apparently Christians, continuing to place "European cupolas over the graves of their

5 See Bonnie S. Ball, "America's Mysterious Race," *Read* 16 (May 1944): 64.
6 See William Allen Dromgoole, "The Malungeons," *The Arena* 3 (1891): 470.
7 See Louise Davis, "The Mystery of the Melungeons," *Tennessee Valley Historical Review* 1 (1972): 27.
8 See Samuel Cole Williams, *Early Travels in the Tennessee Country, 1540–1800* (Johnson City, TN: Watauga Press, 1928), 28–29. Kennedy quotes this source but leaves out the reference to "the many blacks among them" (Kennedy, *Melungeons*, 10–11).
9 See Bonnie Ball, *The Melungeons: Their Origin and Kin* (Big Stone Gap, VA: private printing, 1991), 11.
10 See Kennedy, *Melungeons*, 12.

dead." The fact that English was spoken is something of a dilemma, if one assumes that Portuguese or Spanish was the original idiom of these people; that it was broken, Elizabethan English suggests that an acculturative process was underway and strengthens the claim that these were initially non-English-speaking persons.

The census of 1795 in Tennessee lists 975 "free persons of color," which appears to have been a category that not only included the Melungeons but one that was for the most part comprised by them.[11] They would later be classified as "mulattoes," officially a fusion of African, European, and Native American elements. The evolution of Melungeon identity was not, however, simply a function of genetics; it was very much informed by the struggle for land and the racial politics of the country. Legislation would be passed to legitimize seizures of Melungeon land by anglo-settlers. In the anecdotal and highly instructive recollection of a descendant of these settlers, the latter "knowed the Melungeons, like the Cherokees, had let runaway slaves hide out amongst them. This with their dark skins was enough to make our grandpappies see pretty plain that the Melungeons was a niggerfied people. The more they looked at them good Melungeon bottom lands, the plainer they saw that nigger blood."[12] Thus, the ethnogenesis of the Melungeons was as much a category of imposition from without as it was a transformation from within.

As official mulattoes, the Melungeons would suffer the indignities of other African-descended populations. In 1834, for example, the Tennessee state constitution declared them to be "free men of color" and therefore disfranchised; the Melungeon response was to bring suit before the state supreme court, where it was decided that the Melungeons were not "Negroid" and that they could send their children to white schools.[13] Notwithstanding the legal ruling, the contest over land engendered a process by which Melungeons were forced to seek asylum in "the rocky ridges," thus producing a quality of isolation that, in addition to their physical representations, also defines their corporate identity. As a result, the Melungeons moved higher up the Appalachians, where they "have lived for generations in their secluded valleys and ridges far away from the routes of trade and the centers of population and civilization." Four of "the better-known mountain refuges" are Caney Ridge in Dickenson County, Virginia; Stone Mountain in Wise County, Virginia; the Blackwater area of Lee County, Virginia; and Newman's Ridge in Hancock County, Tennessee. They have also been concentrated in Hawkins and Rhea counties of Tennessee;

[11] See Davis, "Mystery of the Melungeons," 28–29; Will T. Hale and Dixon L. Merritt, *A History of Tennessee and Tennesseans*, 2 vols. (Chicago: Lewis Publishing, 1913), vol. 1, 180. Such a large population by 1795 tends to rule out the theory that Vardy Collins and Buck Gibson were the founding fathers of the Melungeons some time before 1797. For this view, see William Allen Dromgoole, "The Malungeon Tree and Its Four Branches," *The Arena* 3 (1891): 745–51.

[12] See "Melungeon Tales," in James E. Aswell, Julia Willhoit, and Jennette Edrrson eds., *God Bless the Devil! Liar's Bench Tales* (Knoxville: U. of Tennessee Press, 1985), 210.

[13] See Davis, "Mystery of the Melungeons," 22.

Ashe, Yancy, Surry, and Alleghany counties of North Carolina; and Scott and Lee counties of Virginia.[14]

In their navigation of the North American racial terrain, the Melungeons found it in their interest to eschew the term *Melungeon* while wholeheartedly and consistently embracing the appellation *Portuguese*, or more precisely "Portyghee." This is not simply a question of contrivance but rather a cornerstone of long-held tradition. As such, the Melungeons claim descent from those Portuguese "who had either been shipwrecked or otherwise abandoned on the Atlantic coast. It is important to note that, regardless of where the individual pockets of these people dwelled, the same Portuguese (and occasionally Turkish) origin was consistently offered to explain their existence."[15] The disadvantages of an African heritage in a racialized and slaveholding society resulted in assertions of racial purity as early as the late eighteenth century, when Melungeons insisted they were "of Moorish descent being neither Indian nor Negro but having fine European features and claiming to be Portuguese."[16] In response, neighbors and observers noted the Portuguese claim, but in practice used other terms for the claimants, such as *Blackwaters, Ridgemanites,* and *Ramps,* in addition to *Melungeons.*[17]

The rejection of the name *Melungeon* by those it sought to signify is no doubt the consequence of its identification with Africans and their descendants. The association is evident in the formulaic expression of one source, who stated that Melungeons "resent being called 'Melungeon' or 'Ramp' or 'Negro.'"[18] Put in another way, "they especially resent the terms 'Guinea' or 'Guinea Nigger,' which are most generally applied to them by their white neighbors."[19] This resentment has been long-standing, going back at least to the late nineteenth century, when research found that "the pure Melungeons, that is the old men and women, have no toleration for the negro, and nothing insults them so much as a suggestion of negro blood. Many pathetic stories are told of their battle against the black race, which they regard as the cause of their downfall."[20] Clearly, slavery and Jim Crow were of such force as to stimulate an attempt to reverse the conditions of 1674, when blacks were conspicuous, and to deny them a hereditary role in the community. While the question of Native American ancestry is resolved through grudging admission, the connection to Africa is another matter: "Although many of the Melungeons claim a Portuguese ancestry and some admit having Indian blood in their veins they do not like to be called Melungeons or considered as peculiar people.... They

---

[14] See Paul D. Converse, "The Melungeons," *Southern Collegian* (*Washington and Lee University*) 45 (December 1912): 59–69; Kennedy, *Melungeons,* 9, 16.

[15] See Kennedy, *Melungeons,* 9–10.

[16] See Phyllis Cox Barr, "The Melungeons of Newman's Ridge," (M.A. thesis, East Tennessee State U., 1965), 2.

[17] See Davis, "Mystery of the Melungeons," 22–23; Dromgoole, "Malungeons," 473.

[18] See Cox Barr, "Melungeons of Newman's Ridge," 13.

[19] See Gilbert, "Mixed Bloods," 1.

[20] See Dromgoole, "Malungeons," 474–75.

are very sensitive and become angry if accused of having negro blood in their veins."[21] This disclaimer of African ancestry probably explains the derivation of the term *Melungeon* itself. Possibly derived from the French *mélange*, it is more likely from the African-Portuguese (or creolized Portuguese) word *mulango* or *melungo*, which appears to mean "shipmate" or "companion" and points to an African-related origin of the Melungeons, a problem rectified by an insistent oral revisionism.[22] Whatever its original meaning, it soon came to be closely associated with black ancestry; when asked the definition of a Melungeon, a Tennessee Senator replied, "A Portuguese nigger."[23]

Such vigorous insistence on African ancestry, together with an equally vociferous denial, has the effect of attracting even closer scrutiny to the contrasting claims and in turn requires some examination of Melungeon beginnings. It is here, at the site of protestations of racial "purity" and their refutations, that the question of "origins" unavoidably emerges, and it is here that the postulate of an early association with Islam can be offered. Theories seeking to explain Melungeon origins range from the possible to the ridiculous, and they are premised upon information found in genres as disparate as local folklore and detached, independently derived contemporary accounts. Speculation abounds, clarity is distorted, and plausibility a verdict reached by means of a process of an alchemy unique to the dimly lit world of the undocumented, transracial project.

There are a number of competing, yet conceivably complementary, explanations of Melungeon beginnings. The first is that they simply represent instances of small-scale, backwoods fusions of Native American, African, and European elements of no particular, far-reaching significance. Such interactions must have occurred, but the problem with this singular explanation is that it fails to account for the persistence of an insistent Portuguese folkloric tradition, indirectly suggested as early as 1674. A second theory is even less useful in that it maintains the Melungeons are "pure-blooded Carthaginians," or "Phoenicians who after Carthage was conquered by the Romans and became a Roman province, immigrated across the Straits of Gilbrater [sic] and settled in Portugal." The Phoenician claim may have come out of a need to establish an ancient pedigree in the face of southern charges of "mongrelization"; of greater interest is the routing of these Phoenicians through Portugal (and in some accounts Morocco), where they lived for centuries before relocating to the North American Carolinas prior to the American War of Independence.[24]

A third conjecture is that the Melungeons are the descendants of a De Soto expedition that passed through southwestern Virginia. Africans participated in

[21] See Converse, "Melungeons," 63.

[22] See Kennedy, *Melungeons*, xviii; Jean Patterson Bible, *Melungeons Yesterday and Today* (Rogersville, TN: n.p., 1975), 11–12. See also T. B. Irving, "King Zumbi and the Malê Movement," *The American Journal of Islamic Social Sciences* 9 (1992): 397–409, for a brief discussion of the term *mulango* (p. 399).

[23] See Bible, *Melungeons Yesterday and Today*, 13–14;

[24] See Ball, "America's Mysterious Race," 65–66; Cox Barr, "Melungeon's of Newman's Ridge," 4.

De Soto's 1539 expedition through the southeast, including "sub-Saharan and Moorish slaves" who absconded and joined Native American communities.[25] It can be seen as an elaboration of the second theory, but it is clearly related in theme to a fourth notion; namely, that the Melungeons are the offspring of the Santa Elena colony, near what is now Beaufort, South Carolina.[26] As the story goes, in 1566 an allegedly Spanish captain, Juan Pardo, who signed his name "João" and was therefore probably Portuguese, brought approximately 200 soldiers to Santa Elena from the Galician mountains of Spain and Portugal. They were subsequently placed in four or five forts "in northern Georgia, western North Carolina, eastern Tennessee, or a combination thereof, depending on the interpretations of various scholars studying the question."[27] Having left for Spain, Pardo returned two and one-half years later with the soldiers' spouses and children. These military families were then dispersed "in fortifications throughout the hinterland" to facilitate linkages with Santa Elena. However, "they never returned to Santa Elena proper," and there is evidence that "at least some of these settlers were still holding the forts nearby some twenty years later," when in 1587 Santa Elena was destroyed by the remaining settlers under twin pressures from the British and Native Americans. Those who burned the settlement sailed on to St. Augustine, but it is possible that others fled into the interior; those assigned to the outlying fortifications "were certainly left behind." Thus, this is one conceivable source of Melungeon identity.[28]

Of course, these early "Spaniards" and "Portuguese," as Chapter 1 has already indicated, were a hodgepodge of Iberians, Arabo-Berbers, and West Africans. As Braudel mentioned, "in the sixteenth century, Seville and the Andalusian hinterland, still half-Moslem and hardly half-Christian, were engaged in sending their men to settle whole areas of Spanish America."[29] Iberia was not alone in the practice, as Hourani has observed that "European states equally engaged in privateering and used captured Algerians as galley slaves."[30] That at least some of these individuals were Africans and Muslim is fairly obvious; sixteenth-century Portugal "employed large numbers of Muslim/Moorish laborers who called themselves 'mulangos.' These were often West Africans but also Berbers/Moors captured during battle in the Mediterranean."[31] Here, then, is some historical basis for the folkloric equation

---

[25] Ibid. Also see Jane Landers, *Black Society in Spanish Florida* (Urbana and Chicago: U. of Illinois Press, 1999), 13–14.

[26] See Kennedy, *Melungeons*, 103–19.

[27] Ibid., 114, from J. G. Hollingsworth, *History of Surry County, or Annals of Northwest North Carolina* (private printing, 1935), 5, 12.

[28] See Kennedy, *Melungeons*, 117; Daniel J. Weber, *Spanish Frontier in North America* (New Haven, CT: Yale U. Press, 1992), 71–73.

[29] See Fernand Braudel, *The Mediterranean and the Mediterranean World in the Age of Philip II* (New York: Harper & Row, 1972), vol. 1, 84.

[30] See Albert Hourani, *A History of the Arab People* (New York: Warner Books, 1991), 229.

[31] See Kennedy, *Melungeons*, 116.

of "Portuguese" and "Moorish" in Melungeon ancestry. That is, in the collective memory of the Melungeons, there is a seamless, unhyphenated Moorish–Portuguese origin. In the struggle against racialism in the United States, however, a kind of *embraquecimento* occurred, a form of sanitizing that sought to void the African component.

A fifth theory of origin, however, returns the African Muslim to the discursive center. Unfortunately it revolves around the much discussed Lost Colony of Roanoke, but the circumstances are such that it cannot be completely dismissed out of hand. Sailing from England to Santo Domingo and Cartagena with "parts of boats and small ships," Francis Drake busied himself with "collecting men – galley slaves (mainly Moors, but including some Europeans), a few soldiers (again mainly Moors), negro domestic slaves . . . and a substantial number of South American Indians (about 300, including women)."[32] In June of 1586, one year before the torching of Santa Elena, bad weather diverted Drake from his intended destination of Cuba to Roanoke with his assemblage of captives, "as many as five hundred Moors, Turks, South American Indians of both sexes, Spanish and Portuguese soldiers, and a small number of Negro slaves during his South American expedition."[33] The Moors and Turks were said to be "practicing Muslims."

The English soldiers at Roanoke implored Drake to take them back to England; to make room, it is probable that Drake left many captives behind; as many as 300 are unaccounted for in the return to England. It is likely that most were Native Americans, as 100 former galley slaves were sent back to the "Turkish dominions" following their arrival in England and subsequent negotiations. It is unlikely, however, that all of these "practicing Muslims" were so removed. Of course, when Walter Raleigh returned to the island a short time later, the colony was unoccupied. Among other possibilities is that the captives took advantage of a window of opportunity and made for the interior. Kupperman has written this:

> The records are equally silent on their fate. . . . If they succeeded in melting into the Indian population, then they began a tradition that was to have a long history in that part of America. The Algonquians of North America's east coast . . . adopted into their tribes and clans anyone who became culturally one of them, and they did so on terms of equality. It is entirely possible that the people left by Drake lived on and produced descendants who would have been Indians in every sense meaningful to them.[34]

The foregoing discussion by no means establishes the origins of the Melungeons at Roanoke or Santa Elena; it does establish a Muslim presence in North America that is intimately associated with the Portuguese. In this way,

---

[32] See Daniel Beers Quinn, *The Roanoke Voyages: 1584–1590* (London: Hakluyt Society, 1952), ser. 2, no. 104, 251–52.

[33] See Kennedy, *Melungeons*, 120–24.

[34] See Karen Kupperman, *Roanoke: The Abandoned Colony* (Totowa, NJ: Rowman and Allanheld, 1984), 88–92. The Lumbees of North Carolina, for example, claim descent from the Roanoke colonists (Kupperman, 141).

settlements such as Santa Elena may have contributed some or none of the elements that would go into the Melungeon makeup, but they are useful in demonstrating that Spanish and Portuguese forces were operating in parts of what would become the American South, that these forces were very much fortified with Muslim labor and numbers, and that these individuals conceivably passed something of their genes and culture onto progeny who survived. While Melungeons have a number of varying traditions, they all posit Portuguese and Moors as ancestors. The traditions do not specify a particular place of origin (they leave that to the imagination of professional historians), but rather (correctly) point to the vicissitudes of seafaring as source: "The Melungeons have a tradition," according to an early-twentieth-century account, "of a Portuguese ship and a mutiny, with the successful mutineer beaching the vessel on the North Carolina coast, then their retreat towards the mountains."[35] A slightly different version published in 1966 maintains that "a band of shipwrecked Portuguese sailors wandered from the North Carolina coast into the mountains of East Tennessee, intermarried with the Cherokee Indians and lived undisturbed in the tribal fashion until white settlers moved westward."[36] A less sanitized account supports the notion of conflict at sea; that the mutineers rose up against "the captain and his friends," if bearing any relation to historical reality, would suggest that enslaved Muslims and ladinos would have been among the rebels. According to this narrative, the following can be said of the ancestors of the Melungeons:

[They came] from Portugal a long time ago and sailed in a big ship across the wild seas till they reached this country. Then some sort of a hardness sprung up betwixt the captain and the sailormen and they had a bloody scrap and the sailormen won. Soon as they'd hung the captain and his friends, the sailormen set the ship afire and went ashore and hid out in the woods. By and by they found a tribe of Injuns and made off with the women. Then they wandered and they roamed. Where all they went there's no telling. Some time or other they crossed over the high mountains into Tennessee, and set down to stay hereabouts and have been here ever since.[37]

Whatever the precise mechanisms, the Melungeons have preserved an identity that insists on Portuguese ancestry, an ancestry, given the times, that would have required an adjoining Muslim presence. According to the interpretation of one genetic study, there is "an undeniable link between the Melungeon people and the Mediterranean. A 1990 re-analysis of blood samples taken in 1969 from 177 Melungeon descendants concludes that the 'results are consistent with the Melungeon tradition that they are Portuguese.'"[38] Bonnie Ball put it succinctly in 1944: "It is an interesting fact that the 'Moors' of the 'State of Franklin'

---

[35] See Hale and Merritt, *History of Tennessee and Tennesseans*, 184.
[36] See Price, *Melungeons*, 4.
[37] See "Old Horny's Own," in Aswell et al., *God Bless the Devil!*, 208.
[38] See Kennedy, *Melungeons*, 147; James L. Guthrie, "Melungeons: Comparisons of Gene Distributions to Those of Worldwide Populations," *Tennessee Anthropologist* 15/1 (Spring 1990).

called themselves Portuguese; that the Carolina settlers supposedly came from Portugal; that the melungeons still think of themselves today as Portuguese."[39]

There is no evidence that Islam was specifically preserved among the Melungeons for any appreciable length of time, to the extent that it was ever present. By the late nineteenth century they were mostly Baptists, but the affiliation was probably nominal in that by the mid-twentieth century it was observed that "they have no real churches of their own, but like to attend such festivals as basket lunches, and similar church gatherings." By then Melungeons were members of Methodist, Presbyterian, and "Holiness" denominations, but collectively they were still not considered "a church-going people."[40] It may be that this subdued enthusiasm for Christianity reflected an earlier Muslim influence, but indirection is not the only evidence of an Islamic legacy, as will be demonstrated with the potentially related Ishmaelites.

There are parallel claims to Roanoke origins by similar groups, such as the mixed-race Lumbee or Croatan Indians of the Carolinas, who in turn are linked to the Brass Ankles of South Carolina.[41] There are also those who (inconsistently) maintain a sense of distant relationship with the Melungeons and who also make some claim to Portuguese ancestry. The Guineas of West Virginia are held by some to be Melungeons who migrated out of central Virginia and North Carolina, and one of the family names associated with the Guineas is *Male* or *Mayle* (and it is tempting to speculate on the possible relationship to the term *malê* as used in Brazil and elsewhere in Latin America), who lead Guinea families in claiming a "tradition of Portuguese intermarriage."[42] There is disagreement over the derivation of the term *Guinea*, with some arguing that it became a descriptor for Melungeons counterfeiting eighteenth-century English coins of the same name. However, there is the tradition that the Guineas descend from an English nobleman and a West African woman who produced "a large family of crossbreeds" in West Africa, some of whom later came to North America.[43] There are variations on this theme that substitute British, French, or Dutch Guiana for West African territories and intersperse Native American blood with African, but such accounts can all be read as an attempt to describe a process whereby Europeans and Africans created mixed-race communities throughout the Atlantic world.[44] After all, it is not inconceivable that Portuguese-speaking "creoles" in West Africa found their way to North America in the seventeenth and eighteenth centuries.

It is apparent from the case of the Melungeons that the term *Moor* was related to both dark skin and alleged Iberian ties. The use of the term to describe the

---

[39] See Ball, "America's Mysterious Race," 66.

[40] See Dromgoole, "The Malungeons," 475; Ball, "America's Mysterious Race," 67; Cox Barr, "The Melungeons of Newman's Ridge," 30; Davis, "Mystery of the Melungeons," 28–29.

[41] See Adolph L. Dial and David K. Eliades, *The Only Land I Know: A History of the Lumbee Indians* (Syracuse, NY: Syracuse U. Press, 1996), 1–14; Kennedy, *Melungeons*, 48–50, 53.

[42] See Kennedy, *Melungeons*, 34–35.

[43] See Gilbert, "Mixed Bloods of the Upper Monongahela Valley," 1–2.

[44] See Ira Berlin's *Many Thousands Gone: The First Two Centuries of Slavery in North America* (Cambridge, MA: Harvard U. Press, 1998) for a discussion of such phenomena.

Nanticoke Indians and the Cheswold Moors of Delaware also reflects a reaction to physical appearance, but it alternates between the possibility of an African or a Spanish derivation. The Nanticokes are said to have originated in Maryland and subsequently spread to Pennsylvania, Ohio, Indiana, Kansas, Oklahoma, and Ontario, but by 1797 it was said that "of all the northern Indian tribes, the Nantocooks are the darkest as to color."[45] An 1899 publication citing an old legend concerning the Moors of Kent County, Delaware, an apparent relation of the Nanticokes, states that they "are the offspring of Moors shipwrecked near Lewes; a more romantic version gives them only one Moorish progenitor – a captive prince who escaped from his floating prison and found wife and home among the half-Indian population alongshore."[46] In testimony given before the Civil War, an account of Nanticoke origins coincides with the "romantic" story of the Moors. Levin Sockum was accused of selling ammunition to Isaiah Harmon, a Nanticoke, and thereby violating Delaware law prohibiting such a sale to "any negro or mulatto." Eighty-seven-year-old Lydia Clark, also a Nanticoke, was brought in to establish Harmon's pedigree. According to her 1855 statement, "a beautiful lady of Irish birth named Regua" traveled to the site of a shipwreck at Lewes Creek to purchase a slave. "She selected a tall, muscular young fellow of dark gingerbread color who claimed to be a prince or chief of one of the Congo River tribes sold into slavery. Returning to Angola Neck, the two soon married and produced numerous offspring.[47] Clark's version is the most popular, and it could conceivably support Portuguese but not Muslim influence (as the Portuguese constituted a significant force in West Central Africa since the end of the fifteenth century, whereas Islam did not). Other versions give varying identities to the two lovers: the woman is at times a princess, at times Spanish. The gentleman in some accounts is "a handsome, dark-skinned slave who speaks the Castilian tongue." In yet another narrative, a woman purchased a number of slaves to replace those killed by a plague. Arriving at Lewes, "she was impressed by a coterie of seven handsome men and seven beautiful women who stood apart from the other slaves and spoke a different language. Their skins were dark, but their hair was straight and their features as regular as those of white persons. She recognized that they were Moors – not Negroes – and bought the seven couples and took them home."[48] These accounts, while imaginative, may embellish a process whereby certain African groups, already distinguishable from others, formed bonds with Native American and European elements to create novel communities. There are other stories that mention shipwrecked Spanish and Moorish pirates before

---

45 See Clinton Alfred Weslager, *The Nanticoke Indians: Past and Present* (Newark: U. of Delaware Press, 1983), 44.
46 See William Henry Babcock, "The Nanticoke Indians of Indian River, Delaware," *American Anthropologist* 1 (1899): 277–82.
47 See Weslager, *The Nanticoke Indians: Past and Present*, 209–12, 226–37. Apparently Angola Neck was adopted from the claim that many Angolans were imported into the Delaware Peninsula. See Clinton Alfred Weslager, *Delaware's Forgotten Folk: The Story of the Moors and Nanticokes* (Philadelphia: University of P. Press, 1943), 3–4.
48 See Weslager, *Delaware's Forgotten Folk*, 27–39.

America's War of Independence, but for many the Lewes Creek reference is repeated and links the Nanticokes and the Moors to each other and to an Old World location. In all of these versions, however, the suggestion of an Iberian connection never approaches the intensity and conviction of the Melungeon insistence on a Portuguese identity, and there is little sense of an Islamic heritage.

* * *

It is with the Ishmaelites of Kentucky, Indiana, and Illinois, however, that the Islamic dimension is reified. A relatively obscure group concerning whom the scholarship is practically limited to a single source, the Ishmaelite population is estimated to have been around 10,000 at the end of the nineteenth century.[49] Conforming to the triracial model of descent from African, Native American, and "poor white" sources, the Ishmaelites first received attention as an "organized tribe" between 1785 and 1790 in Noble County, Kentucky (now Bourbon County), where they lived in the hills or "refuse land." Their origins are inexact, but they are said to have been fugitives from slavery and the "Indian Wars" from various points in Tennessee, the Carolinas, Virginia, and Maryland, all seeking asylum and converging in Kentucky.[50] Such an explanation suggests that they did not represent splintering branches of previously formed transracial groups in the Southeast (such as the Melungeons), but that the community as a transracial, transcultural project developed in Kentucky itself.

The Ishmaelites are said to have been founded by Ben and Jennie Ishmael, the latter described as "the first queen" and "a warrioress of mighty physique." As legend has it, the couple departed from the community in Kentucky and set out "in the direction of the setting sun" at advanced ages, an apparent euphemism for their demise. It is calculated that some time between 1802 and 1810, their eldest son John led the community across the Ohio River and continued to travel until they settled in "Indian territory" near what is now Indianapolis, a response to the fact that Kentucky had become a slave state. From that time until around 1905, the Ishmaelites engaged in a collective behavior out of the ordinary for most in the Northwest Territory: They followed an annual, triangular pattern of migration from Indianapolis northwest to the Kankakee River (Illinois), then south to the area near contemporary Champaign–Urbana, Illinois, and back to Indianapolis. The fixed migration began every spring, during which whole families and their possessions formed caravans, and it was during one of these movements that the patriarch John Ishmael died (ca. 1846). Speculation over the source of this behavior cites the Shawnees as a possibility, along with the Tinkers (a "gypsy-like" combination of Welsh, Irish, and Scottish elements) and even the Fulbe of West Africa.[51] However, it is also possible that the Ishmaelites had

[49] See Hugo P. Leaming, "The Ben Ishmael Tribe: A Fugitive 'Nation' of the Old Northwest," in Melvin G. Holli and Peter d'A. Jones, eds., *The Ethnic Frontier: Essays in the History of Group Survival in Chicago and the Midwest* (Grand Rapids, MI: Eerdmans Publishing, 1977), 97–141.

[50] Ibid., 98–99.

[51] Ibid., 101–02, 105–06.

reached the decision to remain highly mobile in the face of slavery's continuing threat, along with the ongoing displacement of indigenous persons.

In addition to perennial peregrinations, the Ishmaelites were also unique in that they chose to participate in alternative forms of economy. Originally they hunted, trapped, and farmed gardens, but as white settlement encroached and unclaimed land diminished, the Ishmaelite refusal to enter into wage-labor contracts, along with their rejection of the concept of individually owned land, forced them into such odd jobs as caring for horses, repairing umbrellas, poisoning watchdogs, floating river ice to icehouse chutes, home laundering, and "petty pilfering." Toward the latter part of the nineteenth century, the Ishmaelites became principally known as beggars and scavengers, picking up and disposing garbage, ashes, and scrap for a fee.[52] That the fortunes of the Ishmaelites had rapidly fallen is also indicated by their institutionalization in mental health wards. By the late nineteenth century, "three-quarters of the patients at Indianapolis City Hospital were from the Tribe of Ishmael," a figure that does not include surgical and "acute" cases, nor those from outside the town.[53] This general decline in health is reflected in observations regarding Ishmaelite children: "The number of illegitimacies is very great. The Board of Health reports that an estimate of still-born children found in sinks, etc., would be not less than six per week. Deaths are frequent, and chiefly among children. The suffering of the children must be great."[54]

The Ishmaelites had become the quintessential outsiders in Indianapolis, and a series of measures were taken to enforce their conformity. For example, between the 1840s and the 1880s, local governments passed poor laws that provided for the arrest of "permanent paupers" and their conversion into "bound servants" for employers. Ishmaelite children were taken from their families; adults were frequently incarcerated for "pauperism (chronic unemployment), vagrancy, begging, prostitution, and petty theft." The period between 1880 and 1907 saw a novel phase in the war against the Ishmaelites. Using the new science of eugenics, the Reverend Oscar C. M'Culloch of the Indianapolis Congregational Church led a campaign to end all public and private assistance to the Ishmaelites, advocating their placement in asylums and prisons while legally removing their children.[55] Evoking the image of the "Sacculina," a parasitic crustacean that attaches itself to the hermit crab and "sucks [its] living tissues," M'Culloch went on to more fully express his abhorrence of the original Ishmael family and their descendants:

Since 1840, this family has had a pauper record. They have been in the almshouse, the House of Refuge, the Women's Reformatory, the penitentiaries, and have received

[52] Ibid., 102–05.
[53] Ibid., 102. Data are from Oscar C. M'Culloch, "The Tribe of Ishmael: A Study on Social Degradation," in *Proceedings of the National Conference of Charities and Correction at the Fifteenth Annual Session Held in Buffalo, N.Y., July 5–11, 1888* (Boston: Ellis Press, 1888), 154–59.
[54] See M'Culloch, "Tribe of Ishmael," 156–57.
[55] See Leaming, "Ben Ishmael Tribe," 123–33.

continuous aid from the township. They are intermarried with the other members of this group, as you may see by the marriage lines, and with two hundred and fifty other families. In this family history are murders, a large number of illegitimacies and of prostitutes. They are generally diseased. The children die young. They live by petty stealing, begging, ash-gathering. . . . They have been known to live in hollow trees on the river-bottoms or in empty houses. Strangely enough, they are not intemperate.[56]

Reference to Ishmaelite intemperance will be discussed shortly. At this juncture it is important to observe that M'Culloch's "crusade" was very successful, for within several years of its beginning the annual migrations has ceased, "tribal structure was dissolved, and the Ishmaelites dispersed from their countryside, scattering beyond the reach of regional authorities. Few again admitted to the tribal name they had so proudly borne."[57] Compulsory sterilization, enacted as law in Indiana in 1907 as an option for "confirmed criminals, idiots, rapists, and imbeciles," was also a means of eliminating the Ishmaelite problem. The response of those who still remained in Indiana was to leave the state.

It would appear that the plight of the Ishmaelites was even worse than that of the Melungeons, as they were the very dregs of society, impoverished and marginalized. They also differed from the Melungeons in that the latter developed quite a reputation for producing moonshine and consuming all forms of alcohol, whereas the Ishamelites were teetotalers in the strictest sense. The rationale for their abstention is not obvious, but it may owe something to an Islamic heritage. Indeed, there are several curious factors that point in a similar direction. To begin, the annual migratory route of the Ishmaelites was marked by towns near each end of the triangular route that carried Islamic names: at the northern end was Morocco, Indiana; Mahomet, Illinois was at the southern end; and Mecca, Indiana lay on the path back to Indianapolis.[58] Of course, there are myriad U.S. towns with such names, each adopted for a variety a reasons having little or nothing to do with Islam. In the case of Mahomet, Illinois, however, a historical geography maintains that its founders were of "mixed American Southern extraction," which may well be a description of the Ishmaelites.[59] However, even if Mahomet, or Morocco or Mecca, were not founded by the Ishmaelites, these towns may have been chosen by the Ishmaelites as poles around which their migrations were organized because the names held special significance.

A second factor, just as enigmatic and arguably fragile as the Ishmaelite relationship to certain towns, concerns family names in Mahomet. According to

---

[56] See M'Culloch, "Tribe of Ishmael," 154–55.

[57] See Leaming, "Ben Ishmael Tribe," 130.

[58] Ibid., 137–38.

[59] Ibid., 139; from J. S. Lothrop, *Champaign County Directory, 1870–71* (Chicago: 1871), 232–315. Amir Nashid Ali Muhammad, *Muslims in America: Seven Centuries of History, 1312–2000: Collections and Stories of American Muslims* (Beltsville, MD: Amana, 2001; orig. pub. 1998), says that Mecca, Indiana was founded by Arabs, according to local lore (46–47).

one analysis, some 10 percent of these names as recorded in 1870 were uncommon, and they include the following[60]:

Aimen	Ham	Nebeker
Babb	Hamella	Omey
Barlain	Hayar	Osman
Basore	Hissany	Pankar
Bensyl	Kasheur	Pusha
Booromer	Lahmon	Sherfy
Chadden	Lumen	Swarty
Dalama	Maben	Tapop
Fardy	Manser	Tobaka
Fayant	Mardin	Tomany
Gamel	Mathena	Turk

While unusual for an Indiana context, some of these names possess morphological resonance with Muslim appellations. Some of the correspondences are as follows: Aimen–Amin; Babb–Bab ("door"); Fardy–Fard; Gamel–Gamal; Hissany–Hassan; Manser–Mansur; Nebeker–Abu Bakr; Omey–Umar; Osman–Usuman or Uthman; Sherfy–Sharif; Tomany–Tumane (found in Senegambia); and, of course, Turk. The presence of immigrants from the central Islamic lands and eastern Europe explains many if not most of these names, but not all, as is clear from the example of Sambo Swift, to be discussed presently.[61]

Yet a third consideration is the kind of religion practiced by the Ishmaelites. While the Melungeons were nominally Christian and held church memberships (but did not normally attend services), none of the Ishmaelites were known to belong to any mainline denomination after a brief flirtation with Methodism in the 1830s. The Ishmaelites believed in omens and supernatural signs, and claimed to see "ghosts, demons, witches, 'sperrets' and all the rest of the uncanny and intangible brood that troop about."[62] However, they did not believe in life after death, a concept incompatible with notions of ghosts and spirits unless strictly limited to physical resurrection. Such ideas, together with the fact that the Ishmaelites had among their own spiritual leaders women who also headed clans and supraclans, points to the conclusion that if the Ishmaelites practiced Christianity at all, it was of such variation that it would have been unacceptable to European orthodoxy.

The final bit of evidence suggesting an Islamic heritage for the Ishmaelites, and perhaps the most important, concerns their relationship with the movement of Noble Drew Ali. Noble Drew, the subject of the following chapter, is quoted as having said that the National Temple of his Moorish Science movement should move from New Jersey to the Midwest "because Islam is closer to the

---

[60] See Leaming, "Ben Ishmael Tribe," 139; from Lothrop, *Champaign County Directory*, 232–315.

[61] Amir Muhammad, *Muslims in America*, 46–47, cautions that many had immigrated from lands of the old Ottoman Empire, contradicting Leaming's position.

[62] See Leaming, "Ben Ishmael Tribe," 108–10.

latter region."[63] Was the statement referring to the Ishmaelites? Possibly, but the Ishmaelites were not the only people of African descent in the area with an Islamic connection. At least one other, Sambo Swift, had lived there. Born in 1811, he had been enslaved in Darien, Georgia, right in the epicenter of the Muslim world in coastal Georgia, and was a contemporary of people such as Bilali and Salih Bilali. At some point he moved to Mecca, Indiana, where he is buried, his Muslim grave facing the northeast, his tombstone featuring the symbol of *tawḥīd*, the oneness of God.[64] What drew Sambo to Mecca, Indiana of all places? What was his relationship to the Ishmaelites? Whatever the precise answers, the fact that in the late nineteenth century a Muslim with a clear West African cultural heritage was living in the American Midwest, alongside a group with its own unique relationship to Islam, demonstrates that Islam was not confined either spatially or temporally. In fact, members of the Ishmaelite diaspora from Indiana, arriving in places such as Detroit, encountered the Moorish Science movement and joined. More research is required, but an interview with a black wholesale grocer from Chicago who was a member of Moorish Science underscores the connection. When he joined Moorish Science in 1930, Mr. William Prothro Bey did the following:

[He met] a Mrs. Gallivant, who had joined Moorish Science at Detroit around 1920, when it was first introduced to the Midwest. She had come from downstate Indiana or Illinois and called herself an Ishmaelite. She spoke of the Tribe of Ishmael as a people who had dwelled downstate, and who after moving north were among the first to assist in the establishment of Moorish Science in the Midwest.[65]

This is really an incredible tidbit of information, and it forms one link between twentieth-century Islam among North American blacks and a complicated, multifaceted African Muslim ancestry. In reading the next chapter, one should bear in mind that some percentage of Noble Drew Ali's adherents in the Midwest were recruited from the Ishmaelites, presumably as a result of some resonance between Noble Drew Ali's teachings and the latter's own beliefs and lived experience.

Though little can be proven, it is important to present the possibility that, together with the Melungeons, Nanticokes, Moors, and other transracial communities, the Ishmaelites may very well represent the experience of the archetypal "other" in North America with respect to race and religion, who often underwent cultural transmogrification to survive. Even so, the continuation and progression of Islam did not come to a halt in the United States; rather, the Islamic heritage was in fact strengthened as a result of an ideological restructuring. Much of this was through the pioneering efforts of Noble Drew Ali, and it is to his legacy and the circumstances surrounding his movement that we now turn.

---

[63] Ibid., 137.
[64] See Amir Muhammad, *Muslims in America*, 46–48. According to Muhammad, Sambo had three children: Abrahim (?), Mollie, and Alonzo.
[65] See Leaming, "Ben Ishmael Tribe," 134–35.

PART TWO

6

Breaking Away

Noble Drew Ali and the Foundations of Contemporary Islam in African America

In addition to religious practice and racial composition, Ishmaelite distinctiveness was marked by the fact that their gradual south-to-north trek was stimulated by interests other than industrialization and wage labor. By the early twentieth century, they constituted a collective anachronism, rapidly losing ground to an enveloping urbanization, a people literally and figuratively out of place and time. In contrast, the leader of the successor movement to the Ishmaelites, inheriting the mantle of "Islamism" from them and in fact providing asylum for the ragtag remnant of Ishmaelite survivors in the early twentieth century, was a man initially drawn to the North for economic reasons, and as such served as forerunner to a subsequent, massive relocation of black folk from the South. Noble Drew Ali, as he came to be known, would negotiate a complex set of circumstances in the North, resulting in the creation of a novel ideology and worldview, a metaphysical enunciation that would serve as the essential point of connection between what had been and what was going to be. For, in the final analysis, Noble Drew Ali is necessarily the bridge over which the Muslim legacies of the eighteenth and nineteenth centuries crossed over into the Muslim communities of the twentieth and twenty-first. As his efforts and formulations serve as the foundation for the myriad expressions of Islam among contemporary African Americans, he must be acknowledged as the master builder, a turn of phrase consistent with the multiple interpretive dimensions of such a movement, as will be demonstrated shortly.

Tradition maintains that Noble Drew Ali was born Timothy Drew, January 8, 1886 in rural Simpsonbuck County, North Carolina.[1] As this county did not and does not exist, one can only speculate about the circumstances of his birth, and that he may have come from North Carolina's eastern counties (where

---

[1] See Adib Rashad (James Miller), *Elijah Muhammad and the Ideological Foundations of the Nation of Islam* (Hampton, VA: United Brothers and United Sisters Communications Systems, 1994), 53–54; Peter Lamborn Wilson, *Sacred Drift: Essays on the Margins of Islam* (San Francisco: City Lights Books, 1993), 15–16.

families with the last name *Drew* were concentrated in 1900).[2] Consistent with his shrouded origins, few of the details concerning Noble Drew's childhood and early development are verifiable. That need not deter us here, as our major objective is to examine the ruminations and distillations of Noble Drew Ali, to engage ideas associated with him in such a manner as to qualify the discourse as intellectual history, and to undergo an examination of psychosocial interiority in a search for the modern underpinnings of an orientation toward Islam unique to what has become the African American community. Of course, the contextualization of these concepts will require an adventure through the circumvolutions of social history, but the point is that the beliefs and articulations of Noble Drew Ali deserve, indeed, demand, a level of scrutiny far more serious than has heretofore been provided. Indeed, several early-twentieth-century African American religious communities have attracted the attention of sober scholarship, but so much more remains to be done: To enter the turn-of-the-century black religious world is to enter a realm of kaleidoscopic and seemingly endless variation. Restricting the analysis to Islam allows for a more finite field of possibilities, but even then the possibilities can be surprising with respect to the range of permutations and their impact upon other, arguably more significant, social experiments. Such is the case with Noble Drew Ali, whose contributions to the larger African American social project (or set of projects) have been eclipsed in the literature by the attention given to such luminaries as Marcus Garvey. However, notwithstanding Garvey's enormous significance, there is no embellishment in the assertion that Noble Drew Ali, whose activities actually antedate those of Marcus Garvey in the United States, represents the verifiable beginning of a qualitatively different trajectory in the history of modern, religiously based African American social movements. His ideas reflect the quintessential convergence of Islam, Islamism, Freemasonry, New Thought, Rosicrucianism, anticolonialism in its critique of European imperialism, and nationalism in the rejection of white American racism. Having once formed a coherent stream, subsequent rivulets flowing from the conceptual world of Noble Drew Ali, in the form of organizational principles and philosophical legacies, remain and inform to this day.

* * *

To begin the analysis, it is not unreasonable to postulate that some tangible, organic link between the nineteenth-century Muslim community and Noble Drew Ali may have existed. The obscurities surrounding Noble Drew's early life preclude verifiable evidence, but circumstantial observations suggest intriguing possibilities at the least. After all, he grew up and achieved adolescence in a part of the South in close proximity to coastal South Carolina and Georgia, the gravitational center of the antebellum Muslim community in North America. The context is an interesting one in that, as has been demonstrated, the Islamic

---

[2] See Cheryl McLean, State Library of North Carolina, Raleigh, December 11, 2002, personal communication. There is a Sampson County.

legacy was palpable along the coast and in the Sea Islands, where Sapelo resident Harriet Hall Grovner may well have been a practicing Muslim until her demise in 1922. As late as a decade after that, Lorenzo Turner was collecting names and terms in the coastal area reflecting a profound Muslim influence. Of course, by the 1920s Noble Drew had abandoned the South for the North, and by 1930 he was dead, but the point is clear: If the Muslim legacy extending from enslaved African Muslims was vibrant and undeniable by the 1930s, it was probably even more so during the 1880s and 1890s. That is, a scenario in which Noble Drew may have had some personal contact with Muslims or their descendants, or in which he had at least some familiarity with concepts associated with Islam, cannot be summarily dismissed.

Ironically, traditions produced to establish Noble Drew's connections to an Islamic inheritance constitute the most formidable barriers to an investigation that could in fact lead to testimonies of substance. The dual mythification and mystification of his past, in the attempt to achieve a quality of distinction with respect to both his birth and his upbringing, unnecessarily shrouds the reality and is indeed dubiously didactic in that it invites an analysis racialized in meaning and open to interpretations at odds with the early-twentieth-century project of racial uplift. According to some accounts he was the child of ex-slaves, a reasonable assertion for someone born in the South in 1886. At least one account maintains his father was "of Moorish extraction," which, given preceding chapters, is certainly not out of the question and of import if verifiable.[3] It is with his purported relationship to "Cherokee Indians," however, that stories of his background begin to take on folkloric dimensions. In this regard, either his mother was said to be "of Cherokee ancestry," or he was adopted "among the Cherokee Indians ... so that later in life he always wore a feather in his fez." An alternative story has Noble Drew running away to live with gypsies after his mother dies in his early infancy (a "very small boy"), and he is subjected either to the abuses of a "wicked aunt" or a cruel stepmother, who threw him into a fire: "The Prophet had marks on his face and hands from this attempt on his life."[4]

The association with Cherokees and Moors serves the purpose of establishing an organic link to Islam and nobility, but it could also be read as a device by which Noble Drew's personal heritage is made to be both different from and superior to that of the average African American. Hence the claim of *The*

---

[3] This is reported by Wilson, *Sacred Drift*, 15–16, and is based on the unpublished essay of Ravanna Bey of the Moorish Academy of Chicago. Furthermore, according to Bey, the Drew family had settled in Newark, New Jersey in the early 1880s. There they encountered the "master adept" Jamal al-Din al-Afghani (1838–97), who was visiting the United States in the winter of 1882–83. The Drews were then initiated into al-Afghani's political reform movement known as the Salafiyya, and into the Brethren of Purity or the Ikwan al-Safa. If substantiated, this would obviously radically alter what we know about Noble Drew Ali.

[4] See Wilson, *Sacred Drift*, 15–16; *The Moorish Review*, November 1956, in the Moorish Science Temple Papers, MG 435, Schomburg Center for Research in Black Culture, The New York Public Library; New York.

Moorish Review in 1956: "Our prophet came out of the Cherokee Tribe. The only tribe that produces Nobles."[5] Having presented an atypical childhood, the mythification turns its attention to Noble Drew's call as a prophet, at which point the mystification deepens. Wilson's *Sacred Drift* encapsulates the claims most succinctly, stating that, at age sixteen, Noble Drew did the following:

[He] shipped out as a merchant seaman – some say he took a job as a magician in a traveling circus (he is also said to have worked as a railway expressman) – and somehow ended up in Egypt. There he met the last priest of an ancient cult of High Magic who took him to the Pyramid of Cheops, led him in blindfolded, and abandoned him. When Drew found his way out unaided the magus recognized him as a potential adept and offered him initiation. He received the name Sharif [Noble] Abdul Ali; in America he would be known as Noble Drew Ali. In Egypt his prophecy manifested as a book, the *"Circle Seven Koran"*; or it might have been in Mecca, where he was somehow empowered by Sultan Abdul Aziz al-Sa'ud, ruler [sharif] of the city and later of the whole country.[6]

While the trajectory through Egypt is possible (stranger things have happened) and could in fact represent an allegorical truth, the inquiry here is necessarily informed by the logic of plausibility. It is very plausible that Noble Drew left the South in search of employment and earned a living in some sequence of working for the railroad and in the circus. In this regard Turner has written this: "Perhaps closer to the truth than the legends is the Associated Negro Press's report that 'he [Ali] was accompanying a Hindu fakir in circus shows when he decided to start a little order of his own'," a speculation seemingly supported by a 1927 Chicago flyer promoting "The Great Moorish Drama" in which Noble Drew Ali, scheduled to teach on the principles of his faith, would also divinely heal those in attendance as well as escape the bonds of "several yards of rope, as Jesus was bound at the Temple at Jerusalem."[7]

Whatever the particulars of his circumlocutions, accounts difficult to verify maintain that, in either 1912 or 1913, at the age of 27, Noble Drew established the Canaanite Temple in Newark, New Jersey, preaching "his doctrine in basements, empty lots, and street corners" with the help of one shadowy Dr. Suliman. Short in stature (as were Marcus Garvey, Elijah Muhammad, and Du Bois for that matter), Noble Drew Ali nevertheless had a commanding presence and an eloquence that turned the heads of many in that city. Newark's was the first in a series of worship centers that would collectively come to be known as the Moorish Science Temple. Over the next decade, membership is said to have reached 30,000, constituting a social movement of significance, with temples in such places as Richmond and Petersburg, Virginia and Charlestown, West Virginia, as well as Pine Bluff, Arkansas; Baltimore;

---

[5] See *The Moorish Review*, November 1956.
[6] See Wilson, *Sacred Drift*, 16.
[7] Look closely at the flyer reproduced in Wilson's *Sacred Drift*, 30; see Richard Brent Turner, *Islam in the African-American Experience* (Bloomington: Indiana U. Press, 1997), 92.

Cleveland; and Youngstown, Ohio.[8] Northern centers included Milwaukee, Philadelphia, Pittsburgh, Chicago, and, significantly, Lansing and Detroit, Michigan, the latter the site of Elijah Muhammad's initial encounter with W. D. Fard Muhammad around 1930. Just one year earlier, in nearby Lansing, four-year-old Malcolm Little's house had been firebombed, apparently by white vigilantes, in response to father Earl Little's activism as a minister and member of Garvey's Universal Negro Improvement Association (UNIA).[9] This geography of association is consistent with well-established evidence of close ideological relations between Moorish Science, the Nation of Islam, and the UNIA.

The possible establishment of the Canaanite Temple in Newark, prior to Garvey's 1915 arrival in the United States, places Noble Drew in the midst of momentous change in the African American community, heralding the onset of a major black migration from the South to the urban North, accompanied by blacks' immersion in a veritable plethora of political organizations and social experiments. Noble Drew Ali represents one of the more arresting and novel attempts at rethinking the meaning of the African-descended population in the United States, at breaking out of the conceptual, conventional box. As an individual, he was but a lone statistic in a sea of collective corporeal movement out of the South, where in 1910 some 7 million black folk lived, compared with less than 1 million throughout the rest of the country. Some 78 percent of the 7 million black Southerners lived in rural areas, with another 1.5 million living in urban areas. Altogether, blacks in the South were at a distinct disadvantage in that the region as a whole was comparatively lagging in educational facilities, basic services, and employment opportunities. Interestingly, it would appear that those who left the South for northern environs were disproportionately from urban areas; the typical migrant was between twenty-five and thirty-four years of age and had probably spent an appreciable amount of time in southern towns and cities. This speculation is supported by the fact that, between 1910 and 1920, the literacy rates among northern blacks increased slightly, suggesting that migrants from the South were "of the better educated variety."[10]

Over 1 million blacks left the South for the North during the Great Migration between 1916 and 1930, but nearly half of that number, over 400,000, exchanged addresses during an intense two-year period between 1916 and 1918, coterminous with the United States' involvement in the First World War.[11] The northern interest in black labor is explained, of course, by the precipitous decline in foreign immigration from 1.2 million in 1914 to 110,000 in 1918.

---

[8] Ibid.; also see Clifton E. Marsh, *From Black Muslim to Muslims: The Transition from Separation to Islam, 1930–1980* (Metuchen, NJ and London: Scarecrow Press, 1984), 43; Arna Bontemps and Jack Convoy, *Anyplace But Here* (New York: Hill and Wang, 1966; orig. pub. as *They Seek a City*, 1945), 205.

[9] See Alex Haley, *The Autobiography of Malcolm X* (New York: Ballantine, 1993; orig. pub., 1964), 1–3.

[10] See Carole Marks, *Farewell – We're Good and Gone: The Great Black Migration* (Bloomington and Indianapolis: Indiana U. Press, 1989), 15–19, 34–44.

[11] Ibid., 1–3, 45–59, 121–147; also see Turner, *Islam in the African-American Experience*, 73–75.

Fleeing white criminality and the state-supported terrorism of Jim Crow and his relatives, fleeing economic hardship and the ravages of the boll weevil, heavy infestations of which devastated millions of acres of cotton fields in Alabama, Georgia, and Mississippi, black migrants flooded northern cities, exponentially increasing their presence, with the result that, between 1910 and 1920, the black population rose some 59 percent in Philadelphia, 66 percent in New York City, 148 percent in Chicago, and 611 percent in Detroit; by 1920, nearly 40 percent of the northern black population was to be found in these four cities alone. The black population of New York City, of course, was significantly augmented by the arrival between 1900 and 1930 of some 40,000 black immigrants from the Caribbean, most of whom spoke English. Participating in a scheme largely orchestrated by northern industrialists and encouraged (through strident appeals and employment advertisements) by such black newspapers as the *Chicago Defender* (established in 1905) and the *Boston Guardian* (established in 1901), the mostly "urban, nonagricultural laborers" of the American South often responded to this rather unusual partnership by signing labor contracts with northern companies before actually leaving the South. In the North, most blacks found work in manufacturing jobs in such industries as steel and meat packing, and the initial hope was that they had entered a land of greater possibilities.

But the reality was very different from the promise, and the distinction is crucial to understanding the appeal of Noble Drew Ali. Although many jobs taken by blacks were in manufacturing industries, these positions were at the lowest level and called for unskilled and semiskilled labor. Career choices for black women were particularly constricted, as they were imprisoned in largely domestic occupations as laundresses, maids, and cooks. Altogether, the labor provided by black folk in the North was the "dirty work shunned by the native white population." The strains on these migrant families were tremendous, as the average migrant earned $25.00 for a forty-eight to sixty-four-hour week, although the Bureau of Labor statistics found that, in 1919, a weekly income of $43.51 was necessary to "maintain an acceptable standard of living" for a family of five. Such an estimate did not take into consideration the need to finance the migration itself, a cost often borne by black women working as domestics to help pay for the passage of men in the family as well as their own. Deplorable living conditions were the unavoidable result; deferred dreams translated into a reality in which many blacks lived in impoverished, overcrowded, health-debilitating pockets of northern Jim Crow. This led to outbreaks of smallpox in places such as Cleveland, Pittsburgh, and Philadelphia; pneumonia, venereal disease, and tuberculosis were commonplace maladies. Between 1915 and 1919, the black infant mortality rate was 150 per 1,000, compared with 92.8 per 1,000 for white children. Predictably, the incarceration of blacks soared from 9 percent of the total number of persons incarcerated to 57 percent from 1916 to 1917. These factors, combined with the observation that only 40,000 black soldiers out of 404,384 were allowed to see combat in the war (and in segregated units at that) readily explains the Red Summer of 1919, an explosion of frustration and disappointment informed by both domestic and international considerations, and a poignant indication of the many ways in which the Great Migration was proving a failed experiment.[12]

Black migrant and immigrant disillusionment was heightened by a global context in which people of African descent were everywhere under siege. The Caribbean had long been colonized, with the exception of an isolated Haiti. The occupation of Africa, officially launched with the Berlin Conference of 1884–85, was with few exceptions nearing completion by 1920. The 1896 Ethiopian victory over the Italians at Adwa was a solitary source of solace. So-called race men and women arose here and there, mired in a series of contradictions, declaiming segregation and decrying lynching, intermingling their efforts with the movements of labor while developing a deepening interest in the rationality of Marx.[13] It was heard in the music, it was felt in the dance, it was expressed by stepladder advocates on the street corners and in the literature of the New Negro Movement, as well as in the creativity of négritude and negrismo writers, this aggregate call and response throughout the Diaspora.

In reaction to the virulent nativistic spirit of the period, a spirit targeting Jews and Catholics as well as those of African descent (who were not necessarily distinguished from the preceding two categories), and in an effort to channel the anger and energy manifest in the multiple so-called race riots of the day, various "uplift" organizations were established to aid a burgeoning black population in the urban North.[14] The Niagra Movement, launched in 1905, issued into the National Association for the Advancement of Colored People (NAACP) in 1909 with the attendant strategy of waging struggle in the courts; *The Crisis*, the official organ of the association, achieved a peak circulation of 106,000 between 1910 and 1934. Complementing the NAACP was the Urban League, founded in 1911 and dedicated to the amelioration of working conditions for blacks. Joining these two organizations were the National Association of Colored Women, emerging from the club movement led by such figures as Mary Church Terrell; the National Association of Afro-American Women, under Ida B. Wells, the leader of the antilynching movement; the African Methodist Episcopal Church; the National Baptist Convention; Prince Hall masons (about whom more will be said); and black sororities and fraternities. Working together to achieve racial uplift while laboring under certain contradictions brought about by class pretensions, these "New Negroes" were responding to the changing economic and social circumstances of the country, the so-called fight for democracy, and the rise of empire at the expense of people of color. Inspired by an array of intellectual and artistic leaders of the Harlem Renaissance and the New Negro Movement, these organizations were characterized by the domination of

[12] Ibid.; also see Marsh, *From Black Muslims to Muslims*, 25–29; Tera W. Hunter, *To Joy My Freedom: Southern Black Women's Lives and Labors after the Civil War* (Cambridge, MA: Harvard U. Press, 1997).

[13] See Kevin K. Gaines, *Uplifting the Race: Black Leadership, Politics, and Culture in the Twentieth Century* (Chapel Hill: U. of North Carolina Press, 1996).

[14] Of course the literature on the New Negro Movement is vast, but see Turner's *Islam in the African-American Experience*, 73–80, for an effective synopsis.

upper-class or upper-caste blacks (in relative terms) seeking to raise from the dung heap their less fortunate "brethren," all the while assuming they had the right to interpret and represent the interests of "the folk." No doubt, their intentions were well placed.

However, the rise of myriad, alternative organizations articulating different visions of both the terrain and objectives of struggle speaks to the effective bifurcation of the African-descended people into a class-ridden society, and to the failure of most of the aforementioned associations to experience a profound resonance with the working poor, to really know their aspirations, and to champion their cause. A surfeit of organizations emerged in response to these needs, some of which actually began in the South and not a few of which attempted to wed local and national concerns with international agendas. What is striking about a number of these organizations is that they either trumpeted claims to a connection with Africa of some fundamental sort, or they were centered around a set of religious principles divergent from conventional beliefs and practices, or both. It was an age of unorthodoxy.

So it was that Dupont Bell founded a movement outside of Savannah, Georgia around 1899, in which he was worshiped as a "self-proclaimed son of God."[15] Committed to an asylum, he was soon succeeded by "other self-proclaimed gods or messiahs" who "appeared in various parts of Georgia until 1916." Certainly one of the more colorful persons to follow in the trajectory and tradition of Dupont Bell was Father George W. Hurley, born in 1884 in Reynolds, Georgia (thirty miles southwest of Macon). As opposed to a "jack-leg" (self-trained) preacher, Father Hurley completed high school and attended Tuskegee Institute in Alabama, where he received ministerial training. Raised a Baptist, he would later embrace Methodism until his move with his wife to Detroit in 1919, where he joined a small "Black Holiness sect called Triumph the Church and Kingdom of God in Christ," established in 1904 under the leadership of Apostle Elias Dempsey Smith, who preached that God was in "man." Hurley was apparently on quite the journey of self-discovery, as he again changed his membership in the early 1920s to the International Spiritual Church, after which he founded his own, the Universal Hagar's Spiritual Church, in 1923. By 1941, Father Hurley boasted a membership of 185,000 spread through ninety-five churches, a highly suspect claim. The reference to Hagar in the church's name faintly recalls Noble Drew Ali's own appropriation of biblical tropes and characters in his insistence that African Americans are the descendants of the original Canaanites, a matter into which the study will subsequently look.

Father Hurley was worshiped as "God Incarnate" and the "black God of this Age" until his death in 1943. To briefly elaborate, Hurley maintained that "the spirit of God is embedded in each man" and that "as the 'major god' he [Hurley]

---

[15] See Hans Baer, *The Black Spiritual Movement: A Religious Response to Racism* (Knoxville: U. of Tennessee Press, 1984), 82–96; Rashad, *Elijah Muhammad and the Ideological Foundations of the Nation of Islam*, 43–48.

brought the 'true light into this age,' and his believers in that true light were the minor gods and goddesses." He taught that blacks were the "first people in the world" and the original Hebrews, that they spoke the "original" language of Arabic and were the architects of high civilizations and hieroglyphics, and that they were the most industrious people on earth. Identifying whites as "Gentiles" and the descendants of Cain, "cursed with a pale color because of leprosy," Father Hurley instructed his followers to refer to themselves as "Black" or "Ethiopian" as opposed to the pejorative "Negro," and to eschew interracial marriage. "Contemptuous" of so-called mulattoes, Hurley proscribed swine and alcohol (although he permitted "wine in moderation" for special religious occasions), and he flew his own version of the red, black, and green flag (the colors of the UNIA flag). Given that the Universal Hagar's Spiritual Church was inaugurated some years after the founding of both Noble Drew's Canaanite Temple and Garvey's UNIA (he may have been a member of the UNIA) and spanned the initial period of the Nation of Islam, it is not the argument here that Hurley served in any way as mentor to or model for Noble Drew (or Elijah Muhammad). The point is to convey a sense of the extraordinary context of the times. Indeed, in another similarity with Noble Drew, concerning which more will be stated, Father Hurley's cosmology drew heavily upon Eva S. and Levi Dowling's *Aquarian Gospel of Jesus the Christ*, and contained elements of Catholicism, Protestantism, spiritualism, and hoodoo. A clear example of the Dowlings' influence can be seen in the second and third of Father Hurley's own ten commandments:

2. Thou shall ignore a sky heaven for happiness and a downward hell for punishment.
3. Thou shall believe in heaven and hell on earth.

There are undeniable reverberations between these commandments and the teachings of both Moorish Science and the Nation of Islam, correspondences which will be examined closely. Restricting the deliberation to the Universal Hagar's Spiritual Church alone, we certainly have a melange of religious concepts informed by a political platform of nationalist and pan-Africanist sentiments.

In addition to Father Hurley, there were a number of other spiritual contemporaries operating in eastern cities who similarly claimed either divine or special status. They often had ties to the South, including Georgia and the Carolinas. This was the case with Bishop Ida Robinson, born in Florida and reared in Georgia, who in 1924 founded the Mt. Sinai Holy Church of America in Philadelphia. Then, of course, there was George Baker, a native of coastal South Carolina, who originally came to Baltimore and later to Long Island and Manhattan some time before 1932, where he was transfigured into Father Divine and established the Father Divine Peace Mission Movement with a significant following. Bishop Charles Emmanuel "Daddy" Grace, "said to be Negro and Portuguese" and echoing Melungeon identity, founded the United House of Prayer for all People in Philadelphia in 1925; he likewise acquired a sizeable retinue. The leaders of these churches, while approximating or replicating the prerogatives of divinity assumed by Father Hurley, did not necessarily emulate his association with Africa, a development emblematic of the seemingly ceaseless struggle by the African-descended in North America to achieve a corporate identity that in some way weakens, if not altogether repudiates, links to America. In this vein, Prophet F. S. Cherry's Church of God in Philadelphia was one of many different black Jewish sects in the North; at least eight could be found in Harlem between 1919 and 1931.[16]

*   *   *

The foregoing discussion indicates that very lively and innovative discursive patterns had developed around the conjoined centers of religion and politics in the urban East by the early part of the twentieth century. However, Noble Drew Ali's decision to relocate (or establish) his headquarters in Chicago's South Side in 1925 placed him in an environment no less dynamic. There, an important organization known as the Abyssinian Movement had already blazed a trail. Led by Grover Cleveland Redding and Oscar McGavich, the Abyssinian Movement was "semi-religious and nationalistic," calling for American blacks to repatriate to Africa and specifically Ethiopia, so that "not a few of its converts believed the UNIA and the Abyssinian Movement were at least affiliated." In a parallelism with Noble Drew Ali's reification of Morocco and echoing the message of Father Hurley, Redding taught followers that they were "Ethiopians and not Negroes... an obvious device to avoid the label 'Negro' with all its connotations of inferiority." Further correspondences between Redding and Hurley are evidenced in the former's alleged prescription of "hatred for the white man," as well as in his "esoteric teachings" that maintained a "connection with the 'source' of civilization – curiously enough, Israel via Ethiopia." That Redding would lay claim to both Israel and Ethiopia is hardly curious, however, given the pronounced biblical underpinnings of all of these organizations. Joining Redding to round out the leadership of the Abyssinian Movement were the "Great Abyssinian" Joseph Fernon and his son "The Prince," along with R. D. Jonas, a white "doctor" who may have been involved in organizing for the UNIA in East St. Louis.[17]

Jonas joined Redding and the others in 1920; that same year he turned state's evidence against Redding, who during a June 20 parade drew out an American flag and burned it. A black police officer attempting to impede Redding was shot, perhaps by an Abyssinian follower, and in the ensuing melee a white merchant and a white sailor were killed. Redding and another black male sacrificial

[16] See Arthur Huff Fauset, *Black Gods of the Metropolis: Negro Religious Cults of the Urban North* (Philadelphia: U. of Pennsylvania, 1944), 13–56; Howard Brotz, *The Black Jews of Harlem: Negro Nationalism and the Dilemmas of Negro Leadership* (New York: Schocken Books, 1970).

[17] See Bontemps and Convoy, *Anyplace But Here*, 204–05; E. U. Essien-Udom, *Black Nationalism: A Search for an Identity in America* (Chicago: U. of Chicago Press, 1962), 47–48.

lamb were arrested, convicted, and hanged. Taking the defense during his trial, Redding explained his behavior with millennial invocations:

My mission is marked in the Bible. Even if they have captured me, some other leaders will rise up and lead the Ethiopian back to Africa.... The Ethiopians do not belong here and should be taken back to their own country. Their time was up in 1919. They came in 1619. The time is up. The burning of the flag last Sunday night by me was a symbol that Abyssinians are not wanted in this country. That was the sign the Bible spoke of.

Jonas-turned-informant, either in an effort to save his own life or in keeping with his true undercover calling, would reveal that Redding's activities were by no means confined to Chicago; he had made the circuit in several cities, "handing out blanks which, when properly filled out, would procure membership in the Star Order of Ethiopia and identify the signer as an 'Ethiopian Missionary to Abyssinia.' The signer expressed his loyalty to the 'mother country,' and renounced the name of Negro, given him against his will by a race other than his own." These membership contracts functioned very much like Moorish Science identification cards; as will be seen, Noble Drew would recall Redding's fate at a subsequent, crucial period in the early life of Moorish Science when he carefully navigated around a potentially dangerous confrontation with the state over the display of such cards.[18]

It is not clear to what extent the Abyssinian Movement enjoyed widespread support in the black community either in or beyond Chicago. That the movement's message survived its messenger, however, is supported by the founding of the Peace Movement of Ethiopia in 1932, again in Chicago. Holding meetings at 4653 South State Street, the Peace Movement of Ethiopia was not only ideologically similar but was spatially proximate to the former headquarters of the Moorish Science Temple. As a back-to-Africa movement, its promise was such that a branch of the Ethiopian World Federation Council was formed in Chicago in May of 1938, just after that organization's founding in August of 1937 by Dr. Maluku E. Bayen, a nephew of emperor Haile Selassie, for the purpose of soliciting help and support for the beleaguered state of Ethiopia. A similar effort had been made in June of 1934 in Detroit, when the purported Ethiopian Wyxzewixard ("wise wizard"?) S. J. Challouehliczilczese unsuccessfully tried to reorganize the Nation of Islam as a source of support for Ethiopia. Indeed, the ethiopicentric associations were swimming in a sea of similar formations in Chicago, including the National Movement for the Establishment of the Forty-Ninth State, the World Wide Friends of Africa, the American Economic League, the Garvey Club, United African Federation Council, the Joint Council of Repatriation, the Royal Ethiopian Jews, the Washington Park Forum, and so on. While some were fly-by-night, ephemeral experiments, others achieved relative stability and visibility in otherwise turbulent and unpredictable waters. The point is that the early-twentieth-century black community in Chicago, like

[18] Ibid.

its eastern urban counterparts, was awash in nationalist, pan-Africanist organizations. It therefore falls to the historian to account for the extraordinary
appeal, and relative success, of the Moorish Science Temple in the face of such
steep competition and against seemingly overwhelming odds.[19]

*   *   *

What unites these various and sundry movements was their attempt to rede-
fine the African American position both nationally and internationally. It was
necessary to address both, as African Americans had emerged out of an international context – indeed, that very context was the source of their difficulties in
America, while the black sojourn in North America was so sufficiently mirrored
in Latin America, the Caribbean, and Africa that linkages were apparent and
interpreted as meaningful and instructive. The black diasporic experience had
become an ontological question of the first order, such that religion, ideology,
political discourse, and cultural production were all called upon, sometimes
singularly, often in combinative form, to achieve some degree of overarching,
perhaps totalizing resolution. It was into such a tempestuous swirl of intense
self-examination and energetic reconfiguration that Noble Drew Ali entered.
Indeed, it is possible to argue that, by virtue of his disproportionate impact, he
was a principal architect of early-twentieth-century black social thought and
movement.

The lore maintains that, having launched the Canaanite Temple in 1913,
Noble Drew in the following year faced a serious challenge to his leadership in
Newark by one Abdul Wali Farad Muhammad Ali, "a mysterious teacher of
Islam from the East. Little is known about that man and the early years of his
Newark mission," but it may well be that this encounter informed Noble Drew's
intellectual and spiritual development. If on one hand, the mystery man were an
orthodox Muslim, it would mean that Noble Drew was well aware of orthodox
or Sunni Islam as early as 1914, some thirteen years before the publication of his
Circle Seven Koran. On the other hand, the speculation that this visitor was none
other than Fard Muhammad, the founder of the Nation of Islam, cannot be
summarily rejected, although it would seem unlikely as all indications are that
Fard Muhammad only entered the United States in 1913 and thereafter lived
on the west coast for many years. Purported to be a "Russo-Syrian peddler of
silks and raincoats," the interloper, this tradition claims, "began to lure some
of the Moors away to his own brand of Islam...tainted with race-hatred (the
white man as 'blue-eyed devil')." Such an account must be approached with
caution, as it may be related to the claim, contested by the Nation of Islam, that
Elijah Muhammad was once a follower of Noble Drew Ali and was persuaded
to leave. The question of the relationship between Moorish Science and the Nation of Islam will be addressed in the next chapter, but whatever the reality, the
confrontation with the "teacher from the East" may have had some lingering

[19] See Essien-Udom, *Black Nationalism*, 48–58; Erdmann Doane Beynon, "The Voodoo Cult among Negro Migrants in Detroit," *The American Journal of Sociology* 43 (May 1938): 904.

effects on Noble Drew Ali's early followers, for by 1916 "factionalism" had divided them. Those who remained loyal to Noble Drew reconstituted themselves in Newark as the "Holy Moabite Temple of the World," indicating that Noble Drew chose to maintain his distance from orthodoxy while working out his own philosophical principles. That Noble Drew relocated his headquarters to Chicago from Newark in 1925 suggests escalating tensions between factions. As has been discussed, Chicago was a logical site given the receptivity of many to pan-Africanist (or Ethiopianist, more precisely), nationalist appeals. It must also be remembered that the Ishmaelites had gravitated to the area, so the claim that Noble Drew moved to Chicago because of their prior existence cannot be ruled out. Finally, as will be discussed later on in the chapter, the fact that the Ahmadiyya movement also established its central office in Chicago in 1922 may have affected Noble Drew's decision to relocate. In any event, he set up headquarters in Chicago (see Figure 1). He officially renamed the organization the "Moorish Temple of Science" in 1926 (according to a certificate of corporation filed in Cook County, Illinois), whereas its publications carried the name the "Moorish Holy Temple of Science." In 1928, the Moorish temples were reorganized under a new appellation, "The Moorish Science Temple of America." Organizations antedating Noble Drew's arrival in Chicago had paved the way for Moorish Science in Chicago, unwittingly or otherwise.[20]

Between 1913 and 1929, Noble Drew Ali worked out the tenets of Moorish Science, the centerpiece of which was the *Circle Seven Koran* of 1927. The development of Moorish Science should be seen as a dialectical process involving innovation, reciprocation, and appropriation. That is, Noble Drew certainly initiated some ideas, but he just as certainly borrowed other concepts and was influenced by the whirl of events around him. The lines of demarcation separating original from recycled ideas, however, are not always evident. The congruency of perspective among the various movements, as many were pan-Africanist and religiously premised, allowed for the absorption of multiple influences without necessarily compromising the integrity of the core beliefs and practices. Black social movements in the early nineteenth century were therefore ostensibly and even experientially competitive while concomitantly mutually reinforcing and possibly complementary, given the similarities of their conceptual framework. What follows is a discussion of the more salient principles of the Moorish Science Temple, as promulgated in the most authoritative of the movement's publications, the *Circle Seven Koran*.

To begin, the full title of the *Circle Seven Koran* is in essence a distillation of the central message of Moorish Science: *The Holy Koran of the Moorish Holy Temple of Science 7, Know Yourself and Your Father God-Allah, That You Learn*

[20] See Wilson, *Sacred Drift*, 29–32; Turner, *Islam in the African-American Experience*, 92. According to Turner, the organization was renamed the "Moorish Divine and National Movement of North America, Inc." in 1928. Documents do carry the name "The Moorish Divine and National Movement," but papers filed with Cook County list the official name as given in the text. See the Moorish Science Temple Papers, MG 435.

FIGURE 1. Prophet Noble Drew Ali. Courtesy of the Photographs and Prints Division, Schomburg Center for Research in Black Culture, The New York Public Library, Astor, Lenox, and Tilden Foundations.

to Love Instead of Hate. Everyman Need to Worship Under His Own Vine and Fig Tree. The Uniting of Asia.[21] The title, a reflection of both the masonic signification of the number seven and the apocalyptic signs of the seven seals in the book of Revelation, also points to a logic of progressive revelatory understanding that intertwines the business of religion with the nationalist project. That is, an accurate appreciation of the former is a necessary prerequisite for the eventual attainment of the latter. The progression can be stated somewhat differently: The acquisition of corporate identity is a conjunctive process issuing from the embrace of the appropriate religion, from which flows an adjustment in self-definition and esteem and a reconfiguration of social relations resulting in politics of cooperation and transnational cohesion. Further explication is in order.

To understand the message of Noble Drew Ali, one must engage the context of the times and the import of that context for people of African descent in North America. Put succinctly, they had no home. Two generations removed from slavery, black folk remained locked in combat over their very existence. Southern redemption, Jim Crow, lynchings, race riots, pervasive impoverishment (North and South), and the disillusioning disappointment of the First World War's aftermath had objectively and tangibly demonstrated that they were far from experiencing acceptance in the land of their birth, that they were in but not of America, and that they were Americans only in relation to persons born elsewhere but not with respect to any internal criteria. In very practical terms, they had no country. But they very much wanted one.

In a time of empire, social Darwinism, and pseudo-scientific racism, the question of nationhood and the creation of boundaries simultaneously enfranchising those within while protecting them from competition from without was a preoccupation of restless populations throughout Asia and Africa. African Americans were very much aware of these struggles, and they were generally critical of western imperialism. Noble Drew Ali was also concerned, and, for him, the issue of a viable corporate identity was the most important problem facing people of African descent in the early twentieth century. His solution was unique and creative, and it was national in scope while international in implication.

For Noble Drew Ali, the ambiguity of black corporate identity in early-twentieth-century America was best typified by the unstable nature and application of the racialized nomenclature. African descended people were alternatively identified as coloreds, negroes, and Ethiopians. As ascriptions and New World inventions, none of these terms had any meaningful longevity or historicity, with the exception of the name *Ethiopian*, which for reasons to be explored was just as objectionable. Indeed, these very designations indicated that the person of African descent was adrift and without direction.

---

[21] See Noble Drew Ali, *The Holy Koran of the Moorish Holy Temple of Science 7, Know Yourself and Your Father God-Allah, That You Learn to Love Instead of Hate. Everyman Need to Worship Under His Own Vine and Fig Tree. The Uniting of Asia* (1996; orig. pub., 1927). Henceforth, *Circle Seven Koran.*

Social and political opprobrium in the extreme can lead to etiological crisis. It was Noble Drew's determination that such an emergency had been engendered. As those of African descent were faced with questions of ultimacy, it was his view that only authoritative resolution, extending beyond the ability of the powerful to name their subjects, could serve as remedy. Such authority was to be found in the provenance of the spiritual, for in the general understanding of the day, the spiritual was the final arbiter, transcendent and unchanging, decisive in all matters temporal.

With this in mind, Noble Drew Ali championed the argument that corporate identity, or the identity of nations, was divinely established and therefore unchangeable and unchanging. With the principle of immutability as foundation, Noble Drew enunciated the cornerstone of his claim to prophethood by insisting that the collective identity of the African-descended population was settled long ago and could be found in sacred utterance. For him, those of African descent, and all Africans for that matter, were none other than the "descendants of the ancient Canaanite nation from the holy land of Canaan." The corollary reinforced the claim in a compelling and entirely logical manner: "What your ancient forefathers were, you are today without doubt or contradiction." Far from the coloreds and negroes of western derogation, black folk had a divinely sanctioned identity. Theirs was a dignity and legitimacy derived from the Bible itself.[22]

The use of divine revelation to adjudicate contemporary conflict is certainly far from novel. For some of the African-descended in America, there had long been an identification with the ancient Hebrews in the similitude of their bondage and subsequent wilderness sojourn. The nature of the identification was not always precise: at times it was associative and turned on the notion of parallel experiences; at other times it was appropriative, driven by the conviction that what was recorded was prophetic and predictive of both a time to come and a time that had already come. In the former scenario, the African-descended were like the Hebrews; in the latter, they were the Hebrews. In either case, the essential trajectories were consistent, using similar tropes for the same explicative and interpretive purposes.

Noble Drew Ali changed all of that. Drawing from the same wellspring of biblical imagination, he succeeded in formulating a decidedly different elixir, one meant to satisfy multiple yearnings while sustaining movement in new directions. Rather than being Hebrews, Noble Drew divined that both the African and the African-derived were in reality Canaanites, specifically Moabites. This notion was innovative enough, but Noble Drew went much further by maintaining that the recovery of lineal descent not only conferred a "national" identity but also a religious one. In fact, the national and the political were coterminous, even synonymous, and, just as corporate nationality was unalterably established in antiquity, so too was the shared religion. For Noble Drew Ali, the Moabites of North America were Muslims, as were all Africans:

---

[22] Ibid., chapter 47, 9–12.

This is a fact discernible in the industrious acts of the Moslems of the Northwest and Southwest Africa. These are the Moabites, Hamathites, Canaanites, who were driven out of the land of Canaan, by Joshua, and received permission from the pharaohs of Egypt to settle in that portion of Egypt. In later years they formed themselves kingdoms. These kingdoms are called this day, Morocco, Algiers, Tunis, Tripoli, etc.[23]

This passage specifically claims descent from those displaced by the ancient Hebrews and picks up the story of their dispersal with an expulsion from Palestine back into Egypt, thereby reversing the direction of the exodus account and standing it on its head. Egypt is embraced rather then disparaged, and it serves as asylum and figurative parent for the subsequent nations constituting what is now North Africa. African Americans, therefore, were Muslims who could trace their heritage to Morocco and an even earlier Moabitic origin.

Upon conversion to Moorish Science, initiates took the surnames *Bey* or *El*, their "free national names." The Moorish alteration of the personal name is consistent with conversion custom in orthodox Islam, wherein the convert adopts a new Muslim designation to indicate a spiritual transformation. However, the practice in Moorish Science, while reflecting religious change, simultaneously draws attention to an ongoing existential fallout traceable to the transatlantic slave trade itself. Partial resolution of the loss of original identity is the attempt to approximate that identity, to recover the loss, by as rational a process as possible. With total recovery possibly beyond reach, the reconfiguration of the personal name is nevertheless of tremendous significance, signaling an attempt to reverse the flow of the slave ship's implications while demonstrably rejecting slaveholder characterization. In this reconstruction of the will, the Moors established a precedent that would be readily adopted by the Nation of Islam.

Having provided African-descended people with a new national identity and a new religion, Noble Drew Ali also provided them with a flag, a red Moorish pennant with a green, five-pointed star in the center. He went even further by situating their national identity in a global setting that joined various "people of color," from Asia to the Americas. In this wider perspective, African Americans shared a transnational identity: They were "Asiatics." It would appear that Noble Drew Ali was the first person (at least in North America) to issue such a proclamation, an interpretation of international relations whose echoes would reverberate in the teachings of the Nation of Islam. Alluded to in the full title of the *Circle Seven Koran* as the "uniting of Asia," this version of "Asian" monogenesis is furnished by the document itself:

The inhabitants of Africa are the descendants of the ancient Canaanites from the land of Canaan. Old man Cush and his family are the first inhabitants of Africa who came from the land of Canaan. His father Ham and his family were second. Then came the word Ethiopia, which means the demarcation line of the dominion of Amexem, the first true and divine name of Africa. The dividing of the land between the father and the son. The

---

[23] Ibid., iii.

dominion of Cush, North-East and South-East Africa and North-West and South-West was his fathers dominion of Africa.[24]

There are several items of interest here. First, the *Circle Seven Koran* asserts that the peopling of Africa did not begin with the Moabites but with the postdiluvian settlements of Cush and Ham. Second, Africa was divided between this father and son along a north–south axis; that axis, or line of demarcation, was called "Ethiopia." The reasoning behind this etymological finding is obscure, but it does point to the objective truth that the term *Ethiopia* is of Greek derivation and not an indigenous term. Noble Drew Ali would reject the application of the label *Ethiopian* to the African-derived on the basis that the word referred to the geographics of the continent rather than its people. Third, and in a similar vein, the *Circle Seven Koran* rejected the name *Africa* and replaced it with the heavenly inspired designation *Amexem*. Once again, Noble Drew's challenge of the conventional has some merit, as the etymology of the term *Africa* remains a matter of speculation and dispute. As for *Amexem*, its morphology may refer to Noble Drew's visualization of an African continent that once included what is now the Americas:

Their dominion and inhabitation extended from Northeast and Southwest Africa, across the great Atlantis even unto the present North, South, and Central America and also Mexico and the Atlantis Islands; before the great earthquake, which caused the great Atlantic Ocean.[25]

To the original descendants of Cush and Ham were subsequently added the Moabites, who received pharaonic sanction to "settle and inhabit North-West Africa; they were the founders and are the true possessors of the present Moroccan Empire; with their Canaanite, Hittite and Amorite brethren who sojourned from the land of Canaan seeking new homes."[26] The *Circle Seven Koran* spells out the relationship of the various "Asiatic nations" by way of purported biblical lineage. Beginning with the Moors or "Moorish" of Morocco, who are identified as the "founders of the Holy City of Mecca," the document proceeds to describe the Egyptians as Hamites and the Arabs as "the seed of Hagar, Japanese and Chinese," which seems to suggest that the progenitors of the Arabs, Japanese, and Chinese can all be traced to Hagar, as can her "true" descendants "the Turks." Continuing on, the book refers to the "Hindus of India" as the "descendants of the ancient Canaanites, Hittites and Moabites from the land of Canaan," thus claiming a close affiliation between Africans and Indians. The "Asiatic nations" of the Americas, in contrast, include "the Moorish Americans and Mexicans in North America, Brazilians, Argentinians and Chilians in South America. Columbians, Nicaraguans and the natives of San Salvador in Central America, etc. All of these are Moslems."[27]

[24] Ibid., chapter 47, 1–5.
[25] Ibid., chapter 47, 6–7.
[26] Ibid.
[27] Ibid., chapter 45, 2–6.

As opposed to the Moorish Americans, Indian "Hindus," and Egyptians, the *Circle Seven Koran* does not specify the biblical origins of Native Americans and their hispanicized progeny; rather, they are all designated as Muslims. This technique underscores the conflation of nation and religion in Moorish Science, and it will again be witnessed in the Nation of Islam.

Noble Drew Ali's appropriation and reification of Morocco, as opposed to a country in subsaharan Africa, may be related to the reality that during the early twentieth century there were no independent subsaharan states other than Liberia, itself a western creation. His disdain for the term *Ethiopia* was not necessarily a rejection of Ethiopia or Ethiopians per se but, in addition to what has been stated before, may have been a calculated strategy to distance and distinguish Moorish Science from the various Ethiopianist movements of the day. Certainly, his attempts to locate African identity within both sacred inscription and the ancient "east," although innovative in form, was not without precedent conceptually. Indeed, such attempts can be traced back to West Africa itself, from the eighth through the sixteenth centuries, when ruling elites throughout a wide expanse similarly sought to locate their origins in vintaged cultures; it was in response to the rise of Islam's prestige in the region that the privileged often reinvented competing avenues of descent, all of which invariably converged on lands and communities of revealed religion.

Examples of the foregoing begin with *Ta'rīkh al-Sūdān* ("History of the Blacks") and *Ta'rīkh al-Fattāsh* ("History of the Seeker"), two critical West African documents completed in the seventeenth century (but begun centuries earlier), which contend that the original inhabitants of the ancient kingdom of Ghana (or Wagadu or Kaya-Magha) were *baydān*, a term that can mean "white" but in all probability referred to the Sanhaja or other Berbers.[28] This written record, founded upon preceding oral accounts, is consistent with subsequent oral traditions that speak of the progenitors of the Serrakole (the people of ancient Ghana) coming from "the east."[29] Given the location of ancient Ghana (in the *sāhil* or transitional area between the Sahara and the savannah), there may be some reality behind claims of partial Berber origin, but even in the case of ancient Mali, whose political center was further south and fully in the savannah, there is the assertion that the Keita rulers were the progeny of Bilali Bunama, a probable reference to the Nubian Bilal b. Rabah, the first *mu'adhdhin* and Companion of the Prophet.[30] Similarly, the Zā dynasty of Songhay (ninth through the thirteenth centuries), from which sprang the subsequent Sunni dynasty, is said to have been established by someone from Yemen.[31] Mirroring

[28] See Ibn al-Mukhtār, *Ta'rīkh al-Fattāsh*, ed. and trans. O. Houdas and M. Delaffose (Paris: Librairie d'Amé rique et d'Orient Adrien-Maisonneuve, 1913), 42/78; 'Abd al-Rahmān b. 'Abd Allāh al-Sa'dī, *Ta'rīkh al-Sūdān*, ed. and trans. O. Houdas (Paris: Librairie d'Amé rique et d'Orient Adrien-Maisonneuve, 1900), 9/18–19.

[29] See Charles Monteil, "La legende du Ouagadou et l'origine des Soninkes," *Melanges Ethnologiques* (Dakar: IFAN, 1953).

[30] See *Ta'rīkh al-Sūdān*, 9/18–19.

[31] Ibid., 2–5/4–9. The Sunni dynasty, according to this account, was begun by 'Ali Kolon, son of Zā Yasiboi, a descendant of Zā al-Ayemen. There is evidence, however, of a Sanhaja presence

this approach were the Saifawa rulers of Kanem-Bornu, who alleged descent from the famous Arab Himyarite Arab leader Saif b. Dhu Yazan, who defeated the Ethiopians in Yemen as the *Jahilīyya* (pre-Islamic period) drew to a close. The case of Hausaland is even more incredulous, as various groups claimed descent from a galaxy of pre-Islamic prophets and heroes, ranging from Yusa (Joshua) to Musa (Moses) to Alexander the Great.[32]

Noble Drew Ali, therefore, had drawn upon a strategy of significant historicity. While he may or may not have been aware of West African precedence, he was likewise attempting to reconfigure an identity under assault. Faced with the exigencies of substantially altered social conditions, his solution was to anchor corporate existence in the sands of times and places celebrated by all. His was a quest for the unassailable.

*   *   *

Noble Drew Ali's reformulation is striking in that he chose an identification with both Ham and Canaan, particularly in view of the widely circulating and popularized "Hamitic curse" thesis. The major text for Moorish Science, the *Circle Seven Koran*, addresses neither the curse nor its implications. One is left to speculate that Noble Drew simply rejected the validity of the curse on the basis of a particular exegesis; the fact that Noah is attributed with issuing the pronouncement, rather than God, may have figured in the analysis. There seems, however, to be an anti-Jewish element in Noble Drew's theology, such that the notion of the Jews as a chosen people is eschewed. Indeed, the *Circle Seven Koran* maintains that "'Isa [Jesus] himself was of the true blood of the ancient Canaanites and Moabites and the inhabitants of Africa."[33] Such an assertion enjoys some biblical support in that the book of Ruth identifies David, King of Israel and ancestor of Jesus, as a descendant of Ruth the Moabite. The omission of the Jewish connection, however, is suggestive of its negation.

Although innovative and ontologically modifying, there was a very pragmatic, even conservative aspect to Noble Drew Ali's teachings. Given the emphasis on a reorientation of the collective personality away from North America to Africa, it would have been logical to expect the advocacy of a practical

in the Gao-Sane area by the end of the eleventh century. See J. O. Hunwick, "Gao and the Almoravids: A Hypothesis," in B. K. Swartz, Jr. and Raymond E. Dumett, eds., *West African Culture Dynamics* (New York and The Hague: Mouton, 1980).

[32] For the Saifawas, see Abdullahi Smith, "The Legend of the Saifawas: A Study in the Origins of a Legend of Origin," in B. Usuman and B. Alkali, eds., *Studies in the History of Pre-Colonial Borno* (Zaria: Northern Nigeria Publishing, 1983); Dierck Lange, *Le diwan des sultans du kanem-Bornu: Chronologie et histoire d'un royaume africaine* (Wiesbaden: Steiner, 1977); Louis Brenner, *The Shehus of Kukawa* (Oxford, England: Clarendon Press, 1973). For Hausaland, see Murray Last, "Historical Metaphors in the Kano Chronicle," *History in Africa* 7, pp. 161–178 (1980). For the *Kano Chronicle* in English translation, see H. R. Palmer, *Sudanese Memoirs*, 3 vols. (Lagos: Government Printer, 1928), vol. 3, 92–132. This is a republication of "The Kano Chronicle," *Journal of the Royal African Institute* 38 (1908): 59–98.

[33] Ibid., chapter 46, 2.

implementation involving a physical movement of some sort in parallel with the spiritual. On the contrary, Noble Drew Ali, in anticipation of Elijah Muhammad's subsequent eschatology, envisioned divine intervention into and resolution of the problems of the Asiatic in North America (a projection into which this chapter later delves). In the meantime, it was his argument that the Moor's embrace of his true, free national identity would hasten his acceptance by white America, a position he reiterated in an address on September 28, 1928:

> If you have pride and love your nation, join the MOORISH SCIENCE TEMPLE OF AMERICA and become a part of this divine movement.... Come good people, because I, the prophet sent to redeem this nation from mental slavery which you now have, need every one of you who think that your condition can be better...
> If the European and other nations are helping me, why not you? It is your problem. The "Negro" problem is being solved only as it can and that is by the Moorish National Divine Movement. *If you have a nation you must have a national name in order to be recognized by the nation as an American citizen.* This is what was meant when it was said: 'Seek ye first the kingdom of heaven and all these things would be added unto you.[34] [italics added]

Noble Drew Ali reasoned that there was a connection between the ability of Americans to identify their ethnic heritage and their enjoyment of American citizenship. Once the Moors fully embraced their own background, their circumstances in North America would undergo some degree of amelioration.

Rather than haphazard and undisciplined, Noble Drew Ali's use of biblical authority should be viewed as skillful and perspicacious. The same observation applies to his interpretation of history, at least insofar as it concerns the African experience in North America. In a 1929 editorial and "divine warning" entitled "What Shall We Call Him?," Noble Drew uses history to answer the query:

> Some say "Negro," another will brand him "Race Man," still another will call him "Afro-American," and then comes "Colored," "Dark American," "Coon," "Shine," "The Brethren," and your "Folks."... Is it that these people have no proper name? Did they have a National name when first brought to these shores in the early part of the Seventeenth Century? If so, what was it?

The assigning of these various appellations, according to the analysis, constituted "an act of European psychology." That is, the renaming of the African-descended was not the result of ethnographic ignorance but was a deliberate strategy, such that the various names all signify "something inferior to theirs [Europeans]." With respect to complexion, whiteness is the "color of purity," whereas blackness "represents everything of evil." The reduction of difference to phenotypic divergence is one thing; the full achievement of deprecation, however, requires the African's removal from history:

[34] See Noble Drew Ali, "Prophet Drew Ali Speaks to the Nations – Needs Strong Men and Women," at the end of the 1996 reprint of the *Circle Seven Koran*, x–xi.

The "Negro," as they were called in this nation, have no nation to which they might look with pride. Their history starts with the close of the Civil War or more properly with his being forced to serve some one else. Thus he is separated from the illustrious history of his forefathers who were the founders of the first civilization of the Old World. This matter should be looked into with a hope of correcting it.[35]

Europeans, though responsible for implementing historical erasure, were themselves ultimately the instruments of divine displeasure, since "through sin and disobedience every nation has suffered slavery, due to the fact that they honored not the creed and principles of their forefathers." Loss of historical identity for the Moors, therefore, was a direct outcome of an earlier apostasy:

That is why the nationality of the Moors was taken away from them in 1774 and the word negro, black and colored, was given to the Asiatics of America who were of Moorish descent, because they honored not the principles of their mother and father, and strayed after the gods of Europe of whom they knew nothing.[36]

In Noble Drew Ali's formulation, reference to the "gods of Europe" bears a pagan, pre-Christian imprimatur; European Christianity is polytheistic, while the whole matter of religion is premised as a function of birth and racial affinity:

Therefore we are returning the Church and Christianity back to the European Nations, as it was prepared by their forefathers for their earthly salvation.

While we, the Moorish Americans are returning to Islam, which was founded by our forefathers for our earthly and divine salvation.

Come all ye Asiatics of America and hear the truth about your nationality and birthrights, because you are not negroes. Learn of your forefathers ancient and divine Creed. That you will learn to love instead of hate.[37]

To "love instead of hate," a mantra running throughout Moorish Science literature, was an admonishment not necessarily intended to inform Moorish behavior toward "non-Asiatics." The phrase appears in the title of the *Circle Seven Koran: Know Yourself and Your Father God-Allah, That You Learn to Love Instead of Hate*. This suggests that it is meant to serve principally as a corrective to antisocial behavior and counterproductive activity within the black community and between persons of African descent. The embrace of the true religion, Islam, was therefore foundational to the improvement of the self-perspective, which would positively affect intra-Asiatic relations. Islam would allow the African-descended to overcome self-abnegation and fully embrace themselves.

In contrast, Moorish literature on Europeans and their descendants is more suggestive than explicit. In general, Europeans are not presented in the most flattering of lights. In addition to locating Christian Europe within the vastness of pagan realms, Moorish Science associates a lack of civilization with Europe and endeavors to memorialize a period of history "when barbaric tribes from

[35] This is among the materials found at the end of the 1996 reprint of the *Circle Seven Koran*, xvi.
[36] See *Circle Seven Koran*, chapter 47, 14–17.
[37] See Noble Drew Ali, "The End of Time and Fulfilling of the Prophecies," found at the end of the 1996 reprint of the *Circle Seven Koran*, 141–42.

the North were ravishing all countries...during the days when the burning of libraries was a fad for despotic soldiers."[38] The depiction of Europeans as pagan savages suggests a permanency of character, a condition of the marrow, that is resistant and ongoing. The rejection of Europe therefore is not merely a question of culture but extends to an essentialized notion of their collective nature. Thus:

We, as a clean and pure nation descended from the inhabitants of Africa, do not desire to amalgamate or marry into the families of the pale skin nations of Europe. Neither serve the gods of their religion, because our forefathers are the true and divine founders of the first religious Creed, for the redemption and salvation of mankind on earth.[39]

The abhorrence for "amalgamation" with "pale skin nations" may reflect Garveyite influence, and in that sense was a key component of a racial counter-discourse that sought to reverse the ascending ladder of color hierarchy from black to white. However, Moorish Science appears to go beyond Garveyism in its valuative assessment of whiteness, as can be interpreted from a series of questions and answers in its *Koran for Moorish Children*:

92. What title does Satan give himself? God.
93. Will you define the word White? White means Purity, Purity means God, and God means the Ruler of the Land.
94. To who do we refer to at times, as being the GREAT GOD? ALLAH.
95. Is the devil made in the Image and Likeness of ALLAH? No, he is the shadow of our lower-selves and will pass away.[40]

This rather elliptical passage, having distinguished between God Almighty and another who is in fact "Satan," appears to associate the latter with whiteness and modern empire; at the same time, the identification of "the devil" with the "lower-self" is consistent with earlier passages of the *Circle Seven Koran* in which "the devil" is presented as pre-enlightened human nature and therefore inside of every person, as opposed to some powerful, incorporeal entity.[41] It is therefore possible that the *Koran for Moorish Children* is distinguishing between Satan and the devil, and associating the former with Europe and political, global domination. If so, it would mean that the depiction of whites as the personification of evil did not begin with the Nation of Islam but has more historical roots. Indeed, the next chapter will argue for an even earlier periodization of such a conceptualization.

This assessment of the more significant of the *Circle Seven Koran*'s tenets, while establishing its objectives in relation to the broader social context and concerns, does not at all get to the question of how "Islam" was practiced and

---

[38] See Noble Drew Ali, "Moorish Costume Balls," at the end of the 1996 reprint of the *Circle Seven Koran*, xlvi.
[39] See Nobel Drew Ali, "The End of Time and Fulfilling of the Prophecies," 141.
[40] See *Koran for Moorish Children*, at the end of the 1996 reprint of the *Circle Seven Koran*, questions 92–95.
[41] See for example, *Circle Seven Koran*, chapter 3, 5–7, 17, 19–22; chapter 15, 13.

experienced by the adherents of Moorish Science. The answer to this particular query necessarily begins with a consideration of precisely who Noble Drew Ali claimed to be. In addition to being a prophet, it would appear that Noble Drew Ali saw himself as the reincarnation of Jesus and Muhammad. This may be something of a stretch, but it is based on readings of both the *Koran for Moorish Children* and the *Circle Seven Koran*. In the former can be found the following question:

81. What is the name of the person into whom Jesus was first reincarnated? Prophet Mohammed the Conqueror.[42]

In this formulation, not only are the messages of Jesus, or 'Isa, and Muhammad calibrated, but the messengers themselves become one continuous person. The *Circle Seven Koran* elaborates further:

'Isa himself was of the true blood of the ancient Canaanites and Moabites and the inhabitants of Africa.

Seeking to redeem His people in those days from the pressure of the pale skin nations of Europe, Rome crucified Him according to their law.

The Europe had peace for a long time until Mohammed the First came upon the scene – and fulfilled the works of 'Isa of Nazareth.[43]

"Prophet Mohammed the Conqueror" is identified as "Mohammed the First" in this instance; Muhammad the Second is identified by Moorish Science as the Ottoman ruler Muhammad (who lived 1429–81).[44] This would all suggest that a Muhammad the Third was envisioned, and evidence presented later in this chapter in fact identifies Noble Drew Ali as the one anticipated. In addition, the fact that 'Isa was *first* reincarnated in Muhammad would also suggest 'Isa would be reincarnated again. That Noble Drew Ali was the chosen vessel for that reincarnation is supported by the contemporary appropriation of the John the Baptist–Jesus historical tandem:

In these modern days there came a forerunner, who was divinely prepared by the great God-Allah and his name is Marcus Garvey, who did teach and warn the [v]ile earth to prepare to meet the coming Prophet; who was to bring the true and divine Creed of Islam, and his name is Noble Drew Ali.[45]

The identification with Marcus Garvey is interesting in that it attempts to align Moorish Science with the vision and visibility of the Garvey movement while claiming a far greater authority for Noble Drew Ali by way of analogy with the prophets of old. While Noble Drew clearly thought highly of Marcus Garvey (and even more highly of himself), there is no evidence that Garvey reciprocated the sentiment. Indeed, based on correspondence between Leonard Smith,

---

[42] See the *Koran for Moorish Children*, question 81.
[43] See the *Circle Seven Koran*, chapter 46, 1–5.
[44] This information can be found in a prefatory statement to the 1996 reprint of the *Circle Seven Koran* entitled "From the Renewer," by the Grand Sheik Richardson Dingle-El, iv–v.
[45] See Noble Drew Ali, "The End of Time and Fulfilling of the Prophecies," 140.

the president of the UNIA's Detroit division, and an incarcerated Garvey in September of 1927, the latter had never heard of Noble Drew Ali. Told that Noble Drew was identifying with Garvey and was successfully winning UNIA members over to Moorish Science, Garvey responded:

I know nothing of the man referred to. It is silly for people to allow every unknown person to agitate and influence them on such serious matters. I have spoken and written enough for the people of Detroit to understand [the] purpose of organization and not allow strangers to decoy and exploit them by calling on or using my name.[46]

In fact, concern within the UNIA over Moorish Science extended beyond Noble Drew's death. In a deeply ironic turn of events, UNIA officials, having formerly voiced their suspicions that the NAACP had played a key role in encouraging government harassment of Garvey, now called for the government to take similar actions against the Moorish Science movement. In a May 21, 1935 letter from UNIA Secretary Benjamin W. Jones to Joseph B. Keenan, assistant general in charge of the criminal division of the Justice Department, Jones argues that a deported Garvey should be allowed to return to the United States in order to check the rise of radical black organizations such as the Pacific Movement of the Eastern World (to be discussed in the next chapter) and the Moorish Science Temple. Jones then adds the following:

The Moorish American Science Temples ne[ed] to be checked upon, too, for much of their teachings and activities are subversive to the principles of American ideals; and the[y] are winning the people to their folds under th[e] pretense that they they [sic] are doing Garvey's work, as he no longer can return; then the poor fools[,] not being in touch with Mr. Garvey, accept what they hear and fall in line, and the resul[ts] are, the injustice that was handed down to us, through the deporation [sic] of Mr. Garvey by the Rep[ublicans] is ever put before them, so it makes it rather easy for them to become radical, an[d] there is no one to guide them aright.[47]

The 1927 and 1935 correspondence reflects frustration with the apparent success of Moorish Science's self-presentation as successor to the UNIA. It also provides indirect evidence of the former's growth (at least in profile), an observation further supported by the fact that the Moorish Science movement, along with the Pacific Movement of the Eastern World and other related organizations, was under surveillance by the FBI and the State Department during the 1930s.[48]

If Garvey's apparent ignorance of (or even disdain for) Noble Drew had any impact on the latter's sense of special purpose, it is indiscernible. From every indication, Noble Drew presented his relationship to God in an idiom of

---

[46] See Smith to Garvey, September 19, 1927, and Garvey to Smith, ca. September 21, 1927, Federal Archives and Records Center, East Point, Georgia, Atlanta Federal Penitentiary Records, in Robert A. Hill, ed., *The Marcus Garvey and Universal Negro Improvement Association Papers* (Los Angeles and Berkeley: U. of California Press, 1990), vol. 7, 82, footnote 2.

[47] Ibid., 619–21.

[48] Ibid., 621, footnote 2.

conceptualization analogous to that of the New Testament Jesus (particularly in the book of John), an assessment reflected in the language of a letter written to adherents while Noble Drew was jailed in 1929:

To the Heads of All Temples, Islam: I your prophet do hereby and now write you a letter as a warning and appeal to your good judgment for the present and the future. Though I am now in custody for you and the cause, it is all right and is well for all who still believe in me and my father, God. I have redeemed all of you and you shall be saved, all of you, even with me.... Remember my laws and love one another. Prefer not a stranger to your brother. Love and truth and my peace I leave you all. Peace from your Prophet, Noble Drew Ali.[49]

Whether Jesus reincarnate or not, Noble Drew Ali was at the very least considered a holy prophet. The highest proof of his claim was the *Circle Seven Koran*. There is some confusion, however, over the nature of the document. In the body of the text itself is found the following statement of purpose:

The fallen sons and daughters of the Asiatic Nation of North America need to learn to love instead of hate, and to know their higher self and lower self. This is the uniting of the Holy Koran of Mecca, for teaching and instructing all Moorish Americans, etc.[50]

The "uniting of the Holy Koran of Mecca" is the operative phrase and, while enigmatic, appears to refer to the book's raison d'être: The book was written so that members of this particular branch of the Asiatic nation could achieve the stated objectives. If this is a reasonable reading, then the referenced "Holy Koran of Mecca" is none other than the *Circle Seven Koran*. The question, then, becomes this: Did Noble Drew Ali attempt to pass off his *Circle Seven Koran* as the authentic Qur'ān of orthodox Islam?

A statement that appears in the 1996 reprint of the 1927 original *Circle Seven Koran* suggests that Noble Drew Ali did not make such an attempt:

The Moorish Science Temple of America deriving its power and authority from the Great Koran of Mohammed to propagate the faith and extend the learning and truth of the Great Prophet of Ali [Allah?] in America. To appoint and consecrate missionaries of the Prophet and to establish the faith of Mohammed in America. The Holy Koran Circle 7 is the Book of the Seven Seals, mentioned in the Biblical Scriptures (Revelation, Chapter 5).[51]

The statement is prefatory, the style of writing different from chapters 45 through 47, for which Noble Drew Ali is clearly the author. As a (subsequent) emendation, the statement distinguishes the *Circle Seven Koran* from the "Great Koran of Mohammed." It is entirely possible that Noble Drew intended for the document to be understood as a body of revelation and instruction separate from the Qur'ān of orthodoxy, and that the "Great Koran of Mohammed" (of

49 This appears in Fauset, *Black Gods of the Metropolis*, 43–44.
50 See *Circle Seven Koran*, chapter 45, 1.
51 This appears at the beginning of the reprint of the *Circle Seven Koran*, i.

the preface) should not be confused with the "Holy Koran of Mecca" (in chapter 45). Like the uncertainty surrounding his relationship to the reincarnation of Jesus and Muhammad, ambiguity rather than precision clouds claims of the *Circle Seven Koran*. One must therefore allow for the possibility that such lapses in clarity were part of a conscious strategy of shrouding, designed to heighten mystery and leave open various exegetical avenues.

Perhaps practical considerations can also provide some insight into the relationship between the *Circle Seven Koran* and the Qur'ān. The first major English translation of the latter by Maulana Muhammad Ali became available in 1917; as an Ahmadiyya text, it is known that Noble Drew Ali's disciples obtained copies of this translation and later acquired the translation of Yusuf Ali.[52] Given his prominence, numerous following, and the ten-year span between Maulana Muhammad Ali's translation and the publication of the *Circle Seven Koran*, it is difficult to understand how Noble Drew Ali could not have had some knowledge of the ancient, authoritative tome. What is arresting, however, is that the *Circle Seven Koran* bears no relationship to the Qur'ān of old; as will be discussed, Noble Drew Ali compiled his book from several non-Islamic sources and influences. Two conclusions, equally disturbing from the view of orthodoxy, flow from these observations: Either Noble Drew Ali was in fact quite ignorant of the substance of the Qur'ān and therefore created a "Koran" out of the need for a written revelation (given his claim to head a Muslim community); or, having some knowledge of the Qur'ān, Noble Drew Ali made the determination that it required supplementation, either because it did not sufficiently address the needs of Moorish Americans or because of his own need to establish his claims to prophethood, or both. The existence of the *Circle Seven Koran* and Noble Drew Ali's prophetic office were deeply problematic for Sunni Muslims, emblematic of an often tense relationship between the larger Muslim world and Muslims of African descent in North America that would obtain for most of the twentieth century.

While Moorish Americans may have read the Qur'ān, there is no doubt that the *Circle Seven Koran*, along with several related materials authored by Noble Drew Ali, served as the community's primary source of written spiritual authority. The worship service in a Moorish Science temple, as recorded sometime during the 1930s and 1940s by Arthur Huff Fauset, underscores the centrality of the document. After leading a soft chant joined by the gender-segregated congregation in similar low modulation, the leader of the temple, facing the assembly, read from the *Circle Seven Koran* (or *Holy Koran*), again speaking "barely above a whisper." Continuing in hushed tones, the temple leader "proclaims the reincarnation of their Prophet, Noble Drew Ali, and states that he is in reality Mohammed III, who gave them a nation which he called Morocco."[53] The remainder of the service is taken up with admonishments

[52] See Rashad, *Elijah Muhammad*, 55; Aminah Beverly McCloud, *African American Islam* (New York and London: Routledge, 1995), 17.

[53] See Fauset, *Black Gods of the Metropolis*, 48.

and teachings concerning the true identity of the Moors, the European provenance of Christianity, and the need to follow American laws. There was very
little singing; the few hymns were mostly chants converted from the Christian
context, so that "Give Me that Old Time Religion" became "Moslem's that Old
Time Religion," and so on. Men and women offered prayers with the following
invocation:

Allah, the Father of the Universe, the Father of Love, Truth, Peace, Freedom and Justice.
Allah is my protector, my Guide, and my Salvation by night and day, through His Holy
Prophet, Drew Ali, Amen.[54]

Fauset notes that "there is a complete absence of that emotionalism which
is considered characteristic of Negro [Christian] services," and that the services of the Moorish Science temple "are extraordinarily quiet," beginning and
ending punctually, "a most unusual condition in Negro churches."[55] The emphasis on conservatism and self-restraint was inculcated to further establish
lines of demarcation between Christianity and Moorish Science; the absence
of "emotionalism" should be read as a critique of the energized liturgies of
African-descended Christians, "signifying" upon the latter.

During the period of Fauset's observations, Moorish Americans prayed three
times a day, a practice found often enough among Muslims in West Africa and
transferred to the Americas by means of the transatlantic trade. Facing the
east at sunrise, noon, and sunset, the Moors faced Mecca with uplifted hands;
however, the prostrations and bows that normally accompany prayer were
missing. Friday was the high holy day, a Sabbath, in conformity with orthodoxy, although meetings were held on Sunday, including Sunday School. Other
holidays included "Christmas," celebrated on January 8 in commemoration of
the day on which Noble Drew Ali was "reincarnated," again demonstrating
the intimate connection in Moorish Science between Jesus and Noble Drew.
In greeting one another, the Moors would repeat "Islam" or "Peace" (in their
understanding), with a raised right hand, palm out.[56]

Concerning marriage, monogamy was practiced and divorce was rare among
the Moors. Husbands were expected to provide for their families, while wives
were the primary homemakers and were to obey their husbands; chapters 21
and 22 of the *Circle Seven Koran* provide marital instructions for husbands and
wives, while the next two chapters discuss child rearing and behavior. Marriage
ceremonies were to be carried out by ordained ministers in conjunction with
temple heads; apparently the latter were not licensed by the state to perform
such duties.

---

[54] See Wilson, *Sacred Drift*, 33.
[55] See Fauset, *Black Gods of the Metropolis*, 48–50.
[56] Ibid., 50–51; also see McCloud, *African American Islam*, 15–16. For prayer patterns in West Africa
and North America, see earlier chapters in this volume and also Michael A. Gomez, *Exchanging
Our Country Marks: The Transformation of African Identities in the Colonial and Antebellum South*
(Chapel Hill: U. of North Carolina Press, 1998).

And any man desiring to take unto himself a wife and receive our Moorish rites, he must go to the City Hall and receive his license to be registered in that city, county, and state. It then must be turned over in the hands of the aforesaid ordained minister and head of a temple after it has been properly signed by city official. The price thereby for such administering to man and wife will be five dollars. For all those who have their papers and desire our Moorish marriage ceremony, it is three dollars.

It would appear that there was some confusion in early Moorish Science over the need for the state to sanction Moorish marriages. Noble Drew Ali determined that such sanctions were necessary:

We Moors cannot marry no one; but we obligate you, according to our divine laws and covenant and the lasts [laws] of the land. This must be proclaimed and made known to every temple so that there will be no misunderstanding. There will be no misunderstanding about I, the Prophet, and my teachings because Allah alone binds two hearts together as a unit. These are the marriage obligations and instructions for man and wife.[57]

Regarding dietary proscriptions and other miscellanea, meat of any kind along with eggs and alcohol were prohibited; fish and vegetables were permitted. Sumptuary rules mandated that men wear their red fezzes at all times, including inside the temple. Such requirements were arguably influenced by orthodox Islam. Other "divine laws," however, were more likely influenced by the racial politics of the day. For example, the body was to be kept scrupulously clean by bathing, a probable response to the prevailing view of blacks as perpetually (perhaps incurably) dirty. A strain of puritanism pervaded the movement, as smoking and cosmetics were banned. The banning of tobacco and body paint, while informed by such considerations, was at the same time connected to the project of cleansing the Moors of European cultural contamination, so that all intoxicants, "indulgence in European games," secular dancing, and attending the movie house were also forbidden. Perhaps more interesting was the proscription against chemical straighteners for the hair, clearly enacted for the purpose of encouraging the African-descended to embrace their own natural qualities.[58]

The foregoing information suggests that the adherents of Moorish Science possessed a form or variant of Islam, as is evident by the three daily prayers, the selection of Friday as the holy day, the dietary proscriptions, and the fezzes. As Aminah McCloud has observed, in the absence of orthodoxy's guiding written authorities, Moorish "men and women put into effect the Islamic norms of hospitality, modesty, and gender separateness."[59] The really fascinating question,

[57] See the *Circle Seven Koran*, chapters 21–24; Noble Drew Ali, "Prophet Sends Marriage Law to All Temples," at the end of the 1996 reprint of the *Circle Seven Koran*, xliii–xliv; Fauset, *Black Gods of the Metropolis*, 51.

[58] See Fauset, *Black Gods of the Metropolis*, 51; Wilson, *Sacred Drift*, 33; Marsh, *From Black Muslims to Muslims*, 44–46. The notion that shaving was also prohibited is contradicted by the photos of Moorish Temple men, most of whom were clean shaven.

[59] See McCloud, *African American Islam*, 15–16.

however, is not concerned with the ability of Moorish Science to fashion an Islamic way of life in the void; rather, the truly absorbing query has to do with the extent to which Moorish Science purposely distanced itself from Sunni Islam. Rather than assuming a scenario in which information is unattainable and inaccessible, the question posits the probability of access to at least the Qur'ān, and to the presence of individuals who were practicing a conventional form of religion. That such individuals were known to the Moors will be demonstrated later in the chapter. When combined with Noble Drew Ali's overall preoccupation with the plight of African-descended people, the existence of sanctioned alternatives would support the notion that much of the divergence between orthodox Islam and Moorish Science was consciously achieved and maintained.

*   *   *

What were the sources of Noble Drew Ali's thought, if not orthodox Islam? To answer the question requires a return to the *Circle Seven Koran*. A simultaneously remarkable and unremarkable document, it exemplifies an economy of style, some 139 pages divided into forty-seven chapters. It can be stated with confidence that the book does not suffer from vainglorious boasts of originality. Indeed, the book is more precisely a compilation of previously published New Thought or Rosicrucian texts. This observation need not diminish claims that the *Circle Seven Koran* constitutes divine revelation; however, it does mean that Noble Drew Ali "encountered" most of the revelation indirectly, identifying sacred, arcane utterance rather than receiving it afresh. The real problem with the *Circle Seven Koran*, therefore, does not issue from its mostly derivative nature but from the fact that its sources are unacknowledged. Noble Drew Ali is therefore susceptible to the charge of being one of the more significant plagiarists of the twentieth century.

Beginning with the second part of the book, Chapters 20 through 44 of the *Circle Seven Koran* contain instructions for proper behavior as it applies to young people, young married couples, and children. These chapters are essentially taken verbatim from a book entitled *Unto Thee I Grant*.[60] There are very few

---

[60] See anon., *Unto Thee I Grant* (San Jose: Supreme Grand Lodge of A.M.O.R.C., 1970; orig. pub. 1925 in San Francisco, Oriental Literature Syndicate). The correspondences between the two texts are as follows:

Circle Seven Koran	*Unto Thee I Grant*
Chap. 20	Book Three, Chap. V
Chap. 21	Book Three, "Woman"
Chap. 22	Book Four, Chap. I
Chap. 23	Book Four, Chap. II
Chap. 24	Book Four, Chap. III
Chap. 25	Book Four, Chap. IV
Chap. 26	Book Five, Chap. I
Chap. 27	Book Five, Chap. II
Chap. 28	Book Five, Chap. III
Chap. 29	Book Five, Chap. IV

changes, so much so that the transcription raises some interesting questions. For example, Chapter 28 of the *Circle Seven Koran* represents a whole-cloth adoption of instructions to servants and masters from *Unto Thee I Grant*, passages that support the servile estate. In another, presumably embarrassing instance, the *Circle Seven Koran* uses unaltered language borrowed from the Rosicrucian text regarding a virtuous woman:

But when virtue and modesty enlighten her charms, the lustre of a beautiful woman is brighter than the stars of Heaven. . . . The whiteness of her bosom transcendeth the lily; her smile is more delicious than a garden of roses.[61]

In denigrating the "pale skins" of Europeans and contesting the desirability of "amalgamation" elsewhere in the document, the celebration of the white bosom seems an inconsistency (at least to some), its unmodified transposition to the *Circle Seven Koran* yet another mystery.

Passages borrowed from *Unto Thee I Grant* are for the most part innocuous, filled with witticisms and generalizations cast in proverbial tone. The theological core of the *Circle Seven Koran* is to be found in the first half of the book, and eighteen of the first nineteen chapters are in fact lifted from Eva S. and Levi Dowling's *The Aquarian Gospel of Jesus the Christ.*[62] Except for substituting Allah for God and 'Isa for Jesus to render an Islamic gloss, small and inconsequential differences between the two documents are attributable to errors of reproduction, grammar, and to the need to adjust language descriptive of European phenotype. An example of the latter, for instance, can be found in the *Circle Seven Koran*, Chapter 5, verse 5, which reads as follows:

And Mary asked the guards had they seen 'Isa, a little boy about twelve years old.

Chap. 30	Book Six, Chap. I
Chap. 31	Book Six, Chap. II
Chap. 32	Book Six, Chap. III
Chap. 33	Book Six, Chap. IV
Chap. 34	Book Six, Chap. V
Chap. 35	Book Seven, "Religion"
Chap. 36	Book Eight, Chap. I
Chap. 37	Book Eight, Chap. II
Chap. 38	Book Eight, Chap. III
Chap. 39	Book Eight, Chap. IV
Chap. 40	Book Nine, Chap. I
Chap. 41	Book Nine, Chap. II
Chap. 42	Book Nine, Chap. III
Chap. 43	Book Nine, Chap. IV
Chap. 44	Book Nine, Chap. V

[61] see the *Circle Seven Koran*, chapter 20, 6–7.
[62] See Eva S. And Levi Dowling, *The Aquarian Gospel of Jesus the Christ* (London: C. F. Cazenove and Los Angeles: Royal Publishing, 1909).

In the *Aquarian Gospel*, the verse reads as follows:

And they went up to the temple courts and asked the guards, Have you seen Jesus, a fair-haired boy, with deep blue eyes, twelve years of age, about the courts?[63]

An example of apparent transcription error can be found in the first verse of *Circle Seven Koran's* Chapter 13, which was originally a summary statement in the *Aquarian Gospel* rather than an actual verse.[64]

While appropriated, the passages from the *Aquarian Gospel* that appear in the *Circle Seven Koran* were in fact selected; everything from the former was not transcribed. This means that Noble Drew Ali identified significant meaning in what he borrowed, so much so that he elevated those passages to the plane of the sacrosanct. It is therefore the case that the teachings contained in the borrowed portions shaped the Moorish catechism in fundamental ways. A review of these passages, as relayed in the first nineteen chapters of the *Circle Seven Koran*, reveals that among its more salient concepts is the conviction that evil originates within the human being (as opposed to an externalized "devil"); that heaven and hell are not ethereal, afterlife experiences but, on the contrary, are distinct conditions on earth; and that 'Isa, or Jesus, was closely associated with a clandestine order of mystics whose activities very much resemble those of Freemasonry. All three of these concepts demonstrate the influence of Rosicrucian, New Thought beliefs, as does Noble Drew Ali's declaration that "we honor all the Divine Prophets, Jesus, Mohammed, Buddha and Confucius."[65] Some of these concepts would, in turn, influence the philosophical trajectory of the Nation of Islam.

[63] Ibid., Section VI, Chapter 20.
[64] The correspondences between the two texts are as follows:

Circle Seven Koran	Aquarian Gospel of Jesus the Christ
Chap. 2	Section III, Chap. 7
Chap. 3	Section III, Chap. 8
Chap. 4	Section IV, Chap. 15
Chap. 5	Section VI, Chap. 20
Chap. 6	Section VI, Chap. 21
Chap. 7	Section VI, Chap. 22
Chap. 8	Section VI, Chap. 26
Chap. 9	Section VI, Chap. 27
Chap. 10	Section VI, Chap. 28
Chap. 11	Section VI, Chap. 32
Chap. 12	Section VI, Chap. 33
Chap. 13	Section XI, Chap. 47
Chap. 14	Section XIII, Chap. 61
Chap. 15	Section XIV, Chap. 65
Chap. 16	Section XIX, Chap. 168
Chap. 17	Section XXI, Chap. 178
Chap. 18	Section XX, Chap. 172
Chap. 19	Section XXI, Chap. 176

[65] This is on the back of Moorish Science "nationality and identification" cards as well as other literature; see the Moorish Science Papers, MG 435.

Rosicrucianism is alleged to have begun in seventeenth-century "Germany" and centers around the legend of Christian Rosenkreuz, reportedly born in fourteenth-century Germany, from whence he traveled to Damascus, Egypt, and, interestingly, Morocco, after which he founded his order of mystics. Its spread to the United States is attributed to Paschal Beverly Randolph (1825–75), a self-educated product of a white father and, ironically, a Malagasy mother, such that he found it necessary to continually refute charges that he was a "Negro." He also toured various parts of the world, including Syria, and he wrote a number of books, including *Dealings with the Dead* (1861), later retitled *Soul, The World Soul*; *The Grand Secret*, or *Physical Love in Health and Disease* (1862); and *Ravalette, the Rosicrucian's Story* (1863). Having recruited black soldiers for the Union army, he moved to New Orleans after the war where he taught freedpersons and advocated for their enfranchisement. He wrote several more books during this period, including *Seership* (1868) and *Love and the Master Passion* (1870).[66]

A contemporary of Randolph was Mary Baker Eddy (1821–1910), founder of Christian Science. Born in Bow, New Hampshire, she came to believe that physical healing could take place by "moving below the surface of matter and making contact with the spiritual divine science that was fundamental and eternal" and consistent with scientific principles governing the universe.[67] Christian Science, formed as the Christian Science Association in 1876 and as a church in 1879, is said to have begun as an organized movement in February of 1866, when Baker Eddy (then Mary Patterson) recovered spectacularly from a serious fall. Although she would be opposed by a number of persons who charged her with "appropriating" the ideas of the Portland, Oregon mental healer Phineas Parkhurst Quimby, with whom Baker Eddy first consulted in 1862, she was in the vanguard of a number of like-minded groups largely made up of women. From the 1880s to 1910, these groups called their beliefs "Mental Science, Divine Science, Spiritual Science, Unity, Mind Cure, Science of Being, Home of Truth, and even, until Eddy definitively copyrighted the term in the 1890s, Christian Science."[68] It was at this time that other leaders "united their separate faiths in a loose national alliance and agreed upon 'New Thought' as the umbrella term for the movement." Although technically distinct, both Christian Science and New Thought held certain perspectives in common. They both believed, for example, that the material world is a secondary creation of the mind, and that fact and reality reside in the realm of the mental or spiritual. For both,

[66] See, for example, J. Gordon Melton, ed., *Rosicrucianism in America* (New York: Garland Publishing, 1990); Frances A. Yates, *The Rosicrucian Enlightenment* (London and Boston: Routledge and Kegan Paul, 1972).

[67] See, for example, Gillian Gill, *Mary Baker Eddy* (Reading, MA: Perseus, 1998); Robert Peel, *Mary Baker Eddy, The Years of Authenticity* (New York: Holt, Rinehart & Winston, 1977); Willa Cather and Georgine Milmine, *The Life of Mary Baker G. Eddy and the History of Christian Science* (Lincoln, NE and London: U. of Nebraska Press, 1993).

[68] See Beryl Satter, *Each Mind a Kingdom: American Women, Sexual Purity, and the New Thought Movement, 1875–1920* (Berkeley and Los Angeles: U. of California, 1999), 2–7.

human beings possess "godlike" abilities to order their own worlds through thought, and therefore only need to learn how to control those thoughts to achieve such things as physical healing, accomplished in tandem with prayer for some. While New Thought's lack of rigid structure has allowed it to grow and reformulate itself down to the present, the numerical growth of adherents to Christian Science reached a plateau by 1930, after a phenomenal increase from 26 members in 1879 to 202,000 by 1926.[69]

Noble Drew Ali, like most observers, had to be aware of the rapid emergence of Christian Science, such that "Moorish Science" was a designation most likely inspired by Mary Baker Eddy's success. However, Noble Drew did not appropriate the beliefs of either Christian Science or any other New Thought movement willy-nilly, nor did he borrow indiscriminately from Rosicrucian literature. His selections from these various sources were carefully chosen to support his own, unique articulation of faith and political being. More than any specific doctrine, what Nobel Drew learned from these movements was the notion that the individual was not a prisoner to her or his circumstances, but that, through a disciplined reordering of the understanding, change was possible. The approach qualified as a kind of science in that, if properly applied, it could affect material conditions. In view of the foregoing discussion, it is all the more remarkable that Noble Drew Ali embraced Islamism, for he had every incentive to simply follow in non-Islamic paths already laid. That he grafted elements of the multifaceted world of the cabalistic onto a theory centered upon Islam is highly significant, and once again it may point to a residual, pre-Rosicrucian extension of belief hailing back to Muslims born in Africa.

An example of an idea discussed in Rosicrucian literature but reinterpreted by Noble Drew Ali concerns the relationship between evil and human nature. Mention has already been made of the *Koran for Moorish Children's* reference to the division of the higher and lower selves in the human personality. As a further exploration of this idea, the *Circle Seven Koran's* initial chapter, the only chapter of the first nineteen that does not originate in the *Aquarian Gospel*, maintains that a human being is a "thought of Allah; and all thoughts of Allah are infinite." Physical life is the "plane of the soul," which in turn is "but the ether of the spirit plane vibrating not so fast, and in the slower rhythm of this plane, the essence of life are manifest. . . . And these soul attributes become a body beautiful." Having established human immortality within a sphered continuum, the chapter explains life on earth as a sort of school, in session until all necessary lessons are learned. Dialectically imagined, life's most important lessons are learned through the struggle against the "carnal nature," the successful negotiation of which ends with the removal of the "garb of the flesh" and union with Allah.

Chapter 3 of the *Circle Seven Koran* explores the nature of the struggle against carnality, taking significant departure from the current, commonly held view that human beings struggle against an adversary external to the body:

[69] Ibid.

There are two selves; the higher and lower self. The higher self is the human spirit clothed with soul, made in the form of Allah. The lower self, the carnal self, the body of desires, is a reflection of higher self, distorted by the murky ethers of the flesh. . . . Men seek salvation from an evil that deems a living monster of the nether world; and they have gods that are but demons in disguise all powerful. . . . And yet these gods possess no ears to hear, no eyes to see no heart [sic] to sympathize, no power to save. This evil is a myth; these gods are made of air, and clothed with the shadow of a thought. The only devil from which man must be redeemed is self, the lower self. If man would find his saviour he must look within; and when the demon self has been dethroned the saviour, love, will be exalted to the throne of power.[70]

This principle is applied to the life of 'Isa himself, who, although confronted in the wilderness by "the tempter," did in reality "for forty days . . . wrestle with his carnal self; his higher self prevailed."[71] From Chapters 6 through 12, 'Isa travels through India, initially as a student and eventually as a wise man teaching various truths that are often premised on the dichotomous etiology of the individual. In Chapter 12, the application of the two selves is the basis for the concept of heaven and hell. Identifying the virtues and benefits of labor under optimum conditions as the constituent elements of heaven, 'Isa goes on to correct the misperception of heaven as a place far removed:

My brother man, your thoughts are wrong; your heaven is not far away, and it is not a place of metes and bounds, is not a country to be reached; it is a state of mind!

Allah never made a heaven for man; he never made a hell; we are creators and make our own.[72]

It is the contention here that the Nation of Islam's identification of Europeans as devils was the culmination of a number of contributions, including those of Noble Drew Ali, who prepared the way by relocating the locus of evil from the disembodied to the corporeal. Likewise, the Nation clearly benefitted from the displacement of heaven and hell from the spiritual to the material.

In the various peregrinations of 'Isa throughout India, Egypt, Persia, Greece, and Rome, he invariably encounters an assembly of persons known as "the silent brotherhood," a mysterious group to whom 'Isa usually imparted some facet of esoterica. These encounters build on a discussion of the square, compass, twelve-step ladder, and various other carpentry tools in Chapter 5 of the *Circle Seven Koran.* Though found in the *Aquarian Gospel,* mention of these tools, along with references to the silent brotherhood, suggest a strong connection to Freemasonry. It is probable that the followers of Noble Drew Ali understood these passages as masons, reinforcing a conception of life deeply informed by the principles of Freemasonry. 'Isa presents himself as an imitable example to the silent brethren, repeatedly saying, "What I have done all men can do, and what I am all men shall be."[73] The silent brethren are present at

---

[70] See *Circle Seven Koran*, Chapter 3, 5–7, 17, 19–22.
[71] Ibid., chapter 15, 14–15.
[72] Ibid., chapter 12, 6–10.
[73] Ibid., chapter 17, 45.

his tomb and presage his resurrection from the dead (an unresolved conflict with orthodox Islam), and are the primary audience in Persia (as the "Magian Masters") when 'Isa explains that his revivification had solved "the problem of the ages," to which the brethren respond by describing 'Isa as "the only master of the human race whose flesh has been transmuted into flesh divine. He is the man of God-man of today, but everyone of earth shall overcome and be like Him, a Son of Allah."[74] The elucidation of victory over death, as the most mysterious of mysteries, is delimited to an elect few; the effect of the encounters, therefore, is to strengthen the view that such knowledge is meant for a circle of circumscription. Moorish Science was therefore inextricably intertwined with Freemasonry from its origins, bound together within the pages of a book whose title conveys an implicit claim to a complete and culminating truth capable of protecting its adherents. Reference to encircling is a double entendre, at the least.

* * *

Freemasonry is clearly a major source for Noble Drew Ali and Moorish Science, probably more influential than specifically Rosicrucian literature and New Thought. Indeed, the Rosicrucian texts may have been chosen for their inclusion of and symmetries with masonic principles, whose embrace by the Moors antedates their introduction to theosophy. Freemasonry, however, cannot be construed as solely western in origin, nor can all of the factors compelling persons of African descent to embrace Freemasonry be reduced to developments in the New World. Rather, cultural antecedents in Africa itself also contributed to Freemasonry's popularity among the African-descended population. To be sure, one can only enter the obscure waters of Freemasonry with considerable trepidation and with the caveat that, given the clandestine nature of the phenomenon, arguments are contingent and interpretations open to ongoing debate. However, the subject is unavoidable as it is central to the rise of Islam in twentieth-century North America, and so it must be engaged. While the discussion will therefore begin with Europe, it will eventually move to Africa so that a more comprehensive and reliable context can be established.

There is no agreement concerning the origins of Freemasonry. Speculation extends back to Akenaton and the Isis–Osiris cult of ancient Egypt, or alternatively it focuses on the Essenes, or yet again on the Druids, and so on. A number of traditions date the beginning of Freemasonry, also known as the Craft, to the alleged founding of the Knights Templar order in Jerusalem in 1118 following the first crusade. The name is purportedly derived from the location of the order's first headquarters on the site of Solomon's temple. Pushed out of the holy lands by 1296, crusaders and the Knights Templar supposedly moved to Cyprus, and from there to France and England by the fourteenth century.[75]

[74] Ibid., chapter 19, 35–36.
[75] Literature on Freemasonry is extensive and uneven with respect to scholarly sophistication and reliability. On the origins of Freemasonry, see, for example, Stephen Knight, *The Brotherhood:*

Whatever the historical "truths" of the Craft's origins, it is probable that a medieval guild of practicing stonemasons in Europe constituted the basis for Freemasonry's more contemporary manifestations since the seventeenth century. In seventeenth-century France, for example, the *compagnonnage*, or journeymen's association, was formed to assist the peripatetic in their search for work by providing food and shelter while protecting their joint interests against exploitative masters. At the same time that actual (skilled) laborers were organizing in France, others were joining their ranks in England and Scotland as honorary members. Gentlemen in these two lands were attempting to enter the lodges of practicing stonemasons under the concept that "in becoming a Mason, a gentleman symbolically assumed the identity of a craft worker, a manual worker, albeit a highly skilled one." Such activity was, on the one hand, "part of a general movement toward voluntary association and informal conviviality," but it was also informed by the "widespread European interest in magic and esoteric brotherhood . . . and the more specifically British tradition of collaboration between gentlemen scientists and skilled artisans." As a result, there developed two different yet related forms of Freemasonry: the "operative" wing, composed of actual laborers and skilled artisans responsible for the design and construction of edifices for both church and state; and their "speculative" analogues, gentlemen who created secret lodges "and staged ceremonies or rituals to dramatize important cultural and moral concepts." With respect to speculative Freemasonry, the scholarship ranges between those concerned principally with ritual and the "conspiracists" who view Freemasonry as a cover for eighteenth-century revolutionaries, *philosophes*, and subversives. Drawing from Enlightenment thought, the Bible, and science, it is the speculative branch that would eventually become predominant and serves as the foundation for contemporary Freemasonry.[76]

In 1717, Freemasonry completed its transition from an assembly of veritably covert societies "whose very existence was a secret," to an organizational structure publically recognized yet characterized by an inner archaeology of esoteric knowledge. In that year, the headquarters of the Grand Lodge of England was organized at the Goose and Gridiron Tavern in London; slowly, other lodges (but not all) in and around London revealed themselves and sought affiliation with the Grand Lodge. By the mid-eighteenth century, speculative Freemasonry had spread to other parts of Europe and to what would become the United States. With respect to the latter, although it is alleged that mason John Skene arrived in New Jersey from Scotland in 1682 and that Jonathan Belcher, governor

The Secret World of the Freemasons (London: Granada Publishing, 1984), 15–16; John J. Robinson, *Born in Blood: The Lost Secrets of Freemasonry* (New York: Evans, 1989), xi–xv; Allen E. Roberts, *Masonic Trivia (and Facts)* (Highland Springs, VA: Anchor Communications, 1994).

76 See Mary Ann Clawson, *Constructing Brotherhood: Class, Gender, and Fraternalism* (Princeton, NJ: Princeton U. Press, 1989), 3, 54–56; R. William Weisberger, *Speculative Freemasonry and the Enlightenment* (New York: Columbia U. Press, 1993), 1–3; Lynn Dumeil, *Freemasonry and American Culture, 1880–1930* (Princeton, NJ: Princeton U. Press, 1984), 4.

of Massachusetts and New Hampshire, was made a mason in 1704 while he was in England, the first masonic lodge is recorded to have been formed in Philadelphia in 1730. Varying claims have been made about the subsequent influence of Freemasonry on North American life and institutions, and, as an example, some maintain that fully one-third of the fifty-five signatures on the Declaration of Independence were those of masons who infused the document with perspective and detail learned from the Craft. Such a claim, even if only partially true, indicates the degree to which Freemasonry had already become a force of consequence in the early days of the American republic.[77]

By the middle of the eighteenth century, the general contours of contemporary Freemasonry had taken shape. Consistent with British interest in the supernatural, Freemasonry is essentially concerned with understanding hidden significance. That is, as simple facts, including the mathematical and scientific, serve as allegories for deeper truths, pursuit of the Craft involves a progressive unveiling of these mysteries to the initiated. Bonds are formed between those who share in the secrets, with the result that reciprocities of loyalty, service, and material support are characteristic. In meeting the basic qualification of belief in a supreme being of choice, initiates are systemically introduced to hidden truth as well as standards of moral conduct by way of ritual dramas or staged ceremonies known as "degrees." The catechism of Freemasonry, conveyed through the ritual dramas, tends to be "heavily infused with religious symbolism and allegories," with considerable focus on religious ethics, death, and immortality. For example, Solomon's temple is a principal pedagogical site:

The average Freemason derives his initial knowledge of the history of the Craft from the ritual itself. As he progresses through the ceremonies he learns that at the building of King Solomon's Temple at Jerusalem the skilled masons were divided into two classes, Apprentices and Fellows; that they were presided over by three Grand masters (King Solomon, Hiram King of Tyre, and Hiram Abiff) who shared certain secrets known only to them; that these secrets were lost by the murder of Hiram Abiff – a result of his refusal to divulge the secrets – and that certain substituted secrets were adopted "until time or circumstance should restore the former." The implication in the ritual is that Freemasonry was already established in Solomon's time and has continued as an unchanged system since then. The ritual, however, as the candidate quickly realizes, is

---

[77] See Robinson, *Born in Blood*, 178–79; Knight, *The Brotherhood*, 1–2; Weisberger, *Speculative Freemasonry*, 1–3; Clawson, *Constructing Brotherhood*, 87; Roberts, *Masonic Trivia*, 29; Robert Morey, *The Truth About Masons* (Eugene, OR: Harvest House Publishers, 1993), 73; David Stevenson, *The Origins of Freemasonry: Scotland's Century, 1590–1710* (Cambridge, England: Cambridge U. Press, 1988); Michael Baigent and Richard Leigh, *The Temple and the Lodge* (London: Jonathan Cape, 1989); P. J. Rich, *Chains of Empire: English Public Schools, Masonic Cabalism, Historical Causality, and Imperial Clubdom* (London: Regency Press, 1991); Roy A. Wells, *Freemasonry in London from 1785* (London: Lewis Masonic, 1984); James W. Beless, *Freemen and Freemasons* (New York: Vintage, 1994); Bobby J. Demott, *Freemasonry in American Culture and Society* (Lanham, MD: U. Press of America, 1986), 15. Some of these sources are quite dubious, while others are truly scholarly endeavors. Such is the nature of the literature on Freemasonry.

not literal or historical truth but a dramatic allegory by means of which the principles and tenets of the Craft are handed down.[78]

Initiates advance through three preliminary degrees while in the "Blue Lodge," a conceptual institution equivalent to a masonic elementary school. Successful completion of the three initial degrees, those of the Apprentice, Fellow or Journeyman, and Master Mason, allows the individual to join "higher bodies" or "higher degrees," references to ancillary organizations through which the person could further progress. Such organizations tended to fall under one of two major masonic traditions: the York Rite, and the Scottish Rite. Adhering to the former were such orders as the Royal Arch Masons, the Knights Templar, and the Royal and Select Masons, whereas the Scottish Rite was composed of the Chapter Rose Croix, the Council of Kadosh, and the Lodge of Perfection, among others. The summit of both traditions was the Ancient Arabic Order, Nobles of the Mystic Shrine, commonly known as the Shriners, membership in which required either the successful completion of the thirty-second degree of Scottish Rite, or prior membership in the Knights Templar. It will be necessary to return to a discussion of the Shriners.[79]

The nineteenth century saw an explosion of Freemasonry activity in the United States. The quantitative data are suspect in that they surely fail to include the number of black masons, but they remain useful in that they demonstrate the acceleration of the movement over the course of the century. Beginning in 1800, there were at least 18,000 known masons in the United States; by 1850, that figure nearly quadrupled to 66,142, and in the next ten years (or in one-fifth of the previous period) it tripled to 193,763. By 1870, there were almost half a million (446,000) masons in the United States, belonging to over 7,000 lodges. By the end of the nineteenth century, Freemasonry had become a major phenomenon in the United States; it was a "numerically massive and widely distributed presence." Put another way, the last thirty years of the nineteenth century formed "American fraternalism's golden age. Membership grew exponentially and every year saw the creation of at least one new order." Over 460 orders were launched between 1880 and 1900, and in 1901 it is estimated that over 5 million Americans had joined some 600 orders.[80] The late nineteenth and early twentieth centuries were of course a time in which women's clubs, reform associations, civic organizations, and professional associations proliferated, so

---

[78] See John Hamill, *The Craft: A History of English Freemasonry* (Bedfordshire, England: Crucible, 1986), 15–16.

[79] See Dumeil, *Freemasonry and American Culture*, xii, 9–16; Knight, *The Brotherhood*, 18–20; W. Kirk MacNulty, *Freemasonry: A Journey through Ritual and Symbol* (London: Thames and Hudson, 1991), 6–29; David Bernard, *Light on Masonry: A Collection of All the Most Important Documents on the Subject of Speculative Free Masonry* (Utica, NY: William Williams, Printer, 1829); Richard P. Thorn, *The Boy Who Cried Wolf: The Book that Breaks Masonic Silence* (New York: Evans, 1994); J. Edward Decker, ed., *The Dark Side of Freemasonry* (Lafayette, LA: Huntington House, 1994).

[80] See Dumeil, *Freemasonry and American Culture*, xi, 4–7; Clawson, *Constructing Brotherhood*, 88, 111.

Freemasonry was by no means unique in this regard. What is missing from the historiography, however, is scholarly treatment of Freemasonry of a degree and quality afforded these concomitant organizational strategies that could, in turn, provide a more comprehensive and accurate setting for the circumstances within which Noble Drew Ali developed his ideas.

A more benign reading of Freemasonry in late-nineteenth-century North America characterizes it as a "quasi-religious secret society dedicated to the ideals of fraternity, charity, and moral behavior." This version of morality emphasized "self-improvement, honesty, industry, temperance, and sobriety" in ways that "mirrored Victorian American culture." In one view, the accentuation of morality was a mark of distinction, for while Freemasonry "offered sociability, relief in times of distress, as well as possible financial and political advantages . . . the most important aspect of Masonry was its commitment to moral uplift and self-improvement."[81] However, there was another aspect to Freemasonry, as practiced by whites, and consistent with the earlier experience in England; the lodge cut across class differences while insisting upon a kind of teutonic homogeneity, incorporating materialistically disparate groups into solidarities of whiteness. Indeed, Freemasonry as a principal engine in the creation of American notions of race and gender has yet to be fully investigated, as the analysis of Clawson suggests:

In class terms, American fraternal orders seem to have been quite representative of the population they took for their own: white men of British and Northern European descent. Theirs was an egalitarianism made possible by the exclusion of women, blacks, and ethnic minorities from the relevant social universe, a universe whose boundaries fraternal institutions helped to demarcate and guard. American fraternalism thus heightened the already great social and cultural distinctiveness of those white male workers who were also the most highly skilled and privileged segment of the wage-earning work force. The fraternal order was not, in other words, a neutral social arena in which some people happened, in random fashion, to unite as brothers. Rather, it was a form of association with a particular history and content, based on deeply grounded social and cultural assumptions.[82]

Freemasonry was therefore compromised by antiblack, antifemale, anti-Catholic, anti-Jewish, antiradical, and anti-immigrant sentiments, such that the Ku Klux Klan was "quite successful in recruiting Masons to its ranks."[83] Women, excluded from membership, joined such parallel orders as the Daughters of Isis, Court of Isis for North America, Daughters of the Nile, the Order of the Eastern Star, and so on. As will be argued here, Noble Drew Ali would be influenced not only by those aspects of the Craft emphasizing esoterica, fraternal cooperation, and self-improvement, but also by its racism.

---

[81] See Dumeil, *Freemasonry and American Culture*, xii, 74.
[82] See Clawson, *Constructing Brotherhood*, 110. This is beginning to change; in addition to Clawson, see, for example, Steven C. Bullock, *Revolutionary Brotherhood: Freemasonry and the Transformation of the American Social Order, 1730–1840* (Chapel Hill: U. of North Carolina Press, 1996).
[83] See Dumeil, *Freemasonry and American Culture*, 11–12, 122–24.

Surprisingly, Moorish Science would opt for a more enlightened policy regarding issues of gender and the wielding of power.

For reasons that probably have as much to do with vestiges of African culture as they do with efforts to mimic white society, those of African descent were early on drawn to Freemasonry, undeterred by practices of exclusion. At its inception, Freemasonry among blacks was a multiethnic, transnational undertaking not without its own class pretensions. The founder of "Negro Masonry," Prince Hall, was born in Bridgetown, Barbados in 1748 to an English father and a "free Negro woman of French descent." Arriving in Boston in March of 1765 with leather-tanning skills, he became a freeholder eight years later, exercising the franchise. Converting to Methodism in 1774, he became a minister of the "colored people" before joining the colonial army in 1776. One year later, he and fourteen other Boston blacks began laying the groundwork for a masonic lodge, a group that included one "Cuff Bufform" and "Cato Speain," suggesting an Akan origin for the former and a Latino (Cuban?) derivation for the latter. These fifteen blacks were made Master Masons by an English army lodge during the American War of Independence, but their credentials were rejected by the Grand Lodge of Massachusetts. In response, in May of 1787 Prince Hall founded African Lodge, No. 459 in Boston, having received an official charter from the Duke of Cumberland. He then formed African Lodge, No. 459 in Philadelphia, in which Absalom Jones, the first black priest in the Episcopal Church of America, served as Master and Richard Allen as treasurer. Allen, having moved to Philadelphia in 1786, dedicated Bethel Church in 1794, only seven years after African Lodge, No. 459 was launched in Boston. In a real sense, then, the social and economic framework of Freemasonry provided a foundation for even the African Methodist Episcopal Church.[84]

From 1787 on and in symmetry with developments among whites, Freemasonry spread rapidly within the African-derived community, so much so that, by the first quarter of the twentieth century, many community leaders were in fact masons. As the work of Irma Watkins-Owens demonstrates, the

---

[84] On the subject of black Freemasonry, most of the following references are contemporary and by no means exhaustive: Clawson, *Constructing Brotherhood*, 132–33; Harold van Buren Voorhis, *Negro Masonry in the United States* (New York: Emerson, 1949); Harry E. Davis, *A History of Freemasonry among Negroes in America* (Cleveland: United Supreme Council, Ancient and Accepted Scottish Rite of Freemasonry, Northern Jurisdiction, U.S.A., Prince Hall affiliation, 1946); George W. Crawford, *Prince Hall and His Followers* (New York: The Crisis, 1914); William H. Grimshaw, *Official History of Freemasonry among the Colored People of North America* (New York: Macoy Pub. and Masonic Supply, 1903); William H. Upton, *Negro Masonry, Being a Critical Examination of Obligations to the Legitimacy of the Masonry Existing among the Negroes of America* (Cambridge, MA: The M.W. Prince Hall Grand Lodge of Massachusetts, 1902); Martin R. Delaney, *Origins and Objects of Ancient Freemasonry; Its Introduction into the United States, and Legitimacy among Colored Men* (Pittsburgh: The Crisis, 1853). A useful summary of black Freemasonry's development can also be found in Robert Dannin's *Black Pilgrimage to Islam* (New York: Oxford U. Press, 2002), 17–25, although my sense of the relationship between Freemasonry and the black church diverges from Dannin's view of the former as an institution of the "unchurched."

creation of a Harlem elite for this period was very much tied to the masonic lodges.[85] Freemasonry appears to have functioned as a necessary condition for upward mobility and was rather successful in bridging ethnic and cultural differences among Caribbean, Puerto Rican, and northern and southern blacks, perhaps owing to the Caribbean, African, and Latino origins of Prince Hall and his original fourteen followers. Freemasonry was probably critical to the promotion of a pan-African consciousness for the period and beyond, and, although the relationship between Freemasonry and the black intellectual elite has not been fully mapped out, it is noteworthy that Cyril Briggs, Arthur (Arturo) Schomburg, and Marcus Garvey were all masons. Black Freemasonry, an interlocking nexus of social obligations and economic cooperative ventures, succeeded in forging a sense of expansive community while restricting admission into its inner workings to the circle of those possessing secret knowledge. Largely ignored by the scholarship, Black Freemasonry was in fact a master template into which were poured so many current and successive movements both large and small, providing a cultural lingua franca and a common point of reference. Simply put, it is stunning that at a time of momentous change throughout the African diaspora, at the precise moment within which those so dispersed were organizing transnationally to challenge the vulgarities of empire, so many identified the Craft as ally.

We entered this discussion of Freemasonry by way of observing the interconnections between the Craft, Rosicrucianism, New Thought, and the *Circle Seven Koran*. Given Freemasonry's very strong affiliation with Christianity, especially among black freemasons, it would seem highly unlikely that an initiate's path would ever lead to any form of Islam. And yet, that is precisely what happened in some branches of Freemasonry. An examination of the improbable therefore begins with a group previously mentioned, the Ancient Arabic Order, Nobles of the Mystic Shrine, or Shriners. With their membership restricted to those possessing advanced degrees, the Shrine has been referred to as "the Islamic expression of Freemasonry." The Shrine was founded in New York City in 1870, and the first Shrine Temple was established two years later in that city and was named "Mecca." A second temple was established in Rochester, New York in 1875, and the two temples had a combined membership of forty-three. By 1880, there were forty-eight temples with 7,200 members; twenty years later, the temples had doubled to eighty-two, with a membership of 55,000.[86]

What is interesting for our purposes is the incorporation of certain language and adoption of imagery in the rites and customary greetings of Shriners, language that indicates Islamic influence of a kind. A few examples from the ritual

---

[85] See Irma Watkins-Owens, *Blood Relations: Caribbean Immigrants and the Harlem Community, 1900–1930* (Bloomington: Indiana U. Press, 1996).

[86] See Demott, *Freemasonry in American Culture*, 90–92; Tom C. McKenney, *Please Tell Me ... Questions People Ask about Freemasonry – and the Answers* (Lafayette, LA: Huntington House, 1994), 37–38.

of initiation will suffice. The first to enter the temple are the members, called "nobles," who only gain entrance by whispering the "mystic pass," which is "Mecca." Candidates for initiation are then greeted by an official with these words: "By the existence of Allah and the Creed of Mohammed, by the legendary sanctity of the Tabernacle at Mecca we greet you." The candidate subsequently kneels before the "Altar of Obligation," presumably called a "Muslim" altar because it is covered in black, with a Qur'ān atop (and also a Bible at times) together with the "Black Stone or Holy Stone" of black marble. The rite continues, part of which is as follows:

Grand Potentate: Who is he who hath professed to have conversed in person with the Supreme and maketh himself mightiest of his Mohammed, the Prophet of the Arab's Creed?
Gong, music and short verse.
Chief Rabban: Who but Mohammed mingled his religion with his Hourii and said: Are not these the true source of happiness?
Gong, music, verse.
Assistant Rabban: What shall befall them who have reflected with abhorrence that which the Prophet hath revealed? Wherefore their works shall not avail; do they not travel through the earth and see the end of those who were before them?

The candidate places his hand on the altar and swear a series of oaths followed by this invocation: "May Allah, the god of the Arab, Moslem and Mohammedan, the god of our fathers, support me to the entire fulfillment of the same, Amen, Amen, Amen." In concert with the rite is the entire architecture of Shriner ambience and decor, from the arabesques on the temple walls to the minarets to the red fezzes. A dictum in Shriner ritual underscores the point: "Whoso seeketh Islam earnestly seeks true direction."[87]

To be sure, Shriners are primarily known for their philanthropic endeavors and their love of socializing, and they are often perceived as "wine bibbers." The ritual partially described herein, while somewhat serious in context, did not carry any significance for the participants beyond the initiation itself. No authority on the Shriners suggests that they were or are in any way Muslim, and such is not the argument here. Rather, the issue is one of influence, and the possible conduits through which knowledge of Islam may have come to the attention of Noble Drew Ali. The Shriners, given their expansion and their elite status among masons, may have been one source.

It is more likely, however, that a cognate order drew the attention of Moorish Science's founder. The Ancient Egyptian Arabic Order, Nobles of the Mystic Shrine was founded in 1893, and it appears to have in every way served as an alternative to its white counterpart. The actual origins of this group date back to the first of May, 1893, when the World's Columbian Exposition, or World's Fair,

---

[87] See McKenney, *Please Tell Me*, 39–43; anon., *The Mystic Shrine: An Illustrated Ritual of the Ancient Arabic Order, Nobles of the Mystic Shrine* (Chicago: Ezra A. Cook, 1957), 5–40; George L. Root, *The Ancient Arabic Order of the Nobles of the Mystic Shrine for North America* (San Antonio: George L. Root, 1916).

opened in Chicago, the first such exposition to be held in the United States.[88] Popularly referred to as the "White City" in appreciation of the dazzling buildings constructed for the event (although a double entendre is also conceivable), much of the Exposition was located along the Midway Plaisance, in the midst of what is now the University of Chicago. Some eighty-six countries mounted exhibitions at the Fair, forty-eight of them within the Plaisance, the most popular site of the festivities. Populations represented along the Plaisance included Sudanese, Arabs, "Persians," Turks, and "Moors" (North Africans). The "Street of Cairo" was the greatest attraction of all, with its mosque and *sūq*, where one could find an amazing assortment of goods imported from Islamic lands, including scarves, slippers, and fezzes. Generally speaking, blacks were uninvited, notwithstanding Frederick Douglass's presence as Commissioner from Haiti. However, there were some 15,000 black folk in Chicago at the time, and many of them took great interest and delight in the various exhibitions, especially displays from North Africa and the Central Islamic Lands. Protests were registered to decry the demeaning depiction of subsaharan Africans in the Congo exhibition, and efforts were made to create a more inclusive environment such that more African Americans could participate as vendors as well as spectators. All in all, the Exposition had the effect of further internationalizing the perspective of Americans, especially those of African descent. The Fair also concretized the cultures and beliefs of others of dark hue.

One month after the opening of the Exposition, on June 2, John George Jones, an attorney, a mason, and a member of Chicago's Prince Hall Lodge No. 7, established the Palestine Temple, claiming to have had the "degrees of the Ancient Arabic Order of the Nobles of the Mystic Shrine of Masonry" conferred upon him by a "Noble Rofelt Pasha, a Deputy and Representative from the Grand Council of Arabia," a figure shrouded in mystery. By September 26, Jones had founded the Mecca Temple in Washington, D.C., and the Jerusalem Temple four days later in Baltimore. Jones went on to open the Medina Temple in New York City and the Pyramid Temple in Philadelphia, with a vision of doing the same "in every important city in North and South America." Lieutenants were selected to head up efforts in Ecuador, Uruguay, Venezuela, and Brazil. In December of 1900, representatives of the affiliated temples reorganized themselves as the Imperial Council of the Ancient Egyptian Arabic Order of the Nobles of the Mystic Shrine of North and South America and Its Jurisdictions, a move commensurate with the order's hemispheric-wide ambitions, if not yet its reach. Women, as was true of the white orders, were organized into the Daughters of Isis. The insertion of Egypt into the new appellation therefore signaled an identification with Africa, with the implicit claim of Egypt as an African nation. The Egyptian qualifier also served to distinguish between the

[88] See Root, *Ancient Arabic Order*; Joseph A. Walker, Jr., *History of the Shrine: Ancient Egyptian Arabic Order Nobles of the Mystic Shrine, Inc.* (Detroit: Ancient Egyptian Arabic Order of Nobles of the Mystic Shrine, 1993); Ernest Allen, Jr., "Religious Heterodoxy and Nationalist Tradition: The Continuing Evolution of the Nation of Islam," *The Black Scholar* 26 (1996): 6–7.

new organization and the white Shriners. The movement suffered from serious factionalism, however, as Jones was expelled from Freemasonry by the Grand Lodge of Illinois in 1895; five years later there were several competing imperial councils. By the time Jones died in June of 1914, the factionalism was unresolved.

Among the cities to which the "black" Shriners had migrated by 1901 was Newark. It is therefore probable that while Noble Drew Ali would have been aware of white Shriners, any actual involvement would have necessarily required the presence of their black analogues. That Noble Drew had an intimate knowledge of Freemasonry is certain, as he himself was alleged to be a thirty-second degree mason, which qualified him for membership in the Ancient Egyptian Arabic Order. The name *Noble* was actually the title conferred upon members of both the Ancient Egyptian Arabic Order and the white Shriners, so that Noble Drew's use of the designation in his name suggests a conscious decision to foreground his masonic credentials, as does the existence of photographs in which he is shown wearing a masonic apron and other associated paraphernalia, and demonstrates his understanding of the nature of status and distinction among the African-derived population. It would also appear that he may have been influenced by black Shriner nomenclature in his general use of the term *temple* and the specifications of "Canaanite" and "Holy Moabite," and he certainly would have been introduced to certain symbols (e.g., the fez) and Islamic phrases in the lodge that would be appropriate for Moorish Science.

Noble Drew Ali's immersion in Freemasonry was clearly residual in his subsequent conceptualization of Moorish Science. However, it must be remembered that Freemasonry among those of African descent has complicated roots, as Africans imported into the Americas enjoyed a very intimate knowledge of clandestine organization. Indeed, male and female societies were ubiquitous throughout West Africa during the period of the slave trades, and they are usually referred to as "secret" societies because of the importance of concealment "as an organizing principle." In many West African communities, these male and female societies served as functional equivalents of social, cultural, and even governmental agencies by regulating acceptable standards of behavior and assisting families in material need, providing adulthood training for those on the threshold, and dispensing justice within communities while engaging in diplomacy between them to keep the peace. Of significance is evidence that the operations of such societies as *Poro* and *Sande* of Sierra Leone were maintained in North America by the African-descended population, operations that were classified as instances of Freemasonry by contemporary observers. It was therefore the case that European Freemasonry and West African male and female societies were conceptually similar and structurally parallel, thus explaining the attraction of the former to those of African descent as well as the ease and speed with which they came to navigate its cultural waters. Africans and their progeny returned a quality of Africanness to the lodge, and, as suggested by the reorientation to Morocco and Egypt, Noble Drew Ali infused both Freemasonry and Moorish Science with a sensibility that can only be described as ancestral.[89]

But male and female societies were not the only relevant institutions imported from West Africa that affected the manner in which Noble Drew Ali and others experienced Freemasonry and the rehabilitation of cultural and social meaning, projects always and inextricably tied to the political. Although it is more difficult to demonstrate, it is probable that a number of enslaved African Muslims imported into the New World from the seventeenth through the nineteenth centuries were also practicing Sufis. It therefore follows that Sufism was not unknown among Africans and their descendants in North America, and vestiges of the lifestyle may have played some formative role in the reemergence of Islam in the early twentieth century. The argument admittedly relies much more heavily on what is known about Islam in West Africa, and it is conceded that the quest to find corroborative testimony in North America is somewhat elusive. Nonetheless, incontrovertible evidence for a substantial Muslim presence in antebellum North America, in combination with what is certain about the West African context, allows for responsible and plausible speculation, if tentative and not yet fully verifiable.

Throughout Muslim West Africa and over time, men and women were increasingly organized into brotherhoods and sisterhoods for the purpose of pursuing the experiential dimensions of serving God, moving beyond purely intellectual activity and the codification of behavior. Otherwise known as Sufism, this disciplined approach to the divine was by no means restricted to West Africa but could and can be found throughout the *dār al-Islam*. A characteristic feature of West African Sufism was the gender-segregated assembly of men and women into sessions in which the name of Allah is repeated over and over, together with various *sūras* (chapters) from the Qur'ān. Certain phrases were intoned repetitiously and in a manner consistent with cloaked terminology vocalized by comparable brotherhoods and sisterhoods throughout the Islamic world, arcane formulae that were central to the *wird*, or distinguishing ritual of the particular collective. By the beginning of the nineteenth century, there were two major brotherhoods or *ṭuruq* (singular *ṭarīqa*) in West Africa, the Qadiriyya and the Tijaniyya. Founded in Baghdad in the twelfth century by Shaykh 'Abd al-Qadir al-Jilani, the Qadiriyya had been established in Morocco by the fifteenth century and had begun to spread into West Africa around the same time. The Qadiriyya, with its emphasis on *fanā'* or "absorption" in God, was championed by the Kunta shaykhs near Timbuktu and was quickly adopted by the Hausa, Fulbe, and other West African scholars and persons of piety. The Tijaniyya in turn was founded in eighteenth-century Cairo by Shaykh Ahmad al-Tijani, the son of a woman from the western Sudan. Al-Tijani, originally from North

---

[89] For more on the male and female societies and their continuation in North America, see Michael A. Gomez, *Exchanging Our Country Marks*, 88–105; Margaret Washington Creel, *"A Peculiar People": Slave Religion and Community-Culture among the Gullahs* (New York: New York U. Press, 1988).

Africa, returned to Morocco to establish a religious community or *zāwiya* in Fez, from where the new ṭarīqa diffused into Mauritania and Senegal. It was *al-ḥājj* 'Umar al-Futi, however, who introduced the Tijaniyya into Hausaland in the first quarter of the nineteenth century, after which it became popular throughout West Africa, especially in what would become Senegal and Mali. In addition to variations of practice and interpretation among the ṭuruq, there were also distinctions between scholarly Sufism and its more popular, more accessible analogue among the masses of Muslims, who actively believed in such phenomena as miracles and saint veneration at the site of their tombs. Ṭuruq organized for women appear to have originated in the late nineteenth century and early twentieth centuries, after the transatlantic trade, and therefore they lie outside of the scope of inquiry. Other important brotherhoods such as the Sanusiyya of Muhammad 'Ali al-Sanusi (d. 1859) and the Muridiyya founded around 1886 by the Senegalese Shaykh Ahmad Bamba are similarly beyond the period of analysis.[90]

Given the prominence of organized Sufism in West Africa during the period of the transatlantic trade, it is difficult to imagine that Sufis did not arrive on North American shores. Every indication is that they did arrive, especially in view of the findings of Chapter 5, where it was observed that most of the Muslims in North America were from Senegambia, a region heavily recruited by the Qadiriyya until the rise of al-ḥājj 'Umar al-Futi. The presence of individuals such as Lamine Kaba, a member of the Jakhanke clerisy and therefore a member of a ṭarīqa, adds to the evidence. The Sufi understanding of sacred text, a dichotomous discourse containing an external meaning and a hidden meaning, certainly parallels the perspective of Freemasonry. The Sufi practice of the *bāṭin* or "secret" sciences, which includes numerology and the interpretation of not only words and phrases but the individual letters of the alphabet themselves, not only results in such practical uses as amulet-making but also conditions the overall perspective. Life comes to be seen as an unfolding duality, with meanings and shadings only understood by the initiated, a view in resonance with Freemasonry. Noble Drew Ali, whose personal lineage may indeed include

---

[90] On Sufism, one can begin with A. J. Arberry, *Sufism, an Account of the Mystics of Islam* (London: Allen and Unwin, 1975); Louis Brenner, *West African Sufi: The Religious Heritage and Spiritual Search of Cerno Bokar Taal* (London: Hurst, 1984); N. R. Keddie, ed., *Scholars, Saints and Sufis* (Berkeley: U. of California Press, 1972); Ali Salih Karrar, *The Sufi Brotherhoods in the Sudan* (London: Hurst, 1992); Donal B. Cruise O'Brien and Christian Coulon, eds., *Charisma and Brotherhood in African Islam* (London: Oxford U. Press, 1988); I. M. Lewis, *Religion in Context: Cults and Charisma* (Cambridge, England: Cambridge U. Press, 1986); Jamil Abun-Nasr, *The Tijaniyya: A Sufi Order in the Modern World* (New York: Oxford U. Press, 1965); Lucy C. Behrman, *Muslim Brotherhoods and Politics in Senegal* (Cambridge, MA: Harvard U. Press, 1970); Bradford Martin, *Muslim Brotherhoods in 19th Century Africa* (Cambridge, England: Cambridge U. Press, 1976); Fazlur Rahman, *Islam*, 2nd ed. (Chicago: U. of Chicago Press, 1979); Rex S. O'Fahey, *Enigmatic Saint: Ahmad ibn Idris and the Idrisi Tradition* (Evanston, IL: Northwestern U. Press, 1990); Javad Nurbakhsh, *Sufi Women* (London: Khaniqahi-Nimatollahi Publications, 1990); Jean Boyd and Beverly B. Mack, *Collected Works of Nana Asma'u, Daughter of Usman dan Fodiyo (1793–1864)* (East Lansing: Michigan State U. Press, 1997). See also the journal *Sufi*.

African Muslims, came out of a southern region connected to the core of the African Muslim community, and he grew up during a time when the memory and legacy of those Muslims was strong and vibrant. It may be that Sufism assisted in creating a conceptualization of life and its interior significations in concert with Freemasonry teachings and, in addition to West African male and female societies, helps to explain the rapid diffusion of Freemasonry among those of African descent. Until further investigation either substantiates or vitiates such speculation, it cannot be readily dismissed. A closer examination of the records left by such Muslims as Umar b. Said of North Carolina and Bilali of Georgia may be key. Somewhat ironically, the arrival of a politically infused Sufism in the late twentieth century would provoke a crisis among African American Muslims.[91]

There were therefore several streams that came together in the confluence that was Moorish Science. Garveyism, Rosicrucianism, Freemasonry, gendered African societies, Islam, and possibly Sufism were melded in a unique philosophy that was not without its seams, but was nevertheless novel and distinctive. In fact, one of the more intriguing aspects of its distinctiveness is the identification with Islam. Noble Drew Ali certainly did not follow the example of the masons on this score, for although the Shriners, black and white, evinced Islamic influence in their rituals, they themselves espoused Christianity in their normal lives. Rosicrucianism, in turn, is known for its divergent discourse on the life of Jesus, and for its celebration of the prophets of various religious and philosophical traditions as opposed to any special emphasis on Muhammad. One is therefore pressed to explain Noble Drew Ali's gravitation toward Islam as he understood it; this is a challenge that necessarily leads back to the legacy of enslaved African Muslims as a viable source of inspiration if not an organic foundation. While not conclusive, something moved Noble Drew Ali to declare himself a Muslim, and in doing so establish his personal legacy as a twentieth-century trailblazer, to whom all who would follow, whether orthodox or not, owe an undeniable debt.

* * *

Even those Muslim movements contemporary with Noble Drew Ali and characterized by their dissimilarity with Moorish Science owe their comparatively lesser success, to an appreciable degree, to their ability to distance themselves from the far more established reputation of Moorish Science. The most prominent example of this kind of Islamic counterdiscourse was the Ahmadiyya movement, an important branch of Islam whose North American history is most skillfully presented by Richard Brent Turner.[92] Formally established in 1900, the movement centered on the person of Ghulam Ahmad of Punjab, India (in

[91] I refer here to the rise of al-Fuqra under the Pakistani Syed Gilani. See Dannin, *Black Pilgrimage*, 74–83.
[92] See Richard Brent Turner, *Islam in the African-American Experience* (Bloomington and Indianapolis: Indiana U. Press, 1997). See also Yvonne Yazbeck Haddad and Jane Idleman

1943, Elijah Muhammad would begin serving a prison sentence in Michigan under the name *Gulam Bogans*). In 1890 and 1891, Ghulam Ahmad declared himself to be both the Mahdi (a figure who will appear at the end of time and usher in a new dispensation) and the promised Islamic Messiah (scheduled to appear at the same time), in conflict with the orthodox view that these offices will be occupied by two separate persons. He also claimed to be the *mujaddid* or renewer of the faith sent at the beginning of each new Muslim century. In another breach with Sunni Islam, Ghulam Ahmad espoused the concept of "continuous prophecy"; that is, the prophetic office did not end with Muhammad's death but continued, and that he, Ghulam Ahmad, was a prophet in the same sense that Muhammad had been. This has resonance with Noble Drew Ali, but Noble Drew took it much further by subscribing to the concept of reincarnation; it was not simply the office of the prophet that continued, but the prophet himself.

With Ghulam Ahmad's death in 1908, the Ahmadis split into the dominant Qadian and smaller Lakori factions; the Lakori party came to reject Ghulam Ahmad as a prophet while affirming his claim to be a mujaddid; the Qadian group, in contrast, asserted his prophethood and denounced all those who did not as unbelievers (*kāfirs*). Distancing themselves from the Sunnis by proscribing marriage, prayer, and funerary rites, it was the Qadian faction that launched the proselytizing effort in the West; it was therefore as a movement about which there were serious reservations that the Ahmadiyya sent Mufti Muhammad Sadiq to Philadelphia in 1920 as its first missionary to North America; the following year missionaries were sent to West Africa. Sadiq alternated the Ahmadiyya headquarters between New York City, Detroit, and Chicago from 1920 to 1922, leaving behind small Ahmadi communities as he moved from location to location. From the outset, the Ahmadis sought to distinguish themselves from the Moors by their call for multiracialism and inclusivity. Of course, this is not necessarily in conflict with Noble Drew Ali's imagination of a transnational "Asiatic" family, but if it were achieved it would certainly differ from the homogeneity of the Moors. It is not clear, however, that the Ahmadis were at all successful, at least through the 1920s. The Ahmadis were able to attract some African Americans to the movement, but evidence for their ability to persuade orthodox Muslims to do the same is lacking. The context is interesting. Those Muslims from India and the Central Islamic Lands who were able to get past racist U.S. immigration laws, and who did not repatriate in the face of debilitating experiences with American racism, were often attracted to industrial centers in the Midwest. From 1875 to 1912, and again from 1918 to 1922, Arabs from Syria, Jordan, Palestine, and Lebanon, mostly peddlers and laborers with little western education, landed jobs at such places as the Haskel Railroad Company in Michigan City, Indiana; the Ford Highland Park Plant outside of Detroit, where they were able to put down roots; and the

Smith, *Mission to America: Five Islamic Sectarian Communities in North America* (Gainesville: U. of Florida Press, 1993), 52–65.

Ford Rouge Plant in South Dearborn, Michigan, sites of significance for the subsequent chapter's discussion of Elijah Muhammad. In addition, Muslims from Bosnia and other eastern European areas arrived on the north side of Chicago as well as in Gary, Indiana. Between 1820 and 1860, and again in the early 1900s, Turks immigrated to Chicago and Detroit, as well as to New York City, Philadelphia, and San Francisco. In other words, a small but fairly diverse Muslim universe descended on North America in the early twentieth century, but the vast majority had absolutely nothing to do with the followers of Moorish Science. Arab Muslims and others created their own networks and associations in places such as Highland Park in 1919 and Detroit in 1922. Such was the promise that Mufti Muhammad Sadiq briefly moved his headquarters to Highland Park in the fall of 1920, and began publishing *The Moslem Sunrise* in response to distortions about Islam in the American press and imagination. Appearing every three months, *The Moslem Sunrise* went out of its way to condemn American racism:

There are people fairer than North Europeans living friendly and amiably with those of the darkest skin in India, Arabia, and other Asiatic and African countries. . . . In Islam no church has ever had seats reserved for anybody and if a Negro enters first and takes the front seat even the Sultan if he happens to come after him never thinks of removing him from the seat.[93]

Such rhetoric would appear to be principally aimed at African Americans rather than Arabs, eastern Europeans, or Indians. Indeed, while the Ahmadis' relationship with Sunnis was supposedly "civil," and notwithstanding the observation that Sadiq spoke Arabic and was "highly respected by all Muslims in the United States in the 1920s,"[94] it is nevertheless instructive that Sadiq moved his headquarters to Chicago in 1922, and that between 1921 and 1925, most of the 1,025 converts to the Ahmadiyya (compared with the 30,000 in Moorish Science) were African Americans in Chicago, Detroit, Gary and St. Louis, with converts adopting veils, skullcaps, fezzes and robes, while assuming Muslim names and addressing one another as "Brother Omar," "Sister Ayesha," "Sister Noor," and so on. These developments reflect the Ahmadiyya decision to focus on this demographic; when combined with the fact that few "whites" converted, this strongly suggests that the Ahmadiyya strategy was informed by both its ongoing problems with orthodox Muslim immigrants and by the fact that a variant of Islam had already begun to make significant inroads into the African American community by way of Moorish Science. Whatever Sadiq's personal credentials, he still represented a movement whose tenets were unacceptable to Sunnis; given his lack of success with the orthodox, he turned in a direction already pioneered by Noble Drew Ali.

The Ahmadiyya mission in North America, while espousing heterogeneity, was in reality an Indian-led movement with a mostly African American constituency. That is, it was a black organization for all practical purposes, so

[93] This is quoted in Turner, *Islam in the African-American Experience*, 122.
[94] Ibid., 120.

much so that even a few members of the UNIA joined in the 1920s (seven in Chicago, forty in Detroit), attracted by the anti-imperialist linkages created by Sadiq between pan-Africanism and pan-Islamism and having been primed by their conceptual symmetry with and bonds of affection for the Moors. Interestingly, Sadiq returned to India in September of 1923, and the Ahmadis in North America experienced their nadir between 1924 and 1930, corresponding to the trial, imprisonment, and deportation of Marcus Garvey. This constitutes strong evidence that the Ahmadis in North America were greatly dependent on the fortunes of pan-Africanism and nationalism among the African-derived population.

Having laid a foundation, the Ahmadiyya mission in North America was reinvigorated in the 1930s under the leadership of Sufi Mutiur Rahman Bengalee. Multiracialism was more seriously advocated as opposed to the "radical rhetoric of the 1920s." By 1940, the Ahmadiyya boasted a global membership of almost 2 million, 5,000 to 10,000 of whom were in the United States. It is Turner's contention that, until the 1950s and the emergence of the Nation of Islam, together with the influx of new and significant immigration from the Central Islamic Lands, the Ahmadiyya was "arguably the most influential community in African-American Islam."[95] Perhaps most notably, the Ahmadiyya attracted a number of jazz musicians of African descent, including such luminaries as Art Blakey, Ahmad Jamal, McCoy Tyner, Sahib Shihab, and Yusef Lateef. The dimension of jazz and Islam is fascinating and deserving of a separate investigation, but any viable discussion of the phenomenon would necessarily have to take into account the path-clearing efforts of Noble Drew Ali.

Following Dannin's discussion, Sufi Mutiur Rahman Bengalee's intervention met with mixed results among those of African descent. In one instance, it facilitated such notable conversions as Talib Dawud, an Antiguan musician who came to New York City, played with luminaries Duke Ellington, Louis Armstrong, and Dizzy Gillespie, and who converted to Islam in the meantime. One the other hand, tensions between the Ahmadiyya leadership and African American followers, principally over the former's questionable use of funds, led to the creation of the First Cleveland Mosque, an orthodox community under the leadership of al-ḥājj Wali Akram. Trailblazers such as Imām Wali Akram; Shaykh Daoud Ghani, leader of a Sunni community in rural New York; and Shaykh Daoud Ahmed Faisal, Trinidadian founder of the Islamic Mission to America in Brooklyn, are important examples of African American Muslims entering orthodoxy at an early date and (with the exception of Shaykh Daoud Ahmed Faisal) without an intervening phase through Moorish Science or the Nation of Islam.[96] However, their numbers were minuscule, testimony that most would indeed embrace the teachings of Noble Drew Ali or Elijah Muhammad before the seachange made possible by the career and personal example of Malcolm X.

[95] Ibid., 132–38.
[96] See Dannin, *Black Pilgrimage to Islam*, 35–164.

The Ahmadiyya movement, while not as distinctive in its unorthodoxy as that of the Moors, still faced serious issues of illegitimacy among the Sunni community. That both the Ahmadis and the Moors were viewed with suspicion may account for the former's muted critique of the latter. The reaction of some Sunni Muslims to Moorish Science, however, was by no means tempered. In particular, the response of Sātti Majid Muhammad al-Qadi Suwar al-Dhahab is instructive, coming to light through the scholarship of John Hunwick, R. S. O'Fahey, and Ahmed I. Abu Shouk.[97] Born into a holy family of renown in al-Ghaddar of Old Dongola, Sudan in 1883, Satti Majid probably left the Sudan after 1900 to study at al-Azhar in Cairo, although the duration of his stay is unknown. After a brief period in England, he arrived in New York City in 1904 at the age of twenty-one, and he began a series of efforts aimed at nurturing the fledgling Sunni Muslim community in North America while attracting converts and defending the honor of Islam. He launched four benevolent societies while in New York: the Muslim Unity Society (*jam'iyyat al-ittihād al-Islāmī*), the Islamic Missionary Society (*al-jam'iyya al-tabshīriyya al-Islāmiyya*), the Red Crescent Society (*jam'iyyat al-hilāl al-ahmar*), and the Islamic Benevolent Society (*al-jam'iyya al-khayriyya al-Islāmiyya*). There are lacunae in the accounts of his life, however, so that not much is known about his activities between 1904 and 1921, when he resurfaces through his correspondence.

It is possible that the missionary activities of Satti Majid led to the 1924 establishment of an independent, black Sunni group known as the Islamic Mission of America in New York City. Under the leadership of Shaykh Daoud Ahmed Faisal, the organization was also known as the State Street Mosque and the Islamic Brotherhood. While the orthodox practices of the Islamic Mission of America point to the influence of Satti Majid, its political and cultural declaration that African Americans were "not Negroes but were originally Muslims" indicates an awareness and appreciation for the teachings of Noble Drew Ali, and it suggests that the latter played an important role in preparing the African-descended for orthodoxy. The Islamic Mission in America was a source of Sunnism throughout the 1920s and 1930s, and it continued to serve in that capacity for the remainder of the century.[98]

The Sunni reaction to Moorish Science under Satti Majid was quite different. It is likely that Noble Drew Ali first came to Satti Majid's attention in a serious way after the publication of the *Circle Seven Koran* in 1927. To say that he took an extremely dim view of Noble Drew Ali's claims of prophethood as well as his *Circle Seven Koran* is to frame the matter in an idiom of diplomacy. So incensed was Satti Majid that he apparently wrote to Noble Drew, urging him to both change his name and burn his revelation. He demanded that Noble

---

[97] See Ahmed I. Abu Shouk, J. O. Hunwick, and R. S. O'Fahey, "A Sudanese Missionary to the United States: Sāttī Mājid, 'Shaykh al-Islām in North America', and His Encounter with Noble Drew Ali, Prophet of the Moorish Science Temple Movement," *Sudanese Africa* 8 (1997): 137–91.

[98] See Turner, *Islam in the African-American Experience*, 120; McCloud, *African American Islam*, 21–24.

Drew perform a caliber of miracles (*mu 'jizāt*) that only verifiable prophets could produce. He thereafter attempted to sue the Moorish Science leader in an American court of law for "bringing the Islamic faith into disrepute." Unable to achieve such redress, Satti Majid left the United States for Cairo in January of 1929 to present a formal request, or *istifā'*, to the scholarly community at al-Azhar for a legal ruling, or *fatwā*, that would condemn Noble Drew Ali. Satti Majid never returned to the United States, having failed to receive the appointment of *dā 'ī* or official missionary of al-Azhar to North America for lack of scholarly qualifications. He therefore returned to Sudan in the 1940s and died there in March of 1963, missing one of the most critical periods in the growth and expansion of Islam in North America; one can only speculate as to what impact he would have had on the process had he returned.

Satti Majid was successful, however, in obtaining three fatwās against Noble Drew Ali. Forming "one continuous document," the first was issued at al-Azhar in either 1929 or 1930; the second was written in Omdurman, Sudan in 1930; the third was recorded in Khartoum, Sudan, also in 1930. In his istifā' to the jurists, Satti Majid interprets the name Noble Drew Ali to mean "the noble one descended from 'Ali," a logical deduction although probably unrelated to Noble Drew's own understanding. Satti Majid goes on to attribute to Noble Drew the following statement:

Thirdly, that the Islam that was before him was not true Islam and he claimed that he had garnered his knowledge in the city of Fez and that he had met with leaders of the Islamic religion there and in Egypt, the Hijāz and Iraq, and that all the scholars had testified that he is the prophet promised at the end of time.... Then he said the secret of his prophecy [was] Jesus, peace be upon him. His adoption of Islam was in former times and that they had hidden this from the world. The object of worship in Islam has no eye with which it sees and no intelligence with which it reasons, nor any ear with which it hears, nor does it have power; it is nothing but fantasy, shot through with hocus pocus.[99]

Unless Satti Majid had access to documents no longer extant, it would appear that his representation of Moorish Science was faulty. Certainly the foregoing was not extracted from the *Circle Seven Koran*. Absent corroborating documents, the distortions were either deliberate or based on misunderstanding, the latter possibly a function of linguistic issues.[100]

It would have been enough for Satti Majid to mention the *Circle Seven Koran* and Noble Drew Ali's claim to prophethood. In any event, in language that would have given serious pause to any seeker of Islamic truth, the fatwās were unanimous in their condemnation of Noble Drew Ali. The *'ulamā'* or scholars of al-Azhar wrote the following: "This man of whom you asked . . . is the greatest liar in the world and the man most [guilty] of perverting [the truth]" who

---

[99] See Shouk et al., "A Sudanese Missionary," 157–58.
[100] Ibid., 187–88; here one of Satti Majid's letters to his followers in the United States demonstrates difficulty with the English language.

"deserves eternal and everlasting punishment in Hell." The 'ulamā' who taught at the Ma'had al-ilmī (learnod council) of Omdurman similarly characterized Noble Drew Ali as "a liar (*khadhdhāb*) and a charlatan (*dajjāl*) and an unbeliever (*kāfir*) and an abomination (*mamqūt*).... It is our counsel to every Muslim, indeed, to every person of sound mind, to reject the assertion of this liar and not to give his lies any weight. The liar shall know the outcome of his deeds."[101] There is no evidence that these rulings ever reached the United States. Of course, Noble Drew Ali was already dead by the time the Sudanese jurists issued their verdicts – but it is fascinating to think that his message was so upsetting and his following so impressive that Satti Majid found it necessary to travel all the way to Cairo to address the challenge.

In the November 1956 publication of *The Moorish Review*, a narrative of Moorish Science history is provided in which reference is made to a period of turbulence. Noble Drew Ali founds the Canaanite temple in 1913:

[Then,] after a period of time a man came to Newark from Sudan, Egypt teaching languages. The unbelievers (which are always in the majority) turned from the Prophet to this new comer. Brother told the people that they had a flag, and a nationality. He told them to try and get it. In his last speech in Newark the Prophet said Justice would overtake him (the language teacher) for scattering his children. It did! He was soon arrested in New York City and jailed on charges of being an imposter.[102]

This may or may not be a reference to Satti Majid. On one hand, everything matches save the matter of his detention. The alleged arrest may have something to do with the claim that he was identified by the FBI as a possible agent of Japan, and therefore he was prevented from reentering the United States[103] On the other hand, the turmoil described seems to be a more appropriate fit for the carnage left in the wake of Abdul Wali Farad Muhammad Ali, the "mysterious teacher of Islam from the East." The problem here, however, is that the 1956 account maintains the troublemaker was from Sudan, whereas information surrounding Abdul Wali Farad describes him as "Russo-Syrian." It is always possible, of course, that the 1956 narrative confuses the two men.

It is difficult to gauge the size of Satti Majid following in the United States. If he is the subject of the foregoing 1956 account, then his following seems to have been relatively considerable. On the basis of his actual correspondence, however, the opposite conclusion seems likely. In that correspondence he is often addressed as "Father," and he responds by calling his adherents "sons." The letters hail from Wilkinsburg and Pittsburgh, Pennsylvania, and mention is made of the "Cleveland and New York branches." The letters contain requests that books and magazines sent from Satti Majid be translated into English, presumably from Arabic. In one instance an apology is offered for not being able

---

[101] Ibid., 170, 177.
[102] See *The Moorish Review*, November 1956, in the Moorish Science Papers, MG 435.
[103] See Adib Rashad, *Islam, Black Nationalism and Slavery: A Detailed History* (Beltsville, MD: Writers' Inc., 1995), 141–42.

to send money from the United States. What is more important is that there is clear evidence that Satti Majid had been forced, in the very midst of his Sunni crusade, to reckon with the appeal of pan-Africanism and nationalism. One letter, dated May 18, 1932, states, "Father the idea of establishing a trade between Sudan, Egypt, Abyssinia is very pleasing and I have four men in mind who I think will be able to take care of the matter." Another letter dated September 11, 1935 bears a strong resemblance to the political sentiments of that other orthodox movement, the Islamic Mission of America under Shaykh Daoud Ahmed Faisal, and it indicates that in the proselytizing of African Americans, parts of Garveyism and Moorish Science may have been grafted into the message of Satti Majid himself. Thus, Mohammed Elias wrote the following:

We are searching the newspapers every day to see what the outcome will be in the Ethiopians and Italians dispute. We sympathize for these people as we are a part of them and do hope and pray that these matters will be settled without any injury to these peoples and that great country. We hope some day that we shall be able to return back to our home land Africa, Inshalah. I would be glad if we could colonize in or near Abyssinia as we feel we need a colony.[104]

It is fair to say, therefore, that even the most orthodox of Muslims, summoning all of the zeal for the faith and indignation against innovation that he could muster, probably had to tailor his message to a people thoroughly suffused with the teachings of Garvey and Noble Drew. Indeed, it can be argued that those who eventually embraced orthodoxy had been prepared for it by those very teachings, helping to explain the means by which practitioners gradually negotiated the chasm between what Curtis refers to as the universality of Islam and the "particularism" of black nationalism.[105] Irony of ironies, Satti Majid owed his success, such as it was, to the man he bitterly condemned as a fraud, Noble Drew Ali. In this way, the entire Satti Majid–Noble Drew Ali drama was a forerunner to and a metaphor of the larger movement over time of people of African descent from "Islamism" to orthodoxy, and it suggests the degree to which those who made the journey are indebted to the diminutive man from North Carolina.

* * *

In the consideration of the various conduits through which orthodox Islam was brought to the attention of Noble Drew Ali, the autodidact and polyglot Edward Blyden merits brief mention, not because there is substantial evidence of his direct influence on Noble Drew but in recognition of his contribution to what was generally known about Islam in Africa at the time. Born in St. Thomas, Virgin Islands in 1832, Blyden emigrated to Liberia in 1857, pioneering higher western learning in West Africa while emerging as a principal

[104] See Shouk et al., "A Sudanese Missionary," 183–91.
[105] See Edward E. Curtis IV, *Islam in Black America: Identity, Liberation, and Difference in African-American Islamic Thought* (Albany: State U. of New York Press, 2002).

figure in the formative stages of pan-Africanist thought. In articles written for missionary journals (among others), Blyden, ostensibly a Christian cleric, anticipated Noble Drew's contrast of Moorish identity and Islamic religion for blacks and Christianity for Europeans by asserting that, in relation to Africans, Arabs (and by extension Islam) "belong to a cognate race," while Christianity "has followed chiefly the migrations and settlements of members of the Aryan race."[106] With disregard for ancestral African religions (pervasive for the period), Blyden argued that "whatever may be said of the Koran...no one will doubt that Islam as a creed is an enormous advance not only on all idolatries, but on all systems of purely human origin.... The Koran is an important educator. It exerts among a primitive people a wonderful influence."[107] Islam, Blyden argued, should not be viewed antagonistically but rather as useful preparation for the Christian gospel in Africa. In a rhetorical flourish open to more than one interpretation, he envisioned a reconciliation of the ages on African soil:

It is interesting to feel that the religion of Isaac and the religion of Ishmael, both having their root in Abraham, confront each other on this continent. Japheth introducing Isaac, and Shem bringing Ishmael, Ham will receive both. The moonlight of the Crescent, and the sunlight of the Cross, will dispel the darkness which has so long covered the land. The "Dark Continent" will no longer be a name of reproach for this vast peninsula, for there shall be no darkness here. Where the light from the Cross ceases to stream upon the gloom, there the beams of the Crescent will give illumination; and as the glorious orb of Christianity rises, the twilight of Islam will be lost in the greater light of the Sun of Righteousness. Thus Isaac and Ishmael will be united, and rejoice together in the faith of their common progenitor – Ibrahīm Khalīl Allah – Abraham, the Friend of God.[108]

Whether Blyden remained a Christian or indeed converted to Islam during his many years in West Africa, of his high esteem for the latter there can be no gainsaying. His influence is more discernible on the Garveyites and later generations of Muslims and those of African descent than Noble Drew Ali, some of whose followers may nevertheless have had some familiarity with Blyden's publications, as his work antedates the founding of Moorish Science.[109]

[106] See Edward W. Blyden, *Christianity, Islam and the Negro Race* (Baltimore, MD: Black Classics Press, 1994; orig. pub., 1887), "Sierra Leone and Liberia," 264; "Islam and Race Distinctions," 277–83.
[107] Ibid., "Mohammedanism and the Negro Race," 7–8.
[108] Ibid., "Sierra Leone and Liberia," 267–68.
[109] For more on Blyden, see Hollis R. Lynch, *Edward Wilmot Blyden: Pan-Negro Patriot, 1832–1912* (New York: Oxford U. Press, 1967); Edith Holden, *Blyden of Liberia; an Account of the Life and Labors of Edward Wilmot Blyden, LL.D., as Recorded in Letters and Print* (New York: Vantage Press, 1967); Thomas W. Livingston, *Education and Race: A Biography of Edward Wilmot Blyden* (San Francisco: Glendessary Press, 1975); Edward W. Blyden, *Selected Letters*, ed. Hollis R. Lynch (Millwood, NY: KTO Press, 1978); George J. Benjamin, *Edward W. Blyden, Messiah of Black Revolution* (New York: Vantage Press, 1979); M. Yu. Frenkel, *Edward Blyden and African Nationalism*, trans. from the Russian by E. Mozolkova; ed. E. Bessmertnaya (Moscow: Africa Institute, 1978).

A luminary whose lifework may have had greater impact on Noble Drew Ali was Dusé Mohamed Ali, apparently born in Alexandria, Egypt in 1866 of an Egyptian father and Sudanese mother: "I am, myself, a cross between Arab and Ethiopian, my mother being a Nubian or full-blooded Negress – the two human elements most despised and underrated by European ethnologists."[110] While Dusé Mohamed Ali's very representation would have commended him to Noble Drew, his work as a pioneer in pan-African thought would certainly have endeared him, and it is likely that some among the adherents of Moorish Science came across his writings. Perhaps Dusé Mohamed Ali is most famous for the *African Times and Orient Review* (*ATOR*), a publication featuring a heavy dose of anticolonial critique and pan-Africanist sentiment that ran from 1912 to 1920. The *ATOR* was widely distributed among populations in West Africa, the Caribbean, India, New Zealand, Australia, and Cairo, and it made American ports of call in New York City, Pittsburgh, Los Angeles, Wilmington (North Carolina), and even Guthrie, Oklahoma. While the actual number of subscribers is difficult to determine and may have been unimpressive, contributors to the journal included such visionaries as J. E. Casely Hayford and Booker T. Washington, who (as life would have it) was an advisor to and patron of the *ATOR* from its inception, further complicating his political legacy. The *ATOR* is the obvious forerunner to Garvey's *Negro World*, and in fact Garvey worked in a low-level position, perhaps as a errand runner, for the *ATOR* from 1912 to 1913. In addition to pan-Africanism, Dusé Mohamed Ali was very much interested in Muslim and Asian affairs, something Noble Drew Ali would have supported, and he was a principal author of the Oriental, Occidental and African Society launched in 1912 and succeeded in 1914 by the League of Justice of the Afro-Asian Nations.[111] In 1921, Dusé Mohamed Ali left Britain for the United States, where, in addition to working with Garvey, he pursued various business interests. Wearing his characteristic fez, he made appearances among Detroit's Muslim community in 1922, perhaps preparing the ground in some way for W. D. Fard Muhammad's subsequent advent. The prospect that the Moorish Science Temple may not have been founded in 1913 (as tradition has it) but as

---

[110] See Ian Duffield, "Dusé Mohamed Ali and the Development of Pan-Africanism, 1866–1945" (Ph.D. diss., Edinburgh U., 1971). There is some question about Dusé 's precise origins, as several independent sources who encountered him after his arrival in England in 1876 (the name *Dusé* is taken from the last name of the the French captain who served as his guardian there) maintain that he did not know a word of Arabic, and that although he claimed to be Muslim, he could not recite "the formula of the faith." As he was a relatively dark-skinned person, there were those who believed him to be African American. In his defense, however, his move to England at a tender age, combined with his return to Egypt in 1882 only to see his mother and siblings sent off to Sudan and his father killed under conditions of war, may help to explain his apparent linguistic lapses (assuming the accounts are true). In any event, with his return to London in 1883 he would eventually become a source of solace and advice for young Egyptians traveling in London, and he maintained affiliations with Egyptian organizations there.

[111] Dusé Mohamed Ali in fact contributed to the Ahmadi journal under the leadership of the missionary to Britain Khwaja Kamal ud-Din, whom he met in 1911. Ibid., 420–25.

late as 1925 further raises the possibility that Dusé Mohamed Ali may have had more of a role in Islam's North American development than previously understood. Though not as speculative, the quality of his relationship with Garvey is not readily apparent, nor was it necessarily clarified by his departure from the UNIA in 1925, following Garvey's failed appeal but before his prison sentence began. Returning to West Africa in 1931, he breathed his last in Lagos in 1945, where his remains are buried.[112]

*   *   *

Following the tradition, Moorish Science achieved its definitive structure, and events surrounding it their climax, after the move from Newark to Chicago in 1925. Of the 30,000 members of Moorish Science nationwide, some 10,000 are estimated to have been in Chicago, clearly the epicenter of the movement.[113] With respect to organizational structure, Act One of the Moorish Science *Divine Constitution and By-Laws* describes a pyramidal government at the top of which stood Noble Drew Ali as "Holy Prophet." The power to create and enforce laws was in the hands of the "Grand Sheik and chairman" of the organization, who was to be aided in these matters by an assistant Grand Sheik.[114] It is not clear who occupied the position of Grand Sheik at the time, but it could have been one of the four men (James Lomax, Johnny Reynolds, Eddie Watts, and Sammy Rucker) who signed the 1926 certificate of incorporation as directors along with Noble Drew Ali (who signed as "Drew Alin").[115] Below the Grand Sheik and chairman of the organization were the Grand Sheiks and Sheikesses (or Governors and Governesses) of each branch temple, to whom reported elders and stewards, all of whom were in authority over the regular members (brothers and sisters). Subsequent to Noble Drew's death, structural changes included the creation of a board of directors elected to the national body by delegates from around the nation, and the establishment of grand governors who functioned at the state level.[116]

It would appear that, although the Moorish Science concept of the nuclear family was conventionally patriarchal, it remained possible for women to ascend into the higher levels of organizational management. In a group picture of the Moorish leadership at Chicago headquarters taken in 1928

---

[112] Like Noble Drew Ali, Dusé Mohamed Ali also had a penchant for "borrowing" published materials without attribution. According to Duffield (120–48), Dusé Mohamed Ali's *In the Land of the Pharaohs* (London: Stanley Paul, 1911 and New York: Appleton, 1911) heavily plagiarized the following works: Earl of Cromer, *Modern Egypt*, 2 vols. (London: MacMillan, 1908); Wilfred Scrawen Blunt, *Secret History of the English Occupation of Egypt* (London: T. Fisher Unwin, 1907); and Theodore Aaronovitch Rothstein, *Egypt's Ruin* (London: Fifield, 1910).

[113] See Bontemps and Conroy, *Anywhere But Here*, 207.

[114] See Moorish Holy Temple of Science, *The Divine Constitution and By-Laws*, in the Moorish Science Papers, MG 435.

[115] Ibid., 1926 Certificate of Incorporation.

[116] See Haddad and Smith, *Mission to America*, 98–99.

FIGURE 2. Moorish leadership at the Moorish Science Temple headquarters in Chicago. Courtesy of the Photographs and Prints Division, Schomburg Center for Research in Black Culture, The New York Public Library, Astor, Lenox, and Tilden Foundations.

(see Figure 2), two of the ten persons seated on the same row with Noble Drew Ali (presumably the leading personages in attendance) were women: Sister C. Alsop Bey, a Governess in Chicago; and Sister Lomax Bey, who together with her husband were the Grand Governess and Governor of Detroit.[117] The January 15, 1929 edition of the *Moorish Guide*, in addition, lists thirteen temples, over which there were two Grand Sheiks, nine Governors, one "Bey" (a governor) and one Grand Sheikess, a Sister Whitehead-El, who was in charge of Temple No. 9 at 862 Townsend Street in Chicago. In another edition of the *Moorish Guide* published around the same time, Juanita Mayo Richardson Bey is listed as the managing editor of the bimonthly periodical and Prophet Noble Drew Ali as the owner and publisher. Juanita Richardson-Bey also served as the Secretary-Treasurer of the "Young People's Moorish League" and was culturally very active. One of her poems, published in the *Moorish Guide* and entitled

[117] See the photograph under the heading, "Moorish Science Temple of America," in the Moorish Science Papers, MG 435. The date of the picture would have to be either 1928 or 1929, as the name of the organization was changed as shown in 1928, and Noble Drew Ali, who is in the picture, died in July of 1929.

"Dio de mio," eerily anticipated Noble Drew's demise later that year:

> There's peace within thy walls – Almighty Allah
>   The prayers of Israel's children soothe my mind;
> And all the restlessness of me is calmed;
>   My futile heartaches vanish as I pray
> The loneliness that haunted all my days,
>   E'en when I mingled with the crowds, is gone;
>
> I feel the force and strength of calm companionship,
>   Uniting me with all Thy quiet strength.
> Oh all these years I battled with myself,
>   Denying fiercely there was any God-Allah;
> And all I found was emptiness in life,
>   Until today when something led me here,
> And midst the prayers of Israel I find peace.
>
> My Allah – and Allah of all my fathers
>   Hear my supplication – In the coming year
> Be with me, with me when the road is dark with doubt,
>   Be with me when the haunting loneliness
> Would crush my spirit down to the depths.
>   Oh! Never let me know the emptiness
>   – Juanita Richardson-Bey.[118]

Interestingly, the same publication simply states that Mrs. Pearl Drew Ali, the prophet's wife and the President of the Young People's Moorish League, spoke to that body on January 3, 1929, while "Miss Juanita Richardson Bey held the attention of the members as she very skillfully rendered one of Rudyard Kipling's expressive poems." While the choice of Kipling may be surprising (or lamentable), one can only assume that the space afforded Juanita Richardson-Bey in an official Moorish Science organ must have been commensurate with the prominence she enjoyed.

The *Moorish Guide* was only one of several Moorish Science periodicals, which also included the *Moorish Science Monitor* and the *Moorish Review*, which by the 1950s was published out of Richmond, Virginia.[119] In addition to disseminating periodic messages and instructions from Noble Drew Ali, these papers were also vehicles for advertising businesses owned by the Moors. In particular, the Moorish Manufacturing Corporation ran advertisements for its products, which included the Moorish Antiseptic Bath Compound, "beneficial for dandruff, rheumatism, stiff joints and sore feet. Also skin troubles, when used as a face wash." The antiseptic bath compound cost fifty cents by 1929, the same as the cost of the Moorish Body Builder and Blood Purifier, "beneficial for rheumatism" as was the bath compound, but useful in treating "lung trouble, run-down constitutions, indigestion, and loss of manhood." For fifty cents more, one could purchase a two-ounce bottle of Moorish Mineral and Healing Oil, developed to remedy rheumatism, sore and tired feet, indigestion,

---

[118] See the *Moorish Guide*, 1929, in the Moorish Science Papers, MG 435.
[119] See McCloud, *African American Islam*, 17.

stiff joints, and neuralgia. The oil was to be applied "to the spine" as well as the "lower parts of the stomach" twice daily to treat "loss of manhood." All of these physics carried labels that read, in part, "prepared by Noble Drew Ali, Founder." Sold to anyone interested, the bottom of the newspaper advertisements (and flyers) also ran the following statement: "Live Agents and Dealers Wanted. We pay 50 per Cent Commission," which suggests that one did not have to be a member of Moorish Science to vend their products. The newspapers also published testimonials to the efficacy of these "Moorish herb products"; in one instance, eight out of ten letters were from women (and only two identifiably Moors) who, suffering "with the rheumatism" and "the indigestion" as well as from swelling in joints and sundry other ailments, attested to the wonders of these products, particularly the Mineral and Healing Oil. For example, Beatrice Byrd of 13 West 26th Place, in Chicago wrote this testimonial:

I have been suffering for some time with my throat and I have used everything that I knew of, finally I heard of the Moorish Mineral and Healing Oil, then I purchased one bottle and used it according to the direction, and now I feel like a young girl.[120]

The Moorish Manufacturing Company, maker of the various herbal treatments, was not the only business venture of the Moors. To achieve "economic independence and the sense of self-worth necessary to overcome racist employment patterns," the Moors in Chicago also established restaurants, grocery stores, and variety stores.[121] Although ownership is unclear, it would be logical to assume that the Moorish Science Temple owned at least one of the Chicago properties out of which it operated. There were several addresses: Unity Hall (also called Unity Club), the headquarters of the organization (which "could be rented out for parties, dances, balls, receptions, banquets, etc."), at 3140 Indiana Avenue; the location of the Moorish Manufacturing Corporation, at 3603 Indiana Avenue; and the location of the "Home Office" at 3229 Indiana Avenue, a change from the previous address of 3718 Prairie Avenue. By the 1940s the Moors would acquire farmland, but long before then the idea of establishing living space separate from the rest of America had taken root. Thus, a small article entitled "Moors Endorse Village Idea" appeared in a 1929 edition of the *Moorish Guide* and in part reads as follows:

The following letter is one of the many received by the *Guide* relative to the establishment of a town owned and completely operated by those persons belonging to the Moorish Science Temple of America:
January 29, 1929
Islam:
In response to the question asked concerning the Moors having a town, homes, etc., we will say all honor to the prophet, who is to give us something of our own.
Signed by Bros. E. and D. Jackson Bey
Sister J. Jackson Bey[122]

[120] See the pamphlets, *Moorish Guide*, in Moorish Science Papers, MG 435.
[121] See Haddad and Smith, *Mission to America*, 88.
[122] See the *Moorish Guide*, 1929, in the Moorish Science Papers, MG 435. Regarding the farms, see the *Richmond Times-Dispatch*, April 11, 1943, and the *Berkshire Eagle*, February 10, 1944.

Thus, while the Nation of Islam's indebtedness to Garvey for its mixture of nationalism and capitalism is well known, it would be also be accurate to state that the Moorish Science Temple, also under the sway of Garvey's ideas, provided business models for possible emulation by Elijah Muhammad.

It would appear that, in addition to being a religious innovator and a commercial entrepreneur, Noble Drew Ali was an astute politician as well. His followers in Chicago, for example, were exhorted to participate in the political process:

> Members of the Moorish Science Temple of America who live within the bounds of the Second Ward will give their unqualified support to their friend Ald. Louis B. Anderson, who again will be a candidate for the city council of Chicago.[123]

Although prescriptive, Noble Drew Ali's instructions to the Chicago base points to a quid pro quo arrangement with officials (see Figure 3) that was critical to the unobstructed development of the movement. Cynicism is not necessarily illuminating, however, so that beyond an interest in self-preservation, it is probable that Noble Drew saw civic engagement as an important part of attempting to meet the wide-ranging needs of black folk as a whole. Even his various tonics for the treatment of illnesses can be seen not simply as a money-making scheme but as an effort to address the quotidian concerns of his community. That the Moors were "very active in feeding the poor, providing drug and alcohol rehabilitation, and creating wholesome, disciplined community life" is consistent with this view. Noble Drew's popularity in Chicago was such that even powerful local black politician Oscar DePriest, a member of Congress from 1928 to 1932, was rumored to have joined the Moorish Science Temple.[124]

By 1929, the Moorish Science Temple of America had experienced "meteoric success,"[125] reflected in Figures 4 and 5, but within that success were already embedded the implements of implosion. The first incendiary was set when, according to Fauset, the Moors came to believe "that [a] sign, a star with a crescent moon, had been seen in the heavens, and that this betokened the arrival of the day of the Asiatics, and the destruction of the Europeans (whites)."[126] Augury and budding prosperity were mutually reinforcing, emboldening the membership who, until then, "believed divine intervention would bring about the end of white rule, and therefore cultivated an apolitical, peaceful adherence to the status quo."[127] While such characterization is a simplification of a much more complex response to American racism, the point is that the combined eschatological and material evidence encouraged a sizeable number of Moors

---

[123] See the *Moorish Guide*, January 15, 1929, in the Moorish Science Papers, MG 435.

[124] See McCloud, *African American Islam*, 17. On Oscar DePriest, see St. Clair Drake and Horace R. Cayton, *Black Metropolis: A Study of Negro Life in a Northern City* (Chicago: U. of Chicago Press, 1993; orig. pub., 1945), 342–77.

[125] See Wilson, *Sacred Drift*, 34.

[126] See Fauset, *Black Gods of the Metropolis*, 42.

[127] See Martha F. Lee, *The Nation of Islam, An American Millenarian Movement* (Lewiston, NY: Edwin Mellen Press, 1988), 29.

FIGURE 3. Moorish Science Temple: Noble Drew Ali and guests. Courtesy of the Photographs and Prints Division, Schomburg Center for Research in Black Culture, The New York Public Library, Astor, Lenox, and Tilden Foundations.

to become much more aggressive in their relations with whites. In particular, many began to vigorously identify themselves as Moors by flashing their temple membership cards and lapel buttons on which were Moorish insignia. The cards were in fact "nationality and identification cards," or "passports," emblematic of the Moorish insistence on linkages to Morocco. The front of the card carried Muslim symbols, with the individual's free national or "Asiatic" name written in both English and Arabic, and a warning at the bottom: "The bearer is a registered Moslem. Kindly retain this card and punish of [?] said bearer if found other than righteous." Across the top of the card's back are the words *Islam*, *Unity*, and *Allah*, with corresponding symbols. At the bottom it partially reads, "I do hereby declare that you are a Moslem under the Divine Laws of the Holy Koran of Mecca, Love, Truth, Peace, Freedom, and Justice. "I AM A CITIZEN OF THE U.S.A."[128] According to Fauset, a major problem arose:

A number of disturbances developed. The Moors, made conspicuous by their fezzes, walked the streets, treating white folk with open contempt. In various parts of the Middle West they became anathema to the police.[129]

[128] See the Moorish Science Papers, MG 435.
[129] See Fauset, *Black Gods of the Metropolis*, 42–43.

FIGURE 4. Members of the Moorish Science Temple. Courtesy of the Photographs and Prints Division, Schomburg Center for Research in Black Culture, The New York Public Library, Astor, Lenox, and Tilden Foundations.

In Chicago, "hundreds" of Moors employed the identification card as an amulet, believing that "the mere sight of the card would be sufficient to restrain a white man who was bent on disturbing or harming its holder." Moors were supposedly actually "accosting" whites in public, "singing the praises of their prophet... because he had freed them from the curse of the European." In Detroit, the Moors were becoming odious in the eyes of law enforcement, as is evident in the eyewitness account of one Detroit police officer:

Those fellows! he cried out. What a terrible gang. Thieves and cutthroats! Wouldn't answer anything. Wouldn't sit down when you told them. Wouldn't stand up when you told them. Pretending they didn't understand you, that they were Moors from Morocco. They never saw Morocco! Those Moors never saw anything before they came to Detroit except Florida and Alabama![130]

Noble Drew Ali was facing the crisis of the conflict in his own message. He consistently required his followers to observe the law of the land; on one hand, his argument for the embrace of Moroccan identity as a necessary precursor to full acceptance in North America suggests that he was not interested in a radical political solution to the intransigence of racism. On the other hand, he had created a psychological space, a terrain of the mind, wherein racial separation was envisioned and anticipated. That is, the disequilibria of the society was not a condition to be long endured; its resolution was only a matter of time. For many of his followers, that time had come. Whether disinterested in or unprepared for confrontation with the U.S. government, Noble Drew Ali recalled the 1920 chastening of Redding's Abyssinian Movement and acted to lessen the level of tensions. The January 15, 1929 edition of the *Moorish Guide* carried the following order:

[130] Ibid., 43, footnote.

FIGURE 5. Group photograph of the members of the Moorish Science Temple. Courtesy of the Photographs and Prints Division, Schomburg Center for Research in Black Culture, The New York Public Library, Astor, Lenox, and Tilden Foundations.

PROPHET WARNS ALL MOSLEMS: GOVERNORS ORDERED TO READ PROCLAMATION AT EACH MEETING

I hereby inform all members that they must end all radical agitating speeches while at work in their homes or on the streets. We are for peace and not destruction.

Stop flashing your cards at Europeans; it causes confusion. Remember your card is for your salvation. Failure to obey these orders will be of severe consequence.

We are for Love, Truth, Peace, Freedom and Justice, and when these principles are violated, justice must then take its course.

Any member or group of members who hold malicious feelings toward the temple or the Prophet, or violate the divine covenant of the Moorish Movement will receive their reward from Allah for their unjust deeds.

All true Moors will and must obey the law as laid down to them by their Prophet. If they lose confidence in their Prophets they should turn in their card and button, cease as wearing their turban and fez and return to the state where I, the Prophet found you.

This is a holy and divine movement founded by the Prophet Noble Drew Ali, and if the Prophet is not right, the temple, is not right.[131]

---

[131] See the *Moorish Guide*, January 15, 1929, in the Moorish Science Papers, MG 435; also see Noble Drew Ali, "Divine Warning by the Prophet Noble Drew Ali," at the end of the 1996 reprint of the *Circle Seven Koran*, xxxviii–xxxix.

While the missive may have been issued prior to January 1929, it is clear from its contents that, by that time, there were rumblings of dissension within the ranks of Moorish Science. Noble Drew Ali's response reveals a preoccupation with reestablishing an authority that had apparently come under fire.

What Noble Drew Ali implies in the foregoing order he explicitly expresses elsewhere. Indeed, there were problems developing as early as October of 1928, as is reflected in the following, handwritten "divine warning":

[T]o the members of the moorish science temple of america this is the instruction from your prophet noble drew ali be faithful to your forefathers divine and natio[nal] creed that you will be blessed for your good deeds that you sow in the flesh, allah is the one who judges the world, and his judgement is now on, but "they can comprehend it not the end of time is drawing near, so says allah through his prophet, noble drew ali" and that is why many hearts have been turned to stone, and many have eyes to see and ears to hear. but cannot hear, least they be confounded of their sin, these are trying hours now dear moors and evil spirits is moveing; and they are trying every [illegible] and to over throw. and drag out the true foundation [illegible] of the ones that do believe, but if you have the love of allah and spirit of your forefathers. you [illegible] what you hear or see. but will sacrifice to [illegible] your very life, to protect your movement and your [illegible] watch your enemies dear moors. your enemies are [illegible] speak against your prophet, and ridicu[l]e him to the [illegible] lowest, and the ones that speak against your divine and national principles, of your temple. act according to [illegible] allah will bless you for your good works,

your divine prophet noble drew ali.[132]

While these "enemies of the moors" may have been external to the organization, the likelihood that they were a fifth column is increased when the preceding material is juxtaposed with an undated address entitled "Caveat Emptor":

Moors are men, upright, independent, and fearless who care for their loved ones and follows the Prophet to a destiny which is not unknown.... It is therefore, folly at its greatest height for smelly culprits with their industrious plan to invade such a realm.

They try and try but their own bad planning brings down wrath upon their heads like the sword old Damocles had. I intrigue and scurrilous cunnings find a difficult path to travel within the ranks of the floors. This is so because the Moorish Movement has been well planned by Prophet Noble Drew Ali, whose latent powers are abundant, Unknown and may be called into action, as a matter of defense, at any moment...

A few feet below is another road where schemers walk, where traitors grin, and culprits bask in the sun. They think they are on the same road with true Moors, but the Moors are high above on a pinnacle where they might view the destructionists as they fall for the last time. And their bones bleach in the sultry mid-day sun.[133]

This is clearly a propaganda war, and it indicates that the nature of Noble Drew Ali's opposition was emanating from within the leadership ranks. Thus, Noble Drew issued another stern warning in either 1928 or 1929:

[132] See the letters, 1928–29, 1961, 1964, in the Moorish Science Papers, MG 435.
[133] See Noble Drew Ali, "Caveat Emptor," at the end of the 1996 reprint of the *Circle Seven Koran*, xxviii–xxx.

Forced to make changes. All governors and other officers of the Moorish Science Temple are hereby congratulated for their past loyalty and fidelity, for I know it will be the same in the future. Because of certain incidents that have risen in some of the temples which seem to come from the fact that there are those who do not know where the seat of power is vested in the Prophet Noble Drew Ali And Those Whom He Appoints To Act In The Supreme Body. The Prophet Has Authority and power to expel any officer or member of the Moorish Science Temple of America. . . .

The prophet will positively not tolerate any interference with the operation of this national divine movement from anyone.

BY THE PROPHET, NOBLE DREW ALI.[134]

It is not clear that Noble Drew Ali ever took any punitive actions against these unnamed leaders; given the frequency with which these circulars were issued, it seems that he was hoping that verbal warnings would be sufficient. That he found it necessary to resort to veiled threats in such a public manner, however, strongly indicates that he was losing control over Moorish Science operations.

Some who have written on Noble Drew Ali identify the movement's growing prosperity as the source of its difficulties, and it makes sense that infighting would erupt over increasing revenues. However, the literature tends to be uncritical of this period of Moorish Science history, and it seems to be based on unspecified insider information in the form of a single tradition. According to this view, Noble Drew Ali, recognizing his limitations as a business man, began to recruit and place in positions of financial leadership those individuals with the requisite expertise. Alas, they were in fact "unscrupulous and shady types who achieved high position, milked the faithful, and began to conspire against the Prophet himself." With ulterior motives, they "introduced practices which the prophet had not anticipated. Various methods were employed to exploit the members of the cult, including the sale of herbs, magical charms and potions, and literature pertaining to the cult." With the businesses of the Moorish Science Temple bringing in as much as $36,000 in 1928, some grew "rich." Noble Drew Ali's opposition to their avarice, according to this view, resulted in their attempts to remove him.[135]

Although Noble Drew Ali's own proclamations make it clear that the finances of the movement were in some disarray, they do not point fingers at the business managers. Rather, the problems were emanating from the spiritual leaders (although these and the business managers could have been the same persons). In requiring the leaders of all temples to begin submitting monthly financial reports in October of 1928, for example, Noble Drew directs his attention to the governors and governesses, instructing them "not to charge for membership, or to overcharge for cards, buttons, or for anything issued by

---

[134] See Noble Drew Ali, "Prophet Announces His Authority," at the end of the 1996 reprint of the *Circle Seven Kor*an, xxx–xxxi.

[135] See Wilson, *Sacred Drift*, 34; Turner, *Islam in the African-American Experience*, 99–100; Haddad and Smith, *Mission to America*, 90; Marsh, *From Black Muslims to Muslims*, 48; Fauset, *Black Gods of the Metropolis*, 43.

the prophet. Those who contribute to either of the preceding are not Moors, but robbers."[136] While initial membership was free, monthly dues were fifty cents, and buttons could be purchased for a one-time fee of twenty-five cents. In this way Moorish Science functioned practically as a mutual aid society, further explaining its attractiveness to members who, in addition to spiritual guidance, also received benefits that included such provisions as unemployment and disability assistance.

In addition to charging for initial membership, some leaders were also borrowing money from their parishioners; Noble Drew Ali enjoined temple branch leaders from borrowing "from any member more than five to ten dollars unless by notification of the Prophet." Some were apparently purchasing properties with Temple money, resulting in the following corrective from Noble Drew Ali:

When any said Temple desires to purchase property they must first notify the Grand Body or the Prophet and it must be purchased under the name of the Moorish Science Temple of America or Noble Drew Ali. An individual's name should never be applied. I, Noble Drew Ali, am responsible for all finance, so therefore let I, the Prophet, know what is on me.

There was also an emergency fund that Noble Drew wanted to increase to a total of $91,000. To avoid graft, he demanded that these monies be deposited in a bank under the Temple's name, to be drawn upon only by the treasurer in times of crisis. All of this points to mounting difficulties in the movement, mostly disputes over money with religious leaders, to the extent that Noble Drew was gradually becoming overwhelmed:

Some of you have slipped and slipped drastically, so you had better lace up your shoes before I get there. Everything, every business transaction or anything pertaining to finance is to be transacted in the name of the Moorish Science Temple of America, or Noble Drew Ali. We Moors must maintain a grand treasurer, just as in the days of our forefathers; then you are a nation – until then, you are nothing.[137]

There is no indication that Noble Drew Ali was himself involved with corrupt monetary practices. The matter of the quality of his reception by branch temples was raised on occasion, as it would appear that local temples were responsible for financial arrangements attendant to Noble Drew's visits, but references to the matter may reflect an inattentiveness on the part of the local temples, as opposed to any penchant toward opulence on the part of Noble Drew. The question of his personal finances therefore remains open, as demonstrated by his February 5, 1929 correspondence to a local temple leader:

ISLAM:
Dear Brother:

---

[136] See Noble Drew Ali, "General Laws as Said by the Prophet," October 17, 1928, at the end of the 1996 reprint of the *Circle Seven Koran*, xl–xli.
[137] See Noble Drew Ali, "Think This Over, You Moors," at the end of the 1996 reprint of the *Circle Seven* Koran, xxxiv–xxxvii.

If you desire to see me earlier – you will have to notify your members under a heavy restriction and warning that the more Uplifting Funds they send in to me, the sooner they can see me and the more I know they desire to see me, because I have to raise the finance of a few thousand dollars to place the Nation far beyond their present conditions. It takes finance to Uplift a down trodden people, and place it among the other prosperous Nations of the world. And as a sacrifice to the Moslem Creed, I have sacrificed my life, finance, and labor to place the Nation on an intelligent and financial footing. This matter is to be attended to at once. I will be among those first that appreciate me as Prophet, and the great work that I am doing.[138]

Such a letter can be read cynically; conversely, the need to raise money for any enterprise is ever present, so there is no compelling reason to doubt Noble Drew Ali's motives.

The struggles over local temple autonomy, temple finances, and temple businesses quickly moved from generalized and veiled verbal assaults to open confrontation one fateful day. Apparently convinced that he enjoyed the necessary backing, Sheik Claude D. Greene, Noble Drew Ali's business manager, "small-time politician," and former butler to philanthropist Julius Rosenwald, threw all of Noble Drew Ali's office furniture into the street at 3140 Indiana Avenue, site of the Unity Club, and "declared himself the grand sheik." According to the *Chicago Defender*, Greene had broken with Noble Drew and had directed that all revenues from merchandise and herbal remedies be sent to the Unity Club rather than Noble Drew's home and business headquarters at 3603 Indiana Avenue. On the Ides of March, Greene was killed in retaliation, having been shot and stabbed four times in the neck and body in his Unity Club office by some six to eight assailants. Accounts differ over the whereabouts of Noble Drew Ali at the time of the homicide; some maintain he was out of town, while others contend that he was in hiding two blocks down the street at 3365 Indiana Avenue, "where a feast had been in progress shortly after the word reached him that Greene had been slain." In any event, the pursuant investigation turned up an informant, Small Bey, who told police that Greene was the head of a "breakaway faction," and that Noble Drew had given the responsibility of having him "bumped off" to George (Ira) Johnson Bey (El). Rumors swirled that Greene had embezzled temple funds, had succeeded in drawing temple branch leaders such as Edward Lomax Bey of Detroit after him, and was involved with one of Noble Drew's wives, Pearl Drew Ali.[139]

Noble Drew and nine others were arrested and jailed, and their trial date was set for of May 20. Noble Drew wasted little time trying to reassert

---

[138] See the letters, 1928–29, 1961, 1964, in the Moorish Science Papers, MG 435.

[139] See the *Chicago Defender*, March 16, 1929, March 23, 1929, May 18, 1929, July 27, 1929, and August 2, 1929; also see Wilson, *Sacred Drift*, 34–39; Bontemps and Conroy, *Anyplace But Here*, 207–11; Fauset, *Black Gods of the Metropolis*, 43–44; Turner, *Islam in the African-American Experience*, 100–01; McCloud, *African American Islam*, 18; Haddad and Smith, *Mission to America*, 90–91; Marsh, *From Black Muslims to Muslims*, 48–49.

control over a movement in disarray, and while incarcerated he wrote the following:

To the Heads of All Temples, Islam: I your prophet do hereby and now write you a letter as a warning and appeal to your good judgment for the present and the future. Though I am now in custody for you and the cause, it is all right and is well for all who still believe in me and my father, God. I have redeemed all of you and you shall be saved, all of you, even with me. I go to bat Monday, May 20, before the Grand Jury. If you are with me, be there. Remember my laws and love one another. Prefer not a stranger to your brother. Love and truth and my peace I leave you all. Peace from your Prophet, Noble Drew Ali.[140]

Soon released on bail, Noble Drew Ali never made it to trial. He died on July 20, 1929 from either one or more of the following speculative causes: beatings suffered from the police while in custody; beatings suffered from Greene supporters; tuberculosis; or other health failures.[141] Funeralized at the Pythian Temple (37th Place and State Street) and interred at Burr Oak cemetery, Noble Drew Ali was survived by two wives, the aforementioned Pearl and Mary Foreman Bey.[142] Mary Foreman Bey, who was either fourteen or sixteen years old and pregnant at the time, named two other "girls of tender age" with whom Noble Drew had also been sexually involved. The coroner's inquest into his death seems to verify this, alleging that Noble Drew had been sexually involved with a fourteen-year-old, a sixteen-year-old, and a woman in her twenties, all at the same time and while married, and that he had apparently married the teenagers "in Moorish American ceremonies."[143] If true, the very least that can be stated is that Noble Drew's personal character was one matter, and his official policies (such as elevating women to prominent leadership positions) were another. These allegations point to a seamier side of Moorish Science leadership, an underbelly of licentiousness and exploitation of women and young girls bordering on pedophilia; such behavior seems to turn up with regularity in a number of social, religious, and political movements with populist qualities under charismatic leadership. In each instance, one is faced with the dubious task of decoupling the message from the messenger.

Given the importance of reincarnation in Moorish Science, it was understood by many (but not all) that Noble Drew Ali would "reincarnate" into a chosen successor. With his demise, however, the movement formally splintered into several factions led by various contenders. While the *Chicago Defender* speculated that Aaron Payne, an assistant city prosecutor and a business manager for the Moorish Science Temple, was the likely successor, Kirkman Bey was in fact elected president of the Moorish Science Temple Corporation and Grand Sheik, against whom R. German Ali led a group recognizing only Noble Drew Ali as

---

[140] See Fauset, *Black Gods of the Metropolis*, 43–44.
[141] See Allen, "Religious Heterodoxy and Nationalist Tradition," 8, who maintains that Drew Ali died from tuberculosis on July 20, 1929.
[142] Wilson, *Sacred Drift*, 34.
[143] See the *Chicago Defender*, March 23, 1929; Turner, *Islam in the African-American Experience*, 100.

prophet. Steven Gibbons and George (Ira) Johnson Bey (El), meanwhile, were among several who "claimed that the dead prophet's spirit had entered their bodies." John Givens El, Noble Drew's chauffeur, reportedly fainted shortly after Noble Drew's death while working on his car, and upon examination was said to have "the sign of the star and crescent in his eyes," indicating that "right then he was the prophet reincarnated into his chauffeur," thereafter proclaiming himself "Brother Prophet." In late September, two months after Noble Drew Ali's death, gunplay erupted between the Chicago police and Moors at Temple headquarters. Two officers and one member would remain on the floor, with one officer seriously wounded. Sixty-three Moors were arrested, including George (Ira) Johnson Bey (El), who went to the federal penitentiary for life.[144]

Steven Gibbons eventually founded a new Moorish Temple in Chicago on East 40th Street around 1941, by which time the FBI had filed all black Muslim groups under the heading "Extremist Muslim Groups and Violence." By the mid-1940s, there were at least fifty Moorish Science temples in over twenty-five major urban areas, and together with the Nation of Islam were seen as threats to U.S. security. Turner writes the following:

The basic fear was that these groups were "part of a worldwide organization" and were developing plans with various Japanese organizations in America to unite "the dark races" in order to "take over" the country while white soldiers were away fighting in World War II.[145]

Spurred by such anxieties, the FBI waged a "campaign of harassment" against Moorish Science that included arresting men on charges of sedition and violation of the Selective Service Act, measures that led to women's playing more numerous and more important roles in the organizations. Despite the FBI campaign, the Moors survived, publishing the *Moorish Guide*, *Moorish Science Monitor*, *Moorish Review*, *Moorish Scribe*, *Moorish Voice*, and the *Moorish American Voice* at various times from the 1960s to the present. Multiple branches of Moorish Science, national and international in scope and membership, remain.

* * *

In the early twentieth century, people of African descent in North America were virtually assailed with competing visions of deliverance from all sides. There were numerous organizations springing up here and there with nationalist, pan-Africanist, and uplift philosophies, now filtered through the idiom of religion, then expressed as a much more transparent critique of political economy. The streets and shops and homes and churches and club halls of Chicago and New York City were particularly filled with movement partisans; the air was charged in hopeful anticipation of a desired outcome in the contest between vision and reality. For the Moors to have distinguished themselves from among such a vast messianic host is testimony to the appeal of their message

---

[144] See the *Chicago Defender*, August 3, 1929; Turner, *Islam in the African-American Experience*, 100–01; Haddad and Smith, *Mission to America*, 99; Wilson, *Sacred Drift*, 38–41.
[145] See Turner, *Islam in the African-American Experience*, 101.

as well as the personal charm and dynamism of their founder. Perhaps Noble Drew Ali's most innovative contribution was his attempt to resolve the rootlessness of the African-derived and the absence of a self-defined group identity by the conceptualization of a Moroccan origin and an Asiatic construct. The configuration relocated the source of an immutable black identity to Africa and away from North America while simultaneously erecting a transnational family to which blacks belonged. Blacks were members of both national and international communities, sanctioned by the authority of holy writ.

If such was his most important contribution, perhaps his most salient legacy was establishing the precedent for the promulgation of a variant form of Islam, complete with a different *Koran*, divergent teachings, and religious authority independent of established leadership. Indeed, Noble Drew Ali was the first of a triad of prophets associated with Islam, followed by Ghulam Ahmad and Elijah Muhammad, and thus he paved the way of the acceptability of variance. Noble Drew Ali created an approach to Islam that would deeply influence contemporary and subsequent thinkers who may have more or less conformed to his tradition, like Elijah Muhammad, or may have stood in opposition to it, such as the Ahmadiyya. However, even the orthodox were beneficiaries, as they necessarily built upon the foundation of Noble Drew Ali.

If unorthodox Islam is the principle legacy of Moorish Science, the articulation of a racial ideology is next in line. A careful reading of the *Circle Seven Koran's* final chapters, in conjunction with other Moorish literary publications such as the *Koran for Moorish Children*, reveals an economy of language in which there is the strong intimation of inherent and unresolvable racial polarities that are both expressed and sanctioned in religion. What Elijah Muhammad and the Nation of Islam accomplished was to formalize and make much more explicit the implications of Moorish racialism. The Ahmadiyya, in contrast, represents a fundamental departure from such dichotomized and dichotomizing thought.

Interestingly, Noble Drew Ali was much more conventional when it came to relations with the U.S. government – or perhaps he was not. What he proposed was a form of nationalism that constituted a fraternity of the mind, a psychological frame of reference capable of transcending the very real confinements of Jim Crow and his twin Empire. While claiming Moroccan identity, he apparently never pursued citizenship in that country, nor is there any evidence that he advocated such a strategy for his followers. There is no hint of repatriatory sentiment in his rhetoric, nor, with the exception of several references to purchasing a black town, did he ever evince a vision for the creation of any kind of autonomous black nation on North American soil. Rather, he demanded obedience to American laws and participation in the electoral process while awaiting divine intervention. He seems to have been convinced that Morocco could be used as leverage, persuaded as he was that the African American's fundamental flaw was the absence of a collective image that could command the respect of whites.

Noble Drew Ali's brand of nationalism would certainly be echoed in the Nation of Islam, with clear points of departure. Indeed, there are parallel streams of development among the Moors, the UNIA, and the Nation of Islam, in that all of them adopted pragmatic business policies grounded in capitalist ideology, exhibiting little engagement with critical analyses questioning the relationship between differentiated socioeconomic experience and systemic, overarching mechanisms of production. Such unwillingness to explore underlying principles of social disparity arguably reduced the capacity of such groups to significantly alter fundamental relations of power.

These remarks, however, are incomplete without a few observations concerning the role of class. Indeed, it would not come as a surprise if subsequent research verifies that the makeup of the early Moorish Science community was very much like that of the early Nation of Islam's membership in Detroit: working-class blacks who were overwhelmingly transplants from the South, as were Elijah Muhammad and Noble Drew themselves. Furthermore, although the Garvey movement was perhaps more cosmopolitan in that it was an amalgam of groups from the Caribbean and the North as well as from the South, so that ethnicity and race and gender were concomitantly in negotiation, all three movements drew their strength from working-class populations. In some sense, therefore, these movements, while aspiring to middle-class status, represented a rejection of middle-class leadership. Stated differently, the success of the Moors and the Nation of Islam constituted the establishment of the southern black leader up North, a quality of visionary not only lacking in formal education but almost eschewing it, preferring above all a mastery of the esoteric. This further signifies a chasm of confidence between the membership of these organizations and the leadership of the New Negro Movement. While it is known that such publications as the *Crisis* were read far and wide, the success of the Moorish Science Temple and the Nation of Islam is undeniable testimony to the existence of a profound disjunctive moment in the history of African Americans.

Noble Drew Ali, as the foundation for Islam among African Americans in the twentieth century, may very well be their link to an African Muslim past, as he was born and reared in an area contiguous with Melungeon and Ishmaelite influence at a time when the descendants of verifiable African Muslims may have yet been practicing Islam along the Georgia and South Carolina coasts. These potential connections become even more intriguing in view of his introduction to multiple influences. Rosicrucian literature is hardly a powerful tool of Muslim proselytization, and in any event the two major sources for his *Circle Seven Koran* do not discuss Islam or the Prophet Muhammad. Neither is exposure to Freemasonry sufficiently explanatory, for while it influenced Noble Drew, it also influenced many others, who, despite their initiation into the Craft, never entertained even a fleeting thought of converting to any form of Islam, remaining solidly Christian. So the skeptical will have to answer this question: Why Islam? What motivated Noble Drew Ali to embrace his form of this religion? The answer is by no means as clear as the record of thousands of African Muslims who came to North America in chains, who struggled to maintain their faith against overwhelming odds, and who left their impressions, however imprecise, upon the sands of human hearts and memories.

7

The Nation

According to records internal to the organization, the Lost Found Nation of Islam in America was founded on July 4, 1930.[1] By the time its founder launched the venture, Noble Drew Ali may have been preaching and organizing throughout much of the United States for seventeen years. Indeed, when W. D. Fard Muhammad made his appearance in the streets of Detroit, Noble Drew Ali was already dead, having established Moorish Science as a comprehensive, mature theological articulation. There remains sharp disagreement over the precise nature of the relationship between Moorish Science and Fard Muhammad, if in fact any existed. These disagreements are important as they go to questions of authenticity and claims of divine inspiration, but rather than attempt their resolution, it would be more profitable to simply echo an observation shared by all: Fard Muhammad was a principal beneficiary of a theoretical framework and quality of discourse created by Noble Drew Ali. He was very much aware of the former's influence and stature, so much so that his early message was tailored for ears accustomed to Moorish Science doctrine. To acknowledge as much in no way diminishes Fard Muhammad and his most distinguished disciple, Elijah Muhammad, as originators in their own right and as sources of sacred sentiment.

However, the Nation of Islam would go far beyond the limits of Moorish Science. Indeed, it can be argued that the latter's ideological parameters have essentially remained unchanged, consistent with the initial vision of its founder. In contrast, the teachings of W. D. Fard and Elijah Muhammad evolved over a period of decades in response to changing circumstances and challenges, constituting a significant break with prior patterns of social and religious interpretation while at the same time engaging the legacy of slavery and the Middle

---

[1] See Imam Wallace D. Muhammad, *Religion on the Line: Al-Islam, Judaism, Catholicism, Protestantism* (Chicago: W. D. Muhammad Publications, 1983), 4. See also C. Eric Lincoln, *The Black Muslims in America* (Boston: Beacon Press, 1973); Mattias Gardell, *In the Name of Elijah Muhammad: Louis Farrakhan and the Nation of Islam* (Durham, NC: Duke U. Pres, 1996).

Passage. In the process, it is the Nation that, perhaps surprisingly, provided the multigenerational experience through which the transition from nonorthodoxy to orthodoxy was accomplished. Despite its many detractors, and to their possible chagrin, it is incontrovertible that orthodoxy was achieved for many, if not most, of those of African descent through the steady movement of what became known as the Nation of Islam.

Much has been written on the history of the organization, with emphases on the interlocking stories of W. D. Fard Muhammad, Elijah Muhammad, and Malcolm X. While effort has gone into investigating the shadowy background of Fard Muhammad, even more has been devoted to chronicling and analyzing the development of strained relations between Elijah Muhammad and Malcolm X. As a result of the scholarship, much more is known about the general history of the Nation of Islam. This chapter therefore only recounts this information as needed and in the briefest of summations, focusing on critical elements of the Nation's message instead. The contention here is that, although Fard Muhammad may have launched the Nation, it was Elijah Muhammad who established it and who is primarily responsible for the bulk of its teachings. Those teachings, centered on an elaborate cosmogony and eschatology, challenged all existing conventions concerning race and religions; it was unique for its time.

As was true in the case of Noble Drew Ali, an occlusion of background, of origins, is consistent with the strategy to reify the status of the movement's progenitor. For Noble Drew Ali, this tendency resulted in the creation of several competing myths; for W. D. Fard Muhammad, it has led to the quintessential inquiry into mystery. Recent scholarship has discussed Fard Muhammad's background with confidence, alleging with certainty to have unraveled one of the more intriguing controversies of recent times. These assertions may be credible, but given that much of their data are derived from the archives of the American government, a government often in conflict with the Nation of Islam and not adverse to using both information and disinformation to discredit it, common sense would dictate the need for caution in appropriating such sources. A debt is owed to the arduous, painstaking efforts of such scholars, but a healthy skepticism of uncritical and unreflective use of government issue is also warranted. The following discussion of Fard Muhammad's background is therefore offered with the caveat that it remains more tentative than conclusive.

There is consensus that W. D. Fard Muhammad was born outside of the United States; beyond this, interpretations diverge. In a tone so critical of the Nation as to approximate a polemic, one of the more recent discussions of Fard Muhammad nevertheless presents a plausible reconstruction of his past, notwithstanding the cautionary regarding overreliance on government documents.[2] According to this informed speculation, Fard Muhammad was born Wali Dodd Fard on February 25, 1891 in New Zealand. His father was Zared

---

[2] See Karl Evanzz, *The Messenger: The Rise and Fall of Elijah Muhammad* (New York: Pantheon Books, 1999), 398–417. Evanzz has acquired much more confidence since the publication of his

Fard, an East Indian, and either Zared Fard or his parents came to New Zealand from what is now Pakistan. Fard Muhammad's mother Beatrice was a white Englishwoman living in New Zealand. Such specificity is an improvement over previous inquiries placing Fard Muhammad's birth in either New Zealand or Portland, Oregon to parents who were either Hawaiian or Polynesian and British.[3] Of course, this conflicts with the belief that Fard Muhammad was an Arab from the Middle East, a notion preserved in Fard Muhammad's self-presentation to black folk in Detroit in the early 1930s:

My name is W. D. Fard and I came from the Holy City of Mecca. More about myself I will not tell you yet, for the time has not yet come. I am your brother. You have not yet seen me in my royal robes.[4]

The Meccan theme developed in the nascent Nation, and it held that Fard Muhammad was not only born in Mecca but was a member of the Quraysh tribe and closely tied to the Hashimid sharīfs (physically related to the sixth-to seventh-century Prophet Muhammad).

Prior to his 1930 advent in Detroit, Fard Muhammad apparently spent time in Oregon and California, where he may have married and had children in addition to pursuing various business ventures, not all of which may have been lawful. The probability that he entered the United States from Canada illegally in 1913 with the financial support of his parents, along with the need to anglicize his name, explains his various aliases, including Wallace D. Fard, Wallace D. Ford, and Fred Dodd. Neither his aliases nor his difficulties with life and the law are of concern here, but the possibility that Fard Muhammad, George Farr, and Wallace D. Ford may have been the same person is of great potential relevance. If true, it gives additional insight into the connections between Moorish Science, the Ahmadiyya movement, the UNIA, and the Nation of Islam (hereafter Nation), as George Farr and Wallace D. Ford's activities in the 1920s are of interest. A member of the Theosophical Society in San Francisco by 1921, Farr was also a member in the UNIA there and espoused a philosophy very consistent with the view subsequently promoted by the Nation toward whites. As for Wallace D. Ford, he spent three years in prison before relocating to Chicago in 1929 (before Noble Drew Ali's demise), where he joined the Moorish Science Temple while attending an Ahmadiyya mosque on the city's South Side. The conflation of these three persons suggests that Fard Muhammad was introduced to the teachings of Noble Drew Ali and Marcus Garvey very formally, as opposed to having simply imbibed them from the charged atmosphere of the period.[5] In this way, the possibility of Fard Muhammad's membership in these

book, *The Judas Factor: The Plot to Kill Malcolm X* (New York: Thunder's Mouth Press, 1992), in which he says W. D. Fard Muhammad was born in Hawaii (143–44).
[3] See Claude Andrew Clegg, III, *An Original Man: The Life and Times of Elijah Muhammad* (New York: St. Martin's Press, 1997), 20.
[4] See Erdmann Doane Beynon, "The Voodoo Cult among Negro Migrants in Detroit," *The American Journal of Sociology* 43 (May 1938): 896–97.
[5] See Evanzz, *The Messenger*, 402–07.

organizations is consistent with a Muslim–Jewish–Christian tradition in which various prophetic moments all build on each other while issuing from a single consciousness.

It was as a street merchant that Fard Muhammad initially presented himself to Detroit's black population (approximately 120,000 in 1930), selling wares from house to house in a fashion similar to "other Arab and Syrian peddlers" in the city. It would not have been difficult for blacks to assign Fard Muhammad an Arab identity, given his unique visage and Detroit's small but growing Arab population (discussed in the preceding chapter). Beynon's 1938 sociological study of the early Nation, while reflecting the apprehensions and misconceptions of the day toward the group, is nevertheless valuable in that it may have been the first substantial scholarly treatment of the organization. However, as it was published not long after Fard Muhammad's appearance in Detroit, it is also possible to read Beynon's report as a primary document. From the testimony gathered by Beynon, it is clear that Fard Muhammad's merchant activities were only a means to support his proselytizing mission. According to Sister Denke Majied,

He came first to our houses selling raincoats, and then afterwards silks. In this way, he could get into the people's houses, for every woman was eager to see the nice things the peddlers had for sale. He told us that the silks he carried were the same kind that our people used in their home country and that he had come from there. So we all asked him to tell us about our own country.[6]

Perhaps because of the nature of the sales business, perhaps out of a deliberate strategy, Fard Muhammad's earliest message was directed at black women; they were his initial audience, who then alerted their husbands, fathers, sons, and brothers that a strange man with a new doctrine had come to town. The didactic element in Fard Muhammad's sales pitch established a connection between the apparently beautiful but foreign designs of his goods and the hidden heritage of his customers. He was beginning to address a fundamental need in the collective consciousness of the African-descended population, a deep desire to know something of their days before their humiliation and degradation. That such an interest in their past was shared by an apparent Arab may have been flattering, but it was certainly not an everyday occurrence. This odd combination of messenger and message created a natural curiosity, and people wanted to hear more:

If we asked him to eat with us, he would eat whatever we had on the table, but after the meal he began to talk: "Now don't eat this food. It is poison for you. The people in your country do not eat it. Since they eat the right kind of food they have the best health all the time. If you would live just like the people in your home country, you would never be sick anymore." So we all wanted him to tell us more about ourselves and about our home country and about how we could be free from rheumatism, aches and pains.

[6] See Beynon, "The Voodoo Cult," 894–96.

This is evidence that diet, a central tenet in the Nation of Islam's teaching, was introduced from the very inception of the movement. This beginning discussion of the relationship between food and health was no trivia; it was a major innovation that led to a breakthrough in the ways in which not only members of the Nation but many other black folk (and nonblack folk as well) approached the question and maintenance of the body's well-being. More will be stated about this later, but it is instructive that Fard Muhammad would link issues of diet to a heritage free from food-induced disease, a message most appreciated by a population among whom a range of maladies was endemic. Integral to all of this was the fact that Fard Muhammad seemed to express genuine concern about the details of their lives and how to improve them.

It was only a brief matter of time before several persons began to assemble in this or that home to give greater consideration to Fard Muhammad's novel teachings, which were quickly assuming a radical character:

The former peddler now assumed the role of prophet. During the early period of his ministry he used the Bible as his textbook, since it was the only religious book with which the majority of his hearers were familiar. With growing prestige over a constantly increasing group, the prophet became bolder in his denunciation of the Caucasians and began to attack the teachings of the Bible in such a way as to shock his hearers.[7]

Whatever subtleties there were in Noble Drew Ali's public discourse on whites, Fard Muhammad's private discussions were much more explicit. Their "denunciation" may not have involved their characterization as "devils" as soon as 1930, but the foundation for the eventual conceptualization was clearly being laid. Combined with the attack on Christianity, Fard Muhammad's message deeply disturbed many in the audience, who "ridiculed his attacks against the Caucasians and were angered by his criticisms of the churches and preachers."[8] For others, though, it was an opportunity to finally interrogate an authoritative tome about which there were silences and imponderables. Rather than resolution through faith, Fard Muhammad encouraged rational engagement. Thus, for Challas Sharrieff,

The very first time I went to a meeting I heard him say: "The Bible tells you that the sun rises and sets. That is not so. The sun stands still. All your lives you have been thinking that the earth never moved. Stand and look toward the sun and know that it is the earth you are standing on which is moving."[9]

This "rationalist" approach to the explanation of all phenomena would become the primary hermeneutical lens through which the Nation of Islam would interpret the world, and it represented a sharp departure from the "spiritualism" of many of those of African descent. In this way, the Nation's teachings qualify its followers as materialists. Imam Wallace Muhammad would state it a

[7] Ibid.
[8] Ibid., 897.
[9] Ibid., 895–96.

bit differently: "We believed in a judgement, but it was a judgement that only required us to believe in the physical. It didn't require us to believe in the supernatural, it just required us to believe in the physical. It was a very physical religion."[10]

This new interpretation of the Bible and its apparent misrepresentation of the physical laws of the universe struck a cord with Challas Sharrieff:

Up to that day I always went to the Baptist church. After I heard that sermon from the prophet, I was turned around completely. When I went home and heard that dinner was ready, I said "I don't want to eat dinner. I just want to go back to the meetings." I wouldn't eat my meals but I goes back that night and I goes to every meeting after that. Just to think that the sun above me never moved at all and that the earth we are on was doing all the moving. That changed everything for me.

The mention of food (again) raises the point that while Fard Muhammad called for dietary proscriptions, food as a concept seems to have assumed a venal equivalency early in the Nation's development. A disciplined diet became coterminous with the Nation, quickly constituting an iconographic symbiosis by which the Nation came to be known, or labeled. Beyond diet, however, Fard Muhammad was challenging core beliefs, and nothing could be more rudimentary than one's relationship to the earth and the sun. If preexisting assumptions about something so elementary were wrong, all other assumptions were open to question. In effect, Fard Muhammad had troubled faith in established Biblical truths; he was not eliminating the Bible as a potential source of guidance, but he was underscoring the need for a very different interpretation. In this new and uncertain context, his role as mediator of Biblical truth became essential. That he was at the very least a prophet, increasing numbers had no doubt.

To keep up with the numerical increase in the following, more and more house meetings were scheduled. This soon became untenable, and a hall was rented for the purpose of accommodating everyone. The demographics of this following, as indicated by those interviewed for the Beynon study, are significant.[11] Of the more than 200 families included in the study, all but 6 were recent immigrants from the South – Mississippi, Alabama, South Carolina, and Virginia. Assuming each family represented four persons, the respondents composed only 10 to 16 percent of the estimated 5,000 to 8,000 members of the Nation in Detroit by 1938 (the lower estimate according to the Detroit police department; the latter according to the Nation). Still, this is a fairly large sample, more than sufficient for statistical purposes, and it strongly suggests that, as was true of Moorish Science, the early Nation was composed of black Southerners buffeted by the stiff winds of impoverishment inter alia up North; they were responding to a message that made sense but that did not emanate from the largesse of the black middle class. Indeed, movement toward the Nation can be read as aspiring to middle-class status but rejecting its established leadership.

---

[10] See W. D. Muhammad, *Religion on the Line*, 39.
[11] Ibid., 897–98.

Because the UNIA had a number of southern branches, the early followers of Fard Muhammad could have been knowledgeable of the Garvey movement. More certain, however, is that some "had come under the influence
of the Moorish-American cult," such that following the departure of Fard
Muhammad from Detroit in 1934, the nascent Nation was in danger of being
wholly subsumed by Moorish Science adherents.[12] Given the prominence of
Moorish Science and the lingering impact of Garvey's ideas, Fard Muhammad
necessarily drew upon them and the Bible to provide the idiomatic structure for
his ideas. In addition, he encouraged his followers to read Breasted's *Conquest
of Civilization*, Hendrik van Loon's *Story of Mankind*, and the writings of Judge
Rutherford of the Jehovah's Witnesses. He furthermore asked his followers
to read books on Freemasonry, underscoring that movement's role in providing the Nation with additional language and ideas, though perhaps in a more
derivative fashion than was the case with Moorish Science. Since many could
not read, Fard Muhammad asked that they purchase radios and listen to such
speakers as Rutherford and Baptist preacher Frank Norris. Even though these
sources tended to reinforce each other, their promotion as necessary reading and
listening evinces an engagement with multiple ideas, unsettling the notion of
Fard Muhammad as sole fount of knowledge. For persons acquainted with little
more than Biblical lore, such a source list represented a significant expansion
of the ideological universe as well as a surprising expression of ecumenism.[13]

Although many were clearly familiar with it, there is no evidence that Noble
Drew Ali's *Circle Seven Koran* ever formed part of the canonical matrix. Rather,
the Qur'ān of orthodoxy was elevated above all other materials; Fard Muhammad was said to have "used only the Arabic text which he translated and
explained to the believers."[14] It is conceivable that he knew Arabic, given his
possible Muslim background, and despite reports that he was functionally illiterate (an allegation probably related to English, not other languages).[15] The emphasis on the ancient Qur'ān as opposed to the *Circle Seven Koran* was no doubt
a necessary strategy to distance the inchoate movement from its predecessor;
indeed, followers of Fard Muhammad referred to each other as "Muslims" as
another way to distinguish themselves from the "Moslems" of Moorish Science.
For many years thereafter, Elijah Muhammad and the Nation would be held up
to derision by the "educated" for their alleged malapropism in mispronouncing
the word "Moslem," when in fact their insistence on "Muslim" was consistent
with the Arabic, as opposed to its anglicized derivative.

* * *

As a result of both the post-Depression economic upturn and the Nation's emphasis on disciplined consumerism, many members of the organization began
to experience relative prosperity. It is estimated that, at the time of their initial

---

[12] Ibid., 898.
[13] Ibid., 900.
[14] Ibid., 894, 900.
[15] See Evanzz, *The Messenger*, 401.

encounter with Fard Muhammad, nearly all of them were living in slums, un-employed, and on the dole, but by August of 1937 there was "no known case of unemployment among these people," as most were working in the automobile industry and other factory-related jobs and were living in "some of the best" black neighborhoods.[16] Dietary laws, the avoidance of intoxicants, and the re-jection of certain beauty aids and sumptuary extravagance helped Muslims to rechannel their resources into homes and other property. The rapid rise of their material conditions necessarily served as a source of curiosity and attraction for others; as Essien-Udom subsequently wrote, this would be associated with the Nation's membership for decades to come:

An examination of Muslim behavior suggests rather strongly that upwardly mobile lower-class Negroes join and remain in the Nation.... The pervasiveness of the middle-class spirit and aspirations among the Muslims cannot escape the attention of a keen observer. This spirit differentiates them fundamentally from the vast majority of lower-class Negroes.[17]

The growth of the nascent movement also drew attention from groups out-side of the African-derived community, including those seeking support for their own purposes. There is indication of a significant effort by Marxists to enjoin the help of the Nation in 1932, but the latter responded by embrac-ing a strident antilabor union position. Among others who approached the Nation were the Ethiopian Wyxzewixard S. J. Challouehliczilczese, mentioned in the preceding chapter, and Japanese reserve officer "Major" Satokata (or Satohata) Takahashi, whose efforts at encouraging Muslims to swear allegiance to the Mikado resulted in a complex response difficult to fully decipher. Possibly an agent of the right wing, imperialist Black Dragon Society or Kokuryukai, Takahashi entered the United States around 1930 and was apparently invited to Detroit by someone within the Nation's leadership. His appearance on the black nationalist scene, however, coincided with the rise of schisms internal to the Nation, and it was without doubt a factor in that development. There is deep irony in the fact that this early experiment in Asian–African cooperative venture, representing the praxis of what leaders like Noble Drew Ali and Fard Muhammad preached, proved not only illusive but divisive, and was ultimately no minor element in early internecine conflict among those of African descent associated with some form of Islam.[18]

The Takahashi moment commenced at a time coterminous with other dis-agreements within the early Nation. One debate ostensibly centered around the question of U.S. citizenship; Fard Muhammad insisted that his followers owed allegiance to no other save the "Muslim flag," and that they "did not belong to America" but were citizens of Mecca. Abdul Muhammad, former Moorish

[16] Ibid., 905–06.
[17] See E. U. Essien-Udom, *Black Nationalism: A Search for an Identity in America* (Chicago: U. of Chicago Press, 1962), 104–05.
[18] See Evanzz, *The Messenger*, 904–05; Ernest Allen, Jr., "Satokata Takahashi and the Flowering of Black Messianic Nationalism," *Black Scholar* 24 (1994): 23–37.

Science member Brown El who joined Fard Muhammad after Noble Drew Ali's death and quickly became his leading lieutenant, took issue with this position and broke away from the Nation. In October of 1933 he helped to incorporate, along with George Grimes, the Society for the Development of Our Own whose "cardinal principle" was "loyalty to the U.S. Constitution and flag." The new organization enjoyed the financial support of Takahashi, and if indications that it was in fact operating as early as 1931 prove accurate, it would mean that the Nation was fractured from its very inception, and that Fard Muhammad functioned alongside, and at times in tandem with, the Society for the Development of Our Own, whose membership of reportedly 10,000 in fourteen chapters around the country included individuals from India and the Philippines, as well as those of African descent.[19]

Takahashi's intervention, for all of its importance, does not fully explain the motivations behind the actions of someone like Abdul Muhammad. Rather, a nostalgia for the heyday of Moorish Science as well as personal rivalry are much more convincing. Abdul Muhammad, as life would have it, played a pivotal role in Elijah Muhammad's conversion; months before Elijah Muhammad (then Poole) ever attended a Fard Muhammad meeting, he had heard of the latter through his father William Poole, who, in turn, had previously met Abdul Muhammad. Together with Elijah and his oldest brother Billie, William Poole paid several visits to Abdul Muhammad's home to hear more about Fard Muhammad. By 1932, Elijah Muhammad (who had become Elijah Karriem upon joining the Nation) was a leading official in the Nation, having superseded (if not supplanted) Abdul Muhammad. This may have been a bit much for the latter, as he had been with Fard Muhammad longer and had been responsible for introducing the Nation's teachings to the Poole family. Indeed, given the claim that Fard Muhammad was functionally illiterate (in English), it is conceivable that Abdul Muhammad, with his longer experience in Moorish Science, played a crucial role in the articulation and dissemination of the Nation's early teachings. Elijah Muhammad's rapid rise may have been deeply disconcerting, and probably informed Abdul Muhammad's decision to break away and reembrace the familiar.[20]

Yet another internal squabble concerned the bizarre statement in the Nation's early literature that, in order for Fard Muhammad to return to his Meccan home, each Muslim had to "offer as sacrifice four Caucasian Devils." In an apparent literal (though qualified) reading of the injunction, one Robert Harris, probably not an actual member of the Nation, stabbed John J. Smith to death in November of 1932, while Verlene Ali was arrested in January 1937 for allegedly preparing to "sacrifice" his own wife and daughter for propitiatory purposes. In an effort to defend itself against charges of advocating "human sacrifice"

[19] Ibid.; also see Evanzz, *The Messenger*, 105–11, for a discussion almost wholly dependent on government documents and written in a fashion generating more obscurity than light.
[20] See Clegg, *An Original Man*, 17–18, 23–24, 29; Beynon, "The Voodoo Cult," 903; Evanzz, *The Messenger*, 105–11.

(Beynon in fact claims that Ali was going to "cook" his wife and daughter, language suggestive of a campaign of vilification), the Nation underscored the symbolism of the teaching (reference to four devils concerns the four beasts of the Book of the Revelations, who impede the destruction of the present world and the genesis of the next), and that in any event, Harris and Ali were not in compliance with a literal reading of the teaching since none of the victims (actual or intended) were Caucasian. It would appear that these cases were used by Detroit officials to caricature and discredit a movement that was quickly labeled the "Voodoo Cult." Recoiling from the negative publicity, yet another faction splintered from the Nation and was derisively referred to by those who remained as the "Rebels against the Will of Allah."[21]

Such fracturing of the Nation by August 1937, the point at which Beynon was actually completing findings for publication the following year, depicts an organization in considerable indeterminacy. Fard had been gone for three years, and in his absence there had sprung up a number of competing factions. Beynon, while often tendentious, provides in this pivotal moment an invaluable snapshot of circumstances "on the ground":

From among the larger groups of Moslems there has sprung recently an even more militant branch than the Nation of Islam itself. This new movement, known as the Temple People, identifies the prophet, Mr. W. D. Fard, with the god Allah. To Mr. Fard alone do they offer prayer and sacrifice. Since Mr. Fard has been deified, the Temple People raise to the rank of prophet the former Minister of Islam Rlijah [sic] Mohammed, now a resident of Chicago. He is always referred to as the "Prophet Elijah in Chicago."[22]

This passage is highly instructive in that it indicates developments that project beyond a foundational pedagogy. Reference to "an even more militant branch" points to the fact that the early teachings of the Nation were subject to subsequent interpretation and embellishment; the deification of Fard Muhammad and the elevation of Elijah Muhammad were two key elements of that embellishment, and they underscore the reflection that much of what would come to be known as the Nation's theology was developed after Fard Muhammad's departure. It is the argument here is that it was Elijah Muhammad and not Fard Muhammad who initiated and articulated many of these changes, changes that proved both masterful and troubling in their implications.

A close reading of Nation lore reveals that Fard Muhammad did not emphasize his own divinity. He may have never volunteered anything of the kind, an observation shared by Imam Wallace Muhammad, son of Elijah: "I am convinced that he himself never told anyone that he was God in the flesh."[23]

---

[21] See Beynon, "The Voodoo Cult," 899, 903–04; Essien-Udom, *Black Nationalism*, 227. Clegg expends more energy on the Harris affair (*An Original Man*, 29–32) and insists that "the belief in blood sacrifices was definitely a part of early Muslim doctrine." His evidence, however, does not support the statement.

[22] See Beynon, "The Voodoo Cult," 906–07.

[23] See Imam Wallace D. Muhammad, *As the Light Shineth from the East* (Chicago: W. D. Muhammad Publications, 1980), 11.

Instead, when Elijah Muhammad's recollections of the unveiling are examined, it is always Elijah Muhammad who is pressing the issue and Fard Muhammad acting as respondent. For example, at one of his earliest personal encounters with Fard Muhammad, and apparently before he was even a member of the Nation, Elijah Muhammad is described as asking the teacher: "'You are that one we read in the Bible that he would come in the last day under the name Jesus.... You are that one'?" The more complete background to the question is even more revelatory of the degree to which Elijah Muhammad took the initiative to interpret for himself what he was experiencing:

And I finally met Him, and when I met Him, I looked at Him and He, well, *it just came to me like this*, that this is the Son of Man that the Bible said that or prophesied that will come in the last days of the world, and I couldn't get that out of me. And I shook hands with Him, and I said to Him, I said, you are the One that the Bible prophesies that will come ... under the name of the Son of Man and under the name The Second Coming of Jesus.[24] [italics added]

Fard Muhammad's initial response was "a little stern, then He smiled," and reportedly whispered in Elijah Muhammad's ear was, "'Yes, I am the One, but who knows that but yourself, and be quiet.'" It is instructive that only Elijah Muhammad and Fard Muhammad knew of the latter's true identity, and that it was the former who had to elicit the information. A subsequent private meeting (in continuity with the whispered ear) was represented by Elijah Muhammad as follows:

I asked him: "Who are you, and what is your real name?" He said, "I am the one the world has been expecting for the past 2,000 years." I said to him again, "What is your name?" He said, "My name is Mahdi; I am God, I came to guide you into the right path that you may be successful and see the hereafter."[25]

Once again, it is Elijah Muhammad initiating the exchange that will result in the epiphany, perhaps a rhetorical device used to indicate a quality of spiritual enlightenment in one who had yet to be fully informed; alternatively, the formulaic question-and-answer sequence may unintentionally point to the interrogator's less-than-passive role in fashioning the response. Indeed, Fard Muhammad's putative background suggests he may have provided certain elements of the reply while Elijah Muhammad provided others. It has been speculated elsewhere, for example, that Fard Muhammad's foreparents were from what is now Pakistan, with possible connections to the Ahmadiyya movement.[26] Even if this were not the case, that he would identify himself as the Mahdi suggests

---

[24] See Elijah Muhammad, *History of the Nation of Islam* (Cleveland: Secretarius Publications, 1994), 1–2. This book is apparently a recorded interview conducted by someone whose identity is alluded to in the phrase "since you is of Israel" (p. 79). Also see Clegg, *An Original Man*, 22; Hatim A. Sahib, "The Nation of Islam" (M.A. thesis, U. of Chicago, 1951), 91–93.

[25] See Elijah Muhammad, *Message to the Blackman in America* (Chicago: Elijah Muhammad, 1965), 17.

[26] See Evanzz, *The Messenger*, 398–417.

Ahmadiyya influence, as Ghulam Ahmad presented himself as both Mahdi and Messiah (discussed in the preceding chapter). In this instance, therefore, Fard Muhammad could have simply borrowed the logic of continuous prophecy and interposed himself in the place of Ghulam Ahmad.

It is fascinating to consider that Fard Muhammad may have stated "My name is Mahdi," but that he never uttered what followed, "I am God." Rather, the second statement may have been an attribution, designed by someone with a profound understanding of mimetic device and in position to orchestrate iconographic parallelisms to advantage. This is not to insist that Fard Muhammad did not make the second statement; it is to suggest, however, that the representation of his having made it became crucial to Elijah Muhammad's contention of leadership. Given the vortex of competing claims for control of the Nation, Elijah Muhammad was apparently the only person, or certainly one of the very few, who put forth the startling equation of Fard Muhammad as Allah incarnate. Such was not the general perspective of the membership, as is evident in the testimony of Brother Yusuf Muhammad, who, in discussing Fard Muhammad's troubles with the law over alleged human sacrifice and other activities, related that "when the police asked him who he was, he said: 'I am the Supreme Ruler of the Universe.' He told those police more about himself than he would ever tell us."[27] How Brother Yusuf learned of this unveiling is itself unclear, but that it was disseminated after Fard Muhammad's disappearance and at the instigation of Elijah Muhammad is highly probable.

There was precedent for the development. If nothing else, Elijah Muhammad was a student of the Bible, and was well versed in its various facets in a manner that was critical as well as reverential. He was quite familiar with the life of Jesus, including claims for a corporeal resurrection and ascension, and he must have pondered the dramatic growth of Christianity after the removal of its progenitor. While he did not arrange for the 1934 final departure of Fard Muhammad from Detroit and Chicago (at least there is no evidence to that effect), he made the best of what otherwise appeared to be a catastrophic turn of events. While the claim that Fard Muhammad was Allah in person went far beyond the teachings of Noble Drew Ali, there was sufficient precedent in black religious communities for the notion of divine corporeality, as discussed in the preceding chapter. By establishing Fard Muhammad as such, and by redefining his own office in relation to this disclosure, Elijah Muhammad appropriated the trope of early Christianity and reinscribed it onto an Islamic narrative. It was a strategic move that would prove distinguishing; indeed, it is what made him a "messenger."

* * *

Accounts of Elijah Muhammad's childhood read like hagiography, and they reinforce the notion that he was born for a special purpose. The second male child

---

[27] See Beynon, "The Voodoo Cult," 897.

and the seventh overall of William and Mariah Poole, Elijah was born in October of 1897 either in or near Sandersville, Georgia, in the county of Washington where the population of 25,237 was 59 percent black in 1893.[28] Both his grandfather Irwin, who knew the experience of enslavement, and his father William were preachers as well as sharecroppers, the latter circumstance the fate of 90 percent of all black Georgians by 1890. Both of Elijah's grandmothers, Peggy and Ellen, were "mulattoes," an observation whose significance for Elijah's views on race will require some exploration. It is difficult to determine the extent to which what follows has been molded by the template of the prescient tradition, but it is said that when Elijah's mother Mariah was 7 years old, she believed she would have a male child of "preeminent stature and importance." As one who put tremendous stock in visions and dreams, Mariah saw Elijah as the fulfillment of the promise. Together with her husband, William, she spoiled the infant Elijah, while grandfather Irwin "teasingly called baby Elijah 'the prophet' and predicted he would one day be just that." It may very well be the case, therefore, that from an early age Elijah felt a strong sense of entitlement.[29]

Leaving Sandersville in 1900, the Pooles relocated to Cordele, Georgia, where William continued to preach along with working in various manufacturing jobs and in the mills. According to the tradition, by the age of 4, Elijah was able to absorb something of his father's preaching and was "deeply impressed," and it was not long before he also developed a desire to become a minister. However, he was not interested in simply following in his father's footsteps; rather, from an early age he "determined to become a 'corrector' of the discrepancies and non sequiturs he sometimes discerned in the lessons of his father and other ministers." His father would preach on Sunday, and Elijah would debate with him on Monday, as he "felt that something was missing from the presentations [of his father], some hidden truth that had not been made clear." Elijah would remember such conversations with both father and grandfather, the former of whom would eventually join the Nation of Islam before his demise:

I never believed it like they taught it. My father and I would argue until finally I got him wavering. ... I heard him one day telling My mother, "You know, that boy gets on my nerves." My mother would laugh. She said, "Why don't you answer what He is asking you?" He would laugh and say, "That boy is something, I am telling you."[30]

---

[28] Unconfirmed reports place his birth in Deepstep, Georgia, some eight miles to the west of Sandersville.

[29] See Clegg, *An Original Man*, 3–7; Malcolm X, with Alex Haley, *The Autobiography of Malcolm X* (New York: Ballantine Books, 1965, 1988), 205. Also see Bernard Cushmeer, *This is the One: Messenger Elijah Muhammad, We Need Not Look for Another* (Phoenix: Truth Publications, 1970, 1971); Gregory Parks, *Freedom, Justice and Equality: The Teachings of the Nation of Islam* (Hampton, VA: United Brothers and United Sisters Communications Systems, 1992); Ibrahim M. Shalaby and John H. Chilcott, *The Education of a Black Muslim* (Tucson: Impresora Sahuaro, 1992); Silis Muhammad, *The Wake of the Nation of Islam* (College Park, GA: Silis Muhammad, 1985); Elijah Muhammad, *Our Saviour has Arrived* (Chicago: n.p., 1974).

[30] See Elijah Muhammad, *The Theology of Time*, transcribed by Abbass Rassoull (Hampton, VA: United Brothers and United Sisters Communications Systems, 1992), Book 4, 296, 298–99.

Convinced that the teachings of the church were in error, and as a protest against the "hypocrisy" of its members, Elijah refused to become a member until apparently forced to do so at age fourteen. His discipline and disposition as a seeker of truth is in keeping with the traditions of those undergoing preparation for life-altering revelations.[31] That is, the lore surrounding Elijah Muhammad's early life conforms to the pattern of piety; his encounters with his father resemble those of a young Jesus interrogating the temple scholars. While skepticism is always an option, it is entirely possible that the traditions were not fabricated but rather reflect a historical, prescient Elijah. If the latter is assumed, then this question emerges: What would cause the young Elijah to be so critical and dubious of ecclesiastical doctrine? While highly speculative and lacking in substantiation, a possible response may be informed by the observation that Elijah's parents and grandparents were living at a time and in a place adjacent to coastal Georgia and South Carolina, the historical epicenter of Muslim activity in the American South. Virtually everything characterizing the context into which Noble Drew Ali was born was also true for Elijah Muhammad, who was born only eleven years later but (perhaps) much closer to the coast. It is possible that subsequent investigations will turn up substantive links between the Muslim coastal community and Washington County, Georgia, helping to explain the young Elijah's disposition toward religion. It would be arresting indeed to learn that the message he heard in Detroit only rekindled a far older flame of faith, initially lit in a West African setting long ago, the embers of which had yet to be extinguished.

Having achieved an educational level somewhere between the fifth and eighth grades, Elijah Poole left Cordele around 1913 for Macon, Georgia, where he remained for several years working in sawmills and as a foreman at the Cherokee Brick Company.[32] Taking a job as a gang laborer on the track of the Southern Railroad Company in 1919, he married Clara Evans in March of the same year and soon started a family. In April of 1923 he and his wife and two children, accompanied by his parents, brothers, and sisters, joined the mass exodus of other black Southerners making their way North between 1910 and 1930; credit the conspiracy of Jim Crow, the boll weevil, and new restrictions on foreign immigration for the fateful meeting of Elijah Poole and Fard Muhammad.[33]

The Pooles settled in the largely Polish, independent municipality of Hamtramck outside of Detroit, also known as Paradise Valley. For the first two years, Elijah found steady factory employment, but after 1925 he was in and out of work, which may have included stints as a Baptist preacher.[34] At some unspecified point, perhaps before he left the South, Elijah became a mason, once again indicating the role of the Craft in creating a cognitive framework, a

---

[31] See Clegg, *An Original Man*, 7–13.
[32] See Essien-Udom, *Black Nationalism*, 75–76; Sahib, "Nation of Islam," 89.
[33] See Clegg, *An Original Man*, 14.
[34] So says Essien-Udom, *Black Nationalism*, 74–75.

way of thinking, that was preparatory in the eventual adoption of philosophies in symmetry, correspondences evident in Elijah's own reflection:

I will not go into the history of the Masons since I was a mason Myself once and I swore, too, not to reveal the secrets. Masons who have reached such degrees as 32nd and 33rd are not called Masons. They are called Moslem Shriners. They are reaching up to us [Muslims in the Nation]. When you take the 33rd degree you are taught to greet each other: "As-Salaam-Alaikum." You are taught Islam from then on because you become a Muslim when that degree is conferred on you. At least you are supposed to be a believer in Islam.[35]

The parallels with Noble Drew Ali are rather unavoidable here, as may have been the economic plights of Noble Drew and Elijah Poole upon their initial migration to the North. While little is known about Noble Drew's early employment experiences, Elijah was clearly unable to adequately provide for a growing family. His level of consternation continued to rise until, according to at least one report, he became intimately acquainted with the bottle on a regular, state-altering basis.[36] Having escaped the terror of the South, Elijah Poole had entered a very different dimension, a kind of twilight zone, and he was living the exact antithesis of expectations. He would languish in that condition, far from the life of a divine messenger, until the spring of 1931.

It was then that his brother and father made mention of their interaction with Abdul Muhammad, Fard Muhammad's leading lieutenant. Persuaded that Islam was a "heathen religion," it was months before Elijah decided to go and hear Fard Muhammad in person. His first attempt to hear and then meet Fard Muhammad was frustrated by an overflowing crowd; his second try was nearly as disappointing, although he heard enough of the presentation to grasp the gist of Fard Muhammad's message. It was after this sermon, in the greeting line, that Elijah Poole for the first time shook the hand of the "short, fair-skinned man with dark, straight hair" who could have "passed" for white. It was then that he is said to have asked, "You are the one we read in the Bible that he would come on the last day under the name of Jesus.... You are that one?"[37]

Meditating on the "knowledge of self and others," Elijah returned from the personal encounter with Fard Muhammad occupying the liminal state of self-transformation. In the process of conversion, he began to make as many meetings as possible, reportedly returning from them only to enter his closet and lay prostrate in prayer to Fard Muhammad. The circumstances would suggest that Elijah maintained a regular, more conventional contact with the teacher, and he must have conveyed to the latter an interest in becoming a minister. In a critical tradition that seemingly escapes the mediation of postperiod reconstruction, Elijah's call to the ministry is publicly delivered from Fard Muhammad through the intervention of Elijah's wife Clara. After a teaching

[35] See E. Muhammad, *Theology of Time*, Book 4, 282.
[36] See Steven Barboza, *American Jihad: Islam after Malcolm X* (New York: Doubleday, 1993), 273.
[37] See Sahib, "Nation of Islam," 68, 91–93, 121; Clegg, *An Original Man*, 21–23.

session, Fard Muhammad asked if anyone in attendance knew "the little man who lives in Hamtramck?" Clara responded, "Yes, he is my husband." Addressing Clara, Fard Muhammad went on to perform what amounts to a rather unusual ordination: "You tell him that he can go ahead . . . and start teaching, and I will back [him] up." Elijah, at home with the children at the time, must have experienced something akin to bliss once Clara broke the news. His life as messenger had commenced.[38]

As previously noted, Elijah Poole's name was changed to Elijah Karriem, and the Georgia native moved quickly through the ministerial ranks and became closely associated with Fard Muhammad. Traditions favorable to Elijah Karriem maintain that he was soon designated "Supreme Minister" by Fard Muhammad and second-in-command in the Nation, that they became virtually inseparable for many months, and that Fard Muhammad was a regular visitor to the Karriem home, where he invested significant time in privately teaching Elijah.[39] Seeking to characterize the closeness of their bond, Elijah reported: "He used to teach me night and day. We used to sit sometimes from early part of the night until sunrise and after sunrise. All night long for about two years or more."[40] Elijah would reiterate his claims in much more dramatic fashion:

God came [to] Me in 1931 in Detroit, Michigan. He taught Me for 3 years and 4 months. He taught Me night and day. I used to be glad to get a little sleep but he would tell Me, "I will be back." I would say, "I hope it will be long enough for Me to get a little sleep." He taught Me what you hear Me teach you, for three years, night and day.[41]

While these developments may have some basis in fact, critical distancing requires a consideration of such assertions as echoing the subsequent project of solidifying Elijah Muhammad's power and support. Given the level of competition among lieutenants within the Nation, and the splintering of the movement even before Fard Muhammad's departure (but certainly after it), these traditions may very well conform to that view of history as the provenance of those who won.

The succession struggle following Fard Muhammad's departure was precipitated by the aforementioned "sacrifice" of James Smith by Robert Harris in November of 1932. Fard Muhammad was arrested of November 23 in connection with the murder. Denying any involvement, Fard Muhammad was detained until December 6, by which time the Detroit police had begun to collect information about the organization and its views on race. Fard Muhammad was able to lower his own profile throughout much of 1933, but in May of that year he was rearrested on charges of disturbing the peace, and he was forced to leave the city. His last recorded, physical meeting with Elijah Muhammad

---

[38] See E. Muhammad, *History*, 2–3; Sahib, "Nation of Islam," 92–93; Clegg, *An Original Man*, 22–23.
[39] See Clegg, *An Original Man*, 23–26.
[40] See E. Muhammad, *History*, 4.
[41] See E. Muhammad, *Theology of Time*, Book 1, 84.

took place in Chicago in June of 1934, after which there is an erasure of his whereabouts.[42]

As early as 1931, Elijah Muhammad would visit Chicago on proselytizing missions. The Nation's Temple No. 2 was located there, and with the intensification in factionalism in 1933, his visits to Chicago became more frequent, an indication that he was beginning to view Chicago as a permanent asylum from "the hypocrites," an early designation for opposition from within the movement that would surface decades later in his lethal conflict with Malcolm X. At some point between May of 1933 and Fard Muhammad's final exit in June of 1934, those loyal to Elijah became known as the "Temple People," and with Elijah's decision to officially relocate the Nation's headquarters to Chicago in September of 1934, Temple No. 2 at 3643 South State Street became known as the "Allah Temple of Islam." Brother Theodore Rozier, originally from Haiti, was left in charge of Temple No. 1 in Detroit.[43]

By 1935, matters were unraveling at an alarming rate for Elijah Muhammad. Opposition to him and the Temple People was mounting, symbolized by the opposition's insistence upon calling him Karriem rather than Muhammad, arguing that the latter title was never conferred on him by Fard Muhammad. Consistent with this view was their rejection of both the title "Supreme Minister" and that of "Messenger of Allah." Compounding his struggle with fellow Muslims (who by no means represented a monolithic whole) were conflicts with the Chicago police department in March and April of 1935, reminiscent of earlier encounters with the police in Detroit. The coup de grace was the emergence of a group from within the Allah Temple, itself led by his own, younger brother Kalot, or Kallatt. By the time the dust settled, Elijah Muhammad was in dire financial straits and at the head of a membership that had dwindled from an estimated 400 to 13. Facing threats against his life, he withdrew from Chicago toward the end of 1935. The following year, his trusted aid Theodore Rozier broke ranks in Detroit and established an independent group; his action was emulated by others. Altogether, this was a *fitna* ("time of trials") of a different kind.[44]

Between the end of 1935 and the summer of 1946, Elijah Muhammad's life took any number of twists and turns and reflects a period of dissolution and incoherence in the movement. He made a brief stop in Milwaukee before finding sanctuary in Washington, D.C., where he assumed aliases that included Muhammad Rassoull (or "Muhammad the messenger") and Gulam Bogans (which seems to indicate an awareness of the Ahmadiyya movement), the latter the designation under which he was arrested in September of 1942 for refusing to register for the draft, along with over 100 male followers. The federal

---

[42] See E. Muhammad, *History*, 4–9; Sahib, "Nation of Islam," 70–77, 98; Clegg, *An Original Man*, 29–37.

[43] See Beynon, "The Voodoo Cult," 906–07; Essien-Udom, *Black Nationalism*, 45–46; Clegg, *An Original Man*, 33–37, 80–82.

[44] Ibid.

government, aware of the Nation's rhetoric and engaged in a war with Japan, was already suspicious that the organization was an operative of the Mikado, or at least sympathetic to him. Elijah Muhammad's apprehension was therefore part of the federal government's crackdown on black organizations suspected of pro-Japanese sedition, the most important of which was the Pacific Movement of the Eastern World, founded in Chicago in 1932, with branches in St. Louis, the Mississippi Delta, and elsewhere. From July through October of that same year, organizations such as the Peace Movement of Ethiopia, the Ethiopian Pacific Movement, the International Reassemble of the Church of Freedom League, Inc., the House of Israel, the Colored American National Organization, and the Moorish Science Temple of America all suffered the seizure of members.[45] In federal custody while his fate was being determined, Elijah Muhammad as Gulam Bogans was admitted into the Federal Correctional Institution at Milan, Michigan in July of 1943 along with other constituents. He maintained indirect contact with a diminishing Nation membership through his wife Clara until his postwar release in August of 1946. Given such a dizzying pace of developments, it is unreasonable to believe that his perspective did not undergo change, and that these changes did not find expression in the articulation of the Nation's teachings.[46]

In particular, there are two major developments during the interregnum from 1935 to 1946 that should be interpreted as moments in which Elijah Muhammad took definitive command of the Nation's theological project and placed his personal imprimatur upon it. The first concerns the tradition placing him in the Library of Congress during the Washington, D.C. sojourn, where he is said to have spent most of his days studying from a list of 104 books assigned by Fard Muhammad just before the latter's disappearance. While the secondary scholarship tends to accept this account as literal, a divergent reading would assign a more symbolic significance to the report and underscore its legibility in the realm of implication. In the alternative view, the tradition connotes the further elaboration of Elijah's Muhammad's own views and a deepening of his understanding; the notion that certain books were assigned by Fard Muhammad can be read as a sanctioning device for what emerges from this time of reflection. The second development probably took place near the interregnum's end, so that, by the beginning of 1950, Elijah Muhammad had taken "all of the original pamphlets, or Lesson Books that were given by his teacher, Professor Fard Muhammad. He took those things out of circulation and then he began himself to interpret, to preach, and put the emphasis where he wanted the emphasis to be."[47] This clearly indicates an independence of thought, and it suggests that Elijah Muhammad had so consolidated his base of support that he no longer needed to justify every pronouncement as coming directly from the lips of Fard Muhammad himself. While the sanctioning power

[45] See Allen, "Satokata Takahashi," 23–27.
[46] See Essien-Udom, *Black Nationalism*, 67–67; Clegg, *An Original Man*, 77–108.
[47] See W. D. Muhammad, *As the Light Shineth*, 19.

of the latter would remain critical, by 1950 Elijah Muhammad's position could withstand the realization that he was an innovator in his own right, probably much more so than is currently understood.

Of course, much of Elijah Muhammad's postwar confidence was related to the termination of internecine conflict. In turn, respite from those troubles was directly related to the U.S. government's campaign of harassment against groups such as the Nation for both their nationalist rhetorical positions and for sentiments supportive of Japan; in some sense, the reemergence of the Nation is directly attributable to this campaign as it proved to be one of the few survivors. Events leading up to and during the Second World War proved critical, as the Society for the Development of Our Own could not survive the combination of Takahashi's April 1934 deportation, Abdul Muhammad's death from tuberculosis in 1938, and brother Kalot's alcoholism and bouts of dementia before the war. Other organizations were targeted by the government with the entrance of the United States into the conflict in December of 1941. Takahashi had apparently reentered the country illegally in late 1936 or early 1937, and he had reestablished communications with such groups as the Ethiopian Pacific Movement (or the Peace Movement of Ethiopia) and the Onward Movement of America, organizations whose membership included some persons formerly affiliated with the Universal Negro Improvement Association and the Nation. These groups also supposedly had ties to Ashima Takis, a Filipino (otherwise named Policarpio Manasala) who presented himself as Japanese and may have played a role of some significance in the cause of Asian–African unity. A number of leaders of these and other organizations came under close scrutiny during the war for their alleged support of Japan, and they were either imprisoned or deported. Takis, for example, received a three-year sentence for forgery, while Takahashi was rearrested in June of 1939, convicted of immigration violations and bribery charges, and sentenced to three years in a federal penitentiary. Released in February of 1942, by May he was reassigned to an internment camp along with some 100,000 Japanese Americans, and was later deported (again). Most organizations associated with Japan did not survive the harassment, and with the conclusion of the war, Elijah Muhammad was one of the few with the resiliency to rebuild.[48]

Released from prison in August of 1946, Elijah Muhammad went on to achieve one of the more surprising political recoveries of the period. In tatters just four years earlier, the Nation was soon able to rebound by emphasizing a much more pragmatic strategy of business investment and property ownership. Having purchased a 140-acre farm in White Cloud, Michigan in 1945, the Nation opened the Shabazz restaurant in Chicago at 3117 S. Wentworth,

---

[48] Allen, "Satokata Takahashi," 34–35, maintains that Takahashi was deported from the United States in April of 1934 and that he was in Canada from late 1934 to January of 1939, when he reentered the States illegally. Otherwise, I rely (reluctantly) on Evanzz, *The Messenger*, 111, 122–55, for much of this information; I can only be grateful that, in the need to provide context, this section is not critical to my overall argument.

along with a bakery and grocery store. Chicago became the headquarters of a rejuvenated organization, and, by the 1950s, continued commercial expansion saw the Nation open a laundry, cleaning plant, haberdashery, dress shop, and automobile repair and paint shop, and invest in real estate on Chicago's South Side. Members were expected to patronize these establishments in the name of "doing for self" while moving away from economic dependency on whites. Elijah Muhammad's personal worth is estimated to have reached $75,000 by 1952, a not inconsiderable figure that does not include his home and properties owned by the organization. The renewed stress on economic independence or self-reliance resonated with many in the black community, and temples all across the country experienced growth, especially in Washington, D.C., Detroit, and New York City. The organization was incorporated in November of 1955 as the "Holy Temple of Islam," and while the average convert through the 1940s was a Southern immigrant with less than an eighth-grade education, by the 1950s the Nation was attracting the middle class and professionals. By 1960 there may have been as many as 250,000 members in the Nation, not all active, whereas more conservative estimates place the number of members at 25,000 or fewer.[49] Elijah Muhammad, firmly in control for the first time in his life, was finally in position to shape the central tenets of the Nation in the manner he saw fit.

* * *

Although Elijah Muhammad would credit Fard Muhammad with providing the teachings of the Nation, it was Elijah Muhammad who produced the bulk of the instruction. To be sure, Fard Muhammad initiated the new movement, an improvisation on the foundations of Moorish Science and Garveyism. As Imām Wallace Muhammad explains,

The teacher of the Honorable Elijah Muhammad, who we once identified as a Christ figure, as God in the flesh, Professor Fard Muhammad, envisioned the whole idea and he put together the concept, the FOI, the MGT, the University of Islam, the school for educating us. He put together that whole concept, and he was the one who issued the first identification cards for the members of the movement. . . . The card says, "This person, the bearer of this card, is a Muslim." It was addressing law enforcement. It says that "if anyone finds the bearer of this card other than righteous, take the card, and punish the said bearer." So the organization from its inception believed in obedience to the law of the land and that we shouldn't break the law of the land.[50]

Reference to the use of an identity card by members of the Nation itself underscores Fard Muhammad's indebtedness to the innovations of Noble Drew Ali, as the instructions on the card are identical to those issued by the Moorish Science Temple. Elijah Muhammad would deny that Fard Muhammad was a

---

[49] See Clegg, *An Original Man*, 99–115.
[50] See W. D. Muhammad, *Religion on the Line*, 5–6.

member of Noble Drew Ali's movement, but of the latter's influence there can be no doubt. As Elijah Muhammad stated,

I have always had a very high opinion of both the late Noble Drew Ali and Marcus Garvey and admired their courage in helping our people (the so-called Negroes) and appreciated their work. Both of these men were fine Muslims. The followers of Noble Drew Ali and Marcus Garvey should now follow me and co-operate with us in our work because we are only trying to finish up what those before us had started.[51]

With respect to contributions, then, Fard Muhammad may have fashioned the core beliefs of the Nation, but there was significant secondary and tertiary material that developed well after his 1934 departure, much of which was in response to contemporary challenges and changing circumstances. Even Imām Wallace Muhammad, who assigned Fard Muhammad such a distinctive role as innovator in the beginning of the movement, conceded that "the Honorable Elijah Muhammad changed his teachings [Fard Muhammad's] slightly, and *as he went on he changed many things* – before I started changing things"[52] (italics added). Elijah Muhammad was at the helm of the movement for much of the twentieth century, and he necessarily crafted appropriate responses as well as refined the theology. It is therefore unclear to what extent materials produced within the Nation between 1930 and 1938, the year of Beynon's publication, were solely the creation of Fard Muhammad, particularly after 1934. It is possible that Fard and Elijah Muhammad maintained contact well after the former's exile from Detroit and Chicago, concerning which the latter continued to make allusions as late as 1957:

All the answers are directly from the mouth of Allah (God) in the Person of Master W. F. Muhammad, to Whom all praise is due, the Great Mahdi or Messiah, as the Christians say, and He is also the Son of Man.

   He has taught me and *continues to reveal* His truth to me, although to some it is unbelievable....

   Say: He, Allah, is One God (not three), there is no God but He and I am His Messenger and Servant.[53] [italics added]

While the foregoing material attributes continuing revelation to Fard Muhammad, there is every probability that such communication had long ceased, underscoring Elijah Muhammad's role as the creative force behind much of the post-1934 promulgations. Even so, by 1938 the ideological foundations for all that the Nation would become were more or less established. An exhaustive and detailed investigation of the Nation's doctrine has yet to be achieved, and as it does not constitute the emphasis of the present study, such an analysis will not be attempted here. Instead, what follows is a discussion of select components of the Nation's teachings and practicum.

[51] See Elijah Muhammad, *The Supreme Wisdom* (Newport News, VA: United Brothers Communications Systems, n.d.; orig. pub., 1957), vol. 2, 84; E. Muhammad, *History*, 76–77.
[52] See W. D. Muhammad, *As the Light Shineth*, 14.
[53] See E. Muhammad, *Supreme Wisdom*, vol. 2, 2.

To begin, and in complete concert with the tenets of Moorish Science, the focus of the Nation's early message centered on the problem of identity; one of the most poignant expressions of the profound change in self-perception was the alteration of the personal name to reflect the newfound identity. Both organizations insisted that African-derived persons were not Negroes, but the new names of the Nation went well beyond the custom in Moorish Science, in which *El* and *Bey* were added to the surname. In the early Nation, the new moniker did not necessarily bear any relationship to the old appellation, so that there was no obvious link between Anwar Pasha and Henry Wells, nor was there any indication that Hazziez Allah was the former Lindsey Garrett. Together with a fee of ten dollars, applicants had to submit a written request to receive their "original names" from Fard Muhammad, to whom these names were revealed through an indwelling Spirit of Allah. In an obvious snafu, "the prophet once gave the surnames of Sharrieff, Karriem, and Mohammed to the three Poole brothers. The prophet explained this seeming mistake due to his divine knowledge of the different paternity of the three brothers."[54] The reference is to the family of Elijah Muhammad, formerly Elijah Poole, and the paternity revelation must have caused considerable embarrassment. Even so, there is no gainsaying the importance of the concept itself, as it represented an initial step in a direction away from consequences of acculturation in North America as a historical phenomenon.

In a seeming departure from Moorish Science, the Nation taught that, rather than the descendants of Moroccans, blacks in the North America were actually the scions of members from the lost tribe of Shabazz, who had been stolen from Mecca itself by slave traders approximately 400 years ago. It was Fard Muhammad's divine mission to "find and to bring back to life his long lost brethren," who Fard described collectively as "his uncle," who since their sojourn in "the wilderness of America" were "living other than themselves." Inhabiting an inverse universe, black folk were the disempowered and despised, when in fact they were "the original people, noblest of the earth." Restoration to such lofty heights required a return to their religion and native tongue, Islam and Arabic, which had been taken from them by "the Caucasians." It will be remembered that the Moroccan ancestors with whom Noble Drew Ali was concerned were originally Moabites or Canaanites, and were the founders of Mecca, so that the origin accounts of the Nation and the Moorish Temple converge and can be read as variations on an identical theme.

Whether formerly of Moab or Shabazz, blacks in North America were in need of recovering a culture based on astronomy and advanced mathematics (especially calculus), and acquiring a lifestyle in which their homes were kept clean and their bodies free of all intoxicants (especially liquor) and devoid of such toxic meats as duck, goose, possum, catfish, and, above all, swine. The inculcation of these new values was formalized in the education of the Nation's

---

[54] Beynon, "The Voodoo Cult," 900–01.

youth very early on. Responsibility for housekeeping and cooking food "properly" fell on women and girls, who received formal instruction in these matters in the two related auxiliaries of the Muslim Girls' Training and General Civilization Class, otherwise referred to as MGT and GCC. The University of Islam was created to service children whose enrollment in public schools would clearly pose insoluble problems. Children at the University were taught the "knowledge of our own" as opposed to the "civilization of the Caucasian devils," and they participated in a curriculum that included "higher mathematics" and astronomy. Concerns over the University of Islam reached such a point in the 1930s that the Detroit Board of Education attempted to shut it down and transfer its students to public schools; a "severe riot," however, in which Nation members "stormed the police headquarters" in protest, caused the Board to abort the effort. "Rioters" were released from the court's custody with suspended sentences out of fear that "race riots" would otherwise ensue.[55] As reward for the preservation of the Nation's curriculum, those who had resisted would at some point be transported back to the Paradise from which their ancestors had been pirated – Mecca.[56]

It is not possible to overstate the significance of these teachings, nor the magnitude of their challenges. The Nation's leadership was arguing that all was not what it seemed and urged adherents to embrace a vision in which the world order, or at least that which obtained in the United States, was placed in racial reverse. Like Noble Drew Ali, the Nation's leaders identified the basic problem as one of misidentification. With that addressed, they went on to tell noneducated and barely educated migrants that they had to learn calculus. What was more important was that the acquisition of "higher mathematics" was not some impossible feat but something that would come very naturally, a message that must have comforted people who all their lives had been told that certain forms of learning were quite beyond them. Finally, the leadership exacted a certain discipline, a regulation of personal habits, that required followers to limit meals to once a day and to eliminate such staples as catfish and pork. Beyond the association of certain foods with slavery, these stipulations were consistent with principles of sound health management, something that would not be more fully appreciated until many decades later. In contrast, the Nation's association with and predilection for bean pies, bean soups, and bean salads was not necessarily informed by health issues but by folklore, based on Fard Muhammad's insistence that back in "the East" he had known a man whose secret to longevity (he was allegedly 240 years old) was beans.[57] With the possible exception of this anecdote, Fard Muhammad and his lieutenants were far ahead of their time in calling for changes of mind and habit that were not simply modifications but thoroughgoing transformations.

[55] Ibid., 902.
[56] Ibid., 900–01.
[57] See Benjamin Karim, *Remembering Malcolm* (New York: Carroll and Graf, 1992), 63.

Noble Drew Ali had premised his ideas about black identity on what was known about human history, and he was innovative in linking the histories of Africans with those of Asians, Pacific Islanders, and Native Americans. W. D. Fard Muhammad and Elijah Muhammad, in contrast, dramatically distinguished themselves from Moorish Science by going far beyond the known past, far beyond romanticism, and they offered a rendition of the past radically different from all that had proceeded them. According to their version of history, the people of the lost tribe of Shabazz were physical descendants of the very first Being in all the universe. That Being was God, who formed himself "from an Atom of Life," thus simultaneously inaugurating time. This Atom of water ("because we can't produce Life without water") had been motionless, "hidden in the darkness" for unknown "trillions of years," but its first movement began time, some 76 trillion years ago. Creating himself out of the material surrounding him, "He came out to total darkness and He was dark. He proved that He came out of darkness, because His own color corresponds with the conditions of what is now the Heavens and the Earth, that was nothing then but total darkness. A totally Dark Man came out of total darkness," and chose the earth as his home.[58] There are dual codes in the cosmogony, descriptive and prescriptive: the former, in that in the beginning was the blackest man possible; and the latter, in that just as this original "blackman" emerged out of darkness, so too must his contemporary descendants come out of their confusion. The logic is circular, calling for a return to a divine nature.

Unlike the Christian or Jewish (or for that matter even the orthodox Muslim) imagination of an ethereal, otherworldly Transcendence, the Nation's concept of God or Allah was decidedly corporeal. Allah was a man, a blackman who proceeded to create others like himself along with the stars and planets, having learned "the secrets of light and fire." He decided to chronicle civilization 6 trillion years after his initial act of self-creation, and those he in turn created were also gods, but also men, neither omniscient nor immortal, and on average lived no more than 100 or 200 years, eventually forming thirteen tribes. As scientists, they engaged in experiments, some displaying interests and temperaments inconsistent with and antithetical to the well-being of the majority. One, in fact, tried to destroy the earth 66 trillion years ago when his plan to unify the various languages of the world failed. The result of his effort, which involved unusually powerful explosives, was the cleaving of the earth into two (creating the current earth and moon) and the demise of one of the thirteen tribes.[59] Fantastic to most, the account combines elements from versions of the tower of Babel and the great flood, dividing time into antediluvian and postdiluvian periods.

Reinforcing the image of man as god while reifying his achievements as scientist (in a decidedly masculinist discourse), the Nation taught that trillions of years ago a council of twenty-four scientists-cum-elders was convened, who

---

[58] See E. Muhammad, *Theology of Time*, Book 2, 92–98, 107.
[59] Ibid.; also see Clegg, *An Original Man*, 41–45.

regulate human affairs by writing their history before it happens, and for spans of 25,000 years (a number that "accords" with the approximate circumference of the earth in miles). Toward the end of each 25,000-year period, a different council forms to write the history of the next 25,000 years, and so on. The labor of the council is divided as follows: "The 23 Gods work and One does the analyzation and calculation of what They write."[60] This twenty-fourth god becomes the principal deity, or Allah. While diverging from orthodox ideas about an eternal presence without beginning or end, the significance of this formulation is that it emphasizes the role of black people in determining their own destiny. They write their own history. As will be discussed shortly, even the present experience has been scripted, and because it was scripted by black gods, it will eventually issue into a triumphant conclusion.

Following the catastrophe of the earth's being rent asunder 66 trillion years ago, the tribe of Shabazz was able to recover and relocate to the "best part of our planet (earth) to live on, which is the rich Nile Valley of Egypt and the present seat of the Holy City, Mecca, Arabia."[61] Egypt was located in what was originally "East Asia," or what is now referred to as Africa, an unfortunate development as the earlier descriptor establishes the connections of East Asia to other Asiatic communities throughout the world. However, as Egypt and Mecca carry powerful symbolic meanings as centers of two of the most important achievements known in human history, Elijah Muhammad's identification of them as the original homelands of black folk in North America had the effect of concomitantly linking descendants of the enslaved population with the progenitors of Islam and high civilization.

The foregoing discussion therefore establishes a pedigree for black folk that is virtually timeless, reaching back to the source of life itself, in striking contrast to the mania of theologians whose writings about Hamitic curses have thus far proven much more effective in molding myth into reality. Also embedded in the Nation's cosmology is an approximation of the language of science; these early black folk marshaled the forces of nature and made discoveries through trial and error. They had an advanced understanding of science and mathematics, a didactic message that their contemporary progeny would likewise need to regain mastery over their lives.

The emphasis on the here and now also had profound implications for the Nation's presentation of religion, for it was not at all informed by the same assumptions undergirding other systems of belief. According to Elijah Muhammad, the concept of a "spook God" who lived in some unapproachable "place" and whose existence was spiritual rather than physical was a principal misconception, as were such notions as heaven and hell and life after death:

The so-called Negroes think of God in terms of something without form (spirit or spook) and they believe that His throne is somewhere in the sky. This is due to their ignorance

---

[60] See E. Muhammad, *Theology of Time*, vol. 2, 113–16.
[61] See E. Muhammad, *Supreme Wisdom*, vol. 2, 14–15.

of just what spirit means. The teachings of Christianity have put God out of man into nothing (spirit). Can you imagine God without form but yet interested in our affairs who are the human beings? What glory would an immaterial God get out of a material world? We also learn that a spirit is not self-independent; it is dependent upon air, water and food. Without it, the spirit can have no life. So how can a spirit be God?[62]

It is instructive that Elijah Muhammad's 1965 *Message to the Blackman in America*, a compilation of previous statements with some additions, is organized in such a way that its attack on a "spook" or "mystery" God is the first item of business, indicating the centrality of the tangible as a way of conceptualizing the world.[63] Without doubt, the critique also laid the groundwork for the presentation of Fard Muhammad as God, but the overall objective was far more encompassing. Elijah Muhammad was challenging a way of thinking that posited as authentic such unseen phenomena as ghosts and "haints," hoodoo and related practices, and he was arguing that, together with Christianity, such beliefs were irrational and prevented blacks from making genuine progress in a time–space world.

The assault on belief in spirits and hoodoo is a reminder that Elijah Muhammad was principally engaged in a dialogue with the black community, and on terms internal to that community (or set of communities). He was not concerned about external views of blacks as superstitious; he was interested in dislodging categories that he deemed counterproductive and constraining. In criticizing faith in anything that could not be sensually perceived, he was adopting a kind of empiricism. The Nation's teaching on spirituality was therefore in tension with the African antecedent, as the rejection of the noumenal contradicts much of what characterizes African religions. At the same time, however, the embrace of the time–space dimension can be seen as very African in its displacement of eschatological expectation and insistence on the present as the focus of all activity.

* * *

It was in the schools and homes of the Nation that probably one of the most controversial, and certainly one of the more arresting, tenets of the Nation of Islam's doctrine was systematically communicated: the identification of whites or Caucasians as "blue-eyed devils." It is perhaps a more evocative than provocative assertion in that it tends to generate a visceral, emotive response from all sides, aimed as it is at the moral core of the human personality. The immediacy of the reaction in the form of either acceptance or repudiation, required in light of social and political considerations, does not necessarily lend itself to a mature exploration of the doctrine's historicity and development. Such an investigation is needed if an appreciation of the wide range of interpretations by blacks of their experience in North America (and elsewhere) is to

---

[62] Ibid., vol. 2, 9–10.
[63] See E. Muhammad, *Message to the Blackman*, 1–30.

be achieved. Once the tenet is explored, it will become clear that Africans and their descendants have long debated the meaning of phenotypical difference in light of their subjugation, and that questions concerning the moral nature of whites have been the subject of speculation for quite some time, if not since the fifteenth century and the onslaught of the transatlantic slave trade itself. Such discourse was by no means idle, meaningless cogitation; it was an important if not vital variable for blacks to ponder in attempting to solve the riddles of oppression and freedom. Africans needed to know who or what they were really up against.

The doctrine of the white devil was only a component, albeit an important component, of an overarching, totalizing cosmology whose elements evince a preoccupation with explaining and reversing the relationship between European power and African weakness. Other aspects of the Nation's teachings must continually be borne in mind, as the notion of white-embodied evil was not a self-contained or self-sustaining analysis, in isolation from other principles. However, with respect to the question of whiteness, it was the decided opinion of not a few that something was fundamentally skewed, perhaps unalterably, about the collective character of Europeans; some essential quality was missing, some basic element absent. As Malcolm would characterize it,

You tell that to any Negro. Except for those relatively few "integration"-mad and so-called "intellectuals," and those black men who are otherwise fat, happy, and deaf, dumb, and blinded, with their crumbs from the white man's rich table, you have struck a nerve center in the American black man. He may take a day to react, a month, a year; he may never respond, openly; *but of one thing you can be sure* – when he thinks about his own life, he is going to see where, to him, personally, the white man sure has acted like a devil.[64] [italics added]

Given the litany of atrocities against the African and his progeny, what else could explain the enormity of the inhumanity, an indictment that grew ever more egregious with reports of the European's parallel behavior in Asia and Latin America? Such a question commenced from the very first sighting of the slaver, and it nursed the fear that these "spirits" were cannibalistic in intent (apprehensions not necessarily shared by the victims of African domestic slavery). From the initial encounter, there was trepidation that these foreign captors were entirely dissimilar from their African counterparts. Such fear would only deepen on the other side of the Atlantic.

The doctrine of the "white man as devil" therefore did not begin with Elijah Muhammad. Mention has already been made of Father Hurley of the Universal Hagar Spiritual Church, who taught that blacks were the "first people of the world," whereas whites were Gentiles, the descendants of Cain, and therefore "cursed with a pale color." Similarly, his contemporary Noble Drew Ali viewed the "pale skin nations" of Europe as conjoined lands of paganism, and he seemingly associated whites with Satan and evil. Imām Wallace Muhammad

---

[64] See Malcolm X, *Autobiography*, 186.

concurs with the latter assessment of Noble Drew, as he has asserted that W. D. Fard Muhammad had "studied Noble Drew Ali's approach," and, in Fard Muhammad's attempt to introduce the Qur'ān, he "had to put it in the package of Drew Ali" because of the latter's preceding influence:

The teachings he gave us were very similar to what Drew Ali gave his people. He taught us we were black Asiatics and descendants of a great Islamic Kingdom; Drew Ali taught his people the same. He taught us the Caucasians were devils and Drew Ali taught his people the same. A lot of his people don't know this. He identified white people with the embodiment of evil in scripture, which is Satan. But he was more elusive than Fard Muhammad was. Drew Ali said white people were the rider of the horse – he took that out of the Bible to identify the white man as the pale horse, whose rider is death. He didn't say devil, but the angel of death riding a pale horse is disguised as the devil. Fard Muhammad, because of his comparative religious studies, was able to pick up what the average follower of Drew Ali couldn't pick up – Caucasian race is the embodiment of evil. Fard Muhammad came out in plain language and said they are devils.[65]

In point of fact, and as indicated by the consternation of the enslaved African, speculation over the constitutional nature of white folk long antedates the careers of Noble Drew Ali and Father Hurley. The first in North America to voice such theories in print seems to have been the celebrated martyr David Walker, who in 1829 published his unprecedented, scintillating *Appeal to the Colored Citizens of the World, But in Particular, and Very Expressly, to Those of the United States of America.*[66] Unsurpassed in brilliance in many ways, scathingly unrelenting in its analysis, Walker's *Appeal* constitutes the genesis of multiple intellectual trajectories, among them labor history and capitalist critique, pan-Africanist theory, and the study of Africa and the African Diaspora. In life and death, Walker personified the model of scholar-activist of so much subsequent emulation. His remarkable foresight is displayed in the title of the treatise itself, fully supported by its content. Use of the *Appeal*, deserving of extensive commentary and reflection, is limited here to purposes of the present study.

Hinks, in an investigation that builds on the pioneering work of Sterling Stuckey, offers the possibility that the freeborn David Walker may have been the son of an Igbo father (renamed Anthony Walker) and argues that David was more likely to have been born in 1796 or 1797 rather than 1785.[67] Growing up in Wilmington, a town nearly 70 percent black (and overwhelmingly enslaved), Walker was exposed to a world in which John Kunering and other African

---

[65] See Interview with Imam Wallace D. Muhammad, in Clifton E. Marsh, *From Black Muslims to Muslims: The Transition from Separation to Islam, 1930–1980* (Metuchen, NJ and London: Scarecrow Press, 1984), 106–08 (Appendix).

[66] See David Walker, *Walker's Appeal in Four Articles* (New York: Arno Press and the New York Times, 1969); Charles Wilentz, ed., *David Walker's Appeal* (New York: Hill and Wang, 1965). The former citation will be used and referred to hereafter as Walker, *Appeal*.

[67] See Sterling Stuckey, *Slave Culture: Nationalist Theory and the Foundations of Black America* (New York: Oxford U. Press, 1987), 98–137; Peter P. Hinks, *To Awake My Afflicted Brethren: David Walker and the Problem of Antebellum Slave Resistance* (University Park: The Pennsylvania State U. Press, 1997), 1–21.

cultural expressions were embedded in the quotidian, and where the African-derived were extremely skilled, dominating the trades of both Wilmington and the Lower Cape Fear region. Naval stores (tar, pitch, rosin, turpentine, and tall oil produced from pine trees and stumps) and lumber were the basis of the region's economy through the American Revolution, after which rice cultivation was embraced in response to the loss of the British market for naval stores. Africans and their descendants were the principal workers in all of these various endeavors, including the construction of Wilmington's buildings and infrastructure. Walker's environment was therefore one in which Africans were clearly capable but unjustifiably exploited. Further informing Walker's developing perspective was his move to Charleston at some point between 1815 and 1820, where he remained at least through 1821. He was probably there through the trial of Denmark Vesey and his fellow defendants the following year. Hinks has pointed out the striking symmetry of thought and sentiment between the *Appeal* and the Vesey trial transcripts, and he underscores the likelihood that Walker was deeply influenced by the Vesey conspiracy, if indeed he did not take part.[68] Walker, clearly the beneficiary of a sound education, was highly motivated both by the sufferings of his fellows and the example of resistance by Vesey, and it was with these experiences in mind that he set forth for Boston, from where his *Appeal* was published a scant seven years after the Vesey revolt.

It was therefore as an independent, original thinker that David Walker set forth his views on the plight (and its causes) of his fellow people. In his estimation, those of African descent in the United States were "the most degraded, wretched, and abject set of beings that ever lived since the world began, and I pray God, that none like us ever may live again until time shall be no more."[69] That bondage for the African in America was like that of the Hebrew in ancient Egypt, only worse, was an analogy already popularized by Walker's day; Walker's contribution to the comparison, however, was to complicate the scenario by taking exception to the simplistic identification of slaveholding whites with Egyptians and enslaved blacks with Hebrews:

Some of my brethren do not know who Pharaoh and the Egyptians were – I know it to be a fact that some of them take the Egyptians to have been a gang of *devils*, not knowing any better... For the information of such, I would only mention that the Egyptians, were Africans or colored people, such as we are – some of them yellow and others dark – a mixture of Ethiopians and the natives of Egypt – about the same as you see the colored people of the United States at the present day.[70] [italics added, and so on for all of the direct quotes from the *Appeal*]

The statement is profound, one of the first to posit a correlation between African-descended people in the New World and the ancient Egyptians, a stream of consciousness extending into present discourse, academic and otherwise.

[68] Ibid., 22–62.
[69] See Walker, *Appeal*, 11 (Preamble).
[70] Ibid., 17–18 (Article I).

The current project does not take up this particular trajectory, except to note that Noble Drew Ali and Elijah Muhammad would adopt a similar position. Rather, of greater interest is Walker's use of the term *devils*, a designation associated with the Egyptians in the minds of many. Walker rejects the conjunction, suggesting that slaveholding does not automatically confer the status of devil. To the contrary, Walker argues that the Africanness of the Egyptians supercedes their slaveholding activities, such that the better similarity is between the ancient Egyptians and their more modern African-descended "relations," enslaved though the latter were. Walker's use of the term *devil* is consistent throughout the treatise, and, together with his use of similarly charged terminology and other qualifications of the conventional, forms an invariable perspective.

If one carefully navigates the *Appeal* as it was meant to be read, as a text that gradually unfolds its meaning, one is struck by Walker's lack of equivocation. It is in the same Article One that he introduces yet another concept, that of the "natural enemy." In recounting Moses's rejection of royal privilege and embrace of Hebrew identity, Walker laments: "O! that the colored people were long since of Moses' excellent disposition, instead of courting favor with, and telling news and lies to our *natural enemies*, against each other – aiding them to keep their *hellish* chains of slavery upon us."[71] By so describing their enslaving chains, Walker associates black people's natural enemies with unnatural evil. The qualification of the term *enemy* also indicates that there was something intractable about the constitutive elements of the American slaveholder personality, an idea on which he would further elaborate in a passage remarkable for its weaving together of such themes as the influence of Nilotic valley cultures on Graeco Roman civilizations, the notion and reification of Carthage as an African power, and the call for pan-African unity in view of Haitian and Carthaginian difficulties, ideas that would occupy theoreticians for decades to come:

When we take a retrospective view of the arts and sciences – the wise legislators – The Pyramids, and other magnificent buildings – the turning of the channel of the river Nile, by the sons of Africa or of Ham, among whom learning originated, and was carried thence into Greece, where it was improved upon and refined. Thence among the Romans, and all over the then enlightened parts of the world. . . . I say, when I view retrospectively, the renown of that once mighty people, the children of our great progenitor, I am indeed cheered. Yea further, when I view that mighty son of Africa, HANNIBAL, one of the greatest generals of antiquity, who defeated and cut off so many thousands of the white Romans or murderers, and who carried his victorious arms, to the very gate of Rome, and I give it as my candid opinion, that had Carthage been well united and had given him good support, he would have carried that cruel and barbarous city by storm. But they were disunited, as the colored people are now, in the United States of America, the reason our *natural enemies* are enabled to keep their feet on our throats.

[71] Ibid., 21 (Article I).

Beloved brethren – here let me tell you, and believe it, that the Lord our God, as true as he sits on his throne in heaven, and as true as our Saviour died to redeem the world, will give you a Hannibal, and when the Lord shall have raised him up, and given him to you for your possession, O my suffering brethren! remember the divisions and consequent sufferings of Carthage and of Hayti.[72]

The Romans are depicted as having been murderers, occupying a position similar to the natural enemies of blacks in Walker's day. The invocation of both Carthage and Haiti, from or within which "white" rule was challenged, supports the notion of Vesey's influence, and it indicates the measures Walker envisioned as required to terminate North American slavery.

While it is possible to read Walker's condemnation of his natural enemies as limited to slaveholders, other passages of the *Appeal* suggest that the author himself made no such qualifications. In discussing European behavior in general and over time, Walker offered a historicized analysis:

The whites have always been an unjust, jealous, unmerciful, avaricious and blood thirsty set of beings, always seeking after power and authority. We view them all over the confederacy of Greece, where they were first known to be any thing, (in consequence of education) we see them there, cutting each other's throats – trying to subject each other to wretchedness and misery, to effect which they used all kinds of deceitful, unfair and unmerciful means. We view them next in Rome, where the spirit of tyranny and deceit raged still higher. – We view them in Gaul, Spain and in Britain – in fine, we view them all over Europe, together with what were scattered about in Asia and Africa, as heathens, and we see them acting more like *devils* than accountable men. But some may ask, did not the blacks of Africa, and the mulattoes of Asia, go on in the same way as did the whites of Europe. I answer no – they were never half as avaricious deceitful and unmerciful as the whites, according to their knowledge.[73]

It is instructive that Walker limited his analysis of European behavior, in this instance and for the most part, to events in Europe, and in this way foregrounds the twentieth-century commentaries of W. E. B. Du Bois and Aimé Césaire. For Walker, the behavior of Europeans in Europe was a harbinger of how they would conduct themselves in Africa and Asia. Du Bois and Césaire extend the argument (though they do not subscribe to the notion of whites as devils) by locating the source of mid-twentieth-century atrocities in Europe, especially the assault against European Jews, in that very conduct. Thus, Du Bois asserts that "there was no Nazi atrocity – concentration camps, wholesale maiming and murder, defilement of women or ghastly blasphemy of childhood – which the Christian civilization of Europe had not long been practicing against colored folk in all parts of the world in the name of and for the defense of a Superior Race born to rule the world." Du Bois anticipates Césaire's memorable statement:

People are surprised, they become indignant. They say: "How strange! But never mind – it's Nazism, it will pass!" And they wait, and they hope; and they hide the truth from

[72] Ibid., 29–30 (Article II).
[73] Ibid., 27–28 (Article I).

themselves, that it is barbarism, but the supreme barbarism, the crowning barbarism that sums up all the daily barbarisms; that it is Nazism, yes, but that before they were its victims, they were its accomplices; that they tolerated that Nazism before it was inflicted on them, that they absolved it, shut their eyes to it, legitimized it, because, until then, it had been applied only to non-European peoples; that they have cultivated that Nazism, that they are responsible for it, and that before engulfing the whole of Western, Christian civilization in its reddened waters, it oozes, seeps, and trickles from every crack.

Walker, in his own inimitable way, initiated this line of reason, and, by focusing on the possibly unprecedented levels of violence in European history as precursor to the exportation of that violence, he parallels Cedric Robinson's argument concerning the rise of ethnocentricism in Britain, particularly at the expense of the Irish.[74]

Walker also reduces the glories of ancient Greece and Rome, and by extension all of Europe prior to its Christianization, to so much cruelty and warfare, characteristically so, whose general comportment compares unfavorably to Africans and Asians. They have consistently behaved, in Walker's opinion, more like "devils" than human beings. But what of the impact of Christianity?

But we will leave the whites or Europeans as heathens and take a view of them as christians, in which capacity we see them as cruel, if not more so than ever. In fact, take them as a body, they are ten times more cruel, avaricious and unmerciful than ever they were; for while they were heathens they were bad enough it is true, but it is positively a fact that they were not quite so audacious as to go and take vessel loads and through *devilishness*, throw them into the sea, and murder them in all kinds of ways. While they were heathens, they were too ignorant for such barbarity. But being christians, enlightened and sensible, they are completely prepared for such *hellish* cruelties.[75]

According to Walker, white collective behavior became even worse after the establishment of Christianity in Europe. The depth of his scorn for that behavior is evinced in his condemnation of an enslaved woman who reportedly assisted a wounded slave driver recover the absconded, "for we must remember that humanity, kindness and the fear of the Lord does not consist in protecting *devils*."[76] With such scathing criticism, Walker navigates far beyond the parochial question of slaveholding character, and he moves into streams of "racial" generalization. In light of his own reading of both history and his own observations of enslavement, he invoked the Almighty as witness and rendered his verdict.

I therefore, in the name and fear of the Lord God of heaven and earth, divested of prejudice either on the side of my colour or that of the whites, advance my suspicion

[74] See W. E. B. Du Bois, *The World and Africa: An Inquiry into the Part which Africa has Played in World History* (New York: International Publishers, 1946), 23; Aimé Césaire, *Discourse on Colonialism* (New York: Monthly Review Press, 1972; orig. pub., 1955), 14; Cedric J. Robinson, *Black Marxism: The Making of the Black Radical Tradition* (Chapel Hill: U. of North Carolina Press, 2000; orig. pub., 1983), 29–43.
[75] See Walker, *Appeal*, 27–28 (Article I).
[76] Ibid., 34–36, (Article II).

of them, whether they are *as good by nature* as we are or not. Their actions, since they were known as a people, have been the reverse, I do indeed suspect them, but this, as I before observed, is shut up with the Lord, we cannot exactly tell, it will be prove in succeeding generations.[77]

David Walker, therefore, probably went as far as he could go in his condemnation of whites during the first third of the nineteenth century. It is clear that he raised questions about the very nature of the European. Stuckey has averred, in pointing out some of the inconsistencies in the *Appeal*, that Walker "did not mean literally that whites were the natural enemies of his people."[78] Such a qualification is indeed supported by Walker's less harsh criticism of the English, who were "the best friends the colored people have upon earth," and who, "though they have oppressed us a little, and have colonies now in the West Indies, which oppress us sorely," still did not measure up to the cruelties of North American whites.[79]

The argument here is not that Walker absolutely essentialized Europeans and their descendants as irrevocably evil, but that such a reading is both possible and plausible. Further, it is not the present intention to seek to establish some sort of organic link between David Walker and Noble Drew Ali or W. D. Fard Muhammad and Elijah Muhammad, or to even demonstrate that any of these three individuals ever read the *Appeal*, or even heard of Walker (although both are possible). Rather, discussion of the *Appeal's* treatment of whites is emblematic of an important discursive tradition within the African-derived community. The very nature of whites was a subject of extended conversation and speculation, and, for not a few, it was the determination that something was amiss, so much so that it was in fact evil. In other words, there were many in the black community who referred to whites as devils, long before Elijah Muhammad and probably antedating David Walker. Walker simply echoed and attenuated the conversation, establishing a listening post for the outside. Elijah Muhammad jettisoned the equivocation and presented the suspicion as fact.

Whether Elijah Muhammad ever read the *Appeal* or not, a brief consideration of his early experiences in Georgia demonstrates that he was in no need of a primer on white terrorism from Walker or anyone else. Weaned on his grandmother's stories of extreme brutality suffered by her sister during slavery, ten-year-old Elijah witnessed with his own eyes the lynching of an eighteen-year-old man, an acquaintance, accused of raping a white woman. The sight left an indelible impression on his psyche, only to be reinforced five years later in 1912, when two men were again lynched in Cordele. The town had developed a "special reputation for midnight kidnappings and mob violence," such that the sight and reports of such atrocities were certainly factors in his decision to move to Macon shortly thereafter. In either 1920 or 1921, however, he witnessed yet

---

[77] Ibid., 28–29 (Article I).
[78] See Stuckey, *Slave Culture*, 131–32.
[79] See Walker, *Appeal*, 53 (Article III).

another lynching, so that, by April of 1923, he was on the first thing smoking to Detroit, family in tow. Between 1882 and 1931, Georgia lynched 492 black people, second only to Mississippi's 536.[80] Elijah Muhammad would rarely return to the South after the exodus, having seen "enough of the white man's brutality in Georgia" during that turbulent and traumatic period "to last me for 26,000 years."[81]

It is at this juncture that the earlier *fear* of white cannibalism and the subsequent *fact* of the lynching spectacle come together to form a most arresting if not unnerving image. It is precisely at this juncture that one can discuss figurative or symbolic cannibalism, in that it was often the case that groups of whites would gather to *eat* at the site of the lynching, while *gazing* at the suspended black body. Roediger has elsewhere discussed the lynching *feast* as integral to the production of whiteness or white collective identity; celebratory in nature, the murder of black women and men by means of hanging had become thoroughly ritualized by the last quarter of the nineteenth century.[82] Understood at the political level as a weapon of sheer terror, its psychological meanings have yet to be fully explored. Certainly, the castration ritual of black men says something about white male insecurities at the least, if not about suppressed homoeroticism. However, the introduction of the element of *food* at such a gruesome and otherwise repulsive setting, in which adult family members and their children sat down to *enjoy* a virtual picnic while all along focusing their attention on a mangled black body, must also correspond to some unmentionable atavism. The sensory of sight converged with that of taste, and consumption proceeded literally at the place of the broken black body and was pleasurable. This was figurative cannibalism, justifying the apprehensions of captured Africans.

It is at this point that cannibalism, the fears of such by captured Africans, and the description of black suffering as depicted by Elijah Muhammad coalesce, forming a striking resonance with the foregoing. Elijah Muhammad, descendant of captured Africans and an eyewitness to the lynching feast, gave voice to the victims, repeating ever so eerily that "this black people of America, who have been swallowed symbolically by the white slave-master and his children, must now be brought out of this race of people."[83] The metaphor of predator and prey, and the association of devil and snake, centers around consumption: "[black folk] beg the enemy even for friendship, which is like a frog pleading to the snake not to swallow him after the snake has gotten him in his mouth. The Black people of America have been swallowed by the slave-masters, who are a

[80] See Evanzz, *The Messenger*, 226–27.

[81] See Clegg, *An Original Man*, 10–13.

[82] See David Roediger, *The Wages of Whiteness: Race and the Making of the American Working Class* (London and New York: Verso, 1999). See also Trudier Harris, *Exorcising Blackness: Historical and Literary Lynching and Burning Rituals* (Bloomington: Indiana U. Press, 1984); James Allen, Hilton Als, John Lewis, and Leon F. Litwack, *Without Sanctuary: Lynching Photography in America* (Santa Fe, New Mexico: Twin Palms, 2000).

[83] See E. Muhammad, *Message to the Blackman*, 49, 51.

race of devils." Such sentiments, it should now be clear, were not just invented in 1931 but enjoy a long, transcontinental history.

By the time Elijah Muhammad arrived in what would become Motown, he had certainly participated in speculative conversations about the nature of whites, and he was genuinely puzzled over why they hated and terrorized the African so. The assumption has been that he was at that time exposed to the "white man as devil" doctrine, as opposed to having articulated it himself, so that what he heard in the Nation's early message was an explanation of his experiences, supporting his suspicions and allaying his fears that his re-action to atrocity was abnormal. Once again, though, it is not at all obvious that the *Secret Ritual of the Nation of Islam* or the *Teaching for the Lost-Found Nation of Islam in a Mathematical Way*, the foundational implements of instruc-tion for the nascent movement and initially orally transmitted, were fully de-veloped at the moment of Elijah Muhammad's initial encounters with W. D. Farad Muhammad in 1931, nor by the latter's final departure in 1934.[84] What is clear is that these two sources were available by the time of Beynon's re-search in 1937, as they are quoted in the subsequent 1938 publication of his findings. It is therefore possible, and certainly plausible, that Elijah Muham-mad had more of a hand in fashioning the two documents than previously understood.

In presenting the European as devil, the foundational treatises of the Nation are concerned with the origins of whites, their unrecorded history, and their general character, topics discussed repeatedly in various media and therefore difficult to revisit without some redundancy. With this in mind, the most salient concept about the origins of white people is that they are an invention, "made" (rather than "created," a distinction enjoyed only by black folk) by a black man whose own existence, in contrast, was "natural" and divinely designed. This implies a positional subjectivity of whites to black folk, the realization of which depends to some extent on the "mental resurrection" of the presently subjugated. To be more specific, whites are presented as the consequence of an experiment, conducted by a scientist named Yakub or Yacub (both spellings are used in the documents), and they are therefore referred to as "Yacub's grafted devil."[85] Yakub was an "original blackman" and the "father of the devil," born thousands of years ago and twenty miles outside of the city of Mecca, the center of civilization. Yakub was therefore a descendant of a black people whose beginnings go back 76 trillion years, and in comparison with the

---

[84] The *Secret Ritual of the Nation of Islam* and the *Teachings of the Lost-Found Nation of Islam in a Mathematical Way* have been committed to print and reorganized into the following titles: *Student Enrollment, Actual Facts, English Lesson No. C1*, part three, and *Lost-Found Muslim Lesson Nos. 1 and 2*. The reorganized literature presumably corresponds to the original progression of the oral lessons as found in *Secret Ritual* and *Teachings . . . in a Mathematical Way*, but as the latter were orally transmitted, something may have been lost in transmission and in the process of recording data in print.

[85] See *Student Enrollment*, question 2.

approximate 6,000-year existence of whites, this fact further underscores the former's superiority and effectively circumscribes modernity or postmodernity (in which whites have enjoyed power over blacks and others) as a mere drop in the bucket of time, an anomaly at best.[86]

Born at a time when 30 percent of Meccans were "dissatisfied" with unspecified conditions, Yakub began his formal education at the age of four. Possessing an "unusually" large head, he became known as the "big head scientist" as an adult, all of which conveys the message of being gifted intellectually. At the age of six, Yakub learned the principle of magnetic attraction ("unalike attracts, and alike repels") from playing with steel. Elijah Muhammad explained the significance of the discovery:

It is steel and more steel that his made race (the white race), are still playing with. Steel has become the most useful of all metal for the people. What he really saw in playing with the two pieces of steel was the magnetic power of attraction.

The one attracting the other under its power. In this, he saw an unlike human being, made to attract others, who could, with the knowledge of tricks and lies, rule the original black man – until that nation could produce one greater and capable of overcoming and making manifest his race of tricks and lies, with a nation of truth.[87]

The social implications of magnetic fields, that opposites attract in a way that creates a dominant–subordinate polarity, would be used by Yakub to produce the white race. That whites would use steel as an implement of subjugation, and in conjunction with "the knowledge of tricks and lies," suggests both a close relationship between "western" technology and imperialism (about which more will be stated later) and some sort of affinity or relationship between this metal and the very constitution of whites that extends beyond metaphorical or analogous reasoning. In this way, there is an echo of premodern West African views of metallurgy here, as in many West African societies the process of making metal was seen as a highly dangerous, supernatural endeavor engaged by specialists allied with unseen, spiritual forces; Yakub was similarly involved with abnormal research, whose end result was unnatural and whose progeny would be referred to as "wizards" to emphasize the aberration.[88]

By the age of eighteen, Yakub had completed all of the universities in Mecca, exhausting all existing sources of knowledge. He then made the discovery, through microscopic examination of "the germ of the black man...that there were two people in him, and that one was black, the other brown." Such knowledge gave him the vehicle through which he could manufacture the "unalike" race, and he set out to recruit a following from among the "dissatisfied" 30 percent. Posing a threat to Mecca, Yakub and his 59,999 adherents

[86] See *Lost-Found Muslim Lesson No. 1*, question 4; *Lost-Found Muslim Lesson No. 2*, questions 21–27, 36; see E. Muhammad, *Message to the Blackman*, 103–122.

[87] See E. Muhammad, *Message to the Blackman*, 112.

[88] On West African metallurgy, see, for example, Patrick McNaughton, *The Mande Blacksmiths: Knowledge, Power and Craft in West Africa* (Bloomington: Indiana U. Press, 1988).

accepted banishment to the island of Pelan, or Patmos of the Aegean, where he systemically began a process of "birth control" whereby only brown babies were allowed to live (black babies were fed to wild beasts or otherwise subjected to infanticide). After 200 hundred years, only brown people remained on the island, who had in them "red" and "yellow germs" to complement the brown ones. Another 200 years of such "grafting" resulted in the survival of only red and yellow persons; and after a final 200 years of similar birth control, only whites remained on Pelan. Thus, an "all-pale white race," a society of mutants, had been invented in 600 years. The killing of the darker infants in each successive cycle placed within the disposition of whites a natural desire to lie and murder. The completion of the 600-year cycle took place about 6,000 years ago, and the account of Adam and Eve is in fact a reference to Yakub and the origins of "mankind"; black folk, as the original people, were not a race but a nation, whereas whites were "racing with time."[89]

The foregoing is nothing more than a discussion of genetic engineering, presented by individuals without expertise in the field and at a time when information about DNA material was in its infancy, therefore making this particular "genesis" account all the more intriguing. The specifics of the tradition withstanding, the overall direction of the narrative is not at odds with the general, accepted notion of the movement of prehistoric populations from Africa into Asia and Europe, therefore possibly explaining its attraction to many. Perhaps more cogent was the explanation of how whites came to dominate the earth. Immediately upon their manufacture, this race returned to Mecca and implemented a divide-and-conquer strategy, sowing discord among the Muslims. When their plans were finally exposed, they were driven out of Mecca to the wilds of West Asia, or Europe, where they descended into total barbarity.[90] In contrast to the popular and scholarly opinion of the time, Elijah Muhammad turned the evolutionary model on its head, positing the Caucasian as more closely associated with primates than the African:

They were punished by being deprived of divine guidance, for 2,000 years which brought them almost into the family of wild beasts – going upon all fours; eating raw and unseasoned, uncooked food; living in caves and tree tops, climbing and jumping from one tree to the other. Even today, they like climbing and jumping. The monkeys are from them. Before their time, there were no such things as monkeys, apes and swine. Read the Holy Qur'an (Chapter 18) entitled "The Cave." The Holy Qur'an mentions

[89] See E. Muhammad, *Message to the Blackman*, 111–17; *Lost-Found Muslim Lesson No. 2*, questions 21–31, 38; Essien-Udom, *Black Nationalism*, 12.
[90] See E. Muhammad, *Theology of Time*, Book 2, 181–82:

Our fathers ran him out of the Holy Lands and into the hills and cavesides of Europe, and made monkeys and apes out of him. They even grew animal tails. They tell Me around hospitals that some of them are still born with monkey tails. The monkey is his brother . . . . That is a curse our people put on those of them who refused to listen to Moses. They made him a monkey and made him to eat swine flesh, and he's called apes and swine in the holy Qur'an. He loves swine and he makes you eat swine.

them as being turned into apes and swine as a divine curse, because of their disbelief in Moses. We do know that both of these animals are loved and befriended by the white race, along with the dog.[91]

Moses, a "half-original" man, and Jesus, an original man who was a Muslim and not associated with Christianity, attempted to bring civilization to them, as did the Muhammad of orthodox Islam. For the most part, these attempts at redemption met with failure. As a consequence of Yakub's actions, therefore, whites became "the gods of this world," to whom the naturally created world was to remain in subjection for 6,000 years (as ordered in Genesis 1:26 and 1:28). As it turns out, the era of "white rule" was scheduled to end decades ago, but it was extended: "The time Allah (God) had given the devils to rule the world (6,000 years) was up in 1914. But as long as you [black folk] stay asleep from lack of Knowledge about yourselves, you are extending the time (of their life)."[92]

Not all whites, in Elijah Muhammad's view, were made equal. Described as "pure devils" in one instance, they are distinguished along scales of relative evil ("some are better than others") in another. Unfortunately for blacks in the United States, they happened to live among the most depraved of the lot: "White Americans and Germans – Allah has taught me – are the most wicked of the white race." No doubt, Elijah Muhammad based his assessment in part on his own experiences in North America, which objectively must rank among the highest in the annals of infamy, such that Elijah could make his position on this question unambiguous: "We have lived in a hate that has had the depths of 6,000 years. It was a made hate. It wasn't created in the Creation of God. He did not create hate." The hell that black folk in North America experienced, the hate they inhabited, was not of divine design, contrary to all that they had been taught – a most provocative, consciousness-altering message.[93]

Problems with the Nation's conceptualization of race begin with the beginning, and they center on the indeterminancy of race. Alex Haley, probing the apparent weaknesses of the Nation's teachings, put the question to Malcolm X as early as May of 1963:

Since your classification of black peoples apparently includes the light-skinned Oriental, Middle Eastern, and possibly even Latin races as well as darker Indian and Negroid strains, just how do you decide how light-skinned it's possible to be before being condemned as white? And if Caucasian whites are devils by nature, do you classify people by degrees of devilishness according to the lightness of their skin?

The vacuity of Malcolm's response suggests an unwillingness (or unpreparedness, a rarity for Malcolm) to defend the position on the basis of alleged

---

[91] See E. Muhammad, *Message to the Blackman*, 103–04.
[92] Ibid., 117–22; see E. Muhammad, *Supreme Wisdom*, vol. 2, 32.
[93] See E. Muhammad, *Theology of Time*, Book 3, 191, 209; E. Muhammad, *Message to the Blackman*, 269.

scientific or rational merit; instead, there is a retreat into the verities of social configuration:

I don't worry about these little technicalities. But I know that white society has always considered that one drop of black blood makes you black.[94]

While conveniently dismissed, such flaws in the Nation's "raciology" ultimately could not be ignored, for, ironically, racial indeterminacy was critical to the Nation's origins.

To be specific, W. D. Fard Muhammad's own racial admixture poses interesting questions, suggesting inconsistencies on the order of the irreconcilable. He certainly represents a very different kind of Allah, far from the totally dark divinity at the dawn of time. Quite aside from his Asian father is the question of his Caucasian mother, "Baby Gee" as she is referred to in the traditions, who was "cleaned up" via Islam and therefore able to properly raise her child. Apparently such proclivities as lying and murder were not transferred from her DNA to Fard Muhammad, but why this was so remains unexplained. Perhaps the message is that a rigorous socialization can nullify or counteract characteristics deeply embedded within the genetic code; alternatively, there may be an implicit assumption that any degree of African or Asian derivation is sufficient to vitiate Caucasian behavioral properties. In any event, the fact of the matter is that Fard Muhammad's physical appearance was inconsistent with the core of his message to black folk. Elijah Muhammad attempted an explanation:

Jesus [i.e., Fard Muhammad] is a specially prepared man to do a work of redeeming the lost sheep (the so-called Negro). He had to have a body that would be part of each side (black and white), half and half. Therefore, having been born or made from both people, He is able to go among both black and white without being discovered or recognized. This He has done in the person of Master W. F. Muhammad.[95]

The elucidation does not address the tensions between the ethnogenesis of whites as laid out by the Nation and the observation that Fard Muhammad was the literal embodiment of "racial" antagonism. That such an individual could lead those of African descent, and indeed could be revered as Allah, is deeply problematic for many. Another way to view the matter, however, is to consider the significance of the multiracial background of the founder for his followers. The latter were themselves often of complex origins, hailing back to Africa and Europe as well as Native America, a reflection that includes the grandmothers of Elijah Muhammad and therefore Elijah himself, described as one who "might pass for an Oriental [sic]."[96] That the originator of the movement could have such a lineage would quell any reservations about the suitability of others with diverse family histories. The one-drop rule, sufficient

[94] See Alex Haley, *The Playboy Interviews* (New York: Ballantine Books, 1993), 33–34.
[95] See E. Muhammad, *Message to the Blackman* 19–20.
[96] See Essien-Udom, *Black Nationalism*, 75.

for purposes of identification, also appears to have been all that was needed to negate any undesirable genetic legacy.

Blackness, it would seem, was celebrated in the Nation. In general, and in contradistinction to whites, the Nation taught that black folk (broadly defined) were natural gods, and naturally good, and that Islam was their natural religion: "The people of Islam are the black people, and their numbers are made up of the brown, yellow and red peoples, called races.... By nature, all members of the black nation are Muslims (lovers of peace), whose number is over the billion mark."[97] Elijah Muhammad would clarify the foregoing as follows: "The very nature of the Black Man is a Muslim. He doesn't have to ask Allah to make him a Muslim. But he asks Allah to help him rid himself of the actions and the principles of Satan, and give him his actions and principles of Self which he was created in."[98] This argument of congenital determinism and righteousness as an innate property was a powerful implement in the effort to change behavioral patterns deemed counterproductive and antisocial. With the assimilation of these truths, the Nation taught, the past would be future.

Not only did Elijah Muhammad teach that blackness and righteousness were synonymous, but that the former was aesthetically exceptional:

I imagine you all the time before Me. A great, loving, beautiful people. No one is like you. God told Me Himself that we have the most beautiful people on Earth. When we think we are ugly we are making a mistake. We are not ugly.[99]

The historical (and contemporary, for that matter) record makes it clear that the concept of black beauty has long been viewed, by some blacks as well as whites, as an oxymoron. Such interventions by Elijah Muhammad were therefore critical to the restoration of self-worth, so long assailed in the wilderness of North America: "The Muslims should be proud of themselves and of their black skin and kinky wool, for this kinky woolly hair will be the future ruler (Dan 7:9 and Rev 1:14)."[100]

Given the foregoing statement, how strange and unexpected is the following statement by Elijah Muhammad concerning nappy hair, repeated several times in the various publications of the Nation:

The origin of our kinky hair came from one of our dissatisfied scientists, fifty thousand years ago, who wanted to make all of us tough and hard in order to endure the life of the jungles of East Asia (Africa) and to overcome the beasts there. But he failed to get the others to agree with him. He took his family and moved into the jungle to prove to us that we could live there and conquer the wild beasts and we have.[101]

---

[97] See E. Muhammad, *Message to the Blackman*, 68, 70.
[98] See E. Muhammad, *Theology of Time*, Book 4: 350–51.
[99] Ibid., Book 2, 126.
[100] See E. Muhammad, *Supreme Wisdom*, vol. 2, 54.
[101] Ibid., vol. 2, 16. See also E. Muhammad, *Theology of Time*, Book 2, 115; E. Muhammad, *Message to the Blackman*, 31–32.

There are several items here that invite comment. First, there is the notion that, prior to this experiment 50,000 years ago, black folk had straight hair, perhaps not unlike that of Fard Muhammad. That it grew kinky as a result of people becoming "tough and hard" betrays a fundamental dissatisfaction with tightly coiled hair. Second, according to this account, Africa (or East Asia) is not the original homeland of black folk but rather became inhabited relatively recently. Third, it would appear that Elijah Muhammad's concept of Africa was not terribly far removed from what was conventional at the time – a land of jungle, devoid of civilization. Such an impression was nurtured early in the history of the Nation, as evidenced by an excerpt from the foundational catechism *The Secret Ritual of the Nation of Islam*:

Question – Why does the devil call our people Africans?
Answer – To make our people of North America believe the people of that continent are the only people they have, and are all savages. He brought a trading-post in the jungles of that continent. The Original people live on that continent; they are the ones who strayed away from civilization and they are living a jungle life. The Original people call this continent Asia, but the devil calls it "Africa" to try to divide them.[102]

The perception that Africans were living a "jungle life" congealed as conviction for Elijah Muhammad after he traveled to Africa in late 1959, when he was so disappointed with what he saw and experienced that he embraced the premise of the civilizing mission with a fervor rarely equaled by any Christian missionary:

I have travelled in Africa and Asia. I am not telling you something wrong. I am telling you what I know. If you have been there, you will bear me witness that you saw the same. It is ugly looking. Wives were sitting down under shade trees with their bodies near nude, nursing babies. We have got to civilize people. We must go to Africa. We don't consider the people of Africa's jungle as anything for us to follow. If you are not civilized, you cannot lead a civilized person. If you tell me to go to Africa I will go there, but don't tell me to go there to be civilized. I am already civilized and I am ready to civilize Africa.[103]

To be sure, Elijah could express a more nuanced interpretation, acknowledging the colonial intervention and its delimiting effects while allowing that the continent's contemporary challenges did not flow simply and uninterruptedly from some ancient, unmediated past: "There are many fine scholars and scientists in Africa. But in all the knowledge that they have, it is not from the right source. The white man has taught them."[104] But at the end of the day, the view of Africa as an ugly jungle, an uncivilized condition epitomized by nappy-headed, nursing, nude women, appears to have remained the paramount perspective. In addition to the person of Fard Muhammad, therefore, the apparent disjuncture between the characterization of blacks in North America and the depiction of Africa and Africans represents another area of inconsistency in the Nation's

---

[102] See *Lost-Found Muslim Lesson No. 1*, question 7.
[103] See E. Muhammad, *Theology of Time*, Book 4, 320.
[104] See E. Muhammad, *Theology of Time*, Book 1, 54.

"raciology." As the blackman in North America came from Mecca, Africa's impoverishment did not necessarily reflect on the former.

Imam Wallace Muhammad would later comment that, according to Fard Muhammad, the black man's face "was black but his hair straight" before entering Africa some 50,000 years ago. The antekinkified era was presented, Wallace said, because Fard Muhammad "knew we wanted straight hair. What made your hair kinky, Professor Fard said, was leaving Asia and going into Africa." The preceding posits the anticipation of "Negro aspirations" by Fard Muhammad and the latter's subsequent resolution. As Wallace Muhammad continued his analysis, however, a pattern even more pernicious develops:

He [Fard] said when you went into Africa, you lost civilization and in time your nose got flat, your lips got thick, and your hair got kinky.[105]

With the exception of blackness, therefore, other characteristics of the African phenotype were cast as inferior; the question is, was this assertion also anticipatory on the part of Fard Muhammad, or was he expressing his own aversions, especially in light of the presentation of Africa as jungle in the *Secret Ritual*, a document Fard Muhammad had some role in developing? However the question is answered, it is instructive that Elijah Muhammad and others labored under this rather curious approbation for years; the 1957 embrace of black skin and kinky hair, as stated in *The Supreme Wisdom*, seems to represent growth and independence of thought on the part of Elijah Muhammad.

There is yet another possibility. It may very well be that, while the Nation of Islam was forced to publicly embrace the totality of their blackness (as they could not be impervious to the rise of the Black Power and Black Consciousness movements), some leaders privately clung to privileges created by the superficialities of hair texture and skin tone. Indeed, according to one insider, Elijah Muhammad used color gradation as one of the criteria for the selection of ministers, a completely arbitrary system of preference for the lighter over the darker complected.[106] The elevation of such individuals as Malcolm X and Louis Farrakhan would support this allegation, and it leads to the speculation that Malcolm X may not have had his biological father solely in mind when mentioning his "father's" preference for him because of his light skin.[107] Of course, the association of Islam and privilege with lighter skin is reminiscent of the colonial and antebellum pattern in North America, when these elements were part of the process of stratification among those of African descent. Such exceptionalism was apparently very much a part of the Nation's self-perception and expression.

Beyond color gradations among blacks, the Nation's characterization of non-Muslim black folk was also highly indicative of an exceptionalist perspective.

[105] See Wallace Muhammad, *As the Light Shineth*, 26.
[106] See Yusuf Shah, formerly Captain Joseph X Gravitt, as recorded in the documentary *Making It Plain* (Blackside, Boston, 1993).
[107] See Malcolm X, *Autobiography*, 4.

Already mentally dead, those outside the fold were also "uncivilized," a term loaded with various connotations, not the least of which is the previously described depiction of Africa. Non-Muslim blacks could have simply been seen as unbelievers, or adherents (for the most part) to another faith tradition, or "people of the Book." To insist, however, that they were "uncivilized" is not inconsistent with the most egregious of white racist sentiments, and it conjures up fifteenth-century dichotomies in what would become Latin America between ladinos (enculturated) and bozales ("raw" Africans). Again, this kind of language found its way into distinctions made in North America between Muslim Africans and non-Muslim Africans, and it was correlated with phenotypic differences. How ironic that a movement ostensibly dedicated to the proposition that black folks were deities would concomitantly use an idiom of colonial imposition to categorize those who had yet to convert. How ironic, but how totally in conformity with the historical paradigms.

The Janus face of the Nation's visage, one facing outward and seemingly nondiscriminating, the other internally oriented and perpetuating the very injustice it ostensibly decried, is testimony to the quality of racism as contagion, contaminating all with whom it comes into contact. The ravages of the disease are apparent, having its origins at the origin.

* * *

Race, while indisputably at the center of the Nation's discursive practice, was not its sole framework of social analysis. From the Nation's early days there also existed a means of signification and differentiation based on access to esoteric knowledge. Stated succinctly, the world is divided into three categories in relation to truth as defined by the Nation. The overwhelming majority, 85 percent, are "uncivilized people, poison animal-eaters, slaves of a mental death and power," who are devoid and ignorant of proper religion and are easily misled by a superstratum of persons who account for 10 percent of the global population. This 10 percent, in turn, are those who have amassed wealth from the control of the earth's resources, the "rich slave-makers of the poor who teaches the poor lies to believe that the Almighty true and living God is a spook and cannot be seen by the physical eye." These "blood suckers of the poor" are opposed by the remaining 5 percent of the population, "poor righteous teachers" who reject the false teachings of the 10 percent and who "are wise and know who the true and living God is; who teach that the true and living God is the Son of Man, supreme being, blackman from Asia."[108] While one can assume certain correlations with race, the latter does not enter this particular model in any explicit fashion; rather, the control and dissemination of "knowledges" determine the disequilibria of wealth and power. As Caucasians constitute a minority of the world's population, Asiatics are necessarily part of the confounded majority. Dissatisfaction with the lack of emphasis placed

---

[108] See *Lost-Found Muslim Lesson No. 2*, questions 9–16.

on this doctrine of percentages led to the withdrawal of Clarence "Pudding" 13X and others from the Nation in 1964, and the founding of "The Five Percent Nation," also known as "The Nation of Gods and Earths." Clarence 13X succumbed to a hail of bullets in 1969, but the "Five Percenters" experienced something of a revival in the last two decades of the twentieth century, their message internalized by leading artists of rap music and hip hop culture and assimilated into their aesthetic expression.[109]

As already indicated, the principal means by which the empowered minority control the destinies of the befuddled majority, described as "blind, deaf and dumb to the knowledge of self and kind," is prevarication. Referred to by the Nation as "tricknology," this process of falsification is pervasive, and, as an entire field of endeavor, it is akin to a science, requiring considerable skill and investment of time. Schemes of fabrication cover a wide range of areas, but the principal canard concerns religion and the promulgation of the noumenal. According to this view, the notion of an immaterial supreme deity transfixes the worshiper and diverts his or her attention from the true sources of life and power and the worshiper's own true identity, all of which are to be found in the realm of time and space. The material and the immaterial are vectors heading in opposite directions, the former toward reality and the latter ultimately issuing in sheer fantasy and delusion. As opposed to parallel universes, the corporeal and the numinous are in complete, irreconcilable contradiction. In this way, the foundational error is the very idea of the metaphysical, a premise shared by religions in general, throughout the world, and over time (thus, accounting for 85 percent of the population). This underlying fallacy is compounded, however, by the religion of Christianity, a belief system that targets the African-descended for the express purpose of maintaining their subordinate status. In response, Elijah Muhammad vigorously denounced Christianity, concluding "We know that Christianity came from the white race, and it is not from Allah." He attacked the faith at its seemingly most vulnerable points, arguing with devastating logic that "Jesus was only a prophet and cannot hear you pray any more than Moses or any other dead prophet.... He did his work and is dead like others of his time, and has no knowledge of their prayers to him."[110] On the confluence of a ubiquitous whiteness and the erasure of blackness within the boundaries of the Christian message, resulting in a most objectionable iconography, Elijah Muhammad expressed particular and exacting contempt:

They (the so-called Negroes) hang the pictures of white people on the walls of their homes and one can find these (pictures) also on their mantle shelves, dressers and tables. Some even carry them (the white people's pictures) on their person. They (the so-called Negroes) go to church and bow down to the statues under the names of Jesus and Mary

---

[109] For example, see Yusuf Nuruddin, "The Five Percenters: A Teenage Nation of Gods on Earth," in Yvonne Yazbeck Haddad and Jane Idleman Smith, eds., *Muslim Communities in North America* (Albany: State U. of New York Press, 1994).

[110] See E. Muhammad, *Supreme Wisdom*, vol. 2, 21–22.

and some under the name of Jesus's disciples, which, again, are only the images of the white race, their arch deceiver. My people even worship the white man's names.[111]

Such a critique rings a bit hollow given the preceding discussion of possible internal discrimination within the Nation along with its leadership's apparent aversion to African features, but, absent such considerations, the reasoning is analogous and not easily dismissed. What was the difference, Elijah Muhammad was intimating, between this picture and the historical realities of black folk kneeling before the slaver, the master, the overseer? In fact, did not the religious facilitate the factual?

In confronting what he believed to be the bane of Christianity, Elijah Muhammad paid careful attention to the Bible and the black preacher, identifying them as primary agents in the white man's deployment of tricknology. As for the former, it was a decidedly "poison book" and the "graveyard" of black people, and "who can deny that it is not poison? It has poisoned the very hearts and minds of the so-called Negroes so much that they can't agree with each other." As an originally authentic revelation subsequently altered, a position in accord with orthodox Islam, the Bible was "tampered with" by whites to such a degree that the following could be said:

[I]t is the graveyard for my poor people (the so-called Negroes) and I would like to dwell upon this book until I am sure that they understand that it is not quite as holy as they thought it was. I don't mean to say that there is no truth in it; certainly there is plenty of truth, if understood. Will you accept the understanding of it? The Bible charges all of its Great Prophets with evil, it makes God guilty of an act of adultery by charging Him with being the father of Mary's baby (Jesus) and again it charges Noah and Lot with drunkenness, and Lot with getting children by his daughter. What a Poison Book.[112]

Although Elijah Muhammad would charge that "the enemy" had also tampered with the Qur'ān, his focus was clearly the Bible.[113] Ironically, according to Malcolm X, he would take cover and seek asylum for his own transgressions in the same Biblical accounts he construed as fallacious and ever so toxic.[114]

As for black preachers, Elijah Muhammad's contempt was tempered by his campaign to win them over. He understood them well, as both his father and grandfather were ministers. As leaders in the black community, preachers were the principal obstacle to the Nation's message and growth; conversely, there was nothing more efficacious than the proclamation of the Nation's message through the mouth of a former Christian preacher. Elijah Muhammad's assault on the Christian minister was therefore an important means of recruitment; his constant questioning of their credentials and understanding was not unlike Booker T. Washington's disparagement of the Negro preacher.[115] Washington,

[111] Ibid., vol. 2, 17.
[112] See E. Muhammad, *Message to the Blackman*, 94–95.
[113] Ibid., 90.
[114] See Malcolm X, *Autobiography*.
[115] See Booker T. Washington, *Up From Slavery; an Autobiography* (London: Moring, 1907); Louis R. Harlan, *The Booker T. Washington Papers* (Urbana: U. of Illinois Press, 1972–89).

while subscribing to the tenets of Christianity, lamented the preacher's lack of preparation and unsuitability for leadership. Elijah Muhammad attacked both preacher and profession of faith, and he could reason with considerable force:

If white theologians had something to do with the translation of the Bible and of giving to you your credentials, and if he, himself, the devil blue-eyed Caucasian, says that the Bible is not altogether true, then how can we back him up and say that it is true when he is the one who translated it?[116]

In dueling with the Honorable Elijah Muhammad, the average jackleg was at a serious disadvantage.

Beyond religion, it is possible to conceive of improper diet as part of Caucasian tricknology. As mentioned previously, Elijah Muhammad was a trailblazer in the advocacy of dietary reform, applicable to any person concerned with health and nutrition.[117] Working under the assumption that physical, mental, and psychological spheres of the personality are interconnected, it was Elijah Muhammad's thesis that the consumption of food affects the entire person. The malnutrition of blacks, therefore, began at birth. By some process, the fear of white terror was so powerful that it took on physical dimensions, even chemically altering a mother's breast milk. Suckling black infants were literally nourished on such fear:

He put fear into our parents when they were little babies and they came up nursing that fear from the breast of their mothers. She would nurse her little boy-child with fear of the white man. It went right into the baby. Then the child came up trembling, he is scared of white folks. I am saying to you, Brother and Sister, take it or leave it. It is the Truth.[118]

While many (if not most) would "leave it," the idea of fear being instilled at a tender age, and via the medium of parents, certainly works on the allegorical level. It is plausible that, long before they were conscious of its existence, or understood its basis, black youth subconsciously learned fear. As a consequence, the Nation identified fear as "the number one enemy that is blocking progress and success from coming to the so-called Negroes of America."[119]

From infancy, enslaved black children were immediately exposed to a process by which they absorbed a sustenance of subservience. The process did not end there but only intensified with the consumption of insalubrious provisions. The ingestion of the latter was by no means happenstance according to Elijah Muhammad; it was rather by particular design: "Allah told us that the slave-masters has taught us to eat the wrong food, and that this wrong food was

---

[116] See E. Muhammad, *Theology of Time*, Book 4, 309.

[117] See Elijah Muhammad, *How to Eat to Live*, Book 1 (Newport News, VA: National Newport News and Commentator, 1967 reprint), and E. Muhammad, *How to Eat to Live*, Book 2 (Chicago: Muhammad's Temple of Islam No. 2, 1972).

[118] Ibid., Book 1, 30.

[119] See E. Muhammad, *Message to the Blackman*, 29.

the cause of our sickness and short span of life."[120] The leader of the Nation would go on to distinguish between the healthy and unhealthy, and in the latter category were included such southern, "soul food" standards as collard greens and cornbread, indicating a strategy to jettison all vestiges of enslavement and subsequent systems of racialized oppression.[121] Elijah Muhammad would also recommend eating regimes that included one meal per day or every other day, all of which are beyond the purposes of this inquiry and will go unspecified with the exception of swine. Swine came to symbolize the divide between Muslim and non-Muslim blacks, utterly despised by the former while more or less loved by the latter, from "the rooty to the tooty." Carrying 999 poisonous germs and "grafted" from the rat, cat, and dog, hog meat came to represent enslavement, ignorance, subjugation, impoverishment, and shame. In some ways, the struggle between Christianity and Islam for the allegiance of black folk came down to this animal, and whether one was prepared to do without it; in other ways, the pig was simply emblematic of a much broader and complicated conflict, and it became invested with the values of the opposing camps. That such a momentous decision as religious choice could be decided with this creature as variable is an incredible proposition. Even so, the scientific authority does not currently exist that would quibble with a correlation between black folks' diet and their higher rates of hypertension, heart disease, cancers of various types, and so forth. When Elijah Muhammad was saying this years ago, he was dismissed as a quack.

The essence of tricknology, therefore, was the art of deception, and, according to Elijah Muhammad, white folk were naturally and incurably duplicitous. The deception began with religion, and it branched out to other areas: "The American so-called Negroes are gravely deceived by their slave-masters' teaching of God and the true religion of God. They do not know that they are deceived." White folk had "deceived the whole world," and were "the deceivers and adversaries of Allah."[122] As was true of the tradition of whites as cannibals and devils, their association with cunning and guile spans the continents, and it was certainly true of West Africa, where Europeans first earned a reputation as prevaricators. Traditions of African involvement in the transatlantic slave trade, preserved and disseminated in what would become North America, posits as its central point that European slave traders captured Africans largely through deceit.[123] They came as traders in commodities, but they departed as traffickers in human beings. They were not what they seemed, so said traditions circulating throughout the South. Perhaps this explains in part Elijah Muhammad's exuberance in embracing the message of Fard Muhammad; as a son of the soil,

---

[120] See E. Muhammad, *Supreme Wisdom*, vol. 1, 11.

[121] See Essien-Udom, *Black Nationalism*, 15.

[122] See E. Muhammad, *Message to the Blackman*, 8, 49.

[123] See Michael A. Gomez, *Exchanging Our Country Marks: The Transformation of African Identities in the Colonial and Antebellum South* (Chapel Hill: U. of North Carolina Press, 1998), 154–243.

the notion of whites as archetypal liars would not have been new to Elijah; it would have reverberated with what he long suspected.

* * *

While a comprehensive investigation into the roles and experiences of women in the Nation lies beyond the present scope, their "place" within the organization's ideology certainly requires commentary. To that end, the Nation's project of re-making the world was very much a masculinist enterprise, its dogma thoroughly androcentric. In contrast to many origin accounts throughout Africa, women hardly feature in the drama of creation; the dominant actors are all males. The various councils of god-scientists are all males. Interestingly, it is with the ethnogenesis of Europeans that women are mentioned with any regularity, as they are indispensable to the "grafting" of the white race, but even here they remain anonymous, as so many pawns strategically positioned by Yakub and his male descendants to effect the desired mutations. The Nation, therefore, in both its rhetoric and its policies, epitomized the preeminent fault line in the formulation of nationalist ideology among the African-descended in North America, and in this way it was not dissimilar from nationalist expressions the world over. The agenda, quite simply, was the aggregation of power and pre-rogative among black men; indeed, given their relative disadvantage vis-à-vis white males, the disempowerment of black women became almost essential to the creation of a sense of empowerment within the collective psyche of black men; it was certainly a route more readily available to such an end.

As is true of most nationalisms, the control and appropriation of land is a key preoccupation. The control of land equates with sovereignty and is critical to the question of who is in position to make determinative decisions regarding the meaning, quality, and direction of life. All of this has something to do with "freedom," and the mistake has often enough been made that physical domin-ion over territory is sufficient to achieve such freedom. While it has proven to be insufficient (especially in contemporary Africa), it is nonetheless one of the requisite elements. To this end, Africans and Asians have fought to remove Europeans (and other Asians), as have the Irish to expunge the English in the attempt to reverse the colonial project. In tandem, those of African descent in the diaspora have waged desperate struggles to either procure the sovereignty of the majority (as was true of the islands of the Caribbean), or to arrive at an arrangement by which the land upon which they stood held some sort of significant and far-reaching material as well as symbolic benefits. The African-descended in North America fit into the latter category, as they have mounted any number of efforts to resolve their dilemma, either by becoming full-fledged Americans; or by creating autonomous spaces in order to experience the inverse of what America has come to mean; or by straddling some intermediate position within the continuum. In the end, and quite apart from how it is envisioned, land remains a riveting issue.

To be sure, in what follows Elijah Muhammad says nothing out of the or-dinary or in any way at variance with the conventions of the times (at least through the mid-twentieth century). However, patriarchy requires some form of critique, notwithstanding place and time.

For the architects of the Nation of Islam, land and women are parallel terrain whose convergence in the mind renders them seamless and indivisible. Consider Elijah Muhammad's illustrative language:

The woman is man's field to produce his nation. If he does not keep the enemy out of his field, he won't produce a good nation.[124]

While intended to discourage interracial dating and marriages, the likening of a woman to a field, or more specifically farmland, is instructive and arguably of greater interest than the marriage proscription. Elijah Muhammad has in mind here the black woman's body. It is seen primarily as a tool of procreation and reproduction, as farmland exists for the purpose of raising crops. The issue for him, therefore, is access – who will have the right to "sow seed." As such, his admonition is neither directed toward women nor really stated for their benefit. Rather, his concern is the prerogative of black men and their proprietary rights. Women, like fields, are conceived of in terms relating to questions of ownership. Their reclamation was a prelude, a first step, a necessary exercise in preparation for the more elusive goal of establishing usufructuary in the actual land.

To be sure, the association of women with land is not solely derivative from nationalist thinking; indeed, a conservative reading of the Qur'ān's reference to wives as "arable land" (*ḥarth*) could certainly be used to support the perspective.[125] As a kind of territory, women had to be protected – but for them to be protected, they had to be "respected," or valued for their roles and unrealized potential. To the extent that this constrained domestic violence and abuse of all descriptions, such a call was of great benefit, although falsely premised (in not affording women equal status):

My beloved brothers in America, you have lost the respect for your woman and therefore you have lost the respect for yourself. You won't protect her; therefore, you can't protect yourself. She is our first nurse. She is your teacher. Your first lesson comes from your mother. If you don't protect your mother, how do you look in the eyes of other fellow human beings?[126]

Elijah Muhammad's reference to public opinion underscores the hypocritical tendency in the nineteenth and twentieth centuries for western nations to judge the relative level of civilization of African and Asian societies on the basis of the status and treatment of women.[127] Maternal ties are invoked

---

[124] See E. Muhammad, *Message to the Blackman*, 58.

[125] Qur'ān, sūra 2, 224: "Your wives are your arable land (or tilth) . . . "

[126] See E. Muhammad, *Message to the Blackman*, 59.

[127] For interesting discussions of the relationship of women to civilizational levels, see Joan Wallach Scott, *Feminism and History* (Oxford and New York: Oxford U. Press, 1996); Anne McClintock, *Imperial Leather: Race, Gender and Sexuality in the Colonial Contest* (New York: Routledge, 1995).

for poignancy, the forces against which protection must be afforded then identified:

Stop our women from trying to look like them [white women]. By bleaching, powdering, ironing and coloring their hair; painting their lips, cheeks and eyebrows; wearing shorts; going half-nude in public places; going swimming with them and lying on beaches with men.

Have private pools for your women and guard them from all men. Stop them from going into bars and taverns and sitting and drinking with men and strangers. Stop them from sitting in those places with anyone. Stop them from using unclean language in public (and at home), from smoking and drug addiction habits.[128]

The "enemy" is a category always inclusive of white folk, especially white males, against whom Muslim men are enjoined to defend black women.[129] However, in this circumstance it is western cultural production that must be resisted. The call is therefore to resist cultural contamination, and the injunction against using cosmetics, wearing immodest attire, imbibing strong drink and herb, and socializing with men in public is precisely what Noble Drew Ali taught. This conforms entirely to orthodox Islamic proscriptions, including at least one Qur'ānic injunction that could be interpreted as a command for men to serve as "guardians" over women.[130] It is the political context of white racism, however, that differentiates the appeals of Elijah Muhammad and Noble Drew Ali from otherwise normative sumptuary regulations, the practice of purdah, and routine observance of propriety.

We protect our farms by pulling up our weeds and grass by the roots, by killing animals and birds, and by poisoning the insects that destroy our crops in order that we may produce a good crop. How much more valuable are our women, who are our fields through whom we produce our nation.[131]

In the name of the "good crop," women are most esteemed as mothers and are to be shielded from the powers of corruption.

Given such a perspective, it is by no means surprising that the Nation taught against abortion and birth control. However, while reasons for opposing such practices included issues of morality and the preservation of paternal rights, again they tended to be framed (if not subsumed) by the struggle against racism. Considering the history of the country, anxieties over whites' motivations were not without foundation, so there was certain receptivity to Elijah Muhammad's manifold argument:

To the Lost-Found members of the tribe of Shabazz (the so-called Negroes), I warn you my people and especially the women. Be aware of the tricks the devils are using to instill the idea of a false birth control in their clinics and hospitals.

---

[128] See E. Muhammad, *Message to the Blackman*, 60–61.
[129] See Essien-Udom, *Black Nationalism*, 89–90.
[130] Qur'ān, sūra 4, 35. The operative term is *qawwānūn*.
[131] See E. Muhammad, *Message to the Blackman*, 60.

STERILIZATION IS NOT BIRTH CONTROL, BUT THE END OF ALL POSSI-
BILITY TO BEAR CHILDREN...
     I say beware of being trapped into the kind of disgraceful birth control laws now
aimed almost exclusively at poor, helpless black peoples who have no one to rely on.
     Who wants a sterile woman?
     No man wants a non-productive woman. Though he may not want children for a
time, he does want a woman who can produce a child if he changes his mind. Using
birth control for a social purpose is a sin.
     Using the birth control law against production of human beings is a sin that Allah
(God) is against and for which he will punish the guilty on the Day of Judgment. Both
the Bible and Holy Qur-an's teachings are against birth control.
     So you and I, too, should be against it.

Beyond issues of morality and patriarchy, genocide was an overarching concern. Birth control, in this view, was nothing more than the "grafting" process
invented by Yakub ("the white race is a race that was produced by using the
birth control law") and, in the hands of whites, would inevitably lead to the
destruction of blacks: "The motive behind these schemes is not designed to
promote the welfare of black families, but to eliminate these families in the
future."[132] Such a symmetry of concerns revolved fundamentally around black
women and issues of control.
     That some black women responded to the offer of protection is not nec-
essarily an indictment of their lack of feminist or womanist consciousness; it
could rather be viewed as the choice, among limited options, of a means of negotiating and transcending abusive or undesirable conditions in the home and
larger community. In the 1950s, twenty-two year-old Sister Elaine appreciated
the difference:

Among the dead [non-Muslims] they do not believe in treating you nicely but whenever
they take you out, they want something in return. When you go out with Muslim brothers
they do not make sex demands on you.[133]

As Essien-Udom observed, some women gravitated to the Nation, in part,
to achieve deliverance from "their lowly and humiliating position in Negro
society and from the predatory sex ethos of the lower-class community...a
journey from shame to dignity."[134] Although most Muslim women would
not have suffered from some ignoble and unmentionable past, those who did
were afforded the opportunity to get "cleaned up" and ascend to a moral
altitude so elevated as to be unapproachable by former associations: "We
cannot overemphasize the prestige value to the Muslim women of the newly
acquired sense of self-respect and dignity."[135] Such dignity, however, came with
a price; the quid pro quo was embedded in the social contract. In exchange

[132] Ibid., 64–65.
[133] See Essien-Udom, *Black Nationalism*, 87.
[134] Ibid., 86.
[135] Ibid., 88.

for respect and protection, women yielded autonomy, a reciprocity implicit in Elijah Muhammad's teachings:

We must learn to respect, love and protect our womenfolk. There is no nation on earth that has less respect for and less control of their womenfolk as we the so-called Negroes here in America.... Our women are allowed to walk and stay in the streets all night long, with any man they desire. They are allowed to frequent any tavern or dance hall that they like, and whenever they like. We allow them to fill our homes with children who are other than our own – children who are often fathered by the devil himself.[136]

Women already in the Nation could themselves be the most effective agents of proselytization and, as was true of Sister Levinia X in the late 1950s, often lived sufficiently exemplary lives as to attract others:

A girl in the neighborhood taught us Islam.... I believed her because of the way she dressed, the way she acted and she was different from everyone else.[137]

The way "she acted" would have involved care for the home, and in the cultivation of domesticity, the Nation had few rivals. As Sister Levinia X observed:

It [Islam] teaches women how to raise their children, how to take care of their husbands, how to sew and cook, and several domestic things which are necessary for a family. Islam helps men a great deal because it teaches them how to treat their women. The women are taught to dress decently.[138]

Not everyone subscribed to the emphasis on homemaking, however. With the passage of time, and the rise of successive generations of young women born into the Nation, attitudes could change, challenging patriarchal privilege. Sonsyrea Tate, born around 1966 to parents and grandparents who had been in the Nation for years, complained that, just as her brother was taught from an early age

that our mother and all the rest of us women were put on this Earth to serve him, cook for him, and clean up behind him, I learned that men were here to protect and provide for me.... I knew I'd have to marry somebody since that was the only reason I was on this Earth – to become a good wife and mother.[139]

Tate would eventually experience distance between herself and the teachings of Elijah Muhammad, but her youth in the Nation is a powerful demonstration of the creation of gender within the movement. An important vehicle for the socialization of Muslim women in the Nation was the aforementioned Muslim Girl Training and General Civilization Class (the MGT and GCC) that functioned under the command of a female Supreme Captain. On Saturday mornings, Tate

---

[136] See E. Muhammad, *Supreme Wisdom*, vol. 2, 56–57. In the original wording, the last sentence is actually italicized as follows: "We allow them to fill *our* homes with children who are *other than our own* – children who are often fathered by the devil himself."
[137] See Essien-Udom, *Black Nationalism*, 85.
[138] Ibid., 86.
[139] See Sonsyrea Tate, *Little X: Growing Up in the Nation of Islam* (New York: HarperCollins, 1997), 71.

attended the MGT classes, where she and other girls and women learned a number of skills as well as discipline in drill teams under female supervision. They were given formal instruction concerning the following:

How to Keep a Home,
How to Raise Their Children,
How to Keep Their Husbands,
Sew, Cook, and in General,
How to Act At Home And Abroad.[140]

The emphasis on the family, of course, was a general concern to most elements of the larger society and was not simply a Muslim preoccupation. However, in transforming the lives of black women in conspicuous ways, the Nation enjoyed significant distinction.

*   *   *

The Nation's vision of the resolution of society's contradictions is certainly one of its more curious aspects. Ultimately, the vision relies on an external intervention: Black folk, in this scenario, do not deliver themselves but are rescued by forces totally beyond their control or influence; the contention that the intervention is neither spiritualized or related to "spookism" cannot detract from this rather marked inconsistency. The tension between the Nation's everyday self-reliance and its utter reliance on independent eschatological occurrences is perhaps best explained by Essien-Udom, in a critique not limited to the Nation:

The nationalists tend to become preoccupied with the means of overcoming their sense of powerlessness, but in their preoccupation with the means, the end of building up black power appears to become less important because it seems either unattainable or utopian. Hence, they call upon superhuman or divine intervention for its realization.[141]

As will be demonstrated, the Nation could have served as the paramount model for the foregoing analysis.

The Nation's doomsday scenario unfolds in installments. Preceding the destructive segments are "the Days of Allah," which actually began while Elijah Muhammad was alive and in which Muslims began to reclaim power over "the evil race known as the white race."[142] After that phase, or coterminous with it, begins the countdown to ruin. Claude Clegg, in his comprehensive study, has provided a useful synopsis of the various stages.[143] The "first hell" was initiated in 1965–66 and involves divine warnings in the form of environmental calamities that do not discriminate between whites and blacks. Those blacks who heed the warnings and achieve territorial separation from whites could avoid the "second hell," which would eventually include the total destruction

---

[140] See *Lost-Found Muslim Lesson No. 1*, question 14.
[141] See Essien-Udom, *Black Nationalism*, 55.
[142] See E. Muhammad, *Message to the Blackman*, 22–23.
[143] See Clegg, *An Original Man*, 64–67.

of North America and white civilization. Those few whites who "strove against their nature" and converted to Islam, and who treated blacks well, could also survive, but their reward would be decidedly inferior to that of blacks.

The specifics of the second hell have been discussed elsewhere. They include details concerning the arrival of "angels" or scientists who provide support and direction, the dropping of leaflets in Arabic and English for instructions, and so on. The crux of the matter, for the purposes of this analysis, has to do with the manner in which Allah will rain devastation upon "America" and its allies, and it directly concerns the concept of the Mother Plane, a machine built in Japan by Allah. Envisioned in the prophesies of Ezekiel and John (Ezekiel 10:2–11; Revelations 19:20), it is made "like a wheel" and is a "human-built planet," its dimensions "a half-mile by a half-mile square." The vehicle contains 1,500 "small bombing planes," which altogether will unleash weapons of mass destruction in the form of bombs, poison gas, and fire. In the final hour, the seventh, "dreadful Angel who places one foot on land and one on sea" will lift his hands to the skies and utter words fateful, "Time, time shall soon know no more," and thereafter "cut a shortage into gravity and set the nation on fire." The atmosphere over that portion of the earth will explode into a gigantic fireball; "America" will burn for 390 years, a veritable lake of fire, and will require another 610 years to cool. After this millennium, a population of slightly more than 144,000 will restore the area, obliterating the memory of old America after a mere twenty years. The black inhabitants of this "New World" will enjoy a youthful appearance of sixteen years of age, living for 1,000 years.[144]

As has been pointed out, multiple influences are evident in the Nation's end-of-time imagery: Jehovah's Witnesses theology, science fiction, the Japanese dreadnought, and so on. In other words, there is a convergence of currents at points where intersections were imaginable, not an entirely bizarre exercise in speculations concerning the world's demise. However, the introduction of fancy and fantasy into the equation, precisely at the juncture where concrete plans for overthrowing white rule would have been expected, strongly suggests an inability to conceive of black folk actually establishing a new and different social order, and it raises doubts as to the strength of conviction concerning other teachings of the Nation, such as the whole Yakubian account. Indeed, in consideration of the Nation's very substantive achievements in business and education and rehabilitation of the socially discarded, it is this embrace of both the normative and the fantastic, this tension between the eminently pragmatic and the inescapably preposterous, that significantly adds to the cathartic quality of the Nation of Islam. Perhaps Imām Wallace Muhammad said it best:

This man [Fard] was a mystic, and I think maybe an experimentor who was just experimenting on the minds of the African American people, I think with the hope of challenging the mind of the African American people. And he did. . . . He did challenge

---

[144] Ibid.; also see E. Muhammad, *Theology of Time*, Book 4, 511–32; E. Muhammad, *Supreme Wisdom*, vol. 2, 31; Essien-Udom, *Black Nationalism*, 138–39.

our minds with his mythologies and symbolism. And I think that what he did was to create a big theatre called the Nation of Islam where people were acting out satirically their dislike and rejection for the situation that they were in. The rejection of blacks was changed, reversed, and we rejected whites.[145]

Central to the Nation's critique of Christianity was the latter's "spookism," its embrace of the unreal. But in its eschatology, wherein is situated the settlement and resolution of white racism and black empowerment, the Nation's ideas were just as escapist and illusory, if not more so. This inability to fashion a strategy of direct confrontation, at a time when others in the African American community were laying it on the line, would prove to be a major fault line in the Nation's ideology, one that would play some role in navigating Malcolm X and others along contours of intellectual independence, and defiance.

[145] See W. Muhammad, *Religion on the Line*, 40–41.

8

Malcolm

Interest in the life and times of Malcolm X has, if anything, accelerated rather than diminished in recent years. Since his rise to prominence in the 1950s, there has been a steady production of scholarly and popular materials concerning him by way of books, articles, plays, documentaries, music, and films.[1] Much of the scholarly literature represents quasi-proprietary disputes among nationalists, pan-Africanists, Marxists, loyalists, and those attempting psychoanalytic applications (not necessarily mutually exclusive categories) over a complex and evolving public figure. The present study will not engage many of these debates, and there is little point in exhaustive revisitation of what is already known.

[1] Regarding the literature, see as examples Malcolm X, *Malcolm X on Afro-American History* (New York: Pathfinder Press, 1987); Malcolm X, with Alex Haley, *The Autobiography of Malcolm X* (New York: Ballantine Books, 1993; orig. pub., 1964); Alex Haley, *The Playboy Interviews* (New York: Ballantine Books, 1993); John Henrik Clarke, *Malcolm X: The Man and His Times* (Toronto: Macmillan, 1964); Robert Jabara, *The Word: The Liberation Analects of Malcom X* (Atlanta: Clarity Press, 1994); Kevin Brown, *Malcolm X* (Brookfield, CT: The Millbrook Press, 1995); Sande Smith, *The Life and Philosophy of Malcolm X* (Secaucus, NJ: Chartwell Books, 1993); Jack Rummel, *Malcolm X* (New York: Chelsea House, 1989); Hakim A. Jamal, *From the Dead Level: Malcolm X and Me* (New York: Random House, 1972); Mustafa El-Amin, *Afrocentricity: Malcolm X and Al-Islam* (Newark: El-Amin Productions, 1993); Eugene Victor Wolfenstein, *The Victims of Democracy: Malcolm X and the Black Revolution* (Berkeley and Los Angeles: U. of California Press, 1981); Steven Barboza, *American Jihad: Islam after Malcolm X* (New York: Doubleday, 1993); Bruce Perry, *Malcolm: The Life of a Man Who Changed Black America* (Barrytown, NY: Staton Hill Press, 1991); _____, *Malcolm X: The Last Speeches* (New York: Pathfinder Press, 1992); William Strickland, *Malcolm X: Make It Plain* (New York: Viking Penguin, 1994); David Gallen, ed., *Malcolm X, As They Knew Him* (New York: Carroll and Graf, 1992); _____, ed., *Malcolm A to X: The Man and His Ideas* (New York: Carroll and Graf, 1992); Benjamin Karim, *Remembering Malcolm* (New York: Carroll and Graf, 1992); Benjamin Goodman, ed., *The End of White World Supremacy: Four Speeches by Malcolm X* (New York: Merlin House, 1971); Louis A. De Caro, Jr., *On The Side of My People: A Religious Life of Malcolm X* (New York: New York U. Press, 1996); _____, *Malcolm and the Cross* (New York: New York U. Press, 1998); Clayborne Carson, *Malcolm X: The FBI File* (New York: Carroll and Graf, 1991); Steve Clark, ed., *Malcolm X: The Final Speeches* (New York: Pathfinder Press, 1992); James H. Cone, *Malcolm and Martin and America:*

Rather, the following is a more narrowly defined attempt to place Malcolm X within a context of movement from heterodoxy to orthodoxy; to assess his role in that movement; and to address attendant issues related to that role. The principal argument here is that Minister Malcolm was largely responsible for changing the intellectual climate among African American Muslims, such that orthodoxy became much more palatable, precisely because he was both the leading spokesperson for black nationalism and pan-Africanism, and, as the most dynamic representative of Islam in North America, was best situated to attempt a reconciliation of religious divergence. Malcolm represented the maturation of a process initially articulated by Noble Drew Ali and developed by Elijah Muhammad, a process whose beginnings are at least indirectly related to the presence of enslaved (and free) African Muslims in colonial and antebellum North America. As such, he constitutes a critical link facilitating the passage from an unconventional Islam to one in conformity with a more ancient tradition. Necessarily this required the cultivation of a kind of fluidity, a quality of experimentation, that in the brief time left to him proved insufficient for the completion of a coherent synthesis of political and spiritual expression. Indeed, black nationalism and Sunni Islam are arguably irreconcilable, and in any event certainly contentious, so that ultimately a practicable balance between the two would have proven highly elusive.

The ability of Malcolm to simultaneously represent, or try to represent, nationalism and orthodox Islam is indicative of the observation that Malcolm personified different things to different people. It is not necessarily the case that he intentionally conveyed competing concomitant messages, but it should be borne in mind that Malcolm possessed an expansive intellect, part of which paid careful attention to the perception of his character and mission. It is possible, therefore, that in his quest to mobilize his constituency as well as attract those sitting on the fence, he so skillfully managed his public persona that those of differing perspectives and beliefs within the African-derived community

A Dream or a Nightmare (Maryknoll, NY: Orbis, 1991); Michael Eric Dyson, *Making Malcolm: The Myth and Meaning of Malcolm X* (New York: Oxford U. Press, 1995); Archie Epps, ed., *Malcolm X: Speeches of Malcolm X at Harvard* (New York: Morrow, 1968); Peter Goldman, *The Death and Life of Malcolm X* (New York: Harper & Row, 1973); Zak A. Kondo, *Conspiracy: Unraveling the Assassination of Malcolm X* (Washington, DC: Nubia Press, 1993); Spike Lee, with Ralph Wiley, *By Any Means Necessary: The Trials and Tribulations of the Making of Malcolm X* (New York: Hyperion, 1992); Louis E. Lomax, *When the Word is Given . . .* (New York: Signet Books, 1963); _____, *To Kill a Black Man* (Los Angeles: Holloway House, 1968); _____, *The Negro Revolt* (New York: Harper & Row, 1962); Joe Wood, ed., *Malcolm X: In Our Image* (New York: St. Martin's Press, 1992); William W. Sales, Jr., *From Civil Rights to Black Liberation* (Boston: South End Press, 1994); George Breitman, ed., *Malcolm X Speaks: Selected Speeches and Statements* (New York: Grove Press, 1982); _____, ed., *By Any Means Necessary: Speeches, Interviews and a Letter by Malcolm X*, 12th ed. (New York: Pathfinder Press, 1987); _____, ed., *The Last Year of Malcolm X: The Evolution of a Revolutionary* (New York: Pathfinder Press, 1967); George Breitman, Herman Porter, and Baxter Smith, *The Assassination of Malcolm X* (New York: Pathfinder Press, 1976); Molefi Kete Asante, *Malcolm X as Cultural Hero and other Essays* (Trenton, NJ: Africa World Press, 1993); Oba T'Shaka, *The Political Legacy of Malcolm X* (Chicago: Third World Press, 1983).

focused on those components of his message most suited to their interests. That is, it is not beyond credulity that by 1964 and his official break with Elijah Muhammad, Malcolm had either deliberately or subconsciously achieved a multivalent discourse, a multifaceted glossolalia that, having taken into account the history, struggles, fears, and aspirations of his people, responded with entreaties and behavior targeting specific communities of interest. It is therefore not simply his "militancy" that has and continues to attract admirers, but the multiple values and experiences he has come to represent. Like the apostle Paul, who "became all things to all people, that I may gain some," and with whom analogies were often made, Malcolm's public message and lifestyle were carefully crafted, interwoven, and infused with a series of subliminalities. What follows, therefore, are heuristic rather than definitive ruminations into the covert content of Malcolm's verbal and behavioral representations, as they are key to a clearer understanding of his role in the transformation of Islam in North America.

* * *

Malcolm's discussion of early childhood in the *Autobiography* is as good a place to begin as any, for there he and Haley fashion an account that ostensibly reads as a twentieth-century protest and coming-of-age narrative, but at the same time easily lends itself to a contemplation of the vicissitudes of the transatlantic slave trade, or alternatively the ignominies of plantation slavery. To be sure, elements of the early narrative are inconsistent with a conscious effort at the reorganization of memory for the purpose of conveying a larger story, all the more reason to invest credence in the overall reliability of the account, or at least in the integrity of the attempt. Even so, the various phases and implications of the telling of his childhood carry remarkable correspondences with an earlier and far more inclusive epic, and it is possible that in Malcolm's mind there converged personal and collective memory. In any event, the image of Malcolm as African griot and New World historian is discernible.

When read in this way, Malcolm's account of his early years features principal actors as tropes. Malcolm's father, (possibly) a Baptist minister and organizer of the UNIA, is the quintessential Garveyite warrior and guardian of familial sanctity.[2] As such, Earl Little, a six-foot, 4-inch tall "jet-black" native of Reynolds, Georgia and son of the soil, personifies Africa and is its veritable spitting image. The retelling of his father's life conveys an imbrication of meaning, as it is synchronistic of both the transatlantic slave trade and New World slavery. The association of Earl Little with a precontact African continent, with freedom and independence, is underscored by the transition to the discussion of his constant

[2] Malcolm's older brother Wilfred insists that their father was never a Baptist minister; rather, "sympathetic Black ministers" allowed him to "address their congregations from time to time"and present the Garveyite platform. See Jan Carew, *Ghosts in Our Blood, with Malcolm X in Africa, England, and the Caribbean* (Chicago: Lawrence Hill Books, 1994), ix–x.

travels: We first detect his movement in Montreal, where he met and married his second wife, Grenadian-born Louisa or Louise Langdon Norton, Malcolm's mother and fellow Garveyite, and from where the couple moved to Philadelphia, then to Omaha, then to Milwaukee, and then Lansing, and finally to a location two miles outside of East Lansing. While Louisa's journey to North America reflects substantial Caribbean migrations in various historical periods, and her union with Earl Little is suggestive of the potential of diasporic relations, the movement from the South to successive points in the North speaks to Earl's inability or unwillingness to settle anywhere, his peripatetic lifestyle suggesting an undercurrent of restlessness, of dissatisfaction, revealing a man clearly out of sorts with his environment, unable to reconcile with his surroundings. There is a fundamental incompatibility between his self-image and the limitations of his lived experience. Malcolm informs us that the family's relocation from Milwaukee to Lansing was the consequence of his father's desire "to find a place where he could raise our own food and perhaps build a business," while all the while preaching Garveyism during the week and religion (presumably) on the weekends (according to Malcolm's brother Wilfred, Garvey himself visited the Little family several times, and on one occasion was hidden by their mother to protect him from FBI officials).[3] This equation of restiveness, Garvey, and land coalesces around a vision of return, the core of which is an unfettered Africa.[4]

However, the constant movement of the Little family also has the force of a flight from slavery, Earl's journey from South to North a striking parallelism. Reinforcing this quality is the hostility of his surroundings, the threat of death at every turn. We are told that Earl witnessed the violent expiation of four of his six brothers, three at the hands of white men. He was forced to move his family from Omaha (where Malcolm was born on May 19, 1925) after being threatened by the Ku Klux Klan. The move to East Lansing was occasioned by a stoning from white neighbors; the need to settle outside of East Lansing was the result of a residential prohibition against blacks in that town. Earl Little's world was one of imminent and constant danger, a navigation in a sea of turbulence.[5]

The defining moment of Malcolm's early years was a two-year tumult, beginning with the firebombing of the Little home in September of 1929 and

[3] Carew, *Ghosts in Our Blood*, 118.
[4] See Malcolm X, *Autobiography* (henceforth *Autobiography*), 1–8; Perry (*Malcolm*, 2–3) maintains that Earl and Louisa were married in Montreal and not Philadelphia, as Malcolm recalled. Carew (*Ghosts in Our Blood*, 131) concurs with Perry, stating that the couple were married on May 10, 1919. Carew's information presumably derives from Wilfred. However, Rodnell Collins, son of Malcolm's sister Ella, returns the scene of Earl and Louisa's marriage to Philadelphia. Ella was Earl's daughter from his first marriage to Daisy Mason in 1909, from whom Earl, according to Ella, never legally divorced. Rodnell P. Collins, with A. Peter Bailey, *Seventh Child: A Family Memoir of Malcolm X* (Secaucus, NJ: Birch Lane Press, 1998), 14. Ella died in 1996.
[5] See *Autobiography*, 1–8; Perry, *Malcolm*, 9–11.

ending with his father's death in September of 1931, an aggregation of events so traumatic as to be permanently seared, hardwired, into Malcolm's recollection of the past. Described as "the nightmare night" and Malcolm's "earliest vivid memory," the 1929 firebombing combines with Earl Little's 1931 demise to form a continuum of tragedy, and while it readily lends itself to a cogitation on some scene out of slavery, it also and more poignantly evokes the serial meanings of the Middle Passage. Like some circumstance of initial capture in the interior of eighteenth- or nineteenth-century West and West Central Africa, the 1929 nocturnal attack is recalled by Malcolm in words that capture the tactility and shock and confusion of the moment while conjuring up the trauma of centuries past: Asleep for the night, he was "suddenly snatched awake," surrounded by a cacophony of firearm reports and shouts and fire and smoke. The family "lunged" and "bumped" and "tumbled" in the night, searching for a way out of the conflagration. They barely escaped, only to stand helplessly by as their home was razed in spectacular fashion. Interestingly, most prominent in Malcolm's memory of successive developments over the next two years is the acrimony in the Little marriage: "They seemed to be nearly always at odds. Sometimes my father would beat her." This is an Africa divided, at odds with itself, in response to the demand for captive labor abroad. A slumbering Malcolm would once again be awakened by his mother's screams, this time heralding his father's death. This was calamity at high volume, after which Malcolm's family enters an unknown dimension and unravels with the passage of time. It is a descent into poverty, dependency, dismemberment, and madness. Malcolm recalls hunger's visitation in the form of dizziness, and his mother's resorting to the preparation of weeds for meals. Mrs. Little, under incredible pressure, slowly succumbs, losing her mind in the process. Found incompetent and placed in a mental hospital for the next twenty-five years, Louisa Little's undoing necessarily results in the ruination of the family. The children are parceled out to foster homes and detention facilities.[6] It is clear from the *Autobiography* that the death of Earl Little, determined by Malcolm to have been the work of the Black Legion in retribution for Earl Little's UNIA activities, was identified as the beginning of the end for Malcolm's family, the removal of his protection a metaphor for Africa's inability to defend itself from the ravages of a rapacious external force. Like those African captives separated from their homeland, Malcolm was forcibly removed from the comfort and security of his family and home and expelled into a world of strangers. His personal middle passage would also land him in the "wilderness" of North America, but this time in the urban slave quarters of Boston and New York City. Just like so many enslaved Africans, a fundamental motivation informing every aspect of his subsequent career as a political and

---

[6] After twenty-five years, Malcolm and his family had his mother released from the state mental hospital into his family's care. According to Carew (*Ghosts in Our Blood*, x, 116), Malcolm's mother Louisa went to live with her daughter Yvonne in upper Michigan until her death in 1991, at the age of 91.

religious leader was the reconstitution of his family and the yearning to return home.[7]

* * *

As an adolescent and young adult, Malcolm migrated from the racist environment of Mason, Michigan (near Lansing) to the embrace of black Boston and his half-sister Ella. The former for Malcolm was one characterized by white foster parents, juvenile homes, and predominantly white schools. While maintaining friendships with white students of both sexes, earning high grades, and even becoming elected as his seventh grade's president, Malcolm was nonetheless assaulted on a regular basis by the presumption of white superiority, communicated in so many instances by the referent "nigger" (addressed to him, to his face), and ultimately by learned advice (from a white teacher) that his desire to become a lawyer was no "realistic goal for a nigger," words and experience that would play some role in his conversion to the Nation of Islam ("it was then that I began to change – inside"). Coming under the legal custody of Ella with the completion of eighth grade, Malcolm fell in love with the streets, rejected the black middle-class culture of Roxbury's Sugar Hill (Boston), and began a life of petty crime that extended into his preconversion days in New York City. In the process, he created the persona of "Detroit Red."[8]

Kelley has written insightfully on this phase of Malcolm's life.[9] Part of his argument is that the very culture Malcolm decried in the *Autobiography* as antithetical to his subsequent values as a Muslim minister were in fact contributors to his decision to convert. The phenomenon of the jive-talking, lindy-hopping, conk-headed, urbanized black male youth during the Second World War was obviously cultural but was also infused with political meaning, and therefore it was oppositional to both white-controlled power structures and black middle-class airs. It was this posture of opposition and rejection, this carriage of defiance, that very much permeated all that Malcolm stood for as a political and religious figure. It was the same flavor.

The trajectory of Kelley's analysis, that what Malcolm ultimately became is very much tied to who he was, and that his conversion to Islam was not the total translation that he himself claimed, similarly informs the present

---

[7] See *Autobiography*, 8–35. Space will not permit an examination of Perry's argument that identified Earl Little as being responsible for torching his own home, or his dismissal of the possibility that he was murdered by the Black Legion, or his preoccupation with Louisa Little's moral character. Indeed, Perry's lines of inquiry and analyses consistently take issue with Malcolm's presentation in the *Autobiography*, more suggestive of undeclared commitments than critical scholarship (*Malcolm*, 9–33).

[8] See *Autobiography*, 25–154; Perry, *Malcolm*, 16–83. Perry's pointless speculation on the exact nature Malcolm's relationship with male prostitutes, whether as pimp or client or both, is rather curious, but again entirely consistent.

[9] See Robin D. G. Kelley, *Race Rebels: Culture, Politics, and the Black Working Class* (New York: The Free Press, 1994), 161–81.

discussion. To that end, Malcolm as trickster clearly emerges from his Boston and New York, preincarceration days. The trickster in African-derived folklore in the New World (but not necessarily in Africa itself) represents the triumph of the seemingly weak and disadvantaged over the ostensibly powerful and consequential.[10] The conversion of purported weakness into strength has often been interpreted as a commentary on enslaved–enslaver relations; the struggle is usually resolved by the trickster through means of cunning, stealth, and dissimulation. In this context, and in at least two ways, Malcolm proved the consummate trickster. The first instance involved the draft board, before whom Malcolm appeared after receiving notification to appear in October 1943. Before the board he feigned a convincing level of derangement, having previously spoken of his support for Japan in the hearing of those he believed would relay his sentiment to the authorities. Behaving "high and crazy," Malcolm appeared before the board in a "wild" zoot suit, his blazing red conk matching his "yellow knob-toed" shoes. Playing the clown, he informed the recruiter of a desire to be trained in the South, where he could organize black soldiers and "kill up crackers."[11]

Malcolm's antics merited the 4F, nondraftable status he sought, but his overall performance raises questions concerning the degree to which he was already politicized in his thinking at this early juncture, during his internment "in the grave," long before his joining the Nation of Islam. The conjoining of pro-Japanese sentiment and militant, antiracist rhetoric no doubt represented to Malcolm the most effective means of helping to persuade the draft board of his undesirability, and it was therefore calculated. However, the resonance with the message of the Nation of Islam and the Moorish Science Temple is striking, whose views Malcolm would subsequently espouse. Given that his background included Garveyites as parents, it is not inconceivable that Malcolm really believed what he presented to the draft board in 1943. The idea that he did not, and only came to such conclusions after exposure to Elijah Muhammad, may indicate a revisionism that is itself within the tradition of the trickster.

A second, clear example of Malcolm as trickster concerns his entire lifestyle prior to incarceration. As Kelley has pointed out, Malcolm embraced a culture that was opposed to holding a regular job, deemed another form of slavery

[10] Literature on trickster folklore in North America and Africa includes Harold Courlander, ed., *A Treasury of Afro-American Folklore* (New York: Crown Publishers, 1976); Richard M. Dorson, ed., *African Folklore* (Bloomington: Indiana U. Press, 1972); Isidore Okpewho, *African Oral Literature* (Bloomington: Indiana U. Press, 1992); Bernth Lindfors, ed., *Forms of Folklore in Africa* (Austin: U. of Texas, 1977); Françoise Tsoungui, *Clés pour le conte africaine et créole* (Paris: Conseil International de la Langue Français, 1986); Robert D. Pelton, *The Trickster in West Africa* (Berkeley and Los Angeles: U. of California Press, 1980); Ruth Finnegan, *Oral Literature in Africa* (Oxford, England: Clarendon Press, 1970).
[11] See *Autobiography*, 71.

(and in fact called a "slave"). Having worked as a shoeshine boy and a railway porter, Malcolm gradually moved from supplementing his wage earnings with informal economy activities to becoming fully invested in the latter. Life as a hustler, pimp, drug dealer, and thief was simultaneously a political, social, and cultural commentary. To participate in the informal economy, often but not always synonymous with criminal activity, was to necessarily take on something of a confrontational political posture. However, the informal sector was not only a political training ground; it was clearly an entrepreneurial one as well. While in the grave, Malcolm would learn skills translatable and essential to his resurrected life as a Muslim leader, skills of organization, management, ingenuity, creativity, innovation, and adaptation. The ability to create something out of nothing, to rely on meager resources while pursuing a grander vision, the sheer will to persevere, were all honed in the grave, not in the Nation. Indeed, Malcolm brought these values and attitude *with* him into the Nation, as is clear by an early meeting between him and Elijah Muhammad at the latter's home, presumably in late 1952. Frustrated by the small membership of Detroit's Temple No. 1, to which he belonged, Malcolm asked how many members there should be:

He said, "There are supposed to be thousands."
"Yes sir," I said. "Sir, what is your opinion of the best way of getting thousands there?"
"Go after the young people," he said. "Once you get them the older ones will follow through shame."
I made up my mind that we were going to follow that advice.[12]

Young Malcolm seized the initiative. Obtaining Elijah Muhammad's blessing, he promptly went out and, over the next few years, produced thousands of converts.

*   *   *

There is yet another image of Malcolm that emerges during his preincarceration years, one that is much more difficult to detect, perhaps far less tenable and yet potentially significant. Malcolm as a Shango figure is a subliminal discourse that threads through his entire life. The Yoruba orisha is one of the better known principals of African ancestral religion, and while it is as a shorthand for the broader range of non-Ibrahimic, African religions that he is referenced here, there are elements of Shango's own character that resonate with Malcolm's personality. The legendary fourth king of ancient Oyo (southwestern Nigeria), Shango's smooth eloquence was accompanied by fire when he spoke. Leaving his kingdom as a result of some catastrophe or misfortune, he traveled to Koso, where he appears to have committed suicide by hanging, but in any event was translated into such a celestial existence that his worshipers

---

[12] Ibid., 202–03.

exclaimed, "the king did not hang himself." Capricious, authoritative, belli-cose, destructive, and ardently sexual, this deity of the drums and dance and thunder symbolizes a violent and unpredictable power and is associated with the colors white and red.[13]

While certain of Shango's traits do not apply to Malcolm, the former's pop-ularity, prominent stature, flamboyance, and fiery speech are certainly consis-tent with Malcolm's iconographic status, his high visibility, his regal bearing, and his inimitable oratorical style. While possessing little economic or political power in a conventional sense, Malcolm nonetheless enjoyed a different kind of power, a power of persuasion that grew out of admiration for the absence of equivocation and the presence of integrity. Malcolm was indeed very pow-erful, as evident in the growth of the Nation of Islam during his tenure, in the untold masses who agreed with his message while eschewing membership in

[13] For more on Yoruba religion, see Nicolas Valentin Angarica, *Manual de Orihate: Religión lucumí* (s.l., s.n., 1955?); Sandra T. Barnes, ed., *Africa's Ogun: Old World and New* (Bloomington: In-diana U. Press, 1997); George Brandon, *Santeria from Africa to the New World: The Dead Sell Memories* (Bloomington: Indiana U. Press, 1993); Kim D. Butler, *Freedoms Given, Freedoms Won* (New Brunswick, NJ: Rutgers U. Press, 1998); Edison Carneiro, *Candomblés da Bahia* 3rd (Rio de Janeiro: Conquista, 1961; orig. pub. c. 1948); Carybé, *Iconografia dos Deuses Africanos no Candomblé da Bahia* (São Paulo: Editoria Raizes Artes Gráficas, 1980); Mary Cuthrell Curry, *Making the Gods in New York: The Yoruba Religion in the African American Community* (New York: Garland Publishers, 1997); Agún Efundé, *Los Secretos de la Santería* (Miami: Cubamérica, 1978); Heriberto Feraudy Espino, *Irna: Un encuentro con la santería, el espiritismo y el Palo Monte* (Guadalajara and Jalisco, México: Editorial Conexión Gráfico, 1999); Margarite Fernández Olmos and Lizabeth Paravisini-Gebert, eds., *Sacred Possessions: Vodou, Santería, Obeah, and the Caribbean* (New Brunswick, NJ: Rutgers U. Press, 1997); Tomás Fernández Robaina, *Hablen paleros y santeros* (La Habana: Editorial de Ciencias Sociales, 1994); Manuel Moreno Fraginals, ed., *África en América Latina* (México: Siglo Veintiuno Editores, 1977); Julio García Cortez, *El Santo (la Ocha); secretos de la religió ñ Lucumí* (Miami?: s.n., 1971); Maurice A. Glele, *Le Danxome: du pouvoir Aja á la nation Fon* (Paris: Nubia, 1974); Migene González-Wippler, *Legends of Santería* (St. Paul, MN: Llewellyn Publications, 1994); _____, *Santería: African Magic in Latin America* (New York: Original Products, 1992); _____, *Santería: The Religion, Faith, Rites, Magic* (St. Paul, MN: Llewellyn Publications, 1994); Tabaré A Güerere, *Las diosas negras: la santería en femenino* (Caracas: Alfadil Ediciones, 1995); _____, *Hablan los santeros* (Caracas: Alfadil Ediciones, 1993); _____, *Las planta curativas de los santeros* (Caracas: Editorial Panapo, 1996); Rachel E. Harding, *A Refuge in Thunder: Candomblé and Alternative Spaces of Blackness* (Bloom-ington: Indiana U. Press, 2000); Héctor Izaguirre, *Eleggua, Oggún, Ikú y Ochosi: Guardianes y guerros* (Caracas: Editorial Panapo, 1997); _____, *Orula, Orugán, Chugudú: el triángulo adiv-inatorio en la Santería* (Caracas: Editorial Panapo, 1998); Arturo Lindsay, ed., *Santería Aesthetics in Contemporary Latin America* (Washington and London: Smithsonian Institution Press, 1996); Joseph Murphy, *Santería: An African Religion in America* (Boston: Beacon Press, 1988); Andrés I. Pérez y Mena, *Speaking with the Dead: Development of Afro-Latin Religion among Puerto Ricans in the United States* (New York: AMS Press, 1991); Miguel F. Santiago, *Dancing with the Saints* (Puerto Rico: Inter American U. Press, 1993); Robert Farris Thompson, *Flash of the Spirit* (New York: Vintage Books, 1983); Marta Moreno Vega, *The Altar of My Soul: The Living Traditions of Santería* (New York: One World, 2000); Pierre Verger, *Orixas: Dieux Yoruba en Afrique et au nouveau monde* (Paris: A. M. Métailié, 1982).

the Nation, and in the alarm with which government monitored his activities.[14] Some of the characteristics for which he would become famous were already in formation as early as elementary school, when he was elected class president in seventh grade. His penchant for rhetorical flourish would develop in prison, when his sharp questions and skills in repartee often astonished fellow inmates and authority figures alike. But thoughts of an incarnate Shango prove most irresistible, though conceivably blasphemous to some, when one considers Malcolm as a zoot-suited, fast-talking, streetwise hustler, most identifiable to all by his fire-red conk.

Beyond the specific correlation of Malcolm and Shango is the question of the substratum of Malcolm's belief system; that is, there is the question of what he tended to believe before converting to the Nation's teachings, and continued to believe, perhaps subconsciously, throughout his life. There are at least two indications that, despite the Nation's teachings to the contrary, Malcolm very much subscribed to the notion that a spirit world existed and that there were indeed mysterious forces at work that could not be readily explained, a notion for which he offered no explanation. His description of certain phenomena suggests a residue of pre-Islamic beliefs that Malcolm did not bother to explore, at least publicly, possible reasons for which will be discussed shortly. To the extent that these beliefs share a vision of the noumenal with African ancestral faiths, and may indeed indirectly stem from them, reinforces this competing interpretation of Malcolm as a Shango figure.

The first bit of evidence comes from the birth ordering. Malcolm's emphasis on being his father's seventh child indicates an embrace of the significance of numerology, an alchemy of interpretation informed by Freemasonry, Biblical exegesis, Moorish Science (for example, the *Circle Seven Koran* itself), Islamic and Jewish traditions, and, of course, African cultural influences. Throughout these diverse yet interrelated sources runs the concept of the declaration of divine approbation, even greatness through the association of the person or event with certain numbers. From this perspective, to be the seventh born is a momentous development, indicative of a special calling and purpose. Fully aware that his birth order would be seen as a sign of divine sanction, Malcolm did not shy away from publicizing the matter; indeed, his occasional use of numerology takes on new meaning in this light, as was the case when, in remarks made in 1963 about his former life, he observed that he had "spent 77 months in three different prisons."[15] In fact, numerology in general and the birth order in particular were powerful indications of divine order in the Nation: Wallace Muhammad was the seventh child of Elijah Muhammad, who was in turn the seventh child of his family, facts used to solidify claims to succession and leadership. Such were men of destiny, realizations of

---

[14] For a glimpse into the United States government's anxiety over Malcolm's activities, see Carson, *Malcolm X: The FBI File*.

[15] See Haley, *Playboy Interviews*, 38.

prophecy promulgated not through the spoken word but augured through the womb.[16]

Of course, Malcolm had been exposed to a great many teachings. His brother Wilfred relates that their mother took them to a variety of religious services, including the Seventh Day Adventist Church, where she found support for her dietary proscriptions. The melange of experiences did not lead to a definitive spiritual position but created conditions for the critical reception of orthodox Christianity: "We never set Jesus apart from the other men who had divine inspiration," declared Wilfred, a perspective not unlike that of Nobel Drew Ali.[17] Some deposit of these early experimentations possibly remained with Malcolm throughout life, just as the possibility holds true for Elijah Muhammad himself, who, exposed at a tender age to Christianity, married a "Holiness woman" who sang Christian melodies before her conversion to the Nation, songs long remembered by their son Wallace: "Yes, and my mother sung spirituals. I could hear her every morning."[18] As Pentecostalism is infused with an emphasis on the supernatural and is arguably derivative of African ancestral religion, it would have been a difficult task, growing up in rural Georgia, for Elijah Muhammad to have completely divested himself of all regard for the significance of such matters as birthing orders. His claim to be the seventh child is fairly convincing proof of that.[19]

There is another, more curious indication of Malcolm's acceptance of the supernatural, even while still in the Nation. The occasion involves the apparent apparition of W. D. Fard Muhammad while Malcolm was in prison. De Caro correctly points out that Malcolm mentions the vision without attempting to explain it.[20] In fact, very few commentators have had anything to say about the episode, with the effect of further enshrouding the occurrence in mystery. The relevant passage from the *Autobiography* bears repeating:

It was the next night, as I lay on my bed, I suddenly, with a start, became aware of a man sitting beside me in my chair. He had on a dark suit. *I remember.* I could see

---

[16] See *Autobiography*, 1–2; E. U. Essien-Udom, *Black Nationalism: A Search for an Identity in America* (Chicago: U. of Chicago Press, 1962), 74–81; Louis A. De Caro, Jr., *On The Side of My People: A Religious Life of Malcolm X* (New York: New York U. Press, 1996), 50. Karl Evanzz, *The Messenger: The Rise and Fall of Elijah Muhammad* (New York: Pantheon Books, 1999), observes that Malcolm considered seven his lucky number (285), as does Malcolm's nephew Rodnell (Collins, *Seventh Child*, xii). Claude Andrew Clegg III, *An Original Man: The Life and Times of Elijah Muhammad* (New York: St. Martin's Press, 1997), maintains that Elijah was the sixth born in his family; interestingly, his mother Mariah Poole had a vision that she would have a son who would achieve greatness – she had the vision at age seven (*Original Man*, 6).

[17] See De Caro, *On the Side of My People*, 51–52.

[18] See Imam W. D. Muhammad, *Religion on the Line: Al-Islam, Judaism, Catholicism, Protestantism* (Chicago: W. D. Muhammad Publications, 1983), 67; _____, *As the Light Shineth from the East* (Chicago: W. D. Muhammad Publishing, 1980), 24–25.

[19] On African influences in Christianity, see Michael A. Gomez, *Exchanging Our Country Marks: The Transformation of African Identities in the Colonial and Antebellum South* (Chapel Hill: U. of North Carolina Press, 1998).

[20] See De Caro, *On the Side of My People*, 88–89.

him as plain as I see anyone I look at. He wasn't black, and he wasn't white. He was light-brown-skinned, an Asiatic cast of countenance, and he had oily black hair.
I looked right into his face.
I didn't get frightened. I knew I wasn't dreaming. I couldn't move, I didn't speak, and he didn't. I couldn't place him racially – other than that I knew he was a non-European. I had no idea whatsoever who he was. He just sat there. Then, suddenly as he had come, he was gone.[21] [italics added]

While in prison, before he would even meet Elijah Muhammad, Malcolm was claiming to have been in the presence of W. D. Fard Muhammad, long after he had departed from Detroit and Chicago, never more to be seen: "I would later come to believe that my pre-vision was of Master W. D. Fard, the Messiah."[22]

The passage reads like Elijah Muhammad's initial encounter with Fard Muhammad – there is the same sense of wonder and suspension of critical faculties. What is even more fascinating about the account, however, is the timing and process of its recording. Having received Elijah Muhammad's blessing to begin the *Autobiography* with Alex Haley, Malcolm had broken with the Nation and was at odds with Mr. Muhammad toward its completion. He had opportunities to revise the statement, to explain it, to even remove it. For example, in critiquing the account of Yakub and white ethnogenesis, Malcolm faults orthodox Muslims from the "East" for not doing enough to "make real Islam known in the West. Their silence left a vacuum into which any religious faker could step and mislead our people," an apparent reference to Elijah Muhammad, indicating the passage had been revised after Malcolm's break from the Nation.[23] However, the account of the surreal visitation, only nineteen pages after the thinly veiled denunciation of Elijah Muhammad, remained unedited. We therefore have two options: to either accept the account on its face or to explore the possible reasons for its fabrication. That Malcolm may have genuinely believed what he wrote cannot be discounted, lending further credence to a metaphysical residual of ancestral orientation. The latter possibility, however, suggests the conviction that such a residual permeated the rank-and-file of the Nation's membership, and it constitutes a shrewd manipulation of its potential.

The claim of the W. D. Fard Muhammad vision recalls Paul's encounter with a resurrected Jesus on the Damascus road, and indeed may have been fashioned after it, as in both instances the effect was to distinguish their calls to ministry as unique from the more commonplace promptings of other religious leaders. By relating this incident, Malcolm was certainly making the case that his was a very special, divinely orchestrated place in the Nation's hierarchy of leadership. It was probably not included in the *Autobiography* to threaten Elijah Muhammad's own position, but it could have been interpreted by others in the hierarchy as

---

[21] See *Autobiography*, 190.
[22] Ibid., 192.
[23] Ibid., 167–71.

a bid for succession, others who could have then exploited the insecurities of Mr. Muhammad flowing from a turbulent past, eventually succeeding in turning him against Malcolm.[24] Malcolm also frequently mentioned that, just as Elijah Muhammad had labored "night and day" under Fard Muhammad's tutelage for two years, he too had been personally trained by "for months" by Mr. Muhammad; in combination with the claim of the visitation, such statements could stoke the fires of enormous fear and suspicion.[25] Whatever the truth of the matter, the Fardian apparition could only serve as a vehicle of legitimization, adding to the significance of the birth order. The seventh son had seen God himself, and somewhere in the inner recesses of the collective African-descended memory, Shango stirred.

* * *

If the disintegration and eventual breakup of Malcolm's childhood family mirrors the horrors and destruction of the transatlantic slave trade, and if his life of crime and incarceration is a commentary on slavery and oppression, then his embrace of the Nation of Islam was nothing less than a reclamation of origins, allowing for the symbolic reestablishment of ties to Africa. Indeed, familial connections were critical to his decision to convert.

Malcolm was still quite young, twenty years of age to be exact, when he went to the penitentiary in February of 1946. It was his first experience serving hard time in "the joint," and he would need the support of family and friends on the outside to make it through the difficult process. As is true of life in general, adversity tends to winnow fair-weather friends from the truly loyal, and in Malcolm's case it produced a distillation at the end of which emerged his brothers and sisters among the most prominent of the loyalists. Close friend Malcolm "Shorty" Jarvis provides a most interesting detail: Prior to his initial encounter with the Nation of Islam, both he and Malcolm X had been introduced to the Ahmadiyya movement through the Indian Abdul Hameed, who, according to Jarvis, "spent many hours teaching us" prior to their incarceration, and who continued to visit the two Malcolms at Norfolk Prison Colony.[26] Malcolm therefore had prior knowledge of Islam before accepting the message of Elijah Muhammad, with the Ahmadiyya having played a role in his transformation.

Although Malcolm initially rejected the 1948 letter from Philbert in which the latter introduced his new allegiance to the Nation, he was more receptive to his younger brother Reginald's communications revealing that he, Reginald, had also converted to the same religion. Embedded in Reginald's letter was the

[24] See Clegg, *Original Man*, for a discussion of Elijah Muhammad's early struggles to gain ascendancy over the organization.
[25] See *Autobiography*, 215. Malcolm regularly held private audiences with Elijah Muhammad "for hours" (208).
[26] See Malcolm "Shorty" Jarvis, with Paul D. Nichols, *The Other Malcolm – "Shorty" Jarvis* (Jefferson, NC: McFarland, 2001), 55–56, 124–26.

message: "Malcolm, don't eat any pork, and don't smoke any more cigarettes. I'll show you how to get out of prison." "'Get out of prison,'" Malcolm recalled, "The words hung in the air around me, I wanted out so badly."[27]

While exiting prison was the focus of Malcolm's conscious thought, Reginald's dietary admonitions just as certainly reverberated throughout his subconscious, echoing as they did their mother's earlier regulations ("strong ideas") concerning swine and rabbit ("don't let them feed him any pig," Malcolm recalled his mother exclaiming when state agents removed him from their home).[28] Malcolm was therefore entertaining a message consistent with meritorious elements of his youth, a message that brought him closer to his mother. By the time he began receiving mail daily from a number of converted siblings, Malcolm could not ignore the central truth: His family was being re-constituted before his very eyes. Philbert, Reginald, Wilfred, Hilda – "they were all Muslims," reflected Malcolm. It was not long before these developments burst upon Malcolm's psyche with implications full of meaning and possibility. The Nation, a way out of prison, was also a corridor of reconciliation. It was not long before Malcolm would join the procession.

Resurrection from the grave for Malcolm also involved a transposition of familial roles, in that Malcolm was almost immediately required to choose between his affection for Reginald and his new fidelity to Elijah Muhammad. When Reginald, who was tossed out of the New York temple for an affair with a secretary, began speaking ill of Mr. Muhammad, Malcolm had to make a choice, and in doing so partially transferred expectations of the resumption of familial bonds to the family of Elijah Muhammad himself. The latter did not disappoint. Upon leaving prison in August of 1952, Malcolm began a life of austere allegiance to the Nation, living with Wilfred in Detroit while working a conventional job in a furniture store and attending classes and events held at the Detroit temple. Integrating into the life of the temple, Malcolm eventually met the man with whom he had corresponded while in prison, Elijah Muhammad, on Labor Day of 1952. By the summer of 1953, Malcolm had been named an assistant minister at the Detroit temple, and he began frequenting the home of Elijah Muhammad in Chicago. Their relationship was fast and strong: "I was treated as if I had been one of the sons of Mr. Muhammad and his dark, good wife Sister Clara Muhammad." While Elijah Muhammad had become the dominant father figure in Malcolm's life, it was the former's mother, more so than Clara Muhammad, who served as surrogate mother: "I would spend almost as much time with Mother Marie as I did with him."[29] In and through the Nation, therefore, Malcolm was able to address pressing needs of a personal nature, filling voids created during a turbid childhood. He was home again.

In coming home to the Nation, Malcolm would eventually reemerge as a symbol of reconciliation between a number of competing factors within the

[27] See *Autobiography*, 155–59.
[28] Ibid., 7–8, 20.
[29] Ibid., 186–208.

African-derived community. In the adoption of Elijah Muhammad as paternal head, and in becoming a family man himself, Malcolm successfully melded his religious, professional, familial, and personal lives into an undifferentiated whole. To fully achieve this, though, he had to quickly confront the thorny issue of color consciousness among African Americans. The racialist foundation of the Nation's ideology provided him with the mechanism and the framework within which to address the question, but he appears to have been one of the few (at least among the elite of the Nation) who truly embraced the practical significance of the teachings, committing caste suicide in the process. Even though his light complexion may have initially played some role in his selection as a minister, his eschewing of caste-based privilege became a hallmark of his ministry, and it commended him to many.

In the *Autobiography*, Malcolm, after framing his life story within a context of conflict between white racism and black nationalism (in the person of his father), immediately establishes color caste as a principal issue vexing the African-derived population:

I was among the millions of Negroes who were *insane* enough to feel that it was some kind of status symbol to be light-complexioned – that one was actually fortunate to be born thus. But, still later, I learned to hate every drop of that white rapist's blood that is in me.[30] [italics added]

That Malcolm took time to explore this dimension of blackness in North America indicates its importance to him. Malcolm's own interpretation of his childhood experiences suggests a child who, while not necessarily confused over the issue, was nonetheless troubled by it. With an older brother (Philbert) so dark that he was called "Blackie" by the family, Malcolm's complexion was a near polar opposite, earning him the nickname "Milky." Malcolm discerned a maternal discrimination against him, which is interesting because his mother was often viewed as a white woman, while he believed his father's favoritism was precisely due to the conventional preference for lighter-complected progeny. Until his conversion to Fardian Islam, Malcolm accepted and took full advantage of his complexion, but the conflict he grew up with, concretized by sibling rivalry, remained very much alive and internalized.[31] Resolution came through an even more radical interpretation of the Nation's teachings, perhaps best symbolized by his marriage to brown-skinned Betty, whose beauty he never ceased to extol. By rejecting caste privilege, Malcolm gravitated to the political sensibilities his mother (displayed in her patterns of preference among her children); indeed, Malcolm's mother may have given him "more hell" than his darker siblings not because of her own hangups but precisely because she wanted to discourage color caste privilege among them (if so, the strategy eventually succeeded). While a possible attempt to reconcile with (at least the memory of) his mother, Malcolm's decision certainly endeared him to thousands of dark-skinned

[30] Ibid., 2–3.
[31] Ibid., 4–8; also see Perry, *Malcolm*, 7.

descendants of the continent, who had long tired of a Brahmin-dominated Negro leadership. By rejecting privilege, Malcolm demonstrated an alternative to black racial cohesion through adherence to contradictory, parochial, self-defeating paradigms. In doing so, he exemplified a different process of coalescence, one he was uniquely positioned to lead.

As a locus of conciliation, Malcolm executed his ministerial responsibilities in ways consistent with his quest to recreate a sense of wholeness. There is no gainsaying that the popular image of Malcolm X remains that of a firebrand, an "angry black man" with powers of persuasion. Out of the public eye, however, the image that emerges from close associates of Malcolm is more that of a conscientious shepherd, a dedicated pastor. On the question of Malcolm's personal integrity, critics are few, their voices muted. Benjamin Karim, a close colleague at New York's Temple No. 7, succinctly captured the essence of the matter:

The lessons Malcolm taught were simple ones, ultimately, and he lived his life by them: Be honest. Harm no one, and take nothing that is not yours. Treat others as you would be treated by them. Practice charity. Exercise self-control. Avoid extremes, keep a middle path. Pay your taxes. Obey the law.[32]

According to Karim, by 1962 Malcolm supported his family on a weekly salary of $175.00; all the money he raised from speaking engagements went to Nation of Islam national headquarters in Chicago. It is well known that his house in Queens was owned by the Nation, a fact driven home by the Nation's efforts to have his family evicted following his split with Elijah Muhammad. Whatever one makes of his political views, Malcolm was not the stereotypical opportunistic leader, and from all indications he was resistant to corruption.

Malcolm was therefore in position to trade on his good name for the loyalty and trust of his followers. The ensuing relationship between minister and local temple adherents became predictably familial, notwithstanding Malcolm's ability to be caustically critical of members' shortcomings, an achievement all the more remarkable given national and even international responsibilities that frequently required his absence from New York. Indeed, Malcolm discussed in the *Autobiography* everyday life in the temple, but his recollection does not convey the same quality of nostalgia evident in Benjamin Karim's reminiscence, a perspective tinged if not more fully colored by remorse over Malcolm's passing. At Mosque No. 7 in New York City, where Malcolm was the principal minister from 1952 to December of 1963, there were three public lectures a week – two on weekday evenings and one on Sunday afternoon – before standing-room-only crowds frequently reaching 1,000 in number; as many were often turned away for lack of space. As mentioned in the previous chapter, Monday nights were reserved for the Fruit of Islam, to which all men technically belonged, with sessions in self-defense and martial arts training, instructions in male behavioral conditioning, and court tribunals

---

[32] See Karim, *Remembering Malcolm*, 129.

before whom appeared wayward members. Wednesday and Thursday evenings, in turn, were devoted to Student Enrollment and Muslim Girls' Training and General Civilization Class, respectively. While the pastoral dimension of Malcolm's ministry is discernible in these meetings, it was the care he took in preparing his assistant ministers during his Tuesday night "public speaking class" that more clearly evinced his genuine interest in people. Rather than presenting a course on elocution, Malcolm was much more concerned with the broader education and exposure of aspiring ministers, and he was demanding in the volume and sophistication of the readings he required for the class. His desire to engage people at the level of their humanity was again evident on Saturdays' "Unity Nights," when members gathered to socialize in a controlled but "relaxed" environment where they were served a light fare while listening to African and "Middle Eastern" music as well as selected jazz. However, perhaps the most distinguishable indication of Malcolm's commitment to his immediate flock was that he would gather the children on Saturday mornings and take them on field trips to the museums, the planetarium, and to other enriching experiences. This is a side of Malcolm not well publicized, but his personal participation in the life of the New York temple was no doubt an attempt to recapture his initial, postprison introduction to the temple in Detroit, when and where he first experienced the exhilaration of familial reconstitution:

I had *never dreamed* of anything like that atmosphere among black people who had learned to be proud they were black, who had learned to love other black people instead of being jealous and suspicious. *I thrilled* to how we Muslim men used both hands to grasp a black brother's both hands, voicing and smiling our happiness to meet him again. The Muslim sisters, both married and single, were given an honor and respect that I'd *never seen* black men give to their women, *and it felt wonderful to me.* The salutations which we all exchanged were warm, filled with mutual respect and dignity: "Brother" . . . "Sister" . . . "Ma'am" . . . "Sir." . . . Even children speaking to other children used these terms. Beautiful![33] [italics added]

Having reclaimed his biological family and having found adoptive parents in the persons of Elijah Muhammad and his mother Marie, Malcolm had also succeeded in returning to the village.

* * *

As his life mirrored the vicissitudes of the slave trade and enslavement, survived by using the techniques of the trickster, Malcolm's reclamation of family did not end with his siblings and the Nation. As a Shango figure, he was compelled toward Africa itself in ways unparalleled by any other leader in the Nation. That Malcolm was heeding an inner voice drawing him to the continent is made even more apparent in light of Elijah Muhammad's expressed ambivalence toward things African. In the briefest period of time, Malcolm's vision of liberation

---

[33] Ibid., 90–99; also see Goodman, *End of White World Supremacy*, 10–13; *Autobiography*, 199, 231–32. Benjamin Goodman is Benjamin Karim.

grew to encompass far more than the struggle in North America. Like the prodigal son, Malcolm quickly returned to the politics of his Garveyite father, the embodiment of Africa, and emerged as a leading spokesperson of not only the Nation but pan-Africanism as well.

To be sure, Malcolm's embrace of pan-Africanism, his advocacy of the plight of Africa, was part and parcel of the times. The anti-imperial struggle had reached new heights in the 1950s and 1960s, issuing into a number of politically independent states throughout Africa, Asia, and the Caribbean. Empire was ostensibly in the process of dismantlement everywhere, the result of the collection and surge of powerful currents of resistance throughout the earth. The North American civil rights movement, responding to domestic ignominies, the political implications as well as the economic opportunities flowing from the Second World War, the new international configuration of East versus West, and the agitation of colonized workers and peasants and intellectuals everywhere, acquired a new sense of urgency. Malcolm, perhaps better than any leader of the period, understood the connections between the struggles of oppressed peoples here and there, and he illuminated those relationships in electrifying fashion. He would fight for the translation of these equivalencies from the theoretical and the rhetorical to the practical and programmatic to literally his final hour.

An examination of Malcolm's public speeches demonstrates a progression of thought wherein the concern for the welfare of the African continent, and the relationship of the continent's struggles to the plight of the African-derived in North America and elsewhere in the African diaspora, increasingly began to occupy the center of the discourse, constituting the most incisive components of his analyses. Throughout his presentations, both during his tenure in the Nation and following it, perhaps the most salient element of his pan-Africanism was an astringent critique of the foreign policies of the United States and Europe. Tied to that analysis was the need for people of African descent to respond by organizing and taking any sort of action that would further the cause of liberation. Increasingly, Malcolm turned away from the radical posturing but conservative programmatic of the Nation to embrace a philosophy providing for the use of arms in the defense of life. Critical to his advocacy of freedom "by any means necessary," a position to which he arrived in time, were the examples set by the struggles against empire in Asia, Africa, and Latin America.

As early as 1955, and in keeping with the teachings of the Nation (while echoing those of the Moorish Science Temple), a relatively young Malcolm was making common cause with Asia in New York's Temple No. 7, claiming that the "Chinese Reds are not Communists but are black people," and that the rise of Communist China was part of a global awakening of "black nations." Interviewed by government officials in January of 1955, Malcolm voiced his support of Japan, stating that he would have fought in the Japanese army during the Second World War (boosting the possibility that his performance before the draft board in 1943 was more substantive than formerly understood). Later that year, Malcolm characterized the anticolonial movement throughout the world as a racial struggle, with people of color in China, Egypt, and Japan pressuring "the white man to get out." Malcolm's conceptualization of race was reductive but effective: "There are only two kinds of people," he maintained, "the white and the black, so if you are not white you must be black."[34]

From the mid-1950s to the end of the decade, Malcolm produced a running commentary on the plight of the "dark world," a global configuration of African, Asian, Caribbean, and Latin American societies and populations.[35] The essence of the discourse was that white racism was the thread connecting oppression throughout the world, and that divine judgment was near. Thus, a government informant recorded that, in a February 1959 meeting, Malcolm said the following:

The wars of 1914 and the Second World War have weakened the white race. God bless Japan for bombing Pearl Harbor. We should thank them. The only way Japan was conquered was through the atom bomb. The third and last war is the fight between the darker nations and the white race.[36]

Malcolm's prediction of racial Armageddon was not only informed by the teachings of the Nation but by his rapt attention to the global anticolonial struggle (which seemed to resonate with the Nation's racialism). The 1955 Bandung Conference, to which representatives from a number of nations gathered to promote the fight against empire, was critical to the progression of Malcolm's thinking. Initially interpreted as a validation of the Nation's teaching and a clear indication of the white world's demise, Bandung was a catalyst that would bring Malcolm into direct contact with African and Asian leaders, and it would cause him to rethink the plight of the African-derived in North America as part of an international experience. By July of 1957, Malcolm was able to meet the host of Bandung, Achmed Sukarno, who was visiting Harlem's Abyssinian Baptist Church at the invitation of Adam Clayton Powell, Jr. By April of 1959, Malcolm was calling for a "Bandung Conference of Negro Leaders," by which those of African descent in the United States could adopt the strategies used against imperialism elsewhere in the world. During that same month, Malcolm met with leading pan-Africanists in New York City, an early demonstration of his interest in working with those outside of the Nation. This represented a precursor to his eventual founding of the Organization of Afro-American Unity (the OAAU). By 1959, then, Malcolm had moved from the rhetoric of an imagined Asiatic brotherhood to helping to shape the anticolonial movement in ways that incorporated the plight of Africans in North America.[37]

Malcolm and the Nation were particularly interested in the Muslim world; in turn, Muslim leaders were curious about the Nation. A mutual courtship ensued, culminating in Gamal Nasser's invitation to Elijah Muhammad in May of 1959 to visit Egypt. Because the federal government decided to resist

---

[34] See Carson, *Malcolm X: The FBI File*, 111, 114–15.

[35] Ibid., 141; also see De Caro, *On the Side of My People*, 121–22.

[36] See Carson, *Malcolm X: The FBI File*, 157.

[37] Ibid., 174–77; also see the *Pittsburgh Courier*, July 20, 1957; Evanzz, *The Messenger*, 169, 183–93.

Mr. Muhammad's passport application, he sent Malcolm as his emissary. Leaving for Egypt on July 5, Malcolm was escorted to various audiences by Anwar Sadat before contracting a meddlesome case of diarrhea. Briefly visiting Jerusalem and Damascus, he went on to Saudi Arabia and stayed for two days in Jidda, prevented by illness and scheduling snafus from traveling to Mecca. By July 22, Malcolm had returned to New York, having been unable to visit Ethiopia and Nigeria as was his intention. Elijah Muhammad, accompanied by his sons Akbar and Herbert, eventually left for the Middle East on November 21, 1959. Beginning with Turkey, they would travel to Damascus, Beirut, Jerusalem, Cairo, Khartoum, Ethiopia, Jidda, and Mecca, where he made the minor ḥajj or *'umra*. Briefly stopping in Medina, the entourage arrived in Pakistan at the beginning of 1960, leaving for the United States on January 5. While Elijah Muhammad would return disappointed that the African, Arab, and Asian worlds did not measure up to all that he had been led to believe by W. D. Fard Muhammad, Malcolm had returned with a renewed determination to forge stronger bonds with Africa. Stated differently, the respective 1959 trips resulted in divergent trajectories for Mr. Muhammad and Malcolm: Malcolm was propelled toward Africa, while Elijah Muhammad was repulsed.[38] This development would certainly inform their subsequent split.

His commitment to pan-Africanism reinvigorated, Malcolm would have also noticed in his overseas travels significant differences between Islam in the Muslim world and its practice in the Nation. This was not necessarily a revelation, as orthodoxy had been introduced to the Nation in a formal and sustained way by Jamil Diab, a Palestinian teacher of Arabic at the University of Islam in Chicago, who instructed Mr. Muhammad during the 1950s in a number of areas, including the correct way to pray.[39] However, as Elijah Muhammad did not stray from the teachings of Fard Muhammad, Malcolm in turn remained loyal to his teacher. In fact, Diab's subsequent denunciation of the Nation in the late 1950s as a racist, non-Islamic organization would not have engendered in Malcolm an admiration for the proponents of Sunni Islam. Even so, seeds had been planted.

While Malcolm's pan-Africanism was inclusive of the African diaspora (for example, Malcolm met with Fidel Castro in September of 1960 at the Hotel Theresa in Harlem, expressing his admiration for the Cuban leader), the African continent was clearly the focus.[40] To that end, nothing seemed to have captured his imagination more (while simultaneously firing his indignation) than the brief career and horrific assassination of Patrice Lumumba, independent Congo's first Prime Minister. Assuming office in 1960, Lumumba was turned over to the secessionist leader of Katanga province, Moise Tshombe, who, with the backing of Belgian- and American-supported forces, proceeded to savagely beat and then shoot Lumumba on January 17, 1961, hacking his body to pieces and

---

[38] See Clegg, *Original Man*, 122–45; Evanzz, *The Messenger*, 193–214.
[39] See Clegg, *Original Man*, 122–34.
[40] See Carson, *Malcolm X: The FBI File*, 198–99.

dissolving it in acid. Indeed, Malcolm was not alone in his high regard for Lumumba, as much of the black world was captivated by the youthful, fiery, no-nonsense, autodidactic freedom fighter, in many ways a kindred spirit and counterpart to Malcolm. In speech after speech, in interview after interview, Malcolm denounced the role of the United States and European governments in the Congo in particular and in Africa in general. Malcolm was in fact one of the lone voices to identify the United States as a guilty party in Lumumba's murder, a refrain that would characterize his anti-imperialist platform long after his departure from the Nation itself. An example of how exercised Malcolm had become on the issue of Lumumba is an excerpt from a speech given on November 29, 1964, in which Malcolm articulates a vision of pan-Africanism that questions an uncritical American patriotism:

Also, brothers and sisters, you know Tshombe. You've heard of him. From what I understand, Tshombe arrives in the United States on Tuesday. He's got a whole lot of nerve.... This is the worst African that was ever born. The worst African that was ever born. This is the man who in cold blood, cold blood, committed an international crime – murdered Patrice Lumumba, murdered him in cold blood. The world knows that Tshombe murdered Lumumba. And now he's a bed partner for Lyndon B. Johnson.... It is the Lyndon B. Johnson administration, the man you voted for – you were insane, out of your mind, out of your head, to vote for a man like that; drunk. But I don't blame you, you were just tricked. I told you a fox will always get business.[41]

The intensity of Malcolm's contempt for American foreign policy explains his famous "chickens coming home to roost" statement in late 1963 following President Kennedy's assassination, revealing the consistency of his investment in the anti-imperial struggle.

Having been suspended by Elijah Muhammad in early December 1963, the announcement of Malcolm's official departure from the Nation was publicized by the *New York Times* and other media on March 8, 1964. The African griot of slavery and the slave trade, whose life represented a reenactment of those experiences, echoing as well the characteristics of the trickster and the Shango figure, proceeded to go well beyond symbolism in his embrace of pan-Africanism. That is, with his departure from the Nation, Malcolm attempted to realize a tangible, viable, and practical engagement with the African continent, transcending the limitations of rhetoric and posturing. His strategy, the religious component of which will subsequently be examined, was twofold: to achieve Islamic orthodoxy and to become a full African person, in direct contact with African leaders and involved in their struggles, in exchange for which he sought assistance in the fight against racism in North America. To these ends, Malcolm again set out for Africa and the Middle East. By the end of his travels, he would have acquired an honorific title and a new name, *al-ḥājjī Omowale*, literally meaning

---

[41] See Breitman, *By Any Means Necessary*, 147–48. As additional examples from the same edited volume, see the rest of the November 29, 1964 speech at the Audubon Ballroom (133–56), and the January 18, 1965 interview for the *Young Socialist* (157–66).

"one who made the pilgrimage (al-ḥājjī)," and "the child has come home."[42] The title and name could not have been more appropriate, conjoining Islamic prescription and Yoruba celebration. Malcolm was an Islamized Shango.

On April 13, 1964, Malcolm began a trip to Africa that included the pilgrimage.[43] After performing the ḥājj to Mecca, where he was received as a guest of the state by Saudi Prince Faisal, he flew to Beirut and Egypt and then Lagos, Nigeria on May 6, where he appeared on various television and radio programs. Addressing some 500 students at the University of Ibadan, he then traveled to Accra, Ghana, where he spoke at the university and had the honor of both addressing parliament and meeting with President Kwame Nkrumah. His thirty-ninth birthday (May 19, 1964) found him in Algiers, after brief visits to Senegal and Morocco. In less than two months following his return to New York on May 21, Malcolm was again Africa bound. He left on July 9 for Cairo, where he attended the first and second African Summit Conferences on July 17 and August 21 as the representative of his own organization, the OAAU, its American chapter founded on June 28 and patterned after the Organization of African Unity, further evidence of the profound impact of the initial 1964 African trip. Meeting heads of state, Malcolm also spoke to hundreds of students, some 600 in Alexandria followed by an equal number in Addis Ababa, Ethiopia in early October. By mid-October he was in Dar es Salaam, where he met with the Kenyan President and "Spear of the Nation," the legendary Jomo Kenyatta, after which he was received by Milton Obote, President of Uganda. Returning to Lagos in late October, Malcolm had become a student of African internal affairs; he would remain in Africa until his return to New York on November 24. Malcolm had spent nearly five months in Africa during his second tour, and, together with his first trip, he had spent half of 1964 in Africa and the Middle East. Not that his former pronouncements were ever merely lip service; it was now obvious that Malcolm had come full circle and had succeeded in reversing the direction of the slaver, reconnecting in fundamental, irrevocable ways. When, at the American founding rally of the OAAU on June 28, 1964 Malcolm stated, "There are more Africans in Harlem than exist in any city on the African continent. Because that's what you and I are – Africans," he was claiming an identity shaped by experiences beyond those encountered in the Nation, driven by an imperative in operation long before he had ever heard of Elijah Muhammad.[44] So considerable had Malcolm's interactions with African governments become that officials within the American government seriously contemplated charging him with violating the Logan Act, by which it was illegal for American citizens to seek to influence foreign governments' policies toward the United States.[45] With such extensive contacts and

[42] See Strickland, *Make It Plain*, 155.
[43] See Carson, *Malcolm X: The FBI File*, 57–87, who provides a useful chronology of events. Also see the *Autobiography*, 323–72.
[44] See Breitman, *By Any Means Necessary*, 37–38.
[45] See Carson, *Malcolm X: The FBI File*, 298–99.

notoriety throughout the African world, Malcolm had become even more dangerous, a growing threat to the forces of imperialism. He was a long way from Omaha.

Upon leaving the Nation, Malcolm filed the certificate of incorporation for his Muslim Mosque, Incorporated on March 16, 1964, shortly before the founding of the OAAU. The two organizations worked in tandem, corresponding to both Malcolm's faith and his recognition that not all black folk were going to convert to Islam. While Malcolm's followers were therefore drawn to him for different reasons, there was a seamless quality to the way in which he himself approached politics and religion. For him, they were inseparable, and, if anything, his allegiance to the African world may have been paramount. Malcolm's commitment to the black struggle was certainly no less important than his personal beliefs. McCloud has borrowed concepts from the Islamic world to characterize Malcolm's creation of the two organizations as an attempt to reconcile two warring principles: *'aṣabīyah* ("cohesiveness") an idea introduced by Ibn Khaldūn and recontextualized to represent African American Muslim efforts at nation-building across a wide spectrum of the African-derived community; and the *ummah*, the specifically Muslim community that spanned ethnic, racial, and national differences.[46]

While moved by his post-Nation experiences to abandon the position that whites were devils, Malcolm, it should be remembered, never abandoned his nationalist and pan-Africanist ideologies. His focus remained black people, who constituted the preoccupation of both the Muslim Mosque and the OAAU. Even in launching the Muslim Mosque, Malcolm was explicit in his explanation that its economic, political, and social philosophy would be guided by black nationalism.[47] The need to provide a space for non-Muslims led to the OAAU, its first chapter actually formed on Ghanian soil in May of 1964.[48] With its founding, Malcolm's entire orientation shifted to one of emphasizing international cooperation; his African pilgrimages had made him even more aware of the linkages between oppressed populations, and he now advocated a common cause between the African American struggle and the anticolonial one. Flush with the early successes of such independent states as Morocco, Tunisia, and Sudan (1956), Ghana (1957), various subsaharan, French-held colonies (1958–61), and Algeria (1962), Malcolm sought to emulate their achievements by first identifying areas in which he could cooperate with civil rights and other black organizations, although he remained critical of nonviolence as a liberatory tactic.[49]

[46] See Aminah Beverly McCloud, *African American Islam* (New York and London: Routledge, 1995), 1–5. On Ibn Khaldūn, see *Kitāb al-ibar wa-dīwān al-mubtada' wa'l-khabar*, 6 vols. (Beirut: Dār al-Kitāb al-Lubnānī, 1956–59); _____, *The Muqaddimah. An Introduction to History*, trans. Franz Rosenthal, 3 vols. (Princeton, NJ: Princeton U. Press, 1967); _____, *Histoire des Berbères*, 4 vols., trans. Bn. M. De Slane, new ed. Paul Casanova (Paris: Paul Geuthner, 1968–69).

[47] See Carson, *Malcolm X: The FBI File*, 260–63.

[48] Ibid., 34.

[49] Ibid., 291–92.

Having modeled the OAAU after its African namesake, Malcolm declared that its philosophy would be one of "alignment with Africa." Underscoring his belief in the right to self-defense and related to his advocacy of black rifle clubs, Malcolm issued further indication that he intended to pattern the domestic struggle after that of Africa's by observing that blacks in the United States needed a "Mau Mau," a reference to the brutal guerrilla war in Kenya between colonialists and the Land and Freedom Army in 1952–56.[50] Demonstrating an acute understanding of the nature of the African diaspora, Malcolm determined that membership in the OAAU would not be limited to the United States but would encompass the entire hemisphere:

Once we saw what they [African countries and the OAU] were able to do, we determined to try and do the same thing here in America among Afro-Americans who have been divided by our enemies. So we have formed an organization known as the Organization of Afro-American Unity which has the same aim and objective – to fight whoever gets in our way, to bring about the complete independence of people of African descent here in the Western Hemisphere, and first here in the United States, and bring about the freedom of these people by any means necessary. That's our motto. We want freedom by any means necessary....

So the purpose of the Organization of Afro-American Unity is to unite everyone in the Western Hemisphere of African descent into one united force. And then, once we are united among ourselves in the Western Hemisphere, we will unite with our brothers on the motherland, on the continent of Africa.[51]

Malcolm used a language of inclusion transcending cultural differences and arbitrary political boundaries:

Many of us fool ourselves into thinking of Afro-Americans as those only who are in the United States. America is North America, Central America, and South America. Anybody of African ancestry in South America is an Afro-American. Anybody in Central America of African blood is an Afro-American. Anybody here in North America, including Canada, is an Afro-American if he has African ancestry – even down in the Caribbean, he's an Afro-American.[52]

Garvey's influence is clear. In turning away from Elijah Muhammad, Malcolm was becoming more of his own man, a man who looked philosophically and stunningly like his own, biological father, the Garveyite from Georgia. In the Audubon Ballroom on November 29, 1964, he made it plain:

You waste your time involving yourself in any kind of organization that is not directly connected with our brothers and sisters on the African continent.... Just as a strong China has produced a respected Chinaman, a strong Africa will produce a respected black man anywhere that black man goes on this earth. It's only with a strong Africa,

---

[50] Ibid., 308, 480–81.
[51] See Breitman, *By Any Means Necessary*, 37–38. Comments were made at the Audubon Ballroom, June 28, 1964.
[52] See Perry, *Malcolm X: The Last Speeches*, 152. The speech was delivered at Corn Mill Methodist Church, Rochester, NY, February 16, 1965.

an independent Africa and a respected Africa that wherever those of African origin or African heritage or African likeness go, they will be respected.[53]

In becoming his own original man, Malcolm was connecting to his ancestral origins.

There is no question that Malcolm's plan to bring the United States government before the United Nations, and thereby transform the debate from civil rights to human rights, was a source of concern for the United States. However, the threat of exposure before the United Nations was not the primary source of anxiety; it was the implications of such a development that inspired the true fear. Had Malcolm been able to garner the backing of independent African nations for which he lobbied, it would have meant the dawn of a new era, the realization of a pan-African political project on American soil, in full view of the African American community.[54] There, in New York City, a conflict largely framed as a domestic issue would have been incorporated into a much larger struggle on a global scale, and the African in America would have perhaps understood for the first time the efficacy of waging concomitant war against Jim Crow and apartheid. Malcolm had gone far beyond a discussion of mother planes and moon people. His influence and reach were now global, a very dangerous maturation of potential indeed.

* * *

Malcolm, after leaving the Nation, was becoming his own man, but until the day of his assassination he never quite got there. His life as a minister in the Nation had been an integral part of who he was, and it would continue to influence his way of thinking and world view. Indeed, it would have been impossible for him to have reviewed everything he had learned and come to believe in the brief amount of time (less than a year) between his departure from the Nation and his assassination. While attempting to fashion a movement outside of the Nation, Malcolm maintained a number of conceptual and emotional tethers to it, ties that were never completely severed.

Much has been written about the nature and circumstances of Malcolm's withdrawal from Elijah Muhammad and the Nation of Islam, some of it pure speculation. That discussion will be reengaged at this point, albeit briefly, as it is unavoidably connected to the issue of the migration of significant numbers from heterodoxy to orthodoxy. Essentially, the perspective here is that while Minister Malcolm probably did not plan to attempt the removal of Elijah Muhammad from leadership of the Nation, in all likelihood he saw himself as the logical successor. Concerns within the inner circle of Mr. Muhammad's Chicago headquarters were therefore not simply based on jealousy and envy, but more importantly were fed by anxieties over the practical meaning of a Malcolm-led Nation. The crisis over Mr. Muhammad's numerous relationships

---

[53] See Breitman, *By Any Means Necessary*, 136.
[54] Ibid., 153.

with women and the children issuing from those relationships created the climate within which these tensions bubbled to the surface. In the end Malcolm, forced out of the Nation, remained its reluctant adversary to his death.

Tensions over Malcolm's meteoric rise can be traced back at least to 1959, some seven years after his release from the penitentiary. Several days after Malcolm left the country for Egypt on July 5, Mike Wallace ran the first of a five-part series entitled "The Hate That Hate Produced," a documentary polemic informed by the research of black veteran journalist Louis E. Lomax. Constituting the country's formal introduction to the Nation's existence, the program initially aired on a local New York City television station. News of its content quickly spread to other parts of the country. When Malcolm returned from abroad on July 22, he was greeted by the rebroadcasting of the hour-long feature and the firestorm accompanying it. Civil rights leaders predictably condemned the Nation for its antiwhite stance, but elements within the Nation's leadership were alarmed over the disproportionately greater coverage given Malcolm relative to the Messenger. It was the beginning of a process by which Malcolm received far more media attention, which worked to raise the Nation's visibility and thus increase the number of recruits, but ultimately militated against Malcolm's personal safety as his emergence correspondingly elevated levels of insecurity. Give Malcolm's high oratory and magnetic character, conflict was inevitable.[55]

Malcolm's profile only continued to climb. As minister of New York City's Temple No. 7, Malcolm sought to spread the Nation's message through both spoken and printed word. *Muhammad Speaks*, the newspaper he was responsible for launching in 1960, became the official publication of the Nation after such failed experiments as *The Islamic News* and *The Messenger Magazine*. Crisscrossing the nation, Malcolm electrified his audiences with his speeches, such that his evangelization efforts were a major reason for the dramatic increase in the Nation's membership. While membership is difficult to quantify, the early 1960s may have witnessed a count as high as 250,000, with more conservative estimates placing the figure at 20,000.[56] As far as Malcolm was concerned, he was responsible for increasing the membership one hundredfold, from 400 to 40,000.[57] Unaccounted for, of course, are the thousands (if not millions) who agreed with Malcolm, who enthusiastically received his message, and who regarded him as a leader while never formally joining his organization. In sum, it is irrefutable that Malcolm's ministry was the primary reason for the Nation's rapid rise in the seven years between 1957 and 1964.

The rupture of late 1963 could not have been avoided. Rivalries common to most organizations had by then been exacerbated by government plants inside the Nation, agents of internal dissension who promoted the most invidious

---

[55] See Evanzz, *The Messenger*, 193–202; Clegg, *An Original Man*, 118–36; *Autobiography*, 240–64.

[56] See Clegg, *An Original Man*, 114–15.

[57] See *Autobiography*, 417.

interpretations of Malcolm's motives.[58] The dual governance system established by Mr. Muhammad, by which New York mosque assistant ministers reported to Malcolm (and he to Mr. Muhammad), while Fruit of Islam members reported to East Coast director Captain Joseph, who, in turn, answered to Supreme Captain Raymond Sharrieff in Chicago (and not to Malcolm), suggests that Mr. Muhammad himself was not completely at ease with Malcolm's potential. Indeed, Malcolm would have been very aware of the implications of the dual chain of command, as his efforts to remove Captain Joseph from No. 7 were rebuffed in Chicago.[59]

Thus, the stage was set for tragedy, and the opportunity came with news of Mr. Muhammad's affairs and children out of wedlock. After the smoke cleared, at least seven women, all personal secretaries to the Messenger, and thirteen children were involved in multiple arrangements, defended by loyalists as an expression of Mr. Muhammad's prerogative to maintain four wives (and possibly concubines?).[60] Evanzz, on the basis of government surveillance, has detailed a most sordid, even salacious account of these developments, a story of love nests and serial pregnancies and rumor mills and demands for child support payments and the anguish of Elijah's wife, Sister Clara, who had become "sick of being treated like a dog."[61] Malcolm's response to these events appears to have slowly formed over time; while it is probable that he had caught wind of the rumors at some point in the 1950s, his allegiance to the Messenger and devotion to the message appear to have precluded him from putting much stock in the allegations. He seems to have been unable to seriously entertain the possibility of such scandal.

The atmosphere surrounding the 1963 Saviour's Day celebration in Chicago was the catalyst that forced Malcolm to pay greater attention to the rumors. Suffering from bronchial asthma, Mr. Muhammad was unable to leave his Phoenix residence, leaving Malcolm to officiate. It was at this time that Wallace Muhammad personally informed Malcolm of his father's indiscretions, triggering Malcolm's own discreet investigation into the matter. Contacting several of the women involved, he came to the realization that most had become secretaries to Mr. Muhammad through his own recommendations. Faced with such evidence, Malcolm's enormous disappointment was predictable. His own life, after his redemption from the grave, had been beyond reproach in response to the Messenger's teachings. The inconsistency of the Messenger's lived example must have been a huge blow to Malcolm, a kind of trauma, so much so that he believed his brain was hemorrhaging.[62]

The larger context of the 1963 Saviour's Day event – the growing jealousy and resentment toward Malcolm by the Chicago inner circle, the surge of the

---

[58] See Evanzz, *The Messenger*; Carson, *Malcolm X: The FBI File*.
[59] See Karim, *Remembering Malcolm*, 72; Perry, *Malcolm*, 217.
[60] See Clegg, *An Original Man*, 185.
[61] See Evanzz, *The Messenger*, 214–308; also see Clegg, *An Original Man*, 184–205.
[62] See *Autobiography*, 309–10.

civil rights movement and its direct and dramatic confrontation with a tangible, virulent racism in contrast to the Nation's nonengagement (exemplified by its failure to respond to the murder of Ronald X Stokes and the assault on its Los Angeles mosque in April of 1962), and the pace of decolonization worldwide, especially in Africa – suggests that Malcolm was not simply responding to rumors of infidelity but had become frustrated by the absence of concrete action. His very decision to investigate the rumors by interviewing several secretaries rather than first going to Mr. Muhammad is instructive in that it represents an initial fissure in his faith in Mr. Muhammad.

But it was only a fissure. The fact that Malcolm had already formulated a plan to address the crisis and salvage Mr. Muhammad's leadership may or may not mean he had been convinced of the latter's guilt from his own investigation, but it certainly indicates he intended to be prepared. His effort to protect the Messenger is clear evidence of his firm allegiance, but it was not necessarily devoid of self-interest; in the month's time between Saviour's Day and his meeting with Mr. Muhammad, it would have surely dawned on Malcolm that a scandal as sweeping as this would not only sink the Messenger but everyone associated with him. It was therefore in Malcolm's own interest to place as efficacious a spin as possible on what would have otherwise been seen as yet another instance of the perfidious behavior for which ministers were notorious.

In April, therefore, Malcolm met with the Messenger in Phoenix to discuss the scandal and "ended up," as Clegg has aptly put it, "proposing a plan to cover up Muhammad's indiscretions by shrouding them in biblical allegories." That is, Malcolm was prepared to begin a careful process of apprizing key ministers of the circumstances, instructing them to explain developments as the "fulfillment of prophecy." The Messenger applauded Malcolm's insight into the realm of the oracular, and went on to suggest that his transgressions had been foreshadowed by those of David and Noah. Little did Malcolm realize that in trying to save Mr. Muhammad, he was initiating a catastrophic sequence of events. Mr. Muhammad may have been the offender, but Malcolm would be the sacrificial lamb.[63]

Malcolm, believing he had Mr. Muhammad's approval to broach these matters to key officials, began to do just that. Much turns on precisely what Malcolm said to the East Coast ministers and precisely how he said it, especially in the case of the Boston temple leader, Louis Farrakhan (Louis X at the time). To discuss the sexual life of the Messenger with ministers deeply loyal to him carried tremendous risk in and of itself; a slip of the tongue, an ambiguous phrase, an inflection of the voice, a facial expression and suggestive body language – all could have individually or collectively further disquieted the ministers, raising doubts about Malcolm's motives. That Malcolm may have been organizing some palace coup seems unlikely, as such an effort would not have been supported by the rank-and-file and would have plunged the Nation

[63] Ibid., 298–99; also see Clegg, *An Original Man*, 191–92.

into internecine conflict. That his efforts were represented to Mr. Muhammad as such probably owes more to existing jealousies and rivalries, while others were anxious to shore up their positions at his expense.[64]

Malcolm's reaction to the assassination of John F. Kennedy on November 22, 1963 was the proverbial straw that broke the camel's back. Mr. Muhammad, gauging the popularity of the president and the depth of sorrow over his death, specifically instructed his ministers to limit their comments about the event to expressions of sympathy. Malcolm, when pressed to state his personal feelings on December 1, issued his famous chickens coming home to roost statement. The quintessential pan-Africanist, Malcolm had long been a supporter of struggle against empire, and he had long decried the murder of such individuals as Lumumba. His defiance was not only consistent with a predilection to speak his own mind but was also a deliberate choice to take an unequivocal stand that, uttered on such a historic occasion, would long be remembered.

The egregious nature of Malcolm's offense was underscored by his recall to Chicago the following day, at which point he was notified by the Messenger of his ninety-day suspension, barring him from public speaking.[65] The suspension was made public on December 4, at which point the anti-Malcolm faction gained greater influence and progressively seized control of events. Malcolm X confidant Benjamin Karim provides a glimpse into the growing hostility:

I was in the temple when the call from Chicago came through. We were told that if Malcolm came back to the temple after the suspension, we should give him a job washing dishes in the restaurant.[66]

One month later, on January 2, 1964, Mr. Muhammad's government-recorded telephone call to Malcolm (listened to by two other Nation officials) reveals that a critical juncture had been reached in the crisis between the Messenger and his minister, in that the most salient issues of the day were placed on the table, indicating that they had been conjoined in Mr. Muhammad's mind and clearly understood by him as interrelated. The matter of Malcolm's December 1 pronouncement, the existence of jealousies and ill-feelings toward him by elements in the leadership, and the issue of Mr. Muhammad's sexual affairs came together in a striking reprimand of Malcolm; in particular, Mr. Muhammad now accused Malcolm of helping to promote the spread of the scandal rather than suppressing it, a very different characterization of Malcolm's role than what had been originally envisioned in the April 1963 meeting. Malcolm's contrite posture did nothing to avert the Messenger's decision to extend the suspension indefinitely, nor did it derail Malcolm's January 6 trial in Phoenix before Mr. Muhammad, John Ali, and Raymond Sharrief, at which Malcolm was dressed

---

[64] See Karim, *Remembering Malcolm*, 152–54; Evanzz, *The Messenger*, 265–69; Clegg, *An Original Man*, 191–95. Perry (*Malcolm*, 234–44) supports the view that Malcolm's contact with the East Coast ministers was his "opening gambit" for power.

[65] See *Autobiography*, 301–02.

[66] See Karim, *Remembering Malcolm*, 156.

FIGURE 6. Muhammad Ali at a Nation of Islam gathering, with Elijah Muhammad at the podium and Louis X in the background.

down and instructed to "go back and put out the fire you started," a reference to his attempts to apprize the East Coast ministers of the impending scandal. In the meantime, Mosque No. 7 in New York was placed under Captain Joseph, while James Shabazz was transferred from the Newark mosque to Mosque No. 7. Malcolm, stripped of power, pledged fealty.[67]

In approximately nine months (April of 1963 to January of 1964), relations between Malcolm and the Messenger suffered from the pressures of scandal and national visibility, in the face of which factional disputes required some resolution. By February of 1964, the disintegration was all but irreversible, as three new factors came into play. The first was the Messenger's rejection of Malcolm's appeal for reinstatement. The second was the order given to explosives expert Ana M. Luqman to wire Malcolm's car to explode upon ignition, an attempt that failed as a result of Luqman's decision to disclose the plot to Malcolm. The third factor was the rise of Muhammad Ali (see Figure 6), who as Cassius Clay defeated Sonny Liston for the heavyweight championship of the world on February 25. The bombing plot alerted Malcolm to the fact that his death was planned at the highest levels of the Nation (though the

---

[67] See *Autobiography*, 305–09; Clegg, *An Original Man*, 202–09; Evanzz, *The Messenger*, 274–82.

Messenger himself was probably not suspect in Malcolm's eyes, at least not at this time), while Ali's victory gave Mr. Muhammad a new star, another powerful drawing card, contributing to Malcolm's expendability. The Messenger seized the opportunity and quickly renamed Clay at the Saviour's Day convention, immediately bestowing upon him his divine name rather than a simple X. At the Messenger's insistence on March 6, Ali ended his friendship with Malcolm. Two days later, Malcolm formally broke with the Messenger.[68]

It would appear that both Malcolm and the Messenger went their separate ways with great reluctance. Malcolm, for his part, continued to publicly state his support for Elijah Muhammad, even stating that members of the Nation should remain there. Careful to locate the source of enmity with high officials rather than Mr. Muhammad, Malcolm stated for the record that certain "national officials" in Chicago and New York were behind the campaign to push him out of the organization.[69] His wife, Sister Betty, was also convinced of the intrigue:

As far as Malcolm's suspension from the movement was concerned, if it hadn't happened because of the remarks he is supposed to have made about John Kennedy, it would have occurred for some other reason. Malcolm was told two years before this happened that they were trying to get rid of him. . . . Certain people in the movement felt that he had gotten too big, that he was trying to get a power base for himself.[70]

No matter how high his regard for his spiritual father, Malcolm could not vegetate indefinitely. The global struggle and his personal commitment to it were such that he had to move on, and as early as his March 8 announcement he alluded to establishing a black nationalist organization that would seek to cooperate with the civil rights movement. Still, the thought of what could have been rankled him as late as June of 1964: "Every time I think of how those niggers threw me out of the NOI [Nation of Islam]," he divulged, "I get mad."[71]

For someone consciously creating conditions that would make it intolerable for Malcolm to remain in the Nation, the Messenger's reaction to Malcolm's announcement is rather inexplicable. It was above all visceral; he was personally and deeply wounded. Surprised and stunned, Mr. Muhammad wept in public, expressing his dismay: "I never dreamed this man would deviate from the Nation of Islam." It is probable, therefore, that while those around him may have had serious reservations, Mr. Muhammad remained convinced of Malcolm's fundamental loyalty, and perhaps he hoped for reconciliation once Malcolm had been sufficiently disciplined. His well-publicized departure changed all that, and it was used as evidence by Malcolm's detractors that they had been right all along. From dismay, the Messenger quickly moved to anger, almost immediately condemning Malcolm as a "hypocrite," one of the most

---

[68] See *Autobiography*, 302–09; Clegg, *An Original Man*, 208–13; Evanzz, *The Messenger*, 284–88; Karim, *Remembering Malcolm*, 160–61. Both Karim and Evanzz identify Captain Joseph as the one who ordered the hit (through Luqman) on Malcolm.

[69] See Clegg, *An Original Man*, 212–14; Breitman, *Malcolm X Speaks*, 20.

[70] See Betty Shabazz, "Malcolm as a Husband and Father," in Clarke, *Malcolm X*, 139.

[71] See Carson, *Malcolm X*, 471.

severe pronouncements possible, as it evoked Mr. Muhammad's early difficulties with rivals who were likewise branded. From that point on, peril, already a constant companion, became for Malcolm his most intimate associate.[72]

* * *

Malcolm lived for a little less than a year following his resignation from the Nation; little time was left to embark on an independent path to reengage the struggle for people of African descent in the United States and elsewhere. Critical to that struggle was a reformation of faith, a reembrace of Islam, that would establish him as his own person. It was logical that Malcolm would pursue orthodoxy, but more than logic was involved.

Students of early West African history, in reading about the break between Malcolm X and Elijah Muhammad, will immediately think of its similarities (and differences) with developments in imperial Songhay, as in both instances the transition from heterodoxy to orthodoxy was central to events, and in both cases the consequences were far reaching. Regarding imperial Songhay, the reign of Sunni 'Ali (reg. 1464–92) was characterized by tremendous antagonism between his court at Gao, located toward the eastern buckle of the Niger River, and the community of scholars and merchants in Timbuktu, the commercial center of the empire and slightly north of the Niger's western buckle. The chroniclers of Songhay's history, Muslim scholars with familial and social ties to Timbuktu elites, portray Sunni 'Ali as a tyrannical figure and a prosecutor of Muslims, whose own profession of Islam was seriously compromised by both his continuing adherence to Songhay indigenous religion and by his poor understanding of and failure to properly observe Islamic practices.[73] A closer examination of the record demonstrates that Sunni 'Ali was not necessarily anti-Islamic but was in fact adversarial toward certain families with ties to the Tuareg, powerful Arabo-Berber communities in the Sahara who threatened his control of Timbuktu. In lieu of such families, Sunni 'Ali elevated and patronized other Muslim clerics. His policies were not working, however, as the extensive dislocations of premier families led to momentary commercial decline.

Into this picture strode Muhammad Ture, a high official in the government of Sunni 'Ali and one entrusted with the security of the overland corridor connecting Gao and Timbuktu. It would appear that Muhammad Ture was recruited by disgruntled Timbuktu elites; in any event, he led a coup d'état against the Sunni dynasty, an effort that ended with the death (probably assassination) of Sunni 'Ali and the ousting of his legitimate successor, Sunni Baro, from power by means of a legally declared jihād. Muhammad Ture went on to establish the

---

[72] See Clegg, *An Original Man*, 213–14; Evanzz, *The Messenger*, 287–93.

[73] See 'Abd al-Rahmān b. 'Abd Allāh al-Sa'dī, *Ta'rīkh al-Sūdān*, ed. and trans. O. Houdas (Paris: Librairie d'Amérique et d'Orient Adrien-Maisonneuve, 1900); Ibn al-Mukhtār, *Ta'rīkh al-Fattāsh*, ed. and trans. O. Houdas and M. Delaffose (Paris: Librairie d'Amérique et d'Orient Adrien-Maisonneuve, 1913). For an English translation of *Ta'rīkh al-Sūdān*, see John Hunwick, *Timbuktu and the Songhay Empire* (Leiden: Brill, 1999).

Askia dynasty, but his usurpation meant that he needed to shift the basis of Songhay power from ancestral religion and royal lineage to the *baraka* or communicable spiritual power of the ḥajj. Thus, Askia Muhammad almost immediately went on pilgrimage, a process that could take years and was fraught with political insecurity. When he returned, Askia al-ḥājj Muhammad embarked on a series of reforms that saw the creation of Islamic courts and a more extensive implementation of sharī'a (Islamic law) throughout the empire (but centered in urban areas). He returned to power those families who had suffered under Sunni 'Ali, a move that resulted in the economic prosperity of the entrepot. Askia al-ḥājj Muhammad's reforms were so significant that Songhay acquired an Islamic identity during the sixteenth century. In contrast to their treatment of Sunni 'Ali, Songhay chroniclers lauded Askia al-ḥājj Muhammad, and his reign served as an example to reform-minded Muslim rulers throughout West Africa, especially in what is now northern Nigeria, where imperial Songhay under Askia al-ḥājj Muhammad was an important model for the jihād and subsequent theocracy of Usuman dan Fodio in the early nineteenth century.

By way of analogy, Sunni 'Ali prefigures Elijah Muhammad in that they both represented a form of Islam at odds with the larger orthodox world. In both instances, a brand of Islam was adopted that was deliberately interstitial, attempting to reconcile the principal tenets of Sunni Islam with the traditions and folkways of their constituencies. Both men would be accused of violating the moral codes of Islam, and both would eventually be opposed by trusted lieutenants, who would go on to capture the imagination of the Muslim world and be credited with bringing about sorely needed reform. The fact that Elijah Muhammad was the one to survive the conflict with Malcolm X, as opposed to the victory of Askia al-ḥājj Muhammad over Sunni 'Ali, is a major disruption in the analogy's progression, but it does not alter the view that, in both cases, Sunni Islam is ultimately the victor, and that as a result of the efforts of Askia al-ḥājj Muhammad and al-ḥājj Malik al-Shabazz (Malcolm X).

There is another, critical similarity between the calculations of the late fifteenth century and those of the twentieth. Like Askia al-ḥājj Muhammad, Malcolm made the ḥajj (in April and May of 1964, almost immediately after leaving the Nation) because he needed a new legitimating mechanism. It was not enough to be an intellectual and a gifted orator. He required spiritual sanction, and he achieved it by shifting from the now-useless anointing of Elijah Muhammad to the baraka of the pilgrimage.

Malcolm's detractors aver that he understated his prior knowledge of and experience with orthodox Islam, while in the Nation, in an effort to create distance from Elijah Muhammad and to establish a currency of communication with both the civil rights leadership and the larger Muslim world.[74] According to this view, it was Wallace Muhammad, Elijah's son, who in his rebellious

---

[74] See, for example, Adib Rashad (James Miller), *Elijah Muhammad and the Ideological Foundation of the Nation of Islam* (Hampton, VA: United Brothers and United Sisters Communications Systems, 1984), 15–34.

stage tutored Malcolm in the ways of orthodoxy long before the latter's official break.[75] There is undoubtedly truth in such qualifications, but it is probably reaching too far to suggest that the ḥajj was any less transforming than Malcolm represented it to be. Locating recuperative strength in his African connections, Malcolm had been encouraged to make the pilgrimage by the Sudanese shaykh Ahmed Hassoun and the Egyptian (or Yemeni) Dr. Mahmoud Youssef Shawarbi, and in the battle for preeminence between Egypt and Saudi Arabia he was courted by the latter.[76] Following his sister Ella's example of replacing Fardian Islam with its Sunni version, Malcolm also accepted her offer to pay for the trip. Once in Arabia, Malcolm regretted his failure to learn the proper procedures for performing ṣalāt (prayer), or for properly performing the obligatory ablutions, or for not knowing how to pray in Arabic (did he even know the *Fātiḥa*, the first sūra or chapter in the Qur'ān?).[77] Once in Mecca, his senses, emotions, and intellect were overtaken by the enormity of the experience:

> In my thirty-nine years on this earth, the Holy City of Mecca had been *the first time* I had *ever* stood before the Creator of All and felt like a *complete human being*.[78] [italics added]

Oft-repeated, the aforementioned quote is very significant. That Malcolm had never experienced such affirmation, had never seen himself in this way though all the while proclaiming his humanity, indeed, his superiority, gives great pause, and it cannot be overdramatized.

Malcolm's gravitation to the realm of the orthodox produced immediate results. Although difficult if not impossible to substantiate, the estimate by Karim is that a third of the Nation's national membership left with him, and that a third of New York City's Mosque No. 7 followed him as well.[79] His ties to the *dār al-Islām* deepening, Malcolm would receive twenty scholarships for African American Muslims to study at the prestigious al-Azhar University in Cairo.[80] His travels throughout Africa and parts of the Muslim world, already described, provided him with the kind of international visibility commensurate with his political commitments. While officials in the Nation were busy with their businesses and venal pursuits, Malcolm was actively fashioning a consistency of character and commitment.

Malcolm's entry into orthodoxy would be the signal event in the movement of thousands of others, over time, into the same habitation. To be sure, the successes of the civil rights movement, the growing sophistication of the

---

[75] See, for example, El-Amin, *Afrocentricity: Malcolm X and Al-Islam*, 46–47.

[76] Edward E. Curtis IV, *Islam in Black America: Identity, Liberation, and Difference in African-American Islamic Thought* (Albany: State U. of New York Press, 2002), 92–96 (and Rummel, *Malcolm X*, 95), identifies Youssef Shawarbi as an Egyptian but one allied with the Saudis.

[77] See *Autobiography*, 323–47; De Caro, *On the Side of My People*, 200–42.

[78] See *Autobiography*, 372.

[79] See Karim, *Remembering Malcolm*, 160–61.

[80] See Carson, *Malcolm X*, 296.

FIGURE 7. Malcolm X.

African-derived community, the death of Elijah Muhammad in February of
1975, and an increased presence of immigrant Muslims in the United States
all helped to encourage conversion to Sunni Islam from both the Fardian
tradition as well as from beliefs unrelated to Islam. But as a reenactment of
the African experience of enslavement in America, as a trickster and Shango

figure, as the recoverer of family, and as a champion of pan-Africanism, Malcolm's self-presentation established a compelling model that would long be emulated by many (see Figure 7). Indeed, had there been no Malcolm, Fardian Islam's ascendent position vis-à-vis conventional Islam may well have continued indefinitely.

* * *

While Malcolm may have undergone a religious transformation, it is clear that many of his political views were the same and that he still held psychological and emotional ties to the Nation. For example, his critique of nonviolence at a Paris meeting in November of 1964 includes language that would suggest the Nation's teaching on white "tricknology" continued to reverberate. Speaking on the anti-Apartheid struggle in South Africa, he made this comment:

But at the same time the enemy knows that once eleven million people stop being confined to a nonviolent approach against three million, you're going to have a different situation. They had to use their *new modern tricks*, so they ran down and got one of the Africans and gave him a glorious peace prize for being nonviolent, and it lent strength to the nonviolent image.... And it's the same way in the States. The black man in the States has begun to see that nonviolence *is a trick* that is put upon him to keep him from even being able to defend himself.[81] [italics added]

Regarding black nationalism, the Nation's influence is apparent in remarks made during the same meeting:

I see the time when the black culture will be the dominant culture and when the black man will be the dominant man. And nobody should be against the black man being the dominant man. He's been dominated. I don't think that if we allow ourselves to be dominated it's wrong to pass the ball around once in a while.[82]

Malcolm may no longer have regarded whites as devils, but his nationalism remained intact, as Sister Betty made clear:

Many people base this on his denunciation of racism and they misinterpret this statement to mean that he now endorsed the principles of integration as a solution to America's racial dilemma.[83]

Indeed, the continuity of Malcolm's thought engendered in the Nation of Islam was a source of frustration and disappointment for orthodox Muslims.[84]

As for the psychic tethers, Malcolm made the depth of his devotion to Mr. Muhammad transparent while conversing in a Harlem restaurant with Louis Lomax and C. Eric Lincoln. The latter made this recollection:

In the course of this conversation Lomax, who wrote the book on Muslims called *When the Word is Given*, said to Malcolm, he said, "Look, Malcolm, why don't you stop all

[81] See Breitman, *By Any Means Necessary*, 114.
[82] Ibid., 117–18.
[83] See Betty Shabazz, "Malcolm as a Husband and Father," in Clarke, *Malcolm X*, 141.
[84] See De Caro, *On the Side of My People*, 253–54.

that Mr. Muhammad shit? Why don't you start your own movement and lead your own movement? You got the brains," and so on and so forth. And Malcolm leaped up from the table as if he had been stuck with a hat pin – I had never seen a man so furious – as if he was going to attack Mr. Lomax on the spot, but we were all friends, and he said, "Lou Lomax, don't you *ever* say that to me again. Mr. Muhammad is responsible for everything that I am today. He brought me from nowhere to where I am and as long as I live I will be loyal to him, and I don't want to hear that anymore!"[85]

The sentiment is entirely consistent with Malcolm's emotional response to the entry of the Messenger into a filled auditorium:

Tears would be in more eyes than mine. He had rescued me when I was a convict; Mr. Muhammad had trained me in his home, as if I was his son.[86]

The loss that Malcolm must have felt upon being forced out of the Nation, and his abiding love for the Messenger, is confirmed by the testimony of associate Charles Kenyatta:

I think I'm one of the only ones – in fact, I know I'm one of the only ones – that detected his hurt. And he was going to be, if you could understand how the Nation of Islam was when a member was put out of the mosque. Oh, I've seen older men cry and weep, because they didn't want to go back into what they called the grave; and Malcolm was no different. And the whole crux of the story, I believe, is that ten or fifteen minutes before he was assassinated, if Elijah Muhammad had asked him to come back, he would have come back.[87]

The depth of Malcolm's anguish as reported by Kenyatta is affirmed by brother Wilfred's recollection:

When he broke with Elijah Muhammad, he came to see me, and when he stepped off the plane, I had never seen him looking so devastated. It was as if someone close to him had died.[88]

Perhaps the most important clue to Malcolm's continuing ties to the Messenger lies in his name change following his pilgrimage. In contrast to the far lesser known or used designation "Omowale," the celebrated shift from Malcolm X to al-ḥājj Malik al-Shabazz is usually regaled as symbolic evidence of a spiritual commutation from heterodoxy to orthodoxy, from racialism to tolerance. Why Malcolm's earlier association with this name is overlooked is certainly curious, but in fact he was using the name, or a slight variant of it, almost as soon as he converted to Islam while in prison. By the spring of 1949, Malcolm was signing his letters as "Malachi Shabazz," the name under which he even penned a missive to President Truman in 1950, protesting the Korean War. When Malcolm, still in the penitentiary, made the mistake of signing Malachi Shabazz in a letter sent to Mr. Muhammad, the latter expressed his displeasure

[85] See Gallen, *Malcolm X, As They Knew Him*, 67.
[86] See *Autobiography*, 257.
[87] Ibid., 77.
[88] See Carew, *Ghosts in Our Blood*, 154–55.

that Malcolm had selected his own divine name rather than waiting for it to be revealed through Mr. Muhammad. Malcolm thereafter accepted his "X," but, in his 1963 interview with Alex Haley, he revealed that when traveling and checking into hotels, he used his "real Muslim name, Malik Shabazz." As early as 1962, Malcolm carried a briefcase that "bore in gold letters the name, Malik El Shabazz."[89]

The term *Shabazz* of course refers to the leading tribe of the original black people, a concept introduced by W. D. Fard Muhammad and foreign to Sunni Islam, while *Malachi* may have referred to the belief that a prophecy of Elijah Muhammad could be found in the Book of Malachi. What a strange way for Malcolm to declare his embrace of orthodoxy; the incorporation of *Shabazz* into his postpilgrimage appellation seems to indicate an ongoing identification with the antecedent vision. The transition from Malachi to *Malik*, which literally means "king" or "sovereign," is even more interesting – was Malcolm simply Arabicizing *Malachi*, or was he making a statement about his own aspirations? Given Malcolm's defiant use of *Malachi Shabazz*, even while in prison, was the postpilgrimage name meant to signal to Mr. Muhammad a new era of defiance? Or was the new name, which was in fact not new, deliberately chosen to send the message that Malcolm remained loyal to the Messenger and hoped for reconciliation?

* * *

Whatever the truth of Malcolm's intent, he was not in control of events. Despite his efforts to avoid conflict with Mr. Muhammad and the Nation, he was trapped in a quagmire, and he was a kind of tar baby figure. As the details of his demise have been provided elsewhere, a summary of events will suffice. Within two days of announcing his departure from the Nation on March 8, Malcolm received a letter signed by Captain Joseph and several other officials informing him that his family would have to leave their home, as it was owned by the Nation, and that he was to turn over files and other documents belonging to the organization. The pace quickened with the April 10 edition of *Muhammad Speaks*, in which Malcolm was branded a "hypocrite" and compared with Judas by his own brother Philbert X. The very next month and in June, Louis Farrakhan wrote a two-part editorial excoriating Malcolm for his "treachery," thereby establishing around him an atmosphere of imminent peril. On June 7, Malcolm responded by telling an audience of 500 people that Mr. Muhammad had fathered six illegitimate children, repeating the allegation the next day for journalist Mike Wallace of CBS. In a June 16, 1964 article in the *New York Herald Tribune*, Malcolm declared that "Muhammad was nobody until I came to New York as his emissary," and that "if they had left me alone

---

[89] See Richard Brent Turner, *Islam in the African-American Experience* (Bloomington and Indianapolis: Indiana U. Press, 1997), 188–89; Karl Evanzz, *The Judas Factor: The Plot to Kill Malcolm X* (New York: Thunder's Mouth Press, 1992), 9; Haley, *Playboy Interviews*, 40; Goodman (Karim), *End of White World Supremacy*, 13.

I would not have revealed any of this." Rethinking his strategy, Malcolm published an open letter in the June 26 edition of the *New York Post*, calling for an end to the mounting hostility. Mr. Muhammad responded by calling Malcolm a "red, no-good dog" before a meeting of the Fruit of Islam at New York City's armory. On July 6, Raymond Sharrieff's grandson Hassan called a press conference to announce his resignation from the Nation, calling his grandfather a "fake and a fraud," while Mr. Muhammad's son Wallace was also issuing condemnatory statements to the press. For his part, Malcolm again went on the offensive and persuaded two of the secretaries to be interviewed for the July 11 edition of the *Amsterdam News*. The tit-for-tat involves considerable minutiae.[90]

Encouraged by government operatives and intervention, tensions escalated and time accelerated, reaching a pinnacle with the December 4 edition of *Muhammad Speaks*, in which Louis Farrakhan described Malcolm as a "hypocritical dog." "The die is set," wrote Louis X, "and Malcolm shall not escape.... Such a man as Malcolm is worthy of death, and would have met death if it had not been for Muhammad's confidence in Allah for victory over the enemies."[91] Malcolm's house was firebombed on February 14, 1965 and he was officially evicted from the property on February 18. On February 15, at the Audubon ballroom, Malcolm broadened his critique of Elijah Muhammad, citing the latter's collusion with Georgia's Ku Klux Klan that dated back to December of 1960 and provided an exchange of land for the Nation's continued opposition to the civil rights movement. Malcolm also alleged that Elijah Muhammad was receiving significant financial support from "a rich man in Texas."[92]

With the vitriol ever mounting, words and deeds became one. Malcolm was assassinated at the Audubon on February 21, an event audiotaped by New York's finest.[93] On February 26, Wallace Muhammad appeared on the dais during the Saviour's Day convention and apologized for his "great mistake." Persons were arrested for Malcolm's murder.

* * *

Elijah Muhammad himself breathed his last on February 25, 1975. He was succeeded by his son Wallace, who in October of the following year changed the name of the organization from the Nation of Islam to the World Community of al-Islam in the West (in 1980 he would change it again to the American Muslim Mission). Embarking on a series of decentralizing moves that included disbanding the paramilitary Fruit of Islam and reorganizing the organization's finances, Imam Warith Deen Muhammad (as he would come to be known)

---

[90] See Carson, *Malcolm X*, 322–23; Perry, *Malcolm*, 288; Clegg, *An Original Man*, 214–34; Evanzz, *The Messenger*, 290–335; *Muhammad Speaks*, April 10, 1964, May 8, 1964, and June 5, 1964.
[91] See *Muhammad Speaks*, December 4, 1964.
[92] See Perry, *Malcolm X: The Last Speeches*, 122–25.
[93] See Goldman, *Death and Life of Malcolm X*, 4.

swiftly transitioned thousands of followers from the periphery to the center of Islam, changing the official teachings and practices in conformity with orthodox tenets. The predictable fallout congealed in the person of Louis Farrakhan, among others. Recalled from New York City to Chicago, Farrakhan remained subordinate until 1977–78, when he broke away to reestablish the Nation of Islam.

In developments underscoring the gravitational pull of Sunni Islam, the two leaders began traveling roads of reconciliation with the twentieth century's end. In February of 1999, the two jointly appeared at the annual Saviour's Day celebration in Chicago, a feat repeated at the second International Islamic Conference in the same city the following year. By that time, Louis Farrakhan had made significant changes in the Nation, incorporating much of orthodoxy if not completely eschewing the ideas of Elijah Muhammad, and both organizations have achieved recognition from the international Muslim community (or set of communities), especially those under Warith Deen Muhammad.

Upon taking command following his father's demise, it did not take Warith Deen Muhammad long to change the name of New York City's Mosque No. 7 to Malcolm Shabazz Temple No. 7. The change was more than fitting, as so many owe their spiritual transformation to Malcolm's personal example.

Epilogue

Several aspects of the African and African-descended Muslim experience in the Americas stand out in sharp relief. To begin, the Old World context and set of circumstances molding and impacting Muslim life in Africa and Europe continued to inform conditions in the New World and clearly influenced the ways in which the colonial project unfolded. In what became Latin America, the conflicts and enmities and politics that had evolved for nearly 1,000 years in Iberia were not quickly or easily forgotten in fifteenth- and sixteenth-century Hispaniola, Costa Rica, Puerto Rico, Mexico, Panama, Venezuela, or elsewhere within Spanish-claimed domains. The gelofes (Senegambians) and mandingas (Mande-speakers), among whom were Muslims, were suspected of harboring sustained beliefs in and affiliations with Islam, and they did not disappoint. Rebellion frequently ensued in the sixteenth and seventeenth centuries, often taking the form of marronage. Attempts to bypass these challenges through the importation of ladinos were not always successful, as many ladinos were themselves Senegambian Muslims who had worked alongside the moriscos (purported Christian Moors) in Iberia, circumstances allowing for an acculturative process unanticipated by Christian authorities. When transported to the Americas where they were joined by other Senegambians, many of whom were Muslim, they sought escape from servility, thereby developing a reputation for recalcitrance and revolt. The view of the African Muslim was therefore established by the time Mande-speakers became the predominant representation of Muslims in Spanish-claimed lands into the eighteenth and nineteenth centuries, by which time the notion of *mandinga* had been infused with every negative and evil association. While in some instances they were recognized for their special abilities with livestock, it would appear that many if not most African Muslims in Latin America suffered from a maligning stereotypic view, flowing out of a conflict hailing back to eighth-century Europe, that placed them among the lower strata of the servile estate.

Likewise, it has been argued here that developments in the Old World made some contribution to revolts in Bahia, Brazil. The nineteenth-century reformist

activities of Usuman dan Fodio in what is now northern Nigeria constituted a
large-scale political and social revolution that was seismic in its implications
for West Africa. It is clear that many captives from the Bight of Benin had been
affected by the jihād; many were participants on one side or the another. In the
captives' confrontation of their altered circumstances in Bahia, it would appear
that the response of rebellion was consistent with religiously infused militaristic ventures in West Africa; ideas and experience obtained in the latter were
no doubt called upon to wage war in the former. In this way, these so-called
malê revolts were probably much more than slave insurrections. Reinforcing
the significance of anterior influence was the exclusionary tone of the insurrectionists, a parochial prism through which potential corevolutionists were
recruited, versus the much wider universe of enemies that included not only
Portuguese slaveholders and authorities but Brazilian-born persons of African
descent as well as those African-born whose traditions were deemed antithetical
to and irreconcilable with Islam. The notion that adversaries would themselves
be enslaved suggests that slavery as an institution was not itself under assault.

To be sure, African Muslims imported into anglophone areas, both in the
Caribbean and North America, also brought with them as many of their preexisting values and perspectives as were transferable. However, the English
did not share an ancient hostility with Islam and had not been required to
wage war on their own land for hundreds of years to reacquire sovereignty.
Their receptivity to Muslims was therefore decidedly different. Muslim abilities and atypicality were celebrated, and their divergence from other Africans
was rewarded with less demanding, more highly trained vocational jobs and assignments, which necessarily contributed to the ways in which African-derived
societies were stratified. Runaway slave advertisements include Muslims, so it
is clear that many rebelled. However, Muslim participation in insurrection in
English-claimed lands is not so obvious, their contributions to revolt not at all
distinctive. Indeed, Muslims often enough enforced the status quo as drivers
and supervisors, as was true of Muhammad Kaba of Jamaica, and Bilali and
Salih Bilali in the Georgia Sea Islands. Muslims in Jamaica and Trinidad were
themselves property owners, even slaveholders. Muslim privilege was also apparent in Saint Domingue, governed by another European power without a
prolonged history of critical war with Muslim powers. The evidence suggests
that Muslims did engage in revolt against the French, and they provided some
leadership in the Haitian Revolution of 1791, but they were not necessarily
distinguished in that campaign. In all probability, they were swept away in
its massive reach. More research is required to uncover the possible Muslim
contribution to the composition of the gens de couleur, and how it may have
conditioned the response of the mixed-race buffer category to insurrection. It
is into the broader categories of race and class that such Muslims were probably absorbed, as events in Saint Domingue did not allow for the formation of
recognizable Muslim communities in the fashion of Trinidad.

The experiences of African Muslims in the anglophone world therefore often contrasted sharply with their coreligionists in the lusophone and

Spanish-speaking realms. Ethnocentric pride was also reinforced, ironically, by white preferences and racialism to form an insidious collective hubris, the echo of which reverberates to the present. However, it would be a mistake to conclude that African Muslims so privileged by the English and the Americans were totally or even fundamentally co-opted; the fact that there were repeated attempts on the part of many African Muslims to return to West Africa from both the Caribbean and North America suggests that the Americas were no haven, and that Muslim loyalties remained in the land of their birth, where life was far preferable. That many waited until the Apprenticeship period was nigh is not necessarily a cause for cynicism; that may have simply been the most opportune time to seek repatriation, given that costs associated with transporting so many back to West Africa were prohibitive, together with the dangers. Further, many Muslims, at least in Trinidad, could not have returned to West Africa before this time, as they had only been recently mustered out of the various West India Regiments. Their hearts' desires no doubt resonated with men such as Ayuba b. Sulayman and Abd ar-Rahman, for whom no amount of relative advantage in North America could avert their determination to return home in 1733 and 1829, respectively.

In places such as Trinidad and coastal Georgia during slavery, Muslims practiced their faith openly, and they enjoyed a numerically significant community. The same had been true of Bahia prior to the 1835 revolt, when reactionary forces drove the religion underground. However, it would appear that Muslims in Rio de Janeiro and possibly Alagoas were less fettered and could at least openly purchase Muslim literature. Others, such as Umar b. Said and Abd ar-Rahman of North America, or Muhammad Kaba and Abu Bakr of Jamaica, had to conceal their true beliefs, donning the cloak of Christianity as necessary artifice. Whether they did so publicly or clandestinely, there is every indication that Muslims throughout the Americas attempted a close adherence to the principal tenets of Islam, a serious pursuit that included daily prayers and ablutions, prayer mats and beads, fasting Ramadan, dietary proscriptions, sumptuary observances, high holy days, Qur'ānic instruction, and so forth.

Even so, the demographics were weighted heavily against the Muslims. Very rarely a majority except in very precise, proscribed locales, they were often simply overwhelmed by both the infusion of Africans from other traditions of the continent and by the growth of the American-born population of African descent. Competition with other African religions as well as with Christianity was intense and debilitating, even though aspects of Islam were often absorbed into other liturgical formulae, such as the lucumí or nagô traditions in Cuba and Brazil, or in the approach to Christianity in coastal Georgia. In any event, preservation of Islam's integrity in such hostile (or seductive) environments proved exceedingly difficult.

It did not help that, throughout the Americas, the transmission of Islam tended to be confined to the African-born and their families. Conversions did occur, but the promulgation of Islam was inwardly directed; it was an internal affair, steered away from non-Muslims seemingly as an organizing principle. When combined with the competition of demographics and other religions and cultures, this policy could not augur well for a sustained expression of Islam through the centuries: Islam apparently did not survive the nineteenth century throughout Latin America and Haiti. In Trinidad, a Muslim sensibility was certainly carried forward into the twentieth century; that sensibility also moved forward into early-twentieth-century Brazil, notwithstanding severe repression in Bahia following the unsuccessful nineteenth-century revolts, where there was also a cultural manifestation of Islam, a kind of performance of malê identity, extending into the latter part of the twentieth century. It is not clear to what extent Islam was actually practiced beyond the mid-twentieth century by the African-descended population in Brazil, but it would appear that its followers were relatively few in number by the 1980s.

An Islamic sensibility also transitioned into early-twentieth-century North America, specifically the United States, along with the very real possibility of Islamic practice in coastal Georgia. However, conditions within the United States, in contrast to those obtaining in the Caribbean and Brazil, would allow for a rekindling of the embers of an Islam embedded within that sensibility. That is, there were certainly those who knew that their forebears were Muslims, Moors, or both, and variations of Muslim names and customs were handed down from parent to child. The practice of orthodox Islam itself, though, had been lost in the fading memories of the aged in the faith, who, without Islamic institutions such as schools and mosques and absent access to the Qur'ān (and the clarity to read it), were unable to convey Islam to succeeding generations. The latter had a sense of their heritage, but they lacked its substance.

Social and political currents combined to give the United States its unique or distinctive character (for good or bad), and this proved the means by which those concerned with such matters were able to slowly find their way back to the core of their sensibility. In the United States, there coalesced the related (and often identical) forces of messianic religion, Freemasonry, and traditions of political protest that often enough took aim at the country's pronounced racism. In the struggle against white supremacy and black degradation, black nationalist sentiments acquired coherence, often in an idiom of religious expression. Cause and remedy were both understood to reside in holy unction, while individuals emerged throughout the landscape with visions of their own vaulted roles in the fulfilment of prophecy. There were many organizations exhibiting some or all of these elements that maintained some level of allegiance to Christian principles, while there were others that eschewed all ties to any religion. Experimentation was possible; in the myriad possible combinations of religion and politics, and in the critique of the pervasive effects of racism, there would emerge those formulations that rejected Christianity as accomplice in racial oppression while continuing to embrace the viability of religion. Islam, or some form of it, was one alternative. In contrast, it is not clear that twentieth-century Brazil – steeped in Roman Catholicism (and its variations) and in the simultaneous promotion of a mythical racial democracy, a seductive social arrangement that would have militated against the emergence of race-based nationalism among a population divided along multiple lines of varying racial admixture – or countries in the Caribbean, experiencing their own versions of nationalism, none of which involved struggles against a majority white population on the same soil, would have allowed for the kinds of religious and political permutations witnessed in the United States.

As has been demonstrated, there were many religiopolitical groups vying for the attention of African Americans in the United States through the first half of the twentieth century, some more successfully than others. It is therefore a tribute to the organization and personal magnetism of Noble Drew Ali that Moorish Science emerged from the heap. Able to tap into deep yearnings for personal and collective affirmation, as well as a desire for a home or place of belonging, he also touched a lingering Islamic sensibility.

Noble Drew Ali created both space and respectability for Islam among African Americans, variant though it was. W. D. Fard Muhammad and Elijah Muhammad would embellish those efforts, but it was Malcolm X's ability to effectively and articulately combine nationalism and pan-Africanism with the religious message of the Nation of Islam's teachings, in conjunction with the spirit of the times that was the 1950s and 1960s, that brought thousands into the fold. When he crossed over to orthodoxy, thousands more followed (and have continued to follow). Like the Bornuese Muhammad 'Ali b. Said, who fought in the Civil War against slavery, Malcolm turned from the exceptionalism so characteristic of Muslim attitudes throughout the Americas and across the centuries, and he made common cause with the African-descended of other beliefs and traditions. He reconnected, in very concrete terms, with both Islam and Africa, completing the return to the religion of African Muslim forebears in the process. For his journey, he has Noble Drew Ali to thank, among others.

Index